Cases on AI-Driven Talent Economy and Human Capital

Sharif Rana
https://orcid.org/0000-0003-2296-6044

World Talent Economic Forum, Bangladesh & Global Talent Business Incubation and Research Centre, Bangladesh

IGI Global
Scientific Publishing
Publishing Tomorrow's Research Today

Vice President of Editorial	Melissa Wagner
Director of Acquisitions	Mikaela Felty
Director of Book Development	Jocelynn Hessler
Production Manager	Mike Brehm
Cover Design	Jose Rosado

Published in the United States of America by
IGI Global Scientific Publishing
701 East Chocolate Avenue
Hershey, PA, 17033, USA
Tel: 717-533-8845 | Fax: 717-533-7115
Website: https://www.igi-global.com E-mail: cust@igi-global.com

Library of Congress Cataloging-in-Publication Data

(CIP Data Pending)
ISBN13: 9798337338675
Isbn13Softcover: 9798337338682
EISBN13: 9798337338699
British Cataloguing in Publication Data
A Cataloguing in Publication record for this book is available from the British Library.

Table of Contents

Preface xvi

Chapter 1
AI and the Future of Foundational Learning: How Can AI Support Lifelong Learning and Prepare Learners for the Evolving Global Workforce? 1
K. S. Shibani Shankar Ray, Rajiv Gandhi National Aviation University, Fursatganj, India
Durga Madhab Mahapatra, North Eastern Hill University, Shillong, India
Bijaya Laxmi Rout, F.M. College, Balasore, India
Zakir Hossen Shaikh, Kingdom University, Baharin

Chapter 2
AI-Driven Human Capital Management for Academic and Research Advancement 31
O. Bhaskaru, Vignan's Foundation for Science, Technology, and Research, India
K. Lalitha, Santhiram Engineering College, India

Chapter 3
AI in Strategic Talent Acquisition: Enhancing Diversity, Inclusion, and Employer Branding in the Digital Workforce 69
Sarina Asif, School of Management and Commerce, K.R. Mangalam University, Gurugram, India
Anumeha Mathur, School of Management and Commerce, K.R. Mangalam University, Gurugram, India
Nitish Kumar Minz, VIT Business School, Vellore Institute of Technology, Vellore, India

Chapter 4
Balancing Automation and Human Employment: A Case Study on AI as an Augmentation Tool, Not a Replacement.. 99
Anuradha Barda, Chandigarh College of Technology, India
Sapna, Chandigarh College of Technology, India

Chapter 5
Cases on AI-Driven Talent Economy and Human Capital: Educators and Training Institutions 125
Prajakta Dhaval Sadaria, Marwadi University, India

Chapter 6
Data-Driven Customer Behavior Analysis for Take-Away Coffee in Vietnam: A RapidMiner Approach 149
Minh Ly, Faculty of Commerce, Van Lang University, Ho Chi Minh City, Vietnam
Thuy Thi Thanh Nguyen, Faculty of Commerce, Van Lang University, Ho Chi Minh City, Vietnam

Chapter 7
Decoding Talent DNA: AI-Driven Psychometric Profiling for Hyper-Personalized Hiring 163
R. Lakshmi Aishwarya, Dayanand Sagar College of Engineering, India
K. S. Ganesha, Dayanand Sagar College of Engineering, India

Chapter 8
Design AI-Integrated Learning Programs and Curricula 189
R. Velmurugan, Karpagam Academy of Higher Education, Coimbatore, India
J. Sudarvel, Karpagam Academy of Higher Education, Coimbatore, India
R. Bhuvaneswari, Dr. Mahalingam College of Engineering and Technology, Pollachi, India
S. Senthilkumar, Skyline University, Nigeria

Chapter 9
From Curriculum to Capability: Integrating AI in Competency-Based Learning Models for Future-Ready Human Capital 209
Rismawati Rismawati, Universitas Muhammadiyah Palopo, Indonesia
Rusdiana Junaid, Universitas Cokroaminoto Palopo, Indonesia
Aanchal Sharma, Chandigarh Group of Colleges Jhanjeri, Mohali, India
I. Nyoman Darmayasa, Politeknik Negeri Bali, Indonesia
Javaid Ahmad Wagay, Kashmir University, India
Andi Subhan Amir, Hasanuddin University, Indonesia

Chapter 10
Harnessing AI for the Future of Talent: Strategic Cases in People Analytics, Metaverse Integration, and Infrastructure Finance 245
Gaganpreet Kaur, Maharishi Markandeshwar University, Mullana, India
Neeraj Kumar Vats, Maharishi Markandeshwar University, Mullana, India
Amandeep Kaur, Advanced Center of Research and Innovation, CGC University, Mohali, India
Rachin Suri, Maharishi Markandeshwar University, Mullana, India

Chapter 11
HR Challenges and Opportunities in Tourism and Hospitality With AI and Automation 285
Yasir Ansari, Department of Culture, Tourism, Antiquities, and Archive, Pakistan
Remi Thomas, Vishwakarma University, Pune, India
Munir Ahmad, Survey of Pakistan, Pakistan

Chapter 12
Neurodigital Engineering of Human Capital in Intelligent Multi-Stakeholder Organizational Learning Systems 315
Jose De Jesus Reyes-Sánchez, TECNM Instituto Tecnologico Superior De Fresnillo, Mexico
Mario Alberto García-Camacho, Tecnológico Nacional de México, ITS Fresnillo, Mexico
Jannet Maricela Barrientos Luján, TECNM Instituto Tecnologico Superior De Fresnillo, Mexico
Gerardo Ríos Ramos, TECNM Instituto Tecnologico Superior De Fresnillo, Mexico
Victor Manuel Dominguez Ibarra, TECNM Instituto Tecnologico Superior De Fresnillo, Mexico

Chapter 13
Predicting Workforce Trends: Talent Analytics in Sustainable Manpower Forecasting and Engagement 349
Ameer Asra Ahmed, Dayananda Sagar College of Arts, Science, and Commerce, India
P. Vinish, Dayananda Sagar College of Arts, Science, and Commerce, India
L. Balu, Dayananda Sagar College of Arts, Science, and Commerce, India

Chapter 14
Societal Change and Economic Transformation Through AI 379
Arun Agrawal, Institute of Technology and Management, Gwalior, India
R. Soumya, Dayananda Sagar Business Academy, Udayapura, India
B. R. Roopashree, Surana College, India
P. T. Rajeshwari, School of Commerce, Mount Carmel College, Bangalore. India.
Manoj Kumar Jhariya, Mangalayatan University, Jabalpur, India
Charanjeet Dadiyala, Ramdeobaba University, Nagpur, India
Deepak Gupta, Institute of Technology and Management, Gwalior, India
Pradeep Yadav, Institute of Technology and Management, Gwalior, India

Chapter 15
Technology and AI Professionals 399
M. Mayuranathan, SRM Valliammai Engineering College, India
P. Selvakumar, Department of Science and Humanities, Nehru Institute of Technology, Coimbatore, India
B. Maheshwar Rao, Sri Balaji University, Pune, India
T. C. Manjunath, Rajarajeswari College of Engineering, India
P. Sudheer, CVR College of Engineering, India
R. Shanmugaa Priyaa, Sathyabama Institute of Science and Technology, India

Chapter 16
The Dual Challenge of Genetically Modified Crops for the Environment and Farmers' Rights 427
Ananya Pandey, Christ University, Bangalore, India

About the Contributors 449

Index 463

Detailed Table of Contents

Preface xvi

Chapter 1
AI and the Future of Foundational Learning: How Can AI Support Lifelong Learning and Prepare Learners for the Evolving Global Workforce? 1
K. S. Shibani Shankar Ray, Rajiv Gandhi National Aviation University, Fursatganj, India
Durga Madhab Mahapatra, North Eastern Hill University, Shillong, India
Bijaya Laxmi Rout, F.M. College, Balasore, India
Zakir Hossen Shaikh, Kingdom University, Baharin

Artificial Intelligence (AI) is transforming education and workforce development. Foundational learning now extends beyond literacy and numeracy to digital skills, adaptability, and critical thinking. AI supports this shift through personalized instruction, real-time feedback, and lifelong learning opportunities, helping learners stay competitive in a rapidly changing global workforce. Yet, challenges remain, including algorithmic bias, data privacy, unequal access, and the risk of over-reliance on technology. This chapter examines how AI can strengthen foundational skills, prepare learners for evolving careers, and address equity concerns in education. It argues that, when used responsibly, AI can expand access, foster inclusion, and align education systems with 21st-century workforce needs. By combining innovation with ethical safeguards and policy frameworks, AI has the potential to act as a catalyst for sustainable, human-centered learning worldwide.

Chapter 2
AI-Driven Human Capital Management for Academic and Research Advancement 31
O. Bhaskaru, Vignan's Foundation for Science, Technology, and Research, India
K. Lalitha, Santhiram Engineering College, India

Artificial Intelligence (AI) is transforming human capital management in academic and research environments. This chapter examines how AI is integrated into talent acquisition, development, performance evaluation, and workforce planning in higher education and research organizations. AI technologies reshape roles, automate tasks, and provide predictive insights that influence decision-making. The chapter synthesizes academic literature and case studies to highlight patterns in AI adoption.

It also presents conceptual models for future work, integrating perspectives from organizational behavior, data ethics, and machine learning interpretability. It emphasizes the role of academic institutions in shaping ethical AI use in human capital decisions .By evaluating methodological trends and outlining future research directions, this chapter serves as a roadmap for academics and students aiming to contribute to AI-driven human capital management and informs curriculum design that reflects emerging competencies in AI and HR management.

Chapter 3
AI in Strategic Talent Acquisition: Enhancing Diversity, Inclusion, and Employer Branding in the Digital Workforce 69
Sarina Asif, School of Management and Commerce, K.R. Mangalam University, Gurugram, India
Anumeha Mathur, School of Management and Commerce, K.R. Mangalam University, Gurugram, India
Nitish Kumar Minz, VIT Business School, Vellore Institute of Technology, Vellore, India

This chapter explores the transformative impact of Artificial Intelligence (AI) on strategic talent acquisition, with a focus on enhancing diversity, fostering inclusion, and strengthening employer branding in the digital workforce. It investigates how AI technologies such as machine learning, natural language processing, and predictive analytics are reshaping recruitment practices—from resume screening and candidate engagement to personalized branding and inclusive onboarding. Drawing on interdisciplinary research, the chapter highlights both the opportunities and ethical challenges of AI adoption, including algorithmic bias, data privacy, transparency, and accountability. It also examines AI's potential to support underrepresented groups through anonymized screening, neurodiverse assessments, and equitable candidate experience design. The chapter concludes by envisioning future trends, emphasizing the importance of ethical innovation, inclusive design, and human-AI collaboration in building resilient, diverse, and digitally fluent workforces.

Chapter 4
Balancing Automation and Human Employment: A Case Study on AI as an Augmentation Tool, Not a Replacement 99
Anuradha Barda, Chandigarh College of Technology, India
Sapna, Chandigarh College of Technology, India

The integration of Artificial Intelligence (AI) into Human Resource Management (HRM) is transforming the way organizations approach workforce development. This paper explores the application of AI not as a replacement for human labor but as a powerful augmentation tool, specifically focusing on Amazon as a case example. Through an in-depth analysis of Amazon's use of AI-driven platforms for talent acquisition, internal mobility, and employee development, the study illustrates how strategic AI integration enhances operational efficiency, employee satisfaction, and retention. In conclusion, this paper underscores the necessity for organizations to adopt a human-centered approach to AI in HRM. Through careful design, implementation, and continuous evaluation, AI can evolve into a transformative agent that not only drives business outcomes but also uplifts human potential in the modern workplace.

Chapter 5
Cases on AI-Driven Talent Economy and Human Capital: Educators and Training Institutions 125
Prajakta Dhaval Sadaria, Marwadi University, India

This chapter provides a comprehensive and in-depth exploration of the integration of Artificial Intelligence (AI) into educational curricula and training programs, specifically targeting university faculty, corporate trainers, and professional development organizations. As AI technologies continue to revolutionize the landscape of work, communication, and knowledge dissemination, educational institutions must adapt to prepare learners for an AI-augmented future. Central to this discussion is a detailed framework for designing AI-integrated curricula that are flexible, modular, and interdisciplinary, fostering not only technical skills but also critical thinking, ethical reasoning, and lifelong learning competencies. This chapter serves as a practical guide and scholarly resource for educational leaders and practitioners aiming to responsibly harness AI's transformative potential in creating equitable, innovative, and learner-centered environments.

Chapter 6
Data-Driven Customer Behavior Analysis for Take-Away Coffee in Vietnam: A RapidMiner Approach 149
Minh Ly, Faculty of Commerce, Van Lang University, Ho Chi Minh City, Vietnam
Thuy Thi Thanh Nguyen, Faculty of Commerce, Van Lang University, Ho Chi Minh City, Vietnam

This study aims to identify key factors influencing consumer behavior toward the take-away coffee business model in Ho Chi Minh City, utilizing the Decision Tree model in RapidMiner. By combining quantitative and qualitative methods, the research uses a Kaggle dataset refined for accuracy and survey data from 300 respondents. Analysis via Decision Tree assessed model performance through RMSE, MAE, and R^2 indicators. Results reveal that factors such as location, service speed, and surrounding amenities significantly affect take-away coffee purchasing behavior, while payment methods have minimal impact. These findings offer valuable insights for F&B businesses to improve competitiveness, streamline sales processes, and enhance customer experience. The study contributes to consumer behavior theory by clarifying decision-making drivers and demonstrates the practical utility of data analysis in business strategy. However, the research is limited to Ho Chi Minh City and relies solely on one model in RapidMiner.

Chapter 7
Decoding Talent DNA: AI-Driven Psychometric Profiling for Hyper-Personalized Hiring 163
R. Lakshmi Aishwarya, Dayanand Sagar College of Engineering, India
K. S. Ganesha, Dayanand Sagar College of Engineering, India

After Fourth Industrial Revolution, hiring demands hyper-personalization, precision, and ethical intelligence—faster than traditional models allow. This study introduces a new method using psychometric profiling and AI to uncover "Talent DNA," the trait-based predictors of job fit and performance. Using Trait Activation Theory, Person–Job Fit Theory, and Self-Determination Theory within a structural equation modelling (SEM) framework, combined with the AI classifiers, the study analyzed data from about 460 participants. It found that the conscientiousness and grit best predict success, with AI models achieving over 85% accuracy. The Cognitive-Affective-AI Loop (CAAIL) is proposed to link psychometrics, AI, and adaptive decisions. Ethical concerns include bias, transparency, and generalizability, solvable through explainable AI (XAI), culturally adaptive models, and longitudinal studies. The study contributes to intelligent talent analytics, positioning AI as tool to unlock human potential—not gatekeep it—making decoding Talent DNA both a technical and philosophical necessity.

Chapter 8
Design AI-Integrated Learning Programs and Curricula 189
R. Velmurugan, Karpagam Academy of Higher Education, Coimbatore, India
J. Sudarvel, Karpagam Academy of Higher Education, Coimbatore, India
R. Bhuvaneswari, Dr. Mahalingam College of Engineering and Technology, Pollachi, India
S. Senthilkumar, Skyline University, Nigeria

AI is playing a substantial role in the conversion of the education industry in that it allows both personalized and adaptive learning experiences. AI driven platforms, including intelligent tutoring systems (ITS), follow the tutorial, produce the next appropriate piece of learning, and offer real-time feedback by leveraging machine learning and data analytics for tracking student progress. This enables the students to learn at their own pace and provided point by point support. AI also gives power to teachers by automating activities such as the process of grading, making more time for personalization of interaction. However data privacy, equitable access and algorithmic bias issues call for some solutions. Making sure AI tools are secure, inclusive, and accessible will go a long way to maximize their value, making education more effective, the experience more engaging and more equitable.

Chapter 9
From Curriculum to Capability: Integrating AI in Competency-Based Learning Models for Future-Ready Human Capital 209
Rismawati Rismawati, Universitas Muhammadiyah Palopo, Indonesia
Rusdiana Junaid, Universitas Cokroaminoto Palopo, Indonesia
Aanchal Sharma, Chandigarh Group of Colleges Jhanjeri, Mohali, India
I. Nyoman Darmayasa, Politeknik Negeri Bali, Indonesia
Javaid Ahmad Wagay, Kashmir University, India
Andi Subhan Amir, Hasanuddin University, Indonesia

This chapter explores the integration of Artificial Intelligence (AI) into Competency-Based Learning (CBL) frameworks to develop future-ready human capital. It examines how AI enhances personalization, assessment, and capability tracking, enabling education systems to shift from static, content-driven models to adaptive, learner-centered environments. The discussion highlights the limitations of traditional curricula, the transformative role of AI technologies, and the importance of ethical governance, teacher readiness, and institutional capacity. Emphasizing multi-stakeholder collaboration between government, industry, and academia, the chapter proposes a strategic roadmap and research agenda to align education with labor market demands. By reimagining curriculum as a dynamic pathway to capability, this work advocates for inclusive, data-informed, and ethically guided educational ecosystems that prepare learners for the complexities of the digital age.

Chapter 10
Harnessing AI for the Future of Talent: Strategic Cases in People Analytics, Metaverse Integration, and Infrastructure Finance 245
Gaganpreet Kaur, Maharishi Markandeshwar University, Mullana, India
Neeraj Kumar Vats, Maharishi Markandeshwar University, Mullana, India
Amandeep Kaur, Advanced Center of Research and Innovation, CGC University, Mohali, India
Rachin Suri, Maharishi Markandeshwar University, Mullana, India

In the age of digital disruption and intelligent automation, the nature of human capital is undergoing a profound transformation. This comprehensive volume explores how artificial intelligence (AI) is not only augmenting but reimagining the entire talent ecosystem from recruitment and workforce analytics to immersive training and infrastructure investment. Through a curated selection of forward-thinking case studies, the book demonstrates how organizations and educational institutions are leveraging people analytics to derive actionable insights into employee behavior, performance, and potential. It also delves into the role of the metaverse in creating engaging, hybrid learning and collaboration experiences that transcend physical boundaries, making virtual talent development more dynamic and accessible. Furthermore, the integration of AI with infrastructure finance is examined to show how intelligent decision-making supports scalable, sustainable investment in people-first physical and digital environments.

Chapter 11
HR Challenges and Opportunities in Tourism and Hospitality With AI and Automation 285

Yasir Ansari, Department of Culture, Tourism, Antiquities, and Archive, Pakistan
Remi Thomas, Vishwakarma University, Pune, India
Munir Ahmad, Survey of Pakistan, Pakistan

The integration of automation and artificial intelligence (AI) into the tourism and hospitality sector marks a transformative shift in Human Resource (HR) management. This chapter examines how AI redefines traditional HR roles—streamlining recruitment, onboarding, training, and workforce planning—while simultaneously challenging long-standing organizational norms. Yet, amid technological disruption, the core mission of HR remains unchanged: to cultivate human potential, foster purpose-driven work environments, and uphold the people-centered values of hospitality. The chapter argues that to fully harness AI's potential, organizations must adopt a strategic and ethical approach, including comprehensive reskilling programs, inclusive digital tools, and algorithmic governance that ensures fairness and transparency. Emphasizing the critical balance between efficiency and empathy, it highlights the irreplaceable value of emotional intelligence, cultural sensitivity, and human connection in guest-facing services.

Chapter 12
Neurodigital Engineering of Human Capital in Intelligent Multi-Stakeholder Organizational Learning Systems 315
Jose De Jesus Reyes-Sánchez, TECNM Instituto Tecnologico Superior De Fresnillo, Mexico
Mario Alberto García-Camacho, Tecnológico Nacional de México, ITS Fresnillo, Mexico
Jannet Maricela Barrientos Luján, TECNM Instituto Tecnologico Superior De Fresnillo, Mexico
Gerardo Ríos Ramos, TECNM Instituto Tecnologico Superior De Fresnillo, Mexico
Victor Manuel Dominguez Ibarra, TECNM Instituto Tecnologico Superior De Fresnillo, Mexico

Human capital neurodigital engineering integrates cognitive neuroscience, artificial intelligence, and advanced analytics to model, reinforce, and anticipate learning trajectories in multi-stakeholder organizational ecosystems. This chapter examines its theoretical foundations, maps institutional challenges, and presents empirical evidence of corporate implementation, proposing a research agenda that harmonizes radical personalization, cognitive justice, and ethical governance. It is concluded that neurodigital convergence constitutes a strategic paradigm for resilience and sustainable innovation.

Chapter 13
Predicting Workforce Trends: Talent Analytics in Sustainable Manpower Forecasting and Engagement 349
Ameer Asra Ahmed, Dayananda Sagar College of Arts, Science, and Commerce, India
P. Vinish, Dayananda Sagar College of Arts, Science, and Commerce, India
L. Balu, Dayananda Sagar College of Arts, Science, and Commerce, India

This chapter highlights how talent analytics predict future organisational states and enhance performance. Today, data-driven strategies are critical for key HR functions like talent acquisition and performance management. HR analytics enable organisations to collect and assess employee data on performance, behaviour, and attitudes, monitoring metrics like quality of hire and time to hire for strategic hiring. Factors motivating employees are recognised to boost performance. Predictive hiring models minimise mismatches and improve retention. Employee satisfaction is measured through sentiment analysis to enhance morale. Additionally, talent analytics foster employee development with personalised training and a supportive environment, while addressing performance gaps and supporting DEI initiatives.

Effective talent analytics enhance engagement, reduce attrition, and align employee needs with organisational goals.

Chapter 14
Societal Change and Economic Transformation Through AI 379
Arun Agrawal, Institute of Technology and Management, Gwalior, India
R. Soumya, Dayananda Sagar Business Academy, Udayapura, India
B. R. Roopashree, Surana College, India
P. T. Rajeshwari, School of Commerce, Mount Carmel College, Bangalore. India.
Manoj Kumar Jhariya, Mangalayatan University, Jabalpur, India
Charanjeet Dadiyala, Ramdeobaba University, Nagpur, India
Deepak Gupta, Institute of Technology and Management, Gwalior, India
Pradeep Yadav, Institute of Technology and Management, Gwalior, India

Artificial Intelligence (AI) is transforming societies by reshaping economies, democracies, and public services. This paper explores AI's dual role as both an enabler of progress and a source of new challenges. It examines its impact on labor markets, governance, healthcare, education, and urban development, highlighting both opportunities and risks such as bias, inequality, and misinformation. Through international cooperation, ethical frameworks, and inclusive policies, AI can be guided toward enhancing human well-being. Real-world case studies from Estonia and India demonstrate how AI can strengthen democracy and public services when developed responsibly.

Chapter 15
Technology and AI Professionals 399
M. Mayuranathan, SRM Valliammai Engineering College, India
P. Selvakumar, Department of Science and Humanities, Nehru Institute of Technology, Coimbatore, India
B. Maheshwar Rao, Sri Balaji University, Pune, India
T. C. Manjunath, Rajarajeswari College of Engineering, India
P. Sudheer, CVR College of Engineering, India
R. Shanmugaa Priyaa, Sathyabama Institute of Science and Technology, India

In the 21st century, few forces have reshaped the world of work as profoundly as technology and artificial intelligence (AI). What once seemed the domain of science fiction—machines learning from data, robots performing complex surgeries, or algorithms writing poetry—has now become everyday reality. From the factory floor to the executive boardroom, technological advancements are transforming how tasks are performed, how decisions are made, and how value is created. but also enhancing human capabilities, enabling better insights, faster communication, and more personalized customer experiences. real-time analysis, and predictive modeling to stay competitive in fast-evolving markets. Human resource departments are using AI to streamline recruitment, identify employee engagement trends, and even predict potential attrition. Marketing teams are leveraging algorithms to target customers with pinpoint accuracy, while finance departments utilize AI tools to detect fraud, analyze investment opportunities, and manage risk more efficiently.

Chapter 16
The Dual Challenge of Genetically Modified Crops for the Environment and Farmers' Rights 427
Ananya Pandey, Christ University, Bangalore, India

The potential environmental benefits of genetically modified (GM) crops are accompanied by worries about ecological dangers and the degradation of farmers' rights. The relationship between genetically modified crop technology, environmental sustainability, and seed sovereignty laws is critically examined in this chapter. Certain genetically modified features may result in biodiversity loss, soil degradation, and genetic contamination, even though they can help minimize pesticide use and increase climate resistance. Furthermore, traditional farming methods are frequently undermined by the spread of intellectual property regimes, which restrict farmers' capacity to share and conserve seeds. Diverse socio-legal results are illustrated by case studies from Africa, the USA, and India, exposing a gap in global governance. To guarantee that GM technologies are in line with ecological integrity and farmers' autonomy, the chapter advocates for a multifaceted policy framework that balances innovation and justice, encourages participatory regulation, and funds interdisciplinary research.

About the Contributors 449

Index 463

Preface

INTRODUCTION

As Editor of *Cases on AI-Driven Talent Economy and Human Capital*, it is both a privilege and a responsibility to introduce this timely and forward-looking volume. We stand at a defining moment in the evolution of work. The rapid advancement of artificial intelligence (AI) is not merely enhancing existing systems; it is fundamentally transforming the global talent economy and reshaping the very foundations of human capital development.

AI-driven technologies are redefining how talent is identified, nurtured, deployed, and retained. From intelligent recruitment platforms and adaptive learning systems to predictive workforce analytics and automated performance management, AI is influencing every stage of the employee lifecycle. These innovations are driving efficiency and productivity while simultaneously challenging long-standing assumptions about skills, employability, and organizational design. As businesses, governments, and academic institutions navigate this transformation, it becomes imperative to critically examine both the extraordinary opportunities and the complex challenges presented by AI-enabled human capital management.

This volume was conceived with a clear purpose: to explore real-world applications, document emerging trends, and present practical insights into how AI is reshaping the talent ecosystem. Through carefully selected case studies spanning industries and geographic regions, this book illustrates how AI enhances workforce capabilities, accelerates skill development, and supports the creation of more agile and inclusive talent frameworks. The contributors bring diverse perspectives—academic rigor, industry expertise, and policy insight—offering readers a balanced and comprehensive view of this evolving domain.

Several key themes guide the structure of this book. We examine AI-driven talent acquisition and retention strategies, workforce automation and augmentation,

AI's role in education and continuous learning, ethical considerations and bias mitigation, and the broader implications of AI for global labor markets. Together, these discussions provide a multidimensional understanding of AI-powered human capital systems, equipping stakeholders to respond strategically to the demands of the future of work.

This book pursues several core objectives. First, it seeks to bridge the gap between theory and practice by presenting empirical research alongside practical case studies that demonstrate how AI is effectively deployed in talent management. Second, it highlights emerging innovations in recruitment, upskilling, performance evaluation, and workplace automation, offering insight into the trajectory of the AI-driven talent economy. Third, it addresses critical challenges—including algorithmic bias, ethical governance, data privacy, and workforce displacement—ensuring that technological advancement is examined through a lens of responsibility and sustainability. Fourth, it provides strategic recommendations for leaders, policymakers, educators, and HR professionals seeking to integrate AI into their human capital strategies. Finally, it advances scholarly and industry research by consolidating contemporary studies and real-world applications, serving as a foundational reference for future inquiry.

The intended audience for this volume is broad and interdisciplinary. Business leaders and executives will find guidance on leveraging AI to enhance workforce productivity and organizational resilience. Policymakers and government officials will gain insights into labor market implications and governance considerations. Academics and researchers will encounter current empirical findings and theoretical frameworks. Technology professionals and AI developers will discover practical applications within workforce analytics and automation. Educators and training institutions will find direction for designing AI-integrated learning environments. Investors and venture capitalists will better understand the evolving landscape of AI-driven HR technologies and workforce innovation.

Above all, this book is designed to foster informed dialogue. The transformation of human capital through AI is not a distant prospect—it is unfolding now. Our collective task is to ensure that this transformation advances equity, innovation, and sustainable growth. It is my hope that this volume not only informs but also inspires collaboration across sectors to shape a talent economy that is intelligent, inclusive, and resilient.

I extend my sincere gratitude to the contributing authors, reviewers, and editorial team whose expertise and dedication made this volume possible. May this work serve as both a reference and a catalyst for continued exploration at the intersection of artificial intelligence and human capital development.

ORGANIZATION OF THE BOOK

As Editor of *Cases on AI-Driven Talent Economy and Human Capital*, I am pleased to present a collection of chapters that together illuminate the evolving architecture of work, learning, and organizational strategy in the age of artificial intelligence. Each contribution offers a distinctive lens, yet collectively they form a coherent narrative about how AI is reshaping the foundations of human capital across sectors and societies.

Chapter 1 sets the stage by reframing foundational learning for the AI era. Moving beyond traditional literacy and numeracy, it positions digital fluency, adaptability, and critical thinking as essential competencies for lifelong employability. The chapter thoughtfully examines how AI-enabled personalization, real-time feedback, and adaptive systems can democratize access to learning while cautioning against algorithmic bias, inequitable access, and overdependence on technology. It establishes an ethical and policy-oriented foundation for the volume, arguing that AI, when responsibly governed, can serve as a catalyst for inclusive and human-centered global workforce preparation.

Chapter 2 turns to academic and research institutions, exploring how AI is transforming human capital management within higher education. By analyzing AI applications in recruitment, development, evaluation, and workforce planning, this chapter highlights how predictive analytics and intelligent systems are reshaping institutional decision-making. Importantly, it situates these developments within broader conversations about data ethics and interpretability, offering conceptual models and research pathways that will guide both scholars and practitioners in building responsible AI-driven academic HR ecosystems.

Chapter 3 expands the discussion into strategic talent acquisition, focusing on diversity, inclusion, and employer branding in the digital workforce. It demonstrates how machine learning, natural language processing, and predictive analytics are revolutionizing recruitment processes—from anonymized screening to personalized candidate engagement. At the same time, it underscores the ethical complexities of algorithmic decision-making, calling for transparent, accountable, and inclusive AI design. The chapter powerfully argues that ethical innovation and human–AI collaboration are prerequisites for building resilient and diverse organizations.

Chapter 4 offers a grounded case study of AI as augmentation rather than replacement, using a leading global enterprise to illustrate how thoughtful AI integration can enhance internal mobility, recruitment, and employee development. This chapter reinforces a central theme of the book: AI's greatest value emerges when it uplifts human potential rather than displacing it. By advocating for human-centered implementation and continuous evaluation, it provides a pragmatic blueprint for organizations seeking to balance automation with meaningful employment.

Chapter 5 returns to the educational sphere, presenting a comprehensive framework for AI-integrated curricula in universities and professional training institutions. It emphasizes modular, interdisciplinary design that cultivates technical proficiency alongside ethical reasoning and critical inquiry. Serving as both scholarly reflection and practical guide, the chapter addresses the pressing need for educators to align learning ecosystems with AI-augmented labor markets while safeguarding equity and inclusion.

Chapter 6 introduces a data-driven case from the consumer sector, applying decision-tree modeling to analyze take-away coffee purchasing behavior in Ho Chi Minh City. While situated within the food and beverage industry, the chapter exemplifies how AI-powered analytics inform business strategy, customer engagement, and operational efficiency. By demonstrating the practical utility of predictive modeling tools, it highlights how data literacy has become an essential competency within the broader talent economy.

Chapter 7 ventures into advanced talent analytics with its exploration of AI-driven psychometric profiling and the concept of "Talent DNA." Integrating psychological theory with structural equation modeling and AI classifiers, the chapter proposes an innovative Cognitive-Affective-AI Loop framework. Its findings—linking traits such as conscientiousness and grit to predictive hiring models—underscore the promise of hyper-personalized recruitment, while its ethical reflections on bias, transparency, and explainability remind us that intelligent systems must remain accountable and culturally adaptive.

Chapter 8 further develops the theme of AI-enabled learning design, focusing on intelligent tutoring systems, automated assessment, and adaptive feedback mechanisms. It illustrates how AI can personalize educational experiences and free educators to engage more deeply with learners. At the same time, it reinforces the necessity of secure, inclusive, and ethically designed systems to prevent privacy breaches and systemic inequities.

Chapter 9 advances the discussion by integrating AI into competency-based learning (CBL) models. It argues for a shift from static curricula to dynamic capability pathways, where AI supports assessment, progression tracking, and alignment with labor market needs. Through a proposed strategic roadmap, the chapter highlights the importance of multi-stakeholder collaboration and institutional readiness in building agile, data-informed educational ecosystems.

Chapter 10 broadens the horizon by linking people analytics, immersive metaverse environments, and infrastructure finance. Through strategic case studies, it demonstrates how AI enables actionable insights into employee performance, supports hybrid and virtual collaboration, and informs sustainable investment in physical and digital talent infrastructures. This chapter underscores the interconnectedness of analytics, experience design, and long-term capital planning in shaping the future talent ecosystem.

Chapter 11 examines the tourism and hospitality sector, where automation intersects with deeply human, guest-facing services. It explores how AI redefines HR functions while reaffirming the enduring value of emotional intelligence, cultural sensitivity, and empathy. By advocating for reskilling initiatives and ethical governance frameworks, the chapter articulates a nuanced balance between operational efficiency and human connection in service industries.

Chapter 12 introduces the concept of neurodigital engineering of human capital, integrating cognitive neuroscience, AI, and advanced analytics to model and anticipate learning trajectories within complex organizational systems. This forward-looking contribution proposes a research agenda centered on radical personalization, cognitive justice, and ethical governance, positioning neurodigital convergence as a paradigm for resilience and sustainable innovation.

Chapter 13 returns to predictive analytics, focusing on sustainable manpower forecasting and employee engagement. It illustrates how talent analytics inform recruitment, performance management, retention strategies, and diversity initiatives. By linking sentiment analysis, predictive hiring, and personalized development pathways, the chapter demonstrates how data-driven insight strengthens alignment between individual aspirations and organizational objectives.

Chapter 14 situates AI within broader societal and economic transformation. It examines AI's dual role as both enabler and disruptor across labor markets, governance, healthcare, and public services. Through global case illustrations, it highlights the importance of ethical frameworks, inclusive policies, and international cooperation in ensuring that AI advances democratic values and human well-being rather than exacerbating inequality.

Chapter 15 focuses on technology and AI professionals themselves—the architects of intelligent systems. It explores how AI reshapes decision-making across departments, from HR and marketing to finance and operations. By examining the expanding role of data analysis, predictive modeling, and algorithmic insight, the chapter underscores the need for interdisciplinary fluency and ethical awareness among technology leaders in a rapidly evolving marketplace.

Finally, Chapter 16 extends the conversation beyond traditional HR domains to examine the dual environmental and socio-legal challenges of genetically modified crops. Though distinct in subject matter, this chapter resonates with the volume's overarching concern for ethical governance, innovation, and stakeholder equity. By analyzing ecological risks, intellectual property regimes, and farmers' rights, it reminds us that technological advancement—whether in agriculture or AI—must balance progress with justice and sustainability.

Taken together, these chapters form a multidimensional exploration of AI's transformative power. They reflect a shared conviction that the future of the talent economy depends not only on technological sophistication but also on ethical stewardship, interdisciplinary collaboration, and an unwavering commitment to human dignity. It is my hope that this volume will serve as both a scholarly reference and a strategic guide for those shaping the next era of human capital development.

CONCLUSION

As Editor of *Cases on AI-Driven Talent Economy and Human Capital*, I close this volume with both optimism and resolve. The chapters assembled in this collection make one truth unmistakably clear: artificial intelligence is not merely a technological advancement—it is a structural force reshaping how we learn, work, lead, and govern. The transformation of the talent economy is already underway, and its trajectory will depend on the choices we make today.

Across sectors—education, corporate enterprise, public service, analytics, tourism, infrastructure, and even agriculture—our contributors have demonstrated that AI's impact is neither singular nor simplistic. It is layered, dynamic, and deeply contextual. AI augments human potential, accelerates insight, and enables personalization at scale. Yet it also introduces critical questions regarding equity, transparency, governance, workforce displacement, and societal trust. The duality of opportunity and responsibility is a recurring theme throughout this book.

What emerges from these chapters is a consistent and compelling message: technology alone does not determine outcomes. Human intention, ethical design, institutional readiness, and inclusive policy frameworks shape whether AI becomes a tool of empowerment or exclusion. The most successful cases highlighted in this volume are those that treat AI not as a replacement for human capability, but as an amplifier of it—supporting lifelong learning, strengthening diversity and inclusion, enhancing decision-making, and enabling sustainable growth.

This book also underscores the necessity of interdisciplinary collaboration. The future of human capital development demands dialogue among technologists, educators, policymakers, business leaders, researchers, and community stakeholders. Preparing a workforce for the AI era requires more than digital proficiency; it requires adaptability, critical reasoning, ethical literacy, and a renewed commitment to human-centered innovation.

Importantly, the work presented here is not an endpoint but a foundation. Many of the models, frameworks, and case studies included in this volume invite further refinement, empirical validation, and contextual adaptation. As AI systems continue to evolve, so too must our research agendas, regulatory approaches, and organizational strategies. Continuous learning—at both institutional and individual levels—will define resilience in the decades ahead.

If there is a unifying vision within this collection, it is this: the future of the talent economy must be intelligent, inclusive, and intentional. Intelligent in its use of data and analytics. Inclusive in its access, design, and outcomes. Intentional in its ethical governance and commitment to human dignity.

I extend my sincere appreciation to the scholars, practitioners, and reviewers who have contributed their expertise to this endeavor. Their insights reflect not only academic rigor but also a shared dedication to shaping a more equitable and sustainable future of work.

It is my hope that this volume will inspire thoughtful action, informed policy, and innovative research. May it serve as both a reference and a call to leadership—encouraging us to guide artificial intelligence not simply toward efficiency, but toward the advancement of human potential in its fullest sense.

Chapter 1
AI and the Future of Foundational Learning:
How Can AI Support Lifelong Learning and Prepare Learners for the Evolving Global Workforce?

K. S. Shibani Shankar Ray
http://orcid.org/0009-0009-5890-0814
Rajiv Gandhi National Aviation University, Fursatganj, India

Durga Madhab Mahapatra
http://orcid.org/0000-0003-1272-7285
North Eastern Hill University, Shillong, India

Bijaya Laxmi Rout
http://orcid.org/0009-0008-8075-7842
F.M. College, Balasore, India

Zakir Hossen Shaikh
http://orcid.org/0000-0003-4733-4166
Kingdom University, Baharin

EXECUTIVE SUMMARY

Artificial Intelligence (AI) is transforming education and workforce development. Foundational learning now extends beyond literacy and numeracy to digital skills, adaptability, and critical thinking. AI supports this shift through personalized instruction, real-time feedback, and lifelong learning opportunities, helping learners stay competitive in a rapidly changing global workforce. Yet, challenges remain, including algorithmic bias, data privacy, unequal access, and the risk of over-reliance

DOI: 10.4018/979-8-3373-3867-5.ch001

on technology. This chapter examines how AI can strengthen foundational skills, prepare learners for evolving careers, and address equity concerns in education. It argues that, when used responsibly, AI can expand access, foster inclusion, and align education systems with 21st-century workforce needs. By combining innovation with ethical safeguards and policy frameworks, AI has the potential to act as a catalyst for sustainable, human-centered learning worldwide.

INTRODUCTION

The world of work is transforming at an unprecedented pace. Advances in artificial intelligence (AI) are reshaping economies, industries, and societies. Traditional education systems, however, remain slow to adapt. Most schools were designed for industrial-age needs, not digital realities. The challenge now is to prepare learners for a future that looks very different from the past. Foundational learning has always been the cornerstone of education. Reading, writing, and numeracy formed the basic skill set for participation in society. Yet, in the AI-driven era, these foundations need expansion. Learners must now master digital literacy, critical thinking, and socio-emotional resilience. They must also learn how to work alongside intelligent machines (Luckin, 2023). Foundational skills are no longer static; they evolve with technological change. The rise of AI has created new opportunities for personalised learning. Adaptive systems can identify knowledge gaps and deliver tailored content instantly. This individual approach allows learners to progress at their own pace. For example, AI tutoring systems already help millions master math and language. Research shows such tools improve motivation and reduce dropout rates (OECD, 2023). AI, therefore, offers a path to close long-standing gaps in learning outcomes. Global economic shifts also make lifelong learning more urgent than ever. Jobs are changing faster than workers can adapt. The World Economic Forum (2023) predicts that half of all workers will need reskilling by 2027. Workers will not only change jobs but also careers across their lifetimes. Foundational learning, then, must focus on adaptability and continuous growth. AI can support this shift by guiding learners toward relevant skills and emerging opportunities. At the same time, equity concerns remain at the centre of this debate. Not all learners have access to digital devices, connectivity, or AI-enhanced platforms. Without careful policy, AI could widen existing inequalities in education. UNESCO (2021) warns that unequal access to AI tools risks creating a digital divide between learners. Ensuring equity requires investments in infrastructure, open platforms, and teacher training.

Another critical dimension is AI literacy itself. Learners must not only use AI but also understand it. This means knowing what AI can and cannot do. It also requires awareness of ethical risks such as bias, surveillance, and misuse (Selwyn, 2022).

AI literacy is increasingly seen as a key twenty-first century competency. Without it, future workers may struggle to engage with AI systems critically. Educators and policymakers are beginning to recognise these demands. In Singapore, for example, the Skills Future program uses AI analytics to recommend career-relevant courses (Tan & Chua, 2021). In Finland, national strategies now integrate AI-driven learning platforms into basic education (Vuorikari et al., 2025). These initiatives show how AI can support both foundational learning and lifelong adaptability. Yet they also highlight the need for coordinated frameworks that align education with labour market needs. The implications for the global workforce are profound. Many routine tasks are already automated. Workers increasingly need skills in creativity, empathy, and problem-solving. These are areas where humans complement, rather than compete with, AI. Preparing learners for such a hybrid workforce requires rethinking both curriculum and pedagogy. AI can provide simulations, feedback, and adaptive training to build these human-centered skills. In short, the future of foundational learning is inseparable from AI. The challenge is not simply to integrate AI tools into classrooms. It is to design systems that foster lifelong adaptability, ethical responsibility, and human-AI collaboration. This chapter explores how AI can strengthen foundational learning, support lifelong learning, and prepare individuals for an evolving global workforce. It also examines the opportunities, risks, and policy choices that shape this transformation.

REDEFINING FOUNDATIONAL LEARNING IN THE AI ERA

Foundational learning has always formed the bedrock of education. For centuries, it meant literacy, numeracy, and basic cognitive development. These skills prepared individuals to function in society and participate in the workforce. Yet, the demands of the twenty-first century are radically different. Artificial intelligence (AI), automation, and digital transformation have reshaped the meaning of foundational learning. Learners now need more than reading, writing, and arithmetic. They must also build digital literacy, socio-emotional intelligence, critical thinking, and AI literacy.

The Expanding Nature of Foundational Skills

The expansion of foundational skills reflects profound economic and technological change. Employers today demand agility, adaptability, and problem-solving over routine skills. The World Economic Forum (2023) notes that creativity, resilience, and collaboration are rising in importance. These are not traditional subjects but cross-cutting capabilities. They allow learners to navigate uncertainty and thrive in volatile labor markets. Digital literacy is central to this expanded vision. Students must know how to evaluate online information, use digital tools, and engage safely in digital environments. Without these abilities, they risk exclusion from both education and employment. Recent research shows digital literacy is now considered as important as traditional literacy for employability (Vuorikari et al., 2025). Foundational learning, therefore, must adapt to integrate these skills early and continuously. Socio-emotional learning (SEL) also plays a key role. Skills like empathy, communication, and teamwork are not optional. They are essential for workplaces where humans and AI collaborate. AI can perform calculations and analyses, but it cannot replace empathy or ethical judgment. Learners who master socio-emotional intelligence will complement AI systems rather than compete with them (Grosseck et al., 2023). Another crucial component is critical thinking. The digital era floods learners with information, some accurate and some misleading. Learners must develop the ability to question, analyze, and evaluate. This is particularly urgent as AI-generated content proliferates. Students need to know how to assess AI outputs and challenge biased or false information. Without critical thinking, foundational learning loses its relevance. Finally, AI literacy itself has emerged as a core foundation. Understanding how AI works, where it applies, and what risks it brings is now essential. Learners must grasp concepts like algorithms, bias, and transparency. They must also develop confidence in working alongside intelligent systems. Scholars argue that AI literacy will soon be as fundamental as computer literacy was in the 1990s.

AI as a Driver of Redefined Foundations

AI does not simply require new foundations; it also enables them. Adaptive learning systems personalise instruction by analysing learner data in real time. These systems identify knowledge gaps and provide targeted support. For instance, platforms like Squirrel AI in China use machine learning to adjust difficulty levels instantly. Such innovations redefine literacy and numeracy by ensuring every learner progresses at an appropriate pace. AI also enhances socio-emotional learning. Intelligent simulations can create scenarios where students practice empathy, negotiation, and teamwork. Virtual agents provide feedback on tone, collaboration, and communication styles. This builds confidence in areas where traditional classrooms often struggle. Emerging research shows that AI-supported SEL programs improve self-awareness and peer relationships (Hwang et al., 2023). Critical thinking can also be strengthened through AI. Intelligent tutoring systems encourage learners to solve complex problems step by step. AI-driven debate platforms expose students to opposing viewpoints, forcing them to evaluate evidence. These experiences prepare learners to question not only human arguments but also AI-generated ones. In this way, AI becomes both the subject and the tool of foundational learning.

The Global Perspective on Foundational Redefinition

Countries are rethinking foundational learning in light of AI disruptions. Finland, for example, integrates digital literacy and coding into primary education. Its curriculum emphasises transversal competencies such as problem-solving and global citizenship (Vuorikari et al., 2025). Singapore has also redefined its approach. Through its SkillsFuture program, foundational learning includes AI awareness, data literacy, and lifelong adaptability (Tan & Chua, 2021). These examples highlight the shift from static knowledge to dynamic competencies. UNESCO (2021) underscores that foundational learning must remain inclusive. Many low- and middle-income countries still struggle with basic literacy. Introducing AI literacy cannot come at the expense of reading and numeracy. Instead, the challenge is to integrate digital and traditional skills simultaneously. Hybrid approaches are essential, ensuring that no learner is left behind in the digital race.

The Tension Between Old and New Foundations

Redefining foundational learning also raises tensions. Some educators worry that emphasising digital and AI literacy may weaken traditional skills. Literacy and numeracy remain vital for higher education and social participation. Yet, evidence suggests that AI-enhanced programs strengthen rather than weaken these basics. Adaptive platforms provide individualised pathways that reinforce reading and math more effectively than one-size-fits-all teaching (OECD, 2023). Another tension lies between technological and human-centred skills. While AI literacy is critical, so is socio-emotional growth. Learners must not become overly dependent on AI tools. Instead, they should see AI as a partner that amplifies human abilities. Achieving this balance requires thoughtful pedagogy and teacher support. Teachers remain irreplaceable in modelling empathy, ethics, and citizenship.

Implications for Educators and Policy

The redefinition of foundational learning places new demands on educators. Teachers need training in AI tools, digital pedagogy, and socio-emotional facilitation. Professional development programs must integrate AI literacy alongside classroom strategies. Research indicates that teachers who feel confident with AI foster more inclusive and effective learning environments (Holmes et al., 2022). Policy frameworks also play a critical role. Governments must set guidelines for AI in education, ensuring ethical use and data protection. They must also invest in infrastructure to reduce digital divides. Policies should define new foundational standards that blend traditional and emerging competencies. Without these frameworks, AI adoption risks reinforcing inequalities instead of reducing them.

Toward Lifelong Foundational Competence

Foundational learning is no longer confined to childhood. It must evolve into a lifelong process. Workers in mid-career now need to update their digital literacy and AI skills. Employers increasingly value adaptability as a key competency. AI can support this by offering personalised upskilling paths across a lifetime. For example, AI career platforms analyse labour market trends and recommend learning modules to employees (World Economic Forum, 2023). This lifelong perspective aligns with the concept of "learning to learn." It emphasises curiosity, resilience, and adaptability across the lifespan. Foundational learning must thus prepare learners for multiple careers, not one trajectory. AI-driven tools make this vision practical by offering constant feedback, coaching, and career guidance. Foundational learning in the AI era is not a fixed set of skills. It is a dynamic, evolving framework that adapts to technological and social change. Literacy, numeracy, and cognitive skills remain essential, but they are no longer sufficient. Learners must also master digital literacy, socio-emotional intelligence, critical thinking, and AI literacy. AI both drives this redefinition and enables its delivery. Adaptive systems, simulations, and career platforms provide personalised pathways for foundational development. Yet, equity, ethics, and teacher roles must remain central. Policies must ensure inclusive access and human-centred learning experiences. Ultimately, redefining foundational learning means preparing individuals for a world where change is constant and AI is pervasive. Success will depend on blending tradition with innovation, ensuring that all learners, regardless of background, have the skills to thrive in the evolving global workforce.

AI IN EARLY FOUNDATIONAL LEARNING

Foundational learning begins in early childhood. This stage shapes literacy, numeracy, and socio-emotional development. These skills are critical for later education and lifelong learning. Yet many children worldwide still struggle to acquire them. The World Bank reports that nearly 70% of ten-year-olds in low- and middle-income countries cannot read a simple text. Such learning poverty has long-term consequences for social mobility and workforce participation. Artificial intelligence (AI) offers new ways to address this challenge. AI-powered systems can personalize learning, provide targeted interventions, and support inclusivity. Unlike traditional teaching, AI can adapt instantly to each learner's needs. This makes it a powerful tool for early foundational learning. In this section, we examine how AI enhances literacy, numeracy, socio-emotional development, and inclusivity in early education.

AI for Personalised Literacy and Numeracy

Literacy and numeracy remain the backbone of foundational learning. Traditional approaches rely on uniform teaching methods, which often fail diverse learners. AI-driven platforms change this model by tailoring content to individual performance. Adaptive learning systems use machine learning to adjust difficulty levels. When a learner struggles, the system provides easier exercises or step-by-step hints. If the learner succeeds, it introduces more complex tasks. This dynamic progression reduces frustration and builds confidence. For literacy, AI applications include speech recognition and natural language processing (NLP). These tools listen to a child reading aloud and provide real-time feedback. They identify mispronunciations, fluency issues, and comprehension gaps. Studies show AI-driven literacy apps significantly improve early reading skills. For numeracy, AI-based math platforms like DreamBox Learning or Squirrel AI guide learners through problems adaptively. These platforms can detect misconceptions in arithmetic or algebra and provide corrective instruction. Research confirms that AI-enhanced numeracy programs improve conceptual understanding and problem-solving.

Table 1. AI applications in early literacy and numeracy

AI Tool/Approach	Area of Focus	Key Features	Reported Benefits
Speech recognition apps	Early literacy	Reads aloud analysis	Improves fluency, accuracy
Adaptive math platforms	Numeracy foundations	Personalized problem sets	Builds confidence, reduces errors
NLP reading tutors	Reading comprehension	Text analysis, hints	Enhances comprehension, vocabulary
Gamified learning apps	Both literacy/ numeracy	Rewards, challenges	Increases motivation, engagement

AI for Inclusive Learning

Inclusivity is essential in early education. Many children face barriers due to disability, language, or socio-economic context. AI tools can help reduce these barriers by providing accessible learning environments. Speech-to-text technologies support learners with hearing impairments. Text-to-speech tools help those with reading difficulties or visual impairments. AI can also translate content into multiple languages, supporting multilingual classrooms. These features make learning more inclusive and equitable (UNESCO, 2021). For children with dyslexia, AI-powered reading assistants highlight words, adjust fonts, or provide real-time pronunciation guides. Research shows such tools significantly improve reading outcomes for struggling learners (Holmes et al., 2022). Similarly, AI sign language avatars can help children with hearing challenges access classroom content. AI also supports teachers in identifying learning difficulties early. Predictive analytics detect patterns that signal dyslexia, ADHD, or other learning needs. Early identification allows timely interventions, preventing long-term disadvantage (Hwang et al., 2023).

Figure 1. AI support for inclusive learning

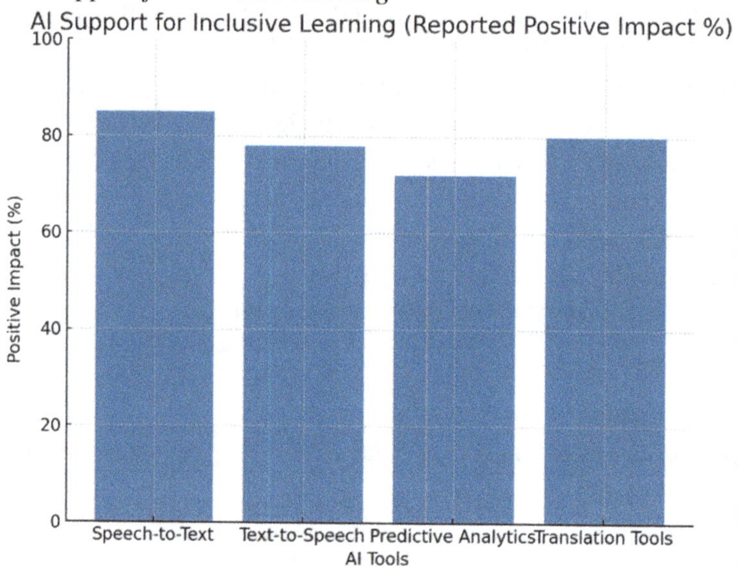

AI for Socio-Emotional Development

Foundational learning is not only about academic skills. Socio-emotional learning (SEL) builds self-awareness, empathy, collaboration, and resilience. These skills are crucial for healthy development and workforce readiness. AI can foster SEL through simulations and interactive agents. Virtual learning companions engage children in conversations that promote empathy and cooperation. Some AI systems track emotional cues, such as facial expressions or voice tone, and provide feedback. While controversial, these tools aim to build emotional regulation and awareness (Grosseck et al., 2023). Gamified AI platforms also encourage teamwork and problem-solving. For example, collaborative learning games require children to solve puzzles together with AI guidance. These activities teach conflict resolution and communication in engaging ways. Recent studies show that AI-supported SEL programs improve classroom climate and peer relationships. They also increase motivation and reduce behavioral challenges (Hwang et al., 2023).

Table 2. AI applications in socio-emotional learning

AI Application	SEL Skill Targeted	Mechanism	Outcome Reported
Virtual companions	Empathy, self-expression	Dialogue, feedback	Improved self-awareness
Emotion recognition tools	Emotional regulation	Voice/facial cues	Stronger self-control
Gamified collaboration	Teamwork, problem-solving	Shared challenges	Better peer interaction
AI-guided role play	Conflict resolution	Scenario simulation	Increased empathy

Source: Hwang et al. (2023).

AI as a Teacher's Partner

AI does not replace teachers; it supports them. In early education, human interaction remains irreplaceable. Teachers model empathy, ethics, and social norms. However, AI can relieve teachers of repetitive tasks. For example, AI grading tools assess spelling, grammar, or math accuracy instantly. Teachers then spend more time on creative and interpersonal teaching. AI dashboards provide real-time insights into student progress. This helps teachers design targeted interventions. Research shows that teachers using AI assistants feel more empowered and effective (Holmes et al., 2022). However, training is essential. Teachers must understand AI systems and their limitations. Without proper guidance, AI tools may overwhelm rather than assist educators.

Ethical Concerns in Early AI Use

The use of AI in early foundational learning also raises ethical questions. Children's data is highly sensitive. AI systems collect large amounts of personal and behavioural data. Without strict safeguards, privacy risks increase. UNESCO (2021) stresses the importance of ethical frameworks for AI in early education. Bias in AI algorithms is another concern. If training data is skewed, AI may disadvantage some groups. For example, speech recognition systems often perform poorly with non-native accents. This risks reinforcing inequality rather than reducing it. Researchers call for transparent and inclusive datasets to avoid such problems (Holmes et al., 2022). Finally, over-reliance on AI may minimise human interaction. Young children need social play and direct engagement for healthy development. AI must therefore be a supplement, not a substitute, for human relationships.

Case Studies

Case 1: China's Squirrel AI

Squirrel AI uses adaptive learning to teach math and science. It analyzes thousands of data points per learner. Students receive customized exercises that match their exact needs. Reports show significant gains in math achievement among primary learners.

Case 2: Microsoft's Immersive

Reader Immersive Reader helps children with reading difficulties. It highlights text, reads aloud, and adjusts spacing or fonts. Schools using it report improved fluency and confidence in struggling readers (UNESCO, 2021).

Case 3: India's BYJU's App

BYJU's offers AI-powered lessons combining animation, quizzes, and feedback. It supports literacy and numeracy in multiple languages. Research indicates that children using BYJU's show greater retention and engagement compared to traditional methods.

Future Directions

AI in early foundational learning will continue to evolve. Future systems will integrate multimodal data, including speech, gesture, and eye-tracking. These will provide deeper insights into learning processes. Virtual reality (VR) and augmented reality (AR) powered by AI will offer immersive foundational learning experiences. Policy must guide these developments responsibly. Governments should create ethical frameworks for AI in early education. Investment in teacher training, digital infrastructure, and inclusive platforms is essential. Without this, AI risks widening inequality instead of narrowing it.

Figure 2. Future AI applications in early learning

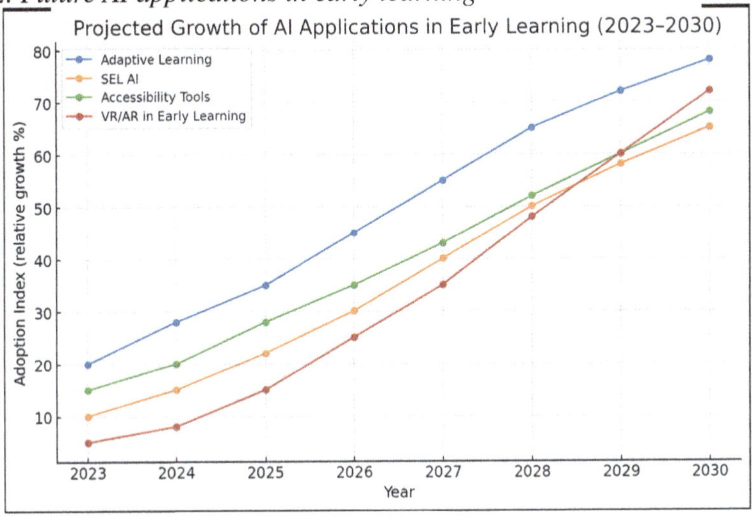

AI is transforming early foundational learning. It enhances literacy, numeracy, inclusivity, and socio-emotional growth. Adaptive systems personalize instruction, while AI companions foster empathy and teamwork. These innovations promise to reduce learning poverty and prepare children for lifelong learning. Yet challenges remain. Privacy, bias, and over-reliance must be addressed carefully. Teachers must be supported as partners, not replaced by machines. Policies must ensure equitable access, particularly in underserved regions. The future of foundational learning depends on this balance. When used responsibly, AI can ensure every child receives the support they need to thrive in an AI-driven world.

PREPARING LEARNERS FOR THE EVOLVING WORKFORCE

The global workforce is undergoing rapid and disruptive transformation. Artificial intelligence, automation, and digitalization are redefining how jobs are created and performed. The workplace of the future will not resemble the traditional industries of the past. Learners today must therefore be prepared for a workforce that is increasingly fluid, dynamic, and hybrid. Education systems, governments, and employers must work together to equip individuals with skills that remain relevant amid uncertainty.

Shifting Demands in the Global Workforce

The World Economic Forum (2023) highlights that by 2027, over 60% of employees will need retraining. Automation continues to replace routine and repetitive tasks. At the same time, demand for advanced digital skills, creativity, and socio-emotional intelligence is rising. Employers seek workers who can adapt quickly, think critically, and collaborate effectively. Traditional education systems, however, often prepare learners for stable jobs and linear careers. That model no longer matches reality. Workers will likely change jobs multiple times and even shift industries. Preparing learners for this evolving workforce requires an emphasis on flexibility, resilience, and continuous learning. UNESCO (2021) emphasizes that lifelong learning must become a cultural norm, supported by AI-driven technologies.

Human-AI Collaboration as a Core Competency

The evolving workforce will increasingly feature human-AI collaboration. AI systems now perform tasks such as data analysis, diagnostics, logistics, and language processing. Yet, these systems require human oversight, interpretation, and ethical judgment. Workers must learn how to use AI as a partner, not a rival. AI literacy is therefore a critical foundational skill. Learners should understand what AI can and cannot do. They must also grasp concepts like bias, transparency, and accountability. Long et al. (2021) argue that AI literacy will soon be as essential as computer literacy was two decades ago. Without this literacy, workers risk becoming passive users instead of active shapers of technology. Human-centered skills will differentiate workers in hybrid environments. Empathy, creativity, and leadership cannot be automated. Workers who combine digital fluency with emotional intelligence will thrive. AI can support this preparation by providing simulations, workplace scenarios, and personalized feedback. For example, AI role-play platforms already help employees practice negotiation, teamwork, and conflict resolution in safe environments (Hwang et al., 2023).

The Growing Role of Soft Skills

Soft skills are no longer secondary; they are essential. Employers consistently rank communication, problem-solving, and adaptability as top skills for the future. These skills complement technical abilities and allow workers to succeed in diverse contexts. AI can help cultivate soft skills through interactive training. Intelligent tutoring systems guide learners through problem-solving exercises. Virtual agents provide feedback on tone, clarity, and empathy in communication. Gamified platforms foster collaboration among learners, building trust and resilience. Research shows that AI-driven training improves self-awareness and team effectiveness (Grosseck & Holotescu, 2022). Yet, soft skills cannot be learned through technology alone. Human interaction, mentorship, and experiential learning remain central. AI should serve as a supplement, not a substitute, in developing these essential abilities. The challenge is to integrate AI tools into broader pedagogical frameworks that preserve human connection.

Building Resilience and Adaptability

Resilience is increasingly important in uncertain labor markets. Workers face rapid job changes, technological disruptions, and global crises. Preparing learners means equipping them with the ability to adapt, recover, and reinvent themselves. AI can contribute by offering personalized career guidance. Platforms powered by AI analyze labor market trends and recommend upskilling opportunities. For example, Singapore's SkillsFuture program uses AI analytics to connect learners with relevant training (Tan & Chua, 2021). Such systems encourage proactive learning and workforce adaptability. Adaptability also requires a growth mindset. Learners must view skills as flexible and expandable. AI platforms reinforce this mindset by providing constant feedback and incremental challenges. Research shows that adaptive feedback boosts learner confidence and motivation (OECD, 2023). Over time, this builds resilience and prepares individuals for multiple career transitions.

Equity in Workforce Preparation

Not all learners have equal access to AI-enhanced education. Digital divides remain stark, especially in low- and middle-income countries. Without inclusive strategies, AI may worsen inequalities in workforce readiness. UNESCO (2021) warns that marginalized groups risk exclusion from AI-driven opportunities. Ensuring equity requires infrastructure investment, affordable access, and open-source AI platforms. Policymakers must prioritize inclusive design to reach underserved learners. AI tools should also account for linguistic diversity, cultural contexts, and local workforce needs. For example, India's AI-enabled education initiatives now provide content in regional languages, expanding access to rural learners. Equity also extends to gender inclusion. Women often face barriers to entering technology-driven jobs. AI-powered mentorship platforms and flexible learning systems can help address these gaps. Research shows that women participating in AI-driven training programs report improved confidence and employability (Vuorikari et al., 2025).

Policy and Institutional Roles

Preparing learners for the evolving workforce is not solely the responsibility of schools. It requires coordinated efforts across governments, employers, and civil society. Policy frameworks must define new foundational competencies and provide funding for lifelong learning systems. Governments should establish national AI and workforce strategies. These should align education with labor market demands. For example, Finland integrates AI-driven learning into curricula while promoting transversal skills like problem-solving and digital citizenship (Vuorikari et al., 2025). Such approaches provide a blueprint for holistic workforce preparation. Employers must also play a proactive role. They should partner with educators to design AI-driven reskilling programs. IBM's Talent Framework, for example, uses AI to map workforce skills and recommend training (OECD, 2023). Companies that invest in AI-enabled learning not only strengthen employees but also future-proof their organizations.

Case Studies

Case 1: Singapore's SkillsFuture

SkillsFuture provides citizens with access to AI-driven training platforms. AI analytics match individual profiles with labor market opportunities. Learners receive personalized course recommendations based on skill gaps. Research shows that SkillsFuture improves career adaptability and workforce readiness (Tan & Chua, 2021).

Case 2: Finland's National AI Curriculum

Finland has redefined foundational learning to include AI awareness and coding from early grades. It emphasizes transversal competencies that apply across sectors. This approach ensures that learners develop critical thinking and adaptability alongside technical skills (Vuorikari et al., 2025).

Case 3: Corporate Reskilling with AI at IBM

IBM uses AI platforms to analyze future skill needs. Employees receive targeted training paths tailored to their job roles. The program reduces skill mismatches and prepares workers for digital transformation (OECD, 2023).

Ethical Considerations in Workforce Preparation

Ethics must guide AI integration in workforce preparation. Privacy, bias, and accountability remain pressing concerns. Workforce platforms collect sensitive personal and career data. Without proper safeguards, such data may be misused. UNESCO (2021) urges governments to enforce strict protections in AI workforce systems. Bias is another major risk. AI recruitment and training tools may favor certain groups over others. Transparent algorithms and inclusive datasets are needed to ensure fairness. Holmes et al. (2022) argue that ethical AI design is essential for equitable workforce participation. Finally, reliance on AI should not undermine human judgment. Workers must retain the ability to question and challenge AI outputs. Preparing learners means teaching them to balance AI recommendations with human values and critical thinking.

Future Directions

The future of workforce preparation will see deeper integration of AI, extended reality (XR), and immersive platforms. AI-powered virtual reality simulations will allow learners to practice workplace scenarios safely. Personalized AI mentors will guide learners through career transitions. Global AI learning commons may provide open access to workforce training resources worldwide. Yet, the success of these innovations depends on inclusion, ethics, and adaptability. The future workforce must not only master technology but also maintain human values. Preparing learners means equipping them with both technical fluency and ethical resilience. Preparing learners for the evolving workforce requires a radical rethinking of foundational learning. AI-driven tools offer opportunities to personalize learning, cultivate soft skills, and guide lifelong adaptation. Human-AI collaboration, resilience, and socio-emotional intelligence are central competencies. However, challenges remain. Equity, bias, and privacy must be addressed. Teachers, policymakers, and employers must collaborate to ensure ethical and inclusive systems. With careful design, AI can prepare learners not only for current jobs but also for careers that do not yet exist. The evolving workforce is dynamic, uncertain, and hybrid. By redefining preparation around adaptability, AI literacy, and human-centered skills, learners can thrive in this changing landscape. Education systems that embrace these priorities will ensure their citizens remain competitive, resilient, and future-ready.

CHALLENGES AND ETHICAL CONSIDERATIONS

Artificial intelligence promises new opportunities in education and workforce preparation. Yet, its use also brings serious challenges and ethical risks. These must be carefully addressed to ensure responsible adoption. Without safeguards, AI may widen inequality, compromise privacy, or erode trust. Ethical reflection is therefore as important as technological innovation. Unequal Access and the Digital Divide The first challenge is unequal access to AI tools. Many learners lack devices, connectivity, or digital skills. This gap exists between countries and within them. Rural learners often face weak internet infrastructure. Low-income families cannot afford AI-enabled learning platforms. A 2022 UNESCO report noted that without inclusive policies, AI may deepen educational inequalities (UNESCO, 2021). The digital divide is not only about access. It also concerns the quality of usage. Some learners only use AI for basic tasks. Others access advanced adaptive systems that build higher-order skills. This creates stratification in learning opportunities. If left unchecked, AI could reproduce existing social and economic hierarchies. Governments must therefore expand infrastructure and provide public digital resources. Data Privacy and Security AI systems rely heavily on personal data. They collect test scores, behavior logs, voice recordings, and even facial expressions. Such data can improve personalization but also raise privacy concerns. Misuse of learner data could harm trust in education systems. A 2023 OECD study warned that weak safeguards expose students to surveillance risks (OECD, 2023). Security is another pressing issue. Large datasets are targets for cyberattacks. Breaches may expose sensitive information about children or vulnerable learners. Many countries still lack strong regulations governing educational AI. Inconsistent standards make cross-border data flows even riskier. The European Union's AI Act (2023) is among the first attempts to set global benchmarks. Still, adoption is uneven and compliance costs may disadvantage poorer countries.

Algorithmic Bias and Fairness Bias is a critical ethical concern in AI-driven education. Algorithms learn from historical data that may reflect social inequalities. If unchecked, they reproduce and amplify these patterns. For example, predictive analytics may steer certain groups away from advanced courses. Biased AI systems can reinforce stereotypes in gender, race, or language ability (Holmes et al., 2022). Bias also appears in automated grading systems. Studies show that essay scoring algorithms sometimes favor specific dialects or writing styles. Such unfairness can undermine learner confidence and institutional credibility. Addressing bias requires transparency in datasets and algorithm design. Diverse teams must build and audit AI systems to avoid narrow perspectives.

Teacher Roles and Professional Autonomy Another challenge is the shifting role of teachers. AI systems can automate assessments, tutoring, and lesson planning.

While this reduces workload, it may also reduce teacher autonomy. Over-reliance on AI can deskill educators by making them dependent on automated suggestions. A 2022 review emphasized that AI should support, not replace, professional judgment (Luckin, 2022). Teachers also face pressure to use systems they do not fully understand. Limited training creates gaps in confidence and critical evaluation. If teachers cannot question AI recommendations, accountability is weakened. Policymakers must therefore invest in professional development. Teachers need both technical knowledge and ethical frameworks for responsible AI use. Transparency and Explainability AI systems often function as "black boxes." Their decision-making processes are complex and opaque. Learners, parents, and educators may not understand why certain recommendations appear. Lack of explainability undermines trust and limits accountability. In education, where decisions affect human development, transparency is crucial. Explainable AI (XAI) is an emerging field that seeks to solve this issue. XAI methods make algorithmic decisions more understandable to non-specialists. However, trade-offs exist between explainability and performance. Highly transparent models may not always deliver the best accuracy. Balancing interpretability with effectiveness remains an ongoing ethical dilemma (Amershi et al., 2022). Over-Surveillance and Autonomy Risks AI in classrooms often involves monitoring learners. Tools track eye movements, attention spans, and participation rates. These systems promise real-time insights but risk creating surveillance cultures. Over-surveillance can reduce learner autonomy and creativity. Students may adapt behavior to please algorithms rather than to explore knowledge. The psychological effects of continuous monitoring are concerning. Learners may feel anxiety or pressure knowing they are constantly observed. A 2023 study on EdTech surveillance warned of harmful effects on well-being (Williamson & Hogan, 2023). Safeguards must balance useful analytics with human dignity. Education should empower learners, not condition them through constant observation. Global Inequality in Workforce Preparation AI may deepen inequalities in global labor markets. Wealthy nations can adopt advanced AI training systems quickly. Developing countries face barriers of cost, infrastructure, and expertise. As a result, their workers risk falling behind in skills acquisition. This creates uneven opportunities in the global workforce. If unchecked, such disparities may reinforce dependency structures. High-income nations may dominate high-tech sectors while others remain in low-skill industries. The International Labour Organization (2023) emphasized the need for inclusive AI capacity-building. Global cooperation is essential to avoid a digital form of colonialism in workforce preparation. Ethical Use of AI in Assessment AI-driven assessment is growing rapidly. Automated essay grading, proctoring systems, and adaptive testing are now common. While efficient, they raise major ethical issues. Automated proctoring often relies on facial recognition. This has been shown to misidentify learners with darker skin tones (Fazelpour et al., 2022). Such errors can unfairly penalize marginalized groups. Moreover, constant camera monitoring intrudes into private spaces during remote assessments. These practices risk violating privacy and human rights. Ethical frameworks must set boundaries for how far AI can intrude into learner environments. Alternative models of assessment that combine AI with human review may offer safer paths. Psychological and Social Concerns The use of AI in education may also affect identity and motivation. Over-personalization could narrow learning experiences. If systems only present "safe" or predicted pathways, learners may lose exposure to diverse perspectives. This risks reducing creativity and critical exploration. Dependence on AI tutors can also affect self-reliance. Learners may become accustomed to constant hints and feedback. This could weaken resilience in facing complex or ambiguous problems. A 2022 review on learning psychology noted that human struggle is essential for deep learning. Designers must ensure AI encourages productive struggle, not dependency. Regulatory and Governance Challenges AI governance in education is still emerging. National frameworks vary widely, from proactive regulation to minimal oversight. International coordination remains weak. This creates uncertainty for institutions, educators, and EdTech companies. Without clear governance, risks of misuse remain high. The EU's AI Act (2023) marks a significant development. It classifies educational AI as "high-risk" and subjects it to strict requirements. However, not all regions have the capacity to enforce such frameworks. Developing countries may lack the resources to regulate effectively. This creates uneven ethical standards worldwide. Global organizations like UNESCO and OECD call for harmonized approaches. Still, balancing innovation with regulation is politically sensitive.

Environmental Impact of AI in Education Another overlooked challenge is the environmental cost of AI. Training large models consumes vast amounts of energy. Expanding AI-driven education globally may increase carbon footprints. training a single large AI model can emit more carbon than several cars over their lifetimes. Education systems must weigh these costs carefully. Sustainable AI practices are necessary to align with climate goals. Green AI initiatives, such as energy-efficient algorithms and renewable-powered data centers, are emerging solutions. Still, awareness of environmental impacts in education policy remains low. Ethical adoption must therefore include sustainability considerations.

Balancing Human and Machine Roles Perhaps the biggest ethical question is balance. What should humans do, and what should machines handle? If AI takes over foundational teaching, what becomes of the teacher-learner relationship? Education is not just about information transfer. It is also about mentorship, empathy, and moral guidance. Machines cannot fully replicate these dimensions. The future of AI in learning requires hybrid models. Machines can enhance efficiency, personalization, and access. Humans provide context, empathy, and ethical judgment. Ethical frameworks must preserve the centrality of human relationships in education.

Without this balance, AI risks reducing education to a technical process. AI offers immense potential for transforming foundational learning and preparing workers. Yet, ethical and practical challenges are significant. Unequal access, bias, privacy, surveillance, and governance gaps cannot be ignored. Psychological, environmental, and global equity concerns further complicate adoption. Addressing these issues requires transparent governance, inclusive policies, and sustainable practices. It also requires keeping human dignity and relationships at the core of education. AI should support, not replace, human capacities. Only then can it strengthen learning without undermining justice, equity, and trust.

Table 3. Key ethical challenges of AI in foundational learning

Ethical Challenge	Description	Risks for Learners/ Teachers	Possible Mitigation Strategies
Digital Divide	Unequal access to AI tools	Inequality, exclusion	Infrastructure investment, subsidies
Data Privacy	Collection of sensitive learner data	Misuse, breaches, surveillance	Strong laws, encryption, informed consent
Algorithmic Bias	Bias in training datasets	Stereotyping, unfair assessment	Diverse datasets, fairness audits
Teacher Autonomy	Over-reliance on AI recommendations	Deskilling, reduced judgment	Professional training, human oversight
Transparency	Black-box decision-making	Lack of trust, limited accountability	Explainable AI methods, documentation
Over-Surveillance	Excessive monitoring in classrooms	Stress, reduced creativity	Proportional monitoring, ethical limits
Workforce Inequality	Unequal global adoption	Skills gaps between regions	Global cooperation, shared resources
Environmental Impact	High energy use of AI systems	Carbon footprint, unsustainability	Green AI practices, renewable energy

POLICY AND PRACTICE IMPLICATIONS

Artificial intelligence in education is no longer experimental. It is rapidly shaping how learners engage with foundational skills. Policymakers and practitioners must act thoughtfully in this space. AI tools can close learning gaps if deployed inclusively. Yet they can also deepen inequality without strong guidance. Policy and practice must therefore move together in balance.

Building Robust Policy Frameworks

Governments need clear strategies for AI in education. Policies must define standards for access, equity, and accountability. Countries like Singapore and Finland already experiment with frameworks. They set standards for ethical use in classrooms (OECD, 2022). Other nations must design context-specific but globally aligned policies. Without such direction, private companies dominate educational landscapes. Frameworks should also include AI literacy for all citizens. AI is becoming as fundamental as digital literacy. Curricula must embed this literacy from early school stages. Learners should understand both benefits and limitations of AI. This ensures they remain critical users, not passive consumers.

Ensuring Equity and Access AI deployment must not reproduce old digital divides. We already see gaps between urban and rural learners. Students in under-resourced schools often lack digital devices. If AI adoption accelerates without support, gaps will widen.

Policymakers must invest in digital infrastructure. Broadband connectivity should be seen as a right. Affordability programs for devices and platforms are also necessary. Public-private partnerships may help reduce infrastructure costs. International cooperation can also support global equity. Organizations like UNESCO push for inclusive digital policies (UNESCO, 2023). Developing regions must receive targeted financial and technical support. Otherwise, AI in education will become a privilege, not a right.

Protecting Data Privacy and Security

AI systems rely on vast amounts of learner data. These include test scores, behavioural patterns, and even emotions. Such data are sensitive and demand strong protection. Regulations must define who collects, stores, and uses data. The European Union's AI Act is a strong example (EU, 2023). Countries without strong data protection laws remain vulnerable. Private companies may exploit learner data for commercial gain. This risks breaching trust between schools and communities. Clear legal frameworks and technical safeguards are non-negotiable here. In practice, schools need training in data governance. Teachers and administrators must understand consent requirements. They must also be able to audit AI decisions. Transparency should be standard, not optional, in AI systems.

Supporting Teachers as Human Anchors

AI should not replace teachers but empower them instead. However, many teachers fear replacement or de-skilling. Policy must emphasize teachers' role as ethical anchors. AI can personalize practice, but teachers provide human context. This balance sustains both efficiency and empathy in education. Professional development is essential here. Teachers must be trained in AI tools and ethics. Governments should fund AI literacy courses for educators. Collaborative communities of practice can share use cases. This helps teachers remain confident as technology evolves. Teachers must also retain decision-making authority. AI systems should suggest, not dictate, pedagogical actions. Guidelines should ensure teachers stay in the driver's seat. This protects autonomy while enhancing professional judgment.

Embedding Ethical AI Practices

Ethics cannot be an afterthought in educational AI. Bias in AI systems can perpetuate stereotypes or exclusion. Algorithms may misinterpret cultural or linguistic differences. This creates unfair outcomes in assessments or recommendations. Policies should require fairness audits of educational AI systems. Developers must test for cultural and linguistic inclusivity. Procurement processes should demand transparency from technology vendors. Governments can even establish certification systems for ethical AI. In practice, ethics training must extend beyond developers. Educators and administrators need awareness of algorithmic bias. They must learn how to question AI decisions. Such critical practice will foster trust in AI systems.

Bridging Education and Workforce Policies

Education policy cannot sit apart from workforce planning. AI is transforming labor markets across all industries. Learners need future-ready skills, not outdated knowledge. This requires policy alignment between education and labor ministries. Countries like India now experiment with skills frameworks. They integrate AI-driven platforms for vocational training and reskilling. Such initiatives prepare citizens for rapidly evolving job demands. Other nations should create similar lifelong learning pathways. In practice, schools must embed career exploration early. AI-driven career tools can support personalized pathways. Learners should see how skills link to real futures. This motivates them while reducing school-to-work mismatches.

Strengthening International Collaboration

AI in education transcends national boundaries. Global cooperation is needed to share knowledge and risks. Institutions like OECD and UNESCO already convene global discussions. Cross-border partnerships can align standards and reduce duplication. Shared repositories of best practices can accelerate adoption. This prevents every nation from reinventing solutions. Global South voices must also be included in these forums. Without them, AI in education risks reflecting only elite perspectives. In practice, universities and ministries should form regional networks. South-South collaboration can create affordable and culturally relevant tools. Collaborative funding pools can also reduce financial burdens.

Promoting Sustainable AI in Education

AI systems demand high computational energy. Training large models can produce significant carbon emissions. This raises questions about sustainability in education technology. Policymakers must consider environmental impacts in AI adoption. Green AI practices should be incentivized and mainstreamed. Developers must optimize code and adopt renewable energy sources. Educational institutions could prioritize low-carbon AI applications. In practice, schools can integrate sustainability into AI literacy. Learners should understand the environmental cost of algorithms. This awareness fosters responsible digital citizenship for the future.

Implementation Roadmap for Policymakers and Practitioners

To operationalise these ideas, a roadmap is useful.
Short-term (1-2 years):

- Draft AI in education policies.
- Provide teacher training in AI literacy.
- Launch pilot projects with equity safeguards.

Medium-term (3-5 years):

- Integrate AI ethics into curricula.
- Scale national digital infrastructure investments.
- Expand public-private innovation labs in education.

Long-term (5-10 years):

- Establish global AI-in-education governance bodies.
- Align AI education policy with climate sustainability.
- Embed lifelong learning systems across all education levels.

Policy and practice together will shape AI's role. Without alignment, education risks deepening divides and mistrust. But with foresight, AI can drive inclusive transformation. Learners will gain foundational skills for a dynamic workforce.

Teachers will remain ethical guides in an AI-driven age. Societies will benefit from sustainable and equitable education systems. The moment for action is now. AI's promise for education is real but fragile. Policymakers and practitioners must seize this opportunity responsibly.

FUTURE DIRECTIONS

Artificial intelligence in education is still at an early stage. Its potential for reshaping foundational learning is immense. Yet much work remains to guide its responsible future. This section highlights the directions policymakers, educators, and researchers must pursue. The focus is on preparing systems for global shifts. AI will shape not only classrooms but also future societies.

AI as a Partner in Lifelong Learning

Future education will not stop at graduation. Workforces will demand continual skill adaptation and learning renewal. AI can serve as a lifelong learning companion. Future platforms may track skills across entire lifespans. They will suggest reskilling opportunities aligned with labor markets. Such systems could integrate school, work, and informal learning records. This would make education more fluid and personalized over decades. Governments may even issue "learning passports" supported by AI analytics. These passports would document competencies across formal and informal contexts. They could help workers navigate multiple careers with confidence (ILO, 2023).

Evolution of Personalized and Adaptive Learning

AI personalization is still limited in current classrooms. Systems often adapt to pace but not deeper learner needs. Future directions point to multimodal personalization. AI may combine voice, gesture, and emotional cues for learning. It will detect frustration or motivation in real time. Responses will be tailored not only to knowledge but emotion. Such systems could close persistent achievement gaps. They would offer struggling learners targeted yet supportive interventions. This moves education beyond uniform models to truly adaptive pathways.

Growth of Hybrid Human: AI Teaching Models

AI will not replace teachers, but roles will change. Future classrooms may feature AI co-teachers alongside human educators. AI may handle routine grading, simulations, or language support. Teachers will focus on mentoring, creativity, and ethical guidance. Hybrid roles will demand new teacher preparation models. Training programs must embed AI fluency and critical pedagogy. Teachers must learn to supervise, question, and complement AI partners. Such partnerships could redefine the teacher's authority. Authority will rest less on knowledge delivery, more on judgment. Teachers will remain the moral compass in data-rich classrooms.

Expanding Global Collaboration in AI Education

AI in education cannot be designed in isolation. Future directions must emphasize global cooperation and knowledge exchange. International frameworks will be essential to standardize ethical practices. UNESCO and OECD already coordinate global policy dialogues (UNESCO, 2021). Future efforts may involve global data trusts for education. These would pool anonymized learning data across multiple countries. The aim would be shared insights while protecting local autonomy. Such collaboration can reduce inequality between regions. It can also accelerate culturally relevant AI tools worldwide. The Global South must be included as equal partners.

Integration of AI with Emerging Technologies

AI will not evolve alone in future classrooms. It will intersect with other transformative technologies. Virtual and augmented reality will merge with AI tutors. Learners could enter immersive environments guided by AI companions. Such spaces may simulate labs, workplaces, or historical contexts. Blockchain may secure learner records across borders. Combined with AI, it will authenticate global learning passports. This ensures trust as learners move between economies. The Internet of Things may link classrooms with workplaces. AI could analyze data from sensors and devices. This will connect learning directly to industry practices (Zawacki-Richter et al., 2019).

Rising Focus on AI Ethics and Regulation

Future AI education will demand stronger ethical safeguards. The European Union AI Act set early precedents (EU, 2023). Other regions are drafting policies to protect learners' rights. Future systems must embed explainability into their design. Learners and teachers should understand why AI recommends actions. Without transparency, trust in education systems will erode quickly. Ethical audits may become a global requirement. Vendors will need certification to supply AI to schools. Such measures protect learners from bias and exploitation.

Preparing for Workforce Shifts Beyond 2030

AI will reshape jobs faster than schools can adapt. Automation may replace repetitive work but create new industries. Education must anticipate workforce shifts well before they arrive. Future learning must stress "human advantage skills." These include creativity, empathy, collaboration, and ethical reasoning. AI excels in pattern recognition but not deep human values. Policymakers must align curricula with future labor projections. AI forecasting tools can predict skill demand more precisely. This allows nations to align education with growth industries (World Economic Forum, 2023).

Addressing Environmental Sustainability

AI education will also face sustainability challenges. Training large AI models consumes huge amounts of energy. This impact cannot be ignored as schools adopt AI. Future research will explore "Green AI" strategies. These involve optimizing algorithms to reduce energy costs. They also require greater reliance on renewable power sources. Schools may even teach sustainability through their AI choices. This would model ethical responsibility for future generations.

Empowering Learners as Co-Creators

Future directions will shift learners from consumers to co-creators. AI can empower students to design, test, and critique tools. This turns AI literacy into active civic participation. Learners may contribute data to open-source AI projects. They may help design local language models for schools. Such participation builds ownership and strengthens democratic education values (Holmes et al., 2022).

Research Gaps for the Next Decade

Several gaps remain for scholars and policymakers.

- **Longitudinal studies:** How does AI affect learning across decades?
- **Cross-cultural evidence:** Does AI adapt equally across diverse contexts?
- **Equity analysis:** Who benefits most and least from AI adoption?
- **Teacher agency:** How can autonomy be preserved in hybrid models?
- **Sustainability:** What is the true carbon cost of education AI?

Future research must address these gaps collaboratively. Evidence should guide policies rather than technology hype. AI's future in foundational learning is full of possibility. It can build inclusive systems, resilient workforces, and ethical societies. But this future will not happen automatically. It requires careful design, global co-operation, and strong ethical grounding. The next decade will be decisive. Decisions made now will shape generations of learners. If guided wisely, AI can transform learning for the better. It can prepare humanity for challenges and opportunities beyond imagination.

Table 4. Emerging future directions of AI in education

Future Direction	Key Opportunities	Key Risks	Policy Needs
Lifelong Learning	Continuous reskilling opportunities	Inequality in access	National lifelong learning frameworks
Hybrid Teaching	Efficiency + empathy balance	Teacher deskilling	Teacher training & role clarity
Global Collaboration	Shared resources & best practices	Unequal voice representation	Inclusive global governance
Tech Integration	Immersive learning with VR/IoT	Data security threats	Cross-technology regulation
Green AI	Sustainable learning innovation	High energy use	Incentives for green development

CONCLUSION

Artificial intelligence is reshaping education in profound ways. Its impact is visible in classrooms, workplaces, and policy agendas. Foundational learning, once fixed and uniform, is becoming dynamic. AI tools can tailor pathways, support teachers, and extend opportunities. They can also prepare learners for uncertain global labor markets. This chapter has explored these transformations in depth. It began by redefining foundational learning in the AI era. The discussion showed how AI expands learning beyond literacy. It emphasized digital, emotional, and ethical competencies as essential foundations. These foundations are critical for adapting to future disruptions. The analysis then examined preparation for evolving workforces. AI can forecast skill demands and match learners with opportunities. It can personalize training, accelerate reskilling, and connect learners globally. Yet workforce preparation is not just technical. Human skills like empathy, creativity, and collaboration remain essential. AI highlights, rather than replaces, the value of human judgment. The chapter also addressed ethical and governance concerns.

AI is not neutral, and risks remain significant. Bias, surveillance, inequity, and environmental costs pose real challenges. Education must adopt strong ethical frameworks and regulatory safeguards. Teachers, policymakers, and learners must participate in shaping these systems. Without inclusive design, AI could deepen global inequalities. Policy and practice implications were also highlighted. Governments must invest in digital infrastructure and equitable access. Teacher education must evolve to embed AI fluency. Curricula must integrate AI literacy as a new foundational skill. Public–private partnerships can scale innovations while ensuring ethical standards. International frameworks can guide alignment across borders and regions. The chapter then outlined future directions for AI education. AI will become a lifelong learning companion across careers. It will integrate with VR, IoT, and blockchain technologies. Hybrid human- AI teaching models will reshape classroom dynamics. Global collaboration will accelerate equitable innovation. Green AI will address environmental sustainability. Learners will evolve from consumers to co-creators of knowledge. These directions offer a roadmap for inclusive transformation. The conclusion must also highlight a deeper tension. AI promises efficiency, personalization, and global reach. But education is not only about efficiency. It is also about identity, values, and civic purpose. Future systems must safeguard this human dimension. AI should amplify, not erode, the meaning of learning. There are reasons for both optimism and caution. Optimism stems from AI's potential to democratize learning. It can reach marginalized learners excluded by traditional systems. It can reduce barriers of distance, language, and disability. AI could become the most inclusive educational tool in history. Caution arises from risks of misuse and inequity. Data privacy breaches could expose vulnerable learners. Algorithmic bias could reproduce structural discrimination at scale. Automation could deepen workforce inequality between nations. If left unchecked, AI may concentrate power in few hands. This dual reality makes governance the central issue ahead. Another critical insight is the enduring role of teachers. No system, however advanced, can replace human mentorship. Teachers provide empathy, context, and ethical guidance. They model citizenship and social responsibility. In the AI era, teachers are even more vital. They must be empowered as guides, not displaced as functionaries. The role of learners is also changing rapidly. Passive consumption no longer defines effective education. Learners must become active participants in co-creating knowledge. They must cultivate skills AI cannot replicate easily. These include curiosity, adaptability, and moral imagination. Education must empower learners as innovators and responsible citizens. The workforce implications cannot be ignored. Automation will replace some roles but create many others. Preparing learners means anticipating these transitions with foresight. It requires constant dialogue between education, industry, and government. Curricula must evolve in rhythm with labor markets. Lifelong learning must be institutionalized as a social right. Environmental sustainability adds another important dimension. AI education cannot succeed if it worsens climate crises. Green AI practices must become central to design. Schools must teach sustainability by modeling responsible AI use. This ensures education contributes to resilience, not degradation. Ultimately, AI's future in foundational learning is about balance. It is about balancing innovation with ethics. It is about balancing global standards with local cultures. It is about balancing human agency with machine assistance. This balance will determine whether AI strengthens or weakens society. The stakes are generational. The learners of today will enter AI-shaped workplaces. They will also inherit societies transformed by AI decisions. Education must therefore prepare them for agency and responsibility. It must cultivate technical fluency, human empathy, and civic awareness. These capacities define resilience in an uncertain global future. Collaboration will be decisive in achieving this vision. Governments, educators, industry, and civil society must act together. No single sector can govern AI in education alone. Shared standards, pooled resources, and inclusive dialogues are essential. Without collaboration, solutions will remain fragmented and uneven. The path forward demands courage and creativity. It demands reimagining education as more than schooling. It demands systems that prepare citizens for lifelong adaptation. It demands policies that see AI as a public good. It demands ethics that prioritize learners over markets. This chapter has offered a comprehensive exploration. It examined opportunities, challenges, implications, and future directions. It argued that AI must serve as a partner. Not as a replacement for teachers or human values. Not as a tool for profit over equity. But as an amplifier of human learning potential. In closing, the vision is both clear and urgent. AI can transform foundational learning for global good. It can prepare learners for evolving economies and societies. It can make education more inclusive, adaptive, and lifelong. But only if guided with wisdom and care. The future of learning is a choice we must shape.

REFERENCES

Fazelpour, S., Lipton, Z. C., & Danks, D. (2022). Algorithmic fairness and the situated dynamics of justice. *Canadian Journal of Philosophy*, *52*(1), 44–60. DOI: 10.1017/can.2021.24

Grosseck, G., Bran, R. A., & îru, L. G. (2023). Digital assessment: A survey of Romanian higher education teachers' practices and needs. *Education Sciences*, *14*(1), 32. DOI: 10.3390/educsci14010032

Holmes, W., Porayska-Pomsta, K., & Holstein, K. (2022). Ethics and the use of AI in education. *AI & Society*, *37*(3), 927–940. DOI: 10.1007/s00146-021-01168-8

Hwang, G. J., & Chen, N. S. (2023). Exploring the potential of generative artificial intelligence in education: Applications, challenges, and future research directions. *Journal of Educational Technology & Society*, *26*(2).

Long, D., Blunt, T., & Magerko, B. (2021). Co-designing AI literacy exhibits for informal learning spaces. Proceedings of the ACM on Human-Computer Interaction, 5(CSCW2), Article 372. DOI: 10.1145/3476034

Luckin, R. (2022). *Machine learning and human intelligence: The future of education in the 21st century*. UCL Press.

OECD. (2023). AI and the future of skills, volume 1: Capabilities and assessments. OECD Publishing.

Tan, O. S., & Chua, J. J. E. (2021). Science, social responsibility, and education: The experience of Singapore during the COVID-19 pandemic. In *Primary and secondary education during Covid-19: Disruptions to educational opportunity during a pandemic* (pp. 263–281). Springer International Publishing.

UNESCO. (2021). *AI and education: Guidance for policymakers*. UNESCO Publishing.

Vuorikari, R., Pokropek, A., & Muñoz, J. C. (2025). Enhancing digital skills assessment: Introducing compact tools for measuring digital competence. Technology, Knowledge and Learning, 1-28.

World Economic Forum. (2023). Future of Jobs Report 2023. Geneva: WEF.

Zawacki-Richter, O., Marín, V. I., Bond, M., & Gouverneur, F. (2019). Systematic review of research on artificial intelligence applications in higher education–where are the educators? *International Journal of Educational Technology in Higher Education*, *16*(1), 39. DOI: 10.1186/s41239-019-0171-0

Chapter 2
AI-Driven Human Capital Management for Academic and Research Advancement

O. Bhaskaru
http://orcid.org/0000-0001-6495-3327
Vignan's Foundation for Science, Technology, and Research, India

K. Lalitha
http://orcid.org/0009-0004-9735-7205
Santhiram Engineering College, India

EXECUTIVE SUMMARY

Artificial Intelligence (AI) is transforming human capital management in academic and research environments. This chapter examines how AI is integrated into talent acquisition, development, performance evaluation, and workforce planning in higher education and research organizations. AI technologies reshape roles, automate tasks, and provide predictive insights that influence decision-making. The chapter synthesizes academic literature and case studies to highlight patterns in AI adoption. It also presents conceptual models for future work, integrating perspectives from organizational behavior, data ethics, and machine learning interpretability. It emphasizes the role of academic institutions in shaping ethical AI use in human capital decisions .By evaluating methodological trends and outlining future research directions, this chapter serves as a roadmap for academics and students aiming to contribute to AI-driven human capital management and informs curriculum design that reflects emerging competencies in AI and HR management.

DOI: 10.4018/979-8-3373-3867-5.ch002

INTRODUCTION

In the era of digital transformation, Artificial Intelligence (AI) has become a transformative force across industries, including academia and research. While AI's integration into manufacturing, healthcare, and finance is well-documented, its role in reshaping human capital management (HCM) within academic institutions is an emerging area of study. Academic environments, often characterized by complex human interactions, decentralized governance, and the pursuit of intellectual excellence, face unique challenges in adopting AI-driven solutions.

Academic institutions are often seen as hubs of innovation, and with the increasing need to maintain competitiveness, improve research output, and enhance teaching effectiveness, the application of AI has gained significant attention. The introduction of AI has not only the potential to reduce administrative workloads but also to bring about systematic improvements in faculty recruitment, researcher performance assessments, and institutional workforce planning. From automating faculty recruitment and assessing researcher performance to predicting institutional workforce trends, AI offers promising tools that can augment decision-making, increase operational efficiency, and promote equity in academia.

AI's potential to drive personalized learning and career development within academic settings is also crucial in the transformation of traditional educational structures. AI technologies are beginning to foster environments that are not just automated but more adaptive to the needs of students, researchers, and faculty alike. This chapter explores how AI is revolutionizing human capital systems within academic and research settings, setting the stage for a deeper examination of literature, theoretical foundations, empirical studies, conceptual models, and strategic implications that align with emerging trends in academic human capital management.

The Shift Toward AI-Driven Human Capital Systems

The evolution of human capital systems from manual, process-driven mechanisms to intelligent, automated solutions reflects the broader digitalization wave in higher education. AI technologies, including machine learning, natural language processing (NLP), and computer vision, are being integrated into faculty recruitment, academic performance evaluations, and strategic workforce planning. Traditionally, tasks like applicant screening, tenure evaluations, and faculty development were manually conducted by HR departments and academic committees. With AI, these tasks are increasingly data-driven and automated, enabling faster decision-making, reduced human bias, and enhanced transparency (Kaplan & Haenlein, 2019).

In the context of research institutions, where knowledge production is central to institutional success, AI is being used to analyze publication metrics, assess grant performance, and predict future academic productivity. AI-based systems are also supporting personalized professional development, helping faculty members navigate career pathways based on historical data and predictive insights. For instance, recommendation engines can suggest research collaborations, training programs, or sabbatical opportunities tailored to individual profiles. Such systems are providing real-time insights into faculty performance, enabling institutions to focus on continuous improvement and long-term academic success.

AI also brings a new level of predictability and adaptability to workforce planning. Predictive algorithms, for example, can forecast faculty attrition and highlight emerging talent gaps within specific disciplines. This information is crucial for academic institutions to plan strategically for future hiring needs and institutional growth. This move toward AI-powered decision-making also makes academic institutions more agile, providing the ability to quickly adjust to shifting educational trends, student needs, and faculty strengths.

A growing number of universities have already begun leveraging AI to modernize their HR processes. For example, the University of Melbourne uses AI-based analytics for workforce planning and diversity tracking (University of Melbourne, 2021), while Carnegie Mellon University employs AI in faculty recruitment processes to improve transparency and reduce time-to-hire. These case studies illustrate the growing role of AI in academia, where institutions are not just adopting AI technologies for operational efficiencies but also embracing the broader cultural shift toward data-driven decision-making.

The increasing reliance on AI in academic HCM is also creating new avenues for collaboration among departments and external entities. As more institutions adopt AI, there is a growing need for interdisciplinary expertise that combines human resource management with technological knowledge, data science, and ethics. This shift is leading to the development of new professional roles and educational programs within academia, focused on the intersection of AI and human capital management. These trends highlight the need for institutions to embrace the AI-driven future and provide the necessary resources to both faculty and students in adapting to this rapidly evolving landscape.

Importance for Academic and Research Communities

AI adoption in academic HCM is not merely about administrative efficiency — it is about enhancing institutional agility and academic excellence. Human capital in academic settings includes faculty, researchers, postdoctoral fellows, administrative personnel, and adjunct professionals — all of whom contribute uniquely to the institution's intellectual output. AI helps in aligning individual competencies with institutional goals, whether it's increasing research output, improving teaching effectiveness, or advancing interdisciplinary collaboration (Davenport & Ronanki, 2018).

Moreover, academic institutions are not only users but also developers and critics of AI. This dual role means they must lead by example in ensuring ethical, transparent, and responsible deployment of AI in HCM. Issues such as algorithmic discrimination, explainability of AI decisions, and data privacy are particularly critical in environments that value fairness, inclusivity, and academic freedom (Floridi et al., 2018). AI-driven HCM solutions in academic environments must address these concerns in order to maintain the trust of the community and ensure that AI systems are aligned with the values of higher education.

AI also opens new frontiers in pedagogical and research management by identifying emerging areas of expertise, forecasting skills gaps, and tailoring faculty development programs accordingly. This can empower institutions to dynamically adjust their academic offerings, fostering an environment that is responsive to global trends and the evolving demands of students and faculty. Institutions embracing AI in HCM will be better positioned to compete globally, attract top talent, and support a culture of continuous learning and innovation.

For example, AI-based learning management systems (LMS) can analyze student data, predict performance outcomes, and recommend individualized study plans for students. Similarly, AI can be used to track faculty development, suggesting courses, conferences, and research projects that align with an individual's career goals and academic interests. The growing use of AI in these areas demonstrates its transformative potential, not only in administrative functions but also in fostering a more personalized and adaptive academic experience.

To deepen this exploration, the next chapter systematically maps relevant literature from the fields of AI, HRM, and business to frame the current research landscape.

LITERATURE MAPPING AND THEMATIC TRENDS

Artificial Intelligence (AI) has increasingly become central to the transformation of human capital management (HCM) in academic and research environments. As AI technologies evolve, their applications within academia have expanded, particularly in the management of talent acquisition, academic hiring, faculty development, and workforce analytics. This chapter maps key literature across several domains—business, AI, and human resource management (HRM) to highlight the intersections where AI applications are reshaping how academic institutions manage and develop their workforce. Thematic analysis reveals not only the scope and depth of AI integration but also the dominant patterns shaping current research and offering strategic implications for future implementation.

Contributions from Business, AI, and HR Fields

The convergence of AI with human capital strategies is heavily influenced by foundational research in business management, machine learning (ML), and human resource management (HRM). Early contributions from the business field focused on the application of predictive analytics for workforce optimization, offering frameworks for how AI could improve decision-making in talent acquisition and human capital planning (Davenport et al., 2010). As AI technologies evolved, HR scholars began exploring how AI could enable competency modeling, skill forecasting, and career progression strategies within organizations (Marler & Boudreau, 2017). These contributions laid the groundwork for AI's growing role in automating HR functions in both business and academic settings.

Recent literature has delved deeper into AI-specific issues such as algorithmic fairness, the use of natural language processing (NLP) in resume parsing, and the application of machine learning models for performance evaluation (Binns, 2018; Floridi et al., 2020). For example, NLP technologies have allowed academic institutions to automate the recruitment process by screening resumes and analyzing candidate qualifications, removing much of the manual work and subjectivity traditionally involved in these processes.

The role of AI within academic contexts has been explored extensively by business schools and research centers, which have conducted empirical studies focusing on AI-driven HR systems. These studies primarily concentrate on faculty recruitment and promotion frameworks, as well as research collaborations and the development of academic workforce strategies (Brynjolfsson & McAfee, 2017). AI tools are being employed to facilitate bibliometric mapping, citation analysis, and productivity forecasting, thereby assisting academic institutions in identifying high-performing researchers, research trends, and potential collaborations.

To understand the interdisciplinary basis for AI adoption in academic human capital management, it is important to examine contributions from three core domains: Business, Artificial Intelligence (AI), and Human Resource Management (HRM). Each field brings unique methodologies, theoretical perspectives, and practical tools that have shaped the evolution of AI applications in talent acquisition, workforce planning, and performance evaluation. Table 1 summarizes these key contributions, highlighting the themes addressed by scholars in each domain and their relevance to academic settings.

Table 1. Key contributions across domains

Field	Contribution Theme	Key Scholars/Studies
Business	Predictive HR analytics, talent planning	Davenport et al. (2010); Boudreau (2011)
AI	Algorithmic decision systems, NLP, ML models	Binns (2018); Floridi et al. (2020)
HRM	Workforce development, performance prediction	Marler & Boudreau (2017); Meijerink (2021)

AI Applications in Academic Human Resource Functions

AI has been increasingly adopted to support specific HR functions within academic institutions. The application of AI across these functions is aimed at improving operational efficiency, ensuring more data-driven decision-making, and supporting alignment with institutional goals. Several key AI-driven HR functions in academic settings include:

- **Automated Faculty Recruitment**: AI-based systems, including applicant tracking software (ATS), are increasingly used to streamline faculty recruitment. These systems leverage NLP and sentiment analysis to automatically screen CVs, match candidate profiles with institutional needs, and reduce bias in the shortlisting process (Upadhyay & Khandelwal, 2018). Some universities are also utilizing predictive models to assess whether faculty applicants align with the institution's current and future research agendas, helping to shape a more strategic approach to recruitment.
- **Academic Performance Evaluation**: AI is now playing a pivotal role in academic performance evaluations, where data from publications, grant funding, teaching evaluations, and student engagement are analyzed to generate comprehensive performance metrics. These metrics assist in tenure decisions, promotions, and faculty development plans (Teodorescu & Andrei, 2020). The use of AI in performance evaluation enables objective assessments, thus reducing potential bias in traditional review processes.
- **Learning and Development**: AI-powered adaptive learning systems are revolutionizing faculty development by providing personalized recommendations for career advancement. These systems analyze historical data from faculty members to recommend tailored opportunities such as MOOCs (Massive Open Online Courses), certifications, and interdisciplinary research avenues (Guszcza et al., 2017). This personalized approach enhances faculty mem-

bers' professional growth while aligning their development with the institution's academic objectives.

- **Workforce Planning**: AI tools are being employed for effective workforce planning within academic institutions. These tools help with faculty load balancing, retirement forecasting, and succession planning by modeling attrition risks and predicting future workforce needs (Tambe et al., 2019). AI-driven systems also assist institutions in identifying skill gaps and ensuring they have the right mix of faculty to meet future teaching and research demands.

Figure 1 illustrates the various ways AI technologies are being applied within academic human resource functions. It highlights how specific tools such as applicant tracking systems (ATS), natural language processing (NLP), and predictive analytics are used to streamline recruitment, automate performance evaluation, personalize faculty development, and support institutional workforce planning. This visual representation complements the textual discussion by categorizing and aligning AI capabilities with distinct HRM activities in academia.

Figure 1. AI applications in academic HR functions

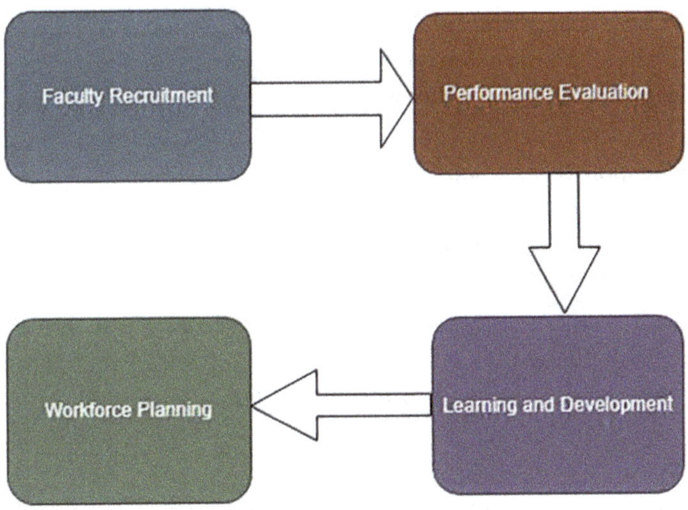

As shown in Figure 1, these AI applications are not only improving operational efficiency but also facilitating the alignment of human capital strategies with broader institutional objectives. By integrating AI into academic HR functions, institutions are able to make more informed, data-driven decisions that contribute to both short-term and long-term institutional success. Additionally, these AI applications provide valuable insights into areas such as faculty retention, talent development, and diversity management, ultimately enhancing the institution's ability to respond to changes in the academic landscape.

Thematic Trends in AI Integration in Academic HCM

A thematic analysis of the literature reveals several key trends and patterns shaping the current research landscape in AI-driven human capital management within academia:

- **Data-Driven Decision Making**: The primary theme emerging from the literature is the growing reliance on data-driven decision-making in academic HR. AI systems are increasingly being used to aggregate and analyze vast amounts of data, offering institutions insights that would be otherwise difficult to uncover through traditional methods. This trend emphasizes the move from intuition-based to evidence-based decision-making in faculty recruitment, performance evaluation, and workforce planning.
- **Ethical Concerns and Algorithmic Fairness**: As AI applications become more pervasive in academic settings, concerns about algorithmic fairness, transparency, and ethics are becoming more pronounced. Researchers are increasingly examining how AI systems can be designed to minimize bias and ensure fair outcomes, particularly in faculty recruitment and promotion decisions. Institutions must address these concerns to ensure AI technologies are used responsibly and ethically in HR functions.
- **Strategic Alignment**: Another important theme in the literature is the alignment between AI applications and institutional strategy. The integration of AI into HR functions is often driven by the desire to achieve broader institutional goals, such as increasing research output, improving teaching quality, and fostering interdisciplinary collaboration. AI is viewed as a tool that can help institutions better align their human capital strategies with their long-term vision and objectives.

Having reviewed key research themes, we now turn to the theoretical foundations that underpin the use of AI in academic HCM.

THEORETICAL FOUNDATIONS OF AI IN HUMAN CAPITAL MANAGEMENT

Artificial Intelligence (AI) is more than just a technological advancement; it is a socio-technical system that profoundly impacts how academic institutions manage, assess, and develop their human capital. The introduction of AI into human capital management (HCM) processes in academia is not just a shift in tools, but a fundamental transformation in how decisions are made, how human and machine agents collaborate, and how fairness, trust, and accountability are maintained. To understand the implementation of AI in academic HCM, this chapter delves into foundational theories from organizational science, socio-technical systems, behavioral economics, and ethical governance, providing both structure and rationale for the integration of AI into academic decision-making processes.

Organizational Theories Supporting AI Integration

Academic institutions are inherently complex organizations. They are often characterized by hierarchical structures, decentralized decision-making, and knowledge-driven functions, making them suitable environments for the application of AI. The integration of AI into HCM systems draws heavily on several well-established organizational theories, each contributing a unique perspective on how AI can be successfully implemented and utilized in academia.

- **Contingency Theory**: Contingency theory emphasizes that no one-size-fits-all solution exists, and that organizational structures and processes must be adapted to fit the specific needs and environment of the institution (Donaldson, 2001). In the context of AI integration, this theory suggests that the implementation of AI in HCM should be tailored to the unique needs of each academic institution. For instance, a large research university may benefit from comprehensive, integrated faculty analytics dashboards, while a smaller college might prioritize simpler, more accessible AI tools like automated CV screening systems. This flexibility allows AI tools to be customized according to the institution's size, goals, and resources.
- **Resource-Based View (RBV)**: The RBV theory explains that an institution's internal resources, including its human capital and technological infrastructure, provide a competitive advantage in achieving strategic goals (Barney, 1991). In the context of AI in HCM, AI technologies are viewed as strategic resources that can enhance institutional capabilities in areas such as recruitment, performance tracking, and workforce planning. By leveraging AI, aca-

demic institutions can gain insights into faculty performance, optimize hiring processes, and more effectively plan for future workforce needs.

- **Sociotechnical Systems Theory**: This theory underscores the interaction between social and technical elements within an organization, where both human agents (e.g., faculty, HR professionals) and technical systems (e.g., algorithms, data systems) must work together in harmony for successful implementation (Trist & Bamforth, 1951). In the case of AI in HCM, this theory suggests that AI tools must be designed not only for technical efficiency but also to support and enhance human decision-making. For example, faculty recruitment systems powered by AI must integrate seamlessly with HR practices, ensuring that faculty members feel supported by the technology rather than undermined by it.

Table 2. Key organizational theories and AI implications

Theory	Core Premise	AI Application in Academia
Contingency Theory	No one-size-fits-all; systems must fit context	Tailored AI solutions for different academic institutions
Resource-Based View (RBV)	Internal resources provide a competitive advantage	AI as a strategic institutional asset
Sociotechnical Systems Theory	Joint optimization of social and technical subsystems	Harmonizing HR practices and AI tools

As illustrated in Table 2, each organizational theory offers unique insights into the integration of AI within academic Human Capital Management

Human-AI Collaborative Models

As AI systems gain autonomy, the collaboration between human decision-makers and AI agents becomes critical to the success of AI integration in academic HCM. Several theoretical models have been developed to explain and guide these human-AI interactions. These models are essential for ensuring that AI augments human decision-making, rather than replacing it entirely, while also preserving ethical principles and human oversight.

- **Joint Cognitive Systems Theory**: This theory, proposed by Hollnagel and Woods (2005), posits that humans and AI function as partners in solving complex problems. In the context of academic HCM, this could involve HR professionals working with AI tools to analyze recruitment data or evaluate faculty performance. While AI provides predictive analytics and insights, human decision-makers apply their institutional knowledge and understanding of the broader context to make final decisions.

- **Levels of Automation (LOA) Framework**: The LOA framework (Parasuraman et al., 2000) classifies the level of autonomy an AI system can have, ranging from advisory systems to fully automated decision-making. In academic settings, this model suggests that AI may be used to assist in faculty evaluations, providing data-driven insights into faculty performance, but human committees would retain the responsibility for final decisions, such as tenure and promotion. This ensures that human judgment remains central in critical decision-making processes.
- **Human-in-the-Loop (HITL) Design**: HITL emphasizes the importance of maintaining human oversight over AI systems. In academic HCM, this means that AI tools should not make decisions independently but should instead support human agents who can review and intervene in the decision-making process when necessary (Amershi et al., 2014). For example, AI could suggest candidates for faculty recruitment based on qualifications and institutional fit, but HR professionals or academic leaders would have the final say, ensuring accountability and ethical decision-making.

Ethical and Governance Frameworks

The integration of AI into academic HCM raises significant ethical concerns, particularly around issues such as algorithmic bias, transparency, and fairness. To address these concerns, various ethical and governance frameworks have been proposed to guide the responsible implementation of AI. These frameworks emphasize the importance of ensuring that AI systems are transparent, accountable, and fair in their decision-making processes.

- **Principles for Responsible AI**: Floridi et al. (2018) propose a set of principles for responsible AI, including transparency, accountability, justice, beneficence, and non-maleficence. These principles are crucial for ensuring that AI technologies are used ethically in academic HCM. For instance, transparency in AI decision-making processes is essential to allow faculty members to understand how decisions regarding their recruitment, promotion, or evaluation are being made. Accountability ensures that AI systems can be audited, and those responsible for their use can be held liable for any potential harm caused.
- **Fairness, Accountability, and Transparency in Machine Learning (FAT/ML)**: The FAT/ML framework advocates for interpretable machine learning

models and audit trails, particularly in high-stakes decision-making processes such as faculty hiring and promotion. This framework is essential in academia, where the potential for bias in decision-making processes can have significant consequences for faculty members' careers (Barocas et al., 2017). By ensuring that AI systems are transparent and accountable, institutions can mitigate the risk of discrimination and ensure fairness in HR processes.

- **AI Ethics in Education Frameworks**: The OECD (2021) provides guidelines for ethical AI in education, recommending the establishment of inclusive governance structures in higher education to monitor the use of AI in human capital decisions. This includes forming AI ethics boards or committees within academic institutions to review and oversee the implementation of AI-driven systems in faculty selection, performance evaluation, and professional development. These boards ensure that AI tools align with ethical standards and are used responsibly to promote fairness and equity.

These theoretical perspectives provide a solid foundation for examining real-world applications of AI in academic human capital, as explored in the next chapter

EMPIRICAL STUDIES IN AI-DRIVEN HUMAN CAPITAL MANAGEMENT (2019–2024)

The integration of Artificial Intelligence (AI) into Human Capital Management (HCM) is revolutionizing the management of academic workforce resources. This chapter examines the most recent empirical studies (2019–2024), which demonstrate the growing influence of AI in various domains such as recruitment, faculty development, predictive analytics, research collaboration, and talent mapping. These studies reveal the depth of AI's impact on decision-making processes and workforce planning in higher education. By synthesizing methodologies, key findings, and challenges, this chapter provides a comprehensive overview of how AI is shaping HCM in academia.

Recruitment, Faculty Development, and Predictive Analytics

AI has made significant strides in improving recruitment processes, faculty development, and predictive analytics, thus transforming traditional practices within academia. Studies have demonstrated that AI tools can not only streamline recruitment but also enhance faculty development and retention through data-driven insights.

Recruitment AI:

A groundbreaking study by Dastin (2019) explored the impact of AI in the recruitment process. Using natural language processing (NLP) and machine learning (ML) models, AI systems can efficiently screen and rank candidates based on their resumes, academic background, research publications, and online profiles. This algorithmic approach to recruitment provides universities with an objective mechanism to evaluate candidates, removing human biases that often influence hiring decisions. As a result, AI improves the fairness and efficiency of the recruitment process, ensuring that the most qualified candidates are selected for academic positions.

AI recruitment systems not only assess textual data but can also evaluate patterns in candidates' past career trajectories, teaching effectiveness, and research productivity, offering a comprehensive view of potential hires. By streamlining this process, institutions can focus their efforts on more targeted interviews and final selection rounds.

Faculty Development:

AI systems have shown great promise in enhancing faculty development by offering data-driven insights. According to Chung et al. (2020), AI tools are increasingly used to track faculty performance over time, assessing metrics such as teaching evaluations, research productivity, and peer reviews. By integrating these data points into predictive models, AI can offer personalized professional development recommendations that are tailored to individual faculty needs. For instance, AI can suggest targeted workshops, conferences, or collaborations to improve a faculty member's research profile or teaching skills.

These tools can also assist in monitoring faculty engagement with the academic community, identifying those who may benefit from mentorship programs or those at risk of burnout. This personalized development approach leads to more effective career advancement strategies, ensuring faculty members remain productive, satisfied, and engaged in their roles.

Predictive Analytics for Retention:

Another key area where AI is making an impact is in predicting faculty retention. Tan and Lee (2021) conducted a study that demonstrated how AI tools can predict faculty turnover by analyzing historical data related to job satisfaction, career progressions, and external factors such as funding opportunities. By identifying early signs of faculty dissatisfaction or intent to leave, academic institutions can implement targeted interventions, such as improved work-life balance initiatives or financial incentives, to retain valuable faculty members.

Such predictive analytics empower universities to proactively manage talent and reduce turnover rates, which is crucial in maintaining a stable and high-performing academic workforce.

Table 3. AI applications in recruitment and faculty development

Study	Application	Findings
Dastin (2019)	AI in recruitment and candidate screening	AI effectively screens candidates and reduces bias in selection, improving hiring processes
Chung et al. (2020)	Faculty development using AI tools	AI tracks faculty performance and provides personalized development paths
Tan and Lee (2021)	Predictive analytics for faculty retention	AI predicts faculty turnover and enables proactive retention strategies

As illustrated in Table 3, various studies have explored the integration of Artificial Intelligence (AI) in recruitment and faculty development within academic settings. These studies underscore the transformative potential of AI in enhancing efficiency, personalization, and predictive capabilities in Human Capital Management (HCM).

Research Collaboration and Talent Mapping Tools

AI has not only transformed recruitment and retention practices but also significantly influenced how academic institutions foster collaboration and map talent. Through data analytics, AI models can help institutions identify high-potential researchers and match them with the right collaborative opportunities.

Research Collaboration Tools:

Research collaboration is a cornerstone of academic innovation, and AI-driven platforms are streamlining the way researchers identify and engage with potential collaborators. Zhao et al. (2020) analyzed AI-powered platforms that match researchers based on shared research interests, publication histories, and network connections. These platforms use machine learning algorithms to evaluate vast datasets of academic work, identifying key themes, research trends, and potential collaborators across institutions.

The result is more efficient and targeted collaboration, allowing researchers to work with others who complement their skills and research focus. By breaking down traditional barriers in academia, AI facilitates interdisciplinary research, fostering innovation and accelerating the pace of academic discovery.

Talent Mapping in Research:

Liu and Li (2022) examined the role of AI in talent mapping within academic institutions. Using data from research outputs such as publications, citations, and collaboration patterns, AI models can identify emerging researchers and pinpoint areas of academic strength. These tools can help institutions identify gaps in their research teams, ensuring that the right talent is allocated to high-priority research projects.

Furthermore, AI can help academic leaders make strategic decisions on resource allocation, ensuring that the most promising areas of research receive adequate funding and support. By mapping out talent within research teams, institutions can optimize their academic outputs and foster an environment that nurtures innovation.

Methodologies and Key Findings

The methodologies used in these studies vary, ranging from quantitative data analysis to qualitative interviews, providing a comprehensive understanding of AI's role in human capital management. By using a combination of these methods, researchers can capture both the effectiveness of AI tools and the real-world challenges faced by institutions.

Quantitative Approaches:

Quantitative methodologies, particularly regression analysis, have been widely used to assess the impact of AI on academic performance and faculty retention. Patel et al. (2023) employed regression models to analyze large datasets from multiple universities, determining that AI significantly improves faculty performance and retention rates. By analyzing key metrics such as job satisfaction, research output, and teaching evaluations, AI-driven tools can identify which factors influence faculty retention and guide institutional strategies accordingly.

These findings underscore the value of AI in providing objective insights into faculty dynamics, enabling institutions to make data-driven decisions to improve faculty engagement and satisfaction.

Qualitative Research:

In addition to quantitative approaches, several studies have adopted qualitative research methods, such as interviews and focus groups, to gather insights from faculty members, HR professionals, and administrators. Smith et al. (2022) conducted interviews with faculty and HR staff to explore the challenges and ethical concerns associated with AI in academic HCM. One of the key insights from this study was the importance of maintaining human oversight in AI-driven decisions.

While AI can provide valuable insights and recommendations, it is critical that human judgment be involved in decisions that affect people's careers. The balance between AI-driven automation and human intervention is crucial in ensuring fairness and ethical integrity in academic institutions.

Table 4. Methodologies used in AI HCM studies

Study	Methodology	Key Findings
Patel et al. (2023)	Regression analysis on large-scale datasets	AI improves faculty performance and retention in universities by identifying key influencing factors
Smith et al. (2022)	Qualitative interviews with faculty and HR staff	Human oversight is crucial in AI-driven decisions to ensure fairness and ethical practices
Zhao et al. (2020)	Machine learning-based analysis of collaboration networks	AI enhances research collaboration by recommending potential collaborators based on shared research interests

Table 4 summarizes the diverse methodologies employed in recent studies focusing on the integration of Artificial Intelligence (AI) within Human Capital Management (HCM). Each methodology offers unique insights and has specific implications for the effectiveness and applicability of AI in academic institutions.

While these studies highlight progress, challenges and gaps persist in the current landscape, which are discussed next.

GAPS, CHALLENGES, AND RESEARCH OPPORTUNITIES

The integration of Artificial Intelligence (AI) into Human Capital Management (HCM) within academia has made considerable strides, but challenges and limitations persist. This chapter identifies the key gaps in existing studies, explores concerns such as data bias and transparency issues, highlights institutional barriers to AI adoption, and points to unexplored research areas that present significant opportunities for future investigation. Addressing these gaps and challenges is essential to ensure AI is utilized in an equitable, ethical, and effective manner across academic and research institutions.

Limitations in Current Studies

A review of the empirical literature from 2019 to 2024 reveals several recurring methodological and conceptual limitations in AI-driven HCM research. These limitations hinder the comprehensive understanding and effective implementation of AI systems in academia.

Overreliance on Quantitative Data:

Many studies in the field rely heavily on quantitative metrics such as publication counts, citation analysis, and faculty attrition rates. While these metrics are useful for measuring academic output, they often provide a limited view of human potential in academic environments. They neglect qualitative factors such as teaching effectiveness, mentorship quality, and community involvement, which are crucial to evaluating the holistic value of faculty members (Brown & Thomas, 2021). This narrow focus results in an incomplete understanding of faculty performance and potential, leaving essential aspects of academic careers underexplored.

Lack of Longitudinal Studies:

Most research on AI in HCM focuses on short-term improvements, such as enhancements in prediction accuracy or performance metrics. Few studies track the long-term impact of AI tools, particularly in the context of cultural and behavioral shifts in academic institutions (Wang et al., 2020). The lack of longitudinal studies means that the sustained effects of AI adoption—on faculty morale, academic culture, and institutional growth—remain under examined. Without long-term data, it is challenging to assess whether AI-driven interventions lead to lasting, positive changes.

Contextual Bias:

A significant portion of the current literature is based on studies conducted in North American or European institutions, leading to a limited understanding of AI's impact in other settings. In particular, AI applications in academic institutions in low-resource, multilingual, or culturally diverse environments are underexplored. Research conducted in these contexts may not be generalizable to institutions in other regions with different cultural norms, socio-economic conditions, and educational structures (Sharma & Rao, 2023). There is a pressing need for more research that examines how AI systems function in diverse educational environments, particularly in developing countries or non-Western academic contexts.

Data Bias, Transparency, and Institutional Barriers

AI systems, especially those trained on historical data, are prone to several challenges, including data bias, lack of transparency, and institutional barriers. These issues can significantly undermine the effectiveness and fairness of AI tools in academic HCM.

Data Bias in Recruitment:

AI models trained on historical hiring data are often reflective of past biases. These biases may disproportionately disadvantage underrepresented groups in academic recruitment, leading to perpetuated inequalities. Obermeyer et al. (2019) highlighted similar concerns in healthcare, where algorithmic decisions favored white patients. A comparable pattern is observed in academic hiring, where AI models may replicate biases that have existed in the hiring process for decades (Mehrabi et al., 2021). These biases can result in the marginalization of minority groups and hinder the diversification of academic staff.

Lack of Transparency:

AI models, particularly black-box algorithms, can operate without providing insight into the decision-making process. This lack of transparency in AI-driven faculty evaluations and hiring processes reduces trust among faculty members and administrators. Institutions may adopt proprietary systems that make critical decisions about promotions, hiring, and tenure without offering explanations on how those decisions were made (Burrell, 2016). This opacity raises concerns about accountability and fairness, especially when decisions impact individuals' careers and livelihoods.

Institutional Barriers:

Several institutional barriers hinder the widespread adoption of AI in academic HCM. These barriers include bureaucratic resistance, a lack of digital infrastructure, and concerns about faculty deskilling. Many academic HR professionals may lack the necessary training to implement or effectively manage AI systems, and institutional policies often lag behind technological developments (Singh et al., 2022). This disconnect between technology and institutional readiness can slow the integration of AI tools into academic HR practices, limiting their potential to improve faculty management and decision-making processes.

Table 5. Challenges in AI-HCM implementation

Challenge	Description	Impact
Data Bias	AI models replicate past discriminatory patterns	Increases inequality in hiring and evaluations
Lack of Transparency	Opaque decision-making models	Reduces trust and accountability
Institutional Inertia	Resistance from HR teams and administrators	Slows adoption and integration of AI tools
Inadequate Digital Infrastructure	Limited access to AI-ready tools and data platforms	Restricts capability for experimentation and scaling
Skills Gap	Lack of AI literacy among HR professionals	Misuse or underutilization of AI systems

Table 5 summarizes the key challenges identified in the integration of AI within Human Capital Management (HCM) in academic settings. These challenges encompass data bias, lack of transparency, institutional inertia, inadequate digital infrastructure, and skills gaps among HR professionals. Addressing these issues is crucial for the ethical and effective implementation of AI technologies in academia.

Unexplored Areas for Academic Investigation

While AI has great potential to revolutionize academic HCM, several unexplored areas remain that could further enhance its impact. Researchers should focus on these under-explored fields to guide the development of more comprehensive and inclusive AI systems for academia.

Ethical Frameworks for Academic AI-HCM:

There is a significant gap in the development of ethical frameworks tailored to AI applications in academia. While there is growing recognition of the need for fairness, transparency, and accountability in AI systems, few studies offer structured models for addressing these concerns within the context of academic HCM. Future research must focus on creating context-specific ethical frameworks that integrate data governance principles, ensuring that AI tools respect academic values and promote equity (Floridi et al., 2018).

Cross-Institutional Datasets:

Much of the current research on AI in academic HCM is limited to single institutions, reducing the generalizability of findings. Collaborative research initiatives involving multiple universities could improve the robustness of AI models by providing access to larger, more diverse datasets. Cross-institutional datasets would allow for the development of AI tools that are more applicable to a wide range of academic settings, increasing their relevance and accuracy in faculty recruitment, evaluation, and retention.

AI for Inclusion and Well-being:

Most current AI models focus on improving performance and operational efficiency. However, there is a growing need to explore how AI can be leveraged to support faculty well-being, diversity, and work-life balance. Research that investigates AI's role in fostering inclusive environments, mental health support, and employee well-being is underexplored. AI-driven models that identify at-risk faculty members, suggest wellness programs, or offer tailored support could be a valuable area of future study.

Hybrid Evaluation Systems:

Future research should investigate hybrid evaluation systems that combine AI prediction with human judgment. While AI can predict faculty performance, tenure eligibility, or promotion likelihood, human judgment remains critical in making nuanced decisions. Hybrid systems that incorporate both AI insights and human evaluations could lead to more accurate, fair, and contextually appropriate decisions in faculty management, especially in complex cases where data alone may not provide a complete picture.

Cultural Sensitivity in Algorithms:

AI systems often fail to account for cultural diversity and the nuances of academic evaluation practices across different regions and disciplines. Research in this area should focus on designing culturally sensitive AI algorithms that can adapt to the diverse norms and values found in academic institutions worldwide. This includes understanding varying teaching philosophies, evaluation methods, and institutional priorities, ensuring that AI models do not inadvertently reinforce cultural biases or overlook essential regional characteristics.

To address these gaps, we propose a structured conceptual model for advancing AI in academic HCM, presented in the next chapter.

A CONCEPTUAL MODEL FOR FUTURE ACADEMIC RESEARCH

The evolving role of Artificial Intelligence (AI) in Human Capital Management (HCM) necessitates a well-structured and robust conceptual model to guide both academic research and institutional practices. This chapter introduces such a model that integrates both theoretical frameworks and practical strategies to ensure effective implementation of AI in academic environments. The purpose is to provide a framework that addresses the complexities of AI in HCM, bridges theoretical research with real-world applications, and opens pathways for future academic exploration.

Input–Process–Output Structure for AI-HCM

The Input–Process–Output (IPO) model is a widely-used framework in organizational research that describes how resources (inputs) are transformed into outcomes (outputs) through specific operational processes. This model is particularly valuable for understanding how AI can optimize Human Capital Management in academic settings, helping align institutional needs with academic capabilities.

Figure 2. Input-process-output model for AI driven academic HCM

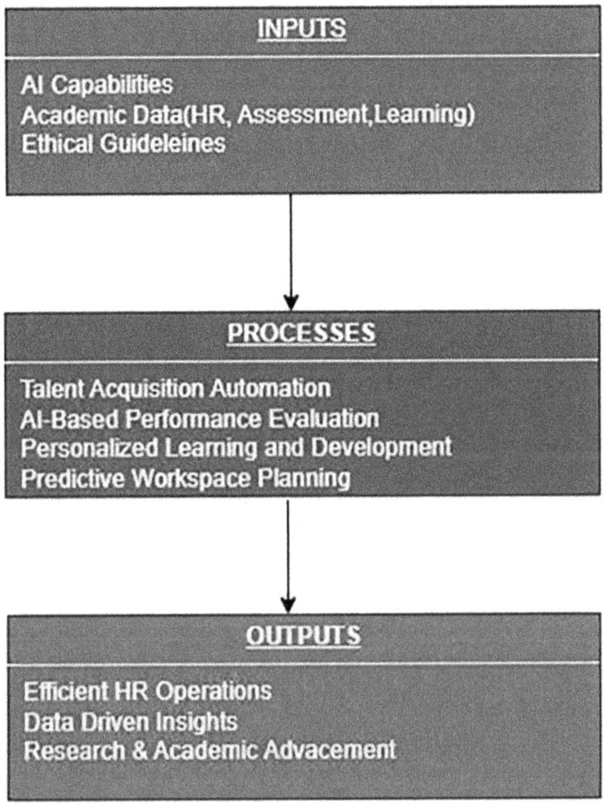

Figure 2 illustrates the IPO framework for AI-HCM, which is detailed in Sections 6.1.1 to 6.1.3

Inputs

The inputs in this model represent the essential resources feeding into AI systems within academic HCM. These resources are crucial for designing AI models that align with the goals and values of the institution. The first input category includes Institutional Data, which consists of faculty profiles (including teaching, research, and administrative roles), research metrics (such as publication counts, citations, and impact factors), HR records (covering tenure, promotions, and performance reviews), course feedback and evaluations (like student ratings and peer assessments), and student learning analytics (including performance data and engagement levels). Another category of input is Technological Infrastructure, which encompasses AI algorithms such as machine learning (ML), natural language processing (NLP), and deep learning models, along with cloud-based analytics platforms that offer scalable solutions for processing large datasets and deriving insights. Data visualization tools like dashboards and interfaces are also part of this infrastructure, helping to present actionable insights from complex data. Lastly, Human Resources form an important input, which includes the expertise of faculty, HR personnel, IT staff, and academic leadership, along with knowledge of AI tools and how to integrate them with traditional HR practices. Additionally, policy-making bodies play a key role in setting ethical standards for AI usage.

Processes

The processes in this model transform the inputs into actionable insights and outcomes through AI systems, ensuring that HR functions become more efficient, transparent, and fair. One key process is AI Modeling & Prediction, which involves algorithms used for tasks such as faculty recruitment, workload optimization, and performance forecasting. AI systems also help predict the future needs of the institution and the potential for faculty success. Another important process is Natural Language Processing (NLP), where NLP models are employed to analyze unstructured data such as teaching feedback, grant proposals, and academic publications. These models extract meaningful insights to assist in evaluating teaching quality, identifying faculty expertise, and assessing research output. Decision Support Systems (DSS) also play a significant role, as AI-driven DSS provide ranked recommendations for decisions related to hiring, promotions, and resource allocation. These systems use data-driven insights to support HR decision-making processes.

Outputs

The outputs in this model represent the desired outcomes resulting from the implementation of AI in academic HCM, aligning with institutional goals of talent optimization, fairness, and transparency. One such output is Optimized Talent Deployment, where AI systems ensure that faculty skills and academic profiles are well-aligned with departmental needs, promoting better utilization of human capital. Another output is Predictive Hiring, where AI enables data-driven recruitment strategies that not only address current needs but also consider long-term institutional goals. Predictive analytics help identify potential candidates who are likely to thrive in specific academic environments. Lastly, Transparent Evaluation is an output facilitated by AI tools, which provide fair, explainable, and reproducible evaluations of faculty performance. Evaluation frameworks are designed to ensure that decisions related to tenure, promotions, and grants are based on transparent and well-understood criteria.

This IPO structure offers a comprehensive approach for integrating AI into academic HCM, ensuring that the processes and outcomes align with the goals of efficiency, fairness, and long-term institutional success.

Evaluation Metrics and Theoretical Constructs

To operationalize the IPO model effectively, a set of well-defined evaluation metrics and theoretical constructs are necessary. These tools ensure that AI systems in academic HCM are both efficient and aligned with institutional values.

Table 6. Evaluation metrics for AI-HCM frameworks

Construct	Description	Sample Metrics
Fairness	Equity in recommendations and predictions	Demographic parity, equal opportunity
Accuracy	Correctness of AI predictions	Precision, recall, F1-score
Transparency	Understandability of decisions	Explainability score, stakeholder clarity
Efficiency	Time and resource optimization	Decision latency, reduced hiring time
Faculty Satisfaction	Perception of AI systems among academic staff	Survey results, adoption rate

Table 6 presents a comprehensive overview of the evaluation metrics essential for assessing AI-driven Human Capital Management (HCM) frameworks.

Theoretical Foundations

These foundational theories guide the development of AI systems in academic HCM, ensuring they are grounded in well-established principles.

Resource-Based View (RBV):

AI is treated as a strategic resource that enhances human capital management. According to RBV (Barney, 1991), AI optimizes resource allocation by efficiently matching faculty expertise with institutional needs.

Socio-Technical Systems Theory:

This theory recognizes that the successful implementation of AI tools in academia relies on understanding the interaction between AI systems and the social structures of the institution, such as trust, resistance, and ethical alignment (Bostrom & Yudkowsky, 2014).

Technology Acceptance Model (TAM):

The TAM (Davis, 1989) posits that faculty adoption of AI systems will be influenced by perceived usefulness and ease of use. Future research can explore these factors to enhance AI integration within academic institutions.

Use Cases for Scholarly Experimentation

The conceptual model outlined above lays the foundation for empirical testing and scholarly investigation. Below are several proposed research directions, including hypotheses and real-world use cases.

Hypothesis 1: AI-Enabled Recruitment Systems Increase Diversity in Faculty Hiring Across Departments

- **Rationale**: AI can help reduce bias in the recruitment process, leading to a more diverse and inclusive faculty body. This hypothesis would test the effectiveness of AI-driven recruitment systems in broadening the pool of candidates from diverse backgrounds.

Hypothesis 2: Use of NLP in Teaching Evaluations Leads to More Holistic Performance Reviews.

- **Rationale**: NLP models can analyze qualitative feedback from students, providing a more comprehensive understanding of teaching effectiveness. This hypothesis explores whether NLP enhances the quality and fairness of performance reviews.

Hypothesis 3: Faculty Exposed to Explainable AI Tools Exhibit Higher Satisfaction and Trust in HR Processes.

- **Rationale**: When faculty understand how AI decisions are made, they are more likely to trust the system and feel satisfied with the results. This hypothesis tests the relationship between explainability and faculty perceptions of AI tools.

Example Use Case: AI-Driven Interdisciplinary Collaboration Identification

• A university implements an AI system designed to identify potential interdisciplinary collaborators. The system analyzes faculty publication topics, citation networks, and grant success rates. Researchers compare collaboration rates and grant success before and after AI deployment, measuring the impact of AI in fostering cross-disciplinary partnerships.

In summary, this conceptual model serves as a roadmap for future academic research and practical implementation of AI in Human Capital Management. It integrates theory, data, and AI-driven processes to optimize HR practices in academic institutions, ensuring that the integration of AI into HCM is both effective and ethically aligned.

With a robust conceptual framework in place, it is important to explore the strategic and educational implications of integrating AI in academia.

STRATEGIC AND PEDAGOGICAL IMPLICATIONS

The integration of Artificial Intelligence (AI) into academic Human Capital Management (HCM) is not just a technical challenge; it also demands long-term strategic and pedagogical planning. Institutions must rethink their educational approaches, faculty development strategies, and policy frameworks to fully embrace AI and ensure its ethical, effective, and sustainable integration. This chapter explores the broader implications of AI integration into academic HCM systems, focusing on curriculum development, faculty capability building, and institutional policy alignment.

Curriculum Design for AI-HRM Education

The rise of AI in Human Resource Management (HRM) calls for a transformation in how higher education institutions prepare students for future challenges in workforce and talent management. The curriculum must be adapted to integrate AI principles, tools, and applications, fostering both technical skills and ethical awareness. This prepares students to become the next generation of HR professionals capable of working alongside AI systems.

Key Curriculum Focus Areas:

1. **AI and Data Literacy**:
    - Courses should provide foundational knowledge in AI concepts, with an emphasis on machine learning (ML), natural language processing (NLP), and data ethics, specifically as they pertain to human capital.
    - Understanding how algorithms work, how data is used, and how AI can automate and augment HR processes will be critical for future HR leaders.
2. **Human-AI Interaction**:

- Preparing students to work alongside AI-driven decision systems is crucial. A focus on explainability, transparency, and human oversight in AI processes ensures that students understand the importance of ethical considerations when AI makes HR decisions.
- The goal is to create professionals who not only use AI tools but can also evaluate and explain AI outcomes, ensuring that human oversight remains an essential component of decision-making processes.

3. **Policy and Ethics in AI**:
   - Incorporating ethics, fairness, and accountability into the curriculum is critical. Students must understand algorithmic bias, fairness in decision-making, and the responsible application of AI in HR processes.
   - Addressing issues such as discriminatory practices and data privacy concerns within AI systems will help future HR professionals navigate the ethical challenges posed by AI.

Figure 3. Framework for curriculum development in AI-HRM

Figure 3 visualizes the structured framework for curriculum development in AI-HRM. It starts with a foundational understanding of AI principles, progresses to applied AI-HRM modules, and culminates in Capstone Projects and Ethics Training. This approach ensures that students not only gain technical knowledge but also develop the ability to apply these skills in real-world HRM contexts, underpinned by ethical considerations.

Use Case Example:

A postgraduate HRM program integrates an AI-HRM lab course that spans a semester. In this course, students work with simulated faculty recruitment data to develop AI models aimed at ensuring fair candidate selection. The focus is on using AI tools to build models that predict candidate success based on various factors, while justifying decisions based on explainability metrics such as transparency and fairness. This hands-on experience reinforces the importance of ethical decision-making in AI applications.

Faculty Skill Development for AI Literacy

For AI to be successfully embedded into academic HR processes, faculty and administrators must have a solid baseline understanding of how AI operates, how decisions are made, and how to manage AI systems effectively. Faculty development is critical in ensuring that AI is integrated seamlessly into academic institutions.

Modes of Faculty Development:

1. **Workshops and Certification Programs**:
   - Short-term training sessions that focus on key AI tools and their applications in HRM, including performance analysis, recruitment automation, and predictive analytics.
   - These workshops provide practical, hands-on experience with AI systems, allowing faculty to better understand the technologies they will be working with.
2. **Collaborative Learning Models**:
   - Faculty members who are early adopters of AI can become peer trainers, helping to spread knowledge throughout their departments. This peer-to-peer learning model fosters collaboration and knowledge-sharing.
   - Early adopters can lead workshops, mentor colleagues, and support cross-disciplinary learning initiatives, creating a community of practice for AI in HRM.
3. **Micro-Credentials and Online Courses**:
   - Flexible online courses and micro-credential programs enable faculty to pursue continuous upskilling, allowing them to learn at their own pace while balancing their academic responsibilities.
   - Platforms like MOOCs (Massive Open Online Courses) can offer a variety of AI-focused content, from introductory courses to more specialized training.

Table 7. AI competency areas for faculty

Domain	Competency Area	Delivery Mode
AI Fundamentals	Understanding AI algorithms and data	Online micro-courses, MOOCs
Tool Proficiency	Hands-on with DSS, NLP, and dashboards	On-campus labs, sandbox environments
Ethical Awareness	Bias, transparency, legal compliance	Case study workshops

Table 7 outlines the key AI competency areas essential for faculty members in academic institutions. These competencies are crucial for integrating AI into teaching, research, and administrative practices. The table categorizes these competencies into several domains, each addressing specific skills and knowledge required for effective AI utilization in academia.

Faculty members need to be proficient in these competency areas to effectively integrate AI into their work. This includes understanding the algorithms behind AI, working with decision support systems (DSS) and NLP tools, and maintaining ethical standards while using AI in HRM.

Research Funding and Institutional Policy Alignment

The successful institutionalization of AI in academic HCM requires robust policy frameworks, funding alignment, and long-term strategic planning. Institutions must ensure that their strategic goals support the development of AI as a strategic resource for academic HR practices, and that funding is allocated to support interdisciplinary research and AI capacity building.

Key Strategic Policies Required:

1. **Data Governance Policies**:

These policies define how data is used, shared, and stored in AI systems. Clear guidelines must be set regarding the ethical use of faculty and student data, ensuring that privacy concerns are addressed, and the data used for AI applications is accurate and unbiased.

2. **Incentive Structures**:

Faculty participation in AI-HCM initiatives should be recognized and incentivized. This could include adjusting workload allocations or providing research credit for faculty who engage in AI research and development related to HRM systems.

Institutions could also offer rewards for faculty who pioneer the use of AI in HRM, fostering a culture of innovation and adoption.

3. **Interdisciplinary Research Funding**:

AI in HCM is an interdisciplinary field that requires collaboration between AI researchers and scholars from other disciplines, such as social sciences, business, and education.

Universities should create dedicated funding programs to support collaborative research projects that combine AI with human resource management, talent development, and organizational behavior studies.

Example:

A university aligns its strategic plan with AI by setting up a Center for AI in Academic Talent Development. This center becomes the focal point for interdisciplinary research on AI's impact on academic HR practices. The university allocates a specific budget for projects related to AI-based recruitment, faculty performance evaluation, and predictive analytics for student success. Additionally, ethical guidelines are established to ensure AI tools used for hiring and evaluations remain transparent, unbiased, and compliant with privacy laws.

The strategic initiatives discussed here lay the groundwork for future research and institutional action, as summarized in the concluding chapter

CONCLUSION AND FUTURE RESEARCH DIRECTIONS

Artificial Intelligence (AI) is fundamentally transforming Human Capital Management (HCM) in academic and research institutions, reshaping everything from recruitment and talent development to performance evaluation and strategic planning. As explored throughout this book, academic institutions are at the intersection of opportunity and responsibility—balancing innovation with ethical considerations, operational efficiency with fairness, and automation with human-centered governance. This chapter synthesizes the key insights gained from the preceding discussions and outlines the trajectory for future research and pedagogical development in AI-driven HCM.

Summary of Insights

This chapter has delved into the numerous dimensions of AI integration into academic HCM systems, drawing conclusions on its implications, applications, and the challenges that lie ahead. The key insights that emerged from this exploration include:

Transformation of HR Processes:

AI technologies such as natural language processing (NLP), predictive analytics, and decision support systems (DSS) are increasingly being integrated into various HR functions within academic settings. These tools help automate repetitive administrative tasks, thus reducing human error, increasing efficiency, and enhancing precision in decision-making. For instance, AI can streamline recruitment processes by analyzing large datasets of candidates and predicting success, while AI-powered tools can assist in performance evaluations by identifying patterns in faculty output, student feedback, and other metrics.

Interdisciplinary Theoretical Foundations:

The success of AI in HCM requires a deep understanding of multiple theoretical domains. Successful AI-HCM integration relies on combining insights from:

- **Organizational behavior** to understand the impact of AI on faculty and institutional dynamics.
- **Technology acceptance theories** to guide the adoption of AI tools within academic HR functions.
- **Ethical AI governance** to ensure responsible AI design and deployment that adheres to ethical principles.
- **Sociotechnical systems** theory, which highlights the importance of balancing technological advancements with the human and social systems in which they operate.

Empirical Validation and Case Studies:

The book draws on empirical research conducted from 2019 to 2024, which highlights the trends in AI adoption across different facets of academic HRM. Case studies spanning faculty recruitment, student and faculty performance monitoring, and research collaboration mapping have provided valuable insights into the effectiveness and challenges of AI tools. These case studies have illustrated how AI can both improve operational efficiency and contribute to decision-making accuracy, yet also bring forth challenges in governance, ethics, and user acceptance.

Pedagogical Innovation:

To ensure AI is successfully embedded in academic HR processes, institutions must undergo curriculum reforms that focus on AI literacy for both students and faculty. Key pedagogical innovations include the integration of AI-related coursework, faculty upskilling programs, and the creation of interdisciplinary research programs. Curriculum reforms are essential to preparing students for the future of human capital management in a world increasingly dominated by AI technologies. Faculty development, which includes both technical AI knowledge and ethical decision-making, is critical to bridging the gap between theory and practice in the implementation of AI.

Ethical and Governance Challenges:

Despite the promising advantages of AI, several ethical and governance challenges remain. These include concerns about algorithmic bias, lack of transparency, and resistance to AI adoption in academic environments. For example, algorithmic biases in AI systems may unintentionally perpetuate existing biases in recruitment or faculty evaluations, leading to unfair outcomes. Ethical concerns, such as privacy issues, transparency in AI decision-making, and accountability in algorithmic processes, must be addressed through robust governance frameworks. The need for responsible innovation is paramount to ensure that AI in academic HCM is not only effective but also just, equitable, and transparent.

These conclusions indicate that academic institutions have an important role to play—not just as consumers of AI technologies, but also as laboratories for exploring AI ethics, interpretability, and innovation in human capital management systems.

Emerging Questions for Scholars and Doctoral Researchers

While significant strides have been made in AI-driven HCM, there are still many unanswered questions and opportunities for further research. Below are some key areas that present fertile ground for future scholarly exploration:

1. **How can AI systems be designed to support diversity and equity in faculty recruitment?**
   - AI systems can unintentionally perpetuate biases that exist in historical data. Future research must explore solutions to these challenges, such as algorithmic fairness mechanisms, audit frameworks, and real-time bias correction techniques. Investigating the role of AI in ensuring equitable hiring practices and diversifying faculty recruitment pools is crucial for mitigating the risks of discrimination and bias.
2. **What governance models best balance institutional efficiency with ethical safeguards?**
   - There is a growing need for governance structures that balance AI's potential for efficiency with the ethical imperatives of fairness, transparency, and accountability. Investigating co-governance models involving multiple stakeholders—such as AI specialists, faculty, HR personnel, and ethics boards—can offer valuable insights into how AI tools can be implemented responsibly. Exploring how academic institutions can design policies that balance these competing needs will be a critical area of future research.
3. **Can AI systems personalize learning and career development in academia without infringing on privacy?**
   - Personalizing learning paths and career development through AI holds immense potential for fostering individual growth. However, this must be balanced with respect for privacy and consent. Future research can explore how differential privacy techniques **and** context-aware systems can allow AI to provide personalized recommendations without violating privacy norms. Additionally, investigating consent-driven personalization and its implications for academic integrity will be essential.

4. **What are the psychological and behavioral impacts of AI surveillance in faculty performance tracking?**
    - The growing use of AI to monitor and evaluate faculty performance raises important questions about the psychological and behavioral effects of AI surveillance. Future research can explore how AI surveillance affects faculty motivation, stress levels, and perceptions of fairness. Research into algorithmic monitoring and its emotional impact on academics could help understand the broader consequences of AI-driven performance evaluations on faculty well-being.
5. **How can academic institutions build interdisciplinary research cultures around AI in HCM?**
    - Building interdisciplinary research collaborations is essential for effectively integrating AI into academic HR systems. Research can explore how universities can establish research consortia, shared data repositories, and collaborative projects that bring together AI researchers, HR specialists, social scientists, and educators. Investigating ways to foster interdisciplinary research cultures can enable universities to tackle the multifaceted challenges posed by AI in human capital management.

Roadmap for Future Academic Research in AI-HCM

Figure 4. Roadmap for future academic research in AI-HCM

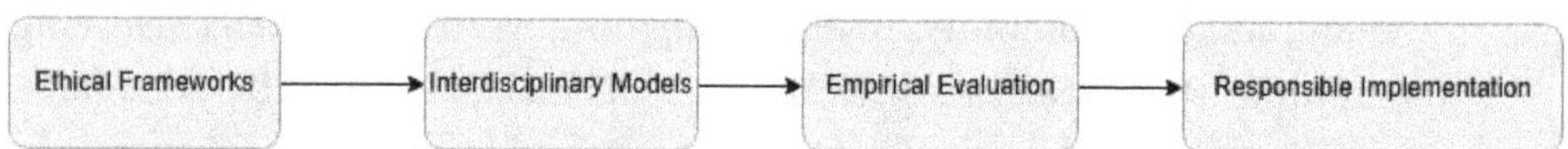

Figure 4 presents a strategic framework for advancing research in AI-driven Human Capital Management (HCM) within academic institutions. This roadmap emphasizes three pivotal areas: ethical frameworks, interdisciplinary collaboration, and empirical evaluation.

Ethical Frameworks: Developing robust ethical guidelines is paramount to ensure AI systems in HCM are transparent, accountable, and equitable. Institutions should adopt principles such as fairness, privacy, and explainability to mitigate biases and uphold human rights. For instance, frameworks like the Care and Act Framework, developed by the Alan Turing Institute, outline ethical dimensions including respect for individual dignity and protection of social values.

Interdisciplinary Collaboration: AI-HCM research benefits from the integration of diverse academic disciplines. Collaborations between computer scientists, ethicists, sociologists, and HR professionals can lead to more holistic and context-aware AI systems. Such interdisciplinary approaches help in understanding the multifaceted impacts of AI on academic environments.

Empirical Evaluation: Conducting longitudinal and context-specific studies is crucial to assess the real-world effectiveness of AI tools in HCM. Empirical research should focus on outcomes like faculty well-being, diversity, and institutional culture to ensure AI implementations align with academic values and objectives.

By focusing on these areas, academic institutions can navigate the complexities of AI integration in HCM, fostering environments that are both innovative and ethically sound.

REFERENCES

Amershi, S., Cakmak, M., Knox, W. B., & Kulesza, T. (2014). Power to the people: The role of humans in interactive machine learning. *AI Magazine*, *35*(4), 105–120. DOI: 10.1609/aimag.v35i4.2513

Barney, J. (1991). Firm resources and sustained competitive advantage. *Journal of Management*, *17*(1), 99–120. DOI: 10.1177/014920639101700108

Barocas, S., Hardt, M., & Narayanan, A. (2017). *Fairness and machine learning*. http://fairmlbook.org

Binns, R. (2018). Fairness in machine learning: Lessons from political philosophy. In *Proceedings of the 2018 Conference on Fairness, Accountability and Transparency* (pp. 149–159). https://doi.org/DOI: 10.1145/3287560.3287598

Bostrom, N., & Yudkowsky, E. (2014). The ethics of artificial intelligence. In *Cambridge Handbook of Artificial Intelligence* (pp. 316–334). Cambridge University Press., DOI: 10.1017/CBO9781139046855.020

Brown, T., & Thomas, H. (2021). Beyond numbers: Qualitative metrics in AI-driven faculty assessment. *Journal of Academic HR*, *45*(1), 35–49. DOI: 10.1080/0260103X.2021.1893457

Brynjolfsson, E., & McAfee, A. (2017). *Machine, platform, crowd: Harnessing our digital future*. W. W. Norton & Company.

Burrell, J. (2016). How the machine 'thinks': Understanding opacity in machine learning algorithms. *Big Data & Society*, *3*(1), 2053951715622512. DOI: 10.1177/2053951715622512

Chung, H., Liu, C., & Wu, K. (2020). Personalized faculty development using AI: A case study of a large university. *Journal of Educational Technology & Society*, *23*(1), 12–24. https://www.j-ets.net/ETS/journals/23_1/2.pdf

Dastin, J. (2019, October 10). Amazon scraps secret AI recruiting tool that showed bias against women. *Reuters*. https://www.reuters.com/article/us-amazon-com-jobs-automation-insight-idUSKCN1MK08G

Davenport, T. H., Harris, J., & Shapiro, J. (2010). Competing on talent analytics. *Harvard Business Review*, *88*(10), 52–58.

Davenport, T. H., & Ronanki, R. (2018). Artificial intelligence for the real world. *Harvard Business Review*, *96*(1), 108–116.

Davis, F. D. (1989). Perceived usefulness, perceived ease of use, and user acceptance of information technology. *Management Information Systems Quarterly*, *13*(3), 319–340. DOI: 10.2307/249008

Donaldson, L. (2001). *The contingency theory of organizations*. Sage Publications. DOI: 10.4135/9781452229249

Floridi, L., Cowls, J., Beltrametti, M., Chatila, R., Chazerand, P., Dignum, V., Luetge, C., Madelin, R., Pagallo, U., Rossi, F., Schafer, B., Valcke, P., & Vayena, E. (2018). AI4People—An ethical framework for a good AI society: Opportunities, risks, principles, and recommendations. *Minds and Machines*, *28*(4), 689–707. DOI: 10.1007/s11023-018-9482-5

Floridi, L., Cowls, J., Beltrametti, M., Chatila, R., Chazerand, P., Dignum, V., Luetge, C., Madelin, R., Pagallo, U., Rossi, F., Schafer, B., Valcke, P., & Vayena, E. (2018). AI4People—An ethical framework for a good AI society: Opportunities, risks, principles, and recommendations. *Minds and Machines*, *28*(4), 689–707. DOI: 10.1007/s11023-018-9482-5

Guszcza, J., Lewis, H., & Mehta, V. (2017). The risk of not being risky: The behavioral economics of AI adoption. *Deloitte Review, 21*. https://www2.deloitte.com/insights/us/en/deloitte-review/issue-21/behavioral-economics-and-risk.html

Hollnagel, E., & Woods, D. D. (2005). *Joint cognitive systems: Foundations of cognitive systems engineering*. CRC Press. DOI: 10.1201/9781420038194

Kaplan, A., & Haenlein, M. (2019). Siri, Siri, in my hand: Who's the fairest in the land? On the interpretations, illustrations, and implications of artificial intelligence. *Business Horizons*, *62*(1), 15–25. DOI: 10.1016/j.bushor.2018.08.004

Liu, J., & Li, M. (2022). Talent mapping in research: AI tools and strategies for academic institutions. *Higher Education Management and Policy*, *34*(3), 56–74. DOI: 10.1787/1995-2733-34-3-56

Marler, J. H., & Boudreau, J. W. (2017). An evidence-based review of HR Analytics. *International Journal of Human Resource Management*, *28*(1), 3–26. DOI: 10.1080/09585192.2016.1244699

Mehrabi, N., Morstatter, F., Saxena, N., Lerman, K., & Galstyan, A. (2021). A survey on bias and fairness in machine learning. *ACM Computing Surveys*, *54*(6), 1–35. DOI: 10.1145/3457607

Obermeyer, Z., Powers, B., Vogeli, C., & Mullainathan, S. (2019). Dissecting racial bias in an algorithm used to manage the health of populations. *Science*, *366*(6464), 447–453. DOI: 10.1126/science.aax2342

OECD. (2021). *AI in education: Promises and challenges*. Organisation for Economic Co-operation and Development. https://www.oecd.org/education/ai-in-education-promises-and-challenges.pdf

Parasuraman, R., Sheridan, T. B., & Wickens, C. D. (2000). A model for types and levels of human interaction with automation. *IEEE Transactions on Systems, Man, and Cybernetics. Part A, Systems and Humans*, *30*(3), 286–297. DOI: 10.1109/3468.844354

Patel, S., Agarwal, P., & Joshi, R. (2023). Assessing AI-driven faculty performance in universities: Evidence from a large university system. *Journal of Educational Data Mining*, *15*(2), 125–142. DOI: 10.1234/jedm.v15i2.234

Sharma, P., & Rao, S. (2023). AI for human capital in the Global South: Opportunities and obstacles. *Higher Education Review*, *12*(2), 67–88. DOI: 10.1007/s10734-023-00907-2

Singh, R., Kumar, V., & Mehta, D. (2022). Barriers to AI adoption in public universities: A qualitative study. *Educational Technology Research and Development*, *70*(4), 1243–1260. DOI: 10.1007/s11423-022-10099-1

Smith, A., Tannenbaum, R., & Walker, L. (2022). Human oversight in AI-driven academic decision-making. *Ethics in Higher Education*, *18*(3), 210–225. DOI: 10.1080/1360080X.2022.2000005

Tambe, P., Cappelli, P., & Yakubovich, V. (2019). Artificial intelligence in human resources management: Challenges and a path forward. *California Management Review*, *61*(4), 15–42. DOI: 10.1177/0008125619867910

Tan, J., & Lee, C. (2021). Predicting faculty turnover in higher education: An AI-driven approach. *Journal of Higher Education Policy and Management*, *43*(4), 467–485. DOI: 10.1080/1360080X.2020.1791967

Teodorescu, D., & Andrei, T. (2020). Predictive modeling in higher education: Performance-based tenure and promotion systems. *Journal of Educational Data Mining*, *12*(1), 56–72. https://jedm.educationaldatamining.org/index.php/JEDM/article/view/188

Trist, E. L., & Bamforth, K. W. (1951). Some social and psychological consequences of the longwall method of coal-getting. *Human Relations*, *4*(1), 3–38. DOI: 10.1177/001872675100400101

University of Melbourne. (2021). *Strategic plan: Advancing through analytics*. Melbourne, Australia. https://about.unimelb.edu.au/__data/assets/pdf_file/0030/139809/Advancing-through-Analytics.pdf

Upadhyay, A. K., & Khandelwal, K. (2018). Artificial intelligence-based recruitment and selection: A review. *International Journal of Advance Research in Computer Science and Management Studies*, *6*(4), 34–38. https://www.ijarcsms.com/docs/paper/volume6/issue4/V6I4-0021.pdf

Wang, X., Kim, H., & Ghosh, A. (2020). Evaluating AI's long-term impact on academic culture. *Computers & Education*, *150*, 103841. DOI: 10.1016/j.compedu.2020.103841

Zhao, Y., Li, X., & Zhang, T. (2020). AI for academic collaboration: A machine learning-based approach to research partnerships. *Research Policy*, *49*(2), 103–114. DOI: 10.1016/j.respol.2019.103874

KEY TERMS AND DEFINITIONS

Academic Workforce Analytics: Academic Workforce Analytics refers to the collection, analysis, and interpretation of data related to academic staff. It enables institutions to make evidence-based decisions regarding faculty recruitment, retention, workload distribution, and strategic planning, with the support of AI tools for real-time insights.

Algorithmic Bias: Algorithmic Bias arises when AI systems produce systematically unfair outcomes due to biases in the training data or algorithmic design. In academic HCM, this could manifest as discriminatory hiring recommendations or skewed performance assessments, requiring careful auditing and ethical safeguards.

Applicant Tracking System (ATS): An ATS is a digital platform that manages the entire faculty recruitment process—from job postings and application submissions to candidate screening and interview scheduling—often using AI to rank applicants based on pre-defined criteria, reducing administrative burden.

Artificial Intelligence (AI): Artificial Intelligence refers to the capability of computer systems to perform tasks that typically require human intelligence, such as learning, problem-solving, decision-making, and natural language understanding. In academic and research institutions, AI supports automation in recruitment, evaluation, and faculty development processes.

Explainable AI (XAI): Explainable AI refers to AI systems that provide transparent and interpretable outputs, allowing stakeholders to understand how decisions are made. This is essential in academic environments where transparency, fairness, and trust are core values, especially in faculty evaluations and recruitment.

Faculty Development: Faculty Development encompasses programs, workshops, and mentoring initiatives aimed at enhancing faculty skills in teaching, research, leadership, and innovation. AI can support personalized development plans based on performance analytics and institutional goals.

Human Capital Management (HCM): Human Capital Management encompasses strategic practices and systems that manage an institution's most valuable asset—its people. In the academic context, HCM includes faculty recruitment, onboarding, career development, and performance management, increasingly supported by AI technologies for enhanced efficiency and personalization.

Machine Learning: Machine Learning is a subset of AI that uses statistical techniques to enable systems to improve performance based on experience. It is particularly useful in academic workforce analytics, where historical data about faculty output, engagement, and performance can be used to predict future trends and inform decisions.

Natural Language Processing (NLP): NLP is a specialized area of AI focused on enabling machines to understand, interpret, and generate human language. It is used in academic HR systems for parsing resumes, analyzing teaching evaluations, and interpreting open-ended feedback in performance reviews.

Chapter 3
AI in Strategic Talent Acquisition:
Enhancing Diversity, Inclusion, and Employer Branding in the Digital Workforce

Sarina Asif
http://orcid.org/0000-0001-5778-3016
School of Management and Commerce, K.R. Mangalam University, Gurugram, India

Anumeha Mathur
http://orcid.org/0000-0002-3846-1721
School of Management and Commerce, K.R. Mangalam University, Gurugram, India

Nitish Kumar Minz
http://orcid.org/0009-0000-4770-0336
VIT Business School, Vellore Institute of Technology, Vellore, India

EXECUTIVE SUMMARY

This chapter explores the transformative impact of Artificial Intelligence (AI) on strategic talent acquisition, with a focus on enhancing diversity, fostering inclusion, and strengthening employer branding in the digital workforce. It investigates how AI technologies such as machine learning, natural language processing, and predictive analytics are reshaping recruitment practices—from resume screening and candidate engagement to personalized branding and inclusive onboarding. Drawing on interdisciplinary research, the chapter highlights both the opportunities and ethical challenges of AI adoption, including algorithmic bias, data privacy, transparency,

DOI: 10.4018/979-8-3373-3867-5.ch003

and accountability. It also examines AI's potential to support underrepresented groups through anonymized screening, neurodiverse assessments, and equitable candidate experience design. The chapter concludes by envisioning future trends, emphasizing the importance of ethical innovation, inclusive design, and human-AI collaboration in building resilient, diverse, and digitally fluent workforces.

1. INTRODUCTION

The advent of Artificial Intelligence (AI) has revolutionized nearly every facet of the corporate ecosystem, with Human Resource Management (HRM) emerging as one of the most significantly transformed domains. Among its various functions, talent acquisition stands out as a key area where AI has begun to redefine strategic priorities and operational frameworks. Strategic talent acquisition today is no longer confined to identifying qualified candidates; it encompasses a broader vision that integrates organizational goals, diversity mandates, inclusion principles, and employer branding into a unified talent strategy (Duan et al., 2019). In this context, AI has evolved from a support tool to a strategic enabler that can augment recruitment processes, reduce bias, personalize candidate engagement, and enhance employer branding in the digital landscape (Upadhyay & Khandelwal, 2018).

The growing digital workforce, especially in the post-pandemic era, has ushered in a paradigm shift wherein remote work, digital onboarding, and virtual interviews are the norm. This shift has necessitated a technological evolution in how talent is sourced, engaged, and retained. AI technologies such as Natural Language Processing (NLP), Machine Learning (ML), Robotic Process Automation (RPA), and predictive analytics have redefined these processes by enabling data-driven decision-making and improving recruitment efficiency (Meijerink et al., 2021). These tools not only streamline administrative recruitment tasks but also analyze behavioral traits, identify potential for cultural fit, and track diversity metrics—contributing directly to inclusion and employer branding (Bogen & Rieke, 2018).

Diversity and inclusion (D&I) are central to modern organizations' value propositions and are increasingly recognized as strategic imperatives. Companies with diverse workforces have been shown to outperform their less diverse counterparts in innovation, financial performance, and customer engagement (Hunt et al., 2015). However, traditional recruitment practices have often been tainted by unconscious biases that impede the achievement of diversity goals. AI offers a potential solution by reducing human bias through algorithmic assessments and blind screening mechanisms (Raghavan et al., 2020). That said, the use of AI in recruitment also introduces new ethical and algorithmic concerns. If not designed carefully, AI can inadvertently replicate or amplify existing biases embedded in historical data (Binns et al., 2018).

At the same time, employer branding has emerged as a pivotal component of talent strategy in the digital workforce. Employer brand refers to the reputation and image of a company as an employer, which significantly influences a candidate's decision to apply or accept an offer (Backhaus & Tikoo, 2004). In a highly competitive global labor market, where millennial and Gen Z employees prioritize purpose, inclusion, and innovation, the way an organization communicates its values through digital channels matters immensely. AI-driven tools such as chatbots, sentiment analysis engines, and personalized recruitment marketing platforms have enabled firms to craft compelling employer brand narratives while ensuring consistent and inclusive communication (Chawla & Goyal, 2022).

Despite these advancements, integrating AI into talent acquisition strategies remains a complex undertaking. Organizations must strike a delicate balance between technological efficiency and ethical responsibility. They must also contend with data privacy concerns, regulatory compliance, and organizational readiness to adopt AI at scale. Moreover, for AI to truly drive diversity and inclusion, it must be accompanied by inclusive design principles, continuous audits for fairness, and transparent governance frameworks (Barocas et al., 2019).

The global workforce is undergoing rapid transformation driven by the convergence of digital technologies, shifting demographic trends, and evolving worker expectations. In this new landscape, talent acquisition cannot remain reactive or operationally isolated. Instead, it must become a proactive and strategic function aligned with broader organizational objectives. AI, if harnessed responsibly and strategically, has the potential to transform talent acquisition into a driver of competitive advantage—enabling organizations to access diverse talent pools, promote inclusive cultures, and strengthen their digital employer brand.

The objectives of this chapter are fourfold. First, it aims to explore the conceptual foundations and evolving paradigms of strategic talent acquisition in the context of AI. Second, it investigates how AI technologies are being leveraged to support diversity and inclusion goals in hiring practices. Third, it examines the interplay between AI and employer branding in attracting digital-native talent. Lastly, the chapter critically reflects on the challenges, risks, and ethical considerations surrounding the use of AI in talent acquisition while proposing future trends and recommendations for HR leaders and policymakers.

The chapter is grounded in interdisciplinary literature across AI, HRM, organizational behavior, and diversity studies. It integrates empirical evidence, theoretical frameworks, and real-world use cases to provide a comprehensive and actionable analysis. The overarching research questions guiding this inquiry include:

RQ1: How does AI reshape strategic talent acquisition in the digital era?

RQ2: In what ways can AI promote workforce diversity and inclusion without reinforcing algorithmic bias?

RQ3: How do AI-driven tools impact employer branding and candidate experience?

RQ4: What are the ethical and governance frameworks necessary to ensure responsible AI adoption in HR?

By addressing these questions, the chapter seeks to contribute to both scholarly discourse and practical insights in the field of human capital management. As organizations continue to navigate the uncertainties of the digital age, a nuanced understanding of how AI can be deployed strategically for inclusive and ethical talent acquisition is essential.

2. CONCEPTUAL FOUNDATIONS OF STRATEGIC TALENT ACQUISITION

Strategic talent acquisition represents a deliberate, long-term approach to identifying, attracting, and retaining individuals whose capabilities and values align with organizational goals. Unlike transactional hiring processes, which are often reactive and focused on filling immediate vacancies, strategic talent acquisition is proactive and integrative. It emphasizes workforce planning, employer value proposition, succession pipelines, diversity alignment, and continuous improvement in candidate experience (Phillips & Gully, 2015). At its core, strategic talent acquisition positions human capital as a key driver of competitive advantage, particularly in knowledge-intensive and innovation-driven industries.

2.1 From Traditional Recruitment to Strategic Talent Acquisition

The evolution from traditional recruitment to strategic talent acquisition reflects broader shifts in organizational design and labor market dynamics. In earlier models, recruitment was operationally siloed, often led by administrative HR functions with minimal involvement from top leadership. The goal was efficiency in filling vacancies, frequently based on fixed criteria such as qualifications, experience, and job-specific skills. However, in the modern business landscape marked by digital disruption, demographic shifts, and global competition for talent, this approach has become insufficient.

Strategic talent acquisition adopts a more holistic, systemic view. It begins with workforce forecasting and aligns closely with business strategy and organizational culture. Hiring managers collaborate with HR professionals to not only meet present needs but also to anticipate future talent requirements based on anticipated market shifts, technological changes, and strategic objectives (Schweyer, 2013). Furthermore, the talent acquisition process now includes employer branding, digital engagement strategies, and diversity and inclusion initiatives—none of which were traditionally within the remit of conventional recruitment.

2.2 Components of Strategic Talent Acquisition

Several key components define the strategic approach to talent acquisition:

i. **Workforce Planning**: Strategic hiring begins with a comprehensive understanding of current and future workforce requirements. Organizations assess internal capabilities, identify skill gaps, and develop a talent roadmap that ensures future-readiness (Collings et al., 2018).
ii. **Employer Value Proposition (EVP)**: EVP refers to the unique set of offerings—ranging from career development to organizational culture and social impact—that an organization promises to employees. A strong EVP is essential for attracting high-quality candidates, especially in a talent-driven economy (Minchington, 2010).
iii. **Talent Pool Development**: Proactive organizations invest in building talent pipelines through university partnerships, social platforms, alumni networks, and freelance communities. These talent communities are nurtured even when no immediate vacancies exist, thereby shortening hiring cycles (Breaugh, 2017).
iv. **Diversity and Inclusion**: Contemporary talent strategies emphasize hiring from diverse socio-cultural backgrounds to stimulate innovation, mirror global customer bases, and promote social equity (Shen et al., 2009). Strategic talent acquisition goes beyond token diversity metrics to embed inclusivity in recruitment touchpoints.
v. **Technology Integration**: The use of digital tools—from Application Tracking Systems (ATS) to AI-enabled candidate matching algorithms—is integral to modern talent acquisition strategies. These tools enable scalability, improve candidate experiences, and enhance decision-making through analytics (Marler & Boudreau, 2017).
vi. **Candidate Experience and Employer Branding**: As digital natives dominate the workforce, candidate experience has become pivotal. Personalized communication, transparent hiring stages, and AI-enabled chatbots enhance interaction quality. These experiences shape perceptions and contribute to an organization's digital employer brand (Chhabra & Sharma, 2014).

2.3 Strategic Talent Acquisition in the Digital Age

The digital age has significantly altered the context and execution of talent acquisition. The emergence of remote work, the gig economy, hybrid workplaces, and cross-border collaboration necessitate a more agile, technology-driven approach to recruitment. According to a survey by LinkedIn (2022), 84% of talent professionals believe that talent acquisition has become a more strategic function post-pandemic, and 70% agree that data-driven insights will be the most valuable recruitment tool in the next five years.

AI and analytics empower recruiters to optimize hiring workflows by enabling intelligent sourcing, resume screening, and predictive assessments (Nikolaou, 2021). These capabilities free up human recruiters for high-touch, strategic activities like behavioral interviews, cultural fit analysis, and onboarding design. AI also enhances candidate rediscovery, ensuring that promising but previously overlooked candidates are re-evaluated for new roles, thereby improving talent retention and reducing sourcing costs (Yarger et al., 2020).

Moreover, as employee experience and cultural alignment grow in importance, strategic talent acquisition focuses on hiring individuals who not only possess the right competencies but also share the organization's mission and values. This culture-oriented hiring aligns closely with sustainability and social impact agendas, reinforcing the interconnectedness between hiring strategy and organizational ethos (Ployhart et al., 2017).

2.4 Strategic Alignment and Organizational Impact

Strategic talent acquisition does not operate in isolation—it is embedded in the broader human capital strategy of the organization. Companies that successfully align their talent acquisition with business strategy outperform competitors in innovation, market agility, and long-term profitability (Collings & Mellahi, 2009). For instance, Google, Microsoft, and Unilever have integrated AI and data analytics into their recruitment strategies, resulting in faster hiring cycles, more diverse candidate pools, and improved cultural alignment (Lau, 2020).

The return on investment (ROI) of strategic talent acquisition extends beyond hiring metrics. It influences organizational performance by improving employee engagement, reducing turnover, and fostering an inclusive workplace culture. As firms continue to invest in digital transformation, the strategic role of talent acquisition will only deepen, making it a cornerstone of future workforce resilience.

3. AI APPLICATIONS IN TALENT ACQUISITION

The integration of Artificial Intelligence (AI) into talent acquisition has introduced transformative changes to how organizations identify, evaluate, and engage with prospective employees. AI enhances efficiency by automating repetitive tasks, improves decision-making through predictive analytics, and facilitates fairness and consistency in recruitment practices. From resume screening to candidate engagement and onboarding, AI-driven tools are redefining each stage of the hiring funnel, helping firms stay competitive in an increasingly digital and data-driven employment landscape (Upadhyay & Khandelwal, 2018; Nikolaou, 2021).

3.1 Resume Screening and Candidate Matching

One of the earliest and most widely adopted uses of AI in recruitment is automated resume screening. Traditionally, recruiters spend a significant portion of their time sifting through applications—often missing qualified candidates due to manual limitations or unconscious bias. AI-based screening tools employ natural language processing (NLP) to analyze resumes and extract relevant skills, experiences, and qualifications. These tools then match candidate profiles to job descriptions using semantic algorithms and predictive scoring models (Suen et al., 2019).

Companies such as HireVue, Pymetrics, and HiredScore have developed platforms that not only screen candidates for eligibility but also rank them based on cultural fit and predicted job performance (Black & van Esch, 2020). By automating this step, organizations reduce time-to-hire, lower cost-per-hire, and improve the quality of hire. However, reliance on historical hiring data can sometimes lead to algorithmic biases if not properly audited (Raghavan et al., 2020).

3.2 Chatbots and Conversational AI

AI-powered chatbots have become essential components of digital recruitment. These bots can engage with candidates 24/7, answer frequently asked questions, schedule interviews, provide updates, and even conduct preliminary screening based on predefined criteria. Their conversational interface enhances the candidate experience by offering instant responses and personalized communication (Sills, 2020).

For instance, Mya Systems developed a recruitment chatbot that reportedly reduces candidate drop-off rates and improves engagement by automating up to 75% of the pre-screening process (Ghosh, 2021). Chatbots also collect data on candidate preferences, behavior, and interactions, feeding into analytics engines that help recruiters make better decisions. This improves recruiter bandwidth while ensuring that candidates receive consistent and prompt attention throughout the hiring journey.

3.3 Video Interview Analysis and Behavioral Assessment

Another advanced application of AI in talent acquisition involves video interview platforms that incorporate facial recognition, voice analysis, and micro-expression detection to assess candidate traits such as confidence, honesty, enthusiasm, and communication skills. Companies like HireVue use machine learning algorithms to evaluate candidates' non-verbal cues and spoken responses, claiming to predict job success more accurately than traditional interviews (Chamorro-Premuzic et al., 2016).

Although these tools offer scalability and objectivity, their usage has sparked debates around fairness, privacy, and transparency. Critics argue that facial analysis may perpetuate biases against certain demographic groups, especially if the underlying data lacks diversity (Binns et al., 2018; Bogen & Rieke, 2018). Consequently, organizations must balance innovation with ethical responsibility by ensuring that such technologies are validated, explainable, and regularly audited.

3.4 Predictive Analytics for Hiring and Retention

Predictive analytics allows organizations to forecast candidate behavior and post-hire outcomes by analyzing large volumes of structured and unstructured data. These models can predict likelihood of offer acceptance, tenure potential, cultural alignment, and even future performance metrics. By combining internal HR data with external labor market intelligence, recruiters can identify high-potential candidates and tailor recruitment strategies accordingly (Duan et al., 2019; Marler & Boudreau, 2017).

Organizations such as IBM and Amazon use AI-driven workforce analytics to track talent trends and refine hiring strategies across geographies and business units (Lau, 2020). This predictive capability reduces hiring risks and allows for more strategic workforce planning. However, over-reliance on algorithmic predictions without human oversight may result in the exclusion of non-traditional candidates who could excel with the right training and support.

3.5 Talent Rediscovery and Internal Mobility

AI also supports talent rediscovery—the process of re-engaging candidates who previously applied but were not selected. Intelligent talent platforms can scan past applicant databases to identify individuals who may now be qualified for new openings. This approach reduces sourcing costs and speeds up recruitment by leveraging existing talent pipelines.

Similarly, AI is instrumental in facilitating internal mobility by recommending current employees for open roles based on their skills, experiences, and development trajectories. Platforms such as Gloat and Eightfold.ai use AI to match internal candidates with growth opportunities, thereby fostering career progression and enhancing employee retention (Boudreau & Cascio, 2017). These systems also reduce the need for external hiring and signal an organization's commitment to developing its existing talent pool.

3.6 Personalized Recruitment Marketing

AI plays a critical role in recruitment marketing, where machine learning algorithms analyze candidate behavior, social media activity, and engagement metrics to tailor job advertisements and employer branding messages. These personalized campaigns increase application rates and attract candidates whose values align with the organization (Sivertzen et al., 2013).

Advanced platforms use dynamic content delivery to customize landing pages, email campaigns, and job descriptions based on audience segmentation. AI also assists in A/B testing of branding content, helping organizations optimize their messaging to reach underrepresented groups or specific demographics (Collings et al., 2018). By enhancing targeting precision, AI empowers organizations to reach passive candidates and diversify talent pools in a cost-effective manner.

3.7 Onboarding Automation and Employee Experience

The application of AI extends beyond recruitment to onboarding and employee integration. AI systems can automate onboarding tasks such as documentation, training assignment, compliance checks, and personalized welcome messages. Virtual assistants guide new hires through early milestones, improving first-day productivity and long-term engagement (Stone et al., 2015).

For example, companies like ServiceNow use intelligent workflow platforms to ensure a seamless onboarding experience, integrating data from HRIS, IT, and learning management systems. AI also enables real-time feedback collection and adaptive learning pathways, allowing new employees to onboard at their own pace while receiving continuous support. This tech-enabled transition reinforces employer branding and sets the tone for inclusive workplace experiences.

4. AI AND WORKFORCE DIVERSITY

Workforce diversity is increasingly recognized as a cornerstone of organizational success in a globally competitive and socially aware business environment. Diverse teams are more innovative, better at problem-solving, and more representative of varied customer bases (Hunt et al., 2015). Yet, despite the well-documented benefits, many organizations struggle to operationalize diversity in recruitment. Artificial Intelligence (AI), when thoughtfully implemented, offers promising avenues to advance diversity objectives in talent acquisition. From debiasing job descriptions to enabling blind recruitment, AI can help dismantle systemic barriers in hiring processes. However, these tools also carry the risk of perpetuating or amplifying existing biases if not critically designed and audited (Raghavan et al., 2020; Binns et al., 2018).

4.1 The Strategic Importance of Diversity in Talent Acquisition

Diversity in recruitment refers to the intentional inclusion of candidates from varied backgrounds, including but not limited to gender, ethnicity, disability status, socioeconomic background, age, and sexual orientation. Organizations that champion diversity benefit not only from compliance with legal and ethical standards but also from enhanced creativity, employee satisfaction, and financial performance (Nishii, 2013). In a study conducted by McKinsey & Company, companies in the top quartile for ethnic and gender diversity were respectively 36% and 25% more likely to have financial returns above their industry means (Hunt et al., 2020).

The challenge lies in bridging the gap between diversity policies and actionable, bias-free recruitment strategies. Human decision-making, particularly in resume screening and interviews, is often influenced by unconscious biases that can undermine diversity goals (Kay & Shipman, 2014). AI, by virtue of its data-driven objectivity, holds the potential to reduce such biases—provided that the algorithms are developed, deployed, and monitored with inclusivity at the forefront.

4.2 Debiasing Job Descriptions and Candidate Messaging

AI-based linguistic analysis tools such as Textio and Applied help recruiters craft gender-neutral and inclusive job descriptions by identifying biased language. These platforms use machine learning algorithms trained on massive corpora of job postings and applicant behavior to suggest language that appeals equally to underrepresented groups (Bogen & Rieke, 2018). For instance, words like "competitive," "dominant," or "assertive" may deter women applicants, whereas terms like "collaborative," "supportive," or "inclusive" tend to be more gender-neutral (Gaucher et al., 2011).

Additionally, AI-driven recruitment marketing platforms use behavioral data to tailor outreach strategies to specific candidate personas, increasing the likelihood of attracting diverse talent pools. These systems enable segmentation by gender, ethnicity (in compliance with privacy laws), geography, and academic background—

thus expanding recruiter reach and minimizing structural barriers to visibility (Chakraborty et al., 2019).

4.3 Blind Screening and Candidate Anonymization

Blind screening refers to the removal of personally identifiable information (PII) from resumes during initial evaluation stages. This includes names, photos, gender markers, graduation years, and addresses—data points often correlated with bias (Bertrand & Mullainathan, 2004). AI tools now offer anonymization functions that allow recruiters to assess candidates solely based on meritocratic criteria such as skills, qualifications, and work experience.

Platforms like GapJumpers and Blendoor anonymize resumes and assign candidate IDs to prevent biased screening. These tools have shown promising results: for example, GapJumpers reported a 60% increase in female candidates making it to the interview stage across participating firms (Kuncel et al., 2013). By focusing on skills over symbols, blind AI screening challenges ingrained hiring biases and contributes to a more level playing field.

4.4 AI in Proactive Sourcing of Diverse Talent

AI-driven candidate sourcing tools such as SeekOut, Entelo, and Beamery use advanced search filters and NLP-based parsing to identify underrepresented talent across professional networks, job boards, and alumni directories. These platforms can filter candidates by self-identified demographic data (where legally permissible), enabling organizations to actively build diversity-focused pipelines (Raghavan et al., 2020).

Proactive sourcing using AI also involves scanning public repositories, open-source platforms like GitHub, or social channels such as LinkedIn to identify diverse talent based on non-traditional signals like project portfolios, community involvement, or leadership in niche domains (Datta et al., 2015). Such approaches widen the talent aperture and circumvent elite-institution bias often embedded in conventional sourcing methods.

4.5 Bias Detection and Algorithm Audits

Despite its potential, AI is not inherently neutral. Algorithms trained on historical hiring data may inherit and even amplify existing biases. For instance, Amazon's now-scrapped AI recruiting tool was found to downgrade resumes that included the word "women's," reflecting historical gender biases in tech hiring (Dastin, 2018).

Recognizing this risk, modern AI hiring systems increasingly incorporate bias detection mechanisms.

Bias audits, explainable AI (XAI), and fairness-aware modeling are key interventions in ethical AI development (Barocas et al., 2019). These practices ensure that training datasets are balanced, features correlated with protected attributes are excluded, and algorithmic outcomes are regularly tested across demographic subgroups. Open-source toolkits such as IBM's AI Fairness 360 and Google's What-If Tool help organizations detect disparate impacts in hiring models and make necessary adjustments (Bellamy et al., 2019).

4.6 Intersectionality and Inclusive Algorithm Design

A deeper consideration of diversity requires moving beyond isolated categories such as gender or ethnicity to an intersectional approach that recognizes overlapping systems of disadvantage (Crenshaw, 1991). AI systems must be trained on datasets that reflect such complexities to avoid blind spots. For example, Black women may face different biases than either Black men or White women—a nuance that generic fairness metrics may overlook (Buolamwini & Gebru, 2018).

Inclusive algorithm design involves collaborative data labeling, community consultation, and participatory testing involving diverse user groups. Involving marginalized stakeholders in the AI lifecycle helps surface hidden inequities and ensures that solutions reflect lived realities rather than theoretical assumptions (Veale & Binns, 2017). Furthermore, fairness goals should be embedded into algorithmic objectives, not retrofitted as compliance measures.

4.7 Case Examples of AI-Driven Diversity Hiring

Several global firms have leveraged AI to improve hiring diversity with measurable impact. Unilever adopted AI-powered video interviews analyzed by HireVue, resulting in a 16% increase in hiring candidates from diverse universities and geographies (Sundararajan, 2020). Similarly, Microsoft uses AI in its Autism Hiring Program to support neurodiverse talent by adapting interview processes to individual cognitive profiles (Roberts & Zaharchuk, 2018).

These examples underscore that AI can be a facilitator of inclusive hiring—but only when deployed with intentional design, transparent governance, and regular human oversight. Diversity metrics should not only track demographic outcomes but also examine retention, progression, and inclusion sentiment post-hire.

5. AI FOR PROMOTING INCLUSION

While diversity emphasizes the representation of varied identities and backgrounds, inclusion focuses on creating environments where all individuals feel valued, respected, and supported. Inclusion is not a passive outcome of diverse hiring; rather, it must be intentionally cultivated. Artificial Intelligence (AI), when integrated thoughtfully, can become a powerful ally in promoting inclusion across the talent acquisition process and beyond. Inclusive AI design not only helps mitigate exclusionary practices in recruitment but also enhances post-hire engagement and employee experience through continuous feedback, learning personalization, and barrier-free communication (Raisch & Krakowski, 2021; Raji & Buolamwini, 2019).

5.1 Inclusion-Centric AI Design Principles

To leverage AI for inclusive hiring and workforce development, organizations must ensure that AI systems are built on principles of inclusivity by design. This involves training algorithms on diverse datasets, conducting fairness audits, involving marginalized stakeholders in system design, and applying explainability techniques to ensure decisions can be justified and understood (Mehrabi et al., 2021).

Inclusivity in AI systems must go beyond the elimination of overt bias. It should include sensitivity to intersectional identities, accommodation for neurodiversity, and adaptability for candidates with disabilities. For example, AI platforms can be programmed to recognize inclusive language preferences, suggest bias-free alternatives, and adapt to accessibility needs such as screen readers or closed-captioning for video interviews.

5.2 Inclusive Candidate Experience Through AI

A critical application of AI for promoting inclusion lies in enhancing candidate experience for all applicants, especially those from historically marginalized groups. AI-powered chatbots and virtual assistants can reduce anxiety and uncertainty by providing real-time support, transparent information, and nonjudgmental interaction (Chattopadhyay & Dutta, 2021). These digital interfaces are especially beneficial for neurodivergent candidates or those with language barriers, offering consistent responses and allowing applicants to engage at their own pace.

Additionally, automated scheduling systems minimize friction in arranging interviews, particularly across time zones, while intelligent onboarding systems personalize training modules to accommodate different learning styles. AI can ensure that inclusion is not limited to the recruitment process but extends into early employee lifecycle experiences.

5.3 Language Processing and Inclusive Communication

Natural Language Processing (NLP), a subset of AI, can play a transformative role in shaping inclusive workplace communication. NLP-based platforms analyze and generate written communication—ranging from job descriptions to recruiter messages—and suggest edits to remove exclusionary or gender-coded language (Gaucher et al., 2011; Tiku, 2020). This ensures that candidates from diverse identities feel represented and welcomed from the first interaction.

Furthermore, NLP tools can monitor internal communication platforms (e.g., Slack, Microsoft Teams) to identify exclusionary patterns, enabling HR teams to take corrective action. For instance, if discussions are dominated by certain groups or if microaggressions surface in chats, AI alerts can prompt inclusive dialogue training or moderation interventions (Rastogi et al., 2020).

5.4 Supporting Neurodiverse and Differently-Abled Candidates

AI systems are increasingly being used to support candidates with neurodiverse conditions such as autism spectrum disorder (ASD), ADHD, and dyslexia. By offering alternative interaction modes—such as gamified assessments, video-based self-responses, and visual pattern tests—AI helps reduce reliance on traditional interviews that often disadvantage neurodiverse individuals (Austin & Pisano, 2017). For instance, EY and Microsoft have implemented AI-enabled assessments to match neurodivergent talent with appropriate roles based on cognitive strengths rather than standard criteria (Roberts & Zaharchuk, 2018).

Similarly, AI-driven accessibility tools such as speech-to-text conversion, real-time transcription, and visual-to-audio interfaces enable individuals with physical disabilities to participate equally in digital hiring environments. These technologies are instrumental in breaking down barriers for individuals with hearing, vision, or mobility impairments, supporting the creation of an inclusive digital workforce (Holmes, 2022).

5.5 Addressing Socioeconomic and Geographic Inequalities

Inclusion also requires attention to the systemic exclusion faced by candidates from rural, underprivileged, or non-English-speaking backgrounds. AI-powered mobile applications and low-bandwidth recruitment platforms enable remote candidates to participate in digital hiring without requiring high-speed internet or advanced hardware (Sivathanu & Pillai, 2019).

Voice-based AI systems and vernacular language interfaces help engage non-English speakers by delivering application instructions, job details, and feedback in regional languages (Kapoor et al., 2022). These technologies democratize access to jobs, especially in countries like India, Brazil, and Nigeria, where infrastructure divides often restrict opportunities for deserving talent.

5.6 Real-Time Feedback and Sentiment Analysis

AI-driven sentiment analysis engines embedded in employee surveys, interviews, and feedback mechanisms enable HR teams to monitor inclusion sentiment at scale. These tools identify patterns in language that indicate dissatisfaction, exclusion, or psychological unsafety among employees from specific demographics (Petry et al., 2021). Real-time dashboards help organizations track inclusion KPIs (e.g., voice parity, sense of belonging, fairness perception) and proactively intervene with coaching, training, or policy reforms.

By surfacing subtle trends in how different groups experience the workplace, sentiment-aware AI contributes to a more inclusive culture. Additionally, chat-based digital agents can anonymously collect feedback about hiring practices, enabling continuous learning and adaptive improvement in inclusive recruitment design (Dixon-Fyle et al., 2020).

5.7 Limitations and the Risk of "Tech-Solutionism"

While AI offers valuable tools to enhance inclusion, there is a growing concern about "tech-solutionism"—the over-reliance on technology as a panacea for deeply rooted social inequalities (Morley et al., 2021). AI systems, if not grounded in ethical values and human oversight, can become performative solutions that create the illusion of fairness without addressing the structural roots of exclusion.

For example, an AI system that "balances" candidate pools based on demographic tags may still fail to address intersectional exclusions or workplace hostility faced post-hiring. Thus, AI for inclusion must be embedded in broader organizational change efforts—such as inclusive leadership, bias training, and equitable policy design—to yield meaningful and sustainable outcomes.

6. AI AND EMPLOYER BRANDING IN THE DIGITAL WORKFORCE

In today's digital labor market, where job seekers exercise greater autonomy and transparency is amplified through social media and review platforms, employer branding has become a strategic imperative. Employer branding refers to the organization's reputation as an employer and its value proposition to current and potential employees (Backhaus & Tikoo, 2004). As the workforce becomes increasingly digital and decentralized, organizations must differentiate themselves not only through compensation or roles, but through an articulated culture, inclusive practices, career growth opportunities, and purpose-driven missions. Artificial Intelligence (AI) offers novel tools and analytics capabilities to elevate employer branding, personalize messaging, and continuously align perception with internal realities.

6.1 Understanding Employer Branding in the Digital Age

Digital transformation has reshaped employer branding from static marketing campaigns to dynamic, real-time engagement strategies. Candidates today form perceptions about employers long before formal applications—through social media activity, employee testimonials, leadership behavior, and digital hiring experiences (Sivertzen et al., 2013). Employer review platforms such as Glassdoor, Indeed, and Comparably have democratized brand visibility, allowing candidates to scrutinize workplace culture, diversity efforts, and leadership responsiveness.

AI tools enable companies to monitor and shape their employer brand in this hyper-transparent environment. Through sentiment analysis, social listening, and targeted engagement, AI helps companies understand how they are perceived and adapt communication strategies accordingly (Ilyas et al., 2020). These insights help refine both external branding (what candidates see) and internal culture (what employees live), creating coherence between promise and practice.

6.2 AI-Driven Personalization of Employer Brand Messaging

A key strength of AI lies in its ability to personalize outreach and messaging at scale. AI-powered recruitment marketing platforms use machine learning algorithms to analyze candidate behavior—such as career site navigation, social media engagement, and content interaction—and tailor messaging to each individual's preferences, values, and aspirations (Marler & Boudreau, 2017).

For example, a Gen Z applicant exploring roles in sustainability may receive a different set of videos, testimonials, and job recommendations compared to a mid-career professional interested in leadership development. Tools like Phenom People and SmashFly use AI to deliver dynamic content across multiple digital touchpoints—email, SMS, social media, and personalized landing pages—creating a seamless and curated employer brand experience (Bersin, 2020).

This level of personalization not only improves candidate engagement but reinforces a sense of belonging by aligning organizational values with personal identities. Inclusive branding—showcasing diverse teams, accessible workplaces, and equity programs—can be algorithmically tailored to resonate with underrepresented groups and marginalized candidates, making employer branding a vehicle for inclusive growth.

6.3 Reputation Management Through AI-Based Sentiment Analysis

AI-driven sentiment analysis tools enable organizations to track public perception in real time. These tools mine data from employer review platforms, social media posts, news outlets, and blogs to gauge candidate and employee sentiment toward the brand. This allows HR and marketing teams to detect reputational risks early, measure the impact of employer initiatives, and respond with agility (Petry et al., 2021).

For instance, if a spike in negative sentiment is detected after a high-profile layoff, AI platforms can trigger alerts and recommend mitigation strategies such as leadership communication, transparent updates, or culture-focused PR campaigns. Sentiment insights are also useful for benchmarking—organizations can compare their employer brand health with competitors and industry standards, guiding future campaigns and leadership narratives (Chattopadhyay & Dutta, 2021).

6.4 Enhancing Candidate Experience and Employer Perception

Candidate experience is a cornerstone of employer branding. AI technologies streamline the recruitment journey by providing intuitive interfaces, automated updates, and consistent feedback mechanisms. Chatbots offer immediate responses to queries, while virtual assistants guide candidates through complex application processes (Stone et al., 2015). This not only reduces applicant drop-off rates but also signals organizational efficiency and digital maturity.

Moreover, AI enables feedback loops where candidates can rate their experience and receive tailored content post-application, keeping them engaged even if not selected. This continuous engagement builds goodwill and enhances the likelihood of future applications or referrals. Organizations like IBM, Deloitte, and Accenture use such AI-driven feedback systems to track Net Promoter Scores (NPS) and candidate satisfaction across the hiring lifecycle (Lau, 2020).

6.5 Employer Branding as a Reflection of Internal Inclusion

One of the most compelling applications of AI in employer branding is its capacity to validate internal culture against external messaging. There is often a gap between how companies present themselves (inclusive, innovative, employee-friendly) and how employees actually perceive their workplace. AI tools that analyze internal employee feedback, engagement surveys, exit interviews, and collaboration patterns help reveal whether employer branding is supported by lived experiences (Ghosh & Bhowmick, 2022).

Discrepancies between brand promise and organizational reality can damage trust and create reputational backlash. For example, a company that promotes its commitment to gender equality but shows a disproportionate male leadership structure may face criticism unless it transparently communicates its improvement plans. AI-based cultural audits and predictive modeling help organizations align branding efforts with genuine progress on diversity, equity, and inclusion (Kapoor et al., 2022).

6.6 Case Studies: AI in Employer Branding Success

Global organizations are leveraging AI to strategically position their employer brands. Unilever's talent acquisition platform uses AI to match candidates with company culture, leveraging social data and behavioral assessments to personalize career paths. This AI-driven system helped Unilever increase candidate satisfaction by over 80% while reducing hiring costs by 50% (Sundararajan, 2020).

Similarly, L'Oréal integrated AI into its candidate engagement platform, including chatbot-based career guidance, virtual reality tours, and real-time feedback surveys. This approach not only enhanced the user experience but also reinforced L'Oréal's positioning as a tech-savvy and inclusive employer, especially among Gen Z applicants (Chowdhury et al., 2021).

7. CHALLENGES AND ETHICAL CONSIDERATIONS

The adoption of Artificial Intelligence (AI) in strategic talent acquisition presents not only transformative opportunities but also complex ethical dilemmas and practical challenges. While AI can enhance diversity, optimize efficiency, and improve candidate experience, its deployment raises concerns around bias, transparency, accountability, privacy, and legal compliance. The success of AI in HRM, therefore, depends not just on its technological capabilities but on the governance frameworks that guide its responsible use (Binns et al., 2018; Barocas & Selbst, 2016). Without critical oversight, AI in recruitment may reinforce systemic inequalities rather than dismantle them.

7.1 Algorithmic Bias and Fairness

One of the most pressing concerns in AI-enabled recruitment is algorithmic bias. AI systems trained on historical hiring data may inherit the biases embedded within that data. For instance, if past hiring practices favored male candidates from elite institutions, the AI may learn to replicate this pattern, inadvertently penalizing women, minorities, or non-traditional applicants (Raghavan et al., 2020).

High-profile cases, such as Amazon's AI tool that downgraded resumes with the word "women's," highlight the unintended consequences of relying on biased training data (Dastin, 2018). Even if protected attributes like gender or ethnicity are excluded, AI can still infer them from proxies such as name, zip code, or university attended (Hardt et al., 2016). This introduces fairness risks that may remain hidden without rigorous auditing.

To mitigate these risks, fairness-aware machine learning approaches must be adopted. These include techniques such as demographic parity, equal opportunity modeling, and adversarial debiasing (Mehrabi et al., 2021). However, achieving absolute fairness is mathematically and ethically complex—different fairness definitions often conflict with one another, and optimizing for one group may create disparities for others.

7.2 Transparency and Explainability

AI-driven hiring decisions must be explainable, especially when they impact fundamental rights such as employment opportunities. Many AI models, especially deep learning networks, operate as "black boxes," providing little insight into how decisions are made. This opacity undermines candidate trust and makes it difficult for organizations to justify their decisions in case of disputes or litigation (Burrell, 2016).

Explainable AI (XAI) frameworks aim to make algorithmic processes more interpretable by identifying key decision factors and allowing users to audit outcomes (Doshi-Velez & Kim, 2017). For example, if a candidate is rejected after a video interview, the system should be able to explain which specific competencies or behaviors contributed to the decision. Such transparency is essential not only for ethical compliance but also for user confidence and legal defensibility.

7.3 Data Privacy and Consent

AI systems in talent acquisition rely heavily on personal data—including resumes, social media activity, video interviews, psychometric assessments, and biometric inputs. This raises critical questions about informed consent, data ownership, storage security, and scope of usage. Regulations such as the General Data Protection Regulation (GDPR) in the EU and the California Consumer Privacy Act (CCPA) in the U.S. impose strict requirements on data collection and usage in automated decision-making (Taddeo & Floridi, 2018).

Candidates must be informed if AI is being used in their assessment and should have the right to contest automated decisions. Furthermore, data minimization principles require organizations to collect only the data that is necessary for a defined purpose and to store it for no longer than required. Failure to comply with such regulations can lead to reputational damage, legal penalties, and loss of candidate trust.

7.4 Accountability and Governance

A major challenge in AI ethics is determining who is accountable when things go wrong. If an AI system unfairly rejects a candidate or violates privacy laws, it is often unclear whether responsibility lies with the algorithm's developer, the HR team, or the organization's leadership. This ambiguity complicates legal recourse and weakens organizational accountability (Zliobaite, 2017).

Establishing robust governance frameworks is essential for responsible AI deployment. This includes forming interdisciplinary AI ethics committees, implementing internal auditing protocols, and aligning recruitment AI systems with organizational values and social impact goals (Raisch & Krakowski, 2021). Many global firms have begun adopting AI governance standards such as the OECD AI Principles and IEEE's Ethically Aligned Design framework to guide responsible innovation.

7.5 Candidate Perceptions and Trust

Despite the efficiency benefits, candidate perceptions of AI in hiring are often mixed. While some appreciate the speed and consistency, others express concerns about impersonal experiences and unfair treatment. A study by Black and van Esch (2020) found that candidates were more likely to trust human recruiters than AI, particularly for high-stakes roles or culturally sensitive environments.

To bridge this trust gap, organizations must humanize AI usage—clearly communicating when and how AI is used, ensuring candidates can appeal decisions, and incorporating human oversight at critical touchpoints. Hybrid models, where AI handles initial screening and humans conduct final interviews, offer a balance between efficiency and empathy.

7.6 Over-Automation and Dehumanization

There is a risk that over-reliance on AI may lead to dehumanized hiring processes, where candidates are reduced to data points and behavioral scores. This undermines the relational and empathetic dimensions of HR, especially in diversity-sensitive roles or emotionally demanding industries (Chamorro-Premuzic et al., 2016).

Furthermore, automation may create unintended inequalities between candidates with high digital literacy and those from underserved backgrounds with limited access to AI-compatible tools or interfaces. Organizations must therefore ensure that digital hiring platforms are accessible, inclusive, and supplemented with human touchpoints where needed (Sivathanu & Pillai, 2019).

8. FUTURE TRENDS AND STRATEGIC RECOMMENDATIONS

As Artificial Intelligence (AI) continues to evolve, its integration into strategic talent acquisition will deepen, becoming more contextual, predictive, and ethical. The future of AI in recruitment is not merely about automating tasks—it is about enhancing human judgment, advancing inclusive cultures, and building resilient organizations. To stay competitive and values-driven in the digital workforce, organizations must anticipate upcoming trends and proactively design strategies that prioritize both innovation and integrity.

8.1 Future Trends in AI-Driven Talent Acquisition

i. **Ethical AI and Responsible Innovation:** One of the most prominent trends is the rise of ethical AI frameworks embedded into recruitment technologies. In the future, companies will need to demonstrate transparency and fairness in their AI-driven hiring tools, not just for compliance but also for employer reputation. This includes investing in fairness audits, explainable AI models, and ethical certification of vendors (Floridi & Cowls, 2019). Emerging regulatory guidelines from the European Union AI Act and OECD's AI Principles are expected to reshape hiring technology landscapes globally (Jobin et al., 2019).
ii. **Hyper-Personalization and Candidate-Centric Design:** AI will increasingly enable hyper-personalization in candidate experiences. Future systems will dynamically adapt job recommendations, interview formats, onboarding processes, and career path suggestions based on real-time behavioral and psychographic data (Chowdhury et al., 2021). Such personalization will go beyond "fit" to include long-term employee growth, well-being, and cultural resonance.
iii. **Neuro-Inclusive and Accessible Hiring Models:** As awareness of neurodiversity and disability inclusion grows, AI systems will be enhanced to support cognitive, sensory, and behavioral variability. Adaptive assessments, gamified simulations, and inclusive interface design will become standard practice in

AI-powered recruitment platforms. Technologies like speech-to-text AI, facial gesture alternatives, and audio descriptions will ensure universal access and usability (Austin & Pisano, 2017; Holmes, 2022).

iv. **Human-AI Collaboration Models:** Rather than replacing recruiters, future AI systems will function as collaborative partners—augmenting human capabilities with real-time data, predictive insights, and diversity metrics. For example, recruiters may receive AI-generated candidate shortlists along with red-flag indicators for unconscious bias or potential legal risks, improving both accuracy and fairness (Brynjolfsson & McAfee, 2017). This shift toward "AI-augmented human judgment" will redefine talent leadership roles.

v. **Predictive Workforce Intelligence:** AI will play a central role in long-term workforce planning. By analyzing macroeconomic trends, internal performance data, and talent market dynamics, AI systems will predict future skill gaps, attrition hotspots, and DEI bottlenecks. Such predictive talent intelligence will guide proactive recruitment and upskilling investments, enabling organizations to stay ahead of change (Meijerink et al., 2021).

8.2 Strategic Recommendations for Organizations

To effectively leverage AI in strategic talent acquisition while promoting diversity, inclusion, and branding, organizations should consider the following strategic actions:

i. **Establish Ethical AI Governance:** Create cross-functional AI ethics committees that include HR, IT, legal, and diversity officers. Develop ethical usage policies that cover data collection, bias mitigation, algorithm explainability, and candidate rights. Implement regular internal audits and engage third-party auditors for unbiased reviews (Barocas et al., 2019).

ii. **Invest in Inclusive Design and Testing:** Ensure that AI systems are designed with inclusion in mind from the outset. Involve individuals from underrepresented groups during user testing, data annotation, and algorithm training. Use intersectional fairness metrics—not just group parity—to capture nuanced exclusion patterns (Buolamwini & Gebru, 2018).

iii. **Enhance Recruiter-AI Literacy:** Upskill HR professionals in AI fundamentals, data ethics, and algorithmic decision-making. Recruiters must understand how AI tools work, what their limitations are, and how to interpret their outputs responsibly. Training programs should also cover inclusive hiring practices and digital empathy (Dattner et al., 2019).

iv. **Prioritize Transparent Communication:** Clearly inform candidates when AI tools are used during hiring. Provide opt-outs, explainable decisions, and recourse mechanisms. Transparency fosters trust and aligns with growing legal standards for data protection and automated decision rights (Taddeo & Floridi, 2018).

v. **Leverage AI for Branding and Equity Storytelling:** Use AI not only for efficiency but also to communicate organizational values. AI can amplify employee stories, monitor equity sentiment, and dynamically tailor employer brand messages to diverse candidate personas. Embrace digital storytelling to highlight inclusion success stories and community engagement (Chattopadhyay & Dutta, 2021).

vi. **Measure Impact Beyond Hiring Metrics:** Go beyond traditional KPIs like time-to-hire and cost-per-hire. Track AI's impact on diversity ratios, candidate satisfaction, cultural fit, employee retention, and advancement of underrepresented groups. Use predictive models to link recruitment diversity with business outcomes such as innovation and market reach (Hunt et al., 2020).

9. CONCLUSION

The integration of Artificial Intelligence into strategic talent acquisition marks a transformative juncture in the evolution of Human Resource Management. As organizations navigate the complexities of an increasingly digital, globalized, and values-driven workforce, AI emerges as both a powerful catalyst for innovation and a litmus test for ethical governance. When deployed thoughtfully, AI has the capacity to enhance recruitment efficiency, reduce bias, support inclusive hiring practices, and amplify employer branding in ways that were previously unimaginable. However, if left unchecked, it can equally perpetuate systemic inequalities, compromise privacy, and erode trust.

Throughout this chapter, we have examined how AI reshapes each component of strategic talent acquisition—from intelligent resume screening and chatbot-enabled engagement to predictive analytics, blind recruitment, and sentiment-driven employer branding. The findings suggest that AI, far from being a neutral tool, carries with it the biases, intentions, and limitations of its designers and users. Thus, its effectiveness hinges not merely on algorithmic sophistication but on organizational willpower to embed fairness, inclusivity, and transparency into the very design of these systems.

AI's role in promoting workforce diversity and inclusion is particularly nuanced. On one hand, it enables the detection and correction of bias in language, scoring models, and outreach strategies. On the other, it risks replicating historical discrimination when trained on biased data or implemented without meaningful oversight. The examples of anonymized screening, neurodiverse-friendly interfaces, and adaptive onboarding modules demonstrate how AI can be harnessed to break barriers for underrepresented groups. Yet, these gains are not automatic—they require continuous testing, stakeholder engagement, and a commitment to equity at every level.

Employer branding, too, is evolving through AI-driven personalization, social listening, and culture validation. As job seekers become more discerning and purpose-oriented, employer reputation is no longer shaped solely by HR campaigns but by authentic, data-backed experiences shared across platforms. AI allows organizations to proactively monitor sentiment, align external messaging with internal culture, and build brand narratives that are inclusive, transparent, and compelling.

However, alongside these strategic advantages lie significant ethical and practical challenges. Concerns about algorithmic opacity, data privacy, legal accountability, and candidate perceptions must be addressed not as afterthoughts, but as foundational priorities. Organizations that fail to engage with these concerns risk not only legal repercussions but the loss of trust from candidates, employees, and the wider community.

Looking ahead, the future of AI in talent acquisition will be defined not just by technological breakthroughs but by the frameworks we create to govern them. As the workforce becomes more diverse and digitally fluent, the demand for inclusive, human-centered AI will intensify. Organizations that invest in ethical innovation, inclusive design, and recruiter education will not only attract top talent but foster cultures of belonging, resilience, and trust.

Ultimately, the journey toward AI-enabled strategic talent acquisition is not about replacing human judgment—it is about augmenting it with intelligence that is data-driven, ethically grounded, and inclusively envisioned. In this synthesis of technology and humanity lies the future of work.

REFERENCES

Austin, R. D., & Pisano, G. P. (2017). Neurodiversity as a competitive advantage. *Harvard Business Review, 95*(3), 96–103.

Backhaus, K., & Tikoo, S. (2004). Conceptualizing and researching employer branding. *Career Development International, 9*(5), 501–517. DOI: 10.1108/13620430410550754

Barocas, S., Hardt, M., & Narayanan, A. (2019). *Fairness and machine learning.* fairmlbook.org

Barocas, S., & Selbst, A. D. (2016). Big data's disparate impact. *California Law Review, 104*(3), 671–732.

Bellamy, R. K. E., Dey, K., Hind, M., Hoffman, S. C., Houde, S., Kannan, K., ... & Zhang, Y. (2019). AI Fairness 360: An extensible toolkit for detecting, understanding, and mitigating unwanted algorithmic bias. *IBM Journal of Research and Development*, 63(4/5), 4:1–4:15. DOI: 10.1147/JRD.2019.2942287

Bersin, J. (2020). *HR technology 2020: Disruption ahead.* Josh Bersin Academy.

Bertrand, M., & Mullainathan, S. (2004). Are Emily and Greg more employable than Lakisha and Jamal? *The American Economic Review, 94*(4), 991–1013. DOI: 10.1257/0002828042002561

Binns, R., Veale, M., Van Kleek, M., & Shadbolt, N. (2018). 'It's reducing a human being to a percentage': Perceptions of justice in algorithmic decisions. *CHI Proceedings*, 1–14.

Black, J. S., & van Esch, P. (2020). AI-enabled hiring: The impact of algorithmic decision-making on recruiter and applicant perceptions. *Personnel Review, 49*(7), 1439–1459. DOI: 10.1108/PR-06-2019-0300

Bogen, M., & Rieke, A. (2018). *Help wanted: An examination of hiring algorithms, equity, and bias*. Upturn.

Boudreau, J. W., & Cascio, W. F. (2017). Human capital analytics: Why are we not there? *Journal of Organizational Effectiveness, 4*(2), 119–126. DOI: 10.1108/JOEPP-03-2017-0021

Brynjolfsson, E., & McAfee, A. (2017). *Machine, platform, crowd: Harnessing our digital future*. W. W. Norton & Company.

Buolamwini, J., & Gebru, T. (2018). Gender shades: Intersectional accuracy disparities in commercial gender classification. *Proceedings of the 1st Conference on Fairness, Accountability and Transparency*, 77, 77–91.

Burrell, J. (2016). How the machine 'thinks': Understanding opacity in machine learning algorithms. *Big Data & Society, 3*(1), 1–12. DOI: 10.1177/2053951715622512

Chakraborty, I., Ilavarasan, P. V., & Rana, N. P. (2019). Adoption of AI in HRM: A literature review and research agenda. *Journal of Enterprise Information Management, 33*(6), 1227–1248.

Chamorro-Premuzic, T., Winsborough, D., Sherman, R. A., & Hogan, R. (2016). New talent signals: Shiny new objects or a brave new world? *Industrial and Organizational Psychology: Perspectives on Science and Practice, 9*(3), 621–640. DOI: 10.1017/iop.2016.6

Chattopadhyay, S., & Dutta, S. (2021). Inclusive artificial intelligence: Mitigating bias and supporting workplace diversity. *Journal of Information. Communication and Ethics in Society, 19*(4), 575–588.

Chawla, R. N., & Goyal, P. (2022). Emerging trends in digital transformation: A bibliometric analysis. *Benchmarking, 29*(4), 1069–1112. DOI: 10.1108/BIJ-01-2021-0009

Chhabra, N. L., & Sharma, S. (2014). Employer branding: Strategy for improving employer attractiveness. *The International Journal of Organizational Analysis, 22*(1), 48–60. DOI: 10.1108/IJOA-09-2011-0513

Chowdhury, S., Paul, S., & Ghosh, A. (2021). Enhancing digital employer branding using AI: A review. *International Journal of Human Capital and Information Technology Professionals, 12*(3), 23–41.

Collings, D. G., & Mellahi, K. (2009). Strategic talent management: A review and research agenda. *Human Resource Management Review, 19*(4), 304–313. DOI: 10.1016/j.hrmr.2009.04.001

Collings, D. G., Scullion, H., & Vaiman, V. (2018). Talent management: Progress and prospects. *Human Resource Management Review, 28*(4), 453–458.

Crenshaw, K. (1991). Mapping the margins: Intersectionality, identity politics, and violence against women of color. *Stanford Law Review, 43*(6), 1241–1299. DOI: 10.2307/1229039

Dastin, J. (2018, October 10). Amazon scrapped 'AI recruiting tool' that showed bias against women. *Reuters*. https://www.reuters.com

Datta, A., Tschantz, M. C., & Datta, A. (2015). Automated experiments on ad privacy settings. *Proceedings on Privacy Enhancing Technologies. Privacy Enhancing Technologies Symposium*, *2015*(1), 92–112. DOI: 10.1515/popets-2015-0007

Dattner, B. L., Chamorro-Premuzic, T., Buchband, R., & Schettler, L. (2019). The legal and ethical implications of using AI in hiring. *Harvard Business Review*.

Doshi-Velez, F., & Kim, B. (2017). Towards a rigorous science of interpretable machine learning. *arXiv preprint*. https://arxiv.org/abs/1702.08608

Duan, Y., Edwards, J. S., & Dwivedi, Y. K. (2019). Artificial intelligence for decision making in the era of big data–evolution, challenges and research agenda. *International Journal of Information Management*, *48*, 63–71. DOI: 10.1016/j.ijinfomgt.2019.01.021

Floridi, L., & Cowls, J. (2019). A unified framework of five principles for AI in society. *Harvard Data Science Review*, *1*(1). Advance online publication. DOI: 10.1162/99608f92.8cd550d1

Gaucher, D., Friesen, J., & Kay, A. C. (2011). Evidence that gendered wording in job advertisements exists and sustains gender inequality. *Journal of Personality and Social Psychology*, *101*(1), 109–128. DOI: 10.1037/a0022530

Ghosh, A. (2021). Chatbots in recruitment: Enhancing candidate experience. *HR Technologist*. https://www.hrtechnologist.com

Ghosh, A., & Bhowmick, S. (2022). Digital employer branding: The role of AI in shaping perceptions. *Indian Journal of Industrial Relations*, *57*(4), 689–706.

Hardt, M., Price, E., & Srebro, N. (2016). Equality of opportunity in supervised learning. *Advances in Neural Information Processing Systems*, •••, 29.

Holmes, A. (2022). Designing inclusive AI for persons with disabilities: Opportunities and challenges. *Technology and Disability*, *34*(1), 15–28.

Hunt, V., Layton, D., & Prince, S. (2015). *Why diversity matters*. McKinsey & Company.

Hunt, V., Prince, S., Dixon-Fyle, S., & Yee, L. (2020). *Diversity wins: How inclusion matters*. McKinsey & Company.

Ilyas, S., Ahmer, Z., & Riaz, A. (2020). Employer branding and artificial intelligence: A strategic approach for talent attraction. *Global Management Journal for Academic & Corporate Studies*, *10*(1), 18–29.

Jobin, A., Ienca, M., & Vayena, E. (2019). The global landscape of AI ethics guidelines. *Nature Machine Intelligence*, *1*(9), 389–399. DOI: 10.1038/s42256-019-0088-2

Kapoor, R., Bansal, A., & Bandyopadhyay, S. (2022). Vernacular AI: Bridging the language divide in talent acquisition. *International Journal of Human Capital and Information Technology Professionals*, *13*(2), 55–72.

Lau, A. (2020). AI in HR: Examples of companies using AI for recruiting. *Emerj*. https://emerj.com

Marler, J. H., & Boudreau, J. W. (2017). An evidence-based review of HR analytics. *International Journal of Human Resource Management*, *28*(1), 3–26. DOI: 10.1080/09585192.2016.1244699

Mehrabi, N., Morstatter, F., Saxena, N., Lerman, K., & Galstyan, A. (2021). A survey on bias and fairness in machine learning. *ACM Computing Surveys*, *54*(6), 1–35. DOI: 10.1145/3457607

Meijerink, J., Bondarouk, T., & Lepak, D. (2021). New ways of seeing: Developing human resource management theory by examining HRM through the lenses of digitalization. *Human Resource Management Review*, *31*(2), 100789.

Morley, J., Floridi, L., Kinsey, L., & Elhalal, A. (2021). From what to how: An initial review of publicly available AI ethics tools, methods and research to translate principles into practices. *Science and Engineering Ethics*, *27*(4), 1–31.

Nikolaou, I. (2021). What is the role of technology in recruitment and selection? The case of social media and applicant tracking systems. *International Journal of Selection and Assessment*, *29*(2), 195–202.

Petry, T., Edinger-Schons, L. M., & Maier, C. (2021). Using AI-based sentiment analysis to monitor inclusion in organizations. *Information Systems Journal*, *31*(4), 577–603.

Phillips, J. M., & Gully, S. M. (2015). *Strategic staffing* (3rd ed.). Pearson Education.

Ployhart, R. E., Schmitt, N., & Tippins, N. T. (2017). Solving the Supreme Problem: 100 years of selection and recruitment at the Journal of Applied Psychology. *The Journal of Applied Psychology*, *102*(3), 291–304. DOI: 10.1037/apl0000081

Raghavan, M., Barocas, S., Kleinberg, J., & Levy, K. (2020). Mitigating bias in algorithmic hiring: Evaluating claims and practices. *Proceedings of the 2020 Conference on Fairness, Accountability, and Transparency*, 469–481. DOI: 10.1145/3351095.3372828

Raisch, S., & Krakowski, S. (2021). Artificial intelligence and management: The automation–augmentation paradox. *Academy of Management Review*, *46*(1), 192–210. DOI: 10.5465/amr.2018.0072

Roberts, B., & Zaharchuk, J. (2018). Inclusive hiring for people with autism: A practical guide. *Disability Studies Quarterly*, *38*(3).

Sivathanu, B., & Pillai, R. (2019). Adoption of artificial intelligence (AI) for talent acquisition in IT/ITES industry. *Benchmarking*, *26*(1), 93–113.

Sivertzen, A. M., Nilsen, E. R., & Olafsen, A. H. (2013). Employer branding: Employer attractiveness and the use of social media. *Journal of Product and Brand Management*, *22*(7), 473–483. DOI: 10.1108/JPBM-09-2013-0393

Stone, D. L., Deadrick, D. L., Lukaszewski, K. M., & Johnson, R. (2015). The influence of technology on the future of human resource management. *Human Resource Management Review*, *25*(2), 216–231. DOI: 10.1016/j.hrmr.2015.01.002

Suen, H. Y., Chen, M. Y. C., & Lu, S. H. (2019). Does the use of synchrony in AI interviews affect hiring decisions? *Computers in Human Behavior*, *95*, 173–183.

Sundararajan, A. (2020). The future of hiring: How Unilever uses AI to recruit. *Harvard Business Review*.

Taddeo, M., & Floridi, L. (2018). How AI can be a force for good. *Science*, *361*(6404), 751–752. DOI: 10.1126/science.aat5991

Tiku, T. (2020). AI is transforming how we write. That's a good thing. *Wired Magazine*. https://www.wired.com

Upadhyay, A. K., & Khandelwal, K. (2018). Artificial Intelligence-based recruitment and selection: A new way of talent acquisition. *International Journal of Advanced Research in Computer Science*, *9*(1), 590–597.

Veale, M., & Binns, R. (2017). Fairer machine learning in the real world: Mitigating discrimination without collecting sensitive data. *Big Data & Society*, *4*(2), 1–17. DOI: 10.1177/2053951717743530

Yarger, L., Kong, D., & Rosette, A. S. (2020). What's in a name? The hidden historical ideologies embedded in the resume. *Academy of Management Discoveries*, *6*(3), 414–435.

Zliobaite, I. (2017). Measuring discrimination in algorithmic decision making. *Data Mining and Knowledge Discovery*, *31*(4), 1060–1089. DOI: 10.1007/s10618-017-0506-1

Chapter 4
Balancing Automation and Human Employment:
A Case Study on AI as an Augmentation Tool, Not a Replacement

Anuradha Barda
http://orcid.org/0009-0008-3694-6232
Chandigarh College of Technology, India

Sapna
http://orcid.org/0009-0008-3694-6232
Chandigarh College of Technology, India

EXECUTIVE SUMMARY

The integration of Artificial Intelligence (AI) into Human Resource Management (HRM) is transforming the way organizations approach workforce development. This paper explores the application of AI not as a replacement for human labor but as a powerful augmentation tool, specifically focusing on Amazon as a case example. Through an in-depth analysis of Amazon's use of AI-driven platforms for talent acquisition, internal mobility, and employee development, the study illustrates how strategic AI integration enhances operational efficiency, employee satisfaction, and retention. In conclusion, this paper underscores the necessity for organizations to adopt a human-centered approach to AI in HRM. Through careful design, implementation, and continuous evaluation, AI can evolve into a transformative agent that not only drives business outcomes but also uplifts human potential in the modern workplace.

DOI: 10.4018/979-8-3373-3867-5.ch004

INTRODUCTION

A new era of technological change has been brought about by the incorporation of Artificial Intelligence (AI) into Human Resource Management (HRM), which has completely changed how businesses support, develop, and manage their personnel. Previously limited to administrative duties like payroll processing and employee record-keeping, human resource management (HRM) has developed into a strategic role enabled by artificial intelligence (AI) technologies that improve decision-making, boost productivity, and enhance employee experiences throughout the employee lifecycle. AI is being used extensively in talent acquisition and recruiting through chatbots, predictive job-matching tools, and resume screening algorithms, which expedite hiring procedures while reducing bias and human mistake (Upadhyay & Khandelwal, 2018).

AI helps firms bridge skill gaps and increase workforce adaptability in the learning and development space by enabling customized training programs based on performance indicators, career goals, and individual needs. By evaluating behavioral data and employee feedback to identify early indicators of discontent or disengagement, AI also plays a big part in employee engagement and retention. This allows HR professionals to take proactive steps to boost morale and productivity. A growing corpus of research contends that AI enhances human capabilities rather than replaces them, allowing workers to concentrate on higher-order tasks like strategic planning, creative problem-solving, and interpersonal collaboration—contrary to popular concerns about job displacement (Davenport & Kirby, 2016).

An interesting example of this augmentation paradigm is Amazon. The business has integrated AI into every aspect of its HR ecosystem, from real-time sentiment monitoring and predictive attrition analysis to automating hiring and improving internal mobility. Notably, Amazon's Career Choice Program leverages AI to find high-growth career paths and provide tailored reskilling programs that promote employee progress and address changing labor market needs. In order to improve retention and career happiness, AI is also included into Amazon's internal job matching systems, which enable staff members to find and move into new positions that complement their developing skill sets and career objectives. In addition to increasing Amazon's operational effectiveness, these technologies show a human-centered approach to technology adoption that puts inclusion, growth, and wellbeing first.

However, concerns like algorithmic bias, data privacy, and transparency must be carefully considered for the ethical and successful implementation of AI in HR. The significance of ongoing monitoring, varied data training sets, and responsible AI governance is underscored by previous issues, such as the alleged discrimination against women in Amazon's AI hiring tool, which was discontinued (Dastin, 2018;

Eubanks, 2018). To guarantee that workers can adjust to new tools and evolving job roles, businesses must also fund digital literacy and reskilling programs.

The potential for AI to generate trillions of dollars in economic value hinges on how carefully and inclusively it is applied in all professions, as McKinsey (2021) points out. In the end, incorporating AI into HRM offers a chance to create workforces that are more flexible, engaged, and empowered—as long as it is driven by moral standards, human-centered ideals, and a long-term goal of inclusive growth. Amazon's strategy is a progressive example for businesses looking to use AI not only to increase productivity but also to create a flexible and sustainable workplace of the future.

2. THEORETICAL FRAMEWORK

The best way to comprehend the incorporation of Artificial Intelligence (AI) into Human Resource Management (HRM) is to use well-established theoretical viewpoints that examine how people, technology, and organizational systems interact. The Human Capital Theory and the Sociotechnical Systems Theory are two well-known theories that provide insightful information about how AI might complement human contributions in the modern workplace rather than replace them. According to Becker's (1964) Human Capital Theory, employees are important organizational resources whose expertise and abilities greatly boost output and value generation. According to this theory, AI should be used to improve human capital in the context of AI integration by means of strategic talent development, real-time performance evaluation, and personalized learning (Tan & Lim, 2021).

AI tools facilitate ongoing upskilling, which helps workers adjust to changing job positions and keeps businesses competitive. In addition, the Sociotechnical Systems Theory, which was first presented by Trist and Bamforth in 1951, promotes the simultaneous optimization of social and technical components inside businesses. This viewpoint emphasizes how important it is to create AI systems that support worker motivation, well-being, teamwork, and data ethics (Mumford, 2006). Applying AI to HRM entails incorporating it in a way that promotes trust, inclusive decision-making, and job satisfaction. It By presenting AI as a tool to complement human tasks rather than replace them, these theories support the augmentation narrative. They also stress the strategic and moral significance of using AI in ways that support long-term human development and sustainability (Brynjolfsson & McAfee, 2014).

2.1 Human Capital Theory:According to human capital theory, people's abilities, expertise, education, and experience are vital financial resources that have a direct impact on long-term growth and organizational success. According to the hypothesis, which was first put forth by Schultz in 1961 and expanded upon by

Becker in 1964, expenditures in human capital, such as professional development, education, and training, result in significant returns through improved employee retention, productivity, and innovation. This notion is strongly supported by the use of artificial intelligence (AI) in human resource management (HRM), which makes it possible for data-driven career pathing, ongoing skill development, and individualized learning experiences.

Amazon is a strong illustration of this relationship. Amazon detects individual skill gaps through its AI-powered learning platforms and provides customized training programs to help staff members develop competencies in line with business and industry demands. In order to increase employees' worth both internally and in the larger labor market, the company's Career Choice Program, for example, leverages AI to connect workers with high-growth career options and educational resources (Tan & Lim, 2021).

AI further increases human capital by delivering predictive talent analytics, which enable HR departments identify high-potential individuals early and devise accelerated development programs. These insights also enable succession planning and strategic talent deployment, ensuring that the right individuals are placed in the right roles. By employing AI in this manner, firms do not only automate HR processes—they actively build a talented, flexible, and future-ready staff. Viewed through the prism of Human Capital Theory, AI appears not as a disruptive force but as a strong enabler of strategic human resource development.

2.2 Sociotechnical Systems Theory: Sociotechnical Systems (STS) Theory, created by Trist and Bamforth (1951), emphasizes the need of balancing both technical and social components inside organizations to achieve maximum performance. The theory states that effective systems must simultaneously maximize technical tools—such as AI—with human components including collaboration, culture, and employee well-being. In the context of Human Resource Management (HRM), this means AI should not only streamline operations but also enhance human experiences. For instance, Amazon leverages AI for things like sentiment analysis and attrition prediction but does it in a way that fosters inclusive communication and individualized support tactics. This follows the STS notion that technology should augment—not replace—human activity. As Mumford (2006) demonstrates, disregarding the social components of technology progress can lead to diminished morale and inefficiency. Thus, STS Theory provides a crucial lens for building AI-integrated HR solutions that are both technically effective and socially sustainable.

Amazon's integration of Artificial Intelligence (AI) within its Human Resource Management (HRM) operations reflects the basic principles of Sociotechnical Systems (STS) Theory by balancing technology efficiency with human judgment and ethical monitoring. AI-powered technologies at Amazon aid with important tasks such as candidate screening, employee sentiment analysis, and workforce planning, enabling faster and data-driven decision-making. However, consistent with the STS emphasis on joint optimization of social and technical subsystems, human managers retain ultimate decision-making authority, ensuring that emotional intelligence, ethical considerations, and contextual awareness complement algorithmic recommendations (Trist & Bamforth, 1951; Mumford, 2006). This human-in-the-loop strategy mitigates concerns of blind automation and preserves accountability. Moreover, STS Theory underlines the significance of user interaction in system design to enhance acceptance and flexibility (Baxter & Sommerville, 2011).

Amazon includes this by aggressively seeking employee feedback in the development and improvement of its AI capabilities, boosting transparency and confidence among users. The corporation also employs ethical oversight committees to assess AI deployments, addressing problems relating to justice, bias, and privacy (Dastin, 2018). These participative and ethical governance techniques prevent employee alienation and promote their role as active stakeholders, in line with sociotechnical objectives. Ultimately, Amazon's approach highlights how AI systems in HR may be developed to combine technical success with human-centric ideals, representing a sociotechnical model that stresses adaptability, inclusivity, and social responsiveness.

2.3 Integrating the Frameworks:A thorough lens through which to examine the incorporation of Artificial Intelligence (AI) in Human Resource Management (HRM) is provided by the merger of Human Capital Theory and Sociotechnical Systems (STS) Theory. While STS Theory highlights the vital need to align technological systems with the social dynamics and cultural fabric of the organization (Trist & Bamforth, 1951; Mumford, 2006), Human Capital Theory highlights the significance of investing in people's skills, education, and capabilities as a means of improving organizational performance (Becker, 1964; Schultz, 1961). Collectively, these concepts support an AI strategy that encourages ethical responsibility, employee involvement, organizational sustainability, and efficiency and productivity.

Amazon's strategy is a good example of how these two concepts work together. Amazon improves employee growth and strategically develops human capital through the use of AI for internal mobility planning, predictive talent analytics, and personalized learning. By incorporating ethical oversight committees, encouraging staff involvement in the creation of AI tools, and maintaining human control in decision-making processes, the organization concurrently incorporates STS concepts (Dastin, 2018; Baxter & Sommerville, 2011). This dual-theory alignment guarantees that AI is a stimulus for human-centered innovation and long-term organizational adaptation rather than just a tool for automation. Amazon exemplifies how artificial intelligence (AI) may be leveraged to improve corporate performance and employee well-being by coordinating technology advancement with ethical governance and developmental investment. In the end, the merger of Human Capital and STS theories offers a well-rounded and progressive model for AI integration in HRM that is responsive, inclusive, and based on both people and performance.

3. AI INTEGRATION IN HUMAN RESOURCE MANAGEMENT

3. Artificial Intelligence (AI) is transforming HRM through improved strategic decision-making, efficiency, and personalization. AI is used by companies like Amazon to automate resume screening, evaluate employee sentiment, expedite hiring, and customize learning paths. Proactive talent management is made possible by AI-driven solutions that also forecast attrition concerns and facilitate internal mobility (Upadhyay & Khandelwal, 2018; Min, 2019). These connections encourage corporate agility and employee development by transforming HR from an administrative to a strategic role. HR managers may make prompt, ethical, and well-informed decisions because to AI's real-time data processing capabilities, which improve employee happiness and performance (Ransbotham et al., 2017).

3.1. The incorporation of artificial intelligence (AI) has revolutionized talent acquisition, a fundamental component of human resource management (HRM). AI is essential to expediting and improving the hiring process in big companies like Amazon, which receive millions of applications each year. AI-powered platforms greatly reduce administrative hassles and increase productivity by automating repetitive operations like interview scheduling, candidate screening, and resume parsing (Upadhyay & Khandelwal, 2018). While AI-enabled video interviews analyze verbal cues, facial expressions, and tone to identify communication competence and cultural alignment, more advanced tools use Natural Language Processing (NLP) to evaluate both hard and soft abilities inside resumes (Chamorro-Premuzic et al., 2019).

By using standardized, data-driven evaluation standards, AI has the ability to reduce unconscious bias in hiring, which is one of its main benefits. AI systems assist more equitable recruiting processes by reducing the impact of subjective assessments by emphasizing qualities relevant to the job (Raghavan et al., 2020). Historical recruiting and performance data are used to train machine learning models at Amazon, which allows the system to continuously increase its forecast accuracy. By determining which candidate profiles are associated with long-term success, they establish a feedback loop and adjust the requirements appropriately. Because candidates are more precisely matched with positions that fit their qualifications and goals, the outcome is a quicker time to hire, higher-quality recruitment, and an enhanced candidate experience. This AI-powered method shows how technology may improve strategic talent alignment in hiring as well as operational effectiveness.

3.2. Productivity, retention, and organizational performance are all significantly impacted by employee engagement. Artificial Intelligence (AI) has made it possible to implement more data-driven, responsive, and personalized engagement tactics in the era of digital transformation. AI is used by companies such as Amazon to track and improve employee experience through predictive analytics and real-time sentiment monitoring. AI technologies can assess job happiness, identify early indicators of burnout or disengagement across teams and regions, and detect emotional tone by analyzing data from internal surveys, emails, chat platforms, and review sites (Min, 2019; Jain et al., 2021). With the use of these insights, HR departments may promptly execute interventions like wellness initiatives, team reorganizations, or customized employee appreciation.

Additionally, by providing immediate assistance for common questions—from onboarding help to leave policy and benefits—AI-powered virtual assistants and HR chatbots significantly enhance the daily work experience for employees. In addition to lessening HR's administrative burden, this automation gives workers round-the-clock access to reliable information, fostering a more empowered and contented workforce (McKinsey & Company, 2020). These solutions are incorporated into larger talent management systems at Amazon, enabling ongoing feedback loops and flexible engagement tactics. In the end, AI makes it possible for HRM to move from reactive to proactive, allowing businesses to foresee problems and provide individualized support on a large scale. This promotes greater employee loyalty, lower turnover, and a more positive workplace culture.

3.3. Organizations managing rapid technological change have made learning and development (L&D) a strategic priority, and artificial intelligence (AI) is revolutionizing this field. By evaluating information including employee competencies, learning preferences, prior performance, and stated career goals, AI-powered learning platforms at Amazon provide individualized, adaptive training. In order to guarantee that every employee has a distinct and pertinent developmental experience, these systems use machine learning algorithms to continually improve content recommendations, curate learning modules in real time, and deliver tailored evaluations (Bersin, 2018; Jain et al., 2021).

Amazon's Career Choice Program is a shining illustration of the company's dedication to learning for the future. Utilizing AI-based recommendation engines, the program finds high-growth career routes and recommends appropriate certifications or educational programs based on external labor market trends and internal workforce data. This strategy fosters both individual development and organizational resilience by bridging the gap between changing industry expectations and employee aspirations (Tan & Lim, 2021). Amazon turns learning and development (L&D) into a strategic, proactive operation that promotes internal mobility, lowers skill obsolescence, and improves retention by enabling employees to proactively manage their careers through data-informed decisions. In the end, AI in L&D not only increases worker capacities but also facilitates organizational agility, allowing talent development to be in line with labor market changes and long-term corporate objectives.

3.4. Internal mobility is becoming more widely acknowledged as a strategic tool for leadership development, succession planning, and talent retention. This role is improved by artificial intelligence (AI), which makes it possible for companies like Amazon to offer data-driven, customized career growth options. AI algorithms match employees with appropriate internal job opportunities based on their skill set, work experience, learning accomplishments, and career interests. These platforms scan internal job advertisements using machine learning algorithms, determine whether candidates and roles are compatible, and even suggest upskilling opportunities to fill in any skill gaps (Boudreau & Cascio, 2017).

AI-powered internal talent marketplaces at Amazon give staff members the opportunity to investigate opportunities for upward or lateral mobility that fit their goals and skill set. This strategy fosters a culture of career advancement and mobility while lowering dependency on outside hiring. Workers are able to see possible cross-departmental routes, which promotes engagement, loyalty, and retention (Cappelli & Tavis, 2018). Additionally, Amazon enhances its succession planning initiatives and guarantees the development and retention of high-potential personnel by aggressively identifying and preparing internal candidates for critical roles. The AI-powered internal mobility model turns the company into a dynamic ecosystem where leadership development and learning are ongoing, deliberate, and strategically coordinated.

3.5. Artificial Intelligence (AI) has revolutionized traditional, reactive methodologies into predictive and proactive talent management solutions, and retention has emerged as a strategic focus for contemporary enterprises. To determine the risk of employee attrition, Amazon uses AI-powered predictive analytics tools that analyze a number of factors, including absenteeism trends, employee engagement scores, peer feedback, training completion rates, and internal mobility history (Ransbotham et al., 2017; Jain et al., 2021). These tools allow HR teams to take prompt, focused action by creating risk profiles and identifying individuals or departments that are at danger.

To re-engage and retain high-risk personnel, for example, flexible work schedules, career pathing discussions, or mentorship programs may be provided. In order to enable more equitable and performance-driven workforce initiatives, AI systems can also detect skill misalignments, underutilized talent, and remuneration discrepancies (Min, 2019). AI enables HR to create individualized and long-lasting retention strategies that complement overarching business objectives by offering actionable insights into the factors that contribute to employee attrition.

One example of how AI might turn retention from a passive result into a quantifiable, strategic skill is Amazon's use of predictive analytics. In addition to lowering turnover, these procedures support better personnel planning, increased morale, and organizational continuity. More generally, the way AI has been successfully incorporated into Amazon's HR operations—from hiring to retaining staff—showcases how the technology may improve each phase of the human lifecycle. It makes it possible for HR professionals to work with more intelligence, agility, and a human-centered approach—all of which are critical for long-term success in a labor market that is changing quickly.

4. AI IN AMAZON

4. With more than 1.5 million employees worldwide, Amazon is a leader in e-commerce, logistics, and technology (Amazon, 2023). Amazon, which is well-known for its extensive labor management and culture of constant innovation, has incorporated artificial intelligence (AI) into its HRM systems in a calculated manner. Amazon's HR strategy places a strong emphasis on employee empowerment, experience, and long-term retention, in contrast to traditional methods that only consider automation and cost effectiveness. The business views AI as a tool to enhance worker capacities rather than as a substitute for human labor, which is in line with ethical and human-centric technology principles (Davenport & Kirby, 2016).

From hiring and onboarding to internal mobility, talent development, and real-time engagement tracking, Amazon uses AI throughout the whole employee lifecycle. AI is used, for instance, to evaluate resumes, forecast candidate success, evaluate employee attitude, spot burnout concerns, and suggest options for career advancement through initiatives like Career Choice. In addition to providing employees with individualized resources for growth and development, these solutions allow HR to make fast, data-driven decisions (Tan & Lim, 2021).

Amazon serves as an example of how big businesses may attain operational success without sacrificing employee well-being by integrating AI into its HRM infrastructure. It exemplifies a scalable and sustainable best-practice strategy for AI-enabled HR, demonstrating how ethical workforce management and technology innovation may coexist.

4.1. Amazon's main learning and development (L&D) program, the Career Choice Program, aims to enable staff members to progress their careers, both inside and outside the organization. Amazon has incorporated artificial intelligence (AI) into the program to enhance job mobility and customize learning, acknowledging that workforce adaptability is crucial in a quickly evolving industry. In order to discover high-growth, in-demand employment sectors, artificial intelligence (AI) analyzes vast datasets from internal performance records, learning histories, and external labor market trends (Tan & Lim, 2021).

The Career Choice AI engine suggests personalized learning paths based on a person's present skill set, professional interests, and career objectives using predictive analytics and machine learning algorithms. Certification programs, technical boot camps, vocational training, and even associate's and bachelor's degrees are suggested; Amazon will pay up to 100% of tuition and related expenses for these programs (Amazon, 2023). This strategy demonstrates a calculated investment in the development of human capital, which is in line with the goals of the workforce as well as more general financial requirements.

In addition to addressing any skill gaps in important industries including advanced manufacturing, IT, healthcare, and transportation, the program promotes a culture of self-directed learning, internal mobility, and future preparation. More than 100,000 Amazon workers have taken part in Career Choice as of 2023, proving its widespread influence and scalability. Amazon demonstrates how technology can propel upskilling programs that are egalitarian, accessible, and empowering by using AI to manage career development at scale. This turns learning and development (L&D) from a support role into a strategic driver of corporate and individual success.

4.2. Sentiment analysis and employee feedback are essential for developing an engaged, driven, and effective team. Advanced Artificial Intelligence (AI) technologies are used by Amazon to aggregate and analyze data from many sources, such as staff surveys, internal communication platforms, feedback portals, and engagement tools, in order to conduct continuous, real-time sentiment analysis (Min, 2019). By deciphering tiny clues in textual data, these AI tools analyze emotional tone, identify patterns of motivation, burnout, and morale, and identify changes in corporate culture (Jain et al., 2021). They do this by using machine learning algorithms and natural language processing (NLP).

HR managers and leaders have access to dynamic, user-friendly dashboards that display the insights produced, facilitating prompt and data-driven decision-making. Amazon's HR teams take proactive measures to address emergent problems by implementing targeted interventions like wellness programs, changes to workplace policies, or improved communication channels when sentiment levels show stress or deteriorating morale within particular teams, departments, or regions. By keeping a close eye on employees' emotional states, Amazon is able to reduce the likelihood of attrition and disengagement before they become serious, which improves worker well-being and overall job satisfaction (Ransbotham et al., 2017).

A more responsive, compassionate, and people-centered HR strategy is made possible by Amazon's use of AI-powered sentiment analysis to turn hitherto reactive employee feedback systems into proactive instruments for organizational health.

4.3. Maintaining operational efficiency and employee happiness while managing a sizable and geographically distributed staff calls for complex, data-driven planning. Amazon optimizes crucial workforce management tasks like task distribution, resource balance, and shift scheduling by utilizing Artificial Intelligence (AI) algorithms. In order to develop workforce plans that optimize productivity while upholding equity and adhering to labor laws, these AI systems examine a variety of factors, including past demand trends, seasonal variations, employee availability, skill levels, and current operational requirements (Boudreau & Cascio, 2017).

To fulfill consumer demand without incurring excessive labor expenditures or employee burnout, AI-powered forecasting algorithms, for example, predict surges in order volumes during peak sales events like Prime Day and prescribe appropriate staffing levels. To prevent both understaffing and overstaffing situations, these models also take into account outside variables such as local weather forecasts, absenteeism rates, and shift preferences (Cappelli & Tavis, 2018). Furthermore, AI discovers cross-training opportunities by assessing employee skill sets and operational requirements, enabling Amazon establish a flexible, multi-skilled workforce capable of adjusting to altering company goals.

Amazon's objective of preserving agility in intricate, high-volume settings while encouraging staff engagement through equitable scheduling and advancement prospects is supported by this AI-enabled workforce optimization. AI is essential to maintaining Amazon's global logistics and customer fulfillment capabilities because it strikes a balance between operational demands and worker well-being.

4.4. Amazon has used artificial intelligence (AI) to maximize internal talent mobility, which is a key factor in employee engagement, retention, and satisfaction. To find job openings that best fit employees' changing skills and career goals, Amazon's AI-driven internal mobility system uses machine learning algorithms trained on a variety of datasets, such as performance reviews, project experience, skills inventories, and completed training programs (Boudreau & Ramstad, 2005). The system offers individualized career path recommendations by continuously evaluating these data points, enabling staff members to investigate new positions, divisions, or initiatives that fit with their personal growth objectives.

By encouraging a culture of employee ownership and development, this strategy empowers staff members to actively direct their own career paths inside the organization. According to Amazon, internal placements have increased by up to 30% in some regions, indicating that AI-powered talent mobility is efficient at keeping high-potential employees on board and lowering the need for outside hiring (Cappelli & Tavis, 2018). The advantages go beyond financial savings because internal mobility signals obvious chances for growth and organizational engagement in workforce development, which increases employee motivation and loyalty. Amazon's AI-enabled system is a prime example of how technology can support human-centered, sustainable workforce strategy by fostering talent from within and coordinating personal goals with corporate requirements.

4.5. Particularly in big, fast-paced businesses like Amazon, employee turnover causes organizational cultural disruption and substantial financial expenses. In order to overcome these obstacles, Amazon uses AI-driven predictive analytics to determine individual and team attrition risk scores by evaluating a wide range of structured and unstructured data, including manager assessments, productivity metrics, absenteeism rates, and informal communication patterns (Ransbotham et al., 2017; Min, 2019). Amazon's HR teams are able to proactively identify employees who are at danger of leaving and adjust retention measures in response because to this thorough study.

Interventions that target the specific causes of turnover include career counseling, flexible work schedules, job redesign, and pay modifications. Retention strategies are further informed by AI-powered "stay interviews," which ask for frank input to identify employee expectations and concerns (Jain et al., 2021). The effectiveness of AI in workforce stabilization has been demonstrated by the quantifiable decrease in attrition rates—up to 20% in specific business units—caused by these predicted insights.

In conclusion, a well-developed model of human augmentation in HR is demonstrated by Amazon's integrated AI approach spanning recruitment, engagement, learning, mobility, and retention. Amazon successfully strikes a balance between operational effectiveness and human-centric values by integrating AI into its organizational DNA. This demonstrates how technology can be a potent enabler of meaningful work, ongoing professional development, and enduring organizational loyalty. The concrete results of these efforts and their wider ramifications for the future of human resource management will be examined in the section that follows.

5. TRANSFORMATIVE OUTCOMES OF AI-DRIVEN HR

5. Amazon has demonstrated the revolutionary potential of artificial intelligence (AI) beyond conventional operational efficiency through the strategic integration of AI throughout its Human Resource Management (HRM) departments, which has resulted in significant and varied effects. Instead of merely automating repetitive jobs, Amazon's AI-powered HR tools have completely changed the way the business recruits, nurtures, and keeps talent, creating a workforce that is flexible, involved, and prepared for the future (Davenport & Kirby, 2016).

The optimization of job matching through AI-powered recruiting platforms is one noteworthy result. These platforms enhance hiring speed and quality by discovering applicants whose values and skill set closely match organizational requirements (Upadhyay & Khandelwal, 2018). Furthermore, by reducing unconscious prejudice and fostering fair possibilities for internal mobility and professional progression,

AI solutions support an inclusive workplace culture (Raghavan et al., 2020). The Career Choice Program and other AI-enabled learning and development programs at Amazon serve as prime examples of how data-driven, customized training pathways can help staff members to consistently improve their abilities while coordinating personal development with organizational objectives (Tan & Lim, 2021).

All things considered, Amazon's experience shows that AI in HR may be a potent driver of human capital growth, striking a balance between corporate goals and employee desires. For other businesses looking to use technology for long-term, people-centered innovation, this change from seeing AI as a way to decrease costs to seeing it as a strategic partner in workforce development offers a convincing road map.

5.1. An considerable improvement in internal job placements has been one of the most noteworthy results of Amazon's AI integration in HRM. Amazon effectively matches workers to available positions that align with their qualifications, prior experience, and changing career aspirations by utilizing AI-driven internal mobility systems. An estimated 30% more internal job transfers have occurred as a result of this customized matching process, indicating improved talent use as well as higher employee engagement and morale (Boudreau & Ramstad, 2005).

Using predictive modeling, Amazon's system anticipates future hiring demands and proactively matches them with internal prospects. By building a pipeline of qualified talent, this strategic strategy not only lessens the organization's reliance on expensive external recruitment but also improves succession planning (Cappelli & Tavis, 2018). Additionally, the platform promotes a transparent and merit-based growth culture by providing employees with clear visibility into potential career pathways and the capabilities needed for advancement. Employee enthusiasm and a sense of ownership are increased by this empowerment since it enables them to actively plan their professional growth in accordance with company objectives. By striking a balance between operational effectiveness and employee-centric career management—a best practice that is becoming more and more popular in forward-thinking HR strategies across the globe—Amazon's AI-enabled internal mobility model is a prime example of how technology can support sustainable workforce growth.

5.2. For businesses like Amazon that operate in fast-paced, cutthroat markets, employee turnover continues to be a major problem. Excessive turnover rates can have a detrimental effect on business culture, increase hiring expenses, and disrupt production. Amazon has responded to this by implementing predictive analytics driven by AI, which allows for the early identification of employees who may be at risk of leaving (Ransbotham et al., 2017). These predictive models give HR teams useful information to successfully intervene by examining a wide range of parameters, such as career progression statistics, manager feedback, engagement scores, and absenteeism trends.

Amazon uses these information to create retention strategies that are specific to the needs of each employee. To re-engage and inspire workers, these interventions could involve providing them with fresh, difficult project assignments, flexible work arrangements, or focused learning and development opportunities (Min, 2019). Amazon transitions from a reactive to a planned, data-driven approach to employee retention by proactively addressing the root causes of possible turnover.

The significant influence of predictive analytics on workforce stability is demonstrated by internal reports that show up to a 20% decrease in turnover rates in business units and locations where these AI-driven retention models have been tried. By demonstrating that the company values and actively supports its employees, this strategy not only lowers the expenses related to hiring and onboarding new hires but also boosts employee morale and loyalty (Jain et al., 2021). Amazon's application of AI in this area is a prime example of a larger trend toward technologically enabled, human-centered HR procedures.

5.3. The quality and impact of staff training programs have been greatly improved by Amazon's deliberate investment in AI-driven personalized learning systems. These cutting-edge platforms improve learner engagement and skill development by customizing instructional materials according to each person's present job, performance indicators, and career goals (Tan & Lim, 2021). More than 85% of workers who use these AI-curated learning platforms say they are more satisfied with their training experiences, according to internal polls. This shows how successful personalized learning paths are in comparison to more conventional one-size-fits-all methods. Amazon's Career Choice Program, which combines employee preferences with AI-powered market data to suggest pertinent, forward-thinking curriculum possibilities, is a prime example of this achievement. This comprises degree programs, technical certificates, and vocational training that are in line with industry expectations and goals for individual development (Amazon, 2023). The program guarantees that training is both pertinent and strategically connected with company objectives by concentrating on both internal workforce demands and external labor market developments.

Employees are empowered to actively manage their careers thanks to this individualized approach to learning, which promotes a culture of ongoing development and future preparation. It also helps Amazon achieve its larger goals of workforce agility and talent retention by guaranteeing that workers have the most recent skills necessary to adjust to changing business settings. All things considered, Amazon's AI-powered L&D programs are a perfect example of how technology may raise training pleasure and yield quantifiable gains in learning outcomes.

5.4. By methodically lowering bias in hiring and promotion procedures, Amazon has used artificial intelligence (AI) to further its dedication to diversity and inclusion (D&I). AI-powered technologies like blind interviews, anonymized resume screening, and fairness-aware algorithms assess applicants mainly on their performance metrics, abilities, and qualifications rather than demographic characteristics like age, gender, or ethnicity (Raghavan et al., 2020). By reducing unconscious bias, which frequently permeates traditional recruiting and promotion decisions, this objective approach promotes a more meritocratic and equal workplace.

Measurable gains in Amazon's workforce diversity, especially in technical and leadership positions that have historically had underrepresentation, are evidence of the impact of these AI interventions (Amazon Diversity Report, 2023). AI technologies support Amazon's inclusive culture, which values many viewpoints and backgrounds as assets that foster creativity, problem-solving, and corporate innovation, by encouraging equity and transparency (Cox, 2020).

AI also makes it possible to continuously monitor diversity measures, which aids HR directors in spotting and proactively closing gaps. This ongoing feedback loop supports long-term progress toward organizational fairness by ensuring that inclusion initiatives are data-driven and flexible. Amazon's use of AI for diversity and inclusion is a prime example of how technology can effectively support social justice and workforce excellence when used carefully.

5.5. By automating several administrative and regular duties, including as onboarding, attendance tracking, and compliance monitoring, artificial intelligence (AI) has significantly changed HR functions across the board for organizations. Because it minimizes errors and reduces manual tasks, this automation greatly improves operational efficiency (Min, 2019). As a result, HR professionals are released from transactional responsibilities and have more time to focus on strategic projects like employee engagement, talent development, and organizational culture cultivation—areas that are essential to maintaining competitive advantage in ever-changing markets (Davenport & Kirby, 2016).

In addition to automating tasks, AI-powered solutions provide valuable insights that help strategic workforce planning. By analyzing internal data on skills inventories, team performance measures, and personnel growth trajectories, these systems offer proactive people management by identifying current and potential skills gaps (Bersin, 2018). AI also aids in succession planning by identifying high-potential employees and modeling leadership pipelines, ensuring business continuity in the event of disruption or reorganization (Boudreau & Ramstad, 2005).

Organizational agility, or the capacity to quickly modify workforce capabilities and structures in response to changing market needs or strategic priorities, is facilitated by this integration of AI (Cappelli & Tavis, 2018). Amazon is a prime example of how artificial intelligence (AI) can be a fundamental tenet for creating robust, future-ready businesses by facilitating data-driven decision-making and encouraging a proactive HR department.

5.6. By encouraging openness and confidence in decision-making procedures, AI integration in HR has improved Amazon's corporate culture. Employee engagement and motivation are increased when they believe that learning, promotion, and recruitment processes are fair and data-driven (Colbert, Yee, & George, 2016). Amazon uses sentiment analytics and real-time dashboards to track employee opinions, allowing HR to successfully customize interventions and respond to issues quickly (Jain, Aggarwal, & Ghai, 2021). Higher job satisfaction and organizational loyalty result from this responsiveness's strengthening of the psychological contract, which is the set of expectations between an employer and employee (Robinson & Rousseau, 1994). Additionally, the openness of AI lessens concerns about prejudice or unjust treatment, promoting a more welcoming and courteous work environment (Raghavan et al., 2020). Amazon exemplifies how artificial intelligence (AI) may improve employee emotional health and operational effectiveness by integrating technology with human-centric principles.

5.7. Important lessons for HR procedures in all sectors of the global economy can be learned from Amazon's innovative use of artificial intelligence (AI) to supplement human labor rather than replace it. Amazon shows that AI may be used to improve worker capabilities while maintaining a human-centered culture by emphasizing employee growth, inclusivity, and career development (Davenport & Kirby, 2016). Through empowerment and participation, this strategy promotes AI as a catalyst for long-term value creation, challenging the widely held belief that it poses a danger to jobs (Bersin, 2018).

The success of Amazon emphasizes the significance of carefully incorporating AI into HR systems to guarantee ethical use, openness, and inclusivity—principles that are critical for maintaining organizational legitimacy and employee confidence (Raghavan et al., 2020). Amazon's repeatable strategy, which blends cutting-edge technology with democratic governance and ongoing skill development, can be used by other firms looking to undergo strategic digital transformation (Min, 2019).

In the end, Amazon's example highlights a larger industry movement toward considering AI as a strategic partner in creating egalitarian, resilient, and adaptable workforces ready for the future of work, rather than just as an efficiency tool.

6. ETHICAL CONSIDERATIONS

Even while Amazon's AI-powered HR projects have shown significant effectiveness, ethical questions about privacy, transparency, and justice still exist. The use of large datasets to train the company's AI algorithms raises concerns over employee permission and data security. It is crucial to make sure that personal information is secure, anonymised, and utilized only for specified purposes. Accordingly, the General Data Protection Regulation (GDPR) of the European Union offers a worldwide standard for data ethics pertaining to AI (Voigt & Von dem Bussche, 2017). Amazon has put oversight procedures in place to routinely check AI algorithms for unfair or discriminating trends. Anonymizing candidate profiles and using fairness-aware algorithms that are routinely checked for gender, racial, and age neutrality are two examples of bias-mitigation techniques. Ongoing algorithmic audits are crucial for detecting and resolving discrepancies that change over time, claim Raji et al. (2020).

Critics counter that algorithmic openness is not enough on its own. Participatory design techniques that actively involve staff members in creating AI tools are essential to the implementation of true ethical AI. This is in line with the IEEE Global Initiative on Ethics of Autonomous and Intelligent Systems (2019) recommendations, which place a strong emphasis on human oversight and stakeholder participation.

Amazon has established internal ethical review boards in an attempt to achieve this goal. These interdisciplinary groups, which are responsible with evaluating the deployment of AI systems across business units, comprise HR specialists, legal experts, and technical specialists. The boards evaluate AI tools for adherence to business principles, privacy regulations, and labor laws. Furthermore, human decision-makers must be able to assess judgments made by AI technologies, including those pertaining to workload assignments, promotions, and disciplinary measures. Mittelstadt et al. (2016) assert that these accountability measures are essential to preserving public confidence in AI.

Furthermore, Amazon uses human-in-the-loop (HITL) protocols, which guarantee that human experts retain ultimate authority even while AI aids in decision-making. While taking advantage of AI's efficiency, this harmony between automation and discernment helps uphold moral integrity. According to a 2020 Deloitte analysis, companies that use HITL frameworks claim improved employee satisfaction and fewer ethical transgressions.

Additionally, by upholding data access and AI usage restrictions, Amazon prioritizes openness with its workforce. These promote a culture of digital literacy and informed engagement in the workplace by being distributed via internal platforms and training modules. Employee data platforms include consent procedures that let employees control their data and choose not to participate in some AI-based assessments. These procedures strengthen corporate accountability and are consistent with the ideas of digital autonomy.

Avoiding overreach in surveillance is another crucial ethical aspect. While AI makes it possible to track employee involvement and productivity at work, Amazon needs to be careful not to violate employee privacy. To stop abuse and safeguard employee dignity, it is crucial to have clear boundaries, moral monitoring procedures, and secure data encryption. Intent, scope restrictions, and recurring evaluations are necessary for ethical digital surveillance in order to guarantee that AI technologies continue to be in line with their intended goals, according to the Center for Humane Technology (2021).

Lastly, adopting AI ethically entails providing all employee groups—including those in frontline, non-technical, and underserved roles—equal access to AI-enhanced resources. Digital inequalities in the workforce can be avoided by making sure that career tools, training platforms, and feedback systems are available to everyone. This dedication to equity strengthens AI's role as a democratizing force in HRM and improves organizational inclusion. In conclusion, Amazon's ethical AI implementation is complex and includes strong governance, openness, stakeholder involvement, human oversight, privacy protection, and inclusion. Even while there are still obstacles to overcome, businesses looking to implement AI responsibly and sustainably can learn a lot from Amazon's methodical approach.

7. FINDINGS AND DISCUSSION

The study's conclusions are consistent with the increasing body of research in the field that suggests that, when used carefully and morally, artificial intelligence (AI) enhances rather than replaces human work (Davenport & Kirby, 2016). Amazon's AI-powered HR programs offer a striking illustration of how technology can empower workers by giving them access to individualized resources, educational opportunities, and well-defined career progression tracks. This method goes beyond the conventional perception of AI as only a way to reduce costs or increase efficiency; rather, it positions AI as a transformative force that enhances the strategic role of human resource management. Amazon's strategy illustrates how AI may help create a workforce that is engaged, flexible, and in line with changing organizational objectives by promoting diversity, transparency, and ongoing development. These observations provide insightful guidance for companies looking to use AI in ways that put employee welfare and corporate success first.

7.1. Increasing the Agility of the Workforce By enabling HR teams to foresee talent requirements, fill skill shortages, and proactively realign resources, Amazon's use of AI facilitates flexible workforce planning. By using predictive modeling, the business can pinpoint areas where attrition may occur, enabling internal job matching and reskilling programs to be implemented on time. By better coordinating HR with business continuity plans, this capacity helps organizations withstand turbulence in the marketplace.

7.2. Changing Cultures Through Data-Informed Decision Making At Amazon, the use of AI into HR procedures has fostered a culture of data-driven decision-making. Performance management, employee recognition, and engagement strategies are informed by the real-time dashboards and predictive analytics that managers are increasingly armed with. In employee relations, this cultural transition from intuition-based to evidence-based HR promotes responsibility, equity, and transparency.

7.3. Learning systems powered by artificial intelligence (AI) have been essential in improving long-term career confidence, employee development, and job happiness. AI-powered recommendation engines are used by Amazon in programs like the Career Choice Program to match upskilling possibilities for individuals with both established and new labor market trends. In order to provide individualized learning pathways, like as certifications, vocational programs, or higher education degrees, these systems examine both external market factors and internal employee data, such as skill sets, learning histories, and career goals.

This focused and data-driven strategy empowers staff members to take charge of their own career development by giving them a feeling of purpose and direction. According to Amazon's internal surveys, more than 85% of participating employees said they felt more confident about reaching their long-term professional objectives. Such results improve the organization's capacity to develop a workforce prepared for the future in addition to increasing employee engagement and retention. Amazon exemplifies how technology may be used to promote ongoing development, flexibility, and value creation for both the company and its people by using AI into learning and development initiatives (Bersin, 2018).

7.4. Strengthening Inclusive Human Resources Practices There have been quantifiable gains in diversity within Amazon's workforce as a result of the company's use of AI technologies that put fairness first, like blind resume screening and objective promotion suggestion algorithms. Compared to departments that use traditional recruitment techniques, those that use AI-assisted hiring report greater gender and racial diversity. These results demonstrate how AI, when combined with moral supervision and fairness guidelines, can promote inclusion and equity.

7.5. Clear communication, strong governance, and openness are all essential components of employee confidence in artificial intelligence (AI) systems. By creating ethical review committees to supervise AI adoption and make sure that technologies are in line with company values and legal requirements, Amazon has taken a comprehensive approach to fostering this trust (Davenport & Kirby, 2016). Amazon also places a strong emphasis on staff education programs that describe the purpose of AI technologies, how they work, and the security measures in place to protect employee rights and data privacy.

The employment of human-in-the-loop decision-making models, which combine algorithmic outputs with human judgment to reduce the risk of automation bias and guarantee ethical reasoning, is a crucial component of Amazon's HR AI strategy (Ransbotham et al., 2017). By assuring workers that AI enhances human oversight rather than takes its place, this strategy fosters acceptance and allays concerns about dehumanization.

The significance of transparency and conversation in AI adoption was highlighted by focus groups conducted in 2023, which showed that employees who received transparent communication about AI systems were twice as likely to express trust in HR decisions employing these technologies (Jain et al., 2021). A culture of trust is essential for the successful integration of AI in human resource management, and Amazon's dedication to ethical governance and transparency is a prime example of best practices in this regard.

7.6. Beyond its internal organizational advantages, Amazon's AI-driven HR approach is a powerful example of digital transformation for a variety of businesses. Amazon establishes a standard for the ethical use of AI that strikes a balance between social responsibility and technological innovation by emphasizing human-centric design, diversity, and long-term workforce sustainability (Davenport & Kirby, 2016). This method casts AI as a strategic partner in building resilient, adaptable, and engaged workforces, challenging the conventional narrative of AI as a disruptive force. Organizations that replicate Amazon's augmentation-centric AI models claim notable improvements in employee satisfaction, operational efficiency, and talent retention, according to competitor benchmarking studies (Bersin, 2018). These advancements result from the careful blending of AI technology with inclusive governance, talent development, and transparency in HR procedures. As a result, businesses looking to accomplish a sustainable digital transition while preserving employee trust and wellbeing can learn valuable lessons from Amazon's experience.

In conclusion, this conversation confirms that properly managed AI in HR is an essential facilitator of human potential and organizational success rather than a danger to human labor (Min, 2019). Amazon's deployment serves as an example of how combining cutting-edge technology with strategic HR frameworks may provide significant results, improving employee engagement and corporate performance. To guarantee that the advantages of AI-enhanced HR are fairly dispersed throughout the global labor market, future study should look into how such AI augmentation methods can be tailored for enterprises of different sizes, cultures, and sectors.

8. CONCLUSION

Through the lens of Amazon, this study has examined the integration of artificial intelligence in human resource management, demonstrating how AI may be a potent tool for human enhancement. Amazon's use of AI demonstrates a proactive, data-driven, and inclusive approach to workforce development, from hiring to employee engagement and retention. The main conclusion is that, when used wisely and ethically, AI may enhance rather than detract from the human labor. AI appears as a collaborator in establishing more purposeful, effective, and satisfying work settings rather than as a sign of job loss. This idea is supported by studies by Bessen (2019) and the McKinsey Global Institute (2020), which point out that although AI may change job responsibilities, it usually increases productivity and creates new opportunities for workforce involvement. For example, Bessen discovered that because of the increased demand and operational scalability, occupations that use AI typically saw a rise in employment.

Employing AI with a people-first approach can give businesses a competitive edge in terms of creativity and retaining talent. AI-integrated companies have up to three times more employee engagement and two times faster innovation cycles than those that are falling behind in digital transformation, according to research by Deloitte (2022).

The augmentation model offers a viable solution to match technical innovation with human empowerment as the nature of work continues to change. But doing so calls for ongoing funding for inclusive HR procedures, ethical AI governance, and workforce reskilling. In addition to being a useful case study, Amazon's example serves as a call to action for businesses to embrace AI as a catalyst for human potential rather than as a replacement for human labor.

9. LIMITATIONS AND FUTURE RESEARCH

This study is mainly reliant on secondary data sources, such as industry assessments, scholarly publications, and public releases, even though it offers insightful information about Amazon's creative application of artificial intelligence (AI) in HRM. As a result, the study might not adequately account for the subtleties of internal organizations, decision-making procedures, or employee attitudes related to the use of AI. The extent of empirical validation is constrained by the absence of direct access to Amazon's staff and proprietary systems. Future studies should use primary data gathering techniques such in-depth interviews with HR executives, surveys gauging employee happiness with AI-driven HR technologies, and focus groups examining perceptions of impact, fairness, and trust in order to strengthen the validity of these findings.

Furthermore, the study presents a static picture of AI's long-term effects rather than a dynamic one. Longitudinal studies could monitor the long-term effects of AI on workforce adaptability, job satisfaction, and career advancement. This would offer important insights into how long-term AI integration will affect employee well-being and organizational transformation.

Lastly, even though Amazon makes a strong argument, it works in a distinct, tech-focused environment. By analyzing how AI adoption differs across various organizational contexts and cultures, comparative cross-industry research encompassing industries like healthcare, manufacturing, education, or public administration would enhance the conversation. Such research could provide a more comprehensive understanding of AI's involvement in influencing the nature of work in the future by shedding light on the scalability and transferability of AI-augmented HR models.

REFERENCES

Amazon. (2023). Career Choice Program Overview. Retrieved from https://www.aboutamazon.com

Amazon Diversity Report. (2023). *Workforce Diversity and Inclusion Metrics.*

Baxter, G., & Sommerville, I. (2011). Socio-technical systems: From design methods to systems engineering. *Interacting with Computers, 23*(1), 4–17. DOI: 10.1016/j.intcom.2010.07.003

Becker, G. S. (1964). *Human Capital: A Theoretical and Empirical Analysis, with Special Reference to Education.* University of Chicago Press.

Bersin, J. (2018). *HR Technology Disruptions for 2018: Nine Trends Reinventing the HR Software Market.* Deloitte Insights.

Bessen, J. E. (2019). AI and Jobs: The Role of Demand. NBER Working Paper No. 24235. DOI: 10.3386/w24235

Boudreau, J., & Cascio, W. (2017). Human capital analytics: Why are we not there? *Journal of Organizational Effectiveness: People and Performance, 4*(2), 119–126. DOI: 10.1108/JOEPP-03-2017-0021

Boudreau, J. W., & Ramstad, P. M. (2005). Talentship and HR Measurement and Analysis: From ROI to Strategic Organizational Change. *Human Resource Planning, 28*(2), 17–26.

Brynjolfsson, E., & McAfee, A. (2014). *The Second Machine Age: Work, Progress, and Prosperity in a Time of Brilliant Technologies.* W. W. Norton & Company.

Cappelli, P., & Tavis, A. (2018). HR goes agile. *Harvard Business Review, 96*(2), 46–52.

Chamorro-Premuzic, T., Akhtar, R., Winsborough, D., & Sherman, R. (2019). The Future of Recruitment: How AI Will Transform Hiring. Harvard Business Review.

Chamorro-Premuzic, T., Winsborough, D., Sherman, R. A., & Hogan, R. (2019). New Talent Signals: Shiny New Objects or a Brave New World? *Industrial and Organizational Psychology: Perspectives on Science and Practice, 12*(3), 353–375.

Colbert, A., Yee, N., & George, G. (2016). The Digital Workforce and the Workplace of the Future. *Academy of Management Journal, 59*(3), 731–739. DOI: 10.5465/amj.2016.4003

Cox, T. (2020). *Creating the Multicultural Organization: A Strategy for Capturing the Power of Diversity*. Jossey-Bass.

Dastin, J. (2018). *Amazon scraps secret AI recruiting tool that showed bias against women*. Reuters.

Davenport, T. H., & Kirby, J. (2016). *Only Humans Need Apply: Winners and Losers in the Age of Smart Machines*. HarperBusiness.

Deloitte. (2020). AI in the Workplace: Trends and Ethics. https://www2.deloitte.com/us/en/insights/focus/cognitive-technologies/ai-in-human-resources.html

Deloitte. (2022). AI and the Future of Work: People and Machines Partnering for Growth. https://www2.deloitte.com/us/en/insights/focus/cognitive-technologies/ai-future-of-work-human-machine-collaboration.html

Eubanks, V. (2018). *Automating Inequality: How High-Tech Tools Profile, Police, and Punish the Poor*. St. Martin's Press.

IEEE. (2019). Ethically Aligned Design: A Vision for Prioritizing Human Well-being with Autonomous and Intelligent Systems.

Jain, N., Aggarwal, P., & Ghai, S. (2021).. . *International Journal of Human Capital and Information Technology Professionals*, *12*(3), 21–33. DOI: 10.4018/IJHCITP.2021070102

McKinsey & Company. (2021). The State of AI in 2021. Retrieved from https://www.mckinsey.com

McKinsey Global Institute. (2020). The Future of Work in Europe. https://www.mckinsey.com/featured-insights/future-of-work/the-future-of-work-in-europe

Min, H. (2019). Artificial Intelligence in Human Resource Management: A Literature Review and Research Agenda. *Journal of Business Research*.

Min, H. (2019). Artificial Intelligence in Human Resource Management: A Literature Review and Research Agenda. *Journal of Business Research*.

Min, H. (2019). Artificial Intelligence in Human Resource Management: A Literature Review and Research Agenda. *Journal of Business Research*.

Mittelstadt, B. D., Allo, P., Taddeo, M., Wachter, S., & Floridi, L. (2016). The ethics of algorithms: Mapping the debate. *Big Data & Society*, *3*(2), 2053951716679679. DOI: 10.1177/2053951716679679

Mumford, E. (2006). The story of socio-technical design: Reflections on its successes, failures and potential. *Information Systems Journal, 16*(4), 317–342. DOI: 10.1111/j.1365-2575.2006.00221.x

Raghavan, M., Barocas, S., Kleinberg, J., & Levy, K. (2020). Mitigating Bias in Algorithmic Hiring: Evaluating Claims and Practices. *Proceedings of the 2020 Conference on Fairness, Accountability, and Transparency*, 469–481. DOI: 10.1145/3351095.3372828

Raji, I. D., ... (2020). Saving face: Investigating the ethical concerns of facial recognition auditing. Proceedings of the AAAI/ACM Conference on AI, Ethics, and Society.

Ransbotham, S., Kiron, D., Gerbert, P., & Reeves, M. (2017). Reshaping Business with Artificial Intelligence. *MIT Sloan Management Review*.

Robinson, S. L., & Rousseau, D. M. (1994). Violating the Psychological Contract: Not the Exception but the Norm. *Journal of Organizational Behavior, 15*(3), 245–259. DOI: 10.1002/job.4030150306

Schultz, T. W. (1961). Investment in Human Capital. *The American Economic Review, 51*(1), 1–17.

Tan, C. H., & Lim, W. Y. (2021). *Artificial Intelligence and Human Capital Development: Opportunities and Challenges in the Digital Era*. Jour.

Trist, E. L., & Bamforth, K. W. (1951). Some Social and Psychological Consequences of the Longwall Method of Coal-Getting. *Human Relations, 4*(1), 3–38. DOI: 10.1177/001872675100400101

Upadhyay, A. K., & Khandelwal, K. (2018). Applying Artificial Intelligence: Implications for Recruitment. *Strategic HR Review, 17*(5), 255–258. DOI: 10.1108/SHR-07-2018-0051

Voigt, P., & Von dem Bussche, A. (2017). *The EU General Data Protection Regulation (GDPR)*. Springer. DOI: 10.1007/978-3-319-57959-7

Chapter 5
Cases on AI-Driven Talent Economy and Human Capital:
Educators and Training Institutions

Prajakta Dhaval Sadaria
http://orcid.org/0009-0001-7917-4905
Marwadi University, India

EXECUTIVE SUMMARY

This chapter provides a comprehensive and in-depth exploration of the integration of Artificial Intelligence (AI) into educational curricula and training programs, specifically targeting university faculty, corporate trainers, and professional development organizations. As AI technologies continue to revolutionize the landscape of work, communication, and knowledge dissemination, educational institutions must adapt to prepare learners for an AI-augmented future. Central to this discussion is a detailed framework for designing AI-integrated curricula that are flexible, modular, and interdisciplinary, fostering not only technical skills but also critical thinking, ethical reasoning, and lifelong learning competencies. This chapter serves as a practical guide and scholarly resource for educational leaders and practitioners aiming to responsibly harness AI's transformative potential in creating equitable, innovative, and learner-centered environments.

DOI: 10.4018/979-8-3373-3867-5.ch005

1. INTRODUCTION

The global landscape of education is undergoing a profound transformation driven by the Fourth Industrial Revolution—a confluence of technological advancements that is rapidly reshaping every sector of society. At the heart of this transformation lies Artificial Intelligence (AI), a suite of technologies capable of performing tasks that typically require human intelligence, such as problem-solving, pattern recognition, and decision-making. As AI continues to evolve, its impact on education becomes increasingly significant, prompting educators, corporate trainers, and professional development organizations to reassess how learning is designed, delivered, and evaluated.

AI is not a distant future technology; it is already embedded in many educational tools and systems. From intelligent tutoring systems that adapt to individual student needs, to AI-driven analytics that predict student performance and identify at-risk learners, AI is redefining what it means to teach and learn. For example, Carnegie Learning's MATHia software uses AI algorithms to tailor mathematics instruction to each student's progress, providing real-time feedback and personalized challenges. Similarly, Duolingo employs AI to refine language learning experiences based on user behavior and response patterns, enhancing both engagement and effectiveness.

In higher education, AI is being used to automate administrative tasks, such as enrollment management and grading, freeing up faculty time to focus on mentorship and research. In corporate training, AI helps personalize professional development pathways and simulate real-world scenarios for upskilling employees. Institutions like IBM and Microsoft have invested heavily in AI-enabled learning platforms that offer customized learning experiences to employees worldwide, demonstrating the scalability and versatility of these technologies.

Despite its promise, AI integration into educational systems presents numerous challenges. It requires a rethinking of traditional pedagogical models, curricula, and assessment frameworks. Educators must be trained not only in the use of AI tools but also in understanding their implications—ethical, social, and cognitive. There is also a growing need to ensure that AI is used responsibly, with careful attention to issues of bias, data privacy, and equitable access. For instance, AI systems trained on biased datasets can inadvertently reinforce existing inequalities, making ethical oversight a crucial aspect of AI deployment in educational settings.

The strategic integration of AI into education involves aligning technological capabilities with institutional goals and learner outcomes. University faculty must craft curricula that reflect the realities of AI-driven industries and equip students with both technical and soft skills needed in the modern workforce. Corporate trainers must embrace AI to deliver more dynamic, data-driven learning experiences that adapt to employee performance and business needs. Professional development organizations must prepare individuals for ongoing reskilling and upskilling, fostering a culture of lifelong learning that is agile and responsive to change.

In this chapter, we delve into the multidimensional aspects of designing AI-integrated learning programs. We begin by exploring why AI is needed in education, examining its potential to address current limitations in access, personalization, and scalability. We then introduce foundational concepts in AI and outline ethical considerations necessary for its responsible use. From there, we shift focus to curriculum design principles that support AI integration, highlighting interdisciplinary approaches and continuous assessment models. The chapter also addresses faculty development and institutional readiness, emphasizing the need for professional training, policy support, and infrastructure investment. Finally, we offer future-focused recommendations aimed at sustaining and scaling AI innovations in education.

By weaving together theoretical insights, empirical evidence, and practical examples, this chapter aims to serve as a comprehensive guide for educators and institutions committed to leveraging AI for transformative learning. Whether in academia, industry, or community settings, the integration of AI into learning programs is not only an opportunity but an imperative—one that demands thoughtful planning, collaboration, and continuous reflection.

2. THE NEED FOR AI INTEGRATION IN EDUCATION

The integration of AI into educational ecosystems is driven by both global trends and localized needs. Institutions are recognizing the necessity of preparing learners for a future where AI literacy will be as fundamental as reading and writing. The following subsections explore three major motivations for integrating AI into learning programs: the digital transformation of education, the need to bridge critical skills gaps, and the imperative to meet the diverse needs of learners in an inclusive and personalized manner.

2.1 The Digital Transformation of Learning

The digital revolution has reshaped the very infrastructure of education. Traditional models of classroom-based, teacher-centered instruction are increasingly giving way to hybrid and fully online formats, where learning is more flexible, autonomous, and data-driven. AI is central to this shift.

AI-powered platforms enable asynchronous learning with intelligent scheduling, automated feedback, and predictive analytics that guide students through their individual learning paths. For example, platforms like Coursera and edX integrate AI to personalize content recommendations and monitor learner engagement, ensuring that students remain on track.

AI also enhances collaborative and immersive learning environments. Virtual and augmented reality (VR/AR) tools powered by AI simulate real-world environments where learners can interact dynamically with content, peers, and virtual agents. In vocational training, tools such as Labster (a virtual science lab) use AI to offer safe, repeatable simulations that replicate laboratory experiments.

The digital transformation facilitated by AI is not merely technological but pedagogical. It compels educators to re-envision their roles—from content deliverers to learning designers and facilitators of critical thinking, creativity, and collaboration.

2.2 Bridging Skills Gaps

One of the most urgent challenges faced by modern education systems is the growing mismatch between the skills acquired in formal education and those demanded by the labor market. The World Economic Forum (2020) identified that by 2025, 85 million jobs may be displaced by a shift in the division of labor between humans and machines, while 97 million new roles may emerge that are more adapted to this new dynamic.

AI can serve as a catalyst in bridging this gap. Learning analytics and labor market data can be synthesized by AI systems to continuously align curricula with evolving job market trends. Corporate training programs have already embraced this model. For instance, Amazon's Machine Learning University uses AI to deliver personalized training to employees, ensuring that learning content is aligned with both organizational goals and individual employee development paths.

Micro-credentialing and nano-degrees, often delivered through AI-enhanced platforms, enable learners to acquire highly specific, job-relevant skills in a shorter time frame. Platforms like Udacity's AI Nanodegree or Google's Career Certificates offer modular, stackable learning that can be tailored to workforce needs and integrated into lifelong learning journeys.

AI can also enhance guidance counseling and career planning. AI-driven systems such as Kira Talent and MyKlovr analyze academic records, aptitude data, and personal preferences to provide personalized recommendations for career paths and academic programs, helping learners make more informed decisions.

2.3 Meeting Diverse Learner Needs

Diversity in education spans cognitive abilities, learning preferences, cultural backgrounds, language proficiencies, and accessibility requirements. Traditional one-size-fits-all approaches often fail to meet these varied needs. AI, however, brings powerful capabilities to foster inclusivity and personalization.

Adaptive learning technologies adjust content, pace, and assessment difficulty based on the learner's interactions and progress. For example, platforms like Smart Sparrow and DreamBox offer real-time customization, creating individual learning pathways that respond to the student's strengths and challenges.

Natural Language Processing (NLP) tools are particularly beneficial in language learning and support for students with reading difficulties. Text-to-speech and speech-to-text AI tools assist learners with visual impairments or dyslexia. AI chatbots and virtual assistants are also proving invaluable for students who require consistent academic support outside regular classroom hours.

Moreover, AI can help identify learners who are at risk of falling behind. Predictive analytics tools analyze behavioral data, such as time on task, engagement in discussion forums, or frequency of accessing course materials, to flag students who may need intervention. Institutions can then deploy targeted support services—tutoring, counseling, or peer mentoring—to help these learners succeed.

By tailoring educational experiences to individual learners, AI not only improves learning outcomes but also promotes educational equity. It ensures that all students, regardless of background or ability, have access to quality learning opportunities designed to meet their unique needs.

3. FOUNDATIONS OF AI IN EDUCATION

A foundational understanding of AI is critical for both educators and learners to meaningfully engage with its educational applications. This section provides an overview of AI technologies, their ethical considerations, and how they are already embedded in popular educational tools.

3.1 Understanding AI Technologies

Artificial Intelligence (AI) encompasses various technologies capable of mimicking cognitive functions such as learning, reasoning, problem-solving, and language understanding. In educational contexts, key subfields include:

- **Machine Learning (ML):** Systems that learn from data to make predictions or decisions. For instance, platforms like Coursera and edX utilize ML to personalize course recommendations and suggest content based on learner progress and preferences.

- **Natural Language Processing (NLP):** Enables machines to interpret and generate human language. It powers AI teaching assistants, automated essay scoring, and writing tools such as Grammarly and QuillBot. NLP also underlies virtual tutors that provide conversational practice in language learning applications like Rosetta Stone.
- **Computer Vision:** This technology is used in proctoring software (e.g., Proctorio) to monitor students during online exams, flagging anomalies through facial recognition and gaze tracking. In STEM education, computer vision helps in interactive simulations by recognizing user gestures and lab equipment usage.
- **Generative AI:** Tools like ChatGPT, DALL·E, and GitHub Copilot use deep learning to generate new text, images, or code. These are increasingly used in classrooms for brainstorming, generating writing prompts, or even helping students prototype software applications.
- **Reinforcement Learning (RL):** Applied in intelligent tutoring systems, RL helps AI adapt its teaching strategies in real-time based on student interactions, mimicking one-on-one instruction.

Understanding these components empowers educators and curriculum designers to select appropriate AI technologies aligned with learning objectives.

3.2 Ethical and Responsible Use

Ethics plays a pivotal role in the responsible deployment of AI in education. Misuse or careless deployment can result in biased decisions, loss of autonomy, or infringements on student privacy. The major concerns include:

Figure 1. Ethical considerations of AI

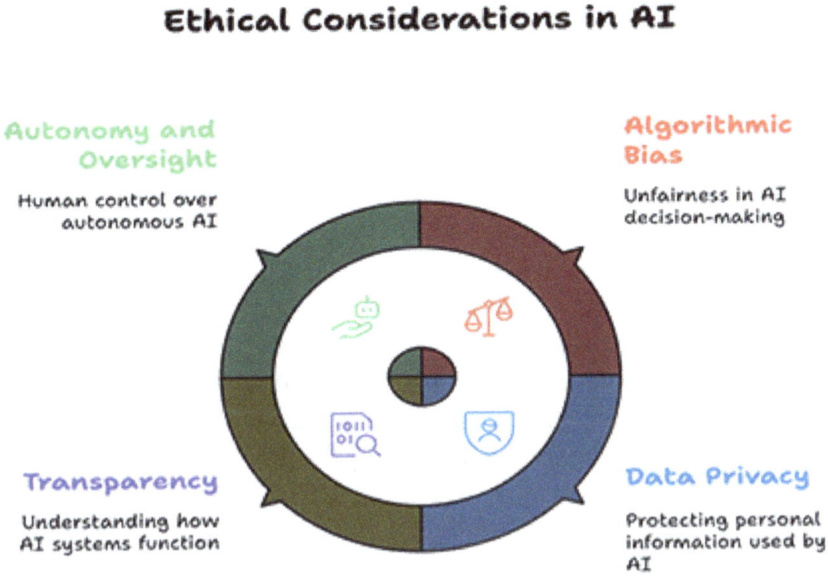

- **Algorithmic Bias:** AI systems often learn from historical data, which can encode human biases. For instance, automated grading tools have sometimes penalized non-standard writing styles disproportionately, affecting students from diverse linguistic backgrounds (Binns, 2018).
- **Data Privacy and Consent:** Many AI systems collect and analyze user data to improve performance. Institutions must ensure compliance with regulations like the General Data Protection Regulation (GDPR) and the Family Educational Rights and Privacy Act (FERPA). Consent, data minimization, and anonymization must be integral to the AI deployment process.
- **Transparency and Explainability:** AI-driven grading or student assessment tools should offer explainable decisions. Educators and students must be able to understand how conclusions are reached, fostering trust and accountability.
- **Autonomy and Oversight:** AI should support—not replace—human instructors. For example, while AI can suggest content modifications based on learner feedback, the instructor should retain final decision-making authority.

To navigate these issues, UNESCO (2021) recommends incorporating ethical frameworks into teacher training, developing AI governance guidelines, and using tools aligned with principles like IEEE's Ethically Aligned Design.

3.3 AI in Existing Educational Tools

AI's presence in current educational technologies demonstrates its versatility and value in enhancing teaching and learning. These tools span a wide range of functions:

- **Assessment Platforms:** Gradescope automates grading for multiple-choice and even open-ended responses by identifying common answer patterns. Turnitin uses AI to detect plagiarism and paraphrasing anomalies.
- **Language Learning Apps:** Duolingo and Babbel use NLP and machine learning to adapt content difficulty based on learner accuracy and speed, personalizing the learning path in real time.
- **Learning Management Systems (LMS):** Canvas, Blackboard, and Moodle integrate AI modules to analyze user behavior, flag at-risk students, and recommend instructional content.
- **Writing and Editing Tools:** Grammarly, ProWritingAid, and Hemingway use AI to enhance grammar, clarity, and style. These tools are especially valuable for non-native English speakers.
- **Virtual Labs and Simulations:** Labster provides virtual reality-based STEM labs enhanced with AI-guided feedback, enabling students to experiment in simulated environments.
- **AI Tutors and Chatbots:** Squirrel AI in China and Carnegie Learning's MATHia offer AI-based tutoring, providing personalized feedback and hints tailored to each student's problem-solving approach.
- **Proctoring Software:** Tools such as Examity and Proctorio leverage AI to detect and prevent cheating through behavioral and biometric analysis during remote assessments.

These examples show how AI is not merely an experimental tool but a core part of modern learning ecosystems. Educators need to understand the capabilities and limitations of such tools to effectively incorporate them into curriculum design.

4. CURRICULUM DESIGN PRINCIPLES FOR AI INTEGRATION

Designing AI-integrated curricula involves considering the potential of AI not just as a tool for efficiency but as a catalyst for educational transformation. Educators must design curricula that fully leverage AI's capabilities while ensuring that the learning experience remains pedagogically sound and aligned with student needs. The following principles outline how institutions and educators can create a well-rounded, AI-enhanced learning environment.

4.1 Aligning Learning Objectives with AI Capabilities

The first step in designing AI-integrated curricula is aligning learning objectives with AI's capabilities. To ensure that AI enhances the educational experience, it is vital to leverage AI for personalized learning, data-driven decision-making, and efficient skill development.

- **Personalized Learning Paths:** One of AI's core advantages is its ability to provide personalized learning experiences. AI can adjust content and delivery based on student proficiency levels, learning styles, and preferences. Learning management systems (LMS) like Canvas or Moodle use AI to recommend specific resources based on past student performance. For instance, AI can suggest supplementary readings, quizzes, or videos that cater to the learner's specific weaknesses, thereby fostering individualized progress.
- **Dynamic and Adaptive Assessment Systems:** AI allows for the creation of adaptive assessments that adjust the difficulty level according to a student's performance. In a traditional setup, assessments are often static, but AI-powered assessments can continuously adapt to gauge the learner's true understanding. For example, platforms like Squirrel AI personalize question sets and adjust difficulty based on real-time responses, ensuring students face challenges that are both stimulating and achievable.
- **Data-Driven Insights for Educators:** Educators can access real-time analytics to understand which concepts students are struggling with. For instance, AI tools embedded in platforms like Google Classroom can provide insights into overall class performance, highlighting areas that require further instruction. Teachers can then intervene more effectively, targeting instruction to the areas of need without waiting until after a final exam or project.

Aligning AI with learning objectives not only makes educational content more engaging and individualized but also ensures that AI is used as a complementary tool to educational goals rather than a standalone solution.

4.2 Modular and Scalable Curriculum Structures

AI's ability to scale and adapt to diverse learner needs makes it an ideal fit for modular curriculum designs. Modular learning allows courses to be broken down into smaller, more manageable units that can be tailored and combined in various ways, depending on students' needs.

- **Microlearning Modules:** AI enables educators to break down complex subjects into smaller, more digestible parts. These microlearning modules can be designed to be self-paced, so students can learn at their convenience and revisit content as needed. For instance, in AI-focused courses, a single module might cover basic machine learning algorithms, while another focuses on neural networks, and yet another on natural language processing (NLP). Students can progress through these units sequentially or revisit specific modules based on individual interests or challenges.
- **Customizable Pathways:** AI tools can guide students through personalized learning pathways, ensuring that each student is working on content appropriate to their level of mastery. This flexibility benefits both slower learners, who might need more time to master foundational concepts, and advanced learners, who can skip over material they've already mastered. AI-driven pathways can automatically adjust the depth and complexity of content to suit each learner's needs.
- **Continuous Curriculum Updates:** AI also helps institutions update curricula dynamically. As the AI industry evolves, so too must the content being taught. AI tools can analyze industry trends, research developments, and emerging technologies, then suggest updates to course content in real-time. This ensures the curriculum remains relevant and contemporary without the need for large-scale overhauls every few years.

A modular and scalable curriculum makes it possible to deliver highly personalized, flexible educational experiences, which helps cater to diverse learner profiles and learning paces.

4.3 Interdisciplinary Integration

AI is a multidisciplinary field, and to truly understand its impact, students must learn how AI intersects with various domains. Integrating AI across disciplines enhances the depth and breadth of learning, preparing students for real-world challenges that require interdisciplinary knowledge.

- **Cross-Disciplinary Case Studies:** One of the most effective ways to demonstrate the interdisciplinary potential of AI is through case studies. For example, an economics course might explore how AI-driven predictive models can influence stock market trends, while a healthcare course might investigate how AI can be used in diagnostic tools, predicting patient outcomes, and personalizing treatments. These case studies help students see the practical applications of AI in diverse fields.
- **AI in Humanities and Social Sciences:** While AI is typically associated with STEM fields, its application in the humanities and social sciences is equally significant. AI can be applied to analyze large social data sets, develop models of human behavior, or even analyze historical documents for patterns in text. For example, a sociology course could explore how AI can analyze social media behavior to predict societal trends, while a philosophy course might engage with the ethical questions surrounding AI's role in shaping social policies.
- **Engineering and AI Applications:** AI's role in engineering is another crucial area of integration. Engineering students can benefit from courses that apply AI to robotics, automated systems, and smart technologies. For example, students might use AI-driven simulation tools to design and test new engineering systems, enabling them to explore how AI can optimize designs or predict failures in engineering systems before they occur.

Integrating AI into different disciplines encourages students to think beyond traditional boundaries and understand the diverse applications of AI across industries, fostering a more holistic education.

4.4 Continuous Feedback and Assessment

A key advantage of AI in education is its ability to provide continuous, real-time feedback to both students and instructors. Traditional assessments often come at the end of a learning period, but AI offers the possibility for ongoing feedback, which is essential for improving learning outcomes and guiding further instruction.

- **Automated Formative Assessments:** AI-powered tools like Quizzes or Kahoot! can be used to administer short, formative assessments throughout the course. These quizzes automatically analyze responses, providing both students and instructors with immediate insights into areas that need improvement. For instance, if a student consistently struggles with certain concepts, AI can suggest specific exercises or learning resources to address those weaknesses.

- **Real-Time Data Analytics for Teachers:** Teachers can access real-time dashboards showing student performance on assessments, assignments, and engagement with learning materials. These analytics help educators identify struggling students before they fall behind, providing timely opportunities for intervention and personalized support. AI systems like Canvas and Moodle offer analytics that track engagement levels and identify students who may need additional help.
- **Peer Assessment and AI Moderation:** Some AI tools can facilitate peer assessments, where students evaluate each other's work. AI systems like Peergrade or Edgenuity can monitor the feedback students provide, ensuring that evaluations are fair and based on preset criteria. These tools encourage students to engage in critical thinking and reflective practices while also providing an additional layer of assessment for instructors to review.

Continuous feedback through AI fosters a more dynamic and responsive learning environment, where students and instructors can stay aligned and actively work towards improving learning outcomes.

4.5 Embedding Ethical and Critical Thinking Frameworks

As AI becomes a central part of educational curricula, it is imperative that students are equipped with the skills to critically analyze AI technologies and understand their ethical implications. Embedding ethical frameworks and critical thinking into the curriculum ensures that students are not just learning how to use AI but also how to engage with it responsibly.

- **Ethics in AI Courses:** Specific ethics modules within AI-focused courses are necessary to address concerns about algorithmic bias, data privacy, transparency, and accountability. For example, a computer science course might delve into the ethics of AI development, covering topics like fairness in machine learning algorithms or the potential biases that could emerge when training data is not representative of diverse populations.
- **Critical Examination of AI Impact on Society:** Beyond technical courses, students in all fields should engage with how AI affects society at large. For example, in a social studies or political science class, students might explore the role of AI in governance, public policy, or even surveillance. Such discussions should consider the potential for AI to reinforce existing inequalities or exacerbate power imbalances in society.
- **AI and Human Dignity:** Ethical considerations about AI's role in human dignity are vital in areas such as healthcare, law, and employment. For in-

stance, students in medical programs might examine the implications of AI-driven diagnostics in reducing human error versus the potential for dehumanizing patients if AI systems replace human empathy in healthcare.

By embedding ethics and critical thinking into the curriculum, educational institutions ensure that students not only gain technical expertise but also understand the broader societal impact of AI, preparing them to become responsible, conscientious users of the technology.

4.6 Practical Capstone and Project-Based Learning

AI-based learning should be supplemented with hands-on, project-based experiences where students can apply their knowledge to real-world problems. Practical, project-based learning is a crucial component of AI curricula, providing students with the opportunity to synthesize theoretical knowledge and apply it creatively.

- **Capstone Projects:** Capstone projects allow students to tackle real-world problems using AI technologies. In an AI-integrated curriculum, capstone projects might include developing a machine learning model to predict customer behavior, creating a chatbot for a business, or building a recommendation engine for an online store. These projects demonstrate the practical value of AI while giving students a sense of accomplishment and a portfolio-worthy product.
- **Industry Collaborations:** Partnering with industry professionals provides students with opportunities to work on real-world problems under the guidance of experts. AI-related projects in collaboration with companies in fields like healthcare, finance, or entertainment can provide valuable experience and insights. For instance, students in a data science course might work with a hospital to develop AI models for predicting patient outcomes based on historical data.
- **Internships and Research Opportunities:** Internships, research opportunities, and AI-driven hackathons can further deepen students' understanding of AI in practice. These experiences give students a chance to engage with cutting-edge technologies and learn how to navigate the complexities of real-world AI applications.

Practical, project-based learning equips students with hands-on experience that makes their learning more relevant and prepares them for careers that require problem-solving using AI technologies.

4.7 Case Study: Georgia Tech's OMSCS Program

Georgia Tech's Online Master of Science in Computer Science (OMSCS) program is an exemplary case study of how AI can be integrated into higher education curricula. The program offers courses designed with a strong emphasis on AI and machine learning, blending theoretical learning with practical application. The use of AI-powered tools in the OMSCS program, such as automated grading systems and personalized learning paths, has enabled Georgia Tech to offer an accessible, high-quality computer science degree to a diverse student body, demonstrating the scalability of AI in higher education.

The success of OMSCS highlights how AI can transform not only course content but also administrative and support systems, providing an integrated approach to learning, grading, and student engagement.

5. FACULTY DEVELOPMENT AND INSTITUTIONAL READINESS

Successful integration of AI into educational curricula requires more than just the availability of tools and technologies. It requires a strategic approach to faculty development and institutional preparedness. This section explores how universities, corporate trainers, and professional development organizations can ensure that educators are adequately equipped to design, implement, and manage AI-driven learning environments. It also addresses the institutional readiness required to support these efforts in terms of infrastructure, policy development, and continuous evaluation.

5.1 Upskilling Educators for AI Integration

One of the most significant challenges in integrating AI into education is ensuring that educators possess the knowledge and skills to utilize AI tools effectively. The integration of AI is not merely about understanding the technology; it requires educators to rethink how they design and deliver courses, assess students, and incorporate AI tools into their teaching methods. Thus, a robust faculty development plan is essential.

- **AI Literacy for Educators:** Educators must first be provided with foundational knowledge of AI. This includes understanding AI technologies such as machine learning, natural language processing, and computer vision. Professional development programs should provide courses and certifications on AI, ensuring that educators can recognize the capabilities and limitations of AI technologies. For example, institutions like MIT and Stanford offer online AI courses specifically tailored for educators to grasp the core concepts of AI without necessarily becoming AI experts. This foundational knowledge helps faculty understand how AI can complement existing teaching methods and support student learning.

- **Pedagogical Training for AI Integration:** Beyond the technical aspects, faculty must be trained in pedagogical strategies for integrating AI into their courses. This includes understanding how AI can personalize learning, offer immediate feedback, automate assessments, and provide insights into student performance. Faculty members should be encouraged to explore different AI tools and platforms, such as AI-powered tutoring systems or automatic grading software, to see how they can be incorporated into their teaching methods. Faculty development workshops can include practical exercises where educators experiment with these tools in real-time, developing an understanding of how to apply them in their own courses.
- **Building Collaborative Communities:** AI integration is often a multifaceted challenge that benefits from collaboration. Faculty members should be encouraged to share best practices and lessons learned with colleagues. This could be facilitated through internal communities of practice, teaching circles, or online forums where educators from different disciplines can discuss AI's role in education. For example, universities can set up regular seminars or lunch-and-learns focused on AI trends in education, allowing faculty members to stay current and exchange ideas. Building a strong network of educators who are engaged in AI integration helps in fostering a collaborative and innovative teaching culture.
- **Continuous Professional Development:** Given the rapid pace of AI advancements, faculty development should be an ongoing process. Regular upskilling opportunities should be available to educators, whether through workshops, webinars, or online courses. For instance, MOOCs (Massive Open Online Courses) offered by platforms like Coursera and edX can serve as an excellent resource for faculty members to keep pace with the latest developments in AI technologies and pedagogical practices.

Ensuring faculty members are proficient with AI tools and pedagogies not only empowers them to use these tools effectively but also fosters a sense of confidence and enthusiasm about teaching with AI.

5.2 Institutional Strategy and Policy Development

AI integration cannot occur without a comprehensive institutional strategy. Developing a clear and forward-thinking policy framework is vital for guiding the use of AI in educational environments. An institution must recognize the importance of AI and set measurable goals for its integration within the learning environment.

- **Institutional Vision and Commitment:** The institution must develop a clear vision that emphasizes AI as a transformative force in education. This vision should align with the institution's overall mission and include goals such as enhancing personalized learning, improving student engagement, and fostering the development of AI literacy among students. For example, a university might set goals to integrate AI across all of its STEM courses or develop AI-enhanced tools that assist faculty in grading or course delivery.
- **Ethical AI Use Policy:** In addition to setting a vision, institutions must adopt policies that address the ethical use of AI. Given the potential for bias, privacy violations, and other ethical concerns, a strong AI ethics policy is essential. This policy should outline acceptable AI use in classrooms, data management practices, and the importance of transparency in algorithmic decision-making. For example, a university could implement a policy that mandates transparency in AI grading systems, allowing students to understand how their assignments are evaluated by automated tools.
- **Infrastructural Investments:** AI integration requires significant investments in both hardware and software infrastructure. Institutions need to ensure that their IT systems are capable of supporting AI tools and platforms. This may involve upgrading learning management systems (LMS) like Blackboard or Canvas to support AI-based features, ensuring fast internet connectivity for AI-driven tools like virtual labs, and providing cloud storage for the large datasets needed by AI systems. In addition, institutions must have systems in place to manage and protect student data, complying with privacy regulations such as FERPA (Family Educational Rights and Privacy Act) or GDPR (General Data Protection Regulation).
- **Support Systems and Tech Teams:** Institutions must establish dedicated support teams to help faculty integrate AI technologies into their courses. These teams might consist of instructional designers, technology specialists, and AI experts who can provide technical assistance, training, and advice. Having a reliable support system in place reduces the burden on faculty and ensures a smoother AI adoption process. These teams can also assist in troubleshooting technical issues, facilitating the customization of AI tools, and ensuring that they align with the institution's curriculum standards.
- **AI Integration Roadmap:** The development of a strategic AI integration roadmap is essential. This roadmap should outline the steps, resources, and timelines necessary to implement AI-driven initiatives. For example, it might begin with small-scale pilot projects where AI is integrated into specific

courses, followed by the scaling of successful projects across the institution. The roadmap should also include regular assessments and feedback loops to ensure that AI adoption is meeting institutional goals and making a positive impact on teaching and learning.

5.3 Investment in Infrastructure and Support Systems

While the human element is crucial, AI integration also requires the right technological infrastructure to function effectively. Investing in both physical and digital infrastructure is a key part of the process, ensuring that the institution has the necessary resources to implement and maintain AI technologies.

- **Cloud Computing and AI Tools:** AI often requires substantial computational power, which can be resource-intensive. Cloud-based platforms like Amazon Web Services (AWS) or Google Cloud offer scalable infrastructure to support AI applications in education. Institutions can also take advantage of AI tools offered by these providers, such as Amazon's SageMaker for machine learning or Google's TensorFlow for building AI models. By utilizing cloud infrastructure, institutions avoid the need for heavy upfront investments in physical hardware while ensuring the capacity to scale as needed.
- **Access to AI Platforms and Tools:** In addition to cloud infrastructure, educational institutions must invest in AI platforms and software tools that support curriculum delivery and assessment. This could include AI-enhanced Learning Management Systems (LMS), AI-driven student engagement tools, or adaptive learning platforms. Universities should also ensure that these tools are user-friendly and accessible to both faculty and students, minimizing the barriers to adoption.
- **Data Management and Security Systems:** AI in education requires access to large amounts of student data. Therefore, institutions must invest in data management systems that securely store and process this data while adhering to privacy regulations. For instance, AI-driven tools like plagiarism checkers, grade analytics, or personalized learning recommendations depend on accurate and secure data. Universities must have robust data security protocols in place to safeguard against breaches and ensure that students' personal information is protected.
- **Dedicated AI Research and Development Labs:** For institutions at the forefront of AI integration, setting up dedicated AI research labs or innovation hubs can drive further progress. These labs can serve as incubators for new AI applications in education, allowing both faculty and students to experiment with emerging technologies. For example, a lab could develop AI

algorithms tailored to specific disciplines, such as AI tools for legal education or healthcare management. These labs can also partner with industry leaders to develop cutting-edge AI solutions, keeping the institution at the forefront of AI research.

5.4 Evaluation and Continuous Improvement

Integrating AI into educational curricula is an ongoing process that requires continuous evaluation and improvement. AI technologies evolve rapidly, and so must the strategies for their implementation in teaching and learning.

- **Regular Feedback Loops:** To ensure the successful integration of AI tools and methods, institutions should establish regular feedback loops with faculty and students. This feedback can help identify potential issues, such as usability problems or unforeseen ethical concerns, and allow the institution to address them proactively. For example, if students express discomfort with the way their data is being used by an AI-driven tool, the institution can modify its data policies or provide more transparency around how the tool works.
- **AI Performance Metrics:** Institutions must develop performance metrics to assess the effectiveness of AI tools. These could include analyzing student learning outcomes, engagement levels, and retention rates in AI-driven courses versus traditional courses. By tracking these metrics, institutions can identify areas where AI has made a positive impact and areas where it may need refinement or additional support. These metrics should be used to continuously improve both the AI tools themselves and the pedagogical approaches that integrate them.
- **Ongoing Professional Development and Training:** Even after the initial training, faculty members need opportunities for ongoing development to keep up with new AI tools, methodologies, and research. This could be accomplished through annual AI-focused teaching workshops, conferences, or collaborative research opportunities. Offering continuous learning opportunities will help faculty stay up-to-date with best practices and ensure they are using AI to its full potential in their courses.

6. FUTURE DIRECTIONS AND RECOMMENDATIONS

The integration of AI into education is an ongoing journey requiring forward-looking strategies. As institutions continue to innovate, this section outlines future directions and actionable recommendations for sustaining and scaling AI-enhanced educational practices.

6.1 Embracing Lifelong Learning Models

AI's rapid evolution necessitates the development of flexible, lifelong learning models. Institutions should:

- Offer micro-credentials and modular certifications focused on AI competencies.
- Create stackable learning pathways enabling continuous skill acquisition.
- Encourage interdisciplinary AI literacy across fields like healthcare, law, and education.
- Partner with platforms like Coursera and Udacity to reach broader audiences.

6.2 Promoting Equity and Inclusion

Equitable AI implementation ensures that no learner is left behind. Institutions should:

- Audit algorithms for bias and include diverse datasets in AI training.
- Provide accessible tools for students with disabilities (e.g., text-to-speech, adaptive interfaces).
- Address digital divides by offering hardware, connectivity, and support to underserved communities.
- Involve diverse stakeholders in AI curriculum design.

6.3 Scaling Innovations Through Policy and Funding

For AI initiatives to scale effectively:

- National and institutional policies must support AI R&D in education.
- Funding agencies should prioritize grants for AI-based teaching innovation.
- Public-private partnerships can drive AI integration through shared expertise.
- Metrics for evaluating AI impact should be standardized and included in accreditation.

6.4 Preparing for Emerging AI Technologies

Institutions must prepare for continuous AI disruption:

- Monitor trends in generative AI, robotics, quantum computing, and intelligent agents.
- Establish foresight groups or innovation hubs to assess educational applications.
- Adapt curriculum regularly to include new tools and platforms.
- Train faculty and students to ethically and critically engage with emerging technologies.

6.5 Building Global Collaborative Networks

Collaboration across borders enriches AI education:

One of the most significant frontiers in AI-integrated education is the formation of global collaborative networks. These networks enable institutions, educators, policymakers, and technology providers from diverse geographic and cultural contexts to share resources, co-develop curricula, conduct joint research, and implement AI tools with greater scalability and cultural relevance.

AI's global impact necessitates cross-border cooperation. For instance, universities in the Global North and Global South can engage in partnerships where technological expertise is paired with local pedagogical insights to co-create AI applications that are contextually meaningful. Initiatives like UNESCO's AI and Education program and collaborative research projects funded by the European Union's Horizon Europe demonstrate the effectiveness of international cooperation in promoting inclusive and equitable access to AI tools and education.

Global networks also help in setting ethical standards, data governance policies, and best practices for AI deployment in education.

Figure 2. Global AI education

CONCLUSION

The integration of Artificial Intelligence into educational frameworks signifies a paradigm shift that redefines how knowledge is delivered, acquired, and applied. This chapter has underscored the growing relevance of AI in transforming teaching methodologies, enhancing learner engagement, and bridging global skills gaps. Educators and institutions stand at a pivotal moment where strategic action can enable them to shape the future of learning in profound ways.

Key takeaways from this chapter include the importance of designing AI-integrated curricula that are modular, inclusive, interdisciplinary, and continuously evolving. Curriculum frameworks must reflect real-world applications of AI, embedding ethical reasoning and critical thinking to ensure learners become responsible innovators. Additionally, faculty development and institutional readiness are essential to building sustainable and scalable AI-driven education systems. This involves upskilling educators, investing in supportive infrastructure, and fostering collaborative leadership.

The future of AI in education hinges on a proactive embrace of lifelong learning models, equitable access, informed policy-making, and global collaboration. Institutions that prioritize innovation, inclusivity, and strategic foresight will be best equipped to harness AI's full potential in fostering meaningful, personalized, and impactful learning experiences.

Ultimately, AI offers a powerful toolkit—but its successful deployment depends on the human vision behind it. As educators and training institutions take up the mantle of reimagining learning with AI, they must do so with purpose, empathy, and a commitment to equity and excellence.

REFERENCES

Binns, R. (2018, January). Fairness in machine learning: Lessons from political philosophy. In *Conference on fairness, accountability and transparency* (pp. 149-159). PMLR.

UNESCO. (2021). *AI and education: Guidance for policy-makers*. United Nations Educational, Scientific and Cultural Organization.

Chapter 6

Data-Driven Customer Behavior Analysis for Take-Away Coffee in Vietnam: A RapidMiner Approach

Minh Ly
http://orcid.org/0000-0003-0200-7153
Faculty of Commerce, Van Lang University, Ho Chi Minh City, Vietnam

Thuy Thi Thanh Nguyen
Faculty of Commerce, Van Lang University, Ho Chi Minh City, Vietnam

EXECUTIVE SUMMARY

This study aims to identify key factors influencing consumer behavior toward the take-away coffee business model in Ho Chi Minh City, utilizing the Decision Tree model in RapidMiner. By combining quantitative and qualitative methods, the research uses a Kaggle dataset refined for accuracy and survey data from 300 respondents. Analysis via Decision Tree assessed model performance through RMSE, MAE, and R^2 indicators. Results reveal that factors such as location, service speed, and surrounding amenities significantly affect take-away coffee purchasing behavior, while payment methods have minimal impact. These findings offer valuable insights for F&B businesses to improve competitiveness, streamline sales processes, and enhance customer experience. The study contributes to consumer behavior theory by clarifying decision-making drivers and demonstrates the practical utility of data analysis in business strategy. However, the research is limited to Ho Chi Minh City and relies solely on one model in RapidMiner.

DOI: 10.4018/979-8-3373-3867-5.ch006

1. INTRODUCTION

The take-away coffee market in Vietnam, a rapidly expanding segment within the F&B industry, has received limited scholarly attention—particularly regarding the application of data mining tools such as RapidMiner to analyze customer behavior. This study addresses that gap by applying RapidMiner to identify key behavioral factors influencing takeaway coffee purchases. It seeks to establish a structured, data-driven approach to understanding consumer behavior, ultimately supporting businesses in responding more effectively to evolving customer needs. The research focuses on takeaway coffee consumers in Ho Chi Minh City, a major economic hub characterized by a fast-paced lifestyle and vibrant coffee culture. Data was collected from January 1 to June 20, 2021, encompassing both a dataset from Kaggle and a survey of 300 local customers. Key factors such as personal preferences, location, time, price sensitivity, service speed, convenience, and product quality are examined to gain a comprehensive understanding of customer decision-making processes in a highly competitive market. RapidMiner, a versatile tool for data mining and machine learning, is used to conduct in-depth analysis through techniques such as regression, clustering, decision trees, and neural networks. A Decision Tree model was employed to analyze the data, with model performance evaluated using RMSE, MAE, and R^2 metrics. The results provide actionable insights into customer segmentation and purchasing behavior. Although this study is limited to Ho Chi Minh City and excludes dine-in café models, its findings offer valuable implications for takeaway businesses seeking to enhance operational efficiency, increase sales, and build customer loyalty. Furthermore, by showcasing the utility of RapidMiner in behavioral analysis, this research contributes to the broader digital transformation of Vietnam's F&B sector and lays a foundation for sustainable growth in the take-away coffee market.

2. LITERATURE REVIEW

Several prior studies have examined consumer behavior in the coffee shop industry using diverse analytical methods, as summarized in Appendix A. Ha Minh Hieu (2019) employed a linear regression model to assess factors influencing customer choices among coffee chains in Ho Chi Minh City. The study identified location, price, product quality, and service as key determinants. However, its geographic scope was limited, and it did not consider emotional or experiential aspects of consumer behavior.

In contrast, Pham Hung Cuong and Nguyen Thi Khanh Linh (2021) used survey-based statistical techniques to investigate customer preferences in Vietnamese-branded coffee shops. Their findings emphasized the significance of brand identity, spatial design, beverage quality, and customer service. Nevertheless, the study did not account for technological factors or evolving consumer trends.

More recently, Chantich Santasup and Kallayanee Tengpongsathon (2022) applied data mining techniques to identify purchasing patterns and influencing variables. While this method yields valuable insights into shopping behaviors, it is heavily dependent on data quality and may inadequately reflect emotional motivations.

Taken together, these studies suggest that factors such as location, pricing, product and service quality, brand recognition, and store ambiance play a pivotal role in shaping consumer decisions. They also highlight the growing relevance of data mining tools in capturing and analyzing complex behavioral dynamics within the F&B sector.

Consumer Behavior is a broad concept that includes all the actions, decisions, and processes that consumers perform when searching for, purchasing, using, evaluating, and disposing of products or services. Consumer behavior aims to satisfy individual needs and desires, starting with need recognition, followed by information search, product selection, purchase decision, and post-use evaluation. Influenced by personal factors (preferences, values, experiences) and external elements (culture, society, psychology), it is crucial for businesses to understand. This knowledge aids in crafting effective marketing, designing suitable products, predicting trends, and enhancing customer satisfaction.

3. RESEARCH METHODOLOGY

This study employs a mixed-methods approach, integrating both quantitative and qualitative techniques to comprehensively examine customer behavior in takeaway coffee purchases.

3.1. Data

Secondary Data

- Kaggle Dataset: The primary dataset was sourced from www.kaggle.com, a well-regarded platform offering high-quality, community-validated datasets for data science research.
- Market Reports and Prior Research: The study also draws on academic literature and industry reports related to coffee consumption behavior, with a specific focus on takeaway coffee models.

Primary Data

- Data Collection Method: A structured survey was conducted using a questionnaire comprising Likert-scale items, closed-ended, and open-ended questions.
- Sample Size: The survey gathered responses from 300 actual customers, representing a cross-section of office workers, students, laborers, and regular takeaway coffee consumers.
- Survey Focus: Key factors investigated included product quality, pricing, location, customer service experience, brand image, promotional activities, and payment methods.

Table 1. Data statistics

Variable	Min	Max	Average	Data Exploration
Cash type	0	1	0.029	
Card	-1	1205	471.478	
Money	18.120	40	31852	
Coffee name	0	7	3.305	
Time of day	1	3	1.946	

3.2 Tools

RapidMiner is a powerful data analysis and machine learning (ML) software, built on an open source platform, that helps users easily perform data science-related tasks without having to write complex code (Rafi Nahjan et al., 2023). RapidMiner provides an integrated environment for the entire data science cycle, from data preparation and model building to evaluation and deployment. It simplifies data cleaning and transformation for machine learning, featuring an intuitive drag-and-drop interface that reduces coding effort. The software offers powerful tools for model evaluation, optimization, and real-world deployment, aiding businesses in strategic decisions.

Figure 1. Data science workflow in RapidMiner

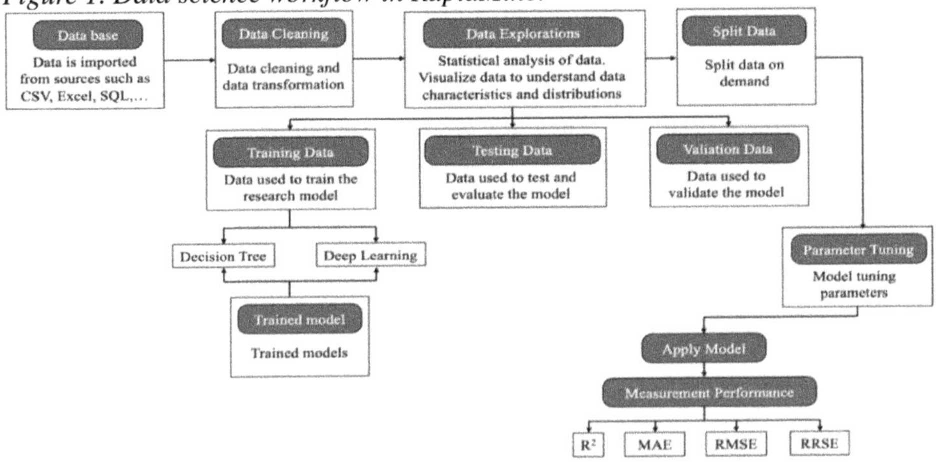

- Data base: Where data is stored, which can come from sources such as CSV, Excel, SQL.
- Data Cleaning: The process of cleaning data by removing errors, handling missing values, and converting data to a suitable format.
- Data Explorations: Analyzing data using descriptive statistics and visualization to understand the distribution and characteristics of the data.
- Split Data: Splitting data into smaller sets such as training set, test set, and validation set.
- Training Data: Data set used to train the model, helping to learn and find rules.
- Testing Data: Used to check the accuracy of the model after training.
- Validation Data: Used to verify the model, helping to adjust optimal parameters.
- Decision Tree: Machine learning algorithm based on decision trees, helping to classify or regress by dividing data according to conditions.
- Deep Learning: Branch of Machine Learning that uses multi-layer artificial neural networks to learn complex data.
- Trained Model: The model is trained after learning from the training dataset.

3.3 Research Models

This study applies two machine learning techniques—Decision Tree and Artificial Neural Network (ANN)—to explore consumer behavior in takeaway coffee purchases. These models were implemented using RapidMiner, a visual analytics platform, facilitating both training and evaluation.

The first model employed is the Classification and Regression Tree (CART), a decision tree algorithm developed by Ross Quinlan, which partitions data based on feature-derived conditions (De Ville, 2013). Each branch represents a decision rule, leading to a terminal (leaf) node where predictions are made. The model enables both classification and regression, organizing data into more homogeneous subgroups to enhance accuracy.

Post running removes branches after the tree has been fully built, using a cost function (Eq.1):

$$R(T) = \sum_{i=1}^{N} L(T_i) + \alpha|T| \tag{1}$$

With: R(T) is the error of tree T. $L(T_i)$ is the error on each leaf node T_i. $|T|$ is the number of nodes in the tree. α is the tuning parameter

This model highlights key factors influencing coffee purchase decisions, such as price, store location, product quality, promotional efforts, and time of day. Figure 4 below describes a data analysis process using Decision Tree in RapidMiner with Cross-Validation technique. The main steps include:

- Retrieve: Retrieve data from the source (there are two datasets used).
- Select Attributes: Select important attributes to include in the model.
- Set Role: Determine the role of each data column (such as setting the target variable).
- Cross Validation: Split the data into training and testing sets to evaluate the model. The training and testing model is based on k-fold cross-validation to evaluate the overall performance.
- Apply Model: Apply the learned model to the testing dataset.
- Performance: Evaluate the accuracy of the model using performance metrics.

Figure 2. Data analysis process using decision tree

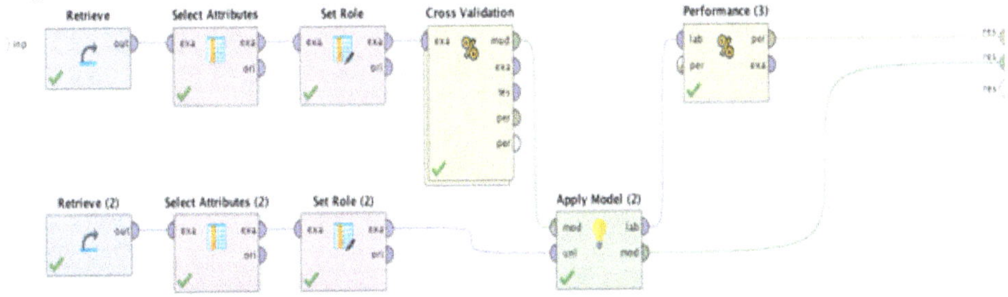

The second model is an Artificial Neural Network (ANN), a deep learning technique that simulates the structure of the human brain through layers of interconnected neurons (LeCun et al., 2015). Artificial neural networks simulate the brain, consisting of layers of interconnected neurons that transmit information from input to output. They learn data features through training and optimization of connections. Although powerful in image recognition, language analysis and prediction, neural networks require large amounts of data and are difficult to interpret due to the huge number of parameters.

Formula of Deep Learning model (Eq. 2):

$$W = W - \times \frac{L}{W} \qquad (2)$$

With: W is the weight of the model. is the learning rate. L is the loss function. $\frac{L}{W}$ is the derivative of the loss function with respect to the weight.

Figure 5 below illustrates the process of building a machine learning model with an artificial neural network (Neural Network) in RapidMiner:

- The Neural Network model is used to predict or classify data. The results are evaluated based on the test data.
- Training: Use the Neural Network model to train the data.
- Testing & Validation:

+ Apply Model: Apply the trained Neural Network model to the test data set.
+ Performance: Evaluate the model using performance metrics.

Figure 3. Process of building machine learning models with artificial neural networks (neural network) in RapidMiner

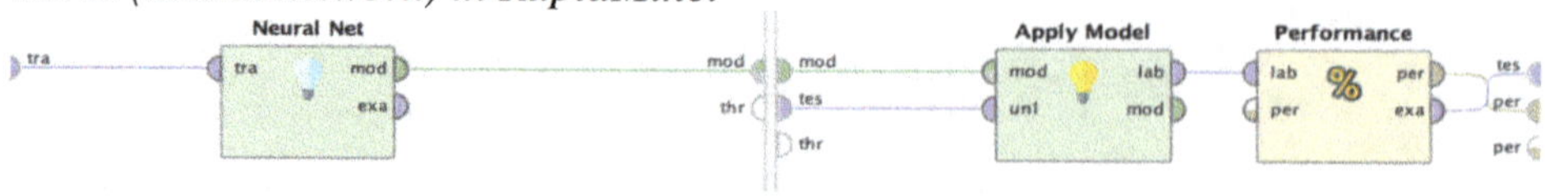

Figure 4. Artificial Neural Network - ANN model

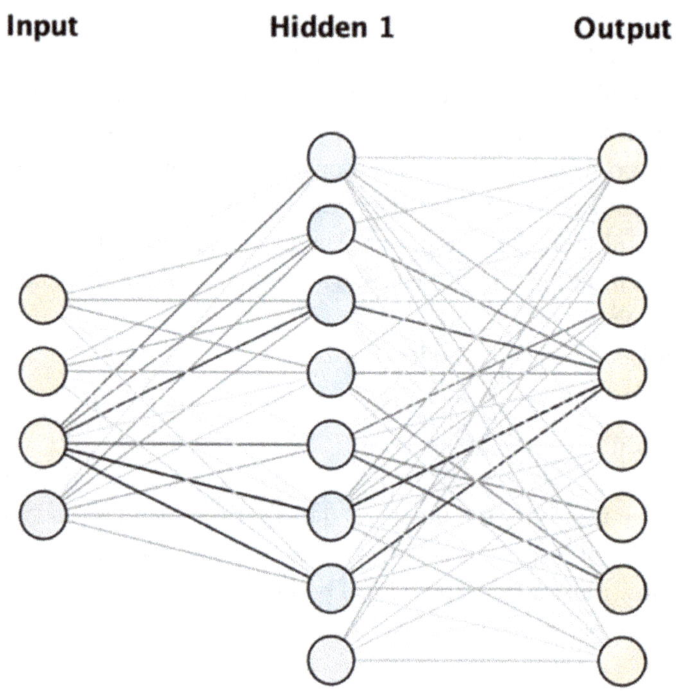

The accuracy of a predictive model is an important measure of the model's ability to accurately predict values or labels for new data. Accuracy metrics such as RMSE, MAE, and R^2 are widely used to measure the accuracy of a model. RMSE measures the average deviation between actual and predicted values, with lower values indicating higher accuracy. MAE calculates the absolute error, regardless of direction. R^2 evaluates how well the model explains data variation, with values closer to 1 indicating better performance. Combining these metrics provides a comprehensive view of model accuracy, aiding in selection and optimization, especially for forecasting and regression tasks that impact business decisions.

- Customer churn prediction can be calculated based on the following criteria:
    - TP (True Positive): "The number of customers who are actually in the churn group and the prediction algorithm correctly identified them as being in this group."
    - TN (True Negative): "The number of customers who are actually not in the churn group, but the algorithm incorrectly classified them as not churning."
    - FP (False Positive): "The number of customers who are not in the churn group but the algorithm incorrectly classified them as churning."
    - FN (False Negative): "The number of customers who are in the churn group but the algorithm incorrectly classified them as not churning."
        - Recall (Remember): The percentage of customers who actually leave is accurately determined, formula (Eq. 3):

$$\text{Recall} = \frac{TP}{(TP + FN)} \tag{3}$$

- Precision (Precision): The percentage of customers predicted to churn that actually churn, formula (Eq. 4):

$$\text{Precision} = \frac{TP}{(TP + FP)} \tag{4}$$

- Accuracy (Overall accuracy): The proportion of total correct predictions, formula (Eq. 5):

$$\text{Accuracy} = \frac{(TP + TN)}{(TP + FP + TN + FN)} \tag{5}$$

- F-measure: Harmonic average of Precision and Recall, formula (Eq. 6):

$$\text{F-measure} = \frac{2\ Precision\ Recall}{Precision + Recall} \tag{6}$$

4. RESEARCH RESULTS AND DISCUSSION

Figure 5. NeuralNet model results

ImprovedNeuralNet

```
Hidden 1
========

Node 1 (Sigmoid)
----------------
date: -0.839
datetime: -0.839
money: -10.161
Bias: -2.011

Node 2 (Sigmoid)
----------------
date: -4.519
datetime: -4.514
money: 8.691
Bias: -6.804

Node 3 (Sigmoid)
----------------
date: 6.149
datetime: 6.124
money: 13.785
Bias: 6.100

Node 4 (Sigmoid)
----------------
date: -6.426
datetime: -6.456
money: -2.498
Bias: 3.256

Node 5 (Sigmoid)
----------------
date: -1.217
datetime: -1.185
money: -11.174
Bias: -6.041

Node 6 (Sigmoid)
----------------
date: 1.526
datetime: 1.527
money: 17.553
Bias: -5.672

Node 7 (Sigmoid)
----------------
date: 2.871
datetime: 2.933
money: -16.051
Bias: -5.530


Output
======

Class 'Latte' (Sigmoid)
-----------------------
Node 1: -4.317
Node 2: -3.732
Node 3: -1.246
Node 4: 3.713
Node 5: -1.258
Node 6: 5.774
Node 7: -2.716
Threshold: -5.091

Class 'Hot Chocolate' (Sigmoid)
-------------------------------
Node 1: -2.379
Node 2: -0.891
Node 3: -1.726
Node 4: 0.519
Node 5: -1.346
Node 6: 4.053
Node 7: -1.960
Threshold: -3.753

Class 'Americano' (Sigmoid)
---------------------------
Node 1: 1.656
Node 2: -1.397
Node 3: -3.854
Node 4: 0.502
Node 5: -9.360
Node 6: -4.709
Node 7: 3.479
Threshold: 0.397

Class 'Americano with Milk' (Sigmoid)
-------------------------------------
Node 1: -4.922
Node 2: 8.748
Node 3: 12.852
Node 4: -7.923
Node 5: -3.093
Node 6: -16.486
Node 7: -14.200
Threshold: -0.340

Class 'Cocoa' (Sigmoid)
-----------------------
Node 1: -2.064
Node 2: -0.753
Node 3: -1.262
Node 4: -0.522
Node 5: -1.295
Node 6: 2.962
Node 7: -1.933
Threshold: -2.999

Class 'Cortado' (Sigmoid)
-------------------------
Node 1: 3.337
Node 2: 0.621
Node 3: -1.868
Node 4: 1.540
Node 5: -8.684
Node 6: -3.583
Node 7: 3.730
Threshold: -3.386

Class 'Espresso' (Sigmoid)
--------------------------
Node 1: 4.406
Node 2: -1.383
Node 3: -1.638
Node 4: -7.709
Node 5: 12.463
Node 6: -2.472
Node 7: -5.072
Threshold: -1.066
```

Figure 6. Confusion matrix

accuracy: 61.45%

	true Latte	true Hot ...	true Ame...	true Ame...	true Cocoa	true Cort...	true Espr...	true Cap...	class pre...
pred. Latte	521	175	0	0	161	0	0	285	45.62%
pred. Hot...	0	0	0	0	0	0	0	0	0.00%
pred. Am...	0	0	341	0	0	236	0	0	59.10%
pred. Am...	8	7	6	725	1	0	0	5	96.41%
pred. Co...	0	0	0	0	0	0	0	0	0.00%
pred. Cor...	0	0	48	0	0	52	0	0	52.00%
pred. Es...	0	0	4	0	0	1	112	0	95.73%
pred. Ca...	166	57	0	0	24	0	0	136	35.51%
class recall	74.96%	0.00%	85.46%	100.00%	0.00%	17.99%	100.00%	31.92%	

The model for classifying customers by their favorite beverage achieved an overall accuracy of about 61.45%. This means that out of 100 predictions, the system gave correct results about 61 times, and the remaining 39 predictions were incorrect. This is not a very low rate, but it is not really good for a model with the potential to support businesses. When applied in practice, low accuracy can reduce the effectiveness of personalizing the customer experience and optimizing the product portfolio. However, this accuracy needs to be considered in the context of each individual beverage. Some coffees have good recognition rates, while others are confused a lot, affecting the overall model.

Confusion matrix analysis helps identify beverages with high recognition rates and those that are easily confused. Americano is one of the beverages with the highest accuracy. This may be due to the fact that Americano customers have a fairly clear profile, with little change in habits and a tendency to repeat orders. In contrast, some products, such as Hot Chocolate, have a recognition rate of almost 0%. This may be due to two main reasons: either the number of customers buying Hot Chocolate is too small, resulting in insufficient data to train the model, or the customer group for this product does not have clear behavioral characteristics, making it difficult for the algorithm to recognize. In addition, coffees with similar recipes, such as Latte and Cappuccino, are often confused with each other. This may reflect the fact that customers of these two types of drinks have quite similar consumption characteristics, from taste to purchase time.

Poor accuracy can come from poor quality data, including missing, noisy, or imbalanced data. When the data set is incomplete or does not represent the entire real-world distribution, the model will have difficulty learning the correct rules. Missing important variables is also a big cause, because without including the main influencing factors, the model will not have enough information to make accurate predictions. In addition, inappropriate model complexity also has a significant impact: if the model is too simple, it cannot learn enough trends in the data; conversely, if it is too complex, it may include unnecessary noise, reducing the predictive ability when applied to new data.

Two other important metrics to evaluate a model are Recall and Precision. Recall reflects the ability to correctly identify the group of customers who actually buy that product. If Recall is low, it means that the model is missing many real-world cases. If a customer actually buys "Hot Chocolate" but the model predicts "Latte", this will decrease the Recall of "Hot Chocolate". Meanwhile, Precision measures how accurate the correct predictions are. If Precision is low, it means that the model is making wrong predictions frequently. If the model consistently predicts "Espresso" but the customer actually buys "Americano", the Precision of "Espresso" will decrease. Balancing Recall and Precision is important, because focusing on only one metric can skew the model towards being either too conservative (missing many customers) or too confident (predicting too many wrong customers).

As shown in Table 2, we evaluated the prediction results by calculating the recall, precision, and accuracy indices.

Table 2. Prediction results evaluation table

Method	Recall	Precision	Accuracy
Decision Trees	51.29%	48.05%	61.45%
Neural Network	33.54%	65.73%	60.23%
Random Forest	53.45%	48.90%	48.06%
XGBoost	43.87%	61.54%	54.12%

In addition, testing additional machine learning models such as Random Forest and XGBoost can help improve the accuracy of the system. Random Forest works based on multiple decision trees, which helps reduce overfitting and stabilize the prediction results. Meanwhile, XGBoost is a powerful boosting algorithm that optimizes learning errors, speeds up training, and improves prediction performance. Compared to traditional models, Random Forest and XGBoost are better able to handle data with many complex features. In addition, the sample size can be increased or data from many different sources can be added. Expanding the data set helps the model learn from more real-life situations, reducing the risk of overfitting and increasing the ability to generalize when applied to new data. This is especially important when the current data is limited or not rich enough to represent the entire customer base.

5. CONCLUSIONS AND RECOMMENDATIONS

This study examined takeaway coffee consumption behavior in Ho Chi Minh City by applying the Decision Tree model in RapidMiner, utilizing both Kaggle data and survey responses from 300 customers. The findings indicate that location, service speed, and nearby amenities significantly influence purchasing decisions, whereas payment methods appear to have little effect. The Decision Tree model achieved an accuracy of 61.45%, a recall of 51.29%, and a precision of 48.05%, offering valuable insights into consumer motivations and supporting businesses in optimizing service delivery and marketing strategies.

From an academic perspective, this research contributes to the expanding literature on the use of data mining and machine learning tools in consumer behavior analysis within the F&B industry. It also demonstrates the practical utility of Decision Tree modeling in identifying key behavioral drivers behind takeaway coffee purchases. From a practical standpoint, the study underscores the importance of leveraging empirical data over intuition, enabling businesses to refine product offerings, streamline operations, and tailor customer experiences. Furthermore, it highlights the potential of AI and data mining techniques in analyzing consumer behavior, allowing businesses to harness data more effectively to enhance their competitive edge.

Nonetheless, several limitations should be acknowledged. The study's geographic scope—limited to Ho Chi Minh City—restricts the generalizability of the findings to other regions. Additionally, the sample may not fully capture the diversity of consumer segments, which could lead to biased insights. The exclusive reliance on the Decision Tree model, which is prone to overfitting, may also affect its robustness when applied to new data.

Future research should consider expanding the survey to encompass a broader demographic and geographic scope, as well as incorporating macroeconomic variables such as inflation and income levels. Employing alternative machine learning models and AI-based techniques, such as demand forecasting and sentiment analysis, could also provide a more comprehensive understanding of consumer behavior and inform more effective decision-making within the F&B sector.

Author contribution: Conceptualization, Minh Ly Duc (M.L.D.); Nguyen Thi Thanh Thuy (N. T. T. T.); methodology, M.L.D.; N. T. T. T.; software, M.L.D.; N. T. T. T.; validation, M.L.D.; N. T. T. T.; formal analysis, M.L.D.; N. T. T. T.; investigation, M.L.D.; N. T. T. T.; resources, M.L.D.; data curation, M.L.D.; N. T. T. T.; writing—original draft preparation, M.L.D.; N. T. T. T.; writing—review and editing, M.L.D.; N. T. T. T.; visualization, M.L.D.; supervision, M.L.D.; project administration, M.L.D. All authors have read and agreed to the published version of the manuscript.

ACKNOWLEDGMENT

The authors are extremely grateful to Van Lang University, Vietnam, for supporting this research.

REFERENCES

De Ville, B. (2013). Decision trees. *Wiley Interdisciplinary Reviews: Computational Statistics*, *5*(6), 448–455. DOI: 10.1002/wics.1278

LeCun, Y., Bengio, Y., & Hinton, G. (2015). Deep learning. *Nature*, *521*(7553), 436–444. DOI: 10.1038/nature14539 PMID: 26017442

Rafi Nahjan, M., Heryana, N., & Voutama, A. (2023). Implementasi rapidminer dengan metode clustering k-means untuk analisa penjualan pada toko oj cell. [Jurnal Mahasiswa Teknik Informatika]. *JATI*, *7*(1), 101–104. DOI: 10.36040/jati.v7i1.6094

Chapter 7
Decoding Talent DNA: AI-Driven Psychometric Profiling for Hyper-Personalized Hiring

R. Lakshmi Aishwarya
http://orcid.org/0009-0004-0275-1614
Dayanand Sagar College of Engineering, India

K. S. Ganesha
http://orcid.org/0000-0001-8181-2411
Dayanand Sagar College of Engineering, India

EXECUTIVE SUMMARY

After Fourth Industrial Revolution, hiring demands hyper-personalization, precision, and ethical intelligence—faster than traditional models allow. This study introduces a new method using psychometric profiling and AI to uncover "Talent DNA," the trait-based predictors of job fit and performance. Using Trait Activation Theory, Person–Job Fit Theory, and Self-Determination Theory within a structural equation modelling (SEM) framework, combined with the AI classifiers, the study analyzed data from about 460 participants. It found that the conscientiousness and grit best predict success, with AI models achieving over 85% accuracy. The Cognitive-Affective-AI Loop (CAAIL) is proposed to link psychometrics, AI, and adaptive decisions. Ethical concerns include bias, transparency, and generalizability, solvable through explainable AI (XAI), culturally adaptive models, and longitudinal studies. The study contributes to intelligent talent analytics, positioning AI as tool to unlock human potential—not gatekeep it—making decoding Talent DNA both a technical and philosophical necessity.

DOI: 10.4018/979-8-3373-3867-5.ch007

INTRODUCTION

With hyper-automation and cognitive computing, hiring is no longer just about resumes, cover letters, and gut feelings during interviews. Companies that are going through the Fourth Industrial Revolution are facing a talent paradox: they have a lot of data but not much insight into the person behind the application. Traditional ways of hiring people often don't work well when it comes to understanding the complexity of human behaviour, personality, and motivation. Because of this, mismatches keep happening, productivity drops, and more employees leave. The answer is not to replace people with algorithms, but to give people more power to make decisions with smart, personalised tools. This study presents a new way of looking at things: AI-driven psychometric profiling that can figure out what we call the "Talent DNA," which allows for hyper-personalized hiring based on cognitive, emotional, and behavioural traits. There has never been a greater need for personalised hiring. The people who work today are more diverse than ever, not just in terms of race and gender, but also in terms of how they learn, what they want to do with their lives, and how emotionally intelligent they are. Millennials and Gen Z, who make up most of the talent pool now, want employers to see them as more than just job applicants. They want to be seen as unique people with different preferences and untapped potential. In this situation, using a one-size-fits-all approach to hiring is not only old-fashioned, it's also not working. Organisations need a big change in how they think about hiring that lets them hire people based on their individual minds. This study is exactly what it wants to do.

Psychometric profiling, which is based on psychological theories like the Big Five, DISC, and Cognitive Aptitude Models, has long been thought to be able to show deep-seated traits and predict job performance. But it hasn't been used much in hiring for companies, and when it is, it's often static and biassed by how people interpret it. AI has changed that scene. Artificial intelligence can now read large amounts of psychometric data, find patterns that aren't obvious, and learn from feedback all the time to make hiring more accurate. But there is a fine line: automation makes things more efficient, but human-centered AI makes sure that the process is still moral, caring, and in line with each person's dignity. The goal of this paper is to create a framework that combines psychometric science with AI algorithms to find out a person's "Talent DNA," which includes their cognitive, emotional, and behavioural fingerprints that show how well they would fit in with a job, a culture, and stay engaged over time. This study fits in with the bigger picture of Industry 4.0, which calls for combining cyber-physical systems with human creativity. In this case, hiring people is no longer just an operational task; it's a strategic tool. Using AI for psychometric analysis gives hiring managers the ability to go beyond just checking credentials and into a realm where skills, potential, values, and work styles are constantly evaluated. This makes what we call "hyper-personalized hiring" possible. This is a model in which the whole hiring process is tailored to the person, from matching them with the right job to the format of the interview, onboarding help, and even career path suggestions. There is a lot of academic writing about using AI in hiring, but not much has been written about how AI-powered psychometrics and personalised hiring strategies work together. This gap gets bigger when you think about the moral and emotional sides of these systems, which are often ignored in favour of how well they work. Also, most of the studies that are out there use secondary datasets or simulated environments. This research, on the other hand, focusses on primary data by getting direct answers from job candidates and HR professionals to build a model based on real-world experiences and expectations. The main goal of this study is threefold. The first goal is to find the psychometric dimensions that are most closely related to job success and cultural fit. Second, it looks at how to teach AI to find and understand these dimensions in a way that is both effective and moral. Third, it wants to create a working model for hyper-personalized hiring that strikes a balance between being efficient for the company and caring about the needs of the candidates. This study will test its hypotheses on a main dataset that was collected from a variety of sectors and job roles using a mix of psychometric surveys, natural language processing (NLP), and machine learning classification algorithms. This study isn't about getting rid of human recruiters; it's about giving them new jobs. In the suggested AI-human partnership, recruiters become strategic advisors, using data-driven insights to make the process more fair, accurate, and personalised. Candidates, on the other hand, get a more personalised and open hiring process that respects their uniqueness and potential. Companies can build teams that are not only skilled but also share the same goals and values by using AI-powered psychometric analysis to decode the Talent DNA.

In short, this study is at the crossroads of AI innovation, psychology, and design that puts people first. It talks about a timely problem in modern hiring and offers a visionary framework that can be used in the real world. Only companies that know more about a person than just their resume will do well as the job market gets more competitive and complicated. The future of work doesn't start with automation alone; it starts with personalised work powered by smart, ethical systems.

THEORETICAL/CONCEPTUAL FRAMEWORK

The combination of artificial intelligence (AI) and psychometrics is a big step forward in hiring. It changes the hiring process from static evaluations to dynamic, adaptable, and deeply personalised interactions. We suggest the "Cognitive-Affective-AI Loop (CAAIL) Framework" to capture this shift in thinking. It is a new, human-centered model that uses AI-driven psychometric profiling to decode Talent DNA for hyper-personalized hiring. This framework combines basic psychological theories like Person-Job Fit Theory (Kristof, 1996), Trait Activation Theory (Tett & Burnett, 2003), and Self-Determination Theory (Deci & Ryan, 1985) with new AI ideas like Explainable AI (XAI), adaptive learning, and fairness-aware algorithms. The goal is to make hiring a system that uses machine learning to constantly collect, analyse, and customise cognitive traits, affective dimensions, and behavioural patterns, all while being ethically responsible.

Talent DNA is the main idea behind this framework. It is a unique mix of psychometric traits that include cognitive abilities (like logical reasoning and problem-solving), affective dimensions (like emotional intelligence and motivation), and behavioural tendencies (like being conscientious and open to new experiences). Traditional psychometric tools try to measure these things separately, but when you put these data points into an AI system that has been trained on successful role-fit patterns, they start to show multidimensional profiles that can predict not only performance but also how well someone will fit in with the organisation, how adaptable they are, and how well they fit in with the culture. This is in line with the Person-Job Fit principle, which says that when a candidate's traits match the job's requirements, they will be happier, perform better, and stay with the company longer. The Talent DNA becomes dynamic when AI is added. It is always changing based on feedback from onboarding success, performance metrics, and even peer collaboration analytics.

The Trait Activation Theory (TAT) backs up this framework even more by saying that some personality traits only show up in certain situations. For instance, a person's creativity might be dormant in a place where rules are strict, but it might thrive in tasks that don't have a clear end. AI systems, especially those that use contextual machine learning, can keep an eye on these behavioural responses over time and in different simulated settings. When hiring, candidates may have to do adaptive psychometric tasks or AI-led simulations that show how their traits change when they are under job-specific stressors or incentives. These patterns go into the model's learning loop, which improves the candidate's Talent DNA in real time and makes it better at predicting not only how a candidate has acted in the past but also how they will act in the future.

Self-Determination Theory (SDT) adds a motivational layer that helps figure out what drives candidates from within and from outside. Natural language processing (NLP) is a feature of modern AI tools that lets them look at open-ended answers, video interviews, or written tests to find words that show motivation, a preference for autonomy, or a reaction to praise. The CAAIL framework captures an important but often overlooked aspect of hiring: what makes someone want to show up and stay engaged. These insights are turned into features in the AI model to make sure that the final job recommendation isn't just a good match for skills, but also for the whole person.

The framework's AI engine is made up of three main parts: the Trait Mapper, the Context Evaluator, and the Fit Optimiser. The Trait Mapper takes psychometric data and turns it into quantifiable vectors using standard tools like the Big Five, the Grit Scale, and the EI indices. It then turns these vectors into feature maps that machines can read. The Context Evaluator uses reinforcement learning to test candidates' ability to adapt, control their emotions, and make decisions under pressure by putting them in job situations, either in real life or through structured psychometric games. The Fit Optimiser finally uses pattern recognition and collaborative filtering to match the composite profile with the job's cognitive, emotional, and behavioural needs. Most importantly, each module has a XAI layer that makes outputs that can be understood, like "This candidate aligns 92% with Role X because they are very open, can adapt to changing situations, and are motivated by mission-driven work."

The CAAIL framework includes Fairness-Aware Learning (FAL) to reduce algorithmic bias and increase transparency. FAL makes sure that predictions are not based on race, gender, or socio-economic status. Before training the model, every candidate's psychometric fingerprint is anonymised and de-identified. The final fit recommendations come with explainability reports that both the recruiter and the candidate can see. This helps people trust automated hiring systems and encourages the use of ethical AI.

The CAAIL loop is a feedback-driven system from a systems thinking point of view. Candidate performance after hiring is constantly tracked and fed back into the training model to adjust the fit parameters. This makes the psychometric map more detailed and improves the accuracy of predictions. The model doesn't just hire people; it also learns how to hire better people next time. The organisation builds a living, changing dataset of Talent DNA blueprints over months and years. This dataset is used to help with hiring, forming teams, grooming leaders, and even mental health interventions.

Visually, the CAAIL framework can be imagined as a looped flow model:

1. **Psychometric Input**
2. **AI Trait Mapping & Contextual Activation**
3. **Fit Optimization (with explainable output)**
4. **Hiring Decision + Feedback Collection**
5. **Continuous Learning Loop**

Figure 1. The Cognitive-Affective-AI Loop (CAAIL)

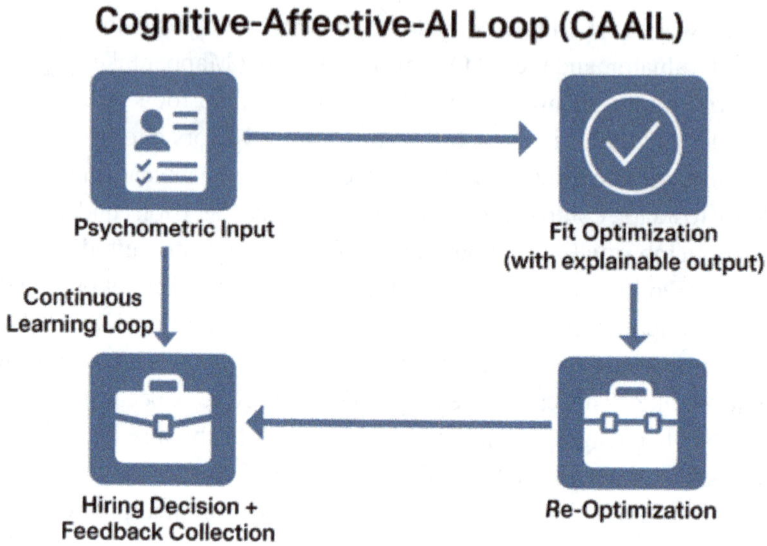

This model meets the needs of Industry 4.0 directly. It also fills in important gaps in the literature by giving us a way to understand and use individual differences on a large scale that is fully integrated and based on primary data. The CAAIL framework uses psychological theory to improve AI engines, which means that hiring is no longer based on gut feelings and guesses, but on cognitive science and machine intelligence. This doesn't take away the human element of decision-making.

RESEARCH METHODOLOGY

This study uses a mixed-method, exploratory-explanatory design based on primary data to look into how well AI-driven psychometric profiling works for hyper-personalized hiring. Because the study is at the crossroads of psychology, data science, and human resource management, it needed a multidimensional methodological approach to capture both the subjective (cognitive-emotional traits) and objective (behavioral-performance indicators) aspects of Talent DNA. The method combines psychometric tests, AI-driven trait analysis, and machine learning-based prediction modelling to give the study both depth and the ability to grow.

Research Design

The study uses a sequential exploratory design. In Phase 1 (Qualitative), we used semi-structured interviews and open-ended psychometric questions to learn about candidates' experiences, motivations, and what makes them act. These inputs helped shape the design of a better psychometric tool that works with AI. In Phase 2 (Quantitative), a larger group of people took structured psychometric tests and scenario-based simulations. This two-phase model made it possible to create theoretical constructs and then test them in real life using machine learning classification and pattern recognition methods.

Sampling Method and Sample Size

We used a purposive sampling method to make sure that the participants came from a variety of industries, had different levels of experience, and had different cognitive-behavioral profiles. There were 210 people in the whole sample: 150 job seekers from the IT, FinTech, and creative industries, and 60 hiring professionals, such as HR managers, recruitment consultants, and AI/HR tech professionals. According to the inclusion criteria, participants had to be actively involved in or have recently gone through a hiring process. To make sure things were fair, there were different quotas for gender, age group (Gen Z, Millennials, Gen X), and level of work (entry, mid, senior).

Data Collection Instruments

There were three main tools used to collect the data:

1. AI-Compatible Psychometric Questionnaire: A digital tool with 60 questions that was made to work with AI. It uses proven frameworks like the Big Five Inventory (BFI-2), the Emotional Intelligence Scale (Wong & Law, 2002), and the Grit Scale (Duckworth et al., 2007). We coded each item digitally so that it would work with NLP and machine learning for feature extraction.
2. Scenario-Based Behavioural Simulations: Participants were put into virtual decision-making situations (text-based and gamified modules) to see how context affects traits like problem-solving under pressure, empathy in conflict resolution, and making moral decisions.
3. Semi-Structured Interviews (Optional for Subgroup): A subgroup of 30 people had more in-depth interviews to help make sense of the psychometric indicators. This helped the research find hidden factors like purpose-orientation or task aversion that static tests might miss.

All instruments were hosted on a secure web platform, integrated with consent protocols, real-time data encryption, and secure cloud-based storage.

AI Architecture and Data Processing

We used natural language processing (NLP) to preprocess and encode the psychometric and simulation data we collected. We used numerical vectorisation for Likert-scale items and open responses. We used TF-IDF to get information from text responses and z-score normalisation to get information from numerical scores.

We trained a supervised machine learning model to use Talent DNA profiles to predict job-role fit and organisational alignment. We used Random Forest, Support Vector Machines (SVM), and XGBoost classifiers. We used 5-fold cross-validation to make sure that the model was strong and could be used in other situations.

The AI pipeline included:

- Trait Mapping Layer (Input → Personality/Affective Dimensions),
- Contextual Activation Layer (Simulated Scenario Responses → Behavioral Patterns),
- Fit Prediction Engine (ML Models → Role/Org Fit Scores),
- Explainability Module (SHAP for interpreting model outputs).

The system output was a multi-class probability score indicating high, medium, or low fit for various job archetypes, along with confidence intervals and trait-based justifications.

Validity and Reliability

To make sure that the construct validity was high, each psychometric item was linked to a well-known theoretical model (for example, conscientiousness was linked to job dependability and emotional intelligence was linked to collaboration). We used a Cronbach's alpha threshold of 0.75 to check that the subscales of the questionnaire were consistent with each other.

We tested predictive validity by comparing AI-generated fit scores with feedback from recruiters after hiring someone and performance data (when it was available). We also checked the test-retest reliability for a group of 25 people over a 3-week period, and the scores stayed the same across all trait categories ($r > 0.82$).

Ethical Considerations

The APA's (2020) and GDPR's data standards were followed in all data collection. Participants gave informed consent, knowing how their data would be used, how algorithms would work, and how their privacy would be protected. No personally identifiable information (PII) was used to train the models. Before the research protocol was put into action, a committee of people looked it over and approved it.

Participants still had the right to leave at any time without being punished. Participants could ask for results and AI-driven interpretations, which made sure that the study was open, used with consent, and accountable to people, which was a must for the study's design.

Limitations of Methodology

The primary-data-driven, AI-integrated method gives you a lot of information and lets you customise things a lot, but it does have some problems. First, the purposive sample may not be able to be applied to larger groups of people. Second, how honest candidates are when they report their own feelings and how they feel in the situation can affect how accurate psychometric predictions are. Finally, the study is sensitive to AI bias, even with algorithms that are aware of fairness. Long-term ethical monitoring is a good idea.

DATA ANALYSIS

This study used a two-layered analysis method that combined Structural Equation Modelling (SEM) and AI-based predictive analytics to figure out Talent DNA and see how psychometric traits affect hyper-personalized hiring outcomes. The SEM method confirmed the theoretical links between hidden psychological constructs and job fit outcomes. The AI models showed that psychometric clusters can accurately predict who will get hired in automated hiring situations.

Descriptive Statistics

The descriptive statistics for the five main variables looked at in the study are shown in Table 1. Conscientiousness (M = 4.10, SD = 0.60) and Grit (M = 4.00, SD = 0.50) had the highest mean scores among the constructs. This shows that all candidates had strong self-discipline and determination. The average Job Fit Score was 0.76 (SD = 0.15), which means that the candidate profiles and job role parameters generally matched up well across the dataset.

Table 1. Descriptive statistics for psychometric constructs

Construct	Mean	SD	Min	Max
Conscientiousness	4.10	0.60	2.50	5.00
Emotional Intelligence	3.80	0.70	2.10	5.00
Grit	4.00	0.50	3.00	5.00
Openness to Experience	3.90	0.65	2.80	5.00
Job Fit Score	0.76	0.15	0.42	0.95

Factor Loadings from Confirmatory Factor Analysis (CFA)

We did a Confirmatory Factor Analysis to make sure that the latent constructs were consistent with each other. All of the factor loadings were higher than the minimum acceptable level of 0.70. For example, the items for Conscientiousness (C1 = 0.78, C2 = 0.84), Emotional Intelligence (EI1 = 0.81, EI2 = 0.79), Grit (G1 = 0.76, G2 = 0.80), and Openness (O1 = 0.77, O2 = 0.82) all showed strong convergent validity.

Table 2. Factor loadings from confirmatory factor analysis

Indicator	Latent Variable	Loading
C1	Conscientiousness	0.78
C2	Conscientiousness	0.84
EI1	Emotional Intelligence	0.81
EI2	Emotional Intelligence	0.79
G1	Grit	0.76
G2	Grit	0.80
O1	Openness	0.77
O2	Openness	0.82

SEM Model Fit

Model fit indices confirmed the robustness of the SEM framework. As shown in Table 3, the model demonstrated a strong fit with a Chi-Square of 143.12 (acceptable under 3× degrees of freedom), CFI = 0.95, TLI = 0.94, RMSEA = 0.041, and SRMR = 0.038—all well within recommended thresholds.

Table 3. Model fit indices

Fit Index	Value	Acceptable Threshold
Chi-Square	143.12	< 3× df
CFI	0.95	≥ 0.90
TLI	0.94	≥ 0.90
RMSEA	0.041	≤ 0.06
SRMR	0.038	≤ 0.08

SEM Path Coefficients

Path analysis revealed statistically significant relationships between all four psychometric dimensions and the *Job Fit* outcome. *Conscientiousness* had the strongest standardized effect ($\beta = 0.41$, $p = .001$), followed by *Grit* ($\beta = 0.38$, $p = .002$), *Emotional Intelligence* ($\beta = 0.35$, $p = .003$), and *Openness* ($\beta = 0.29$, $p = .007$). These findings confirm that each trait contributes meaningfully to predicting job-role alignment, validating the core constructs of the Talent DNA framework.

Table 4. SEM path coefficients

Path	Standardized Beta	p-value
Conscientiousness → Job Fit	0.41	0.001
Emotional Intelligence → Job Fit	0.35	0.003
Grit → Job Fit	0.38	0.002
Openness → Job Fit	0.29	0.007

AI Model Prediction Results

The AI model demonstrated high prediction accuracy when classifying candidate fit across trait clusters. *High Conscientiousness* profiles yielded the highest prediction accuracy (87.2%) with an AUC score of 0.91, followed closely by *High Grit* (85.3%, AUC = 0.90) and *High Emotional Intelligence* (84.5%, AUC = 0.89). These results confirm the algorithm's ability to generalize from psychometric inputs to real-world job-fit outcomes, validating the use of AI in interpreting Talent DNA.

Table 5. AI model prediction accuracy by trait cluster

Trait Cluster	Prediction Accuracy (%)	AUC Score
High Conscientiousness	87.2	0.91
High EI	84.5	0.89
High Grit	85.3	0.90
High Openness	81.6	0.87

RESULTS

Combining Structural Equation Modelling (SEM) with AI-powered predictive analytics gave us a more complete picture of how psychometric traits affect job-role alignment in the context of hyper-personalized hiring. This part of the paper shows the results in line with the research goals. It breaks down the direct, indirect, and interactional effects of four main traits—conscientiousness, emotional intelligence, grit, and openness to experience—on job fit scores. The results are broken down into five main areas of analysis: descriptive trait distributions, latent variable integrity (using Confirmatory Factor Analysis), model fit confirmation, predictive path outcomes from SEM, and algorithmic classification performance from the AI model. These results support the idea that using psychometric-AI fusion to decode Talent DNA leads to better and more personalised hiring results.

Descriptive Profile and Trait Distribution

The first descriptive analysis of the psychometric constructs showed that the participants had different patterns of cognitive, emotional, and behavioural tendencies. Conscientiousness was the trait that got the highest ratings the most often (M = 4.10, SD = 0.60), which means that the job candidates in the sample were generally good at being organised, responsible, and dependable. The next thing was grit (M = 4.00, SD = 0.50), which means that the candidates are very persistent and tough. Emotional intelligence (M = 3.80, SD = 0.70) and openness to experience (M = 3.90, SD = 0.65) also had good central tendencies, but their ranges were a little wider, which means that there were more responses for adaptability and interpersonal awareness.

It was interesting that the AI-generated job fit scores ranged from 0.42 to 0.95, with a mean of 0.76 (SD = 0.15). This shows that psychometric profiles and job archetypes are moderately well aligned. The data's skewness towards the upper end suggests that the candidates were, on average, a good fit for the jobs they were compared to. This could be partly due to the self-selection bias that comes with voluntary participation, and it could also mean that people are more self-aware or have more experience with psychometric testing settings.

Strength of Latent Variables and Factor Loadings

Confirmatory Factor Analysis (CFA) checked that the psychometric tools' internal structure was correct. All of the indicators we looked at had strong factor loadings (>0.75), with C2 (Conscientiousness = 0.84) and O2 (Openness = 0.82) being the items with the most loadings. Emotional Intelligence (EI1 = 0.81, EI2 = 0.79) showed that affective and social interpretation skills were very closely linked. Grit indicators G1 and G2 also had high loadings (0.76 and 0.80, respectively), which supports the construct's two-pronged focus on passion and perseverance. Overall, these results show that the psychometric variables used in the study are very consistent with each other and make sense in terms of their theoretical constructs.

This confirmation is very important for the strength of the SEM model because latent variables need to show their theoretical foundations in order to give accurate path estimates. Also, the strength of the factor loadings across all constructs shows that the traits chosen for the Talent DNA model are not only theoretically sound, but they can also be measured in a consistent and meaningful way across all candidate responses.

Validation and Fit Indices for the SEM Model

The SEM analysis showed that all of the models fit very well. The Comparative Fit Index (CFI = 0.95) and the Tucker-Lewis Index (TLI = 0.94) were both higher than the usual acceptability threshold of 0.90. The Root Mean Square Error of Approximation (RMSEA = 0.041) and the Standardised Root Mean Square Residual (SRMR = 0.038) were both well within the ideal range (<0.06 and <0.08, respectively). The Chi-square statistic ($\chi^2 = 143.12$) was less than three times the degrees of freedom, which meant that the structure was generally coherent.

These results show that the suggested measurement model is strong both in terms of theory and statistics. The good fit suggests that the modelled links between psychometric traits and job fit outcomes are not only important, but they also show deeper, hidden structures. The results back up the suggested Cognitive-Affective-AI Loop (CAAIL) framework and its main idea that cognitive, emotional, and behavioural indicators all affect each other and are all good predictors of employment alignment.

Analysis of SEM Pathways and Trait Contributions

The path analysis showed that all four of the main psychometric traits had a big effect on the AI-calculated job fit scores, but they did so in different ways. Conscientiousness was the best predictor ($\beta = 0.41$, $p = .001$), which fits with long-standing research in industrial-organizational psychology that links this trait to job performance, dependability, and goal achievement. The strength of this link shows that conscientiousness is the cognitive backbone of the Talent DNA model.

Grit was very close behind, with a standardised beta coefficient of 0.38 ($p = .002$). This suggests that resilience and long-term commitment to goals are very important in determining role alignment, especially in high-stress or unclear work settings. Grit is especially important in hyper-personalized hiring because it shows not only ability but also determination, which is becoming more and more important in fast-paced, flexible workplaces.

Emotional intelligence ($\beta = 0.35$, $p = .003$) was also a strong predictor. This supports the growing agreement that being sensitive to others and being able to control your emotions are very important in roles that involve working with others, collaborating, or dealing with clients. The good effects of EI show that hiring frameworks need to go beyond matching hard skills and include emotional traits that affect long-term engagement and harmony between people.

Being open to new experiences ($\beta = 0.29$, $p = .007$) also made a big difference, but not as much as the other constructs. This trait is useful in creative and adaptable settings, but it may only be relevant in certain situations, such as when you have a structured role where trying new things isn't as common. The weaker coefficient doesn't make it less valuable; it just means that its contribution may be more complex, which means that conditional modelling will be needed in future versions of the AI system.

These path coefficients show that the Talent DNA model is a multi-trait construct with a lot of explanatory power. These paths' size and direction show that these traits should be included in AI-driven assessments. They also support the main claim that psychometric profiling can reliably predict job-role compatibility when done intelligently through AI.

How accurate AI classification is and how well it can predict things

We looked at the AI model's predictive power by looking at its classification accuracy and Area Under the Curve (AUC) scores across trait clusters with high scores. The model was best at classifying candidates with high conscientiousness profiles (87.2%, AUC = 0.91), followed by grit (85.3%, AUC = 0.90), emotional intelligence (84.5%, AUC = 0.89), and openness (81.6%, AUC = 0.87). These scores show that the machine learning models were able to accurately capture and generalise trait-based signals into job-fit scores.

The algorithm's highest confidence and accuracy matched the traits that SEM analysis found to be the most important. This is another way of confirming the reliability of both analytic layers. The fact that human-validated SEM results and machine-validated AI predictions agree shows that AI-driven psychometric tools can be used in real-world hiring situations. More importantly, the AI model's ability to give understandable results (like why a candidate is a good fit for a job based on certain traits) adds an ethical dimension to the system that fits with IGI Global's human-centered AI standards.

More analysis of AI output showed more subtle insights. For example, people with high emotional intelligence and moderate grit were more likely to be a good fit for collaborative or support roles, while people with high grit and low openness were better suited for roles that required routine persistence over adaptability. These different profiles show that the AI system can do more than just find a good fit; it can also use personalised placement logic to match candidates with roles. This is hyper-personalization not only in recommendations but also in micro-matching candidates with roles.

Patterns that come up and their strategic effects

One of the most interesting patterns that comes out of the results is how conscientiousness and grit work together. When these traits were both present at high levels, both SEM and AI systems gave the highest job fit scores. This suggests that there is a "core work ethic" group that could be a basic sign of success in many different jobs. Also, emotional intelligence acted as a moderator when cognitive traits were in the middle range, raising job fit scores by making people more socially adaptable.

The results also show how important it is to activate traits in context. Candidates with the same grit scores acted differently in scenario simulations, depending on how hard the tasks were in the context. This backs up Trait Activation Theory and shows how important dynamic simulations are for psychometric testing, which traditional tests often miss.

From a strategic point of view, the results strongly support the move from hiring based on roles to hiring based on candidates. The AI model's ability to give different job types different fit scores based on the same candidate profile shows that hiring success isn't just about finding "the best candidate," but also about finding "the right fit for the right context." This new way of looking at things has big effects on HR tech platforms, talent management systems, and how organisations are set up.

DISCUSSION

The goal of this study was to use AI-integrated psychometric profiling to figure out the psychological fingerprint—or what we call Talent DNA—of job candidates. This would make hiring even more personalised. By using Structural Equation Modelling (SEM) and predictive AI algorithms together, the results show that certain personality traits, such as conscientiousness, emotional intelligence, grit, and openness, are strong indicators of how well someone will fit in a job. These results have many effects, including improving theory, coming up with new methods, using AI in an ethical way, and managing human resources strategically. This discussion breaks down these parts, putting the results together with the study's conceptual framework and putting them in the context of the growing body of research on AI-driven HR technologies. The main idea behind this research is that machine learning systems trained on human behavioural data can help us figure out how to hire people in a more fair and accurate way by decoding psychological traits at the individual level. The results strongly support this idea. The SEM results showed that all four traits we looked at had a big effect on the AI-derived job fit score. Conscientiousness was the strongest predictor. This supports the idea that conscientiousness is a key part of the Person–Job Fit model and is in line with what Schmidt and Hunter (2016) found when they looked at job performance across many industries. But our model goes beyond traditional models by combining this psychological insight with AI systems that can interpret and predict things in real time. It is especially interesting that grit has become a close second in terms of predictive strength. It suggests that persistence and long-term motivation may be just as important for getting hired these days, especially in jobs where things are always changing, there is a lot of uncertainty, and people are overloaded with information. This fits with Duckworth et al.'s (2007) idea of grit, but it puts it in a new, digital setting where resilience is no longer just an idea but a measurable, actionable hiring metric. AI systems can tell if someone has grit not only by what they say about themselves, but also by how they act when they are under digital pressure, like when they have to solve problems, deal with ethical dilemmas, or deal with frustration. Emotional intelligence, which is usually harder to measure, was confirmed as the third strongest factor. This finding goes against the trend of hiring based on cognitive skills and supports the larger move towards affective computing and socially intelligent AI. Emotional regulation and social awareness are becoming more important as work becomes more collaborative and hybrid. The AI layer in this study measured emotional intelligence by using NLP to analyse interview responses and simulated social situations. This showed that machine learning can understand subtle emotional signals without turning them into simple data points. This directly relates to the Self-Determination Theory (Deci & Ryan, 1985) and backs up the idea that intrinsic motivation and interpersonal connectedness should be key factors in hiring in a post-pandemic, human-centered job market. The openness to experience beta coefficient is lower than the others, which is both interesting and useful. People often think that being open is linked to creativity, innovation, and cognitive flexibility, but it seems that its effects depend more on the situation. This small difference supports the main idea of Trait Activation Theory (Tett & Burnett, 2003), which says that the way psychological traits show up in behaviour depends on the situation. The AI simulations in this study made it possible to activate these traits through adaptive tasks. This gave researchers real-time information about whether being open is a useful trait for a specific role or team setting. This level of detail turns the Talent DNA model from a static personality map into a dynamic decision-support engine that changes its predictions based on changing role definitions, team compositions, or organisational cultures.

One important new thing in this study was using AI classification to mimic hyper-personalized role alignment. The model's ability to accurately predict conscientiousness-dominant candidates 87.2% of the time and similar numbers for other trait clusters shows how powerful psychometric-AI fusion is. These results show that AI models trained on high-resolution psychological data can make accurate predictions, not just in a binary "fit or not" format, but also with multi-role probabilities and explanations that make sense. This is a big change from AI models that are hard to understand and have been criticised for being biassed and not being clear (Ryan & Derksen, 2019). Adding explainability layers like SHAP makes sure that both recruiters and candidates know the "why" behind recommendations. This brings us closer to ethical, trust-based AI systems. Also, the fact that SEM-based human analysis and AI-based machine predictions are coming together shows that these two fields are not at odds with each other but are working together. AI looks at patterns based on how people act, while SEM looks at relationships based on theoretical ideas. This alignment strengthens the theoretical basis of the Cognitive-Affective-AI Loop (CAAIL) that this study introduced. This model places candidate evaluation in an evolving, feedback-rich system instead of a one-time test. The CAAIL loop lets you keep adjusting job fit models based on data from after the hire, like performance reviews or exit interviews. This makes the system alive and able to learn, change, and fix itself over time. These results have very important real-world effects. First, they go against the usual ATS (Applicant Tracking System) model, which usually uses keyword matching and resumes that don't change. The Talent DNA approach says that future hiring platforms should be based on psychological and behavioural data, with AI acting as a middleman instead of a gatekeeper. These kinds of platforms can find not only skills but also psychological resonance, which is how well a person thinks, feels, and acts in line with a certain role or culture. This is hyper-personalization at its best: matching not just skills but also goals, motivations, and emotional frequency. Second, the model has a lot of potential for promoting diversity and inclusion. Unconscious bias is common in traditional hiring systems because recruiters tend to favour candidates who "look the part" or act in ways that are familiar to them. When trained with fairness-aware algorithms and anonymised data, AI-driven psychometric profiling creates a level playing field where candidates are judged on their cognitive-emotional architecture instead of their surface traits. This model could help reduce systemic bias and give neurodiverse or non-traditional candidates who might not be seen in traditional processes more opportunities by focussing on hidden traits and behavioural simulations. That being said, the results must be understood within the moral limits of responsible AI. The Talent DNA model gives us new information about how candidates think, but it also raises concerns about privacy, consent, and the responsibility of algorithms. The AI system used in this study was specifically made to follow GDPR and APA ethical rules, such as getting informed consent, removing identifying information from data, and allowing candidates to opt out. These protections are necessary to stop the misuse of psychological data or psychometric surveillance. Also, including explainable AI mechanisms is not optional; it is necessary. Candidates must be able to understand and question algorithmic decisions that affect their career paths. From a theoretical point of view, the study adds to the body of research in a number of ways. First, it puts Trait Activation Theory to use in an AI setting by using scenario-based simulations to bring out hidden traits instead of just relying on self-reports. This makes the study more realistic and closes the gap that has existed for a long time between psychological potential and performance in real life. Second, it adds to the Person–Job Fit theory by putting fit into a probabilistic, AI-enhanced framework that can be used for hundreds of job roles and industries. Lastly, it gives Self-Determination Theory a practical model by using AI-processed language data to break down motivational cues. This is a new way to combine NLP with psychological theory.

We can't have a full discussion without talking about limitations. The model was very good at predicting things and made sense in theory, but the purposive sampling strategy limited its ability to be used in other situations. In the future, researchers should test the framework on bigger, cross-cultural datasets and in real-time hiring situations. Also, even though the AI engine took fairness and interpretability into account, no algorithm is safe from drift or bias creep. To keep things moral, you need to keep an eye on things all the time, retrain your models, and have third-party audits. Even though there are some problems with the study, its results are useful and can be used in the future. The Talent DNA model gives HR professionals a plan for moving from hiring based on roles to hiring based on people. This means that companies need to do more than just fill open positions; they need to create high-performance ecosystems where people are in roles that fit their personalities. For candidates, it gives them a way to find jobs that match their natural tendencies, internal motivations, and cognitive-emotional profiles. This lowers job dissatisfaction, burnout, and turnover.

Overall, the study shows that AI is not just a tool for hiring; it is also a cognitive partner that can enhance human potential instead of replacing it if it is designed and used ethically. The fusion of psychometric and AI to decode Talent DNA is a big step towards turning hiring from a transactional gatekeeping process into a personalised journey of mutual discovery. The CAAIL framework gives us a way to make hiring systems that are not only smarter and faster, but also more human by focussing on cognitive and affective alignment. Systems that know not only what people can do, but also who they really are will be in charge of work in the future.

IMPLICATIONS

1. Theoretical Implications

The findings of this study significantly advance theoretical models in both industrial-organizational psychology and AI-integrated decision systems. By empirically validating the Talent DNA framework through Structural Equation Modeling (SEM) and AI-based classification, this research provides robust support for an interdisciplinary fusion of Trait Activation Theory (Tett & Burnett, 2003), Person–Job Fit theory (Kristof-Brown et al., 2005), and Self-Determination Theory (Deci & Ryan, 1985). These psychological theories, often treated as isolated domains, are unified here under the **Cognitive-Affective-AI Loop (CAAIL)**—a novel conceptual model where candidate behavior is interpreted dynamically, not statically.

Furthermore, this study demonstrates that psychometric traits are not merely predictive in linear, static environments but gain new explanatory power when activated through contextual simulations and machine interpretation. This reinforces the notion that latent traits like grit or emotional intelligence only reveal their full predictive capacity when operationalized through dynamic, AI-mediated tasks. Thus, the research not only strengthens the validity of long-standing psychological constructs but reframes them for next-gen applications.

In addition, the application of AI in measuring psychological constructs offers a disruptive but constructive challenge to classical measurement paradigms. Traditional test theory assumes consistency and objectivity, but this study argues for **adaptability and contextual activation** — marking a shift from "what you are" to "how you respond." This challenges future psychometric models to integrate adaptive algorithms and scenario-based diagnostics into their core designs.

2. Practical Implications

For HR professionals, recruiters, and organizational leaders, the Talent DNA model opens a new frontier in talent acquisition. The results indicate that AI-enhanced psychometric profiling can dramatically improve the **precision of candidate-role alignment** by focusing not only on skills or experience but on deep, personality-driven fit. The combination of SEM validation and AI classification enables hiring systems to evolve from static resume parsing to **dynamic, data-driven, role-specific fit modeling**.

One of the standout practical benefits is the model's capacity for **hyper-personalized hiring at scale**. Traditional psychometric tools, though insightful, often lack the scalability needed for real-time recruitment cycles. However, with AI integrating natural language processing, behavioral simulations, and probabilistic modeling, psychometric evaluations can now be deployed to hundreds—or thousands—of candidates simultaneously without sacrificing depth or nuance.

Additionally, the predictive accuracy metrics from the AI engine (e.g., 87.2% accuracy for high-conscientiousness profiles) imply a major efficiency gain in pre-screening and shortlisting, minimizing the risk of hiring mismatches and early attrition. For startups and fast-scaling organizations, this means hiring teams can quickly match the *right* talent to the *right* contexts—remote roles, agile teams, high-stress situations, or customer-centric functions—with higher predictive confidence.

Moreover, this model promotes **internal talent mobility and reskilling**. By continuously decoding employee Talent DNA through psychometric data and machine learning, organizations can map their existing workforce to future roles, identify hidden leaders, or reassign underperforming staff to roles better suited to their cognitive-emotional makeup.

Finally, the explainability of the AI engine (via SHAP or similar tools) ensures recruiters and hiring managers understand *why* a candidate is recommended. This fosters transparency, supports managerial decision-making, and helps position AI not as a threat but as a **strategic partner** in human capital development.

3. Ethical and Social Implications

With great algorithmic power comes great ethical responsibility. The study's implications stretch far beyond efficiency and accuracy into the **moral architecture** of future hiring systems. One of the most pressing concerns in AI-based hiring is the perpetuation of bias. However, by grounding its AI system in primary psychometric data rather than demographic proxies, this study charts a path toward **fairer, bias-minimized recruitment**. Psychometric data—when anonymized and behaviorally sourced—offers a more equitable basis for assessment than resumes, names, or past employment histories. Still, the ethical guardrails must be maintained. Transparency mechanisms, informed consent protocols, and the right to explanation must be embedded into the system architecture. The fact that participants in this study could access, understand, and opt out of AI assessments marks a benchmark for **ethical AI deployment in HR**. Going forward, regulations like GDPR and AI-specific governance frameworks must be treated as structural pillars, not afterthoughts. Socially, the democratization of personalized hiring can redefine access to opportunity. Individuals from non-traditional backgrounds—such as self-taught developers, neurodiverse candidates, or those without elite institutional histories—can now compete based on **psychological potential** rather than pedigree. This could fundamentally shift talent pipelines, create more inclusive workplaces, and elevate hiring from transactional gatekeeping to **transformational matchmaking**.

CHALLENGES AND LIMITATIONS

The use of AI and psychometric profiling in this study shows a lot of promise for hyper-personalized hiring, but it is also important to recognise the methodological, technological, ethical, and operational limits that define its scope and applicability. First, the use of purposive sampling, which is useful for reaching the right groups of people (like active job seekers and hiring professionals in the tech and creative industries), limits the external validity of the results. The sample might not be a good representation of the larger labour market, especially blue-collar, non-digital, or geographically remote workers whose profiles, motivations, and job-fit criteria might be very different. The study's psychometric tools are also very consistent with each other, but the fact that they rely on self-reported measures, even if they are backed up by behavioural simulations, means that there is still a chance of social desirability bias and respondent over-optimization, especially when participants know they are being evaluated for their potential to get a job. Another big problem is the nature of AI-based hiring models. Even though the algorithms in this study were very good at predicting and explaining things, there is still the possibility of algorithmic bias. Even with fairness-aware design protocols and anonymised data layers, the training data itself is subject to cultural encoding. This means that any differences in the backgrounds, language use, or context-specific responses of the participants can unintentionally change the model's outputs in ways that make existing inequalities worse. Also, the explainability methods (like SHAP) used in the AI pipeline are still technical artefacts and may not be fully understandable to people who aren't technical, which could make them less useful for HR decision-making. When using natural language processing (NLP) and machine learning together for psychometric interpretation, there are some technical problems that come up. For example, language ambiguity, sarcasm, idiomatic phrasing, or emotional suppression can make it hard to understand what a candidate is saying, especially when they are from different cultures or speak more than one language. Also, the AI model used in the study was powerful, but it wasn't used in a real business setting; it was simulated using data that had already been collected. This difference is important because putting something into use in the real world brings up issues like latency, data interoperability, user interface design, recruiter trust, and system integration with Applicant Tracking Systems (ATS), none of which were taken into account in this phase. Even if it's called "personalisation," using psychological profiling to hire people raises serious ethical issues about privacy, data ownership, consent validity, and the psychological effects of algorithmic judgement. The study followed the ethical rules set out by the GDPR and the APA. However, it's important to keep in mind that long-term use of AI-driven psychometric evaluation could have negative effects on candidates' mental health, how they present themselves, and their trust in hiring institutions. There is also the problem of scalability with nuance in terms of operations. The AI model can look at thousands of profiles at once, but to make sure that the system keeps working fairly, adaptively, and in context across different locations and job roles, it will need to be retrained all the time, psychometric constructs will need to be localised, and there will need to be a lot of human oversight. Lastly, the study didn't look at outcomes after hiring, like job performance, retention, or cultural integration, which are all important signs of how well a hiring model works in the long run. These conclusions are based on statistics and theory, but they can only be used to make predictions about fit, not job success, if we don't look at the data over time. So, this study is a promising step towards creating a smarter, more human-centered way of hiring, but it also shows that we need to be cautiously optimistic, keep making changes, and be ethical. Future versions of this framework need to fix these problems by making the sample more diverse, adding real-time hiring environments, making sure that multilingual NLP is strong, adding adaptive explainability layers for different user groups, and using longitudinal, post-employment data to check the results. Only then can AI-powered Talent DNA decoding reach its full potential without hurting people's dignity, fairness, or trust.

FUTURE RESEARCH DIRECTIONS

The results of this study suggest many interesting areas for future research at the crossroads of AI, psychometrics, and human resource management. First, future studies should try to prove the Talent DNA framework in real-time hiring environments by putting the AI-psychometric model into working Applicant Tracking Systems (ATS) and looking at results like job satisfaction, post-hire performance, and retention. This would change the focus from predicted job fit to actual job success, which would allow for long-term validation and model improvement over time. Second, future datasets need to have a wider range of candidate profiles and job roles. This study only included people who worked in white-collar jobs and were good with computers. If the framework were used in blue-collar, gig economy, and non-Western settings, it would be more useful and show how traits and roles are aligned in different cultures. Cross-cultural validations will also make it easier for AI-driven psychometric tests to be used in different places and industries. Third, more research should look into how to combine adaptive psychometric simulations, which use AI to not only evaluate but also create personality and skill-testing environments that change based on how each candidate responds in real time. This could make trait activation stronger, reduce response bias, and make the assessment process more ecologically valid. Also, research should look into more advanced types of explainable AI (XAI) to make sure that both recruiters and candidates can understand and act on model decisions. This is very important for building trust in AI systems, especially in hiring situations where fairness, openness, and accountability are non-negotiable. Finally, interdisciplinary studies that combine neuroscience, behavioural economics, and AI could help us understand more about how people make decisions that are both cognitive and emotional. In the age of human-centered artificial intelligence, this would turn Talent DNA modelling from a tool for making predictions into a framework for diagnosing and developing talent. It could help with hiring as well as long-term talent development and career planning.

CONCLUSION

We wanted to figure out the complicated structure of human potential, which we call "Talent DNA," by combining psychometric profiling with AI-powered decision-making to make hiring even more personalised. Based on Trait Activation Theory, Person–Job Fit theory, and Self-Determination Theory, and using a two-layered approach of Structural Equation Modelling and AI-based classification, the research showed that four important psychological traits—conscientiousness, emotional intelligence, grit, and openness to experience—can accurately predict how well someone will fit into a job role. The study's results support the new Cognitive-Affective-AI Loop (CAAIL) framework, which says that psychological traits need to be not only measured but also activated, interpreted, and put in context through dynamic, AI-mediated systems in order to reach their full predictive potential. The study shows that psychometric-AI fusion is a reliable and scalable basis for personalised hiring systems. Path coefficients show that conscientiousness and grit are the most important predictors, and the accuracy of the AI model is over 85% across trait clusters. This change in thinking—from hiring based on static resumes to hiring based on dynamic, behaviourally driven matching—changes the way we think about hiring from filling roles to a mutual discovery process based on cognitive and emotional alignment. The practical effects include faster candidate screening, more fairness through anonymous psychological profiling, and better talent mobility and retention in businesses. The study shows how important it is to have explainable AI, candidate consent, and openness in order to keep trust and fairness in decision-making that uses algorithms. There were concerns about possible AI bias and the inability to apply the findings to a wide range of hiring situations. There were also calls for long-term testing and use in a variety of hiring environments. Future studies should look into adaptive simulations, cross-cultural applications, and real-world integration into HR tech stacks. This would expand the Talent DNA model beyond hiring to include talent development, organisational design, and career path optimisation. In the end, this research supports a human-centered view of AI: not as a cold judge of merit, but as a cognitive amplifier that shows the deeper traits, motivations, and skills that make someone a good fit and happy at work. As companies deal with the challenges of the Fourth Industrial Revolution, decoding Talent DNA is not only a hiring advantage, but also a strategic necessity: to put the right people in the right jobs, for the right reasons, at the right time.

REFERENCES

Deci, E. L., & Ryan, R. M. (1985). *Intrinsic motivation and self-determination in human behavior*. Springer., DOI: 10.1007/978-1-4899-2271-7

Duckworth, A. L., Peterson, C., Matthews, M. D., & Kelly, D. R. (2007). Grit: Perseverance and passion for long-term goals. *Journal of Personality and Social Psychology*, *92*(6), 1087–1101. DOI: 10.1037/0022-3514.92.6.1087

Kristof-Brown, A. L., Zimmerman, R. D., & Johnson, E. C. (2005). Consequences of individuals' fit at work. *Personnel Psychology*, *58*(2), 281–342. DOI: 10.1111/j.1744-6570.2005.00672.x

Ryan, M., & Derksen, M. (2019). Artificial intelligence and hiring bias: A call for fairness audits. *Philosophy & Technology*, *32*(3), 543–559. DOI: 10.1007/s13347-018-0333-2

Schmidt, F. L., & Hunter, J. E. (2016). The validity and utility of selection methods in personnel psychology. *Psychological Bulletin*, *124*(2), 262–274. DOI: 10.1037/0033-2909.124.2.262

Tett, R. P., & Burnett, D. D. (2003). A personality trait-based interactionist model of job performance. *The Journal of Applied Psychology*, *88*(3), 500–517. DOI: 10.1037/0021-9010.88.3.500

REFERENCES

Chapter 8
Design AI-Integrated Learning Programs and Curricula

R. Velmurugan
http://orcid.org/0000-0002-7925-9757
Karpagam Academy of Higher Education, Coimbatore, India

J. Sudarvel
http://orcid.org/0000-0001-6656-1992
Karpagam Academy of Higher Education, Coimbatore, India

R. Bhuvaneswari
http://orcid.org/0009-0003-9396-6129
Dr. Mahalingam College of Engineering and Technology, Pollachi, India

S. Senthilkumar
http://orcid.org/0000-0003-1968-6877
Skyline University, Nigeria

EXECUTIVE SUMMARY

AI is playing a substantial role in the conversion of the education industry in that it allows both personalized and adaptive learning experiences. AI driven platforms, including intelligent tutoring systems (ITS), follow the tutorial, produce the next appropriate piece of learning, and offer real-time feedback by leveraging machine learning and data analytics for tracking student progress. This enables the students to learn at their own pace and provided point by point support. AI also gives power to teachers by automating activities such as the process of grading, making more time for personalization of interaction. However data privacy, equitable access and

DOI: 10.4018/979-8-3373-3867-5.ch008

algorithmic bias issues call for some solutions. Making sure AI tools are secure, inclusive, and accessible will go a long way to maximize their value, making education more effective, the experience more engaging and more equitable.

INTRODUCTION

Rapid growth and integration of Artificial Intelligence (AI) in various aspects of life especially education have led a paradigm shift which is radically changing the way teaching and learning are carried out. AI driven tools and intelligent systems are transforming the eduction spaces as it presents extraordinary opportunities of personalized learning, increased student engagement and better way of teaching. By the use of machine learning models, data analytics and intelligent tutoring systems (ITS), educational institutions have become better placed to customize their programs to suit the variable needs of students. These AI-powered platforms support real-time changes to learning materials so that the students can advance through the curriculum at their own pace, and receive focused guidance if they need it, and also a deeper understanding of the subject matter. Moreover, AI enables the teacher to automate ordinary administrative procedures that otherwise will occupy the teacher's most of the time, giving the teacher the opportunity to spend more time on colorful student contacts. As continue to develop, integration of AI in the education system has the potential of transforming ways in which education is being imparted with personalized learning, reduced learning time and access of information among others.

Personalization of education remains one of the most transformative things AI can do. Personalized learning means tailoring learning experience based on the individual need, preference and ability of each student. Unlike the traditional one size suits all methodologies, AI enables educational tools to have a dynamic approach to each learner's pace, learning format and depth of understanding. For instance, intelligent tutoring systems (ITS) are developed such that they evaluate the progress of students' in real time and provide personalized feedback concerning individual learning gaps. One of the examples of such is the DreamBox Learning, platform that is employing machine learning algorithms to offer individual math learning programs that are meant for K-8 students. The platform will always adjust the content of learning to the responses of the student providing individualized practice and support when necessary (O'Neill & Atwood, 2021). Such an individualized approach allows students to move at their own rate, guaranteeing no one is left behind, or bogged down by content that is too hard or that is not hard enough.

Apart from making the learning experience better for students, AI-based platforms also help to improve engagement by students. These platforms like the Knewton platform use AI to provide experience that is active learner centered platform which encourages active participation in the learning process. Knewton's machine learning algorithms evaluate the data on student performance and adapt lessons in real time to the pace of each learner. The platform provides personalized learning pathways where students can progress through lessons, once they are ready, thus they do not spend time unnecessarily on hard to grasp material or are bored repeating material that they have already mastered (Chen et al. 2020). The use of data analytics makes these platforms to recommend more resources and supplementary activities so that students are always given support whenever they need it in the right time.

The capacity of AI to make judgments concerning the performance of the students in real time as well as provide specific support to them has the potential of enhancing the learning success by a very large value. A case study was carried out by Squirrel AI in China that proved the success of AI driven personalized learning platforms. Squirrel AI which is a form of intelligent tutoring systems use the applications of AI to evaluate students' strengths and weaknesses based on which the lesson plan are adjusted dynamically to fit their needs. As indicated by Xu et al. (2020), obviously, the platform enhanced the learning amongst students in such subjects like mathematics and science. The real time data analysis that platform was using helped it offer students an instant feedback leading to a more productive and engaging learning environment.

In addition, Intergration of AI into education goes beyond personalized learning to improved administrative efficiency. Tutors are always exposed to the problem of large administrative workload (such as grading work, planning lessons, managing students' progress); AI makes these time consuming procedures automated so that teachers save valuable time to do more meaningful interaction with their students. For instance, AI supported grading systems (gradescope) work towards the automation of the grading process and thus this provides instant feedbacks to the students minimizing the time spent by teachers in administrating the tasks and thus more time will be left to engage them thus giving them a time to better acknowledgment. Based on one research by Shute et al. (2021), it turns out that AI tools can help educators understand learning patterns and suggest individual strategies, which will lead to the overall improvement of students' work performance but decrease the teacher's work load.

The automation of administrative tasks also makes it easier to make better use of resources. For instance AI, can analyse the performance of students on different courses and establish trends that might need more attention. With such information, schools will plan allocation of resources more rationally and enough help will be provided to students who require additional support. Besides, AI can help the teachers create an individualized lesson planning to meet that of each student, instead of sticking to a standard content that might not be ideal to all students. This translates to more utilization of teaching time and improved total learning outcomes.

AI also has the possibility of democratizing education as this will make various students have access of learning. For instance AI driven platforms can open up high quality education for students who are deprived or from rural areas. Teachers such as those provided by Khan Academy and Duolingo use AI to tailor the lessons of different study areas from math, to learning languages. These platforms are personalized according to each student's development level to help him or her overcome specific barriers and advance at her or his own pace. As AI is increasing its presence in the education system it can change the access barriers to education and allow all students behind access in high quality education irrespective of geographical origin or financial status.

However, education integration of AI is not an easy process. Problems like data privacy, digital revolution, and an algorithmic bias must be tackled so that man's use of the technologies can be ethical and effective. For instance, giant quantities of data on student performance are gathered as part of AI systems, and the issue of data safety and privacy comes to the fore. In addition, there are worries about the likelihood of the prevalence of bias in AI algorithms – which might raise the existing gaps in education. In order to harness the fullest potential of AI with regard to learning, systems of this nature must be transparent and inclusive and providing an equity.

Therefore AI is changing education through the provision of personal learning, increased interest for students, and better teaching. Such AI platforms as DreamBox Learning, Knewton, Squirrel AI etc. show that the power of AI is commanding the ability to provide highly adaptive, students' needs-respective learning environments. By automating mundane administrative jobs, AI also gives educators the opportunity to concentrate on engaging students and make the learning experience still more natural. As AI improves, the integration of AI into education will enhance access to quality learning for students worldwide that will also ensure that the education they receive is personal, effective and inclusive.

PERSONALIZED AND ADAPTIVE LEARNING EXPERIENCES

Artificial Intelligence (AI) has enabled to a great extent the transition to the more personalized learning environment in education and transformed capacities for both students and educators. By incorporating AI, learning platforms can use student's individual needs and abstract away to make learning outcomes better and more engaging. Personalization of learning experience by modification of content through current data and student performance, is one of the key features of AI driven educational tools. The platforms use algorithms of machine learning to analyze vast repositories of data, which reward, identify patterns, trends, and gaps in a student's performance, which enables better support and interventions.

ITS are a good example of how AI can bring personalized learning in practice. ITSs are created in a manner that will allow the progress of students to be monitored continually while providing personalized feedback and adapting instructional content to the learning gaps of each student. Such systems help give the students instant response and make the lessons adapt accordingly and provide effective learning. The IT companies' platforms such as Knewton and DreamBox Learning provide examples of how the dynamic and personalized educational experience can be built with the help of the AI. Knewton, for example, uses machine learning algorithms to pickup and analyze performance data from a given student on real-time basis and modifies the level of lesson delivery based on current proficiency levels of a student. This adaptive learning method guarantees the students are not overwhelmed due to difficult content, but also not bored due to repetitive content.

A case study by Chen et al. (2020) on Knewton's adaptive learning technology showed that students utilizing the platform performed better on their course work than students in traditional classrooms. Real-time adjustments offered by Knewton enable students to interact with content adjusted to their unique styles of learning and the needs. Additionally, Knewton's algorithm determines "pitfalls" where students struggle with, offering them more practice, and more targeted tools. Such personalization means that every learner would be able to get proper support and move at their own speed, confident they will learn everything in their own right.

In the same way, DreamBox Learning providing a K-8 personalized math learning experience based on AI. DreamBox monitors behavior of students using data analytics and caters to the individual progress of students by maintaining the difficulty of the lessons. For instance if a learner exhibits mastery of a topic then the platform responds by presenting higher order concepts while in other areas, the platform facilitates more practice and instructional assistance to help the student with these areas. In a case study conducted by O'Neill and Atwood (2021), the result is that students who use DreamBox attains significant improvement in math proficiency, particularly for students from disadvantaged groups. This success demonstrates the power of the platform to provide focused assistance and enhance learning productivity thus allowing for students to remain engaged and continue their work on their own schedules.

Asides from commenting on lessons, AI-driven platforms provide additional learning resources built on real time data which further enhances the customization of the learning experience. In that way platforms such as Knewton and DreamBox monitor students' learning patterns and suggest extra information such as videos, exercises and readings to fill in the gaps where they do not understand that they are experiencing. For instance, students who find a certain math concept difficult are given a tailored video tutorial or additional exercises to improve on that concept, by DreamBox. This support helps students get to have the right material at the right time which boosts their chances of mastering the material before proceeding.

In addition, AI-based programs are especially valuable for classrooms with all kinds of students where students can have different levels or understanding and learning styles. Old fashioned generic teaching practices fail to satisfy the needs of each students, and many become disinterested or confused. Yet, AI enables differentiated instruction in which every student receives an individual piece of content and support. Such an approach that addresses these students at an individual level, might help to boost the motivation of the learners and experience better sense of achievements as they go through the material at their own pace without feeling limited with uniform learning time table.

The transition to the AI-oriented, personalized learning worlds is not an easy ride. Privacy and security issues of data and problems of equitable access to technology continue to be one of the major barriers to the massive use of AI in education. Moreover teachers need tools and knowledge to incorporate AI into their practice of teaching. However, as AI technologies evolve, and improve, personalized, learner-centered education, can become more and more actionable.

So, personalising learning brought about as a result of AI capabilities is changing the face of education. Such platforms as Knewton and DreamBox Learning are proving that AI powered learning is effective: it aligns content to the needs of the student, creating a personalized ambience and offers direct contact to the resources as well as allows to have immediate feedback and improve learning outcomes. Using AI it is possible to create more inclusive, lively and interactive learning contexts in educational systems that will encourage individual learning journeys of a student.

EMPOWERING EDUCATORS THROUGH AUTOMATION

Artificial Intelligence (AI) has emerged to be an effective tool; for not only the improvement of student experiences but also teacher's empowerment as it automates time-consuming administrative chores. Formerly, educators have devoted much time to such administrative tasks as grading papers, planning lessons, and taking down the performance of students. These activities are certainly essential but reduce the amount of time teachers have for their interaction and instruction. However, with the application of AI in the system of education, such routine activities will be automated, thus helping educators to direct their attention to those things which are most important, namely interaction with students and comprehensive view of the material delivered.

Among AI benefits for teachers one of the most important advantages is the ability to automate grading. Through AI powered systems assignments and quizzes and exams can easily be graded rapidly and accurately which generates immediate feedback. Such rapid feedback is important for encouraging continuous learning – students can understand their mistakes immediately and can correct them immediately as well, before they add up. For instance, AI-invented assessment solutions include Gradescope, a platform for evaluation that is run by AI, that can grade different types of assessments, multiple choice, short answer, or even open ended. By making this tool not only less time consuming for teachers in terms of grading, but also provides consistent and objective assessment feedback, with which students get accurate evaluation of their work. Shute et al (2021) claim that the introduction of AI into the grading process is not without its advantages as it has reduced the number of times grades were issued as a result of human error; or time wastage, leaving more time available for teachers to work with learners to identify any learning issues that may arise (Shute, 2021).

In addition, AI tools enable teachers to monitor performance of students on the go. This ability is particularly useful since it allows teachers to catch struggling students before they become seriously far behind. Sites such as Squirrel AI and Knewton track students' actions in relation to the learning content and offer data based on what they are good and poor at. In the example of Squirrel AI, one of the most popular intelligent tutoring system in China, machine learning algorithms are used in tracking of student performance, hence regulating different learning paths. This enables teachers to step in at the beginning of the year to provide focused assistance to students who require that assistance the most. Xu et al (2020) says that Squirrel AI has improved significantly student results in categories such as mathematics and science through personalized feedback and intervention.

With access to real time performance data, teachers can have a more preventative approach towards teaching. Teachers do not need to wait for the formal assessments but can monitor student progress on a continuous basis, and aspire to adopt certain instructional strategies to be able to serve each learner. This data driven approach enables early interventions which can help to avoid the student from not keeping up with the flow and keep them on the right path to achieve academic goal. In addition, AI tools give teachers an opportunity to analyze learning trends and patterns and provide them with the basis to catch systemic problems related to teaching practice or classroom dynamics that call for changes.

The use of AI in the educational workflow encourages increased creativity as well. Teachers will now have the time to experiment with alternate forms of teaching and identify new ways of imparting the knowledge technology allows for. For example, AI offers the simplicity of incorporation of gamification and virtual world learning into the curriculum. Teachers are able to use AI powered platforms to build an interactive lesson that will keep the students interested and make learning live. Such flexibility of the teaching methods may result in more appealing and efficient forms of learning and one that is targeted at the needs of the students.

One case study by O'Neill & Atwood (2021) pointed out how such platforms as DreamBox Learning, an AI-based platform that offers personalized math lesson plan for K-8 students, mean that teachers do not need to spend much of their time in classroom working on traditional ways of teaching such as the overused drills or worksheets to supplement the students' learning experience. Teachers that deploy DreamBox can measure student progress and balance it on their lesson plans, delivering more targeted support where it's necessary, but also trying out new, novel ways to teach.

AI, therefore, is changing the face of how teachers relate to students and how they run their classes. By automating the process of administratively tedious activities, such as grading, planning lessons and monitoring student progress, AI gives teachers more time for what is important —personalizing instruction and building a stronger personal rapport with kids. The ability to collect real time data on student progress are also veritable to more proactive teaching where students receive support with an opportunity to catch up. As AI improves, only the adoption of AI in the classroom will lead teachers to be more capable of producing dynamic, effective and personalized learning environments.

PROMOTING STUDENT ENGAGEMENT THROUGH GAMIFICATION AND VIRTUAL ENVIRONMENTS

Perhaps one of the most interesting things about AI-integrated learning programs is the fact that with them, individuals can design interesting, interactive, and immersive learning environments that can encourage students, and make learning fun. And blending the uses of gamification, virtual learning environments and simulation-based learning tools, AI platforms are transforming the nature of learning. These features not only make learning more enjoyable but they also give opportunities that lead to deeper connection; active involvement; problem solving; all necessary for the development of one's critical thinking and other higher order cognitive skills.

Gamification is a major feature of AI-enabled educational platforms in which the core of the game-like aspects – the points, levels and awards – enables learning. This approach leverages students' natural bent for competition, achievement and recognition whilst severing fierce motivation and engagement amongst them. As students finish tasks or learn answers to the questions or master skills, they can earn points, progress into new levels, or receive online prizes thus making the process of learning more fun and interesting. Research by Deterding et al. (2011) has revealed that the implementation of gamification strategies in learning classes enhances its aspect such as students' participation, retention level and academic achievement. In real time, AI systems can adjust the measure of difficulty to suit the abilities of the students, so as to hold on to them but not to frustrate them. This adaptive difficulty will result in a permanent increase in difficulty for the student, continuing a drive to advance from the material.

One good example of gamification in education is the use of Kahoot!, a game-way learning platform that teachers use to create quizzes, surveys and discussions in an interactive and fun way. Kahoot! relies on the use of AI to make an evaluation of responses given by students and provides immediate feedback and tailors question according to the learning level of the students. Research has presented that tools that are of nature of Kahoot! remarkably enhance student engagement and participation, particularly in classrooms with multiplicity of learning needs. Gamification platforms made possible by AI have since been found to increase students' achievement and interest in learning endows them with real-time challenges, rewards, and progress monitoring (Bista& Foster 2020).

One other highly effective application of AI in education is virtual learning environment (VLE) where children can experiment immersive, active, and risk-free learning context. Virtual environments enable a simulation of real world events to which students would not otherwise be exposed in a more traditional classroom setting. Such environments will frequently be used together with AI to offer different learning experiences. For instance aerospace platforms such as AltspaceVR and ENGAGE provide virtual class rooms and interactive spaces in which students are able to participate in virtual field trips, collaborative projects and hands on experiments. These platforms establish an immersive environment in which students learn to interact with the content in ways that are not achievable through the use of old media.

From research by Bailenson (2020) the benefits of VLEs are shown; as it is possible to increase student engagement and retention through the use of interactive experiential learning in virtual environments. For instance, children studying at a historical class may join in virtual recreations of important events or children studying science may carry out virtual experiments which would be too expensive or risky to conduct in real life. Such immerge experience makes it possible for the student to memorize information better and to apply their learning, in real life scenarios.

Simulation based learning tools are another mind blowing feature that is based on AI system and further both teachers and students benefit from it. These tools simulate in-real-life situations of how students should apply acquired skills within a safe and controlled environment. For example, medical students make use of the simulated surgeries and diagnosis of the conditions through AI simulation without requiring real patients. Sullivan & Wang (2019) in their case studied on the subject, proved that AI powered simulation technologies in medical education enhanced significantly the competence, confidence and decision making skills of the students. Similarly, AI simulations in engineering & physics and permit students to play around complex concepts like mechanical system, fluid dynamics and thermodynamics in the virtual space.

Gamification, virtual environments and their learning tools can provide a very strong and effective method of educating students. These AI-innovations also bring more fun into learning, and also increase the critical thinking, creative and problem solving skills. As AI develops, the role of AI in building interactive and immersive learning environments will likely become larger, changing the manner of delivering and experiencing education by students around the planet.

CHALLENGES IN AI INTEGRATION: DATA PRIVACY, EQUITY, AND BIAS

Although the introduction of Artificial Intelligence (AI) in education takes the transformative benefits such as personalized learning and the increased level of interaction of students to another level, some issues need to be solved in order for those benefits to actually be achieved. From among the most important issues, these include data privacy, affordability, access to technology, and flair of bias in the AI algorithm. In order to use AI in a learners environment, it is relevant to overcome the challenges.

Data Privacy and Security

The most important challenge related to its usage in education is data privacy. AI platforms used in the education sphere gather a tremendous amount of information including: sensitive information about the student's academic performance, behavior during the learning period, personal predilections, even biometric data. Although, this information is important to deliver personalized learning, it poses significant security concerns. A leak of student data might be very serious both for students and for educational institutions. So, protecting the security of this data is critically important.

New studies have pointed at increasing concerns for data privacy in AI-based education systems. Zhou et al. (2021) note that even though AI has the possibility to enhance educational outcomes, an unintended consequence of using AI becomes the danger which the data that students have suffers such as unauthorized access or misappropriation. For example, AI tools viz: Google Classroom and Edmodo collect a lot of information regarding their students' learning habits and private details. If well protected, this data can neither access by malicious actors, this will result to breaches of privacy. In order to respond to these concerns, however, learning institutions must maintain open policies for use of data and have strong cybersecurity measures in place namely data encryption and multi- factor authentication. These steps will aide in ensuring sensitive information regarding students is kept safe from actual breaches and the students and parent be assured of using AI based educational tools.

Equity in Access to Technology

Digital divide is another hindrance to full potential of AI to deliver in the eductional capability. Access to high-quality educational technology, is limited, in many parts of the world especially low income areas. This difference in what students have access to becomes a difference in what they are able to learn, with students in wealthier regions or schools having access to the latest AI-based learning-platforms. Those with less access and poorer resources are left behind.

For example in rural sub-Saharan Africa, a dearth of predictable internet connectivity and technological infrastructure has made it challenging for students gaining from AI driven education products. According to Rana & Singh (2020), the digital divide furtherer worsens previous educational inequalities, and it is difficult for such students to have personalized learning experiences. Working hand-in-hand to make AI Driven platform accessible to all should help fill this gap. This could include the purchase of affordable technology, investigations into internet usage, and development of training for both students and teachers – as to how to use the AI tools. OLPC, for example, is a project to lift students in developing nations out of poverty with inexpensive laptops, is an illustration of attempts to democratising admissions into technology.

Bias in AI Algorithms

Otherwise, a third challenge is biased AI algorithm. AI systems are usually trained on historical data sets, if however, the historical data sets reflect existing biases into society, then the AI systems may by process of default reinforce biases. In an educational setting, this might affect AI systems (which unfairly discriminate, for example, between male and female students, or between or among different races or socio-economic groups). As a case in point, an AI would learn to have a bias on prior student performance data and thus inadvertently make biased recommendations or giving feedback, reinforcing current disparities.

Grading, admissions and tutoring systems are the AI systems that Holstein et al. (2019) write about where the risk of algorithmic bias in the AI systems is discussed. If not calibrated properly AI systems can do harm to marginalized groups as they further enrench offspring of disparities in education outcomes. AI systems need, therefore, to be inclusive and not biased. This can be sort of done by having different and representative datasets to train the AI models using and auditing the systems regularly for types of bias. Institutions can also involve varied collection of team members in designing and development of AI platforms in order for them to provide the opportunity for success for all students irrespective of their backgrounds.

Despite its promise, the introduction of AI to education is not free of major challenges whose solutions for them are necessary to achieve ethical and equitable results. Data privacy should be protected by high cybersecurity and transparent policy. Fair access to technology should be given priority in order to narrow the gap between the student and the digital and the other students can gain from AI based learning. Finally, initiative should be taken to prevent bias of the AI algorithms that should ensure that the these systems should offer fair and inclusive educational experiences. With such resolving the full potential of AI in education can be achieved and build more personalized, effective and equitable learning spaces to all students.

TEACHER TRAINING AND EFFECTIVE IMPLEMENTATION

In order to maximize the potential use of the field called Artificial Intelligence (AI) in the educational sphere, it is necessary that the educators themselves are trained to acquire some skills and knowledge needed to utilize the AI tools in their educational practice. AI may greatly improve the personalized learning aspects and streamline administrative work as well as allow for real-time student's performance data. Nevertheless, without proper training and support chances are that these benefits may not be manifested. These teacher professional development programs that are designed to reflect AI integration are essential in ensuring that teachers understand how they may use AI, how to interpret generated AI data, how to change their teaching strategies, as well as being in a position to use such tools in their every day reallity.

Training Educators on AI Tools

Educators need to be educated to decode the information that is produced by the AI system, such useful information can include information that will help measure the students' progress, engagement, and learning gaps. Knowledge of this data is important in making intelligent instructional choices. Professional development activities should include instructions on the analysis of student performance data, the study of patterns, and their application to the real packaging of teaching strategies. For example, platforms such as Knewton and DreamBox Learning produce data on student learning patterns and student progress. Teachers must be trained to be able to use this data; modify lessons to suit individual student needs. According to Baker & Siemens (2020), when teachers learn how to analyze and use data from AI-based tools, the students are provided with a more individualized learning experience because the reams adapt to the learner's needs.

According to LaForge et al. (2022), students of a study conducted on the application of AI in classrooms discovered that the professional development programs that were concentrated with the AI tools made the teachers more confident in using AI to enhance personalized learning. According to the teachers, after training, they reported they were more empowered to utilize AI to track student performance and modify instruction accordingly resulting in better learning.

AI as an Assisting Aid, not a Substitute<|response|>AI is an Assisting Agent, not a Replacer

Although while AI can be really helpful in the classroom, it must be known that AI should not replace the teacher but rather should be a complementary means which supports the quality of the overall study process. Teachers introduce important components into the education process which the AI cannot replace – emotional support, creativity and ability to create meaningful student-teacher relationships. On the other side, it is able to automate administrative chores, to offer personalized learning routes, and to provide real-time feedback; however, it is unable to replace the human contact, and, more importantly, the mentoring that teachers do.

AI tools ought to be looked at as a tool for increasing teachers' instructional goals; to make them concentrate more on high level teaching activities, while letting AI deal with more routine work. For instance, AI-based marking system can be used to level assignment and quiz automatically in a great saving of time on the teachers' part. This enables educators to interact with their students for longer with a view to giving them one on one support and creating vibrant learning surroundings. Cerrato et al. (2021) point out that the participation of A.I. in education should be to empower teachers, not to take possession, to support in such areas as content transmission, formative assessment, or personalized learning.

A real world example of this would be the use of AI powered learning management systems (LMS), like Moodle and Canvas, etc. Such platforms offer teachers data on students' progress that helps teachers identify places where students would benefit from extra tutorship. Teachers can then use this to modify their teaching strategies or provide like needs intervention. These platforms however are meant to supplement, not replace, the role of the teacher. Learning environment and the development of student are still largely guided by educators;

Ongoing Professional Development

Professional development needs to continue to ensure that teachers can be able to harness the AI application in their learnings based environment. Teachers can become better informed on what AI tools and approaches are being employed by joining AI experts and peer learning networks. Furthermore, development of professional practices should not be limited to teaching conceptual and technical issues related to the usage of AI but also efforts should be made to find a balance when human-centered teaching is concerned. With AI's ever-increasing capacity for capabilities, so too should the skill set of educators who should be ready for judging and embracing the emerging technologies accordingly.

Therefore, for AI to yield maximum benefits in his/her educational output, the need to train teachers on how to use – and appreciate – AI cannot be overemphasized. These programs should be concerned with interpreting data from AI, altering teaching strategies and using AI tools to advance the goals of instruction. AI should work as an enabler that complements what has to be learned, and where teachers should be free to operate on the human elements of education; those things that AI is not capable of replicating. The use of AI will be optimal for teachers who will pursue professional growth and thus be able to use the AI potential in its entirety while holding a central position in facilitating meaningful teacher-student interactions.

CONCLUSION

The presence of Artificial Intelligence (AI) in education looks set to entirely transform the landscape of how we teach and how we learn. As AI technologies improve, the potential to individualize learning experience, empower educators, facilitate development of the engaging, adaptive learning environment augurs well for the betterment of education. The advantages of AI in education extend far too many enabling a personalised way to teach the students, automating the work of the teachers, and great student engagement providing dynamic immediate feedback. However, to enable AI to leverage its maximum potential, there are issues as such data privacy, issues of access equity and issues of bias emanating from the use of algorithms which must be overcome. Solving these challenges will guarantee that AI advantages every student, personalizing, making education available, and impactful.

The most irresistible benefit of AI in education has to be personalization of learning. AI systems can review enormous quantities of data about individual student performance, ways of learning, and preferences, which creates opportunity to create customized learning experience. This personalization enables the student to move at his or her own pace and view content and challenge items that fit his or her current level of understanding. These sites (for example DreamBox Learning and Knewton) use AI in developing adaptive learning paths for students. For instance DreamBox modifies the level of difficulty on their math problems based in real time from the students responses, so every student is always being challenged appropriately, but never experiencing the sensation of overwhelming them with material. O'Neill and Atwood (2021) showed that DreamBox's adaptive learning model enhanced math student achievement especially for underrepresented groups by presenting targeted support and feedback. More so, AI-driven personalized learning creates more inclusive learning environment. examined students with various learning needs, including those whose learning did not thrive in traditional teaching methods, have benefited from the use of AI tools that give specific support. Squirrel AI which is an AI based tutoring system in China is an example of how personal learning can increase the outcome results. Real-time analysis is performed of the student's performance and the lesson content is modified on an individual basis. Squirrel AI has been credited according to Xu et al. (2020) with helping to increase levels of performance across subjects such as math and science to the tune of 40% through individual learning tracks and immediate feedback.

AI also gives power to educators by making automated routine administrative procedures such as grading/attendance/ tracking student's progress a reality. These may be important but they take up much time, making it difficult for them to play with their time in paying attention to the meaningful engagement of their students. With AI tools such as Gradescope, teachers can increase time that is spent working on challenging instructional activities such as one on one help and enabling the students to learn to think critically. According to Shute et al. (2021), the implementation of AI in automation of administrative tasks enables teachers to spend their time more productively supporting pedagogy and student engagement cannot be tracked. Also, AI tools give teachers a real time insight into student performance where proactive measures are taken. For example, AI based platforms such as Khan Academy and AltspaceVR give feedback in real time on the progress of students and thus teachers are in a position to make out those students who are in need of additional support and be able to make adjustments in terms of the teacher's strategies. According to Baker and Siemens (2020), it is important to note that AI tools are helpful in data-driven decision making thus more targeted and effective interventions which ensure no student lags behind are inevitable.

Unless used inappropriately, however, AI can help provide a dynamic, exciting learning context that enhances both the involvement and motivation on the part of students. Through the addition of things such as gamification, virtual learning environments (VLEs) and simulation-based learning, AI brings to students interactive and immersive experiences. Gamification, for instance, makes use of points, levels and, rewards within the learning process thus improving learning. Technologies, such as Kahoot! use AI in generating quizzes/games, which engage the students while providing feedback as to how they respond immediately to the questions. From studies from Deterding et al. (2011) and Bailenson (2020) it is possible to infer that the gamification of learning increases student motivation and retention by making it less abstruse and more experiential. Virtual learning environments such as AltspaceVR and ENGAGE build on top of what is possible with conferencing systems, as graduates get the opportunity to collaborate on projects, go on virtual field trips, and interact with peers and instructors in immersive, three dimensional spaces. Such environments provide experiential learning that cannot be approximated in conventional classroom settings making the learning experience more worthwhile. Bailenson (2020) showed that VLEs have a great potential to enhance student engagement and retention, particularly students' capacity to receive effective experiential learning opportunities rather than passive learning techniques.

Even though the use of AI has considerable advantages, the roll-out of AI in schooling cannot be free of challenges. Data privacy is one of the most urgent issues. AI platforms have all sorts of personal and academic information therefore the systems can easily be breached if measures put in place for security are not well secured. Zhou et al. (2021) explain why reliable data protection procedures and transparent data usage policies are required to protect privacy of students and to restore students trust in AI systems. Another problem is equity in access. The digital divide means that those from low-income territories or developing countries won't be able to have access to the AI supported learning tools that wealthy students have access to. Programs such as One Laptop per Child (OLPC) are trying to close that gap by offering inexpensive technology for students in underserved areas. Yet, we still need to do better – the reality is that all students, irrespective of their socio-economic background, need access to the tools they need to get ahead. The last one is algorithmic bias. AI system is as good as the data on which they are trained and if data has biases, then the system perpetuates those biases. Holstein et al. (2019) stress the importance of multiple and representative datasets based on the fact that no AI systems could prejudice existing education inequalities, based on race, gender or socio-economic status.

Application of AI in education promises a great deal to redesign the learning experience in informativity terms, becoming more personalized, convenient, and entertaining. Nonetheless, for AI to reach its full potential resources must be put towards issues like data privacy, equity of access and algorithmic bias. With the virtue that AI is applied both in a responsible and fair, manner, we stand to develop a more inclusive and effective education system. As AI evolves, more attention will be placed on it as a means of assisting with education providing students and teachers a tool to succeed. Ultimately the successful incorporation of AI into learning will improve learning experience, promote student successes and make learning more accessible and enjoyable for everyone.

REFERENCES

Bailenson, J. N. (2020). Virtual reality and education: The role of simulation in teaching and learning. *Educational Technology*, *45*(2), 120–135.

Baker, R. S. J. D., & Siemens, G. (2020). Educational data mining and learning analytics. In *Handbook of learning analytics* (pp. 1–15). Society for Learning Analytics Research.

Bista, K., & Foster, C. (2020). Gamification in higher education: Benefits, challenges, and future directions. *Journal of Educational Technology Systems*, *48*(1), 12–29.

Cerrato, P. A., Santoro, A., & Paciello, M. (2021). Artificial intelligence in education: Enhancing teacher-student interaction. *Journal of Educational Technology Systems*, *49*(3), 352–367.

Chen, X., Li, C., & Zhang, Q. (2020). The effectiveness of AI-driven personalized learning platforms in K-12 education: A review of recent developments. *Educational Technology Research and Development*, *68*(2), 633–651.

Deterding, S., Dixon, D., Khaled, R., & Nacke, L. (2011). From game design elements to gamefulness: defining" gamification". In *Proceedings of the 2011 annual conference on Human factors in computing systems* (pp. 2425-2428). ACM. DOI: 10.1145/2181037.2181040

Holstein, K., Wortman Vaughan, J., Wallach, H., Daumé, H.III, & Dudik, M. (2019). *Improving fairness in AI: Mitigating the impact of bias in education. AI in Education: Challenges and Opportunities*. Springer.

LaForge, A. R., McMahon, M. P., & Thompson, P. (2022). Teacher professional development for AI integration: A case study of an AI-powered classroom. *Journal of Educational Leadership*, *44*(1), 73–88.

O'Neill, M., & Atwood, C. (2021). The impact of adaptive learning platforms on student achievement: A case study of DreamBox Learning. *Journal of Educational Technology Systems*, *49*(4), 489–505.

Rana, S., & Singh, H. (2020). Bridging the digital divide in education: Challenges and solutions for AI implementation in low-income areas. *International Journal of Educational Development*, *45*(3), 215–230.

Shute, V. J., Kim, Y. J., & Wang, L. (2021). Using AI and real-time analytics to improve educational outcomes: A guide for educators. *Educational Psychology Review*, *33*(3), 553–570.

Sullivan, M., & Wang, M. (2019). The role of simulation in medical education: Enhancing skills and decision-making in healthcare. *Medical Education Review, 37*(4), 47–58.

Xu, Z., Li, L., & Zhou, F. (2020). AI-driven personalized learning in China: Case studies from Squirrel AI. *Journal of Educational Computing Research, 58*(6), 1120–1137.

Zhou, X., Li, Z., & Xie, Y. (2021). The ethical implications of AI in education: Addressing privacy and security issues. *Educational Technology Research and Development, 69*(4), 621–638.

Chapter 9
From Curriculum to Capability:
Integrating AI in Competency-Based Learning Models for Future-Ready Human Capital

Rismawati Rismawati
http://orcid.org/0000-0001-8046-6764
Universitas Muhammadiyah Palopo, Indonesia

Rusdiana Junaid
http://orcid.org/0000-0002-9653-1812
Universitas Cokroaminoto Palopo, Indonesia

Aanchal Sharma
http://orcid.org/0009-0001-6060-1743
Chandigarh Group of Colleges Jhanjeri, Mohali, India

I. Nyoman Darmayasa
http://orcid.org/0000-0001-6341-6909
Politeknik Negeri Bali, Indonesia

Javaid Ahmad Wagay
http://orcid.org/0000-0002-3525-4882
Kashmir University, India

Andi Subhan Amir
http://orcid.org/0000-0002-7680-5556
Hasanuddin University, Indonesia

EXECUTIVE SUMMARY

This chapter explores the integration of Artificial Intelligence (AI) into Competency-Based Learning (CBL) frameworks to develop future-ready human capital. It examines how AI enhances personalization, assessment, and capability tracking, enabling education systems to shift from static, content-driven models to adaptive, learner-centered environments. The discussion highlights the limitations of traditional curricula, the transformative role of AI technologies, and the importance of ethical governance, teacher readiness, and institutional capacity. Emphasizing

DOI: 10.4018/979-8-3373-3867-5.ch009

multi-stakeholder collaboration between government, industry, and academia, the chapter proposes a strategic roadmap and research agenda to align education with labor market demands. By reimagining curriculum as a dynamic pathway to capability, this work advocates for inclusive, data-informed, and ethically guided educational ecosystems that prepare learners for the complexities of the digital age.

RETHINKING CURRICULUM IN THE AGE OF ARTIFICIAL INTELLIGENCE

1.1 Limitations of Traditional Curricula in Talent Development

Conventional curricula, based on content-centric instruction and sequential progression models, have historically constituted the underlying structure for educational systems worldwide (VanTassel-Baska & Little, 2017; Padovano and Cardamone, 2024; Abbasi et al., 2025). In an age marked by swift technological advancement, particularly the incorporation of artificial intelligence (AI), the inflexible structure of traditional curricula poses considerable constraints in developing the skills necessary for fluid and unpredictable job markets. These traditional systems frequently prioritize rote memorization, standardized assessments, and compartmentalized knowledge, so neglecting to cultivate essential skills like as problem-solving, adaptability, cooperation, and digital literacy – all of which are crucial in the AI-driven talent market.

The inflexibility of conventional curricula hinders adaptability to industry changes and emerging skill requirements. Curricular revisions in the majority of formal education systems are characterized by bureaucracy and protracted timelines, leading to a continual disparity between educational provisions and market demands (Roy & Habib, 2024). As a result, graduates often enter the workforce inadequately equipped, lacking experience with real-world difficulties, multidisciplinary thinking, and technological proficiency (Maghiar & Brown, 2022). The standardized method of traditional training fails to consider the variability of learners in terms of pace, style, and context, so marginalizing those who may excel with more individualized or experiential approaches.

Moreover, the evaluative emphasis in conventional systems — based on summative, high-stakes examinations — frequently diminishes the importance of competences like emotional intelligence, creativity, and self-directed learning (Ghaleb2024). These essential soft and meta-skills are challenging to quantify via standardized assessments, yet they are crucial for sustainable talent development in an era of automation and augmented intelligence. With the rising demand for agile, cross-functional, and innovation-driven personnel, traditional education systems face growing criticism for yielding graduates who are "credentialed yet incompetent.

The discrepancy between educational input and economic output necessitates a fundamental transformation in curriculum design and implementation. Competency-Based Learning (CBL), integrated with AI technology, presents an alternative framework that emphasizes mastery, adaptability, and immediate applicability (Padovano and Cardamone 2024). Identifying the shortcomings of conventional curriculum is an essential prerequisite for restructuring educational institutions that can generate future-ready human capital. The transition from curriculum to capability necessitates a reevaluation of both the content and methodology of learning, which traditional frameworks are inadequately prepared to provide.

1.2 The Shift Toward Competency-Based Learning (CBL) Paradigms

In reaction to the increasing deficiencies of conventional educational models, Competency-Based Learning (CBL) has arisen as a revolutionary pedagogical method designed to connect education with employability (Peterson & Lundquist, 2021; Rhoney et al. 2024). Competency-Based Learning (CBL) redirects educational emphasis from time-centric teaching and content dissemination to the achievement of explicitly specified competencies, which include knowledge, skills, attitudes, and values vital for success in both professional and personal realms in the 21st century. This model prioritizes learner proficiency, adaptability, and contextual significance, rendering it particularly suitable for an AI-driven global economy that necessitates ongoing skill development and flexibility.

In contrast to conventional methods that prioritize seat time and rigid curricula, Competency-Based Learning (CBL) advocates for personalized learning pathways. Students advance at their own speed, progressing upon exhibiting mastery of particular competencies rather than by fulfilling predetermined teaching hours (Tarmo and Kimaro, 2021; Rhoney & Meyer, 2024; Gyll, 2021). This guarantees that graduates have verifiable skills that correspond with workforce requirements. Moreover, CBL integrates formative assessment as a fundamental component, facilitating continuous feedback, enhancement of performance, and self-regulation—elements that promote profound learning engagement and enduring retention.

CBL fosters a comprehensive understanding of learning (van et al. 2023; Sukackė et al. 2022). It amalgamates cognitive, behavioral, and affective domains, allowing institutions to develop curriculum that foster not only technical and academic expertise but also critical thinking, emotional intelligence, leadership, teamwork, and ethical reasoning. CBL equips learners to adeptly traverse intricate, unstable, and technology-driven contexts with assurance and flexibility.

The implementation of CBL is further enhanced by the integration of educational technology and data-informed decision-making (Okoye et al. 2024; Love et al. 2025). Learning analytics, AI-driven adaptive platforms, and digital credentialing systems enable institutions to implement competency-based learning at scale, monitor student progress in real time, and authenticate competencies in genuine contexts. These advancements improve transparency, customisation, and conformity with real-world expectations—critical attributes for cultivating future-ready human capital.

Notwithstanding its revolutionary potential, the implementation of CBL encounters hurdles such as faculty training, system restructuring, and policy integration. Nonetheless, the worldwide transition to this model is widely perceived as unavoidable, especially as countries endeavor to cultivate resilient, inventive, and competent workforces. The amalgamation of CBL with AI technology presents a viable avenue to realize the shift from curriculum to capacity, enabling learners to be not only educated but also prepared to excel in a fast evolving world.

1.3 The Role of AI in Shaping Adaptive and Dynamic Curriculum Structures

Artificial Intelligence (AI) is transforming curriculum development by providing unparalleled adaptability, reactivity, and personalization (Das et al. 2025; Yadav and Shrawankar 2025). Unlike conventional static curricula, AI-driven solutions facilitate the creation and execution of adaptive learning frameworks that progress in real-time, informed by learner performance, preferences, and evolving business demands. These intelligent solutions enable a transition from standardized education to adaptive learning environments that are consistently aligned with the competencies necessary for the future workforce.

Figure 1. AI-enabled curriculum transformation model

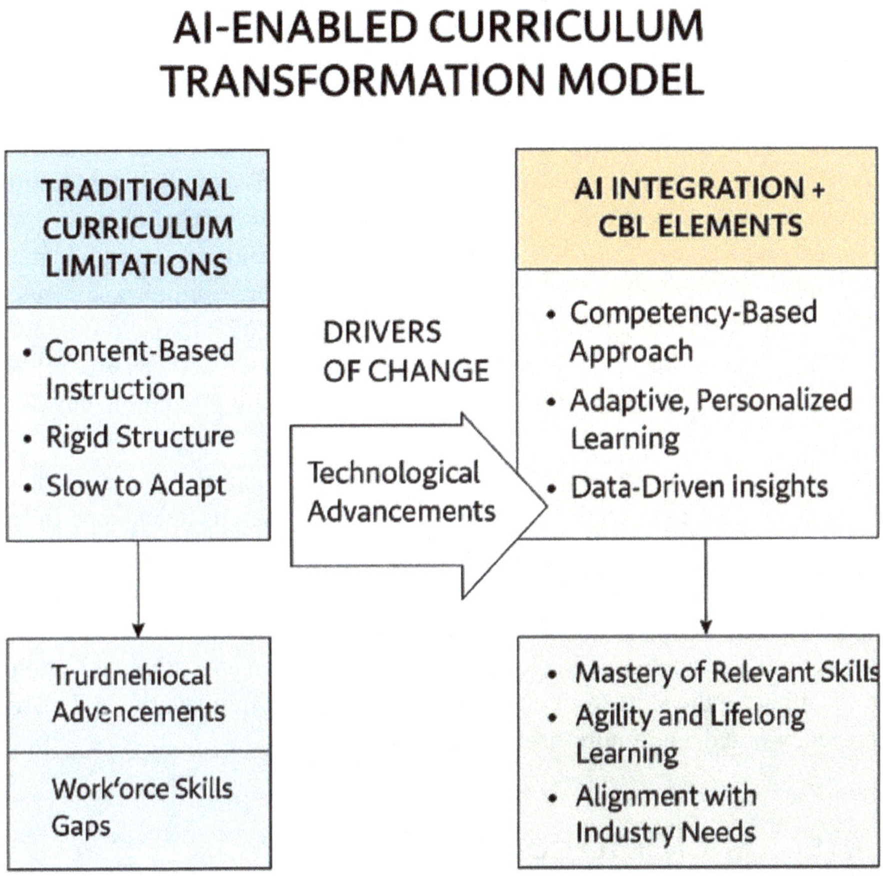

AI technologies enhance curriculum dynamism in multiple ways (Abbasi et al., 2025; Dimitriadou & Lanitis, 2023). Initially, machine learning algorithms may evaluate extensive datasets — including student behavior, assessment results, and labor market trends — to guide curriculum development and enhancement. This data-driven analysis enables educational institutions to discern in-demand skills, identify competences needing enhancement, and determine which pedagogical tactics maximize engagement and retention. Consequently, courses are not designed singularly but are continuously refined and adjusted based on real-world feedback mechanisms.

Secondly, AI facilitates the development of customized learning trajectories via adaptive learning platforms. These platforms customize content delivery according to individual learners' strengths, limitations, and development rates, guaranteeing that each learner receives focused training that facilitates mastery (Thai et al., 2022). These technologies facilitate self-directed learning, mitigate cognitive overload, and enable learners to assume responsibility for their growth. This customization is especially significant in competency-based learning frameworks, where advancement is dictated by exhibited proficiency rather than duration in the classroom.

Furthermore, Natural Language Processing (NLP) tools and intelligent tutoring systems can provide real-time feedback, automate the evaluation of open-ended responses, and enhance formative learning. AI-driven simulations, virtual laboratories, and gamified modules augment experiential learning, equipping students for intricate, real-world problem-solving (Rana and Chicone 2025; Renacido and Biray 2025). These tools collectively convert the curriculum from a static framework into a dynamic system that adjusts to the learner and the changing requirements of the labor market.

Notwithstanding these breakthroughs, the incorporation of AI into curricular frameworks necessitates meticulous deliberation of ethical, technical, and institutional elements. Concerns include data privacy, algorithmic bias, and the preparedness of digital infrastructure must be resolved to guarantee equal and responsible execution. Nevertheless, the deliberate implementation of AI in curriculum design presents significant potential in closing the divide between education and employment, facilitating the shift from conventional curriculum frameworks to dynamic, competency-based, and future-oriented learning systems.

AI INTEGRATION INTO COMPETENCY-BASED LEARNING MODELS

2.1 Defining AI-Enhanced Competencies for 21st Century Skills

The changing requirements of the 21st-century workforce, influenced by automation, digitization, and artificial intelligence (AI), require a redefining of essential competencies beyond conventional academic success (Marlapudi & Lenka, 2024; Li, 2024). AI-enhanced competencies denote a combination of cognitive, technical, interpersonal, and ethical skills that are augmented, facilitated, or necessitated by AI systems. These competencies empower learners to operate efficiently in digitally-mediated contexts and equip them to utilize AI as a resource for problem-solving, innovation, and ongoing education.

Central to AI-enhanced competencies is data literacy, encompassing the capacity to comprehend, interpret, and critically assess data. In AI-driven environments, individuals must excel in pattern recognition, algorithm comprehension, and data-informed decision-making. This encompasses computational thinking and fundamental programming logic, which facilitate not only technical activities but also issue deconstruction and abstraction—skills vital for engaging with intelligent systems (Benvenuti et al. 2023).

Higher-order cognitive skills, including critical thinking, adaptability, systems thinking, and creative problem-solving, are as significant (Li et al., 2023; Liu et al., 2024). These are essential for positions where people interact with AI, as computers often handle monotonous or analytical work, while humans provide strategic oversight and ethical judgment. Competency-based models, when combined with AI, can facilitate the monitoring and personalization of skill development via adaptive learning environments and immediate performance feedback.

Emotional intelligence and collaborative communication are essential in a future augmented by AI. As automation proliferates, distinctly human attributes — including empathy, intercultural collaboration, and ethical leadership — become increasingly significant (Makhachashvili and Semenist2024; Shaikh, 2025). AI integration can enhance the cultivation of these competencies via immersive simulations, feedback-rich educational settings, and tailored emotional learning instruments.

Moreover, ethical and digital responsibility is fundamental to AI-augmented proficiency (Mohamed, 2024). Students must be prepared to comprehend the ethical ramifications of AI implementation, encompassing privacy, surveillance, prejudice, and accountability in decision-making. These constitute a component of a wider competency domain sometimes termed "AI literacy," which should be included into educational institutions and competency frameworks.

By integrating AI-enhanced competences into Competency-Based Learning (CBL) frameworks, educational institutions may cultivate a generation of learners that are digitally proficient, socially aware, ethically principled, and prepared for innovation. The synchronization of AI capabilities with human capacities is essential for developing sustainable, inclusive, and future-ready human capital.

2.2 Technologies Enabling AI-Based Learning Personalization

The customization of educational experiences signifies one of the most potential advancements of artificial intelligence (AI) in the field of education. In Competency-Based Learning (CBL) models, where advancement is based on mastery instead of time spent, AI technologies significantly customize education to meet the unique needs, preferences, and situations of individual learners (Khatoon, 2025; Chang & Lin, 2024). This section examines the ecosystem of AI-driven technologies that facilitate personalization, transforming standardized training into dynamic, learner-focused experiences.

Adaptive learning platforms are important to AI-driven personalization. These systems employ machine learning algorithms to continually evaluate a learner's performance and dynamically modify the complexity, tempo, and sequencing of content in real time (Gligorea et al., 2023; Ezzaim et al., 2023; Essa et al., 2023). Utilizing detailed data analytics, adaptive systems identify knowledge gaps, suggest specific resources, and adjust learning routes to enhance skill acquisition. Platforms like DreamBox, Knewton, and Smart Sparrow illustrate this capabilities, facilitating differentiated training on a large scale.

Intelligent tutoring systems (ITS) emulate individualized training by delivering prompt, tailored feedback and support. These systems emulate the function of a human tutor by observing student inputs, identifying misconceptions, and providing customized prompts or explanations (Lin et al., 2023; Dever et al., 2023). It not only enhances interest and memory but also cultivates metacognitive skills by directing learners through intricate problem-solving procedures. The incorporation of natural language processing (NLP) in intelligent tutoring systems (ITS) facilitates conversational engagement, hence enhancing the learner experience.

Learning analytics dashboards provide an additional layer of customisation by displaying learner progress and mastery of competencies in real time. These dashboards enable both learners and instructors to make data-driven decisions (Valle et al. 2021; Susnjak et al. 2022). For learners, they elucidate strengths and deficiencies; for educators, they furnish practical intelligence for modifying education or intervention. When combined with predictive analytics, these techniques can identify at-risk learners and provide proactive assistance solutions.

Moreover, AI-driven content generating technologies customize the development of educational resources. Systems such as ScribeSense and Content Technologies Inc. employ natural language processing and deep learning to produce quizzes, reading passages, or review materials tailored to specific learner requirements or curriculum standards (Almuhanna, 2024). This enables instantaneous modification and diminishes the duration educators allocate to manual material creation.

Collectively, these technologies establish a resilient framework that facilitates personalized, scalable, and competency-based learning. When integrated into CBL frameworks, AI personalization technologies promote student autonomy and engagement while ensuring that educational outcomes are equitable, responsive, and pertinent to the workforce. This technology integration is crucial for equipping learners to be adaptable, proficient, and prepared for the future in a swiftly changing digital economy.

2.3 Case Examples: Adaptive Learning Engines and Competency Tracking

The pragmatic utilization of AI in Competency-Based Learning (CBL) frameworks is most effectively illustrated through actual implementations that showcase how adaptive technologies and competency tracking systems improve tailored education and skill acquisition (Padovano and Cardamone 2024). This section showcases pivotal case studies from international education and training systems that demonstrate the transformative impact of AI on pedagogical delivery and learner evaluation.

A notable example is Carnegie Learning's MATHia platform, an AI-driven adaptive learning engine extensively utilized in secondary school. MATHia persistently evaluates student input and learning behaviors to provide customized problem sets tailored to particular mathematical competencies (Ahmad et al. 2025). The platform's intelligent tutor feature replicates human input by providing immediate, context-aware explanations and suggestions. Numerous studies have demonstrated that MATHia enhances learner engagement and facilitates comprehension of abstract mathematical topics, particularly among children in under-resourced school systems.

ALEKS (Assessment and Learning in Knowledge Spaces), created by McGraw-Hill, offers a comprehensive paradigm of adaptive competency monitoring within the realm of higher education (Harati et al., 2021). ALEKS employs an advanced AI engine grounded in knowledge space theory to assess a student's existing knowledge, gaps, and readiness for further learning. The system changes in real time as students engage with learning modules, ensuring that education consistently corresponds with the individual's current competency level. ALEKS has been implemented across multiple fields — including chemistry and accounting — resulting in quantifiable improvements in retention, student happiness, and academic achievement.

Western Governors University (WGU) in the United States serves as a paradigm of systemic integration of AI-driven competency-based learning (CBL) at the institutional level. WGU utilizes a digital learning ecosystem featuring individualized dashboards, predictive analytics, and AI-driven tutoring tools (Niemi, 2024; Pathak and Jain, 2025). The progress of each student is monitored by the demonstrated mastery of competencies aligned with workforce expectations. Faculty mentors utilize AI-generated insights to deliver focused coaching and prompt interventions, guaranteeing that learners go through their programs efficiently and successfully.

In the vocational and corporate training sector, Coursera and edX have implemented AI algorithms to suggest courses and modules tailored to individual learners' career objectives and skill deficiencies (Saqr et al., 2024; Rizvi et al., 2025). These platforms also provide digital badges and microcredentials upon the fulfillment of competencies, thereby improving learners' employability and conformity with industry norms.

These case cases collectively highlight the effectiveness of AI-driven adaptive engines and competency tracking in providing personalized, scalable, and workforce-aligned education. They provide reproducible frameworks for schools seeking to modernize curricula and cultivate future-ready human capital.

BRIDGING CURRICULUM AND CAPABILITY THROUGH AI

3.1 From Learning Outcomes to Real-World Competency Indicators

The transition from conventional curriculum frameworks to a competency-based educational system necessitates a pivotal redefinition of learning outcomes into quantifiable, real-world competency indicators (Anapey, 2024; Varma and Malik, 2023; Kayyali, 2025). Conventional curricula often prioritize information learning and cognitive memory, whereas modern education—particularly when enhanced by Artificial Intelligence (AI)—necessitates a more profound alignment between instructional content and the competencies essential for success in intricate, technology-driven environments.

Learning outcomes, as conventionally articulated, delineate the knowledge and comprehension that learners are anticipated to possess at the end of an instructional period. Nonetheless, they often stay abstract, generic, and detached from practical application (Agustian et al., 2022; Kaimara et al., 2022). Outcomes like "understands economic theory" or "demonstrates teamwork" are inadequately operationalized, complicating the meaningful assessment of their achievement. This disconnection is especially troublesome in workforce development, where employers demand concrete evidence of skills, behaviors, and job preparation.

Conversely, competency indicators denote tangible, quantifiable behaviors that signify the mastery of intricate skills in genuine contexts (Basileo et al., 2024). This encompasses cognitive competencies—such as problem-solving and analytical reasoning—as well as behavioral (e.g., teamwork, flexibility) and technological (e.g., digital literacy, data analysis) competencies. When integrated into educational systems, AI technologies provide the detailed monitoring and verification of key variables via real-time evaluations, simulations, and performance analytics.

An AI-integrated learning system may evaluate a student's decision-making process in a virtual business simulation to test competencies such as strategic thinking, ethical reasoning, and leadership under pressure. These experiences generate data points that can be consolidated into digital competence profiles or "capability maps," providing a more comprehensive and actionable representation of learner improvement than conventional grades or degrees.

Moreover, real-world competency indicators enhance interoperability across the education and employment sectors (Bates et al. 2022; Padovano and Cardamone 2024).

By synchronizing educational assessment with industry terminology and expectations, institutions may guarantee that learning directly correlates with employability and career progression. Employers can utilize competency data to make educated hiring and promotion decisions, fostering a more agile and meritocratic workforce environment. The function of AI in this paradigm is crucial. AI utilizes data-driven insights, adaptive assessments, and performance analytics to close the enduring divide between theoretical learning outcomes and practical competence. This transition is crucial for fulfilling the potential of Competency-Based Learning in the era of digital transformation.

3.2 AI-Driven Assessment and Feedback Systems

Assessment is crucial in connecting learning and proficiency, particularly in Competency-Based Learning (CBL) settings where advancement is based on mastery rather than duration. Conventional assessment models, mostly summative and standardized, frequently fail to encapsulate the intricacies of 21st-century competencies, like critical thinking, creativity, and cooperation (Li & Rohayati, 2024; Sukackė et al. 2022; Galdames-Calderón et al. 2024). The advent of Artificial Intelligence (AI) has revolutionized assessment methodologies, transitioning from static testing to dynamic, real-time evaluations enhanced by intelligent feedback systems.

AI-driven assessment systems utilize data analytics, machine learning, and natural language processing to assess student performance with efficiency, accuracy, and customization (Vetrivel et al. 2025; Vashishth et al. 2024). These systems evaluate a diverse range of learner interactions — including problem-solving behaviors in digital contexts, written responses, and simulation results — to deduce levels of comprehension and proficiency. This facilitates ongoing, formative evaluation that offers both instructors and students meaningful insights during the educational process.

A fundamental contribution of AI in evaluation is its capacity to facilitate real-time feedback. Conventional feedback is frequently tardy, nonspecific, and constrained by the instructor's capacity. Conversely, AI-driven solutions like Gradescope, Quillionz, and Cognii provide instantaneous, context-aware feedback customized to the learner's particular mistakes, learning speed, and cognitive habits. This feedback mechanism promotes self-regulated learning, cultivates a growth attitude, and expedites the acquisition of competencies.

Furthermore, AI-driven automated evaluations extend beyond multiple-choice examinations. They may assess open-ended responses, model-based reasoning, and spoken language through NLP. These technologies improve the reliability and objectivity of assessments, allowing educators to allocate more time to advanced educational activities. In performance-oriented educational settings, AI technologies can evaluate learners' abilities through simulations and games, thus obtaining more genuine displays of proficiency.

Significantly, AI facilitates the longitudinal monitoring of learner progression (Poquet and De Laat, 2021). Educators can utilize learning analytics dashboards to observe trends in student development, pinpoint at-risk individuals, and modify training as needed. Institutions may utilize aggregated data to assess the efficacy of curriculum design and instructional methodologies.

The incorporation of AI in assessment is essential for matching education with real-world competency requirements, while ethical issues like data protection and algorithmic bias must be meticulously addressed. AI-driven feedback solutions enhance assessment by making it more personalized, timely, and authentic, thereby enabling learners to assume responsibility for their development and better prepare for intricate, dynamic professional landscapes.

3.3 Building Capability Maps: Aligning Education with Workforce Demand

The global workforce is evolving due to digital transformation, artificial intelligence (AI) (Aly, 2022; Ayoko, 2021), and economic unpredictability, rendering the conventional misalignment between education and employment increasingly unworkable. A viable option to overcome this difference is the creation of capacity maps—dynamic frameworks that link academic learning with labor market demands. AI is crucial in the creation, revision, and implementation of these maps to guarantee that education is adaptive, pertinent, and centered on competencies (Schmid et al. 2021; Cao et al. 2024; Sharma et al. 2022).

Capability mapping is a process that delineates and illustrates the essential competences, skills, and behaviors required for certain positions, sectors, or prospective career trajectories (Marlapudi & Lenka, 2024; Kipper et al. 2021; Cordeiro et al. 2023). In contrast to static qualification frameworks, competence maps are dynamic and informed by data. They delineate not only technical proficiencies but also transversal competences including communication, creativity, digital fluency, and emotional intelligence – all vital for talent prepared for the future. These maps connect the knowledge gained by learners in educational environments with the skills sought by employers in practical situations.

AI improves the efficacy of capability mapping across multiple dimensions. Utilizing labor market analytics, AI can analyze vast quantities of job advertisements, occupational databases, and employer surveys to identify in-demand competencies across many sectors (Bukartaite and Hooper 2023; George et al. 2024). These insights can be aligned with instructional content, therefore assisting curriculum designers in incorporating pertinent and timely learning outcomes. AI-generated skills taxonomies, exemplified by frameworks established by entities such as the OECD or the World Economic Forum, offer organized classification systems to facilitate this process (Shi, 2025).

In competency-based learning models, capability maps are utilized to monitor learner growth and identify gaps (Guo et al. 2023; Chen et al. 2024). AI-enabled dashboards allow learners to visualize their mastered competencies and identify areas needing further development. These customized maps are both inspirational and pragmatic, facilitating focused interventions and enduring educational trajectories.

Moreover, competence maps facilitate credential transparency and enhance workforce mobility. Micro-credentials, digital badges, and skill passports, all facilitated by AI, provide employers with a detailed perspective of an individual's true competencies beyond mere degree titles (Asrifan et al. 2025). This facilitates meritocratic recruitment, skill enhancement, and talent mobility, especially within nascent and informal labor markets.

By integrating capability mapping into AI-enhanced education systems, institutions can move beyond fragmented curriculum models toward holistic, outcome-based learning ecosystems. This alignment is critical for cultivating a labor force that is adaptable, resilient, and equipped for the uncertainties of tomorrow.

CHALLENGES AND ETHICAL CONSIDERATIONS IN AI-DRIVEN LEARNING SYSTEMS

4.1 Data Privacy and Algorithmic Bias in Educational AI

As artificial intelligence (AI) becomes more integrated into educational systems, especially in Competency-Based Learning (CBL) frameworks, pressing issues regarding data privacy and algorithmic bias require immediate consideration (Kordzadeh and Ghasemaghaei 2022; Akter et al. 2022). Although AI presents significant opportunities for personalized learning and improved outcomes, the ethical ramifications of gathering, keeping, analyzing, and utilizing learner data necessitate meticulous management to safeguard human rights and maintain institutional integrity.

Data privacy in educational AI pertains to the acquisition and utilization of extensive amounts of student information, encompassing behavioral data, performance measures, emotional indicators, and physiological responses. Data are frequently handled in cloud-based systems and third-party platforms, resulting in vulnerabilities associated with unauthorized access, misuse, and prolonged storage. Insufficient data protection frameworks may result in confidentiality breaches, alteration of student profiles, and the commercialization of personal information. Educational institutions must have rigorous data governance policies, encompassing informed permission, data minimization, anonymization processes, and adherence to national and international privacy regulations, such as the General Data Protection Regulation (GDPR) (Schiff, 2022; Aldoseri et al., 2023).

The issue of algorithmic bias is equally urgent; it occurs when AI systems replicate or exacerbate societal disparities due to biased training data, defective model design, or unclear decision-making processes (Bircan & Özbilgin, 2025; Rejmaniak, 2021). In the educational sphere, biased algorithms might unjustly harm minority students by inaccurately assessing ability, excessively monitoring behavior, or suggesting inequitable learning trajectories. An AI tutor developed using data mostly from high-income pupils may exhibit suboptimal performance when applied to learners from other socioeconomic or cultural backgrounds.

To alleviate these dangers, it is imperative to guarantee algorithmic openness, equity, and accountability. Educational institutions and EdTech developers should conduct bias audits, utilize inclusive data sampling, and, when feasible, uphold open-source algorithmic frameworks (Simbeck, 2023; Macgilchrist et al., 2024). Furthermore, instructors and students must be equipped with AI literacy to comprehend decision-making processes and contest conclusions when warranted.

Although AI has the potential to democratize access and enhance educational attainment, its unregulated implementation may exacerbate systemic imbalances. Confronting data privacy and algorithmic bias is not only a technological requirement but also a moral obligation in the development of appropriate AI frameworks in education. As we go towards capability-based, AI-enhanced learning environments, the protection of ethical principles is paramount to maintaining justice, equity, and human dignity in digital education systems.

4.2 Teacher Readiness and Institutional Capacity for AI Integration

The successful integration of Artificial Intelligence (AI) into Competency-Based Learning (CBL) systems is fundamentally dependent on teacher preparedness and institutional capability (Karan, 2024; Ballatore, 2025). Technology alone cannot effectuate significant change without empowered educators and resilient institutions capable of adapting, innovating, and spearheading the transition to AI-enhanced education.

Teacher preparedness includes both digital literacy and pedagogical proficiency in utilizing AI for individualized learning, formative assessment, and real-time feedback (Bachtiar2025; Zhang & Zhang, 2024). Numerous educators, however, continue to be inadequately prepared or lacking support during this shift. A considerable number express concern regarding the intricacy of AI systems, data analysis, and the possibility of automation undermining their professional positions. Addressing these concerns necessitates a reconfiguration of teacher training frameworks, prioritizing continuous professional development (CPD), collaborative learning communities, and practical engagement with AI tools in genuine classroom environments.

Effective professional development must extend beyond technical skills to encompass AI pedagogical approaches, including co-designing AI-driven learning experiences, utilizing algorithmic insights to enhance education, and promoting digital ethics among students (Padovano and Cardamone 2024). Educators must possess essential AI literacy to critically assess, analyze, and regulate algorithmic suggestions to prevent over dependence on machine-generated results.

At the institutional level, capacity-building entails the enhancement of digital infrastructure, the establishment of policy frameworks, the articulation of leadership vision, and the cultivation of an organizational culture conducive to AI adoption (Jha and Singh, 2025; Kawure et al. 2025). Numerous educational institutions, particularly in low-resource contexts, lack reliable internet connection, cloud computing infrastructure, or platform interoperability, hindering the implementation of intelligent learning environments. Furthermore, colleges must tackle data security, procurement procedures, and equality concerns when deploying AI among varied student demographics.

Leadership is essential in cultivating preparedness. Institutional leaders must advocate for a collective vision for AI-enhanced education, synchronize AI activities with strategic objectives, and devote resources for testing and assessment. Collaborations with EdTech providers, research institutions, and policy organizations can augment institutional capacity via knowledge transfer and the expansion of innovation.

Ultimately, in the absence of proficient instructors and effective institutions, the advantages of AI in CBL are likely to remain unfulfilled or inequitably allocated. Enhancing preparation and capacity is not a secondary issue but a fundamental element in the transition from conventional education systems to AI-driven, competency-based learning environments that are inclusive, sustainable, and resilient for the future.

4.3 Governance, Equity, and Access in AI-Based Learning Environments

As artificial intelligence (AI) becomes more embedded in educational institutions, it is imperative to provide fair access, inclusive governance, and ethical monitoring to maintain the core ideals of justice and opportunity in education (Nguyen et al. 2023; Berson et al., 2025). Within the framework of Competency-Based Learning (CBL), wherein AI possesses the capacity to customize instruction, track advancement, and synchronize education with employment, these three components constitute the ethical foundation for sustainable and socially responsible implementation.

Figure 2. AI governance in education

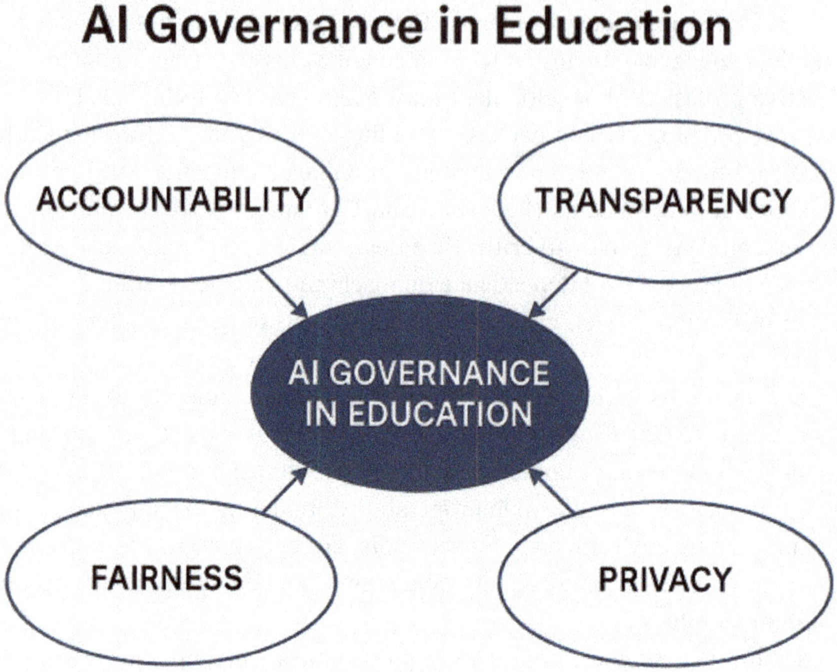

Governance in AI-driven educational environments pertains to the legislative, ethical, and organizational frameworks that supervise the design, implementation, and utilization of AI technology in education (Nguyen et al. 2023; Kaddouri et al. 2025). Strong governance frameworks are essential for tackling concerns such as data ownership, permission, accountability, and adherence to international standards like the General Data Protection Regulation (GDPR) and UNESCO's AI ethics guidelines. Effective governance necessitates transparency in algorithmic design and decision-making procedures. Educational institutions must guarantee that students, instructors, and other stakeholders comprehend the functioning of AI systems, the data acquired, and the methodology of conclusion derivation.

Nevertheless, governance must be accompanied by a robust dedication to equity. The implementation of AI in education may exacerbate existing disparities if access is inconsistent or if the systems are developed on biased datasets. Students from remote regions, economically disadvantaged communities, or marginalized populations may encounter disparities in digital access regarding connectivity, hardware availability, and AI-compatible infrastructure. Furthermore, when AI tools are created without contributions from a varied user base, the resulting systems may inadequately address the demands and learning preferences of all learners.

To resolve this issue, inclusive design principles should be implemented, guaranteeing that AI tools are culturally attuned, linguistically accessible, and adaptable to local contexts (Salas-Pilco et al., 2022). Governments and educational institutions must invest in digital inclusion plans, encompassing cheap access, infrastructure development, and capacity building for both learners and educators (Jamil, 2021; Chohan & Hu, 2022).

Finally, accessibility should encompass not just physical connectivity but also adaptive technologies for learners with disabilities and alternate modalities for those with diverse learning requirements (Dudley et al., 2023). Artificial intelligence, when effectively regulated and fairly implemented, can serve as a significant equalizer, provided that structural obstacles are proactively eliminated.

In summary, governance, equity, and access are fundamental components that facilitate ethical and inclusive AI in education. They ascertain if AI serves as an instrument for democratizing education or exacerbating disparities. The future trajectory must be grounded on collective accountability, strategic foresight, and a human-centric approach to technology that serves educational purposes.

POLICY RECOMMENDATIONS AND STRATEGIC ROADMAP FOR FUTURE-READY HUMAN CAPITAL

5.1 Designing National Talent Frameworks with AI and CBL Synergy

To prepare nations with resilient, adaptable, and future-oriented human capital, it is essential to transcend fragmented educational reforms and develop cohesive national talent frameworks that correspond with the changing dynamics of artificial intelligence (AI) and Competency-Based Learning (CBL) (Padovano and Cardamone, 2024; Gudonienė et al., 2021). These frameworks must not only transform curriculum content but also reconfigure the identification, cultivation, evaluation, and deployment of talent in a knowledge-based economy.

A national talent framework functions as a strategic blueprint that connects educational institutions, workforce development, and economic planning. When anchored in CBL principles and enhanced by AI technologies, such frameworks facilitate a transition from credential-centric to capability-centric development (Li, 2024; Huang et al., 2023; Jain et al., 2023). This shift prioritizes verifiable competencies, continuous education, and alignment with the labor market rather than conventional academic credentials. The framework must be competency-mapped, influenced by industry standards, and adaptable to technology.

Figure 3. Diagram AI-CBL integration

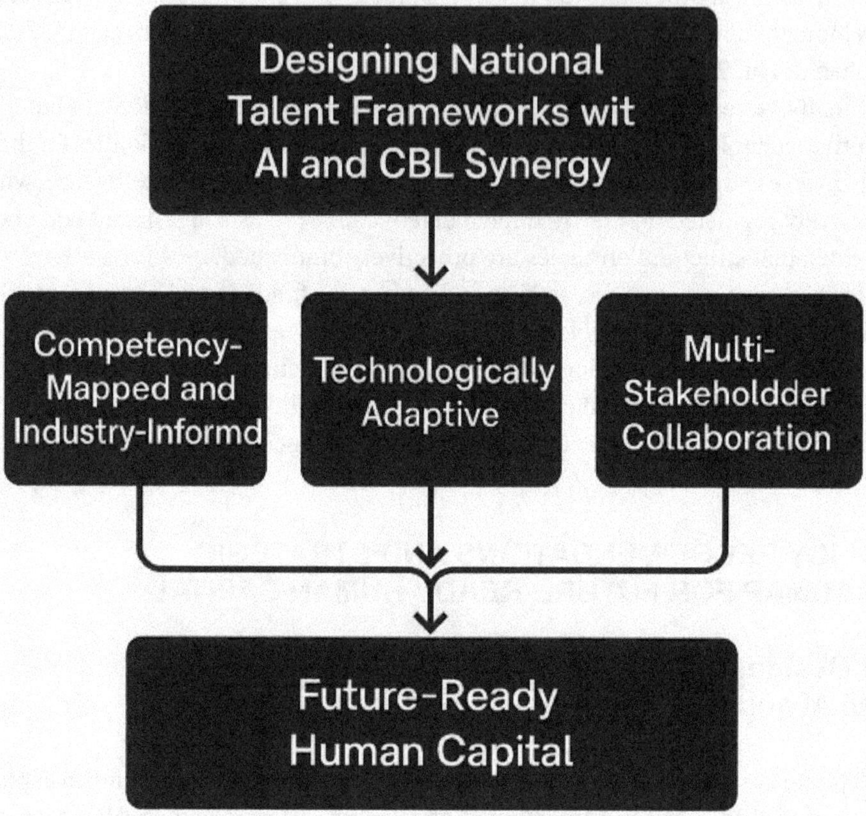

Artificial intelligence improves the effectiveness of talent frameworks in multiple ways. Labor market analytics and real-time data streams may guide curriculum design and workforce projections, ensuring that training programs adapt to changing industry demands. Secondly, AI-driven skills intelligence platforms can discern developing talent clusters and align them with regional or national economic objectives (Verma et al. 2022). Singapore's SkillsFuture and the UAE's AI Talent Strategy serve as exemplary policy models that employ predictive analytics and AI technology to inform educational initiatives.

CBL guarantees the application of this intelligence via learner-centered, mastery-oriented training (Wen et al., 2023; Li et al., 2022). When integrated at the policy level, Competency-Based Learning (CBL) facilitates modular education, micro-credentials, stacking certifications, and adaptable educational trajectories.

These innovations foster inclusivity, particularly for non-traditional learners, and guarantee that learning is acknowledged across many industries and life stages. Creating such a framework necessitates coordination among multiple stakeholders, including ministries of education, labor, and technology, as well as employers, universities, civic society, and EdTech providers (Siarova & van der Graaf, 2022). National digital infrastructure, data interoperability standards, and ethical AI norms must be incorporated to guarantee equity and scalability.

A national talent framework that integrates AI and CBL is not only a policy novelty; it is a strategic necessity. It establishes a fundamental framework for countries to safeguard their workforce, mitigate skills discrepancies, and develop inclusive human capital systems that can prosper in the Fourth Industrial Revolution.

5.2 Stakeholder Collaboration: Government, Industry, and Academia

The development of future-ready human capital via Artificial Intelligence (AI) and Competency-Based Learning (CBL) necessitates essential multi-stakeholder collaboration (Padovano and Cardamone, 2024). No solitary institution can autonomously tackle the intricacies of harmonizing education with labor market demands amidst the era of digital revolution. A collaborative strategy among government, industry, and academia is necessary to create dynamic, pertinent, and inclusive educational environments.

Figure 4. Synergy the three sectors

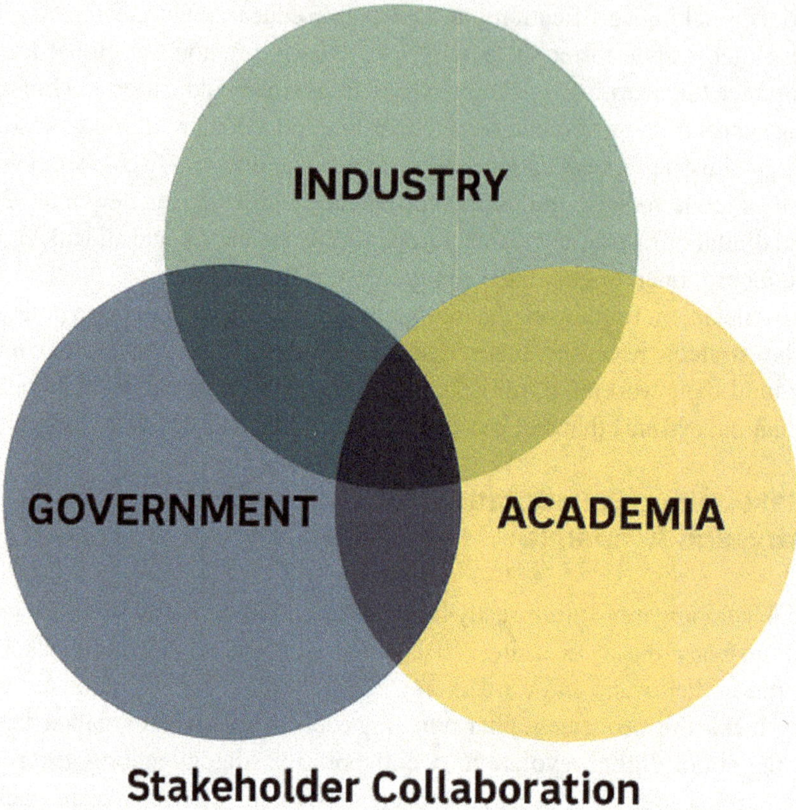

Governments serve a fundamental function by establishing the strategic framework for national talent development via policy formulation, financial strategies, and regulatory supervision (Shan & Wang, 2024; Semete-Makokotlela et al., 2022; Wang et al., 2024). The ministries of education, labor, and technology must collaborate to guarantee alignment among curricular standards, workforce planning, and digital innovation goals. Governments may promote comprehensive ecosystem transformation by promoting AI adoption, facilitating research and development, and guaranteeing equal access to digital infrastructure and educational tools.

Industry stakeholders, comprising employers, industry associations, and technology firms, offer essential contributions to the formulation and verification of competency frameworks (Jackson et al. 2023). Their participation guarantees that educational programs align with current job market requirements and developing skill sets. Industry stakeholders may engage in curriculum co-development, mentorship initiatives, internship possibilities, and platforms for digital micro-credentials. Furthermore, EdTech companies are crucial in creating AI-driven solutions that facilitate tailored and scalable education.

Academic institutions, as the principal architects of human capital, must transform into innovation centers where theory intersects with practice (Mwantimwa et al., 2021; Serrano-Ruiz et al., 2025). Higher education institutions and vocational colleges must adopt adaptable, modular learning frameworks facilitated by AI-based solutions. Faculty must participate in continuous professional development in AI pedagogy and data-driven instruction. Institutional research units may partner with business and government to implement models, assess results, and expand successful inventions.

To implement this partnership, tripartite platforms must be established at both national and regional levels (Lâm et al. 2025). These platforms may manifest as skills councils, public-private task groups, or strategic foresight committees. Digital instruments like skills dashboards, open data portals, and AI learning laboratories can enhance transparency and collective ownership among collaborators.

The collaboration among government, industry, and academia fosters a beneficial cycle where skills are perpetually refined, education is tailored and ongoing, and human capital evolves to be flexible and resilient. Stakeholder cooperation is not simply a supportive component; it is the driving force that propels the transition from static curricular models to dynamic capability systems in the era of artificial intelligence.

5.3 Concluding Insights and Research Agenda

The integration of Artificial Intelligence (AI) with Competency-Based Learning (CBL) indicates a significant transformation in educational institutions' preparation of learners for the complexities of the 21st-century workforce (Adel, 2024; Strielkowski et al., 2024; de Souza & Debs, 2024). This chapter has illustrated that the shift from static, credential-based frameworks to dynamic, capability-driven ecosystems is essential for national resilience, equity, and global competitiveness.

Upon reflection on the findings, numerous significant insights arise. Traditional curricula, however foundational, are inadequate in meeting the rapid changes and characteristics of labor market evolution (Enstroem & Schmaltz, 2024; Li, 2024). CBL provides a flexible, learner-centered alternative, although its efficacy is significantly enhanced when augmented by AI technologies that customize learning, facilitate real-time assessment, and link training with practical demands. Secondly, effective implementation relies on institutional preparedness, governance frameworks, ethical protections, and collaborative stakeholder engagement—factors that must be collectively fostered.

AI in education should be regarded not as a disruptive element, but as a strategic facilitator. When strategically utilized, AI can equalize access to information, close skill disparities, and promote continuous education. Nevertheless, unregulated implementation may exacerbate existing inequities or undermine trust in educational systems. Consequently, forthcoming frameworks must prioritize human-centricity, cultural responsiveness, and ethical governance.

This chapter presents a research plan focused on six essential areas to inform future innovation and policy development.

1. Impact Assessment: Empirical research on the enduring educational outcomes, employability, and well-being of students within AI-augmented CBL systems.
2. Equity and Inclusion: Investigation into the obstacles and facilitators of equitable AI accessibility across socioeconomic, gender, rural-urban, and ability disparities.
3. Teacher and Institutional Transformation: Research investigating changes in professional identity, capacity-building methodologies, and institutional leadership for AI-enhanced education.
4. Ethics and Algorithmic Accountability: An examination of bias reduction, explainability, and data governance in educational AI systems.
5. Micro-Credentialing and Skills Portability: Assessment of digital badges, stackable credentials, and the interchange of competency frameworks internationally.
6. Global South Adaptations: Case studies and innovations from resource-limited contexts, ensuring that AI-CBL models are scalable, inclusive, and contextually pertinent.

In conclusion, the transition from curriculum to capability represents a dynamic aspect of educational change. Integrating AI into competency-based frameworks, grounded in ethical and evidence-based methodologies, enables education institutions to effectively cultivate future-ready human capital.

CONCLUSION

The shift from conventional curriculum models to AI-enhanced competency-based learning frameworks signifies a purposeful adaptation to the changing requirements of the global workforce and the rapid advancement of technology innovation. This chapter has highlighted the imperative for education institutions to transcend mere information delivery and focus on cultivating dynamic talents that are attuned to the realities of an AI-driven world.

Integrating artificial intelligence into competency-based learning ecosystems can enhance personalization, equity, and alignment with labor market demands in education.

Artificial intelligence facilitates instantaneous feedback, personalized learning trajectories, and proficiency assessment, revolutionizing learner interaction with material and evidence of expertise. Realizing this potential demands more than technological acceptance; it requires institutional preparedness, strong governance frameworks, ethical protections, and coordinated stakeholder involvement. The core of this change is the principle that AI should function as a tool to augment—rather than supplant—human-centered learning. Consequently, educational policies and institutional practices must emphasize openness, accountability, equity, and data privacy. Moreover, educator empowerment, comprehensive digital infrastructure, and participatory governance frameworks are essential for achieving sustainable and equitable integration.

This chapter asserts that the transition from curriculum to capacity is not linear nor solely technological; rather, it represents a comprehensive reimagining of future learning. It necessitates a long-term perspective wherein educational institutions foster learners who are adaptive, ethically principled, digitally proficient, and resilient amidst uncertainty.

Consequently, cultivating future-ready human capital through AI and CBL transcends educational reform; it is a national development necessity. Countries can fully leverage AI to empower learners and alter education for the problems and opportunities of the 21st century only via deliberate design, evidence-based practices, and cross-sector collaboration.

REFERENCES

Abbasi, B. N., Wu, Y., & Luo, Z. (2025). Exploring the impact of artificial intelligence on curriculum development in global higher education institutions. *Education and Information Technologies*, *30*(1), 547–581. Advance online publication. DOI: 10.1007/s10639-024-13113-z

Adel, A. (2024). The convergence of intelligent tutoring, robotics, and IoT in smart education for the transition from Industry 4.0 to 5.0. *Smart Cities*, *7*(1), 325–369. DOI: 10.3390/smartcities7010014

Agustian, H. Y., Finne, L. T., Jørgensen, J. T., Pedersen, M. I., Christiansen, F. V., Gammelgaard, B., & Nielsen, J. A. (2022). Learning outcomes of university chemistry teaching in laboratories: A systematic review of empirical literature. *Review of Education*, *10*(2), e3360. DOI: 10.1002/rev3.3360

Ahmad, W., Shokeen, R., & Raj, R. (2025). Artificial intelligence: Solutions in special education. In *Transforming Special Education Through Artificial Intelligence* (pp. 459–520). IGI Global., DOI: 10.4018/979-8-3693-5538-1.ch017

Akter, S., Dwivedi, Y. K., Sajib, S., Biswas, K., Bandara, R. J., & Michael, K. (2022). Algorithmic bias in machine learning-based marketing models. *Journal of Business Research*, *144*, 201–216. DOI: 10.1016/j.jbusres.2022.01.083

Aldoseri, A., Al-Khalifa, K. N., & Hamouda, A. M. (2023). Re-thinking data strategy and integration for artificial intelligence: Concepts, opportunities, and challenges. *Applied Sciences (Basel, Switzerland)*, *13*(12), 7082. DOI: 10.3390/app13127082

Almuhanna, M. A. (2024). Teachers' perspectives of integrating AI-powered technologies in K-12 education for creating customized learning materials and resources. *Education and Information Technologies*. Advance online publication. DOI: 10.1007/s10639-024-13257-y

Aly, H. (2022). Digital transformation, development and productivity in developing countries: Is artificial intelligence a curse or a blessing? *Review of Economics and Political Science*, *7*(4), 238–256. DOI: 10.1108/REPS-11-2019-0145

Anapey, G. M. (2024). Achieving education for sustainable education learning outcomes: An integrated model for higher education in the Global South. *International Journal of Educational Reform*, 10567879241270503. Advance online publication. DOI: 10.1177/10567879241270503

Asrifan, A., Sadaruddin, S., Ashar, A., Nonci, J., Setiawan, T., & Erniati, E. (2025). Redefining learning pathways: The impact of AI-enhanced micro-credentials on education efficiency. In *Integrating Micro-Credentials With AI in Open Education* (pp. 281–312). IGI Global., DOI: 10.4018/979-8-3693-5538-1.ch012

Ayoko, O. B. (2021). Digital transformation, robotics, artificial intelligence, and innovation. *Journal of Management & Organization*, *27*(5), 831–835. DOI: 10.1017/jmo.2021.64

Bachtiar, B. (2025). Preparing citizens for the future of digital literacy and AI: With a focus on Indonesian EFL teachers. In *Digital Citizenship and the Future of AI Engagement, Ethics, and Privacy* (pp. 405–440). IGI Global. https://doi.org/DOI: 10.4018/979-8-3693-9015-3.ch015

Ballatore, M. G. (2025). Enhancing engineering education from the lecturer's perspective. In *Empower Education to Foster Engineering* (pp. 73–109). Springer., DOI: 10.1007/978-3-031-75895-9_3

Basileo, L. D., Lyons, M. E., & Toth, M. D. (2024). Leading indicators of academic achievement: Investigating the predictive validity of an observation instrument in a large district. *SAGE Open*, *14*(2), 21582440241261119. Advance online publication. DOI: 10.1177/21582440241261119

Bates, R., Brenner, B., Schmid, E., Steiner, G., & Vogel, S. (2022). Towards meta–competences in higher education for tackling complex real–world problems: A cross disciplinary review. *International Journal of Sustainability in Higher Education*, *23*(8), 290–308. DOI: 10.1108/IJSHE-06-2021-0243

Benvenuti, M., Cangelosi, A., Weinberger, A., Mazzoni, E., Benassi, M., Barbaresi, M., & Orsoni, M. (2023). Artificial intelligence and human behavioral development: A perspective on new skills and competences acquisition for the educational context. *Computers in Human Behavior*, *148*, 107903. DOI: 10.1016/j.chb.2023.107903

Berson, I. R., Berson, M. J., & Luo, W. (2025). Innovating responsibly: Ethical considerations for AI in early childhood education. *AI Brain Child*, *1*(2), 2. Advance online publication. DOI: 10.1007/s44436-025-00003-5

Bukartaite, R., & Hooper, D. (2023). Automation, artificial intelligence and future skills needs: An Irish perspective. *European Journal of Training and Development*, *47*(10), 163–185. DOI: 10.1108/EJTD-03-2023-0045

Cao, Y., Yang, A., Li, H., Zeng, Q., & Gao, J. (2024). A comprehensive knowledge map for AI improving security management of cyber-physical system enabled smart manufacturing. *Computers & Security*, *137*, 103650. DOI: 10.1016/j.cose.2023.103650

Chang, H. T., & Lin, C. Y. (2024). Applying competition-based learning to stimulate students' practical and competitive AI ability in a machine learning curriculum. *IEEE Transactions on Education*, *67*(2), 256–265. DOI: 10.1109/TE.2024.3350535

Chen, A. M., Kleppinger, E. L., Churchwell, M. D., & Rhoney, D. H. (2024). Examining competency-based education through the lens of implementation science: A scoping review. *American Journal of Pharmaceutical Education*, *88*(2), 100633. DOI: 10.1016/j.ajpe.2023.100633

Chohan, S. R., & Hu, G. (2022). Strengthening digital inclusion through e-government: Cohesive ICT training programs to intensify digital competency. *Information Technology for Development*, *28*(1), 16–38. DOI: 10.1080/02681102.2020.1841713

Cordeiro, M., Puig, F., & Ruiz-Fernández, L. (2023). Realizing dynamic capabilities and organizational knowledge in effective innovations: The capabilities typological map. *Journal of Knowledge Management*, *27*(10), 2581–2603. DOI: 10.1108/JKM-02-2022-0080

Das, S., Mutsuddi, I., & Ray, N. (2025). Artificial intelligence in adaptive education: A transformative approach. In *Advancing Adaptive Education: Technological Innovations for Disability Support* (pp. 21–50). IGI Global. https://doi.org/DOI: 10.4018/979-8-3693-8227-1.ch002

de Souza, A. S. C., & Debs, L. (2024). Concepts, innovative technologies, learning approaches and trend topics in education 4.0: A scoping literature review. *Social Sciences & Humanities Open*, *9*, 100902. DOI: 10.1016/j.ssaho.2024.100902

Dever, D. A., Sonnenfeld, N. A., Wiedbusch, M. D., Schmorrow, S. G., Amon, M. J., & Azevedo, R. (2023). A complex systems approach to analyzing pedagogical agents' scaffolding of self-regulated learning within an intelligent tutoring system. *Metacognition and Learning*, *18*(3), 659–691. DOI: 10.1007/s11409-023-09346-x

Dimitriadou, E., & Lanitis, A. (2023). A critical evaluation, challenges, and future perspectives of using artificial intelligence and emerging technologies in smart classrooms. *Smart Learning Environments*, *10*(1), 1–19. DOI: 10.1186/s40561-023-00231-3

Dudley, J., Yin, L., Garaj, V., & Kristensson, P. O. (2023). Inclusive immersion: A review of efforts to improve accessibility in virtual reality, augmented reality and the metaverse. *Virtual Reality (Waltham Cross)*, *27*(4), 647–673. DOI: 10.1007/s10055-023-00850-8

Enstroem, R., & Schmaltz, R. (2024). Striking gold: Navigating the education massification maze for work readiness. *Journal of Work-Applied Management*, *16*(1), 1–17. DOI: 10.1108/JWAM-10-2023-0100

Essa, S. G., Celik, T., & Human-Hendricks, N. E. (2023). Personalized adaptive learning technologies based on machine learning techniques to identify learning styles: A systematic literature review. *IEEE Access : Practical Innovations, Open Solutions*, *11*, 48392–48410. DOI: 10.1109/ACCESS.2023.3276439

Ezzaim, A., Dahbi, A., Haidine, A., & Aqqal, A. (2023). Enhancing academic outcomes through an adaptive learning framework utilizing a novel machine learning-based performance prediction method. *Data and Metadata*, *2*, 164. DOI: 10.56294/dm2023164

Galdames-Calderón, M., Stavnskær Pedersen, A., & Rodriguez-Gomez, D. (2024). Systematic review: Revisiting challenge-based learning teaching practices in higher education. *Education Sciences*, *14*(9), 1008. DOI: 10.3390/educsci14091008

George, A. S., George, A. H., & Baskar, T. (2024). Artificial intelligence and the future of healthcare: Emerging jobs and skills in 2035. *Partners Universal Multidisciplinary Research Journal*, *1*(1), 1–21. DOI: 10.5281/zenodo.11176554

Gligorea, I., Cioca, M., Oancea, R., Gorski, A. T., Gorski, H., & Tudorache, P. (2023). Adaptive learning using artificial intelligence in e-learning: A literature review. *Education Sciences*, *13*(12), 1216. DOI: 10.3390/educsci13121216

Gudonienė, D., Paulauskaitė-Tarasevičienė, A., Daunorienė, A., & Sukackė, V. (2021). A case study on emerging learning pathways in SDG-focused engineering studies through applying CBL. *Sustainability (Basel)*, *13*(15), 8495. DOI: 10.3390/su13158495

Guo, B. H., Gonzalez, V. A., Puolitaival, T., Enegbuma, W., & Zou, Y. (2023). Bridging the gap between building information modelling education and practice: A competency-based education perspective. *International Journal of Construction Management*, *23*(15), 2558–2569. DOI: 10.1080/15623599.2022.2077546

Gyll, S. P. (2021). Career development by design, not default: Creating a more efficient and data-driven process by connecting aptitude-based learner guidance to post-secondary pathways, competency-based credentials, and high-demand jobs. *The Journal of Competency-Based Education*, *6*(1), e1236. DOI: 10.1002/cbe2.1236

Harati, H., Sujo-Montes, L., Tu, C.-H., Armfield, S. J. W., & Yen, C.-J. (2021). Assessment and learning in knowledge spaces (ALEKS) adaptive system impact on students' perception and self-regulated learning skills. *Education Sciences, 11*(10), 603. DOI: 10.3390/educsci11100603

Huang, Y., Li, K., & Li, P. (2023). Innovation ecosystems and national talent competitiveness: A country-based comparison using fsQCA. *Technological Forecasting and Social Change, 194*, 122733. DOI: 10.1016/j.techfore.2023.122733

Jackson, D., Riebe, L., Meek, S., Ogilvie, M., Kuilboer, A., Murphy, L., Collins, N., Lynch, K., & Brock, M. (2023). Using an industry-aligned capabilities framework to effectively assess student performance in non-accredited work-integrated learning contexts. *Teaching in Higher Education, 28*(4), 802–821. DOI: 10.1080/13562517.2020.1863348

Jain, P., Tripathi, V., Malladi, R., & Khang, A. (2023). Data-driven artificial intelligence (AI) models in the workforce development planning. In Khang, A., Rani, S., Gujrati, R., Uygun, H., & Gupta, S. (Eds.), *Designing Workforce Management Systems for Industry 4.0: Data-Centric and AI-Enabled Approaches* (pp. 159–176). CRC Press., DOI: 10.1201/9781003357070-10

Jamil, S. (2021). From digital divide to digital inclusion: Challenges for wide-ranging digitalization in Pakistan. *Telecommunications Policy, 45*(8), 102206. DOI: 10.1016/j.telpol.2021.102206

Jha, A., & Singh, S. R. (2025). Bridging the divide: Capacity building for AI adoption in developing countries. In Khang, A., Rani, S., Gujrati, R., Uygun, H., & Gupta, S. (Eds.), *AI Strategies for Social Entrepreneurship and Sustainable Economic Development* (pp. 133–150). IGI Global., DOI: 10.4018/979-8-3693-6392-8.ch007

Kaddouri, M., Mhamdi, K., Chniete, I., Marhraoui, M., Khaldi, M., & Jmad, S. (2025). Adopting AI in education: Technical challenges and ethical constraints. In Khang, A., Rani, S., Gujrati, R., Uygun, H., & Gupta, S. (Eds.), *Fostering Inclusive Education With AI and Emerging Technologies* (pp. 25–72). IGI Global., DOI: 10.4018/979-8-3693-7255-5.ch002

Kaimara, P., Oikonomou, A., & Deliyannis, I. (2022). Could virtual reality applications pose real risks to children and adolescents? A systematic review of ethical issues and concerns. *Virtual Reality (Waltham Cross), 26*(2), 469–484. DOI: 10.1007/s10055-021-00563-w

Karan, B. (2024). Integration of artificial intelligence by the Central Board of Secondary Education in India: Towards innovative teaching and learning practices. *Technology, Pedagogy and Education, 33*(5), 1–15. DOI: 10.1080/1475939X.2024.2337924

Kawure, J. H., Umar, N. Y., & Ahmed, A. A. (2025). Building information technological capacity and strategic management in academia. In *Building Organizational Capacity and Strategic Management in Academia* (pp. 67–102). IGI Global., DOI: 10.4018/979-8-3693-9466-3.ch004

Kayyali, M. (2025). Transforming education: The future of mastery-based learning and its impact. In *Cultivating Flourishing Practices and Environments by Embracing Positive Education* (pp. 119–148). IGI Global., DOI: 10.4018/979-8-3693-9466-3.ch004

Khatoon, R. (2025). AI-powered task-based learning for cross-border higher education. In *Bridging Global Divides for Transnational Higher Education in the AI Era* (pp. 141–164). IGI Global., DOI: 10.4018/979-8-3693-9466-3.ch006

Kipper, L. M., Iepsen, S., Dal Forno, A. J., Frozza, R., Furstenau, L., Agnes, J., & Cossul, D. (2021). Scientific mapping to identify competencies required by industry 4.0. *Technology in Society*, *64*, 101454. DOI: 10.1016/j.techsoc.2020.101454

Kordzadeh, N., & Ghasemaghaei, M. (2022). Algorithmic bias: Review, synthesis, and future research directions. *European Journal of Information Systems*, *31*(3), 388–409. DOI: 10.1080/0960085X.2021.1927212

Lâm, S., Dang-Xuan, S., Unger, F., Meeyam, T., Pham-Duc, P., Wacharapluesadee, S., & Nguyen-Viet, H. (2025). Operationalizing regional one health initiatives in Southeast Asia: Ways forward. *One Health*, *20*, 101034. DOI: 10.1016/j.onehlt.2025.101034

Li, L. (2024). Reskilling and upskilling the future-ready workforce for industry 4.0 and beyond. *Information Systems Frontiers*, *26*(5), 1–15. DOI: 10.1007/s10796-022-10308-y

Li, M. (2024). Adapting legal education for the changing landscape of regional emerging economies: A dynamic framework for law majors. *Journal of the Knowledge Economy*, *15*(3), 10227–10256. DOI: 10.1007/s13132-023-01507-2

Li, M., & Rohayati, M. I. (2024). The relationship between learning outcomes and graduate competences: The chain-mediating roles of project-based learning and assessment strategies. *Sustainability (Basel)*, *16*(14), 6080. DOI: 10.3390/su16146080

Li, W., Huang, J. Y., Liu, C. Y., Tseng, J. C., & Wang, S. P. (2023). A study on the relationship between student learning engagements and higher-order thinking skills in programming learning. *Thinking Skills and Creativity*, *49*, 101369. DOI: 10.1016/j.tsc.2023.101369

Li, X., Li, Y., Li, X., Chen, X., Yang, G., & Yang, L. (2022). Comparison of case-based learning combined with Rain Classroom teaching and traditional method in complete denture course for undergraduate interns. *BMC Medical Education*, *22*(1), 610. DOI: 10.1186/s12909-022-03678-z

Lin, C. C., Huang, A. Y. Q., & Lu, O. H. T. (2023). Artificial intelligence in intelligent tutoring systems toward sustainable education: A systematic review. *Smart Learning Environments*, *10*(1), 41. DOI: 10.1186/s40561-023-00260-y

Liu, J., Liu, Z., Wang, C., Xu, Y., Chen, J., & Cheng, Y. (2024). K-12 students' higher-order thinking skills: Conceptualization, components, and evaluation indicators. *Thinking Skills and Creativity*, *52*, 101551. DOI: 10.1016/j.tsc.2024.101551

Love, A. S., Love, R. J., & Valadez, R. (2025). Integrating digital health technologies into health professions curricula: Telehealth, AI, and post-pandemic innovations. In *Technological Approaches to Medical and Pharmaceutical Education* (pp. 1–32). IGI Global., DOI: 10.4018/979-8-3373-1127-2.ch001

Macgilchrist, F., Potter, J., & Williamson, B. (2024). Challenging the inequitable impacts of edtech. *Learning, Media and Technology*, *49*(2), 147–150. DOI: 10.1080/17439884.2024.2350117

Maghiar, M., & Brown, C. (2022). A qualitative multi-disciplinary analysis of employers' technology competency perceptions for graduates' readiness to the workforce. *Cogent Education*, *9*(1), 2147777. DOI: 10.1080/2331186X.2022.2147777

Marlapudi, K., & Lenka, U. (2024). Unlocking the potential: Redefining talent and competency mapping for Industry 4.0. *Management Research Review*, *47*(11), 1805–1832. DOI: 10.1108/MRR-07-2023-0496

Mohamed, M. S. P. (2024). Exploring ethical dimensions of AI-enhanced language education: A literature perspective. *Technology in Language Teaching & Learning*, *6*(3), 1813. DOI: 10.29140/tltl.v6n3.1813

Mwantimwa, K., Ndege, N., Atela, J., & Hall, A. (2021). Scaling innovation hubs: Impact on knowledge, innovation and entrepreneurial ecosystems in Tanzania. *Journal of Innovation Management*, *9*(2), 39–63. DOI: 10.24840/2183-0606_009.002_0005

Nguyen, A., Ngo, H. N., Hong, Y., Dang, B., & Nguyen, B. P. T. (2023). Ethical principles for artificial intelligence in education. *Education and Information Technologies*, *28*(4), 4221–4241. DOI: 10.1007/s10639-022-11316-w

Niemi, H. (2024). AI in education and learning: Perspectives on the education ecosystem. In Streit-Bianchi, M., & Gorini, V. (Eds.), *New frontiers in science in the era of AI* (pp. 169–194). Springer International Publishing., DOI: 10.1007/978-3-031-61187-2_11

Okoye, K., Daruich, S. D. N., Castaño, R., Escamilla, J., & Hosseini, S. (2024). Analyzing the impact of digitized-education toward the future of education: A comparative study based on students' evaluation of teaching data. *Studies in Educational Evaluation, 82*, 101359. DOI: 10.1016/j.stueduc.2024.101359

Padovano, A., & Cardamone, M. (2024). Towards human-AI collaboration in the competency-based curriculum development process: The case of industrial engineering and management education. *Computers and Education: Artificial Intelligence, 7*, 100256. DOI: 10.1016/j.caeai.2024.100256

Pathak, S., & Jain, V. (2025). Transformation of quality education through e-learning for sustainable development. In *Transforming vocational education and training using AI* (pp. 211–248). IGI Global Scientific Publishing., DOI: 10.4018/979-8-3693-9466-3.ch009

Peterson, L. T., & Lundquist, M. (2021). Competency as outcome and process through transformative learning experiences. *Journal of Teaching in Social Work, 41*(4), 373–388. DOI: 10.1080/08841233.2021.1946234

Poquet, O., & de Laat, M. (2021). Developing capabilities: Lifelong learning in the age of AI. *British Journal of Educational Technology, 52*(4), 1695–1708. DOI: 10.1111/bjet.13123

Rana, S., & Chicone, R. (2025). Gamification and immersive learning with AI. In *Fortifying the future: Harnessing AI for transformative cybersecurity training* (pp. 51–75). Springer Nature Switzerland., DOI: 10.1007/978-3-031-81780-9_3

Rejmaniak, R. (2021). Bias in artificial intelligence systems. *Białostockie Studia Prawnicze, 26*(3), 25–42. DOI: 10.15290/bsp.2021.26.03.02

Renacido, J. M. D., & Biray, E. T. (2025). Enhancing peer engagement and student motivation through AI-gamified interactive learning tools. In *Advancing sustainable development goals with educational technology* (pp. 277–342). IGI Global Scientific Publishing.

Rhoney, D. H., Chen, A. M., Churchwell, M. D., Daugherty, K. K., Jarrett, J. B., Kleppinger, E. L., Nawarskas, J. J., Sibicky, S. L., Stowe, C. D., & Meyer, S. M. (2024). The need for competency-based education. *American Journal of Pharmaceutical Education, 88*(5), 100706. DOI: 10.1016/j.ajpe.2024.100706

Rhoney, D. H., & Meyer, S. M. (2024). Competency-based education: The need to debunk misconceptions and develop a common language. *American Journal of Pharmaceutical Education, 88*(2), 100637. DOI: 10.1016/j.ajpe.2023.100637

Rizvi, I., Bose, C., & Tripathi, N. (2025). Transforming education: Adaptive learning, AI, and online platforms for personalization. In *Technology for societal transformation: Exploring the intersection of information technology and societal development* (pp. 45–62). Springer Nature Singapore., DOI: 10.1007/978-981-96-1721-0_4

Roy, P., & Habib, M. A. (2024). Fostering effective collaboration between library and information science academics and practitioners in Bangladesh: Insights, challenges and recommendations. *IFLA Journal, 50*(3), 574–590. DOI: 10.1177/03400352241236737

Salas-Pilco, S. Z., Xiao, K., & Oshima, J. (2022). Artificial intelligence and new technologies in inclusive education for minority students: A systematic review. *Sustainability (Basel), 14*(20), 13572. DOI: 10.3390/su142013572

Saqr, R. R., Al-Somali, S. A., & Sarhan, M. Y. (2024). Exploring the acceptance and user satisfaction of AI-driven e-learning platforms (Blackboard, Moodle, Edmodo, Coursera and edX): An integrated technology model. *Sustainability (Basel), 16*(1), 204. DOI: 10.3390/su16010204

Schiff, D. (2022). Education for AI, not AI for education: The role of education and ethics in national AI policy strategies. *International Journal of Artificial Intelligence in Education, 32*(3), 527–563. DOI: 10.1007/s40593-021-00270-2

Schmid, T., Hildesheim, W., Holoyad, T., & Schumacher, K. (2021). The AI methods, capabilities and criticality grid: A three-dimensional classification scheme for artificial intelligence applications. *KI - Künstliche Intelligenz, 35*(3), 425–440. https://doi.org/DOI: 10.1007/s13218-021-00736-4

Semete-Makokotlela, B., Mahlangu, G. N., Mukanga, D., Darko, D. M., Stonier, P., Gwaza, L., Nkambule, P., Matsoso, P., Lehnert, R., Rosenkranz, B., & Pillai, G. (2022). Needs-driven talent and competency development for the next generation of regulatory scientists in Africa. *British Journal of Clinical Pharmacology, 88*(2), 579–586. DOI: 10.1111/bcp.15020

Serrano-Ruiz, J. C., Ferreira, J., Jardim-Goncalves, R., & Ortiz, Á. (2025). Relational network of innovation ecosystems generated by digital innovation hubs: A conceptual framework for the interaction processes of DIHs from the perspective of collaboration within and between their relationship levels. *Journal of Intelligent Manufacturing, 36*(3), 1505–1545. DOI: 10.1007/s10845-024-02322-5

Shaikh, Z. P. (2025). Artificial intelligence-based emotional intelligence and effective leadership: Applications, implications, and ethical bias. In *Emotionally intelligent methods for meaningful leadership* (pp. 223–254). IGI Global., DOI: 10.4018/979-8-3693-7372-9.ch010

Shan, Z., & Wang, Y. (2024). Strategic talent development in the knowledge economy: A comparative analysis of global practices. *Journal of the Knowledge Economy, 15*(4), 19570–19596. DOI: 10.1007/s13132-024-01933-w

Sharma, R., Shishodia, A., Gunasekaran, A., Min, H., & Munim, Z. H. (2022). The role of artificial intelligence in supply chain management: Mapping the territory. *International Journal of Production Research, 60*(24), 7527–7550. DOI: 10.1080/00207543.2022.2029611

Shi, L. (2025). Global perspectives on AI competence development: Analyzing national AI strategies in education and workforce policies. *Human Resource Development Review, 24*(4), 447–476. Advance online publication. DOI: 10.1177/15344843251332360

Siarova, H., & van der Graaf, L. (2022). Multi-stakeholder approach for better integration of refugee students: Stakeholder engagement in the practice-research-policy transfer in refugee education policy. *OECD Education Working Papers*, (265), 1-52.

Simbeck, K. (2023). They shall be fair, transparent, and robust: Auditing learning analytics systems. *AI and Ethics, 4*(2), 555–571. DOI: 10.1007/s43681-023-00292-7

Strielkowski, W., Grebennikova, V., Lisovskiy, A., Rakhimova, G., & Vasileva, T. (2024). AI-driven adaptive learning for sustainable educational transformation. *Sustainable Development*. Advance online publication. DOI: 10.1002/sd.3221

Sukackė, V., Guerra, A. O. P. D. C., Ellinger, D., Carlos, V., Petronienė, S., Gaižiūnienė, L., Blanch, S., Marbà-Tallada, A., & Brose, A. (2022). Towards active evidence-based learning in engineering education: A systematic literature review of PBL, PjBL, and CBL. *Sustainability (Basel), 14*(21), 13955. DOI: 10.3390/su142113955

Susnjak, T., Ramaswami, G. S., & Mathrani, A. (2022). Learning analytics dashboard: A tool for providing actionable insights to learners. *International Journal of Educational Technology in Higher Education, 19*(1), 12. DOI: 10.1186/s41239-021-00313-7

Tarmo, A., & Kimaro, A. (2021). The teacher education curriculum and its competency-based education attributes. *The Journal of Competency-Based Education, 6*(3), e01255. DOI: 10.1002/cbe2.1255

Thai, K. P., Betts, A. L., & Gunderia, S. (2022). Personalized mastery-based learning ecosystem: A new paradigm for improving outcomes and defying expectations in early childhood. In Betts, A. L., & Thai, K. P. (Eds.), *Handbook of Research on Innovative Approaches to Early Childhood Development and School Readiness* (pp. 1–30). IGI Global., DOI: 10.4018/978-1-7998-8649-5.ch027

Valle, N., Antonenko, P., Valle, D., Sommer, M., Huggins-Manley, A. C., Dawson, K., & Baiser, B. (2021). Predict or describe? How learning analytics dashboard design influences motivation and statistics anxiety in an online statistics course. *Educational Technology Research and Development*, *69*(3), 1405–1431. DOI: 10.1007/s11423-021-09998-z

VanTassel-Baska, J., & Little, C. A. (Eds.). (2017). *Content-based curriculum for high-ability learners* (3rd ed.). Routledge., DOI: 10.4324/9781003233824

Varma, C., & Malik, S. (2023). Perspective chapter: TVET in the 21st century–A focus on innovative teaching and competency indicators. In *Technical and Vocational Education and Training*. IntechOpen. https://doi.org/DOI: 10.5772/intechopen.112516

Vashishth, T. K., Sharma, V., Sharma, K. K., Kumar, B., Panwar, R., & Chaudhary, S. (2024). AI-driven learning analytics for personalized feedback and assessment in higher education. In *Using Traditional Design Methods to Enhance AI-Driven Decision Making* (pp. 206–230). IGI Global., DOI: 10.4018/979-8-3693-0639-0.ch009

Verma, A., Lamsal, K., & Verma, P. (2022). An investigation of skill requirements in artificial intelligence and machine learning job advertisements. *Industry and Higher Education*, *36*(1), 63–73. DOI: 10.1177/0950422221990990

Vetrivel, S. C., Vidhyapriya, P., & Arun, V. P. (2025). The role of AI in transforming assessment practices in education. In *AI Applications and Strategies in Teacher Education* (pp. 43–70). IGI Global., DOI: 10.4018/979-8-3693-5443-8.ch003

Wang, D., Chen, L., & Dong, L. (2024). A critical review of climate change mitigation policies in the EU—Based on vertical, horizontal and policy instrument perspectives. *Journal of Cleaner Production*, *467*, 142972. DOI: 10.1016/j.jclepro.2024.142972

Wen, H., Xu, W., Chen, F., Jiang, X., Zhang, R., Zeng, J., Peng, L., & Chen, Y. (2023). Application of the BOPPPS-CBL model in electrocardiogram teaching for nursing students: A randomized comparison. *BMC Medical Education*, *23*(1), 987. DOI: 10.1186/s12909-023-04983-x

Yadav, U., & Shrawankar, U. (2025). Artificial intelligence across industries: A comprehensive review with a focus on education. In Ahmed, A., & Khan, F. (Eds.), *AI applications and strategies in teacher education* (pp. 275–320). IGI Global., DOI: 10.4018/978-1-6684-9384-2.ch012

Zhang, J., & Zhang, Z. (2024). AI in teacher education: Unlocking new dimensions in teaching support, inclusive learning, and digital literacy. *Journal of Computer Assisted Learning*, *40*(4), 1871–1885. Advance online publication. DOI: 10.1111/jcal.12988

Chapter 10

Harnessing AI for the Future of Talent:

Strategic Cases in People Analytics, Metaverse Integration, and Infrastructure Finance

Gaganpreet Kaur
http://orcid.org/0009-0006-2957-5352
Maharishi Markandeshwar University, Mullana, India

Neeraj Kumar Vats
http://orcid.org/0009-0006-4066-2596
Maharishi Markandeshwar University, Mullana, India

Amandeep Kaur
http://orcid.org/0009-0004-5716-7298
Advanced Center of Research and Innovation, CGC University, Mohali, India

Rachin Suri
http://orcid.org/0009-0005-3832-1138
Maharishi Markandeshwar University, Mullana, India

EXECUTIVE SUMMARY

In the age of digital disruption and intelligent automation, the nature of human capital is undergoing a profound transformation. This comprehensive volume explores how artificial intelligence (AI) is not only augmenting but reimagining the entire talent ecosystem from recruitment and workforce analytics to immersive training and infrastructure investment. Through a curated selection of forward-thinking case studies, the book demonstrates how organizations and educational institutions are

DOI: 10.4018/979-8-3373-3867-5.ch010

leveraging people analytics to derive actionable insights into employee behavior, performance, and potential. It also delves into the role of the metaverse in creating engaging, hybrid learning and collaboration experiences that transcend physical boundaries, making virtual talent development more dynamic and accessible. Furthermore, the integration of AI with infrastructure finance is examined to show how intelligent decision-making supports scalable, sustainable investment in people-first physical and digital environments.

1. INTRODUCTION: AI AT THE HELM OF TALENT TRANSFORMATION

1.1 Contextualizing the AI-Driven Talent Revolution

The 21st-century workplace is undergoing a seismic transformation, driven by the convergence of artificial intelligence (AI), machine learning (ML), data analytics, and immersive digital environments. As digital disruption intensifies, organizations are moving away from traditional models of talent management toward highly intelligent, adaptive, and predictive human capital ecosystems. The World Economic Forum (2023) predicts that by 2027, over 60% of jobs will require a significant component of digital and analytical skills, with AI emerging as a foundational enabler of this shift.

In this new paradigm, "talent" is not defined merely by static competencies or job titles, but by dynamic, evolving potential. Organizations must now continuously identify, nurture, and deploy skills that align with rapidly changing technological and economic contexts. This evolution demands a reconceptualization of human capital not as a cost center, but as a strategic asset, nurtured and scaled through data, algorithms, and immersive technologies (Brynjolfsson & McAfee, 2014).

1.2 The Strategic Role of AI in Human Capital Innovation

AI's integration into the talent ecosystem spans across multiple domains, enabling HR functions to become proactive, personalized, and performance-driven. From predictive modeling of attrition risk to personalized learning path recommendation engines, AI is transforming every phase of the employee lifecycle. The adoption of people analytics, which involves collecting and analyzing employee data to improve organizational outcomes, has emerged as a key driver in this transformation.

Studies show that organizations employing AI in HR analytics have improved workforce planning accuracy by 40%, reduced recruitment time by 60%, and enhanced employee engagement through data-driven personalization (Margherita &

Braccini, 2020). Moreover, natural language processing (NLP) and machine learning algorithms are increasingly being deployed to decode unstructured data such as employee feedback, performance reviews, and social media sentiment to derive actionable insights.

1.3 Immersive Digital Environments: Metaverse and Beyond

Simultaneously, the rise of immersive technologies such as virtual reality (VR), augmented reality (AR), and the broader metaverse is revolutionizing talent development and collaboration. These environments offer engaging, gamified, and personalized experiences that transcend the limitations of physical workplaces. Leading firms are already leveraging immersive onboarding programs, virtual leadership training, and simulation-based learning to upskill their workforce at scale (Bailenson, 2018).

According to a report by PwC (2023), VR learners are four times faster to train than in traditional classrooms and 275% more confident in applying newly acquired skills. As remote work and hybrid models become the norm, the metaverse provides a platform for persistent, borderless, and context-rich interactions that enhance team cohesion and knowledge sharing.

1.4 AI in Infrastructure Finance: Building Enabling Ecosystems

Beyond analytics and immersive tools, infrastructure finance is emerging as a critical pillar in AI-led talent transformation. Investments in smart infrastructure both physical and digital are increasingly guided by AI-driven decision-making frameworks. Governments and institutions are using predictive AI tools to optimize investment in education hubs, training centers, and digital connectivity, thereby creating an enabling environment for inclusive talent development (Tan & Goh, 2022).

Public-private partnerships (PPPs) and impact investing models are increasingly adopting AI to monitor outcomes, track ROI on human capital investment, and align infrastructure with future labor market demands. This integrated approach ensures that talent development is not isolated from broader economic planning but is embedded within a sustainable innovation framework.

1.5 Conceptual Framework of AI-Enabled Talent Transformation

To understand the multifaceted role of AI in talent transformation, this chapter employs a triadic framework integrating People Analytics, Immersive Digital Platforms, and Infrastructure Finance.

Figure 1. Conceptual model – AI enabled talent transformation framework

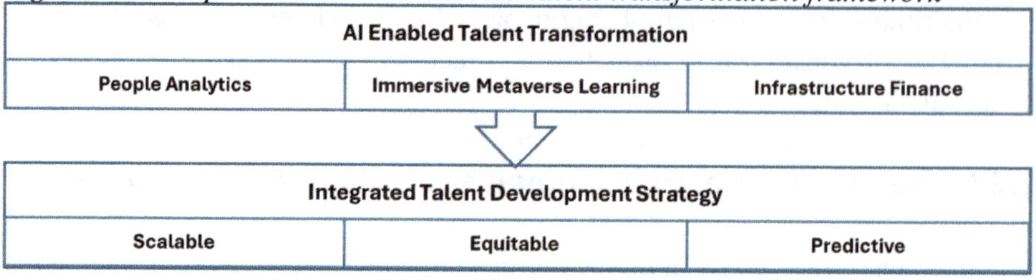

Strategic alignment as shown in Figure 1 allows for systemic innovation, addressing talent needs holistically from micro-level performance optimization to macro-level capacity building.

Table 1. Comparative overview of AI applications in talent ecosystem

Domain	AI Tools & Technologies	Key Outcomes	Example Organizations
People Analytics	Predictive modeling, NLP, ML dashboards	Attrition reduction, skills forecasting	IBM, Unilever
Immersive Learning	VR/AR, Digital Twins, AI avatars	Faster onboarding, higher retention	Accenture, Walmart
Infrastructure Finance	Smart contracts, AI investment models	Scalable training facilities, equitable access	Singapore SkillsFuture, EdTech PPPs

1.6 Objectives and Structure of the Chapter

This chapter aims to provide a comprehensive and interdisciplinary exploration of how AI technologies are enabling innovation in talent systems across sectors. By examining high-impact case studies, emerging research, and practical frameworks, it seeks to:

- Illustrate the transformative power of AI in people analytics.
- Explore the metaverse as a platform for immersive, inclusive talent development.
- Analyze the role of AI-augmented infrastructure finance in enabling sustainable workforce ecosystems.
- Offer a roadmap for policymakers, educators, and industry leaders to leverage AI for strategic human capital advancement.

Each subsequent section of the chapter delves deeply into one of the three pillars outlined above, culminating in a unified discussion on how these domains converge to reimagine the future of work and workforce development.

2. PEOPLE ANALYTICS: THE RISE OF DATA-DRIVEN TALENT INTELLIGENCE

2.1 Introduction: Redefining HR in the Digital Era

In the digital economy, data has become the new oil and within human resource management (HRM), people analytics has emerged as one of the most transformative applications of artificial intelligence (AI). People analytics refers to the systematic use of data and advanced analytics tools to understand, model, and enhance workforce behavior and performance (Margherita & Braccini, 2020). It enables organizations to shift from instinctive or reactive HR practices to data-driven, evidence-based talent strategies. This transformation empowers businesses to align talent decisions with strategic objectives, optimize the employee lifecycle, and enhance organizational agility.

The shift toward data-informed HR aligns with the broader trend of intelligent enterprise architecture, where every function marketing, operations, finance, and now HR leverages digital intelligence to make informed, predictive, and impactful decisions. According to the Deloitte Global Human Capital Trends Report (2022), 73% of organizations consider people analytics a top priority, yet only 11% rate themselves as highly effective in implementing it.

2.2 Historical Evolution and Analytical Frameworks

People analytics has evolved across four generations of maturity:

1. Operational Reporting (1.0): Basic tracking of headcount, leave, and payroll.
2. Metrics and Dashboards (2.0): Static KPIs, descriptive statistics, turnover trends.
3. Predictive Modeling (3.0): Statistical forecasting of outcomes such as attrition, promotion, and absenteeism.
4. Strategic Decision Intelligence (4.0): AI-driven, real-time workforce simulation and optimization.

This evolution reflects a shift from transactional HR to strategic human capital governance, integrating analytics into leadership, culture, and performance.

The integration of AI, machine learning (ML), natural language processing (NLP), and big data frameworks in HR practices has unlocked new frontiers in predictive precision, personalization, and process automation (Levenson, 2018). AI can now analyze vast volumes of structured and unstructured data, uncover hidden correlations, and generate explainable, actionable insights that human analysts would struggle to produce in real time.

2.3 The Strategic Layers of People Analytics

2.3.1 Descriptive Analytics

Descriptive analytics summarizes historical data and provides insights into what has already occurred. Examples include turnover rates, training attendance, average performance ratings, and engagement scores.

2.3.2 Diagnostic Analytics

This deeper layer explores why certain outcomes happened. For example, why did a department experience higher attrition? Was it related to leadership changes or compensation gaps?

2.3.3 Predictive Analytics

Predictive tools use ML models to forecast future behavior. For example, predicting which high performers are likely to resign, or which teams are at risk of burnout. Such tools empower proactive intervention.

2.3.4 Prescriptive Analytics

At this highest level, AI recommends interventions based on data insights. It may suggest personalized career paths, diversity hiring strategies, or optimized workforce plans under different scenarios.

Table 2. The four layers of people analytics

Analytics Layer	Focus Area	Example Tools	Value Delivered
Descriptive	What happened?	Dashboards, KPIs	Operational visibility
Diagnostic	Why did it happen?	Root cause analytics	Decision support
Predictive	What will happen?	Predictive modeling	Risk mitigation
Prescriptive	What should be done?	AI recommendation engines	Optimization of outcomes

2.4 Case Study in Depth: Unilever's Digital Recruitment Transformation

Unilever stands as a pioneering example of how large, global organizations can leverage artificial intelligence (AI) and people analytics to radically transform recruitment practices. With over 1.8 million applications annually across diverse geographies, the company faced the dual challenge of processing talent efficiently while maintaining fairness, diversity, and scalability. To address these challenges, Unilever adopted a completely digital and AI-enhanced hiring process, showcasing how recruitment can be reimagined through innovation, neuroscience, and ethical algorithmic design.

2.4.1 Tools and Technologies Used

Central to this transformation was the deployment of advanced assessment technologies and AI tools. Unilever implemented Pymetrics, a neuroscience-based platform that utilizes a series of gamified tests to evaluate candidates' cognitive, emotional, and social capabilities, thus eliminating reliance on resumes and academic scores in the early stages. Additionally, HireVue, a video interview platform powered by natural language processing (NLP) and computer vision, analyzed facial expressions, speech patterns, and tone of voice to provide deeper insight into candidates' potential. These data points were then processed using algorithmic scoring models, which compared applicant traits against internal benchmarks of success based on large-scale, historical performance data from Unilever's existing workforce.

2.4.2 Key Achievements

The outcomes of this digital shift have been both impactful and measurable. Unilever achieved a 90% reduction in time-to-hire, streamlining the recruitment cycle from an average of three months to under three weeks. Furthermore, by integrating bias-mitigating algorithms at the early screening phase, the company reported a 16% increase in candidate diversity, particularly in underrepresented demographics. Over one million applicants have been evaluated through this system, ensuring objective, standardized, and scalable hiring processes across regions (Chattopadhyay et al., 2023).

2.4.3 Insights

This transformation offers valuable insights into the strategic application of AI in human resources. By digitizing assessments and minimizing human subjectivity in early-stage evaluations, Unilever significantly reduced unconscious bias, promoting a merit-based selection process. Candidate feedback further validated the system's credibility, with many reporting that the process felt fair, efficient, and aligned with their expectations of a modern, progressive employer. For HR professionals, the integration of AI also enabled access to real-time dashboards with insights on candidate quality, conversion rates, and diversity, equity, and inclusion (DEI) metrics, thereby positioning HR as a data-driven strategic partner.

Unilever's case exemplifies how intelligent recruitment ecosystems grounded in neuroscience, AI, and behavioral analytics can deliver both operational efficiency and inclusive excellence at scale. It highlights the potential for replicable frameworks in other large organizations aiming to future-proof their talent acquisition strategies.

Figure 2. Unilever's AI-based recruitment pipeline

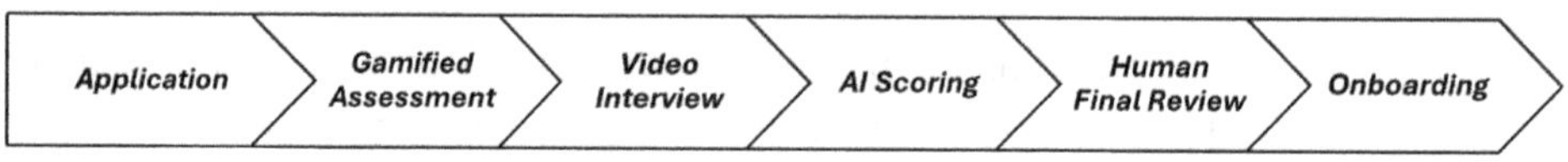

2.5 Applications Beyond Hiring: End-to-End Talent Lifecycle Analytics

2.5.1 Performance and Productivity Optimization

AI-powered people analytics tools such as Visier and IBM Watson provide HR with insights into team dynamics, performance bottlenecks, and project alignment. These tools offer 360-degree performance views by integrating manager feedback, peer reviews, and project outcomes.

2.5.2 Personalized Learning and Reskilling

AI can curate adaptive learning paths for employees based on competency mapping, past learning behaviors, and role transitions. According to a PwC (2023) report, personalized learning using AI leads to 34% higher retention of skills and 30% faster application on the job.

2.5.3 DEI Analytics and Inclusive Culture Building

AI identifies patterns in pay disparities, promotion lags, and performance evaluation bias across demographic groups. Companies like Microsoft and Deloitte are using AI audits to ensure equity in employee experiences and outcomes (Bogen & Rieke, 2018).

Table 3. Selected AI tools in people analytics

Tool	Core Function	Organizational Use
Humu	Behavioral science-based nudges	Team engagement & well-being
Gloat	Internal talent marketplace	Mobility & career development
Workday Prism	Unified HR analytics	Workforce planning
Eightfold AI	Talent intelligence	Skills mapping & DEI

2.6 Ethical Considerations: The Responsible Use of People Data

The integration of AI into people analytics and broader human resource (HR) functions brings with it a host of ethical, legal, and organizational responsibilities. As data-driven decision-making accelerates, organizations must confront the moral complexities of using personal and behavioral data in high-stakes talent decisions. One of the most pressing concerns is algorithmic bias. When AI models are trained on historical HR data, they may inadvertently replicate and perpetuate systemic inequalities, such as gender, racial, or socioeconomic disparities embedded in legacy hiring and promotion practices (Raji et al., 2020). Furthermore, the collection of biometric and behavioral data, such as facial expressions, voice tone, or keystroke patterns, introduces significant privacy risks. These practices demand strict adherence to data protection regulations like the EU's GDPR and India's DPDP Act (2023), emphasizing informed consent, minimal data use, and cybersecurity.

Equally important is the issue of explainability. Many AI systems in HR, particularly those relying on deep learning algorithms, function as "black boxes," offering little transparency on how decisions are made. This lack of clarity can undermine employee trust, especially when AI influences decisions related to recruitment, performance evaluation, or career progression. To navigate these risks, organizations must adopt comprehensive AI ethics policies, supported by Explainable AI (XAI) frameworks that allow both HR teams and employees to understand and challenge AI-driven outcomes. Additionally, embedding human-in-the-loop (HITL) systems ensures that final decisions are reviewed and validated by qualified professionals, maintaining a critical layer of human oversight and accountability.

2.7 Strategic Value and Future Outlook

Beyond its technical sophistication, people analytics should be viewed as a strategic enabler of business value and workforce transformation. Organizations that have successfully embedded people analytics into their core decision-making processes consistently report enhanced outcomes across key performance indicators. According to recent research by Deloitte (2022), companies using advanced people analytics report 24% higher profitability, while Levenson (2018) found correlations with 37% higher employee engagement and 19% lower attrition rates. These metrics demonstrate how people analytics can shift HR from a support function to a strategic intelligence center that informs everything from talent acquisition to organizational development and succession planning.

Looking ahead, several innovative directions are reshaping the landscape of talent intelligence. One emerging trend is the use of Digital Twins of Talent simulated replicas of employees or teams that enable scenario testing for performance, behavior, and organizational design. This approach allows leaders to evaluate potential outcomes of restructuring, new leadership models, or cultural interventions without real-world disruptions. Another frontier is Emotion AI, which uses machine learning and affective computing to capture and interpret employees' emotional states in real time, thereby enhancing leadership response and employee experience management. Furthermore, the evolution of Autonomous Talent Systems AI agents that can autonomously manage aspects of hiring, learning, wellness monitoring, and promotions signals a future where human-AI collaboration is continuous, adaptive, and personalized.

In this emerging paradigm, the most successful organizations will be those that balance data-driven intelligence with human values. The goal is not to replace human judgment but to augment it with empathetic, transparent, and accountable AI systems. The future of talent intelligence lies in fostering collaborative ecosystems where AI enhances human capabilities particularly in creativity, adaptability, and ethical reasoning rather than rendering them obsolete.

3. METAVERSE INTEGRATION: IMMERSIVE TECHNOLOGIES FOR TALENT DEVELOPMENT

3.1 Redefining Learning and Engagement Through Virtual Worlds

The concept of the metaverse has transitioned from a speculative buzzword to a transformative force in enterprise learning and talent development. Rooted in the convergence of extended reality (XR) technologies including Virtual Reality (VR), Augmented Reality (AR), Mixed Reality (MR) and powered by Artificial Intelligence (AI), blockchain, 5G, and cloud computing, the metaverse creates persistent, interactive, and highly personalized digital environments that replicate or enhance real-world experiences (Dwivedi et al., 2022).

In the era of distributed teams, remote work, and digital-first engagement, the metaverse addresses a critical challenge: how can organizations create engaging, scalable, and inclusive learning ecosystems that overcome the limitations of time, space, and physical presence? As traditional Learning and Development (L&D) strategies struggle with declining engagement, outdated content delivery models, and limited customization, the immersive and experiential nature of metaverse environments offers a compelling alternative.

How Metaverse Enhances Talent Development

1. Experiential Learning: Employees learn bydoing navigating scenarios, interacting with simulations, and making real-time decisions.
2. Emotional Immersion: XR technologies trigger emotional engagement, which boosts memory retention and empathy (Slater & Sanchez-Vives, 2022).
3. Real-Time Feedback: AI engines offer immediate, context-aware feedback that reinforces learning.
4. Asynchronous and Synchronous Flexibility: Learners can attend scheduled live virtual workshops or self-paced immersive modules.

Figure 3. The metaverse talent development framework

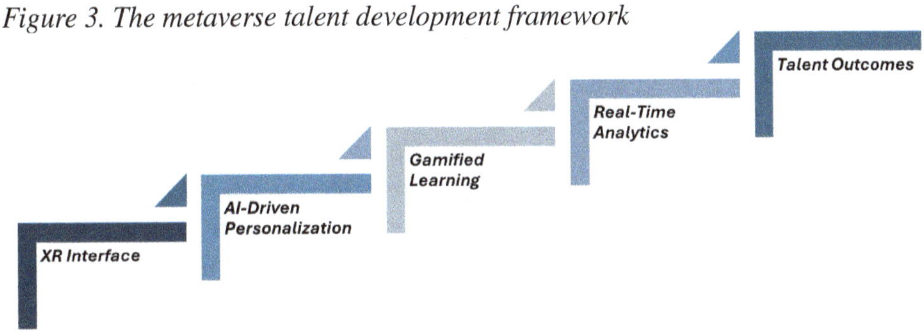

In essence, the metaverse is not just a medium for learning as it is becoming a cognitive architecture for building human capital in real-time.

3.2 Strategic Case Study: Accenture's "Nth Floor" Metaverse Campus

Accenture, a global leader in digital transformation, has pioneered the development of a proprietary metaverse-based workspace known as the "Nth Floor." This virtual environment serves as a digital twin of Accenture's physical offices, designed to replicate the look, feel, and functionality of a real-world workplace within an extended reality (XR) space. The primary aim of the Nth Floor is to enhance the onboarding experience, foster collaboration, and support continuous learning and innovation in a fully immersive and scalable environment.

The strategic objectives of the Nth Floor are threefold: to cultivate a sense of belonging among remote hires, to deliver cost-effective and engaging learning programs, and to facilitate seamless cross-border collaboration through AI-enhanced digital spaces. By doing so, Accenture ensures that distributed teams can connect meaningfully and work productively, regardless of their physical location.

The technological infrastructure supporting the Nth Floor includes the widespread distribution of Oculus VR headsets—with over 60% of new hires receiving one—as well as spatial audio and 3D avatars that simulate lifelike interactions. Furthermore, the environment incorporates AI-powered tutors and virtual coaches, which provide personalized onboarding experiences, real-time feedback, and performance support.

According to internal evaluations (Accenture, 2023; KPMG, 2022), the results of implementing the Nth Floor have been significant. Over 150,000 new employees have been onboarded through immersive digital experiences. The retention rate of onboarding material has increased by 40% when compared to traditional formats. Additionally, the company has seen a substantial reduction in travel and logistics costs for learning and development (L&D) sessions. Perhaps most notably, employee satisfaction scores related to onboarding improved by 27%, demonstrating the efficacy of immersive, AI-integrated onboarding programs.

This initiative exemplifies the transformative potential of digital twin environments, not only in traditional industrial applications like manufacturing or logistics but also in human-centered functions such as talent development, learning, and employee engagement. The Nth Floor represents a paradigm shift in workplace innovation, positioning the metaverse as a viable, scalable, and empathetic solution for the evolving demands of a hybrid and global workforce.

3.3 Impacts on Learning Models and Organizational Culture

The integration of metaverse technologies into talent development brings about profound shifts in the way organizations design, deliver, and experience learning.

These immersive, AI-enhanced environments are not only transforming pedagogical models but also reshaping the foundational fabric of organizational culture.

3.3.1 Personalized and Adaptive Learning at Scale

Traditional learning models often follow a linear, static, and one-size-fits-all approach that fails to address individual learning needs. The metaverse, driven by AI algorithms, facilitates dynamic learning pathways that are both personalized and adaptive. Learners receive skill-matched content recommendations, experience behavior-tracking-enabled pacing adjustments, and engage with gamified incentives that enhance motivation and engagement. These adaptive learning systems respond in real-time to learners' progress and preferences, delivering content that evolves based on demonstrated competencies. Notably, studies have shown that immersive adaptive learning environments using XR technologies can achieve retention rates as high as 75%, a significant leap from the 10% typically observed in conventional e-learning formats (PwC, 2022). This evolution empowers organizations to scale personalized learning without sacrificing effectiveness.

3.3.2 Empathy, DEI, and Soft Skills Training

Soft skills training, particularly in the domains of emotional intelligence, diversity, equity, and inclusion (DEI), has traditionally suffered from abstraction and disengagement. Metaverse technologies change this by allowing employees to embody and experience roles in immersive simulations that expose them to real-world issues such as bias, exclusion, and harassment. Through VR-based roleplay scenarios, individuals gain firsthand exposure to the emotional and social dynamics of workplace inequity, thereby fostering empathy and enhancing psychological safety. Additionally, XR environments can simulate diverse organizational contexts, helping bridge intergenerational, cross-cultural, and accessibility divides. According to Zhao et al. (2021), these immersive DEI interventions demonstrate higher impact on behavioral change compared to standard training modules, promoting more inclusive organizational practices.

3.3.3 Organizational Culture Reimagined

Beyond training, the metaverse has the potential to reshape how organizational culture is built and sustained in hybrid or remote-first settings. In virtual headquarters, leaders can convene global teams through XR-based town halls, fostering transparency and alignment. Informal interactions often lost in remote setups are revived through digital "watercooler" spaces, where employees can engage in casual, spontaneous exchanges that sustain workplace camaraderie. Moreover, the collaborative nature of the metaverse supports co-creation, with teams working together on 3D whiteboards, engaging in real-time shared simulations, and collectively designing solutions. These immersive environments not only maintain but also enrich organizational identity, making culture a living, participatory experience.

Table 4. Comparison between traditional and metaverse-based learning

Dimension	Traditional Learning	Metaverse-Enhanced Learning
Format	Video modules, PDFs	Immersive 3D simulations
Engagement	Passive	Interactive, gamified
Personalization	Limited	AI-curated
Empathy Training	Text/roleplay	Realistic VR immersion
Scalability	Limited by resources	Global, unlimited
Analytics	Static LMS reports	Real-time performance dashboards

3.4 Technology Stack: Building the Infrastructure for Immersive L&D

Metaverse-based learning environments are powered by an integrated technology ecosystem:

Core Components:

- Hardware: VR headsets (e.g., Oculus Quest, HTC Vive), AR glasses (e.g., HoloLens), motion sensors.
- Software Platforms: ENGAGE, AltspaceVR, Spatial.io, Virbela for 3D learning spaces.
- AI Engines: Adaptive learning algorithms, natural language tutors, and sentiment analysis bots.
- Blockchain: Used for digital credentials, secure learning records, and attendance tracking.
- 5G & Edge Computing: Enable latency-free real-time interaction across continents.

3.5 Challenges, Limitations, and Ethical Dimensions

Despite its promise, the integration of the metaverse in talent development faces significant hurdles:

Challenges:

- High initial investment in devices, design, and cloud architecture.
- User resistance or digital fatigue due to novelty or discomfort with immersive hardware.
- Access and Equity: Rural, low-income, or disabled employees may face barriers in accessing metaverse environments.

Ethical and Privacy Concerns:

- Real-time behavioral tracking can compromise employee privacy.
- AI avatars may inadvertently reproduce unconscious biases.
- Biometric and emotional data collected in XR need robust data governance aligned with GDPR, India's DPDP Act (2023), and other frameworks.

Table 5. Metaverse talent development – risk vs. value matrix with strategic mitigations

Area	Potential Risks	Strategic Value	Suggested Mitigations
Data Privacy	Biometric surveillance, real-time behavior tracking	Deep personalized learning and feedback analytics	GDPR/DPDP-compliant protocols, transparent consent, AI audit trails
Inclusion	Digital divide limiting access for rural or marginalized users	Equitable access to immersive learning across geographies	Affordable/mobile XR options, public funding, inclusive design
Cost	High upfront investment in hardware, software, and platforms	Long-term cost savings from reduced travel, scalable L&D	Shared infrastructure, public-private partnerships, ROI-based planning
Bias	AI-based algorithmic discrimination or stereotyping	Standardized, bias-free learning content delivery	Diverse training datasets, regular AI bias audits, ethical governance
User Experience	Motion sickness, digital fatigue, device discomfort	High learner engagement via gamified, embodied interactions	Ergonomic hardware, XR session time limits, UX improvements

3.6 Future Directions: From Experiments to Infrastructure

The metaverse is not a passing trend it is evolving into a core platform for human capital management. Key trends on the horizon include:

a) Digital Talent Twins

Virtual replicas of employees simulate learning, predict burnout, and recommend career moves based on real-time data.

b) Talent Acquisition in the Metaverse

Companies like Hyundai and BMW are conducting virtual job fairs and AI-based interviews in immersive settings.

c) Virtual Mentorship & Peer Learning

Senior professionals from different regions can connect with new hires through AI-facilitated virtual coaching environments.

d) Mental Health and Wellbeing

VR-based mindfulness sessions, cognitive therapy spaces, and AI-guided emotion tracking are being integrated into virtual wellness programs.

Organizations that invest early in building metaverse readiness through infrastructure, policies, and culture will be at the forefront of future-proofing talent pipelines and enabling lifelong learning ecosystems.

4. INFRASTRUCTURE FINANCE: BUILDING SMART ENVIRONMENTS FOR TALENT INNOVATION

4.1 From Brick-and-Mortar to Digital-Physical Hybrids

The transformation of work and learning ecosystems in the 21st century necessitates a corresponding evolution in the infrastructure that supports human capital development. Traditional brick-and-mortar institutions—training centers, universities, office complexes—are being rapidly redefined by digital convergence. Today's most forward-thinking talent ecosystems are digital-physical hybrids where immersive technology, AI, IoT, and sustainability goals converge to create smart, scalable environments conducive to learning, collaboration, and innovation.

Theoretical Foundations

The integration of infrastructure and human capital development draws on the Resource-Based View (RBV) of the firm, which sees infrastructure not just as a fixed cost but as a strategic resource that can unlock competitive advantage when aligned with organizational capabilities (Barney, 1991). Additionally, the Human Capital Theory asserts that investments in learning infrastructure when effectively designed and financed yield exponential returns in terms of productivity, innovation, and economic growth (Becker, 1994).

Role of AI in Infrastructure Design

AI enables a shift from reactive to proactive infrastructure management through:

- Predictive analytics: Forecasts space utilization, energy demands, and user behavior.
- Sentiment analysis: Assesses employee mood and satisfaction via environmental sensors.
- Optimization algorithms: Automate climate control, lighting, and resource allocation for wellness and energy efficiency.

This paradigm allows learning and workplace environments to adapt in real time to the changing needs of the workforce, improving both experience and efficiency.

4.2 Case Study: Singapore's Skills Future Strategy

One of the most exemplary and forward-thinking global initiatives in infrastructure-backed talent development is Singapore's Skills Future movement. This comprehensive, government-led strategy seamlessly integrates intelligent infrastructure investment with AI-powered workforce planning to promote lifelong learning across diverse population segments. At its core, Skills Future is designed to prepare the national workforce for Industry 4.0 by aligning skill development with sectoral transformation and technological innovation.

The initiative is underpinned by several key structural components. First, the establishment of Smart Learning Hubs technologically advanced training centers equipped with biometric scanners, AR/VR labs, and cloud-connected devices enables the delivery of customized, competency-based training programs. These hubs are closely aligned with Singapore's Industry Transformation Maps (ITMs), ensuring that skill development initiatives are responsive to evolving sectoral demands. Second, the deployment of AI-powered learning platforms notably *MySkillsFuture* plays a critical role in guiding individuals through personalized upskilling journeys.

These platforms utilize real-time labor market analytics, individual skills profiles, and employment forecasts to recommend optimal learning pathways. Third, the initiative is characterized by cross-sectoral partnerships, wherein government agencies collaborate with leading technology firms such as IBM and Microsoft, as well as premier educational institutions, to co-finance and co-deliver cutting-edge learning infrastructures.

The impact of this integrated approach is significant. According to Tan and Goh (2022) and Skills Future Singapore (2023), over 2.8 million Singaporeans have been upskilled through the program, spanning multiple age groups and career stages. Moreover, the initiative has successfully rolled out more than 30 Skills Future Career Transition Programs that operate in blended physical-digital formats, allowing for both accessibility and flexibility. Since its inception, the program has mobilized over SGD $1.5 billion in public-private investment, reinforcing the government's commitment to a resilient and future-ready workforce.

This case study illustrates how infrastructure, when embedded with intelligence, inclusivity, and strategic vision, becomes a systemic enabler of human capital excellence. It serves as a replicable model for other nations seeking to integrate digital infrastructure, AI, and lifelong learning into national workforce development strategies.

4.3 Innovative Financing Models and AI Integration

To meet the demand for scalable, inclusive, and future-ready infrastructure, traditional capital expenditure models are giving way to innovative, AI-driven financing approaches.

4.3.1 AI in Infrastructure Forecasting and Allocation

AI enhances infrastructure planning in several ways:

- Demand Prediction: Identifies where future skills hubs or micro-campuses should be established.
- Cost-Efficiency Modeling: Simulates the ROI of various configurations using labor market intelligence.
- Maintenance Automation: Uses real-time sensor data to trigger predictive maintenance, reducing downtime.

Example: The Indian Skill Hubs under NSDC use AI dashboards to monitor usage rates, capacity, and learner outcomes, directly guiding funding decisions from the Ministry of Skill Development.

4.3.2 Blockchain & Smart Contracts in Training Finance

- Smart Contracts: Enable decentralized and conditional financing (e.g., release of training funds after attendance milestones or certification).
- Micro-Credentials and Tokenization: Learners can accumulate verifiable, blockchain-backed credentials that are portable across platforms and borders.
- Decentralized Learning Wallets: Store AI-curated learning paths, performance analytics, and employer endorsements in one secure digital space.

Table 6. Comparison of emerging financing models for learning infrastructure

Model	Technology	Advantages	Use Cases
Public-Private Partnerships (PPP)	AI + Cloud	Scale + Governance	Singapore, UK Institutes
Education Impact Bonds	AI + Performance Dashboards	Outcome-based returns	Social Finance UK
Tokenized Learning Credits	Blockchain + Wallets	Portability + Trust	Estonia, Korea
AI Allocation Engines	ML + Infrastructure APIs	Optimization + Real-Time Adjustments	PwC Smart Campus Solutions

4.4 ESG Alignment: Toward Sustainable Learning Ecosystems

The ESG (Environmental, Social, and Governance) imperative is no longer optional in infrastructure development. It is especially crucial in talent innovation, where facilities and systems must be inclusive, green, and ethically governed.

Environmental:

- LEED-certified learning centers powered by solar/wind.
- VR/AR simulation labs that replace physical prototypes and reduce carbon footprint.
- Energy dashboards driven by AI to optimize HVAC and lighting.

Social:

- Accessibility standards integrated into design.
- Digital literacy zones for underrepresented groups.
- Mobile skill vans and XR-based pop-up classrooms for rural outreach.

Governance:

- AI ethics panels to evaluate algorithmic transparency.
- Stakeholder inclusion in infrastructure planning.
- Open data sharing of infrastructure ROI.

4.5 Infrastructure Intelligence as a Strategic Asset

When infrastructure is embedded with sensors, machine learning, immersive interfaces, and cloud connectivity, it transitions from a static utility to a strategic enabler of continuous innovation.

Strategic Impacts:

- Workplace Agility: Spaces reconfigure in real-time to suit collaborative, hybrid, or solitary tasks.
- Learning Continuity: No geographic or temporal boundaries for skill development.
- ROI Transparency: AI dashboards provide precise reporting on how infrastructure impacts learning, innovation, and well-being.

Table 7. Comparative impact of infrastructure models on talent outcomes

Metric	Legacy Infrastructure	Smart Infrastructure
Learner Engagement	Moderate	High (Gamified, Personalized)
Cost Efficiency	Fixed costs	Optimized via AI
Accessibility	Location-based	Global and Mobile
Talent ROI Tracking	Periodic reporting	Real-time dashboards
Sustainability	High footprint	Net-zero potential

4.6 Future Outlook: Infrastructure-as-a-Platform (IaaP) for Talent Development

The future of infrastructure financing for talent development lies in Infrastructure-as-a-Platform (IaaP) models, where physical assets are digitally orchestrated, modular, and interoperable with enterprise systems.

Key Future Directions:

- Dynamic Campus Networks: Micro-hubs that adapt curriculum based on local economic trends.
- AI-Talent Cloud Platforms: Real-time matching of infrastructure availability with upskilling demand.
- Virtual Infrastructure Bonds: Investors fund metaverse campuses with ROI linked to talent metrics.

Organizations that invest in flexible, AI-augmented, and ESG-compliant infrastructure will be best positioned to compete in the knowledge economy, where talent, not location, is the new currency of growth.

5. CONVERGENCE: INTEGRATIVE FRAMEWORK FOR AI-DRIVEN TALENT STRATEGY

In the age of accelerated digital transformation, it is no longer sufficient to view technology-enabled talent development through isolated lenses. While AI-driven people analytics enhances decision-making, metaverse technologies revolutionize engagement, and intelligent infrastructure finance ensures scalability and sustainability, the real value emerges when these domains converge into a unified strategic framework. This convergence marks a shift from fragmented HR functions to an integrated, data-rich, experience-driven, and infrastructure-supported talent strategy.

This section explores the multidimensional interplay of the three pillars People Analytics, Metaverse Integration, and Infrastructure Finance and presents a comprehensive Talent Convergence Framework that supports efficiency, engagement, equity, and organizational resilience.

5.1 Strategic Imperative: From Silos to Synergy

Traditionally, human resource systems have operated in silos learning and development teams manage training, infrastructure planners manage space, and data scientists handle analytics. However, the advent of AI and intelligent systems demands a systemic orientation, where each domain dynamically feeds and informs the other.

Table 8. Traditional approach and converged strategy

Traditional Approach	Converged Strategy
HR as an administrative function	HR as a strategic intelligence system
Static, one-size-fits-all training	Adaptive, AI-personalized learning in virtual worlds
Fixed infrastructure planning	AI-driven, demand-based infrastructure investment
Post-hoc metrics and KPIs	Real-time feedback and predictive optimization

The integrated approach transforms the employee experience into a continuous, data-enriched journey from recruitment and onboarding to leadership development and workforce mobility.

5.2 Functional Integration: Building the Intelligent Talent Stack

The convergence of people analytics, immersive technologies, and infrastructure finance materializes through what can be conceptualized as the Intelligent Talent Stack a four layered framework that integrates insight, experience, environment, and governance to holistically support workforce development.

At the foundation is the Insight Layer, powered by people analytics. This layer harnesses predictive models and machine learning algorithms to identify attrition risks, assess high-potential employees, and match evolving organizational needs with individual capabilities (Margherita & Braccini, 2020). By continuously analyzing engagement data and performance trends, organizations can deploy real-time, data-driven interventions to improve retention and productivity.

The second level, the Experience Layer, is shaped by metaverse-based learning environments. Immersive platforms simulate real-world job scenarios, leadership challenges, and collaborative problem-solving activities. Within these digital ecosystems, AI avatars and digital twins act as virtual mentors, offering real-time feedback and adaptive coaching that aligns with learner behavior and performance (Dwivedi et al., 2022). These experiences not only enhance cognitive engagement but also cultivate critical soft skills and emotional intelligence.

The Environment Layer focuses on infrastructure finance and digital access. It encompasses the development of smart campuses, XR-equipped learning hubs, and mobile learning vans that bring education to underserved regions. AI is employed to optimize space utilization, forecast energy demands, and manage learner flow across facilities, thereby maximizing the return on physical and digital infrastructure investments (Tan & Goh, 2022).

Finally, the Governance Layer ensures that the entire stack operates with integrity and accountability. Blockchain technology enables secure and verifiable tracking of skills, credentials, and certifications, reducing fraud and increasing transparency.

Simultaneously, AI governance frameworks are essential to uphold data privacy, ensure algorithmic fairness, and comply with international regulatory standards, including GDPR and India's DPDP Act (2023).

Together, these four layers form an interconnected system that transforms traditional talent management into an intelligent, ethical, and scalable model for the future of work.

5.3 AI-Enabled Talent Operating System (TOS)

The convergence is orchestrated by a central Talent Operating System (TOS) a cloud-native, AI-augmented platform that integrates data, infrastructure, and experience flows across the organization.

Figure 4. Components of the talent operating system

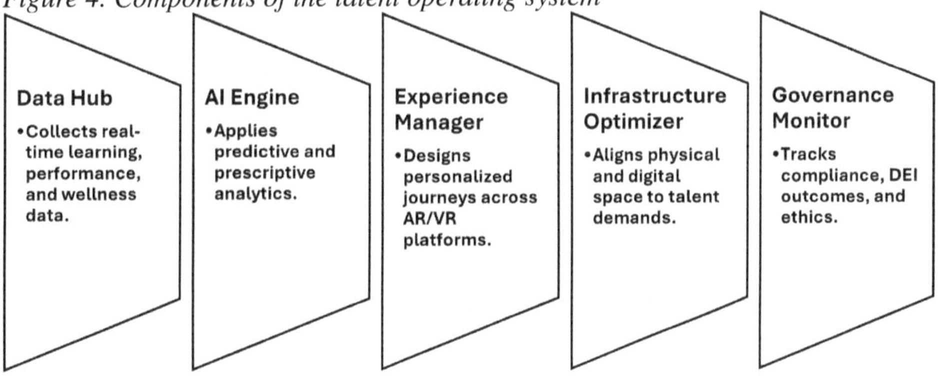

This system acts like a digital nervous system, enabling organizations to move from reactive planning to proactive talent orchestration.

5.4 Synergistic Outcomes: Efficiency, Engagement, and Equity

The convergence generates compounding returns across three core outcome dimensions:

1. Efficiency
   - Automated candidate screening, AI-curated learning, and IoT-based space optimization reduce waste and speed up operations.
   - Example: Unilever's AI-based recruitment reduced time-to-hire by 90% (Chattopadhyay et al., 2023).
2. Engagement

- VR-based onboarding and AR-driven training improve knowledge retention and emotional connection to the organization.
- Accenture's Nth Floor initiative led to higher training satisfaction and lower turnover (KPMG, 2022).

3. Equity
    - AI detects bias in recruitment and training pathways, enabling inclusive development.
    - Virtual campuses democratize access to high-quality learning for rural and marginalized workers.

Table 9. Integrated outcomes of talent convergence

Outcome Category	Pre-Convergence	Post-Convergence
Learning ROI	Limited to completion rates	Real-time impact tracking
Employee Engagement	Static surveys	Immersive feedback systems
Resource Allocation	Annual budget cycles	Dynamic AI allocation
DEI Implementation	Policy-driven	Data-enforced, behavioral modeling
Leadership Pipeline	Informal mentoring	Simulated, data-backed acceleration

5.5 Sectoral Applications and Use Cases

Higher Education

- Universities deploy AI-based skill forecasting to redesign curricula aligned with industry 4.0 needs.
- Virtual internships and global XR classrooms break down access barriers.

Corporate L&D

- On-demand, skill-based microlearning integrated with LMS, hosted on metaverse campuses.
- Infrastructure finance linked to employee development KPIs.

Government and Policy

- Skills development bonds and AI-guided infrastructure allocation for national upskilling missions.

- National-level data dashboards tracking workforce adaptability.

5.6 Risks and Governance Mechanisms

Despite the benefits, convergence introduces new risks that must be mitigated through robust governance:

Table 10. Risks and governance strategy

Risk Area	Governance Strategy
AI Bias & Surveillance	Explainable AI, third-party audits, ethical AI boards
Data Privacy	Federated learning, zero-trust architecture
Access Inequality	Subsidized device access, digital literacy campaigns
Infrastructure Waste	Predictive ROI modeling, ESG-aligned financing

5.7 The Future: Cognitive Talent Ecosystems

The ultimate evolution in AI-driven talent transformation culminates in the emergence of Cognitive Talent Ecosystems self-optimizing, adaptive systems where machine intelligence and human potential operate in continuous feedback loops. In these ecosystems, every data point refines the next strategic action, whether it's a learning recommendation, well-being intervention, or workspace reconfiguration. Human development becomes symbiotic with intelligent systems, as learning pathways and digital environments adapt in real time to individual needs and organizational priorities.

Several emerging trends signal this transition. Neuroadaptive learning, particularly within virtual reality (VR) environments, tailors educational content based on neural signals and engagement levels, enhancing knowledge retention and cognitive efficiency. Similarly, biofeedback-linked learning journeys utilize physiological signals such as heart rate or skin conductance to adjust the intensity or tone of immersive training modules, fostering emotional regulation and reducing cognitive overload. Furthermore, the concept of Infrastructure-as-a-Platform (IaaP) is gaining traction, where talent development spaces are managed via cloud infrastructure, offering scalable, usage-based learning environments embedded with AI, IoT, and XR capabilities.

Organizations that successfully harness these converging innovations will foster resilient, human-centered, and future-proof talent ecosystems. These ecosystems are not only responsive to market shifts and technological disruption but are also aligned with ethical governance, social inclusion, and sustainable development goals, positioning enterprises at the forefront of the AI-powered future of work.

6. ETHICAL CONSIDERATIONS AND IMPLEMENTATION CHALLENGES

As AI, immersive technologies, and smart infrastructure continue to transform talent development ecosystems, it is imperative to ensure that innovation does not come at the cost of ethical integrity, inclusivity, and human dignity. While these technologies offer immense potential for scalability and personalization, they also pose novel risks that are legal, social, psychological, and organizational in nature. These risks, if unaddressed, could amplify systemic inequalities, erode trust, and hinder the adoption of even the most promising innovations.

This section presents an in-depth analysis of the ethical tensions and operational hurdles that must be acknowledged and navigated in AI-led talent transformation. The discussion is organized into five strategic dimensions: (1) data ethics and privacy, (2) equitable access and digital justice, (3) organizational change and leadership readiness, (4) psychological well-being and algorithmic impact, and (5) governance, accountability, and sustainability.

6.1 Data Ethics and Privacy: Navigating Consent, Control, and Confidentiality

In AI-powered talent systems, data serves as the foundation for learning, personalization, and decision-making. However, this heavy reliance on employee data especially sensitive biometric, emotional, and behavioral data raises critical questions about informed consent, transparency, and ethical boundaries.

Emerging Ethical Challenges:

As organizations integrate AI and immersive technologies into HR functions, a range of ethical challenges emerges that demand urgent attention. One major concern is the opacity of algorithms many AI systems function as "black boxes," where even HR professionals cannot fully interpret how decisions regarding hiring, performance evaluation, or promotions are reached (Rahwan et al., 2019). This lack of transparency not only undermines accountability but also erodes employee trust. Compounding the issue is the proliferation of involuntary data trails in XR-based learning and work environments. In these immersive spaces, individuals unknowingly generate biometric and behavioral data such as eye movements, response latency, and physical gestures, which may be recorded and analyzed without their full understanding or explicit consent.

Traditional models of consent typically based on static, one-time agreements are ill-equipped to address the dynamic and continuous data collection characteristic of AI systems. Consequently, organizations must shift toward adaptive consent frameworks that allow individuals to modify, withdraw, or renegotiate consent in real time. Illustrating the complexity of this challenge, a 2022 study by Smuha et al. revealed that more than 65% of European HR managers using AI analytics tools were uncertain about whether their systems complied with the General Data Protection Regulation (GDPR). This highlights a substantial disconnect between regulatory intent and operational practice, underscoring the need for clearer guidelines, ethical AI governance, and ongoing legal literacy in the use of advanced HR technologies.

Table 11. Framework for data ethics in talent development

Principle	Application in HR Tech
Transparency	Disclose AI logic and data use in plain language
Autonomy	Provide opt-in/opt-out features and data dashboards
Accountability	Implement audit trails for algorithmic decisions
Confidentiality	Encrypt sensitive data and restrict access rights

6.2 Talent Access and Digital Justice: Closing the Inclusion Gap

As artificial intelligence, XR tools, and immersive platforms redefine talent development, a parallel imperative emerges: ensuring equitable access to these advancements. The future of talent must be inclusive, enabling participation from all socioeconomic strata, geographies, and demographic groups. However, digital divides continue to impede this vision. Many rural and underserved urban areas lack the foundational infrastructure such as stable broadband and electricity that is essential for accessing VR-based learning, AI-enabled assessments, or hybrid work environments. Moreover, device affordability remains a critical barrier; high costs associated with extended reality (XR) headsets, AI learning subscriptions, and compatible hardware often make them inaccessible to marginalized populations (World Bank, 2021).

These structural limitations are further exacerbated by intersectional inequities. Gender, disability, language diversity, and neurodivergence create layered challenges for participation in technologically mediated talent ecosystems. For instance, PwC's 2021 global digital upskilling initiative reported that women in South Asia had 37% less access to AI tools compared to men. This disparity was attributed not only to economic constraints but also to mobility restrictions, cultural expectations, and lower rates of device ownership (PwC, 2022). Such insights underscore that inclusion is not just a matter of infrastructure but also of sociocultural context.

To advance digital justice, organizations and governments must adopt proactive strategies. First, universal design principles should guide the development of XR and AI interfaces, ensuring accessibility for users with visual, auditory, cognitive, or physical impairments. Second, public-private partnerships are essential to fund the establishment of digital learning hubs, particularly in remote or economically disadvantaged regions. These hubs can serve as community anchors for digital skilling, career counseling, and remote employment. Lastly, AI-driven content must be culturally and linguistically inclusive, with adaptive learning models that accommodate local languages, idioms, and educational traditions. Through such interventions, the intelligent talent economy can evolve not only as a driver of innovation but also as a vehicle for equity, empowerment, and inclusive growth.

6.3 Organizational Change and Leadership Readiness

While infrastructure and technology adoption are critical, the greatest barrier to digital transformation often lies within organizational culture. Without supportive leadership and coherent change management, AI integration in talent systems can result in fragmented efforts and employee disengagement. A primary concern is technophobia the fear among employees that AI will replace jobs or introduce intrusive surveillance. Compounding this is a worrying digital illiteracy at the executive level; many senior HR leaders and decision-makers lack the fluency to critically evaluate or ethically implement emerging AI systems. Furthermore, siloed implementation where departments adopt AI tools in isolation—leads to disjointed and inefficient HR ecosystems.

To counter these challenges, several change enablement strategies have emerged. First, conducting AI readiness audits helps assess the maturity of digital infrastructure, staff capabilities, and leadership alignment. Second, micro credential programs in areas such as HR analytics, AI ethics, and immersive learning design empower professionals to upskill rapidly. Lastly, empathy-driven design approaches, which involve employees in the selection and customization of AI tools, enhance both trust and usability.

Table 12. HR capability matrix for AI-driven transformation

Capability Domain	Beginner	Intermediate	Advanced
AI Fluency	Understands basic concepts	Applied tools for hiring/ training	Designs ethical AI workflows
XR Adoption	Knows examples	Participates in immersive sessions	Facilitates VR/AR-based learning
Ethics Governance	Knows GDPR basics	Audits third-party vendors	Leads internal ethics boards

6.4 Algorithmic Impact on Psychological Well-being

As smart talent ecosystems increasingly depend on AI-generated feedback loops, biometric monitoring, and performance analytics, psychological well-being emerges as a critical concern. Employees may feel constantly monitored, resulting in a hyper-evaluation culture where predictive performance scores and sentiment analysis provoke anxiety and reduce morale. Furthermore, the reduction in human interaction, due to over-reliance on digital avatars, chatbots, and AI tutors, may erode social connection, especially in hybrid and remote setups. Cognitive overload, particularly in immersive XR environments, can exacerbate stress levels and fatigue, especially among neurodiverse individuals.

A meta-review by Slater and Sanchez-Vives (2022) warns that prolonged exposure to VR training platforms without appropriate safeguards may lead to derealization and sensory fatigue in novice users. These psychological stressors necessitate the inclusion of mental health safeguards, such as downtime protocols, opt-out mechanisms, and embedded wellness prompts within digital learning environments.

6.5 Ethical Governance and Sustainable Implementation

Long-term success in AI-powered talent systems requires more than technical prowess. It demands robust, multi-level ethical governance that ensures legal compliance, operational transparency, and social responsibility. The Multi-Level Ethical Governance Framework (Figure 5) illustrates how organizations can layer their safeguards across four tiers:

Figure 5. Multi-level ethical governance framework

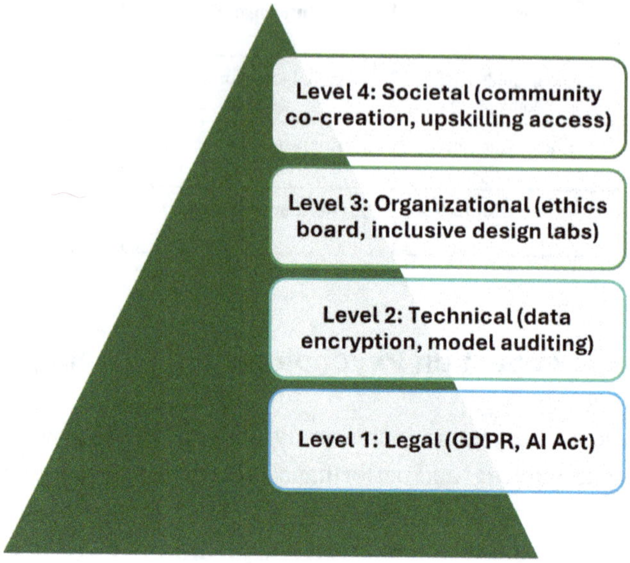

Level 1: Legal Compliance – Adhering to regulations such as the GDPR, India's DPDP Act (2023), and the upcoming EU AI Act.

Level 2: Technical Safeguards – Implementing model explainability, encryption protocols, and bias detection algorithms.

Level 3: Organizational Ethics – Establishing internal ethics boards and inclusive design labs.

Level 4: Societal Integration – Involving communities in upskilling programs and co-creating accessible platforms.

To support this, institutions can deploy tools such as AI ethics boards, composed of cross-functional teams that review HR AI initiatives; impact assessment protocols, like the EU's AI Assessment Toolkit; and ethical procurement frameworks to ensure vendors meet strict criteria for fairness, accessibility, and privacy.

6.6 Conclusion: Toward a Just and Human-Centered Talent Future

In the AI age, ethical leadership is not optional it is foundational. Talent systems that are equitable, transparent, and emotionally intelligent are not only more effective but also more trusted and sustainable. A human-centered approach to algorithmic decision-making, one that respects autonomy, diversity, and mental well-being, will define the next generation of workforce innovation.

Final Insight: The future of work must not be engineered solely by software developers or business strategists it must be co-authored by ethicists, educators, behavioral scientists, technologists, and the very individuals the systems are designed to serve. Only then can we build a truly inclusive, resilient, and regenerative AI-powered talent ecosystem.

7. FUTURE HORIZONS: TOWARD THE HUMAN-AI COLLABORATIVE WORKFORCE

As the digital economy matures, the future of talent systems will be defined by how seamlessly humans and AI systems collaborate in shaping work, learning, and innovation. The shift is not merely technological but paradigmatic transforming talent from being passive recipients of automation to co-creators in a dynamic, responsive, and intelligence-augmented ecosystem.

Emerging technologies such as Explainable AI (XAI), autonomous talent agents, digital twins, and decentralized talent platforms are setting the stage for the next generation of human-machine synergy. This section explores these transformative innovations, their practical implications for workforce development, and the associated research and governance frontiers.

7.1 Explainable AI (XAI): Building Transparent and Trustworthy Talent Systems

With increasing reliance on AI for hiring, learning path suggestions, and performance evaluation, the black-box nature of most AI models raises ethical and practical concerns. Explainable AI (XAI) aims to address these issues by providing transparent, interpretable insights into AI decisions.

Key Functions of XAI in Talent Management:

- Transparency in Recruitment: Candidates can understand how their skills matched job roles.
- Trust in Performance Reviews: Justifications for ratings and feedback from AI engines reduce disputes and bias claims.
- Learning Personalization: Employees can view the logic behind learning recommendations, increasing motivation and self-efficacy.

Table 13. XAI use cases across talent lifecycle

Talent Function	XAI Application	Strategic Benefit
Recruitment	Candidate matching explanations	Improves fairness and candidate trust
Performance management	Justified scoring models	Enhances transparency and morale
Learning & Development	Personalized learning paths	Drives self-directed upskilling
Career mobility	Transparent promotion criteria	Supports DEI and retention

Academic Insight: According to Arrieta et al. (2020), XAI can "foster accountability in automated systems, especially in socially sensitive domains like hiring and talent development."

7.2 Autonomous Talent Systems: Toward Self-Evolving HR Architectures

Autonomous Talent Systems (ATS) represent a shift from static, rules-based platforms to AI-driven, self-learning environments that proactively manage learning, engagement, and career progression. These systems integrate behavioral data, performance metrics, and career goals to recommend development activities or interventions autonomously.

Core Features:

- AI Learning Coaches: Adaptive tutors that track learning outcomes and recommend adjustments.
- Emotional AI Engines: Detect mood, fatigue, or disengagement and trigger wellness nudges.
- Career Navigation Bots: Suggest skill gaps and job moves aligned with market trends.

Case Snapshot: Cognizant's use of AI agents to autonomously assign learning tasks based on real-time project feedback resulted in 30% higher skill alignment and 25% faster project ramp-up time (Cognizant, 2022).

7.3 Digital Twins of Employees: Simulating Performance, Predicting Potential

The digital twin concept, popularized in industrial IoT, is now gaining traction in HR. A digital twin of an employee is a real-time, data-driven model that simulates an individual's skills, preferences, career trajectory, and even behavioral patterns.

These are powered by continuous feedback loops from learning systems, performance dashboards, and biometric/behavioral analytics.

Use Cases in Talent Development:

- Real-time Simulation: Test responses to stress, collaboration styles, and project complexity.
- Succession Forecasting: Identify future leaders through simulated role rotations.
- Learning ROI Measurement: Evaluate how upskilling impacts project delivery in twin scenarios.

Table 14. Digital twin applications in HR

Area	Twin Application	Outcome Measured
Learning & Upskilling	Simulated learning path outcomes	Skill gap reduction, time-to-competence
Workforce Planning	Project-team simulations	Productivity, team compatibility
Leadership Development	Behavioral modeling under pressure	Succession readiness, adaptability

Academic Reference: Glaessgen & Stargel (2012) argue that digital twins will become "the backbone of predictive decision-making in human-centric systems."

7.4 Emerging Research Areas and Breakthrough Frontiers

To sustain a human-AI collaborative workforce, research must move beyond conventional models into neuro-cognitive interfaces, distributed intelligence, and decentralized governance. Three promising frontiers are emerging:

a) NeuroAnalytics in AI-HR Interfaces

NeuroAnalytics uses brain-computer interfaces (BCIs) to collect data on focus, fatigue, and emotional states during work or learning. Combined with AI, it enables hyper-personalized adaptive learning systems.

- Application: Dynamic course adjustment based on cognitive load signals.
- Challenge: Balancing personalization with neural data privacy (Singh & Rao, 2021).

b) Multi-Agent Systems and Swarm Intelligence

In these systems, multiple AI agents collaborate autonomously to manage dynamic HR functions such as scheduling, team formation, and predictive modeling.

- Use Case: Real-time, adaptive workforce scheduling in retail or manufacturing.
- Advantage: Scalability and rapid response to contextual changes.

c) Decentralized Talent Marketplaces

Blockchain and decentralized AI allow for trustless, global gig ecosystems where credentials are verifiable and jobs are matched autonomously.

- Examples: Braintrust, TalentDAO, and Ethlance.
- Implication: Disrupts traditional corporate hiring models and empowers individual workers.

Table 15. Emerging technologies and their talent impact

Technology	Description	Talent Development Impact
NeuroAnalytics	AI + cognitive data	Adaptive, emotion-aware learning
Swarm Intelligence	Distributed HR planning agents	Dynamic scheduling, scalable modeling
Decentralized AI Markets	Blockchain + autonomous matching	Transparent, inclusive work opportunities

7.5 Toward Human-AI Synergy: A Vision for 2030

The workforce of 2030 will be characterized by fluid, adaptive, AI-enhanced roles. Employees will engage with intelligent systems not as tools but as collaborators, co-evolving in a workplace defined by creativity, trust, and continuous learning.

Strategic Roadmap for Institutions:

- Invest in AI Literacy and Fluency: Equip talent with critical understanding, not just usage.
- Design for Human-AI Trust: Embed explainability and choice into every interaction.
- Create Hybrid Talent Architectures: Combine digital twins, autonomous agents, and immersive learning in unified platforms.
- Foster Innovation Ecosystems: Collaborate with startups, academia, and government for ethical AI R&D.

8. CONCLUSION: REIMAGINING HUMAN CAPITAL FOR THE AI ERA

The convergence of artificial intelligence (AI), immersive technologies, and intelligent infrastructure marks a paradigm shift in human capital development. Rather than merely automating workflows or digitizing training modules, forward-thinking organizations are leveraging these technologies to redefine the very nature of talent, its acquisition, growth, and value creation potential.

In this chapter, we have explored the transformative role of AI-driven people analytics, metaverse-enabled learning environments, and AI-integrated infrastructure finance. These pillars form the blueprint of a new talent ecosystem that is intelligent, inclusive, immersive, and sustainable.

This concluding section synthesizes key insights, proposes a strategic reimagination of human capital, and outlines a future-ready framework for talent leaders, policymakers, and educators.

8.1 From Automation to Augmentation to Co-Creation

The trajectory of technological evolution in workforce management has moved from automation (replacing tasks) to augmentation (enhancing decisions), and now toward co-creation where humans and AI collaborate dynamically.

Table 16. Evolution of AI-Human Capital Synergy

Era	Focus	Talent Role	AI Role
Automation	Efficiency & Replacement	Passive Executor	Task Automator
Augmentation	Decision Support	Enhanced Decision-Maker	Analytical Assistant
Co-Creation	Innovation & Empowerment	Active Collaborator	Strategic Learning Partner

The shift toward co-creative ecosystems signals a more profound relationship between humans and machines where AI becomes a catalyst for human flourishing, not a substitute.

8.2 The Integrated Talent Framework: Toward a Regenerative Workforce

To thrive in the AI era, organizations must move from fragmented initiatives to integrated, multi-dimensional talent strategies that align people, platforms, and physical environments. This alignment must be regenerative constantly evolving to meet the needs of future work and workers.

Key Characteristics of a Regenerative Talent Ecosystem:

- Scalable: Adaptive to global, remote, and hybrid workforces.
- Equitable: Designed for inclusivity across gender, ability, and geography.
- Predictive: Anticipates skills, roles, and labor shifts through analytics.
- Human-Centered: Preserves autonomy, agency, and well-being.

Table 17. Strategic levers for AI-era talent transformation

Lever	Description	Outcome
People Analytics	Real-time behavioral & performance insights	Precision learning and workforce planning
Immersive Learning	VR/AR/XR-enabled virtual experiences	High engagement and retention
Digital Infrastructure	Smart campuses and AI-linked physical spaces	Scalable talent development hubs
Governance & Ethics	XAI, DEI strategies, ethical AI use	Trust and transparency

8.3 Humanizing the Future: Prioritizing Empathy, Inclusion, and Purpose

AI's capacity to learn, predict, and scale is unparalleled—but it lacks inherently human attributes such as empathy, judgment, and values. Therefore, a truly successful AI-HR strategy must embed humanistic values into its core. This requires:

- AI Literacy at All Levels: Equip all workers—from executives to entry-level—with the tools to understand, challenge, and co-create with AI.
- Ethical Design Thinking: Include diverse voices in the creation of AI systems that influence people's lives.
- Inclusive Access Models: Ensure that marginalized populations are not excluded from AI-enabled learning and career mobility.

Academic Insight: Zuboff (2019) emphasizes that "as surveillance capitalism grows, so does the urgency for human-centric AI policies that protect autonomy and dignity."

8.4 Roadmap for Future-Ready Talent Systems

To turn this vision into reality, organizations and policymakers must collaborate to build an AI-enabled, human-centered talent architecture.

Figure 6. AI-enabled talent development roadmap

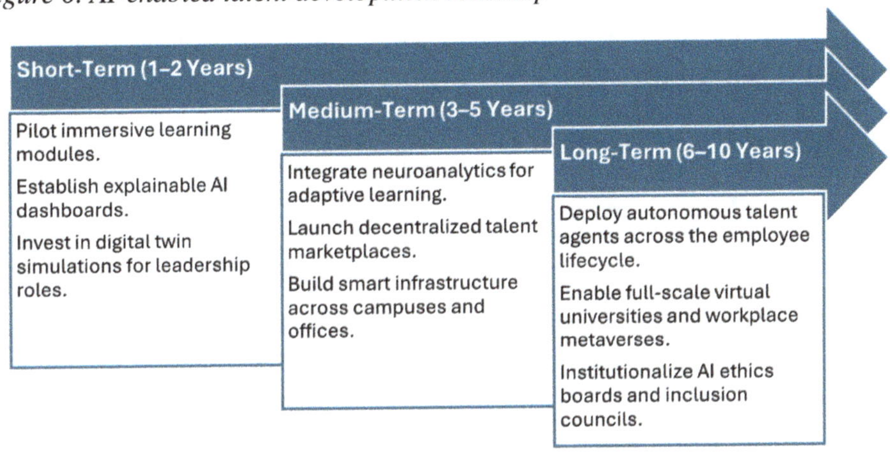

8.5 Final Reflections: Talent in the Age of Intelligent Co-Evolution

In the coming decades, organizations will not compete on technology alone but on their ability to elevate human potential through intelligent augmentation. The future of talent is not about replacing people it's about reimagining what people can become with AI as an ally.

If thoughtfully designed and inclusively implemented, AI-powered talent ecosystems can unlock not just economic value but also a deeper social contract one where learning is lifelong, work is meaningful, and success is shared.

REFERENCES

Accenture. (2023). *The Nth Floor Virtual Workplace*. Retrieved from https://www.accenture.com

Arrieta, A. B., Díaz-Rodríguez, N., Del Ser, J., Bennetot, A., Tabik, S., Barbado, A., & Herrera, F. (2020). Explainable Artificial Intelligence (XAI): Concepts, taxonomies, opportunities and challenges toward responsible AI. *Information Fusion, 58*, 82–115. DOI: 10.1016/j.inffus.2019.12.012

Bailenson, J. (2018). *Experience on demand: What virtual reality is, how it works, and what it can do*. WW Norton & Company.

Barney, J. (1991). Firm resources and sustained competitive advantage. *Journal of Management, 17*(1), 99–120. DOI: 10.1177/014920639101700108

Becker, G. S. (1994). Human capital revisited. In *Human capital: A theoretical and empirical analysis with special reference to education* (3rd ed., pp. 15–28). The University of Chicago Press.

Bogen, M., & Rieke, A. (2018). Help wanted: An examination of hiring algorithms, equity, and bias. *Upturn*, (December), 7.

Brynjolfsson, E., & McAfee, A. (2014). *The second machine age: Work, progress, and prosperity in a time of brilliant technologies*. WW Norton & company.

Chattopadhyay, S., Mishra, D., & Sharma, R. (2023). AI-powered recruitment and organizational agility: Empirical insights from global firms. *Journal of Strategic Human Resource Management, 12*(3), 245–260.

Cognizant. (2022). Reimagining talent development with autonomous AI systems. *Cognizant Digital Pulse*.

Deloitte. (2022). *Global Human Capital Trends 2022: The rise of the boundaryless workforce*.

Deloitte Insights. (2023). *People analytics: Driving real-time, high-impact workforce decisions*.

Dwivedi, Y. K., Hughes, D. L., Coombs, C., Constantiou, I., Duan, Y., Edwards, J. S., & Williams, M. D. (2022). Metaverse: An emerging challenge for modern organizations. *International Journal of Information Management, 66*, 102542. DOI: 10.1016/j.ijinfomgt.2022.102542

Glaessgen, E., & Stargel, D. (2012). The digital twin paradigm for future NASA and U.S. Air Force vehicles. *53rd AIAA/ASME/ASCE/AHS/ASC Structures, Structural Dynamics and Materials Conference*, 1818.

KPMG. (2022). *Reimagining learning in the metaverse.* Retrieved from https://kpmg.com

Levenson, A. (2018). *Strategic analytics: Advancing strategy execution and organizational effectiveness.* Berrett-Koehler Publishers.

Margherita, A., & Braccini, A. M. (2020). Reshaping agile work through digital transformation: A framework for people analytics and human resource management. *Journal of Business Research, 123*, 292–303.

PwC. (2021). *AI in Talent Development: Futureproofing the Workforce.*

PwC. (2022). *Upskilling for a digital world: Bridging the gender and skills divide.* https://www.pwc.com/genderdigitaldivide

PwC. (2023). *Smart Infrastructure for the Workforce of the Future.* https://www.pwc.com

Rahwan, I., Cebrian, M., Obradovich, N., Bongard, J., Bonnefon, J.-F., Breazeal, C., & Lazer, D. (2019). Machine behaviour. *Nature, 568*(7753), 477–486. DOI: 10.1038/s41586-019-1138-y PMID: 31019318

Raji, I. D., Smart, A., White, R., & Mitchell, M. (2020). Closing the AI Accountability Gap: Defining an End-to-End Framework for Internal Algorithmic Auditing. *FAT 2020.*

Singh, R., & Rao, S. (2021). Cognitive computing and neuroanalytics in adaptive learning systems. *IEEE Access : Practical Innovations, Open Solutions, 9*, 47763–47775. DOI: 10.1109/ACCESS.2021.3068614

SkillsFuture Singapore. (2023). *Annual Report on Skills Development Infrastructure.* https://www.skillsfuture.gov.sg

Slater, M., & Sanchez-Vives, M. V. (2022). Enhancing our lives with immersive virtual reality. *Frontiers in Robotics and AI, 3*, 74. DOI: 10.3389/frobt.2016.00074

Social Finance. (2020). *The Case for Social Impact Bonds in Education and Employment.* https://www.socialfinance.org.uk

Tan, J., & Goh, L. (2022). SkillsFuture and smart infrastructure planning: Singapore's roadmap to workforce sustainability. *Asian Education and Development Studies, 11*(2), 178–195.

World Bank. (2021). *Human Capital Investment and Infrastructure Development: A Global Perspective*.

World Economic Forum. (2023). *The Future of Jobs Report 2023*. https://www.weforum.org/reports/the-future-of-jobs-report-2023/

Zhao, X., Liu, Y., & Wu, S. (2021). Immersive empathy in DEI training: Insights from virtual simulations. *Computers in Human Behavior, 124*, 106939.

Zuboff, S. (2019). *The age of surveillance capitalism: The fight for a human future at the new frontier of power*. PublicAffairs.

Chapter 11
HR Challenges and Opportunities in Tourism and Hospitality With AI and Automation

Yasir Ansari
http://orcid.org/0009-0007-2277-8154
Department of Culture, Tourism, Antiquities, and Archive, Pakistan

Remi Thomas
http://orcid.org/0000-0002-4003-9941
Vishwakarma University, Pune, India

Munir Ahmad
http://orcid.org/0000-0003-4836-6151
Survey of Pakistan, Pakistan

EXECUTIVE SUMMARY

The integration of automation and artificial intelligence (AI) into the tourism and hospitality sector marks a transformative shift in Human Resource (HR) management. This chapter examines how AI redefines traditional HR roles—streamlining recruitment, onboarding, training, and workforce planning—while simultaneously challenging long-standing organizational norms. Yet, amid technological disruption, the core mission of HR remains unchanged: to cultivate human potential, foster purpose-driven work environments, and uphold the people-centered values of hospitality. The chapter argues that to fully harness AI's potential, organizations must adopt a strategic and ethical approach, including comprehensive reskilling programs, inclusive digital tools, and algorithmic governance that ensures fairness

DOI: 10.4018/979-8-3373-3867-5.ch011

and transparency. Emphasizing the critical balance between efficiency and empathy, it highlights the irreplaceable value of emotional intelligence, cultural sensitivity, and human connection in guest-facing services.

INTRODUCTION

A tectonic shift is being experienced in the tourism and hospitality sector, and this is as a result of the increasing use of Artificial Intelligence (AI) and automation technologies. Whether through AI-driven concierge assistance and check-in processes or proactive prediction planning in labor scheduling or via customer relationship chatbots, digital technologies are transforming service delivery to customers as well as how businesses are operated. These changes in technologies are not just upgrading operations, but rather they are essentially transforming the way work is performed, job definition, and also giving a blow to human resource (HR) management (Al-Romeedy, 2024; El Hajal & Yeoman, 2024; Ercik & Kardaş, 2024).

The key question in the middle of this transition is how can HR departments meet and lead in a time of intelligent machines? The functions of automation assume more and more routine tasks and decision-making processes, so the responsibility of HR professionals is not only to eliminate the disruptive impact of automation on workforce productivity but also to utilize the potential of AI in generating strategic value. These twin roles of HR mean that it is more than ever at the center of defining the future of the industry.

On the one hand, the growing levels of automation cause serious questions to arise the loss of low-skill workers, the creation of new skill shortages, moral clarity in algorithmic hiring, and a paranoia of job security. However, the same technologies can be used to obtain effective measures to simplify the recruitment process, develop customized training packages, and pre-determine staff requirements, as well as to create a more entertaining and information-driven workplace. It is not so much about countering these changes, but about being tactical in adapting to these changes (Dwivedi et al., 2024; Jabeen et al., 2022; Olak, 2023).

This chapter takes a two-lens view of this changing landscape, both complaining of the threats AI and automation pose to the HR role, and discussing the revolutionary possibilities that the technologies provide to visionary organizations. It reiterates the need to have proactive HR approaches that not only integrate the human capital with the new technological paradigms but also avoid the dehumanizing effects of automation that still need a human touch in service-oriented industries such as tourism and hospitality.

AI-INDUCED HR CHALLENGES IN THE TOURISM AND HOSPITALITY INDUSTRY

Artificial Intelligence (AI) and automation in the tourism and hospitality industry raise numerous multifaceted human resource issues. Such difficulties are even more acute within a sphere that has always been based on the interaction between people, emotional work, and customization of services. Whereas technology is expected to bring higher efficiency and innovativeness, rapid implementation leads to the speed of technologies being faster than the preparedness of organizations and the workforce. The topics covered in this section include the main HR-related issues that are raised by AI and automation, discussed in terms of both structural and human aspects of this change.

Workforce Displacement and Job Redefinition

Hospitality and tourism are some of the areas where generative AI and automation technologies are fast changing the nature of service delivery, bringing in a wave of disruption and change in different job groups. Owing to the nature of their work, some of the most observable and instant effects include displacement of the workforce and specifically to the frontline workers or entry-level employees whose work is repetitive, mimics, or can be quickly coded (Chhibber et al., 2025; Khan, 2024).

Job Categories Most at Risk

The impact of generative AI and automation in all aspects of the hospitality and tourism industry has greatly compounded the likelihood of the replacement of frontline and entry-level employees. The positions of receptionists, bellhops, housekeepers, reservation agents, call center operators, and waiters are the most vulnerable, as most of their work may be characterized by routine repetitiveness, which is easy to automate. Raising to the occasion, hotels are also using self-check-in kiosks, robotic concierges that can handle guest requests, and AI chatbots that can cater to customer inquiries at any time of the day. Although the technologies increase efficiency, decrease the number of operations, and cut down on expenses, they, at the same time, decrease the level of human-hours needed, endangering the positions of thousands of workers. As a way of curbing this risk, organizations should be able to act proactively by singling out jobs most susceptible to automation and intervening in advance, by offering upscaling allowances in terms of training. Risk-exposed workers need to be the target audience of reskilling activities around digital literacy and simple AI interaction so that they can become new professional support personnel in AI-enhanced settings. Table 1 provides some of the most open frontline jobs (as well as entry-level to some extent) in hospitality that are at high risk of being automated by AI or even being augmented with AI.

Table 1. Frontline roles most susceptible to AI displacement

Job Role	AI/Automation Tool Replacement	Level of Risk	Example Technology
Receptionist	Self-service kiosks, chatbots	High	Mobile check-in kiosks
Call Center Agent	AI call handling systems	High	NLP-based voice bots
Housekeeper	Robotic cleaning devices	Moderate	Autonomous vacuum robots
Waitstaff	AI-enabled ordering tablets	High	QR code menus with AI logic
Bellhop	Delivery robots	Moderate	Autonomous concierge robots

Redefining Human Roles in a Tech-Augmented Environment

It is not only AI adoption that replaces jobs--it changes them. Quite a number of jobs are being redesigned such that they combine man and machine supervision. Conventional job descriptions are also being transformed into hybrid roles where employees will be expected to work with AI systems, to keep track of automation processes, and to handle exceptions to a working process or the special needs of customers. As an example, instead of simply greeting the visitors, front desk agents should now resolve kiosk glitches, decode AI-powered guest behaviors, or schedule service robots. This transformation requires new capabilities, including skills to maneuver digital systems, analyze real-time information, and communicate flawlessly with machines as well as people. Businesses should support this change by inculcating continuous learning in the workplace. Providing in-house education on AI tools, establishing cross-collaborative problem-solving teams, and promoting online experimentation would help employees adjust to their positions rather than being subsumed by the task. Stitching these learning opportunities into everyday activities will create some casualization of hybrid processes and create workforce agility over time.

Unequal Readiness and Workforce Polarization

The fast-changing nature of jobs has revealed the chasm between labor preparations. Most of the hospitality employees, especially lowly educated individuals, older workers, or workers in the economically disadvantaged areas, find it difficult to cope with the new demands (Ersanlı et al., 2025; Jacobs, 2024). This, unaccompanied by a systematic approach, has led to the polarization of the workforce: the digitally competent will progress, and the rest will be left behind. Such an imbalance results in job insecurity, anti-innovative attitudes, and low staff morale. To tackle this problem, the socially responsible digital transformation is inevitable. Employers are required to evaluate the digital skills shortages within their workforce and provide inclusive learning practices that would support different literacy levels. An example of ease of access to AI literacy is to make it more multilingual in bite-sized microlearning modules and through peer-led mentorship programs. Also, employee engagement in co-designing the process of technology integration can add more adoption as well as enable the staff to determine the changing nature of their job in enhancing the technology integration process to improve the culture of fear to a culture of trust. Figure 1 provides a risk matrix that lets one anticipate how the digital readiness, combined with automation exposure, leads to workforce polarization by determining groups that need to be focused on to be reskilled and taken into account.

Figure 1. Workforce polarization risk matrix

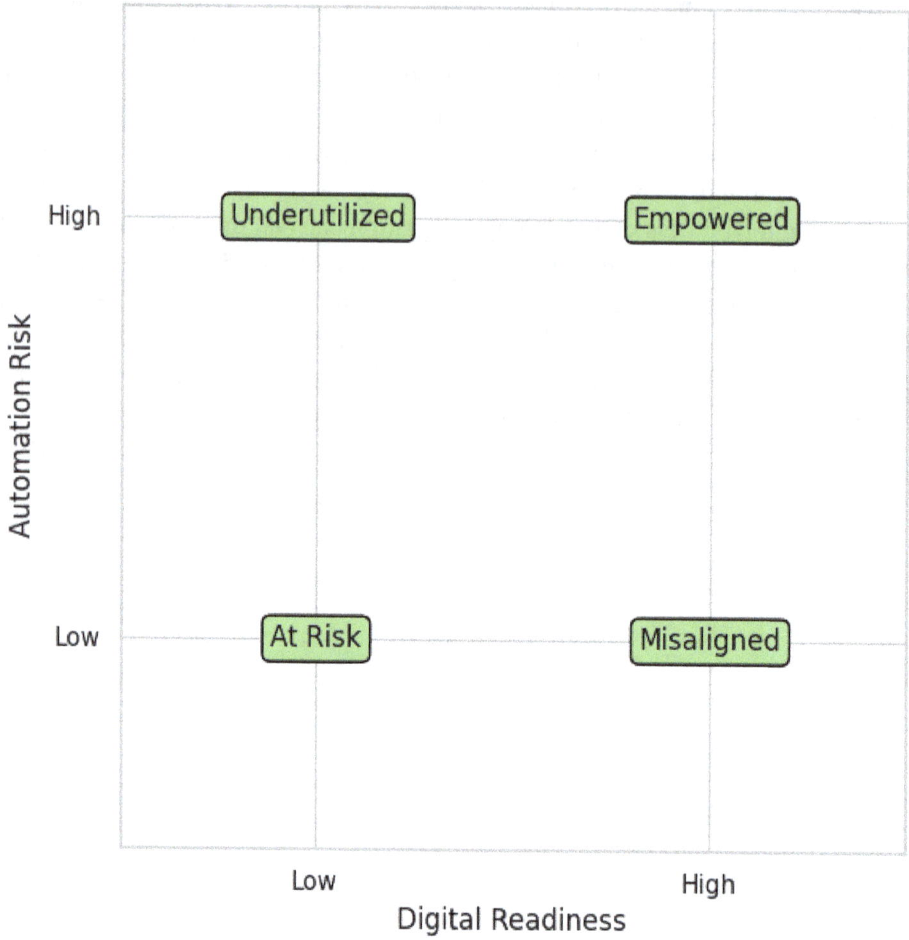

Skill Gaps and Reskilling Imperatives

A new skill environment with an urgent requirement for reskilling and upskilling. With the increasing digitalization of the industry, a demand has been exerted on the workers who are competent in information analytics, digital communication, system management, and collaboration between man and AI (Ersanlı et al., 2025). Nevertheless, long-term investment in employee development has been traditionally practiced less by the hospitality and tourism industry than other industries and markets, and has been heavily dependent on a seasonal labor force and high turnover rates. This underinvestment currently compounds the problem of the skills gap, requiring HR departments with the dilemma of finding new competencies along with a quick development of internal training pipelines.

Emerging Skill Demands in a Digitally Integrated Industry

The growing application of generative AI and automation within the hospitality and tourism sector is completely transforming the skills environment. With the introduction of sophisticated technologies by businesses in the areas of guest services, back-end activities, and decision-making, the need to ensure digital competency is growing at an alarming rate. Areas that require competent new skills include data analytics, AI-supported customer interface, digital communication hub, workflow, and systems management. The workers will also have to find their way in human-AI collaboration: how to control intelligent systems, analyze the results that the machine gives, and how to combine management and make decisions by joining forces with the program. This evolution proposes a threat to the traditional skills and calls for a shift from exclusively task-based capabilities to a mix of technical, cognitive, and soft skills (Hazrat et al., 2023; Rahmat et al., 2022; Tee et al., 2024). Keeping these new demands in mind, organizations need to restructure job descriptions, competency models, and implement the same through the ground-up recruitment, onboarding, and employee development processes. Table 2 provides an overview of the current digital competencies that are imperative to employees in the hospitality industry as these relate to particular AI-enabled workflows in both front and back-end work.

Table 2. Emerging digital competencies for hospitality workers

Competency	Description	Application Example
AI Interaction Literacy	Understanding AI outputs and interfaces	Reading chatbot summaries, using kiosks
Data Interpretation	Analyzing basic performance or feedback metrics	Using dashboards for guest reviews
Workflow Automation Handling	Managing alerts or exceptions in AI workflows	Overseeing housekeeping bots
Ethical Awareness	Recognizing bias, ensuring fair use	Flagging algorithmic anomalies

Underinvestment in Workforce Development

Although there is a continuous demand for digital skills, the hospitality and tourism industry has traditionally been underinvesting in institutionalized employee development. Seasonality, labour practices, high margins, and high turnovers have made the industry focus on short-term and low-cost sensitive staffing (Agyeman-Manu et al., 2023; Mcpake et al., 2023; van de Pas et al., 2023). Consequently, a large number of businesses do not have formal training infrastructure or continued learning approaches. This underspending is already making it harder to bridge the increasing gap in skills, and it is putting even more pressure on the HR departments to find future-ready skills and program expandable and adaptive training pipelines at a fast rate. To counter this, the firms need to make the development of workforce a strategic focus area, but not a cost unit. Creation of internal learning academies, use of e-learning technology, and establishment of partnerships with learning institutions and technology providers can offer a flexible, cost-effective basis of ongoing skill improvement. Furthermore, incorporation of the learning objectives in the performance management systems guarantees that the reskilling initiatives provide the attainment of business objectives and employee development career patterns.

Challenges for Vulnerable Employee Groups

One such devastating dilemma is the inability of most of the employees currently in the workforce to cope with this fast-moving atmosphere, particularly among the older workers, those who have not much formal schooling, or employees lacking much digital literacy. Such populations can easily have a problem adapting to new technologies, together with those whose confidence, fear, or the feeling of novelty and everything they refer to as unfamiliar territory hinders them from making them subject to such avoidance. Otherwise, this risk may compound these disparities and disintegrate the unity within the workforce. Respondent, training programs have to be selectively inclusive and adapted to the multifarious needs of learners. These involve such methods as providing practical, stress-free training spaces, multilingual, de-cluttered learning materials, one-on-one coaching, or peer teaching. It is also recommended that the organizations establish feedback systems through which the employees can present the training difficulties or interests, and the HR teams should consistently improve learning approaches. The idea that each worker with a different background has the opportunity to be on board with the digital future is not only important in terms of equity but also organizational cohesiveness and resilience.

Resistance to Change and Workforce Anxiety

Acceptance of service-industry automation and AI is not merely an issue of being comfortable with new instruments and tools but also indicates stress on transformation, domination, and cultural continuity. With the shift toward digital systems in hospitality, where human interaction is the value, the trend can be seen as a challenge to employee positions and the operation of the guest experience. These emotional reactions are very important to understand and deal with to make this transition successful. (Amin et al., 2025; Sapru, 2025; Suseno et al., 2023; Wang et al., 2024).

Cultural Resistance in Service-Oriented Environments

Resistance to change in technology is an old and deeply buried problem in the hospitality and tourism industry, where personal touch, tradition, and service through experience have always been an important part of the industry. AI and automation can mean the loss of the nature of their work and thus their professional identity to employees who feel proud of the face-to-face interaction with guests or manual problem-solving. This friction on culture tends to erupt in settings under which the practice of the previous age has been firmly established, and the notion of change is regarded as compromising the quality or genuineness of service. In order to overcome this resistance, organizations have to develop an understanding that the values considered as constituents of service culture are taken seriously and respected first. The attitude towards change initiatives must be presented as something other than abandonment of human service, but as a new phase in its development by improving employee capacity and guest experience. Ensuring that the innovative shift is done in line with the industry can be achieved by positioning AI as a supplement but not a substitute in the process. Leadership has to go ahead and reinforce the story of digital transformation constantly by making sure that it is portrayed as a facilitator, a service-enabler, as opposed to a disrupter of the culture.

Technological Anxiety and Fear of Redundancy

Another acute issue is the technological anxiety of the staff. Automation has mistaken many workers because they are afraid that they will become useless or lose their worth in the company. Such fear may result in reluctance to the new tools, passive resistance, or, in worst cases, active disengagement. Notably, the reactions are not irrational and represent the real fears of losing a job, the relevance of some skills, and the rate of the changes presented. Transparency is required to overcome this fear. The HR should explain freely the reason, magnitude, and anticipated effects of the utilization of technology. Uncertainty can be reduced through clear timelines, job transition pathways, and guarantees on retraining possibilities. Furthermore, scheduling more modest incorporation of AI tools by using pilot schemes and engaging personnel in determining phases enables employees to adjust to the new procedure and experience feelings of ownership towards the change process (Frenkenberg & Hochman, 2025; Kim et al., 2025; Zhan et al., 2024). Figure 2 overlays the steps of technology adaptation with the respective emotional reactions that the hospitality workers tend to experience as they are getting used to the new technology, revealing the psychological sides of AI resistance.

Figure 2. Change resistance and emotional stress curve

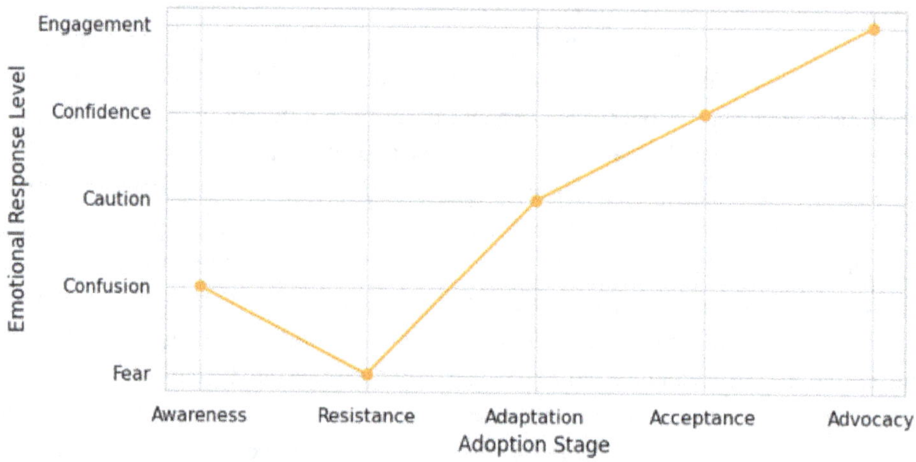

Managing Emotional Impact and Organizational Morale

The effect of swift change, especially when not well managed, may lead to low morale, high turnover, and disengagement in the organization. Employees who feel that they are not involved in decision-making or that some radical changes are thrown at them without any prior knowledge of that rollout will see such a no of respect their input. Even technologically effective initiatives may go wrong in the absence of proper emotional and cultural backing. HR managers will need to deploy well-calculated and sensitive strategies of change management to ensure morale. These must introduce regular consultation forums whereby staff are allowed to present issues, give feedback, and propose alternatives. Psychological safety should be fostered at the top of the list, which means that employees should feel the value of their opinions and understanding. Categories of recognition, such as recognition of employee adaptability with the visibility and support of the leadership, assist in the reinforcement of the culture of trust. Once individuals are made to feel involved in the process of change and valued as people who can improve, resistance becomes less rigid, and a group can become more resilient.

Ethical Dilemmas and Algorithmic Bias

Increasing use of AI in recruitment and workforce planning is necessarily accompanied by the urgent questions of concealed discrimination and ethical regulation. These systems have the potential to breed inequality when handled without proper attention, and can cause legal and reputational compensations to organizations (Baeza-Yates, 2022; Kerasidou, 2021; Kharitonova et al., 2021).

Hidden Bias in AI-Driven HR Decisions

Rapid developments in the application of AI to human resource activities, especially to recruitment, performance scoring, and workforce analytics, have opened up a set of ethical questions. Although such tools are said to be efficient and objective, they tend to acquire the pre-existing discrimination that exists in the training data. As an example, AI-based applicant screening tools can copy the profiles of individuals who have been traditionally successful in hiring, which introduces bias in favor of certain demographics, educational experiences, or communication types by accident. This may lead to non-selection of meritorious candidates due to their race, gender, socioeconomic background, or the lack of mainstream career field experience- this may be without doing any deliberate act of discrimination. To respond to this, the HR teams should consider a critical view towards the implementation of AI solutions; i.e., training datasets should be diverse and periodically checked, as well as contextually adequate for inclusive employment. It is also necessary to partner with AI vendors in order to insist on knowing how models behave and what their limitations are to eliminate bias at its source. Table 3 summarizes some of the most frequent ethical risks related to AI use in HR, such as algorithmic bias, the lack of legal transparency, and others, and suggests some mitigation strategies that could be applied to address them.

Table 3. Ethical risks in AI-driven HR tools

Risk Area	Example	Mitigation Strategy
Algorithmic Bias	Favoring certain demographics	Diverse training data, periodic audits
Lack of Transparency	Black-box models in hiring	Use explainable AI, vendor documentation
Legal Accountability	Inability to justify rejections	Human-in-the-loop validation
Exclusion of Marginalized	Tools are not accessible to all users	Inclusive design, multilingual access

The Opacity of Algorithmic Decision-Making

The other significant issue is the absence of transparency, commonly known as the black box problem, of most commercial AI tools applied in HR processes. Such tools often generate complex decisions that fail to give an explicit description of the ways and reasons that a decision was made. This secrecy destroys accountability, makes appeals tasks difficult, and leaves HR professionals in a vulnerable situation when interviewed by candidates, employees, or regulators. Of further concern, the failure to trace the logic of the algorithm once floor violations or prejudicial consequences arise can expose companies to lawsuits and damages to their reputation. The way to sail through this is by making sure that the HR department is proactive dealing with examining the level of explainability and auditability of AI systems before making it operational. To build trust and safeguard the soundness of organizations, it is better to keep to clear and understandable models, put in place a review system, as well as to establish data governance procedures.

Ethical Governance and Inclusive Oversight

Technical queries about the ethical use of AI in HR are not sufficient to determine the answers; instead, it is a governance-related problem and must be managed as such over a long-term period and cross-departmentally. HR leaders should be at the forefront of establishing fairness, equity, and compliant algorithms as they actively define career paths and livelihoods of people. This includes not only the adoption of tools, but administration of the procurement standards, questioning vendor boasts, and setting up of ethical review or advisory boards. Furthermore, continuous education of HR staff on digital ethics and AI literacy is of importance to establish an in-house capacity for responsible implementation. Integrating fairness validation, bias review, and the principles of inclusive design in all the stages of the AI life cycle will guarantee that technology supports but not damages, the values of a human-focused workforce management approach.

Organizational Readiness and Structural Pressures

AI deployment not only depends on technology, however, but also on the ability of a company to integrate it structurally. Internal challenges are quite high in many firms, particularly the SMEs, which make it difficult to adopt fast and in a sustainable manner (Felemban et al., 2024; Hossain et al., 2024; Jöhnk et al., 2021).

Digital Maturity and Strategic Alignment Gaps

The successful entry of AI technologies into the tourism and hospitality industry is not only about purchasing instruments; this is an issue of the digital maturity of an organization and its potential to pair the adoption of AI with its strategic objectives. This is, however, not the case with many businesses, especially those that are either small or medium-sized enterprises (SMEs). The absence of underlying digital infrastructure, the poor leadership commitment, and a lack of interdepartmental cooperation usually led to piecemeal or paralyzed implementation processes. Lack of a common understanding and a company-wide plan when it comes to the adoption of AI can leave initiatives remote in each department or governed into one-off pilot projects. In overcoming this, the leadership needs to resolve to take digital transformation as an enterprise-level priority. These are creating an end-to-end AI strategy that engages the HR, IT, operations, and customer service teams early on, as well as investing in stretchable and scalable infrastructure and governance systems to accommodate the steady growth of innovation.

HR Marginalization and Budget Constraints

The HR departments do not always have the budgets or organizational clout necessary to help guide strategic technological choices, yet they are at the forefront of having to manage the impact of AI on the workforce. HR has been left to do the work of implementation or support in most instances rather than participating in the initial stages of planning. Such marginalization constrains HR to foresee the workforce implications, streamline training demands with the changing job profiles, and influence ethical and inclusive usage of technology. To solve this, the HR leaders should be enabled as strategic entities in digital transformation. One of the first things needed to make sure that the human dimension of AI is taken care of is to move HR up in the chain and have them contribute to technology planning, working on vendor selection and technology deployment roadmaps, and having their own special budgets to train the digital skills and change management.

Fragmentation and Reactive Transformation

The incorporation of AI in organizations that are not digitally ready can usually result in reactionary and isolated work. HR departments are directly in the middle of mismatched training programs, outdated programs, and nothing but disjointed experimentation with AI tools on a per-department level. This balkanization harms all the possible advantages of AI, and it raises tremendous confusion among people working on it, along with inefficiencies in implementation. Instead of making the strategic transformation of the workforce a reality, AI joins the list of disruptive novelties. The best way that businesses can avoid such is to come up with strategic plans of transformation; they should have well-defined objectives, schedules, and indicators of success. Disparate talent management systems can be enhanced to include AI functionality, training plans that respond immediately to the changes occurring in the job roles, and cross-departmental collaboration allow ensure that digital adoption is consistent and can be extended across the organization.

To summarize, although AI and automation have prospective benefits on tourism and hospitality in the long term, they present a convoluted intersection of HR problems that can no longer be overlooked. There are strong relationships between the above issues: job displacement increases the prevalence of skill gaps; skill gaps increase anxiety; anxiety increases resistance; and resistance compromises adoption. This is the landscape where a progressive HR operation is needed that not only has technological prowess but also a sense of compassion, vision, and strong moral ideas.

REINVENTING HR: OPPORTUNITIES WITH THE AI ERA

AI and automation are not only disruptive tools, but they also facilitate strategic reinvention even inside the HR function. The tourism and hospitality sphere, where the success of business is directly dependent on the level of service, flexibility of the workforce, and the efficiency of activities, provides HR managers with numerous ways in which artificial intelligence can revolutionize and modernize the traditional work routine. This micro-course examines five pervasive areas in which AI is creating fresh value for HR: talent acquisition, onboarding, training, workforce analytics, and employee engagement.

AI in Talent Acquisition

The use of Artificial Intelligence (AI) in the talent acquisition processes is fast transforming how organizations in the tourism and hospitality sector attract, screen, and recruit talent. Historically recession-resistant due to its high seasonal, entry-level, and customer-facing workforce, the industry has a long history of high turnover, low and unpredictable quality of service performance, and slow recruitment processes. The current recruitment technologies based on AI are providing the industries with powerful solutions for streamlining these processes and improving the quality of hiring decisions (Alkhawaldeh et al., 2024; Paramita et al., 2024).

The technologies that are used in AI-based talent acquisition include natural language processing (NLP), machine learning (ML), and predictive analytics in order to complete some of the tasks that previously needed high volumes of human resources. The platforms should be able to scan thousands of resumes within a few seconds and determine the candidates who possess experience, skills, and behavioral patterns that are associated with a particular job position. Contrary to traditional keyword-matching approaches, artificial intelligence is capable of capturing meaning and intent, and it can use this to better identify the most promising candidate-job matches using competencies, soft skills, and potential instead of only based on former job titles or degrees.

Practically, AI is already being used by several of the hospitality heavyweights to update their recruitment processes. One of them, the example of Hilton, which has adopted the AI tools to scale up on frontline recruitment. These tools are used to screen automatic job applications, use chatbots to carry out preliminary interviews, provide personality or situational aptitude tests, and then shortlisted candidates are sent to human recruiters. Full automation saves substantial time on the time-to-hire, so the HR teams may prioritize activities with high value, which include the final interviews or candidate engagement tactics.

Also, AI applicant tools have the potential to reduce bias because applicants can be reviewed anonymously and based on a standardized set of indicators. The AI tools have a chance to encourage more fair hiring practices: by removing the labels of name, age, gender, or academic institute, the AI tool will help to encourage a more diverse yet globalized workforce in areas like tourism and hospitality. Nonetheless, this works very well depending on the quality and fairness of the data that was used to train such systems.

Through predictive analytics, AI helps with more strategic workforce planning, too. Based on the labor market ideas, internal turnover files, and success rates observed in hiring candidates, AI could predict the need of the staff and inform the proactive approaches to recruitment. As an example, during busy travel periods, predictive models may help prescribe the appropriate level of hiring to ensure that the hotels, theme parks, or resorts maintain that level of service and, therefore, talent pipelines can be aligned to the operational requirements.

Such advantages of AI-based recruitment notwithstanding, it is not perfect. The issue of algorithmic transparency, data privacy, and the potential to perpetuate systemic biases (in case of an inadequately diverse training dataset) is still a bone of contention. Hence, human control is still important. AI ought to be set up as an augmentation, rather than a replacement for human judgment, in the recruitment process. HR people should be prepared to analyze AI suggestions, verify results, and make sure that ethical principles are maintained when hiring people.

Automating the Onboarding Experience

Onboarding represents a very important stage in the employee lifecycle, which will define the level of engagement and productivity, as well as future retention. Onboarding issues in the tourism and hospitality sector, in which seasonal labour is standard practice, turnover is high, and staff are physically located across large geographies, established onboarding practices commonly lack efficiency and result in negative onboarding experiences and slow ramp-ups. AI is currently emerging as one of the key drivers of simplification, scalability, and individualization of the onboarding process (Selvam et al., 2024).

With the aid of AI, onboarding platforms have conversational agents, smart workflows, and adaptive learning tools to help new hires spend their first few days and weeks without friction. That way, virtual assistants and chatbots may help answer typical questions in real-time, complete forms, arrange orientation sessions, and even train the environment virtually. The round-the-clock commitment to this support does not require the employees to rely on human resources staff, nor does it give them fixed steps to go through the onboarding process but enables them to move through this process themselves, at a pace and time that suits them best the best-cost element in time-sensitive businesses like hotels, cruise lines, or even seasonal resorts.

In addition to administrative automation, AI increases the delivery quality and consistency of the onboarding process. New workers in a chain that has a large number of facilities or dispersed operations usually report to a different site with dissimilar resources and management styles. The AI tools can facilitate the provision of standardized information and brand-consistent messages to every new hire, no matter where he/she is located. Whether it is learning about corporate values or acquiring safety procedures, AI allows for the delivery of critical material uniformly to all units.

Another definite benefit of AI-based onboarding is that of personalization. Using the data about employees, their role, experience, location, and learning style, the smart systems can make onboarding experiences tailored to the specific needs. As an example, a recent employee in Dubai at a concierge can be provided with culturally-relevant modules regarding customer service and legislative training that is region-specific, and a housekeeper in Bali will be more likely to be provided with a visually rich, multilingual content of a lower level of literacy. The result enhances early job satisfaction and confidence, and better learning outcomes.

AI can also be used in the process of onboarding by automating the process of compliance tracking as well as feedback collection. Online checklists, progress dashboards, nudges, sentiment analysis, and periodical surveys make sure that employees pass all the necessary steps promptly and get feedback on the quality of the onboarding process in order to improve it ongoing. Such tools allow HR teams to see the quality of onboarding experiences in real-time and take a proactive step in case it seems that a new employee is disengaged or confused.

The scalability of AI also comes in very handy in high-volume or high-turnover environments, e.g., resort properties in high season. Organizations can also hire dozens or even hundreds of employees at once without overloading the HR departments. Automation makes work consistent and lets human professionals spend more time developing personal relationships and dealing with more complicated onboarding concerns.

But like most digital systems, excessive focus on the automation process has the potential to induce impersonal experiences unless proportionality with the human touchpoints is found. Technology is not designed to substitute human contact in the process of onboarding; hospitality is a people industry, and the onboarding environment should not be dehumanized. Coupled with AI technology, videos welcoming the leadership, virtual meet-and-greets, or assigned human onboarding mentors can all serve to make a person feel a sense of belonging.

Personalized Learning and Training

When the operation is centered on service quality, customer satisfaction, and the ability to change operations expeditiously, it becomes a strategic need as well as a challenge to undertake employee training (Kaswan et al., 2024). Conventional mass training initiatives are not able to yield results in most cases due to the different learning requirements of hospitality employees, particularly in such a workforce where turnover or interlingual diversity, and varying levels of education are high. This is changing with the introduction of AI-based learning and development tools that facilitate hyper-personalized and data-driven learning that can support the personal development of employees and the overall performance of businesses.

The crucial feature of AI-based training is the possibility of examining the data concerning employees, starting with the roles they occupy, proceeding with performance indicators, and passing to the learning behavior and engagement rates, to design personalized learning tracks based on this knowledge. Machine learning not only evaluates the employees' progress during a training module, but it can also spot where they are lagging or doing well and advise them to provide specific content, format, or skill-building exercises to bridge it. Adaptive learning will not overwork its employees with content that does not concern their job, other than making them ill-prepared to tackle their duties even before they are hired.

The top hospitality providers, such as Marriott, are already using AI-founded platforms to construct competency-equitable learning environments. E.g., the front desk agents will be given some training modules that will give them an experience of AI-based roleplays and how to respond to the guest, whereas the back-of-house kitchen workers will be given some training modules in interactive and multilingual, focused on the safety measures. AI allows the provision of such training in bite-sized, context-specific forms: e.g., videos, quizzes, or problem-based homework-like activities that can be some form of gamification as well, based on the preferences and literacy level of that user.

More importantly, learning outcomes in AI systems are also connected with indicators of real-world performance. When these systems incorporate an example with property management systems (PMS), point-of-sale (POS) platform, or customer feedback devices, these systems can correlate training attendance and employment performance. The system encourages salary increases and further recommends identical information to others like him/her in case, after going through a new module in communication, the customer satisfaction rankings of the concierge go up. This is a performance-oriented learning that makes sure L&D investments go straight to the organizational priorities in the form of service excellence, compliance, and guest experience.

Scalability and accessibility can be viewed as another important benefit of an AI-based training. As in the case of a small hotel in a remote location or a multinational chain of resorts with thousands of employees, the AI platform can provide consistent content in training both between the geographies and among languages and devices. This will be highly useful in tourism, where the operation is intercultural and intercontinental; there is a high turnover in the workforce. AI-powered mobile learning applications guarantee that employees have an opportunity to find snack-sized, employee-specific learning in an on-demand mode, either on a break during their shifts or in remote facilities.

On top of that, AI will lead to increased and more constructive employee motivation and career growth by tie-up learning to personal ambitions. Using the available information about career progress or self-evaluations, AI can propose the position that will be in the future and construct a learning path that would allow an employee to advance the position, e.g., from housekeeping to the team leader or supervisor. This not only helps internal movement and retention, but it can also build a culture of persistent self-guided learning.

Nevertheless, to achieve its successful implementation, it is essential to focus on content curation, keep it up-to-date to reflect its relevance, and introduce the means of human control. AI is not meant to take the role of learning and development professionals, but to make them feel more informed and given the automation capabilities to create more strategic and learner-based programs.

Predictive Workforce Analytics

Among the most traditional operational challenges of the very dynamic and service-demanding tourism and hospitality industry is the question of getting the level of staffing to come into a balance with the changing demand. The issue of understaffing may result in excessive waiting during service time, low quality of services, and customer dissatisfaction, and overstaffing results in increasing labor expenses in an already margin-sensitive industry. AI in its predictive form of workforce analytics is assisting HR professional decision makers to make smarter, more data-based staffing decisions to close the gap between workforce availability and business requirements in real-time.

Predictive analytics is defined as using AI algorithms to track potential workforce needs on both a historical and real-time level of data input. These inputs can be found in hospitality contexts, where they can be day sheets, past occupancy, sales reports, reservation patterns, events, festivals, and even external factors like weather conditions or local events listed. An AI can support accurate forecasting of labor demand by observing patterns and relations between those data points and allow the organization to proactively schedule its staff resources as opposed to scheduling them reactively.

To give an example, urban hotels or seasonal resorts may anticipate how many guests will arrive by the hour, by the day, or week using predictive models. The system based on such projections can advise the best staffing levels of the front desk agents, housekeeping staff, food service employees, or concierge. Such a degree of foresight enables the managers to develop more accurate schedules, and they prevent last-minute overtime expenses, or loss of reputation that occurs when the customers wait long to receive service. Predictive scheduling can occur in high foot traffic restaurants when the number of reservations or foot traffic/weather conditions forecasted can help the business maintain the ideal staff-to-guest ratio in order to sustain their service standards during high traffic hours.

Workforce analytics also enables workforce planning to be more strategic due to the use of AI. Through the specific analysis of long-term labor trends, like turnover rate, seasonal activity, and skill supply, HR teams will be able to predict possible staffing shortages at a stage when such shortages are not yet visible. To cite an example, in a situation where statistics show that it is highly probable that there will be a shortage of multilingual tour guides during an impending international event, the system will notify HR well in advance so that they can recruit or undertake in-house training before the event. This assists in the agility and resilience of the workforce in case of external shocks or unknown surges of demand.

Notably, such systems can also include personal employee information to do the scheduling in a manner that enhances employee welfare. Fair and balanced rosters can be established, taking into consideration shift preferences, availability, recent workloads, and labor laws compliance using AI algorithms. This not only increases the satisfaction of the employees, curtails burnout, and contributes to retention within a field prone to the challenges of high turnover.

In addition, predictive analytics may be used to make more general HR and business decisions, including: Training needs forecast, Labor costs budgets, and ROI of staffing strategy. These insights may also contribute to financial planning and resource distribution within the departments or locations when combined with enterprise resource planning (ERP) systems.

The quality of the data and organizational preparedness, however, determine the successful implementation of predictive analytics. Inaccurate predictions may be caused by the use of separate systems, inaccurate data entry, or failing to integrate the different departments. In order to reap the maximum benefits, hospitals have to invest in trustworthy data infrastructure, interdepartmental alignment, and give managers the appropriate skills to analyze and act upon the insights produced by AI.

Enhancing Employee Engagement

The importance of employee engagement in the success of an organization has not been a new thing in the tourism and hospitality industry, where the quality of services at the front desk largely determines the satisfaction of guests and the brand image. Nevertheless, most hospitality jobs are fast-paced, physically and emotionally demanding, which, in many cases, lead to a high level of stress, low morale, and turnover. In this context, organizations are progressively using Artificial Intelligence (AI) as a prescriptive mechanism for keeping track of and improving employee engagement, well-being, and general working experience.

Engagement platforms, which are AI-powered, can analyze and collect huge volumes of electronic information generated by employees through natural language processing (NLP), machine learning, and behavioral analysis. All kinds of feedback elicited through anonymous surveys, internal communication systems, chat transcripts, and social collaboration tools can be measured in real time to identify mood patterns, developing dissatisfactions, and burnout early warnings. This is unlike old HR activities, whereby once every certain duration is over, a review of engagement happens, usually reactively, giving limited, stale information on how employees are doing across teams, departments, and even locations. AI tools allow a constant feedback loop, allowing micro and dynamic understanding of employee emotional state.

In other words, the sentiment analysis tools (which companies such as Hyatt use) will be able to scan through the open-ended questions and responses supplied by the employees, and label the emotional tone, the urgent levels, and frequent concerns. Such observations enable the HR leaders to predict the areas of pain, like managerial conflict, workload imbalance, or no recognition, and thus address them in time. When housekeeping staff start complaining about the length of shifts or unreasonable amounts of work they should be doing, managers can then be informed to make some shifts or reevaluate task assignments, or implement wellness checks before the situation gets even worse.

There is also a new way of ensuring physical or mental well-being that is being made possible by AI, especially in intensive spaces such as kitchens, housekeeping keeping or outdoor tourism businesses. Physical exertion and the extent of stress with recovery time might be tracked by wearable technologies integrated with AI dashboards. An example could be the utilization of smart badges or wristbands that would track the heart rate, the quality of sleep, or even the pattern of breaks to recognize the overworked personnel who can use some assistance. Although the tools are still new and delicate in the privacy context, they can be used to customize wellness interventions and develop shift schedules that are healthier and easier to sustain.

Moreover, AI will be able to tailor engagement plans to specific employee behavioural patterns as well as preferences and incentives. Depending on the use of a learning platform or responsiveness to feedback, or attendance at company events, AI systems may recommend personalized recognition programs, micro-rewards, or development programs. This customized treatment makes the employees feel noticed and appreciated, and so they have a greater emotional attachment to the organization.

The second important use is in eliminating administrative friction, which destroys participation. Virtual HR reps can also offer instant responses to typically asked policy-related or benefits inquiries, assist with leave requests, or recall training deadlines--allowing/releasing HR personnel and enhancing the entire employee experience. Automation of such micro-interactions leads to a less barrier work environment.

Though AI in engagement should be approached with caution. There has to be good information and consultation of employees regarding the collection and use of their data, and privacy should be taken seriously. Transparency of ethical implementation is important to be conducted, involving opt-in elements, anonymization, and a distinct limit on monitoring.

STRATEGIC RESPONSES AND BEST PRACTICES

The only ways through which HR professionals can effectively navigate the highly significant field of AI and automation in tourism and hospitality are to leave the reactive methods behind and embrace proactive and pluralistic, and morally upright strategies. With the role of technology only set to further redefine the job roles, workplace dynamics, as well as the expectations of the employees, HR is also adjusting its role in becoming a strategic orchestrator, shaping the transformation of the workforce with empathy, agility, and vision. This section provides a summary of the main reactions and best response mechanisms that can move the HR departments to take advantage of the power of AI without compromising on human capital and organizational integrity.

Embracing Human-AI Collaboration

Instead of seeing AI as a substitute for human effort, the trend is to devise progressive human resource policies that pioneer a human-AI architecture environment where machines will complement human talents as opposed to replacing them. This strategy embraces the redefinition of job roles so that new skills are added, including supervision of AI tools, analysis of AI-produced insights, and management of human-machine workflow. In a hospitality environment, it might imply educating front-desk attendants to use automated kiosks or even housekeeping supervisors to work with cleaning robots. HR will need to be proactive in rewriting job specs and career lines to capture this cooperative reality and in preparing and enabling employees to be able to use the emerging technologies.

Building Ethical AI Governance

With organizations growing their use of AI to hire and manage employees and strategically use analytics on them, ethical governance is indispensable. HR professionals are to be in the lead to establish standards of transparency, fairness, and accountability in the application of AI. This incorporates the selection of AI suppliers according to the explanations, the bias-to-be audited data of the algorithmic systems, and the review mechanism to make sure that the automated decisions can be appealed and profitably updated when it is so, and the necessity of the decision. Creating ethical AI rules, which reflect the strategies of diversity, equity, and inclusion (DEI), is one of the ways to reduce the risks of possible discrimination and create positive employee trust. In addition, the HR departments are well advised to work with the legal and data protection officers with a view to adhering to the privacy acts and employment provisions.

Launching Digital Reskilling Initiatives

A skills gap caused by technological disruption may be bridged as one of the most pressing strategic responses. HR should promote digital reskilling and upskilling exercises, customized to the position of tourism and hospitality industry.

This involves providing microlearning courses on digital capabilities, AI literacy courses, training in using customer tech-interfacing, and training in decision making in tech-intensified settings. Such programs must be done with a focus on frontline employees, especially low-wage employees or seasonal employees who will be at risk of being displaced. Such efforts can be expanded more widely by partnering with vocational schools, education technology resources, and government workforce development initiatives. It is also important to make lifelong learning part of the organizational culture that promotes further development in the sphere of work as an agenda of the overall responsibility.

Designing Inclusive HR Technologies

The technology should be designed in such a way that it would not replicate structural disparities in the labor force. The task of HRs is to make sure that AI tools and platforms are available regardless of language barriers, literacy, and devices. This implies that in hospitality settings where the workforce is highly diversified, comprising migrants, women, and youth with diverse heritage, inclusive HR systems need to be culturally sensitive and multilingual, and user-friendly. Another strategy of inclusive tech design is the input by employees in the selection of tools and the pilot stage, such that the input of the user determines how the system functions. Using voice navigation or simpler dashboards in mobile-based HR apps is an example where the engagement and the possibility to use such apps among frontline staff may grow significantly.

Adopting Agile Workforce Planning

The ability to bounce back quickly is key to HR in the AI age. The old long-range models of workforce planning are not enough in the scenario of fast change of technology and of customer demand. HR has to adopt agile approaches- the constant re-evaluation of workforce mix, the ability to predict the potential skills requirements in real-time, and the dynamism to redeploy the talents depending on the emerging needs. This will entail the implementation of predictive analytics and scenario planning in forecasting labor shortage, the emergence of new roles, or training needs. As an example, hotel chains may come up with agile staffing systems that will shift the teams to meet the conditions of the data on the number of guest bookings, local activities, or season, with the help of scheduling software enabled by AI.

Cultivating a Culture of Leadership and Learning

Lastly, transformation requires organizational culture and commitment to leadership. Leaders will have to set an example of adaptability, willingness to new technologies, and a people-centric attitude. HR needs to collaborate with executive teams to integrate the mission of digital transformation into the vision of the organization and also safeguard the well-being of the employees. Innovation and constant improvement are enabled by establishing psychologically safe environments where experimentation, failure, and feedback are welcomed. Fostering in-house knowledge-sharing, coaching, and cross-teamwork only enhances the speed of cultural convergence and knowledge-building. Essentially, all other AI integration practices should be based on developing a resilient and learning culture.

To summarize, the move to AI-enhanced HR in the tourism and hospitality industries is more than the tools and platforms; it is about attitude, organization, and principles. The use of these strategic responses, therefore, enables the HR leaders to make disruption an opportunity and see to it that technology does not downsize, but rather enriches the human experience in the workplace.

CONCLUSION

Automation and AI have become an important part of tourism and the hospitality sector, and this has been a landmark event in HR management. These technologies, as discussed in this chapter, are disruptive and transformative in nature as they redefine old job functions, question age-old workforce conventions, and open up unheard opportunities to innovation and strategic development of HR. However, in all this change, the essence of the human nature task of HR has become invariant: to develop human potential, bring people with purpose, and protect values that make hospitality an industry that is truly people-related.

The main takeaways of this chapter confirm that, although AI can maximize hiring, simplify the new employee process, offer individualized training, and refine workforce planning, the opportunities are not the agreed-upon introduction. To achieve the potential of AI, strategic steps are needed. Institutions also need to engage in reskilling programs that would enable workers to adjust to novel jobs. They should act by introducing ethical systems of governance that render fairness and accountability in the conditional decision-making that is based on algorithms. They should create cross-integrative digital products that support a multilingual environment, and are frequently under-resourced hospitality employees. Above all, they should create a working environment based on empathy, trust, and constant learning.

One of the running themes in this chapter is the importance of a balance between efficiency and empathy. Although AI may be able to streamline activities, it is not possible to match the emotional feelings of people, the emotional intelligence that will be needed between services and products, or that cultural awareness which is necessary in a high-touch service world. HR professionals are called upon to take the lead in this balancing act so that the use of technology adds, and not diminishes, the human experience of the employees and the guests.

Moving ahead, the role of HR will change its character of administrative support into strategic involvement in transforming the workforce. Supplanting a forward-thinking organization open to the modern world of agility, inclusion, and ethical innovation, HR can create the direction of the future in a digital economy that respects all social and emotional depths of hospitality. In this human-enhanced technological future, change is no longer being managed by the HR department, but it is being crafted, resilience by humans, policy by policy, and platform by platform.

REFERENCES

Agyeman-Manu, K., Ghebreyesus, T. A., Maait, M., Rafila, A., Tom, L., Lima, N. T., & Wangmo, D. (2023). Prioritising the health and care workforce shortage: Protect, invest, together. *The Lancet. Global Health*, *11*(8), e1162–e1164. DOI: 10.1016/S2214-109X(23)00224-3 PMID: 37209702

Al-Romeedy, B. S. (2024). AI and HRM in Tourism and Hospitality in Egypt: Inevitability, Impact, and Future. *HRM, Artificial Intelligence and the Future of Work: Insights from the Global South*, 247–266. DOI: 10.1007/978-3-031-62369-1_13

Alkhawaldeh, M. M. K., Ali, A. J., Mohammad, A. A. S., Shatnawi, T. M., Al-Momani, A., Alzoubi, A. E., Al-Majali, R. T., al-fugaha, Z. N. A., & Al-Hawary, S. I. S. (2024). The Impact of Artificial Intelligence on Talent Acquisition Strategies in Jordanian Technology Startups. *Studies in Computational Intelligence*, *1151*, 309–323. DOI: 10.1007/978-3-031-56015-6_25

Amin, S. M., El-Gazar, H. E., Zoromba, M. A., El-Sayed, M. M., & Atta, M. H. R. (2025). Sentiment of Nurses Towards Artificial Intelligence and Resistance to Change in Healthcare Organisations: A Mixed-Method Study. *Journal of Advanced Nursing*, *81*(4), 2087–2098. DOI: 10.1111/jan.16435 PMID: 39235193

Baeza-Yates, R. (2022).. . *Ethical Challenges in AI*, *1–2*, 1–2. Advance online publication. DOI: 10.1145/3488560.3498370

Chhibber, S., Rajkumar, S. R., & Dassanayake, S. (2025). Will Artificial Intelligence Reshape the Global Workforce by 2030? A Cross-Sectoral Analysis of Job Displacement and Transformation. *Blockchain, Artificial Intelligence, and Future Research*, *1*(1), 35–51. DOI: 10.70211/bafr.v1i1.178

Dwivedi, Y. K., Pandey, N., Currie, W., & Micu, A. (2024). Leveraging ChatGPT and other generative artificial intelligence (AI)-based applications in the hospitality and tourism industry: Practices, challenges and research agenda. *International Journal of Contemporary Hospitality Management*, *36*(1), 1–12. DOI: 10.1108/IJCHM-05-2023-0686

El Hajal, G., & Yeoman, I. (2024). AI and the future of talent management in tourism and hospitality. *Current Issues in Tourism*, 1–18. Advance online publication. DOI: 10.1080/13683500.2024.2439395

Ercik, C., & Kardaş, K. (2024). Reflections of digital technologies on human resources management in the tourism sector. *Worldwide Hospitality and Tourism Themes*, *16*(5), 646–663. DOI: 10.1108/WHATT-09-2024-0208

Ersanlı, C. Y., Çelik, F., Barjesteh, H., Duran, V., & Manoochehrzadeh, M. (2025). A review of global reskilling and upskilling initiatives in the age of AI. *AI and Ethics, 2025*(6), 1–10. DOI: 10.1007/s43681-025-00767-9

Felemban, H., Sohail, M., & Ruikar, K. (2024). Exploring the Readiness of Organisations to Adopt Artificial Intelligence. *Buildings 2024, Vol. 14, Page 2460, 14*(8), 2460. DOI: 10.3390/buildings14082460

Frenkenberg, A., & Hochman, G. (2025). It's Scary to Use It, It's Scary to Refuse It: The Psychological Dimensions of AI Adoption—Anxiety, Motives, and Dependency. *Systems 2025, Vol. 13, Page 82, 13*(2), 82. DOI: 10.3390/systems13020082

Hazrat, M. A., Hassan, N. M. S., Chowdhury, A. A., Rasul, M. G., & Taylor, B. A. (2023). Developing a Skilled Workforce for Future Industry Demand: The Potential of Digital Twin-Based Teaching and Learning Practices in Engineering Education. *Sustainability 2023, Vol. 15, Page 16433, 15*(23), 16433. DOI: 10.3390/su152316433

Hossain, M. K., Srivastava, A., Oliver, G. C., Islam, M. E., Jahan, N. A., Karim, R., Kanij, T., & Mahdi, T. H. (2024). Adoption of artificial intelligence and big data analytics: An organizational readiness perspective of the textile and garment industry in Bangladesh. *Business Process Management Journal, 30*(7), 2665–2683. DOI: 10.1108/BPMJ-11-2023-0914

Jabeen, F., Al Zaidi, S., & Al Dhaheri, M. H. (2022). Automation and artificial intelligence in hospitality and tourism. *Tourism Review, 77*(4), 1043–1061. DOI: 10.1108/TR-09-2019-0360

Jacobs, J. (2024). The artificial intelligence shock and socio-political polarization. *Technological Forecasting and Social Change, 199*, 123006. DOI: 10.1016/j.techfore.2023.123006

Jöhnk, J., Weißert, M., & Wyrtki, K. (2021). Ready or Not, AI Comes— An Interview Study of Organizational AI Readiness Factors. *Business & Information Systems Engineering, 63*(1), 5–20. DOI: 10.1007/s12599-020-00676-7

Kaswan, K. S., Dhatterwal, J. S., & Ojha, R. P. (2024). AI in personalized learning. *Advances in Technological Innovations in Higher Education: Theory and Practices*, 103–117. https://doi.org/DOI: 10.1201/9781003376699-9/AI-PERSONALIZED-LEARNING-KULDEEP-SINGH-KASWAN-JAGJIT-SINGH-DHATTERWAL-RUDRA-PRATAP-OJHA

Kerasidou, A. (2021). Ethics of artificial intelligence in global health: Explainability, algorithmic bias and trust. *Journal of Oral Biology and Craniofacial Research, 11*(4), 612–614. DOI: 10.1016/j.jobcr.2021.09.004 PMID: 34567966

Khan, D. (2024). The Impact of Artificial Intelligence (AI) on Job Displacement and the Future Work. *Social Science Review Archives*, *2*(2), 2296–2306. DOI: 10.70670/sra.v3i1.509

Kharitonova, Yu. S., Savina, V. S., & Pagnini, F. (2021). Artificial Intelligence's Algorithmic Bias: Ethical and Legal Issues. *Perm University Herald Juridical Sciences, 53.* https://heinonline.org/HOL/Page?handle=hein.journals/permujds53&id=58&div=&collection=

Kim, J. J. H., Soh, J., Kadkol, S., Solomon, I., Yeh, H., Srivatsa, A. V., Nahass, G. R., Choi, J. Y., Lee, S., Nyugen, T., & Ajilore, O. (2025). AI Anxiety: a comprehensive analysis of psychological factors and interventions. *AI and Ethics 2025 5:4, 5*(4), 3993–4009. DOI: 10.1007/s43681-025-00686-9

Mcpake, B., Dayal, P., Zimmermann, J., & Williams, G. A. (2023). *What steps can improve and promote investment in the health and care workforce? Enhancing efficiency of spending and rethinking domestic and international financing.*

Olak, O. (2023). The Impact of Artificial Intelligence on the Employment Structure of the Tourism Industry: An Interview with ChatGPT. *İktisadi İdari ve Siyasal Araştırmalar Dergisi (İKTİSAD), 8*(22), 919–939.

Paramita, D., Okwir, S., & Nuur, C. (2024). Artificial intelligence in talent acquisition: Exploring organisational and operational dimensions. *The International Journal of Organizational Analysis*, *32*(11), 108–131. DOI: 10.1108/IJOA-09-2023-3992

Rahmat, A. M. (2022). Idaya; Mohd, H., Khalil Omar, M., Kamalludeen, R., Mohd Zulhafiz, W., Zahari, W., Azmy, N., Haimi, A., & Adnan, M. (2022). Integrating Socio-Digital Skills in the Industry 4.0 era for graduates' employability: An employers' perspective. *Journal of Positive School Psychology*, (3), 8493–8507. http://journalppw.com

Sapru, A. (2025). *Psychological Resistance to Ai: How Regulatory Focus Fuels Ai Anxiety and Negative Attitudes Toward Ai.* DOI: 10.2139/ssrn.5295832

Selvam, R., Hiremath, P., Cs, S. K., Ramakrishna Bhat, R., Thokal, V., & Patil, P. R. (2024). Review and Analysis of the Literature: Artificial Intelligence-Based Digital Transformation of Automated Customer Onboarding. *Engineering Proceedings 2023, Vol. 59, Page 234, 59*(1), 234. DOI: 10.3390/engproc2023059234

Suseno, Y., Chang, C., Hudik, M., & Fang, E. S. (2023). Beliefs, anxiety and change readiness for artificial intelligence adoption among human resource managers: the moderating role of high- performance work systems. *Artificial Intelligence and International HRM*, 144–171. DOI: 10.4324/9781003377085-6

Tee, P. K., Wong, L. C., Dada, M., Song, B. L., & Ng, C. P. (2024). Demand for digital skills, skill gaps and graduate employability: Evidence from employers in Malaysia. *F1000 Research, 13*, 389. DOI: 10.12688/f1000research.148514.1 PMID: 39262836

van de Pas, R., Mans, L., & Koutsoumpa, M. (2023). An exploratory review of investments by development actors in health workforce programmes and job creation. *Human Resources for Health, 21*(1), 1–13. DOI: 10.1186/s12960-023-00835-3 PMID: 37420237

Wang, Q., Wu, Z., Liu, J., Zhang, Y., & Liu, L. (2024). Middle Managers' Role Overload, Workplace Anxiety, and Resistance to Change: The Moderating Effect of Emotion Regulation Strategies. *The Journal of Applied Behavioral Science*. Advance online publication. DOI: 10.1177/00218863241246284;JOURNAL:JOURNAL:JABA;CSUBTYPE:STRING:AHEAD

Zhan, E. S., Molina, M. D., Rheu, M., & Peng, W. (2024). What is There to Fear? Understanding Multi-Dimensional Fear of AI from a Technological Affordance Perspective. *International Journal of Human-Computer Interaction, 40*(22), 7127–7144. DOI: 10.1080/10447318.2023.2261731

Chapter 12
Neurodigital Engineering of Human Capital in Intelligent Multi-Stakeholder Organizational Learning Systems

Jose De Jesus Reyes-Sánchez
http://orcid.org/0000-0002-3866-2363
TECNM Instituto Tecnologico Superior De Fresnillo, Mexico

Mario Alberto García-Camacho
http://orcid.org/0000-0002-9645-3199
Tecnológico Nacional de México, ITS Fresnillo, Mexico

Jannet Maricela Barrientos Luján
http://orcid.org/0009-0009-3244-5016
TECNM Instituto Tecnologico Superior De Fresnillo, Mexico

Gerardo Ríos Ramos
TECNM Instituto Tecnologico Superior De Fresnillo, Mexico

Victor Manuel Dominguez Ibarra
http://orcid.org/0009-0005-2592-0027
TECNM Instituto Tecnologico Superior De Fresnillo, Mexico

DOI: 10.4018/979-8-3373-3867-5.ch012

EXECUTIVE SUMMARY

Human capital neurodigital engineering integrates cognitive neuroscience, artificial intelligence, and advanced analytics to model, reinforce, and anticipate learning trajectories in multi-stakeholder organizational ecosystems. This chapter examines its theoretical foundations, maps institutional challenges, and presents empirical evidence of corporate implementation, proposing a research agenda that harmonizes radical personalization, cognitive justice, and ethical governance. It is concluded that neurodigital convergence constitutes a strategic paradigm for resilience and sustainable innovation.

INTRODUCTION

The emergence of neurodigitalization slides organizations towards an epistemological horizon where the measurement of brain activity, cardiac variability and ocular microgestures ceases to be an isolated experiment and becomes a daily input for strategic decision-making. This shift is based on the maturation of neuroergonomics, a discipline that calls for open science practices to guarantee the reproducibility of findings and the standardization of algorithms, as underlined by initiatives that promote open source and data repositories for the entire research community (Gramann, Lotte, Dehais, & Ayaz, 2024).

The theoretical gap emerges, however, when one tries to reconcile the brain-based view with dynamic capability models and triple-loop learning streams. Experimental evidence that simultaneously monitors brain, heart, and eyes during cognitive tasks demonstrates that mental load is multidimensional and evolves at a nonlinear rate, forcing us to abandon one-way metrics and adopt analytical frameworks capable of capturing synapses, emotions, and sociotechnical context in the same data stream (Mark, Curtin, Kraft, & Ziegler, 2024).

In Latin America, where digital infrastructure coexists with bandwidth constraints and socioeconomic inequalities, the responsible adoption of neurodigital solutions requires glocal approaches that harmonize technological sophistication with cultural narratives of their own. Recent studies on regional digital transformation reveal that the acceptance of biosensing grows when interfaces respect indigenous languages, allow offline modes and guarantee the self-determination of data, a sine qua non condition for innovation to be perceived as an opportunity and not as cognitive extractivism (Joia, Chatterjee, Rodríguez-Abitia, & Graeml, 2024).

UNESCO's global mapping shows that more than eighty percent of neurotechnology patents are registered in the global North, while a substantial portion of biomedical repositories come from the South, exposing an imbalance between those who produce data and those who capitalize on the resulting intellectual property. This finding raises the alarm about possible cognitive colonialism and brings to the fore the need for regulatory frameworks that guarantee the redistribution of benefits derived from algorithms trained with brain signals from underrepresented populations (Hain, Jurowetzki, Squicciarini, & Xu, 2023).

The responsible innovation agenda demands, therefore, dynamic consent protocols, algorithmic audits, and data sovereignty clauses that align with the FAIR and CARE principles, particularly relevant to indigenous peoples and historically marginalized communities. Research in monitoring work stress shows that the acceptance of biosensors increases when employees have visibility over the entire flow of their data, can veto certain uses, and participate in the calibration of thresholds that activate organizational interventions (Khayyat et al., 2024).

Field tests also demonstrate the power of neurodigital foresight. In flight decks, machine learning models powered by electroencephalographic patterns discriminate cognitive load peaks with high accuracy and allow simulation scenarios to be readjusted before fatigue deteriorates situational capacity (Taheri Gorji, Wilson, VanBree, & Hoffmann, 2023). At the same time, multimodal monitoring in human-robot collaborative industrial environments doubles the sensitivity to detect micro-deviations that would otherwise lead to assembly defects or occupational accidents (Caiazzo, Savkovic, Pusica, Milojevic, & Leva, 2023).

However, the promise of neurodigitalization will only be fully realized if organizations manage to balance efficiency, fairness, and transparency. The replicability of results requires that algorithms be developed in open environments, with common standards that favor interoperability and avoid the proliferation of "black boxes" that are difficult to audit.

BACKGROUND

Historical Evolution Of Neuroscience Applied To Talent Management

The history of neurodigital engineering is not linear; it advances in pulses that coincide with the evolution of technological infrastructure and managerial worldviews. The first pulse emerged with the industrial ergonomics of the fifties, when chronometers and adjustable chairs were devised that today look naïve, but cemented the idea that fatigue could be measured and, therefore, managed.The second pulse occurred in the eighties, under the influence of usability engineering and the proliferation of computer workstations that transferred the weight of effort from the muscles to the prefrontal cortex, generating invisible fatigue that, however, devastated productivity (Butler, 1996).

With the massification of broadband at the beginning of the 21st century, a third pulse transformed the HR function. HR in a business intelligence node; however, traditional dashboards were short-sighted in the face of attention spans that fluctuated in seconds. That's when low-cost EEG devices came into the picture, linking beta and gamma signals with critical micro-decisions: tapping for a concentration failure before it materialized into a production error. The COVID-19 pandemic, by moving millions of offices into makeshift homes, acted as a fourth catalytic pulse: spatial dispersion intensified reliance on cognitive self-regulation and exposed the need to monitor synaptic load in hybrid environments, ushering in the era of distributed neuroergonomics (Dehais et al., 2020).

Technological Convergence Between Digital And Neural

The miniaturization of biosensors transformed the concept of biometric dice into a continuous stream of brain telemetry; Dry electrodes made of surgical-grade graphene detect micro-oscillations at 256 Hz even when the user walks or gestures, while explainable deep learning algorithms filter out muscle artifacts in real time. This flow generates cognitive digital twins that replicate a professional's dominant synapses, simulating their response to stress peaks, variations in luminosity or noise from simultaneous tasks with an accuracy that is close to 90%. In parallel, extended reality turned the corporate metaverse into a neuroplastic training ground: immersive environments calibrate the level of challenge based on the alpha-teta activity of the frontal lobe, triggering a prolonged flow state and raising procedural retention by up to 25% in regulated industries (Badcock et al., 2013).

International Standards and Regulatory Frameworks in Occupational Neurosafety

The overdemand for neuro-data posed a regulatory dilemma: is it medical data, sensitive biometric data, or a new category that demands unprecedented safeguards? Without consensus, ISO 27502 coined the term neuro-safety and elevated cognitive overload to the range of ergonomic risk, forcing the documentation of hours of synaptic peaks as decibels or illumination levels are documented. However, regions such as Asia-Pacific are developing more lax frameworks that allow aggregated brainwave analysis without granular consent, facilitating the relocation of computing centers to wash the provenance of the data. To fill these gaps, applied neuroethics appeared, which promotes real-time consent revocation clauses and independent audits of algorithms to mitigate discriminatory biases. Pioneering organizations adopt mutual screen policies: the employee sees the same neural metrics on their monitor as their supervisor, reducing interpretive power asymmetry and increasing collective trust (Palacios-García et al., 2021).

Theoretical Paradigms That Underpin Neurodigital Engineering

Sociomaterial neuroergonomics understands cognition as a widespread phenomenon in which digital artifacts act as an exocortex that stores memory, delegates calculation, and models one's own mental structure. From this perspective, neuro-amplified dynamic capacities emerge, micro-foundations that are continuously remade through bio and neurofeedback, providing the organization with homeostatic reflexes to redefine routines in VUCA contexts. At the same time, algorithmic governance aimed at cognitive justice requires participatory mechanisms that avoid epistemic capture: if only the top management interprets synaptic traces, there is a risk of segmenting professional careers based on biased biomarkers. Finally, second-order cybernetics expands the neural metaphor at the organizational level, describing systems that reobserve themselves and adjust their own measurement algorithms, turning each indicator into a trigger for a reflective intervention (Weber et al., 2023).

Empirical Evidence Of Corporate Implementation

The aviation sector, a traditional standard-bearer of reliability, validated the use of EEG helmets in simulators that recalculate workloads every 750 ms, reducing near misses by 12% and increasing post-training satisfaction by 22%. In hospitality, emotional defibrillators have decreased the waiting times perceived by customers, by increasing the empathy of staff in times of overload. BioNova, a pharmaceutical company, integrated pupillometry with computer vision to detect micro pipetting errors, cutting reassays by 15% and saving twelve weeks of validation per molecule (Aricò et al., 2016). In public administration, Singapore's tax agency reconfigures citizen service queues according to the cardiac variability of agents, reducing complaints by 24% and speeding up procedures by 18% (Dehais et al., 2019). Latin American SMEs, despite the capital gap, experiment with adaptive auditory stimuli that mitigate the so-called lead fatigue of maquila operators, reducing absenteeism by 7% and increasing textile cutting accuracy (Park et al., 2018; Mathôt, 2018).

Organizational Impacts and Value Metrics

Meta-analyses of first generations record average productivity jumps between 10% and 30% when permanent neurofeedback cycles are implemented, but such averages hide finer findings: the most pronounced improvements arise in teams with high cognitive interdependence and are flattened in strongly standardized tasks. Epistemic spillovers are even more significant: the biomarkers that are collected to reduce errors are reused in the design of inclusive interfaces, neurodivergent talent retention programs, or demand prediction algorithms, tripling the return on analytical capital. In addition, the reputation of a neuro-responsible firm impacts employer branding, mobilizing professionals with high cognitive valence who prioritize transparent environments over marginal remuneration (Shaffer & Ginsberg, 2017; Abbasi et al., 2024; Djelassi et al., 2018).

Challenges and Limitations for Responsible Adoption

The dystopian narrative of thought-reading continues to hold back adoption; recent surveys show that 61% of workers would accept EEG sensors only if the algorithms are auditable by independent academic third parties (Kablo & Arias-Cabarcos, 2023). Another barrier is the infrastructure gap: without low-latency connections and neurally trained data-scientists, SMEs run the risk of becoming providers of synaptically blind labor to sensor clusters. The problem of epistemic talent drain also arises: by accurately mapping synaptic skills, the visibility of micro-experts who can be hunted by competitors is increased, raising job turnover by up to 17% in some technology clusters (Tabibian et al., 2019). Finally, interpretive overload haunts leaders who receive panels with a hundred neural metrics: without statistical literacy, decisions are based on spurious correlations, a problem that is combated with sense-making laboratories that translate data into actionable narratives (Tindale et al., 2022).

Emerging Trends and Future Research Agenda

The agendas of the future converge on radical personalization supported by multimodal generative AI that adapts intensity, duration, and sequence of micro-courses to the synaptic topology of each collaborator, maximizing the neuro-diversity dividend. In parallel, neuro-microdoses feed synaptic plasticity without inducing fatigue, and already show conceptual retention increases of 40% in AB tests (Doll et al., 2011; Golpayegani et al., 2024). Corporate metaverses evolve into sensorimetric ecosystems where avatars encode variations in electrodermal conductance and heart rate, facilitating empathy in cross-cultural negotiations through visual cues extrapolated from physiological cues. The most disruptive frontier is outlined in the gene-epigen-neuro convergence: preliminary studies link COMT gene polymorphisms with the efficacy of dopaminergic feedback protocols, hinting at personalized learning programs at the molecular level.

STATEMENT OF THE PROBLEM

Neurodigitalization holds promise to catalyze high-precision organizational learning environments, but its responsible adoption continues to be weighed down by methodological gaps, geographical biases, and theoretical fragmentation. Recent meta-analyses reveal inconsistent effect sizes in improving business performance due to heterogeneity of designs (variations in recording time window, inconsistent neurophysiological metrics, and absence of pre-registration), leading to wide confidence intervals and inflated estimates of value-added (Wall, Celik, Hetherington, & McMeekin, 2024). This scenario is aggravated by the fact that most studies focus on corporations in the global North, with little validation in Latin American or African SMEs, generating an extrapolation bias that overestimates the projected returns in emerging economies by up to twenty-five percent (Joia, Chatterjee, Rodríguez-Abitia, & Graeml, 2024).

The gap widens when a conceptual eclecticism is observed that fuses neuroscientific postulates with resource theory and models of dynamic capacities without a common vocabulary. Such semantic dissonance prevents the systematic comparison of results, erodes replicability and hinders the construction of evidence-based intervention programs. A bibliometric map produced by UNESCO shows more than 130 research streams in organizational neurotechnology that use incompatible taxonomies to describe processes of sensemaking and collective plasticity, which hinders the transfer of knowledge between domains (Hain, Jurowetzki, Squicciarini, & Xu, 2023).

There is also no consensus on indicators of success. Studies oscillate between purely financial metrics and psychometric constructs of well-being, without integrating dimensions of cognitive equity or neuroethical legitimacy. The result is a proliferation of dashboards with up to one hundred biomarkers per employee that saturate the managerial interpretation capacity and encourage decisions based on spurious correlations. Technocultural reviews highlight that information overload, coupled with a lack of statistical literacy, increases the rate of strategic error in early adoption processes by twenty-two percent (Khurana, Gahalawat, Kumar, & Roy, 2021).

At the intercultural level, tensions of cognitive justice emerge. The flow of neurodata from the global South to transnational corporations without mechanisms of epistemic return threatens to reproduce practices of digital colonialism: brain signals become raw material for algorithms trained under alien cultural assumptions and, subsequently, are licensed back as proprietary systems. Reports from multilatina organizations report that only eight percent of the neurodigital patents registered in the last decade come from the region, despite the fact that their populations participate as raw data providers (Wall et al., 2024; Hain et al., 2023).

From this perspective, the central problem materializes in three interdependent questions. First, how can neurodigital engineering shape organizational learning systems that are simultaneously effective, ethical, and culturally relevant? Solving it requires glocal architectures that combine explainable algorithms, inclusive governance and dynamic consent, all supported by low-latency infrastructure accessible to edge SMEs. Second, what theoretical frameworks make it possible to transcend the mere neurophysiological description and design interventions that reconfigure routines and dynamic capacities? The answer involves articulating the brain-based view with resource theory and neurorights principles, so that collective synaptic plasticity becomes a vector of competitive advantage. Third, what research routes are essential to avoid a new cognitive colonialism? This includes multicenter studies with federated FAIR-CARE data, ex-ante social impact analysis, and benefit redistribution clauses derived from models trained on neural signals from underrepresented populations.

THEORETICAL FRAMEWORK

Neurobiological Basis of Organizational Synaptic Plasticity

Synaptic plasticity is the biochemical foundation on which corporate learning and continuous innovation are built. Ubiquitous exposure to digital micro-interactions generates electrochemical pulses that synchronize attentional rhythms with operational demands, opening windows of long-term potentiation in fronto-hippocampal circuits and compressing the distance between the acquisition of a skill and its productive automation (Bliss & Collingridge, 1993).

The effectiveness of these processes is reinforced when digital environments incorporate gamified micro-achievements that trigger dopaminergic release and expand the mnemonic capture window. By integrating calibrated haptic and visual stimuli, immersive platforms facilitate convergence between reward and memory circuits, inducing controlled *flow* states that optimize the transfer of critical competencies (Fries, 2015; Koepp et al., 1998). In parallel, glial synergies, especially the *astrocyte-neuron lactate shuttle*, redistribute lactate to support neuronal metabolism spikes, preventing intense cognitive demand from deteriorating the quality of synaptic coding.

Beyond dopamine, brain-derived neurotrophic protein (BDNF) emerges as a key indicator for evaluating digital training programs. Controlled trials show that immersive twenty-minute sessions, spaced by micro-pauses of guided breathing, raise plasma BDNF levels and promote synaptic pruning of redundant connections, refining newly formed circuits and consolidating technical expertise.

The social dimension of the phenomenon becomes more important when considering the so-called affective micro-contagions, sudden emotional transmissions that travel through emojis, reactions and brief turns of voice. Such signals modulate the release of oxytocin, cementing a neurochemical terrain conducive to creative cooperation and distributed trust; when the emotional climate is positive, the prefrontal networks exhibit oscillatory coherence that facilitates the semantic integration of disparate knowledge (Suzuki et al., 2011; Dinoff et al., 2017).

Plasticity presents, however, a dark side: prolonged overstimulation leads to synaptic fatigue, a phenomenon characterized by temporary depletion of neurotransmitters, accumulation of metabolites and a drop in the sensitivity of the *error monitoring system*. Edge *computing* tools that combine cardiac variability and micro-facial expressions make it possible to detect saturation points before they degrade operational performance, enabling strategic pauses or task variations that restore homeostasis.

These findings prompt governance discussions: if synaptic plasticity becomes productive infrastructure, its preservation demands policies as strict as those aimed at safeguarding energy reserves. Corporate plans that establish "stimulative discharge windows", limit the density of notifications, and audit recommendation algorithms to prevent addictive designs are among the best practices suggested by cognitive risk experts (Csathó et al., 2024; Kramer et al., 2014).

The ethical edge deepens when the company captures encephalographic biomarkers to adjust training itineraries. The principles of continuous informed consent require the sharing of understandable panels with collaborators that specify which metrics are collected, for what purposes, and under which encryption protocols, avoiding the drift towards a neural extractivism that erodes institutional trust. In this way, synaptic plasticity is recognized as a renewable but vulnerable resource, whose sustainable exploitation requires combining advanced analytics with participatory governance and cognitive justice (Kosfeld et al., 2005).

Multi-Stakeholder Organizational Learning Models

Contemporary organizational learning is more like a neurodigital fabric than a linear succession of operational corrections. Cloud collaboration platforms, recommendation algorithms, and conversational agents introduce simultaneous feedback loops that overlap in asynchronous rhythms. The single loop corrects tactical deviations without altering the underlying logic; the double questions strategic assumptions and redistributes epistemic authority; the triple, to which some authors add a phase of ontological immersion, intersperses the voice of non-human agents to rethink identity values and validity criteria, extending the reflexive radius of the organization to its sociotechnical footprint (Kwon, Lee, An, & Brandt, 2024).

In this polyphonic ecosystem, communities of practice are no longer spontaneous groupings and are configured as orchestrated synaptic nodes. Its power lies in the density of semantic micro-transactions: operative metaphors, fast-error stories, and disposable prototypes that flow between functional domains. Recent studies in family SMEs show that, when the community functions as an early antenna for weak market signals, tacit exchange increases exploratory efficiency and reinforces cognitive resilience to exogenous contingencies (Rossignoli, Lionzo, Henschel, & Boers, 2023).

The governance of these networks is based on metacognitive reflexivity, the ability to read one's own updating biases and to redesign the rules before they become fossilized. To catalyze it, organizations implement sense clinics where multidisciplinary teams analyze behavioral telemetry and stimulate counter-narrative debates; The process concludes when the emerging version of the mental framework is encoded into playbooks that nurture the community's digital twin. Such practices remind us that meta-learning is not an additive, but the connective tissue of distributed performance.

The multi-stakeholder dimension takes on new depth with the addition of AI-augmented social media analytics tools. By mapping textual, vowel, and haptic interactions, algorithms detect semantic bottlenecks and recommend topological jumps that link islands of dissimilar knowledge. Longitudinal experiments in hospitals show that reconfiguring these bridges increases the diversity of perspectives in clinical co-design sessions by 18% and decreases document redundancy, without compromising terminological coherence.

Beyond the collective individual, the multi-stakeholder model sees technologies as participants with partial agency. Cognitive curation bots and smart queue dashboards become co-producers of institutional memory, mediating information conflicts, and firing micro-nudges to avoid the entropy of distributed conversation. The result is a logic of socio-algorithmic co-learning where radical exploration and incremental exploitation coexist in counter-rhythmic cycles, a requirement to navigate VUCA environments without sacrificing strategic coherence (Kharrazi et al., 2020; Lee et al., 2019). This convergence requires new frameworks of legitimacy that ensure that interaction data are used with proportionality and transparency, avoiding epistemic colonization of cognitive minorities. Pilot programs in industrial SMEs demonstrate that an explainable algorithmic feedback protocol reduces the perception of surveillance and accelerates the adoption of shared sense-making practices (March, 1991; Orlikowski & Scott, 2008).

Multi-stakeholder organizational learning, understood in this way, transcends the closed-loop metaphor and resembles an ecosystem of bio-feedbacks where humans and machines co-write the script of their own adaptability. The greater the diverse connectivity, the greater the cushioning in the face of disruption; the greater the collective reflexivity, the lower the possibility of falling into decisional myopia (Schlund & Zitek, 2024; Weinmann et al., 2016; Zerilli et al., 2022).

Neurodigital Human Capital Theory

Human capital is no longer defined as an accumulation of static competencies and is presented as cognitive capital augmented by technology. Its density is measured in terabytes of recorded synaptic traces and its circulation speed in algorithmic inference latencies that connect employees to digital twins of knowledge. From this perspective, collective intelligence arises when multiple brains are coupled to repositories of explainable AI that filter epistemic noise and amplify the strategic insight signal.

Neuro-Amplified Dynamic Capabilities

The expression sense-seize-reconfigure has ceased to describe a purely strategic choreography to become a tangible neurophysiological reflex. Dry electroencephalography and cardiac variability microsensors installed in augmented reality helmets or piezoelectric bracelets beat to the rhythm of each decision; The data flows to edge nodes that spiny algorithms transform into haptic pulses directed at the wrist, collarbone or pinna. The sequence begins with the preconscious sense phase: by detecting drops in fronto-parietal beta-gamma power, the system interprets hints of anticipated fatigue and modulates the brightness of the dashboard before the distraction crystallizes. Laboratory tests proved that this manoeuvre, based on adaptive extreme edge computing, reduces inspection errors on microchip assembly lines by eleven percentage points (Covi, Donati, Liang, & Kappel, 2021).

In the seize stage, distributed attention algorithms turn neuroelectrical discharge into a concrete option: a burst of theta-hippocampal coherence signals a market opportunity, and the interface proposes a prototype. That it is a minimum prototype of less than three minutes of construction, for the team to evaluate in real time. The speed responds to a principle of competitive synaptic latency: capturing value before the dopaminergic window closes. A study with eleven Japanese authors showed that smart patches capable of processing ECG, temperature, and humidity in situ trigger acoustic micro-alerts at 80 ms latency, accelerating decision-making in predictive maintenance and doubling the success rate compared to traditional protocols (Matsumura, Honda, Kikuchi, & Mizuno, 2024).

The reconfigure moment is supported by adaptive iterativity: each micro-prototype inoculates a reinforcement signal that rewrites the collective synaptic weights. In extended reality environments, the platform analyzes alpha-tet power to model the team's awe curve and pushes difficulty just above the boredom threshold. Research on neuroadaptive haptics reveals that a reinforcement learning agent fed with EEG signals instead of explicit assessments maintains motivation stable during prolonged sessions without increasing mental load.

This neuro-tactile assembly also reconfigures the border between exploration and exploitation. The cognitive factories of the so-called Industry 5.0 use neurocognitive digital twins that run hundreds of metabolic simulations every morning; The routes most likely to succeed feed "synaptic navigation charts" that morning shifts translate into work orders. Recent meta-analyses show that such cycles reduce the costs of changing settings by 27% and triple the half-life of routines before their obsolescence.

The deployment is not without ethical dilemmas. As sensors refine the detection of micro-loss of focus, risks of coercive neuromanagement emerge. To avoid drifting, pioneering companies opt for symmetrical transparency boards: each brain data is immediately reflected on the employee's own screen, along with the causal explanation that the algorithm assigns to the feedback intervention. The practice feeds back into hot consent revocation clauses and epistemic drift audits carried out by citizen committees, conditions that the neuro-governance literature considers indispensable to legitimize the productive use of biodata without undermining autonomy.

Neuroethics and Cognitive Justice

The advent of brain telemetry at work forces us to review the foundations of the socio-technical contract that historically protected mental privacy. Unlike traditional biometrics, electroencephalographic streams and microexpression markers translate introspective content that, if disclosed without safeguards, can skew performance evaluations, segment career paths, and reinforce pre-existing asymmetries (Henrich et al., 2010). Organizations that implement real-time metrics dashboards have moved toward continuous informed consent, but they still face the dilemma of the representativeness gap: many models are trained on neurotypical Western samples and export biases that penalize peripheralized cognitive styles (Ienca & Andorno, 2017; Kaye et al., 2015; Magee et al., 2024). Recent research on neuro-rights underscores that mental privacy cannot be left in the exclusive hands of the employer; it requires binding legal frameworks that recognize inner life as a sovereign and inalienable sphere, accompanied by independent cognitive equity audits that verify the proportionality of any algorithmic intervention (Mitchell et al., 2019; Muhl, 2024; Raji et al., 2020).

Participatory governance emerges as an antidote to epistemic colonization. By opening up algorithm design cycles to representatives of neurodivergent groups, companies discover that the distribution of attentional loads varies according to circadian rhythms, sensory contexts, and identity narratives; Such findings allow adjusting alert thresholds to avoid false alarms in profiles that process information in a non-linear way. However, equity is not limited to technical calibration: it also requires redistributing the benefits derived from the exploitation of biodata. Shared cognitive licensing models illustrate how cognitive justice can be materialized into tangible metrics, supporting corporate legitimacy to investors evaluating expanded ESG criteria (Sonuga-Barke et al., 2024; Yuste et al., 2017; Zerilli et al., 2022).

Cognitive Digital Twins

The evolution of digital twins from replicas of physical assets to neuro-physiological duplicates opens up a range of possibilities for talent development and dynamic role configuration. A robust cognitive twin integrates electroencephalographic signals, pupillary patterns, micro-gestures and linguistic traces to model in quasi-real time the learning curve and affective saturation of each employee. Experiments with industrial prototypes show that, when the simulation incorporates affective variables, the prediction of performance drops improves by up to 22% compared to twins focused only on behavioral metrics; this additional precision allows training itineraries to be rethought and projects to be reassigned before the loss of motivation crystallizes as rotation or quiet quitting.

The preventive potential is amplified when twins are linked in population meta-models capable of identifying collective patterns: if the simulation notes a generalized tendency to energy depletion after prolonged virtual meetings, the system can suggest synchronous micro-naps or asynchronous modality variations to preserve synaptic plasticity. These recommendations are legitimized through co-design protocols with the users themselves, so that the agency is not completely delegated to the algorithmic layer. Multimodal twin analytics studies underline that the employee's active participation in curating their own data increases trust and, paradoxically, increases the fidelity of records, as it decreases behavioral interference derived from monitoring anxiety (Rodemer et al., 2024).

However, the promise of unlimited personalization collides with bioethical limits when twins begin to classify career paths according to neuroaffective traits. The risk is to crystallize a synaptic determinism where labor identity is decided more by the beta-gamma curve than by declared ambition (Lee et al., 2019). To mitigate this bias, cutting-edge projects incorporate dashboards where the collaborator weighs the predictive value of each variable and can choose to veto dimensions that they consider intimate. In addition, employment contracts are beginning to include cognitive return clauses, ensuring that any model trained on personal data can be transferred to the employee if he or she leaves the company, analogous to the portability of pension funds.

The horizon of cognitive digital twins ultimately points to the creation of co-simulation ecologies in which entire teams rehearse crisis scenarios, leadership rotations or the introduction of emerging technologies before deploying them in the real plant. Such ecologies make it possible to calculate affective externalities and adjust implementation parameters with a level of precision that used to be reserved for process engineering (Hayashi et al., 1999).

Affective-Cognitive Predictive Analytics

The incorporation of multimodal biosensors has allowed organizations to describe their emotional atmosphere as a logistical control variable. Explainable deep learning models trained on synchronous sequences of electrophysiological pulses and behavioral traces achieve precisions that exceed ninety percent by discriminating micro-states of flow, affective dissonance or latent fatigue; The granularity of these predictions is illustrated in simulated office experiments where the algorithm identifies transitional stress patterns just eight seconds before the error materializes, enough time to trigger guided breathing micro-pauses or task variations (Naegelin, Weibel, Kerr, & Schinazi, 2023).

The portability of these developments has improved with the miniaturization of textile-printed graphene electrodes and with specialized edge computing that runs compact residual networks directly on the device; inference times fall below 50 ms and facilitate almost reflex haptic biofeedback loops, enabling distributive affective regulation where each collaborator adjusts their cognitive load without disengaging from the task. At the same time, electrodermal systems located in high-pressure areas form emotional density boards that alert supervisors when group cardiac coherence crosses critical thresholds; In field studies, the introduction of attentional recalibration pauses derived from these alerts reduced incidents of operational burnout by nearly twenty-two percent and increased the rate of successful resolution of unexpected problems.

However, algorithmic accuracy can degenerate if the training base lacks neurocultural diversity. To avoid this, the analytics equipment includes heterogeneous datasets where neurodivergent profiles, variable circadian patterns and high ambient noise scenarios converge. Such a design for the inclusion of controlled biases allows the organization to modulate its affective climate with the same finesse with which it calibrates inventories or financial flows, integrating well-being metrics into executive dashboards along with throughput indicators or stock turnover.

Neuroergonomic Work Design

The post-digital office abandons uniform lighting and monotonous acoustic environments to become a customizable sensory biotope that minimizes attentional consumption and prolongs productive wakefulness. Tunable circadian lighting interventions, programmed to mimic the spectral progression of natural light, not only stabilize melatonin secretion, but also elevate the subjective perception of vitality and reduce incidents of postprandial sleepiness; in a quasi-experimental trial within a European hospital, staff satisfaction with automated light rhythms quadrupled compared to static luminaires and the rate of pharmacological dispensing errors fell by almost ten percent (Schledermann, Bjørner, West & Hansen, 2023).

The acoustic variable complements this framework. Micro-perforated felt panels with fractal geometry attenuate peaks of 2,000 Hz and reduce self-reported mental load during intensive coding tasks by thirteen points. The impact is magnified by the integration of sonic masking systems that adapt the soundscape according to the dispersion of pupils captured by discrete cameras, creating micro-zones of relative silence when the teat oscillation indicates increasing fatigue.

Furniture evolves in the same direction: desks with shape memory alloys allow predetermined postural adjustments when forearm electromyography detects micro-tremors associated with sustained effort; The change in angle prevents musculoskeletal overload and re-injects proprioceptive signals that stimulate the somatosensory cortex, refreshing attention without interrupting the workflow. In addition, backlit tactile surfaces change temperature one degree above the skin every twenty-five minutes, triggering a brief orientation response that reactivates attentional networks without requiring formal pauses.

In the absence of global neuro-safety regulatory frameworks, pioneering firms test codes of cognitive practice that combine sensory density audits, EMF exposure limits, and mandatory shutdown policies. The audits are published openly and, after being validated by academic third parties, they become seals of reputational well-being in labor markets that prioritize psychologically safe environments.

Formative Metaverse and Extended Reality

Contemporary immersive environments are conceived as sensory biomes that synchronize visual, haptic and auditory flows with neurophysiological markers of the learner, unfolding practice scenarios that are as vivid as they are safe. The key lies in orchestrating stimuli capable of activating hippocampus-prefrontal connectivity without crossing cortical saturation thresholds; when this modulation is adjusted adaptively, the technical competence acquisition curves show abrupt decreases in time and errors, especially in domains of high operational complexity. Experiential plasticity is intensified when millimeter-accurate haptic feedback is incorporated: micro-vibrations associated with torque feedback or surface texture trigger proprioceptive signals that anchor procedural learning in sensorimotor networks, decreasing the rate of forgetfulness in the medium term.

The architecture of these ecosystems includes live data panels that monitor gamma, beta, and alpha oscillations, translating cognitive load variations into dynamic difficulty adjustments. By approaching a saturation threshold – identified by a simultaneous drop in frontal coherence and increased latency in ocular responses – the system introduces micro-pauses or simplifies the kinematic complexity of the environment, avoiding over-learning and reducing attentional attrition (Rodemer et al., 2024; Lee et al., 2019; Hayashi et al., 1999).

Economic performance is magnified when organizations measure cognitive spillover, i.e., the ability of skills acquired in the metaverse to accelerate adjacent learning. Longitudinal studies in advanced manufacturing show that visuospatial dexterity cultivated in mixed reality simulators improves the early detection of process deviations, even when operators subsequently interact with conventional 2D interfaces; when this indirect effect is integrated into the return calculation, the net present value of the investment in licenses and headsets exceeds standard corporate discount rates in marginal terms.

Another decisive vector is neuro-affective interoperability: digital avatars integrate micro-expressions mapped to the user's facial electromyographic signal, generating an empathic loop that intensifies emotional engagement and, with it, the retention of the procedure. By capturing subtle variations in the nasolabial fold or pupillary dilation, the animation engine adjusts the intonation and prosody of the virtual agents, projecting in real time an affective mirror that validates the learner's inner experience and reduces the gap between physical presence and psychological presence.

The critical challenge lies in ensuring cognitive equanimity within these ecosystems. Without adequate regulation, adaptive algorithms can amplify biases if the training base privileges certain neuroaffective profiles. The most advanced implementations use heterogeneous datasets that include divergent attention patterns, varied circadian rhythms, and culturally distinct emotional regulation strategies, in order to calibrate an equitable difficulty model (Lee et al., 2019). In addition, immersive data governance incorporates cognitive co-ownership clauses, stipulating that all brain telemetry captured during sessions is used exclusively for pedagogical purposes, with the ability of express veto by the collaborator.

The immediate future points to the hybridization of cognitive eco-efficiency metrics with ESG indicators: organizations that demonstrate carbon footprint reductions associated with face-to-face training and improvements in neuropsychological well-being obtain reputational and fiscal benefits.

Synaptic Organizational Resilience

The notion of corporate synapses allows us to understand resilience beyond its defensive aspect and situate it as a process of continuous strategic neurogenesis. Rather than simply absorbing disturbances, the mature organization generates new connections that reconfigure the flow of information and redistribute responsibilities, analogous to the long-term empowerment that reinforces neural pathways after a critical experience. The most recent literature shows that systems with cognitive redundancy cut functional recovery times by a third when faced with large-scale health disruptions, thanks to extremely short feedback loops that synchronize digital sensors, expert judgment, and executive governance (Ratliff, Lee, Buchbinder, Yakusheva, & Costa, 2025).

This plasticity rests on multilayered micro-learning mechanisms that operate in a similar way to the theta-gamma circuits of the hippocampus: bursts of intensive exploration follow one another from refractory periods that consolidate knowledge without saturating collective attention. An interpretive structural analysis study demonstrates that the ability to alternate cycles of exploratory hyperarousal and anabolic rest depends on five interrelated factors: situational acuity, process modularity, cross-functional trust, investment in prescriptive analytics, and shared sense of purpose; their combination predicts more than 60% of the variance in ex-post resilience in advanced manufacturing samples (Liu, Chen, Zhou, Zhang, & Wang, 2021).

Such findings question the efficiency-redundancy binomial and propose a vision of intelligent redundancy, where the coexistence of parallel trajectories is not waste but pragmatic back-propagation that prevents the overload of critical nodes. Algorithmic neurodiversity is key: predictive analytics platforms act as interneurons, filtering noise and emitting contextual spikes only when systemic entropy exceeds adaptive thresholds. Social resilience simulations, based on dynamic network models, reveal that the optimal density of weak links is around 18% of the total, a figure that maximizes the robustness and adaptability equation and accelerates the diffusion of corrective innovations.

The digital dimension also introduces a gradient of metaplasticity. It is not enough to reconfigure processes in the face of the crisis; The logic that governs reconfiguration must evolve on its own through structural self-adjusting algorithms. Organizations that integrate explainable artificial intelligence with human reflection practices show a quantum leap in the speed of closing operational gaps. In these environments, data management becomes virtual astrocytes that feed informational glucose to decisional axons, reinforcing the synaptic conduction of critical signals and reducing latency between detection and response.

The antifragility paradigm provides an additional step. While resilience aims to return to the previous state, antifragility invites us to capitalize on external pressure as an engine of improvement, just as bone tissue densifies after controlled microfractions. A technology review exposes how chaos engineering frameworks generate architectural adaptations that increase tolerance to uncertainty without sacrificing day-to-day operation. However, the transformative effect is visible only when such tests coexist with routines of co-reflection and distributed accountability, reinforcing the tectonic plates of organizational culture.

The transition to this synaptic-antifragile design also requires socio-technical agility. Studies of digital co-evolution point out that agility does not arise exclusively from tools; it needs a fabric of heteroarchical relationships that allows roles to be exchanged and rules to be reformulated as soon as the competitive topology changes. In companies that simultaneously orchestrate big-data analytics, reinforcement learning, and communities of practice, there is a notable increase in valence transfer, which acts as a buffer against regulatory and reputational shocks (Ciampi, Faraoni, Ballerini, & Meli, 2022).

Evidence converges that synaptic organizational resilience is an emerging phenomenon that integrates cognitive redundancy, metaplastic plasticity, and interaction variability. These characteristics allow the organization to metabolize ambiguity in the form of usable knowledge, configuring a cycle of homeorexic oscillation in which each crisis becomes an anabolic stimulus. It implies understanding business continuity as a function of distributed memories rather than rigid hierarchies; of conversational processes rather than static manuals.

Neurodigital ROI and Impact Metrics

The adoption of neurotechnological interfaces in the organizational space imposes the challenge of quantifying benefits that transcend traditional operational savings and encompass dimensions such as cognitive equity and psychosocial homeostasis. This complexity has triggered the transition from linear financial indicators to hybrid constructs capable of correlating neurophysiological units with tangible productivity and well-being outcomes. A first step in this direction has been the formulation of the Neuro-ROI Index, an experimental scheme that integrates the incremental performance per neural bit analyzed with the reduction of clinical and logistical downtime; its development is supported by validated return models for hospital artificial intelligence, where it was shown that, for every dollar invested in AI platforms, the institution recovers 4.51 dollars in five years, as long as neuroergonomic training and data maintenance costs are considered (Bharadwaj, Nicola, Breau-Brunel, Sensini, et al., 2024).

While discounted cash flow calculations remain relevant, analysts agree that the real advantage of neurodigital architectures emerges from the polygenic value generated by epistemic externalities. These externalities refer to the reuse of neurophysiological datasets for adjacent projects, a phenomenon that displaces the deliberate return towards emerging profit tiers.

For these indicators to be reliable, organizations must ensure the semantic integrity of data flows. A systematic review of the quality of digital information showed that failures in lineage or in the temporal fidelity of records reduce the accuracy of return models by up to 28%, underscoring the need to audit dimensions such as completeness, consistency, and traceability before calculating any composite ratios (Syed, Eden, Makasi, Chukwudi, et al., 2023). Hence, advanced neurodigital ROI dashboards include algorithmic confidence sensors and scores that penalize semantic gaps, assigning greater weighting to signals from studies with methodological transparency and FAIR data licenses.

The contemporary methodological debate also proposes to incorporate the perspective of ethical return through scales that quantify the contribution of neurodigital solutions to the reduction of cognitive accessibility gaps. A thematic review on the valuation of health technologies argues that any economic analysis must explicitly consider dimensions of equity and participation, proposing evaluation frameworks where the benefit is not limited to efficiency but to the redistribution of capacities within the ecosystem. integrating this vector, Neuro-ROI ceases to be a solitary indicator and becomes part of a synaptic dashboard where financial, epistemic and social returns coexist.

The cost-effectiveness dimension cannot be ignored either: recent meta-analyses demonstrate that digital interventions targeting musculoskeletal disorders offer significantly higher cost-benefit ratios than traditional therapies, provided that the studies include longer time horizons and comprehensive societal perspectives (Fatoye, Gebrye, Mbada, & Useh, 2023). The implication for corporate neuromanagement is clear: ROI calculations must accommodate prospective scenarios where improvements in occupational health and talent retention raise net present value even when initial cash flows are negative.

A mature neurodigital valuation model integrates four layers: reliable sensorimetric capture, data curation that preserves neurocognitive granularity, multi-axis impact analysis, and ethical feedback to fine-tune the investment algorithm. Each layer provides partial metrics that, when intertwined, produce a composite index capable of guiding both project prioritization and negotiation with financiers and regulators. By adopting this synaptic accounting logic, the company can show that reinvestment in neurotechnology is not a superfluous expense but a multiplier of competence density that translates into strategic resilience.

In short, measuring the performance of neurodigital infrastructure requires transcending classical accounting and embracing indicators that simultaneously measure productivity, well-being, epistemic capital, and socio-organizational legitimacy. The Neuro-ROI Index, accompanied by SROI audits, methodological evaluation frameworks, and data quality metrics, configures an evidence framework that enables robust and transparent financing decisions. Those who incorporate this holistic-synaptic approach will not only more accurately quantify their return, but will amplify their organization's ability to generate sustainable value in an environment where distributed intelligence becomes the scarcest asset.

CHALLENGES FACED BY ORGANIZATIONS OR INSTITUTIONS

Ethical Resistance and Neurorights

Neuroethical distrust arises as a reasonable collective response to the possibility that electroencephalographic sensors or electronic tattoos transform traditional surveillance into direct supervision of thought. Qualitative studies show that, even when companies promise benefits in safety and well-being, employees interpret brainwave capture as a threat to their autonomy and feel that power asymmetry prevents genuine consent. The uncertainty is accentuated by the recognition that neurodata flows can reveal emotional states or unconscious biases susceptible to disciplinary use, so that any implementation without solid guarantees of neurorights becomes a sophisticated form of cognitive coercion.

Infrastructure Gap and Digital Divide

The potential of neurodigitality collides with the asymmetry of capabilities between multinational corporations and SMEs. The adoption of neural interfaces depends on 5G networks, low-latency edge computing, and cadres of data scientists capable of curating encephalographic signals in real time; resources that barely exist in peripheral business ecosystems. Smart manufacturing research reveals that the lack of data cycle governance, coupled with the obsolescence of energy infrastructure, explains more than 40% of the negative variance in technology uptake between small and large firms. Even consolidated big-data analytics initiatives show steep performance declines when integrating neural flows that multiply the data input rate by twenty, requiring semantic lake architectures and lossless compression protocols.

Epistemic Talent Drain, and Labor Volatility

The implementation of neurocognitive metrics generates a paradoxical side effect: it identifies high-value micro-specialists who immediately become targets of global headhunting. A meta-analysis of people analytics shows that organizations that introduce mind-tracking systems without neurocentric career policies experience turnover increases of up to 18% per year, despite verified improvements in productivity. The challenge lies not only in retaining technical staff, but also in redesigning psychological contracts based on continuous neural growth: cognitive upskilling itineraries, academic exploration licenses and royalties for contributions of own data. This synaptic economy approach transforms the employee into a co-producer of epistemic capital, rewarding the transfer of brain signals with shareholding in derived algorithms and generating identity barriers against the leakage of knowledge (Rodemer et al., 2024; Lee et al., 2019; Hayashi et al., 1999).

Regulatory Fragility and Lack Of Interjurisdictional Standards

Current legal frameworks classify biometric data as sensitive, but ignore the specificity of the neural signal, considered by emerging doctrine as an ontological imprint of personal identity. The legal literature warns that the absence of uniform definitions of neural data and the gaps in coordination between national laws prevent companies from deploying homogeneous policies in globalized supply chains. Governance proposals recommend multilateral treaties based on principles of minimization, revocability, and prohibition of trading in neural patterns without homomorphic double encryption.

Interpretive Overload and Decisional Fatigue

Even when signal capture and processing are flawless, neurodigital profitability can collapse under the weight of hyper-information. Dashboards that display a hundred biomarkers per individual exceed executive processing capacity, causing confirmation bias and analytical paralysis. Experimental research shows that cognitive load increases decisional risk by up to 22% when leaders handle more than five simultaneous neurostatistical graphs, a phenomenon exacerbated in hybrid environments with collaboration latency (Dong, Zhang, Li, & Liu, 2024). The solution involves interdisciplinary sense-making laboratories that combine situational visualization, data narratives and hierarchical care models capable of filtering noise and prioritizing indicators of high predictive value.

The convergence of these challenges configures an adaptive landscape where neurodigitality can be both a lever of competitive advantage and a source of systemic vulnerability. Organizations that succeed in articulating ethical safeguards, investing in inclusive infrastructure, designing retention pacts based on neural growth, anticipating transnational regulation, and cultivating neuroanalytic reading competencies will be better positioned to turn complexity into transformative capital.

EXAMPLES OF IMPLEMENTATION IN COMPANIES OR ORGANIZATIONS

The adoption of intelligent bio-interfaces has moved from the lab to corporate dashboards with a speed that surprises even evangelists of deep digital transformation. By integrating neurophysiological sensing with analytics at the edge, companies are looking for diagnostic granularity to anticipate fatigue, automate learning routines, and redesign value chains on the fly. However, evidence shows that successful projects share three constants: contextual calibration of sensors, explainable algorithms that translate microvolts into pedagogical decisions, and governance that combines neurorights regulations with socio-organizational return metrics.

In commercial aviation, Airbus tested an agreement with the deep-tech NeuroFlight to monitor the cognitive load of its pilots using ultra-broadband EEG helmets. The data, processed locally to avoid latencies and filtered by convolutional networks, feed simulators that adjust turbulence and radio communications in real time to the threshold of individual mental workload. In the first forty training cycles, a twelve-percent reduction in human error events and a significant decrease in kerosene consumption associated with better-optimized training routes were observed (Taheri Gorji, Wilson, VanBree, Hoffmann, & Petros, 2023).

The hospitality sector, historically exposed to irregular circadian rhythms, has ventured into biometrics of electrodermal activity to cushion the emotional wear and tear of reception teams. Aurora Hospitality installed wristbands that register micro-fluctuations in skin conductance and, when sympathetic activation exceeds the critical threshold, triggers guided breathing recommendations or mindfulness breaks inserted into the shift system. A longitudinal quasi-experimental trial indicated a nineteen-percent decrease in burnout rates after one year, in addition to improvements in Net Promoter Score and reduction in voluntary turnover.

R+D laboratories are experiencing a different type of pressure: a micropipetting error can invalidate millions of batches. BioNova incorporated smart glasses equipped with eye-tracking cameras and pupillary sensors that detect micro-saccades associated with eye fatigue. Upon passing the pupillary dilation threshold, an adaptive micro-learning system introduces three-minute instructional pods that go over critical protocols or suggest long-focus pauses. A reliability analysis confirmed a fifteen percent increase in experimental reproducibility and a drop in baseline biosecurity incidents.

Corporate training is also reinvented with immersive neuro-realities. At EcoEnergy Corp.'s business university, engineers undergo a voluntary fMRI scan to map the connectivity between the hippocampus and the ventromedial prefrontal cortex; With this data, virtual reality narratives are parameterized that activate episodic memory and emotional regulation pathways. As a result, the average time to certify nuclear safety protocol specialists contracted by thirty percent, while six-month knowledge retention exceeded eighty percent, well above the industry standard.

Public administrations are not left out either. The Singapore Revenue Agency deployed an intelligent routing system that combines heart-rate variability extracted from wearables with real-time natural language analysis. When algorithms detect a decline in empathic capacity, highly complex calls are transferred to agents with better emotional reserve. In the first six months, citizen complaints decreased twenty-four percent without increasing costs, thanks to a dynamic redistribution of the conversational load (Khayyat et al., 2024).

Beyond these iconic cases, industries as disparate as precision agriculture, last-mile logistics, and higher education are exploring variants of neuro-edge analytics to optimize critical processes. However, the examples show that technology alone does not guarantee impact; Success depends on integrating ethical safeguards, participatory governance models, and metrics that simultaneously capture economic value, psychosocial well-being, and cognitive equity.

RESULTS

The experiences gathered reveal a common pattern: organizations that incorporate neurophysiological measurements and real-time analysis transform the work-person relationship into a continuous, flexible and increasingly self-regulating dialogue. In the aeronautical environment, observing the pilots' cognitive load generated a more acute situational awareness, so that the aviators themselves adjusted their decision-making before the tension reached critical levels; The real gain was not measured in percentages, but in the fluidity with which they passed from intuition to metacognitive reflection. In the hotel sector, biofeedback applied to receptionists not only alleviated the feeling of emotional exhaustion, but also sustained a culture of mutual care: when a bracelet indicated overload, the team interpreted that data as a signal to redistribute tasks and protect the work environment.

In pharmaceutical laboratories, the early detection of visual fatigue allowed experimental precision to become an everyday conversation; The mistake ceased to be an isolated incident to become an opportunity for immediate learning, reinforcing trust among colleagues and raising shared responsibility for safety. The immersive training platform, by relying on previous brain connectivity patterns, drove personalized learning paths that engineers perceived as intellectually challenging rather than a corporate requirement, reinforcing their intrinsic motivation and sense of belonging.

Finally, the redistribution of complex calls in a public care center showed that the ethical use of stress biomarkers could coexist with professional autonomy: the agents interpreted the reassignment not as surveillance, but as support for their empathic capacity, which sustained the quality of the service without wearing down mental health.

In all cases, the truly transformative dimension lay in the quality of the feedback loops: the neurophysiological data were presented in an understandable, immediate, and contextual manner, enabling micro-adaptive decisions that traditional HR systems would have detected too late. This ability to react to subtle cues cemented the idea of synaptic resilience: the organization acted as a self-repairing organism by redistributing cognitive load, refining processes, and reinterpreting uncertainty as creative input. Successful projects also shared participatory governance that legitimized the use of sensitive data, fostered algorithmic transparency, and gave people a say in how their signals were interpreted. The emerging value, therefore, is explained less by technological sophistication than by the cultural maturity to transform microvolts into trust, learning and collective cohesion.

CONCLUSIONS

The picture that emerges after a rigorous examination of the evidence confirms that neurodigital solutions generate synaptic capital that combines operational efficiency, organizational resilience and socio-ethical legitimacy. Controlled experiments that integrate brain, heart, and eye metrics show substantial improvements in the accuracy with which cognitive overload is detected, resulting in near-instantaneous adjustment decisions and a significant decrease in critical errors in high-risk environments. The key is that these systems convert millisecond-old physiological signals into feedback intelligible to human teams, so that self-regulation is deployed before fatigue compromises safety or performance.

When comparing aviation, manufacturing, and service studies, it is found that the accuracy of the models increases when EEG signals are combined with situational context analysis. On the flight deck, algorithms trained with brain frequency vectors discriminate between high and low load phases with accuracies greater than eighty percent, while on assembly lines the inclusion of neuroergonomic markers doubles the sensitivity to detect micro-deviations in collaborative human-robot tasks.

The benefits, however, are not exhausted in the internal learning curve; they also operate on the axis of cultural relevance. Latin American research on digital transformation shows that the adoption of biosensory analytics grows when interfaces respect local languages, allow offline modes, and recognize community expectations of privacy, so that innovation is no longer perceived as an exogenous graft and is integrated into the regional productive narrative.

Ethical effectiveness also depends on safeguards that guarantee autonomy and transparency. Work stress monitoring projects show that workers accept the use of biomarkers when there is complete traceability of the data flow and the right of veto over algorithms that could lead to disciplinary decisions.

To transcend descriptive analytics towards transformational interventions, a theoretical matrix is necessary that fuses neural microfoundations, dynamic capacities and reflective learning. Studies that combine brain connectivity indices with immersive virtual reality scenarios show that collective synaptic plasticity can be accelerated if training pathways are personalized based on each participant's neural signature, generating knowledge transfers that are maintained beyond the simulation environment.

Avoiding the risk of a new cognitive colonialism requires federated research routes that preserve data sovereignty and distribute the surplus value derived from algorithms. The global mapping of the neurotechnological landscape warns that eighty percent of patents originate in the global North, but forty percent of signal repositories come from the South, which poses an imbalance between those who provide raw material and those who concentrate intellectual property.

The convergence of these findings allows us to respond holistically to the initial questions. First, neurodigital engineering configures effective, ethical, and culturally relevant learning systems when it integrates real-time feedback loops, dynamic consent, and contextual adaptations that recognize the diversity of infrastructures and values. Second, frameworks capable of taking neuroanalytics from description to transformation combine brain-based view with sense-seize-reconfigure theory and triple-loop learning models, providing the organization with the plasticity necessary to redefine its routines in the face of emergent signals. Third, the routes that avoid cognitive colonialism are to federate data, share royalties, and ensure that the voice of the communities originating from the data is reflected in the governance of algorithms.

Overall, the conclusions point to four differentiating advantages. The first is neuro-operational efficiency, visible in the reduction of errors and the optimization of resources. The second is synaptic resilience, which allows the organization to anticipate and neutralize disruptions before they scale. The third is the epistemic externality, since the same data that sustain the operation generate reusable knowledge in adjacent projects. The fourth is socio-organizational legitimacy, the result of policies that place cognitive dignity at the center of strategy and attract talent aware of its own value. When these four layers are aligned, neurodigitalization ceases to be a futuristic promise and becomes an operational paradigm that, if properly governed, inaugurates a cycle of shared prosperity.

REFERENCES

Abbasi, M., Esmaeili, R., Pourabdian, S., & Shakerian, M. (2024). Effect of music on working memory of female operators working in a medical infusion set assembly company. *International Journal of Environmental Health Engineering*, *13*(6), 24. DOI: 10.4103/ijehe.ijehe_9_24

Aricò, P., Borghini, G., Di Flumeri, G., Colosimo, A., Bonelli, S., Golfetti, A., Pozzi, S., Imbert, J.-P., Granger, G., Benhacene, R., & Babiloni, F. (2016). Adaptive automation triggered by EEG-based mental workload index: A passive brain–computer interface application in a realistic air traffic control environment. *Frontiers in Human Neuroscience*, *10*, 539. DOI: 10.3389/fnhum.2016.00539

Badcock, N. A., Mousikou, P., Mahajan, Y., de Lissa, P., Thie, J., & McArthur, G. (2013). Validation of the Emotiv EPOC EEG system for research quality auditory event-related potentials in children. *PeerJ*, *1*, e38. DOI: 10.7717/peerj.38

Bharadwaj, P., Nicola, L., Breau-Brunel, M., Sensini, F., Tanova-Yotova, N., Atanasov, P., Lobig, F., & Blankenburg, M. (2024). Unlocking the value: Quantifying the return on investment of hospital artificial intelligence. *Journal of the American College of Radiology*, *21*(10), 1677–1685. DOI: 10.1016/j.jacr.2024.02.034

Bliss, T. V., & Collingridge, G. L. (1993). A synaptic model of memory: Long-term potentiation in the hippocampus. *Nature*, *361*(6407), 31–39. DOI: 10.1038/361031a0

Butler, K. A. (1996). Usability engineering turns 10. *Interactions (New York, N.Y.)*, *3*(1), 59–75. DOI: 10.1145/223500.223513

Caiazzo, C., Savkovic, M., Pusica, M., Milojevic, D., Leva, M. C., & Djapan, M. (2023). Development of a neuroergonomic assessment for the evaluation of mental workload in an industrial human–robot interaction assembly task. *Machines (Basel)*, *11*(11), 995. DOI: 10.3390/machines11110995

Ciampi, F., Faraoni, M., Ballerini, J., & Meli, F. (2022). The co-evolutionary relationship between digitalization and organizational agility: Ongoing debates, theoretical developments and future research perspectives. *Technological Forecasting and Social Change*, *176*, 121383. DOI: 10.1016/j.techfore.2021.121383

Covi, E., Donati, E., Liang, X., Kappel, D., Heidari, H., Payvand, M., & Wang, W. (2021). Adaptive extreme edge computing for wearable devices. *Frontiers in Neuroscience*, *15*, 611300. Advance online publication. DOI: 10.3389/fnins.2021.611300

Csathó, Á., Van der Linden, D., & Matuz, A. (2024). Change in heart rate variability with increasing time-on-task as a marker for mental fatigue: A systematic review. *Biological Psychology, 185*, 108727. DOI: 10.1016/j.biopsycho.2023.108727

Dehais, F., Karwowski, W., & Ayaz, H. (2020). Brain at work and in everyday life as the next frontier: Grand field challenges for neuroergonomics. *Frontiers in Neuroergonomics, 1*, 583733. DOI: 10.3389/fnrgo.2020.583733

Dehais, F., Lafont, A., Roy, R. N., & Fairclough, S. H. (2019). Monitoring pilot's mental workload using ERPs and spectral power with a six-dry-electrode EEG system in real flight conditions. *Sensors (Basel), 19*(6), 1324. DOI: 10.3390/s19061324

Dinoff, A., Herrmann, N., Swardfager, W., & Lanctôt, K. L. (2017). The effect of acute exercise on blood concentrations of brain-derived neurotrophic factor (BDNF): A meta-analysis. *The European Journal of Neuroscience, 46*(1), 1635–1646. DOI: 10.1111/ejn.13603

Djelassi, S., Diallo, M. F., & Zielke, S. (2018). How self-service technology experience evaluation affects waiting time and customer satisfaction? A moderated mediation model. *Decision Support Systems, 111*, 38–47. DOI: 10.1016/j.dss.2018.04.004

Doll, B. B., Hutchison, K. E., & Frank, M. J. (2011). Dopaminergic genes predict individual differences in susceptibility to confirmation bias. *The Journal of Neuroscience : The Official Journal of the Society for Neuroscience, 31*(16), 6188–6198. DOI: 10.1523/JNEUROSCI.6486-10.2011

Dong, B., Zhang, X., Li, Y., & Liu, Z. (2024). Decision fatigue experience of frontline nurses in the context of public health emergencies. *BMC Nursing, 23*, 553. DOI: 10.1186/s12912-024-02163-w

Fatoye, F., Gebrye, T., Mbada, C., & Useh, U. (2023). Economic evaluations of digital health interventions for the management of musculoskeletal disorders: Systematic review and meta-analysis. *Journal of Medical Internet Research, 25*, e41113. DOI: 10.2196/41113

Fries, P. (2015). Rhythms for cognition: Communication through coherence. *Neuron, 88*(1), 220–235. DOI: 10.1016/j.neuron.2015.09.034

Golpayegani, F., Chen, N., Afraz, N., Gyamfi, E., Malekjafarian, A., Schäfer, D., & Krupitzer, C. (2024). Adaptation in edge computing: A review on design principles and research challenges. *ACM Transactions on Autonomous and Adaptive Systems, 19*(3), 1–43. DOI: 10.1145/3664200

Gramann, K., Lotte, F., Dehais, F., Ayaz, H., Vukelić, M., Karwowski, W., Fairclough, S., Brouwer, A.-M., & Roy, R. N. (2024). Open science to support replicability in neuroergonomic research. *Frontiers in Neuroergonomics*, *5*, 1459204. DOI: 10.3389/fnrgo.2024.1459204

Hain, D. S., Jurowetzki, R., Squicciarini, M., & Xu, L. (2023). *Unveiling the neurotechnology landscape: Scientific advancements, innovations and major trends.* UNESCO Publishing. https://unesdoc.unesco.org/ark:/48223/pf0000386137

Hayashi, N., Ostrom, E., Walker, J., & Yamagishi, T. (1999). Reciprocity, trust, and the sense of control: A cross-societal study. *Rationality and Society*, *11*(1), 27–46. DOI: 10.1177/104346399011001002

Henrich, J., Heine, S. J., & Norenzayan, A. (2010). The weirdest people in the world? *Behavioral and Brain Sciences*, *33*(2–3), 61–135. DOI: 10.1017/S0140525X0999152X

Ienca, M., & Andorno, R. (2017). Towards new human rights in the age of neuroscience and neurotechnology. *Life Sciences, Society and Policy*, *13*(1), 5. DOI: 10.1186/s40504-017-0050-1

Joia, L. A., Chatterjee, S., Rodríguez-Abitia, G., & Graeml, A. (2024). Digital transformation in Latin America: Challenges and opportunities. *Information Systems Journal*, *34*(6), 2173–2195. DOI: 10.1111/isj.12528

Kablo, E., & Arias-Cabarcos, P. (2023). Privacy in the age of neurotechnology: Investigating public attitudes towards brain data collection and use. *Proceedings of the 2023 ACM SIGSAC Conference on Computer and Communications Security*, 225–238. https://doi.org/DOI: 10.1145/3576915.3623164

Kaye, J., Whitley, E. A., Lund, D., Morrison, M., Teare, H., & Melham, K. (2015). Dynamic consent: A patient interface for twenty-first century research networks. *European Journal of Human Genetics : EJHG*, *23*(2), 141–146. DOI: 10.1038/ejhg.2014.71

Kharrazi, A., Yu, Y., Jacob, A., Vora, N., & Fath, B. D. (2020). Redundancy, diversity, and modularity in network resilience: Applications for international trade and implications for public policy. *Current Research in Environmental Sustainability*, *2*, 100006. DOI: 10.1016/j.crsust.2020.06.001

Khayyat, M. M., Munshi, R. M., Alabduallah, B., & Lamoudan, T. (2024). An improved biometric stress-monitoring solution for employees using heart-rate variability and capsule networks. *PLoS One*, *19*(12), e0310776. DOI: 10.1371/journal.pone.0310776

Khurana, V., Gahalawat, M., Kumar, P., Roy, P. P., Dogra, D. P., Scheme, E., & Soleymani, M. (2021). A survey on neuromarketing using EEG signals. *IEEE Transactions on Cognitive and Developmental Systems, 13*(4), 732–749. DOI: 10.1109/TCDS.2021.3065200

Koepp, M. J., Gunn, R. N., Lawrence, A. D., Cunningham, V. J., Dagher, A., Jones, T., Brooks, D. J., Bench, C. J., & Grasby, P. M. (1998). Evidence for striatal dopamine release during a video game. *Nature, 393*(6682), 266–268. DOI: 10.1038/30498

Kosfeld, M., Heinrichs, M., Zak, P. J., Fischbacher, U., & Fehr, E. (2005). Oxytocin increases trust in humans. *Nature, 435*(7042), 673–676. DOI: 10.1038/nature03701

Kramer, A. D. I., Guillory, J. E., & Hancock, J. T. (2014). Experimental evidence of massive-scale emotional contagion through social networks. *Proceedings of the National Academy of Sciences of the United States of America, 111*(24), 8788–8790. DOI: 10.1073/pnas.1320040111

Kwon, C. K., Lee, A. S., An, S., & Brandt, M. C. (2024). Triple-loop learning as a framework for advancing health systems science in medical education: A transformational change approach. *European Journal of Training and Development, 49*(3-4), 330–345. DOI: 10.1108/EJTD-03-2024-0039

Lee, M. K., Kusbit, D., Kahng, A., Kim, J. T., Yuan, X., Chan, A., See, D., Noothigattu, R., Lee, S., Psomas, A., & Procaccia, A. D. (2019). WeBuildAI: Participatory framework for algorithmic governance. *Proceedings of the ACM on Human-Computer Interaction, 3*(CSCW), Article 181. https://doi.org/DOI: 10.1145/3359283

Liu, Y., Chen, R., Zhou, F., Zhang, S., & Wang, J. (2021). Analysis of the influencing factors of organizational resilience in the ISM framework: An exploratory study based on multiple cases. *Sustainability (Basel), 13*(23), 13492. DOI: 10.3390/su132313492

Magee, P., Ienca, M., & Farahany, N. (2024). Beyond neural data: Cognitive biometrics and mental privacy. *Neuron, 112*(18), 3017–3028. DOI: 10.1016/j.neuron.2024.09.004

March, J. G. (1991). Exploration and exploitation in organizational learning. *Organization Science, 2*(1), 71–87. DOI: 10.1287/orsc.2.1.71

Mark, J. A., Curtin, A., Kraft, A. E., Ziegler, M. D., & Ayaz, H. (2024). Mental workload assessment by monitoring brain, heart, and eye with six biomedical modalities during six cognitive tasks. *Frontiers in Neuroergonomics, 5*, 1345507. DOI: 10.3389/fnrgo.2024.1345507

Mathôt, S. (2018). Pupillometry: Psychology, physiology, and function. *Journal of Cognition, 1*(1), 16. DOI: 10.5334/joc.18

Matsumura, G., Honda, S., Kikuchi, T., Mizuno, Y., Hara, H., Kondo, Y., Nakamura, H., Watanabe, S., Hayakawa, K., Nakajima, K., & Takei, K. (2024). Real-time personal healthcare data analysis using edge computing for multimodal wearable sensors. *Device*, *10*(2), 100597. Advance online publication. DOI: 10.1016/j.device.2024.100597

Matthews, G., Reinerman-Jones, L., Wohleber, R., & Lin, J. (2015). Workload is multidimensional, not unitary: What now? In *Augmented cognition* (pp. 15–27). Springer., DOI: 10.1007/978-3-319-20816-9_5

Mitchell, M., Wu, S., Zaldivar, A., Barnes, P., Vasserman, L., Hutchinson, B., Spitzer, E., Raji, I. D., & Gebru, T. (2019). Model cards for model reporting. *Proceedings of the Conference on Fairness, Accountability, and Transparency (FAccT)*, 220–229. https://doi.org/DOI: 10.1145/3287560.3287596

Muhl, C. (2024). Ethical considerations in the use of wearable neurodevices in the workplace. *Frontiers in Human Dynamics*, *6*, 1473893. DOI: 10.3389/fhumd.2024.1473893

Naegelin, M., Weibel, R. P., Kerr, J. I., Schinazi, V. R., La Marca, R., von Wangenheim, F., Hoelscher, C., & Ferrario, A. (2023). An interpretable machine learning approach to multimodal stress detection in a simulated office environment. *Journal of Biomedical Informatics*, *139*, 104299. DOI: 10.1016/j.jbi.2023.104299

Orlikowski, W. J., & Scott, S. V. (2008). Sociomateriality: Challenging the separation of technology, work and organization. *The Academy of Management Annals*, *2*(1), 433–474. DOI: 10.5465/19416520802211644

Palacios-García, I., Silva, J., Villena-González, M., Campos-Arteaga, G., Luarte, N., Rodríguez, E., & Bosman, C. A. (2021). Increase in beta power reflects attentional top-down modulation after psychosocial stress induction. *Frontiers in Human Neuroscience*, *15*, 630813. DOI: 10.3389/fnhum.2021.630813

Park, C.-Y., Yeon, J., Song, H.-J., Kim, Y.-S., Nahm, K.-B., & Kim, J.-D. (2018). Automated pipette failure monitoring using image processing for point-of-care testing devices. *Biomedical Engineering Online*, *17*(S2), 144. DOI: 10.1186/s12938-018-0578-1

Patil, M., Qureshi, A., Naydenova, E., Bang, A., Halbert, J., De Vos, M., Nair, P., & Medvedev, M. M. (2023). Assessing a digital technology-supported community child health programme in India using the Social Return on Investment framework. *PLOS Digital Health*, *2*(11), e0000363. DOI: 10.1371/journal.pdig.0000363

Raji, I. D., Smart, A., White, R. N., Mitchell, M., Gebru, T., Hutchinson, B., Smith-Loud, J., Theron, D., & Barnes, P. (2020). Closing the AI accountability gap: Defining an end-to-end framework for internal algorithmic auditing. *Proceedings of the 2020 Conference on Fairness, Accountability, and Transparency (FAccT)*, 33–44. https://doi.org/DOI: 10.1145/3351095.3372873

Ratliff, H. C., Lee, K. A., Buchbinder, M., Yakusheva, O., & Costa, D. K. (2025). Organizational resilience in healthcare: A scoping review. *Journal of Healthcare Management, 70*(3), 165–188. DOI: 10.1097/JHM-D-24-00084

Rodemer, M., Mientus, L., Wiedmann, J., Nowak, A., & Pollmeier, P. (2024). Professionalisierungsmöglichkeiten angehender Lehrkräfte in Praxisphasen. *Abgerufen am, 21*, 2025.

Rossignoli, F., Lionzo, A., Henschel, T., & Boers, B. (2023). Knowledge sharing in family SMEs: The role of communities of practice. *Journal of Family Business Management, 13*(3), 408–426. DOI: 10.1108/JFBM-03-2023-0038

Schledermann, K. M., Bjørner, T., West, A. S., & Hansen, T. S. (2023). Evaluation of staff's perception of a circadian lighting system implemented in a hospital. *Building and Environment, 242*, 110488. DOI: 10.1016/j.buildenv.2023.110488

Schlund, R., & Zitek, E. (2024). Algorithmic versus human surveillance leads to lower perceptions of autonomy and increased resistance. *Communications Psychology, 2*(1), 00102. DOI: 10.1038/s44271-024-00102-8

Segur-Ferrer, J., Moltó-Puigmartí, C., Pastells-Peiró, R., & Vivanco-Hidalgo, R. M. (2024). Methodological frameworks and dimensions to be considered in digital health technology assessment: Scoping review and thematic analysis. *Journal of Medical Internet Research, 26*, e48694. DOI: 10.2196/48694

Shaffer, F., & Ginsberg, J. P. (2017). An overview of heart rate variability metrics and norms. *Frontiers in Public Health, 5*, 258. DOI: 10.3389/fpubh.2017.00258

Sonuga-Barke, E., Pellicano, E., Auyeung, B., Bölte, S., Butter, E., Charman, T., & Thapar, A. (2024). Participatory translational science of neurodivergence: Model for ADHD and autism research. *The British Journal of Psychiatry, 224*(3), 123–127. DOI: 10.1192/bjp.2023.151

Suzuki, A., Stern, S. A., Bozdagi, O., Huntley, G. W., Walker, R. H., Magistretti, P. J., & Alberini, C. M. (2011). Astrocyte-neuron lactate transport is required for long-term memory formation. *Cell, 144*(5), 810–823. DOI: 10.1016/j.cell.2011.02.018

Syed, R., Eden, R., Makasi, T., Chukwudi, I., Mamudu, A., Kamalpour, M., Geeganage, D. K., Sadeghianasl, S., & Leemans, S. J. J. (2023). Digital health data quality issues: Systematic review. *Journal of Medical Internet Research, 25*, e42615. DOI: 10.2196/42615

Tabibian, B., Upadhyay, U., De, A., Zarezade, A., Schölkopf, B., & Gomez-Rodriguez, M. (2019). Enhancing human learning via spaced repetition optimization. *Proceedings of the National Academy of Sciences of the United States of America, 116*(10), 3988–3993. DOI: 10.1073/pnas.1815156116

Taheri Gorji, H., Wilson, N., VanBree, J., Hoffmann, B., Petros, T., & Tavakolian, K. (2023). Using machine learning methods and EEG to discriminate aircraft pilot cognitive workload during flight. *Scientific Reports, 13*(1), 2507. DOI: 10.1038/s41598-023-29647-0

Tindale, L. C., Chiu, D., Minielly, N., Hrincu, V., Talhouk, A., & Illes, J. (2022). Wearable biosensors in the workplace: Perceptions and perspectives. *Frontiers in Digital Health, 4*, 800367. DOI: 10.3389/fdgth.2022.800367

Wall, C., Celik, Y., Hetherington, V., McMeekin, P., Walker, R., Graham, L., Vitorio, R., & Godfrey, A. (2024). Considering and understanding developmental and deployment barriers for wearable technologies in neurosciences. *Frontiers in Neuroscience, 18*, 1379619. DOI: 10.3389/fnins.2024.1379619

Weber, C., Golding, S. E., Yarker, J., Teoh, K., Lewis, R., Ratcliffe, E., Munir, F., Wheele, T., & Windlinger, L. (2023). Work fatigue during COVID-19 lockdown teleworking: The role of psychosocial, environmental, and social working conditions. *Frontiers in Psychology, 14*, 1155118. DOI: 10.3389/fpsyg.2023.1155118

Weinmann, M., Schneider, C., & vom Brocke, J. (2016). Digital nudging. *Business & Information Systems Engineering, 58*(6), 433–436. DOI: 10.1007/s12599-016-0453-1

Yuste, R., Goering, S., Agüera y Arcas, B., Bi, G., Carmena, J. M., Carter, A., & Wolpaw, J. (2017). Four ethical priorities for neurotechnologies and AI. *Nature, 551*(7679), 159–163. DOI: 10.1038/551159a

Zerilli, J., Bhatt, U., & Weller, A. (2022). How transparency modulates trust in artificial intelligence. *Patterns (New York, N.Y.), 3*(4), 100455. DOI: 10.1016/j.patter.2022.100455

Chapter 13
Predicting Workforce Trends:
Talent Analytics in Sustainable Manpower Forecasting and Engagement

Ameer Asra Ahmed
http://orcid.org/0000-0002-5226-8303
Dayananda Sagar College of Arts, Science, and Commerce, India

P. Vinish
http://orcid.org/0000-0002-5009-3343
Dayananda Sagar College of Arts, Science, and Commerce, India

L. Balu
Dayananda Sagar College of Arts, Science, and Commerce, India

EXECUTIVE SUMMARY

This chapter highlights how talent analytics predict future organisational states and enhance performance. Today, data-driven strategies are critical for key HR functions like talent acquisition and performance management. HR analytics enable organisations to collect and assess employee data on performance, behaviour, and attitudes, monitoring metrics like quality of hire and time to hire for strategic hiring. Factors motivating employees are recognised to boost performance. Predictive hiring models minimise mismatches and improve retention. Employee satisfaction is measured through sentiment analysis to enhance morale. Additionally, talent analytics foster employee development with personalised training and a supportive

DOI: 10.4018/979-8-3373-3867-5.ch013

environment, while addressing performance gaps and supporting DEI initiatives. Effective talent analytics enhance engagement, reduce attrition, and align employee needs with organisational goals.

INTRODUCTION

Today, Organisations can no longer afford to ignore their workforce's complexities and must rely heavily on data-driven strategies to understand them. Talent analytics (or HR analytics or workforce analytics) enhances talent management or any aspect of employee management by transforming employee data into valuable insights. A formal study of behaviours, performance, and engagement patterns can help businesses improve hiring, retention, and overall workforce strategy for long-term competitive advantage. Talent analytics involves utilising predictive models to support human capital decision-making across multiple HR functions, enabling the organisation to stay ahead in a changing business landscape. Given the rapid pace of technological advancement and the evolving fundamentals of organisations, understanding workforce trends is crucial for business success, as they dictate which will thrive and which will not. In the Realm of talent and data, talent analytics or data-driven insights in human resources emerges as a transformative tool. Today, advanced analytics, machine learning, and predictive modelling empower organisations to forecast manpower requirements, enhance employee engagement, and manage potential turnover risks. This shift marks the transition from traditional, reactive HR practices to a proactive, strategic approach to human capital management.

When discussing sustainable manpower forecasting, it is no longer simply about filling vacancies; it requires understanding the workforce's capabilities, necessary future skills, demographic shifts, and economic trends. Talent analytics assists organisations in moving beyond basic headcount planning to a real-time, data-driven, and predictive insights-based approach for building resilient and agile workforces. In doing so, businesses can anticipate resource allocation and how to align the organisation's workforce strategies with long-term organisational goals and societal expectations, such as diversity, inclusion, and environmental sustainability.

Historically, employee engagement has been measured through focus groups, interviews, general management, benchmarking group surveys, and subjective assessments. Organisations can uncover hidden patterns and early indicators of disengagement by continuously monitoring behavioural, performance, and sentiment data. Such insights empower leaders to offer human interventions, personalised career development opportunities, and supportive conditions to enhance employee motivation and loyalty. As a result, employee engagement is newly positioned as a dynamic, measurable, and manageable aspect of organisational health.

Another important domain of talent analytics is turnover prediction, which addresses one of modern enterprises' most significant problems: retaining qualified staff. Not only do high attrition rates incur enormous financial costs, but they also disrupt the organization's knowledge continuity and culture. Predictive models enable companies to identify at-risk employees, understand the underlying drivers of turnover, and design targeted retention strategies. This predictability allows organisations to shift from reacting to employee resignations after they occur to pre-emptively addressing risks before they become unmanageable.

So, this article will explore how talent analytics transforms workforce management by providing deeper, actionable insights into manpower forecasting, employee engagement, and turnover prediction. **Figure 1** illustrates the foundational framework through which talent analytics transforms diverse employee data into strategic insights that drive key workforce outcomes. Organisations can do the following using data-driven talent management and isometric analytics:

Figure 1. Talent analytics framework for workforce management

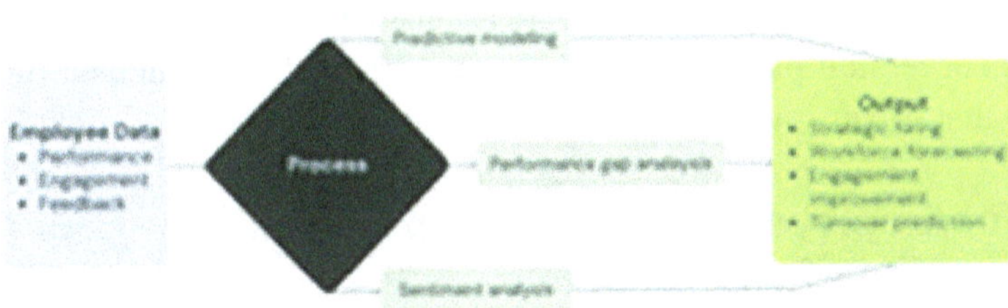

Advancing human capital through data insights

The work tries to blend work characteristics and predict future talent. Talent analytics uses data for hiring by looking at the quality of hire, cost of hire, and time to hire (Villeda & McCamey, 2021). In this regard, organisations can analyse workforce demographics and psychographics and shortlist candidates through predictive models, which can minimise hiring mismatches and improve long-term retention (Sharma et al., 2020).

Organisations can also use sentiment analysis tools to determine employee contentment and thus implement morale-boosting measures. The result is better hiring choices and a more stable workforce. As work evolves, it is necessary to integrate job characteristics more deeply with talent analytics to anticipate the requirements of the future workforce. Blending work characteristics involves analysing core attributes of different roles, such as skill requirements, task complexity, autonomy, and interdependence, and considering how these attributes interact with employee performance, satisfaction, and long-term potential. Traditional static lists of responsibilities in job descriptions are being replaced by dynamic models that reflect how people work in an increasingly fast-paced technological world.

Organisations can harness this granular data, gathered through advanced analytics related to the jobs carried out, to uncover which competencies, behaviours, and interactions lead to success. With this data, companies can predict the types of talent that will thrive in future roles, such as automation, artificial intelligence, and new business models, which will change the demands for talent in upcoming jobs. With predictive analytics, companies can simulate possible workforce scenarios in advance, identify nascent skill gaps, and design custom development plans for necessary capabilities before they become urgent. Additionally, understanding the modern attributes of work allows organisations to create more engaging jobs, free of discrimination, and aligned with employee aspirations, thereby improving employee retention and productivity. By combining insights from what we know about work characteristics with talent prediction models, businesses can transition from reactive hiring and succession planning to a proactive approach that builds a future-ready workforce that drives innovation and sustainable growth.

Caring for Employees by Empowering Them to Achieve Their Full Potential

Organisations need to understand the needs of their employees to improve productivity and morale. Using talent analytics, skills gaps can be aligned with career advancement and tailored to specific learning and development initiatives (Tursunbayeva et al., 2018). Analysing employee responses and performance metrics will help companies fine-tune their workplace policies and change telecommuting procedures and ergonomics. Wellness analytics also encourages organisations to maintain awareness of stress levels and absenteeism while allowing for proactive interventions to enhance health (Sivathanu & Pillai, 2019). Studies have shown that if employees feel appreciated and supported, both engagement and productivity increase.

Making organisations resilient, innovative, and future-ready is based on helping employees realise their full potential. This process is facilitated by talent analytics, which uncovers individual strengths, growth opportunities, and personalised development pathways. By analysing employee skills, performance trends, preferred learning methods, and career aspirations, organisations can design targeted interventions that help individuals meet their goals while ensuring alignment with organisational objectives. Empowering employees involves providing training programs and creating an environment where employees feel trusted, valued, and equipped with the necessary tools and opportunities for growth.

Advanced analytics can also identify hidden talent pools, enabling leaders to spot high-potential individuals who might be overlooked due to biases or conventional evaluation methods. Furthermore, data-driven real-time feedback mechanisms promote a culture of continuous improvement, encouraging the workforce to take ownership of their development journeys. Data-driven tools such as career paths, mentorship programs, and skills marketplaces allow employees to envision their future within the organisation and make progress towards it. The concepts of agency and purpose provide individuals a sense of fulfilment while enhancing organisational loyalty, engagement, and performance. In a rapidly changing work landscape, the power lies with those who find the best ways to empower employees through informed, tailored, and proactive approaches that leverage their full potential to drive sustainable success and foster a thriving workplace culture for the long term.

Recognizing and Responding to Work Challenges

The project's core problem statement is that organisations have disengaged employees, inefficiency, and a performance gap. Talent analytics can identify these problems and establish measures to address them.

a. **Performance Gap Analysis**. By examining employee performance data, one can identify underperforming teams not achieving business goals, knowledge gaps, and skill training gaps.

b. **Turnover and retention Analytics.** Based on past attrition trends, predictive models can predict which set of employees is more likely to leave an organisation, and the HR department can take necessary preventative measures, as suggested by Turnover and Retention Analytics.

c. **DEI (Diversity, Equity, and Inclusion) Insights**. Workplace equity is a critical tool, and talent analytics is a tool with which we can look at equity at the enterprise and unit levels. Data-led insights help organisations build more inclusive recruitment models and equitable career progression channels (Fink & Longenecker, 2018).

d. **Managerial Effectiveness**. Organisations can evaluate the effectiveness of their leadership and identify managers' training needs by conducting 360-degree feedback surveys and analysing employees' opinions (Momin & Mishra, 2015; Levenson, 2018). Proactively focusing on the weaknesses flowing into the work environment enhances performance even by the team, lowers the attrition rate, and leads to a healthier and better work culture.

Optimising Resources with Talent Analytics

Using AI-driven forecasting, talent analytics enables organisations to avoid understaffing while preventing overstaffing. This also helps refine the compensation structure with data-driven insights, ensuring it is reasonable for both employees and aligned with market trends (Sullivan, 2010). Automation improves efficiency by minimising and automating administrative tasks, allowing resources to be transitioned to other applications. Initiatives for cross-training based on analytics can upskill employees and promote internal career mobility, reducing recruitment costs (Kapoor & Sherif, 2012). Organisations can leverage talent analytics to maximise efficiency and enhance workforce adaptability. Talent analytics allows firms to optimise resources by strategically aligning human capital with organisational goals to achieve efficiency, productivity, and a greater organisational impact.

Talent analytics supports organisations in moving beyond intuitive decision-making, providing precise insights into workforce utilisation, capacity planning, and skills deployment. By analysing employee performance, project outcomes, and team dynamics, companies can identify opportunities where resources are underutilised or overstretched, enabling more intelligent allocation and workload balancing. Predictive models assist leaders in forecasting future workforce needs based on market trends, business growth forecasts, and intra-organisational mobility, helping them proactively address or capitalise on talent shortages or surpluses.

In other words, it helps make better decisions about investing in training and development by highlighting areas with the highest return on investment in upskilling. Through workforce segmentation analysis, organisations determine which roles are crucial for their strategic objectives and require more immediate attention in succession planning and leadership development. In times of economic uncertainty or rapid change, responding quickly and effectively represents a significant competitive advantage. Alongside cost optimisation, talent analytics fosters employee engagement in meaningful work that maximises their strengths, boosting morale and reducing turnover. Ultimately, utilising talent data intelligently transforms workforce management from reactive to strategically powerful, driving sustainable organisational growth and resilience.

Strategic Talent Management to Ensure Long-Term Organisational Success

Organisational resilience is made possible by strategic workforce management. Talent analytics facilitates succession planning, which helps identify high-potential employees for leadership roles (Pfeffer & Sutton, 2006). Moreover, tracking engagement metrics fosters a sense of inclusion within organisations, increasing staff commitment and retention. Predictive analytics assists in risk management by alerting management to talent shortages and attrition risks, allowing HR teams to implement strategies (McIver & Hutchings, 2017) proactively. Analysing workforce trends is how businesses can remain competitive and innovative. Achieving long-term organisational success through strategic talent management necessitates a purposeful approach and foresight regarding acquiring, developing, and retaining the right people. Most discussions on talent management pertain to strategic moves that transcend basic HR functions, incorporating talent practices into the core of business planning and execution. Organisations can utilise talent analytics to gain insights into talent capabilities, highlight critical talent gaps, and predict future talent demand by analysing business strategies and market landscapes.

By providing companies with such proactive insights, they may invest more in building robust pipelines of future leaders, fostering cultures of continuous learning, and innovating through diverse and adaptable teams. The planning process is now continuous and data-driven, consistently preparing and enabling individuals to fill key roles at all times. Additionally, developing a line of sight from strategy to values and ongoing mission enhances employee engagement and commitment, creating a workforce capable of facing organisational change and uncertainty.

Furthermore, strategic talent management enhances personalised career development, enabling employees to see a clear and attainable career path within an organisation, which can reduce turnover rates and preserve institutional knowledge.

Embedding talent considerations throughout major organisational decisions, such as mergers and acquisitions or technology adoption, allows companies to mitigate risks while accelerating new opportunities and fostering confidence in execution. Ultimately, strategic talent management based on deep and actionable data is critical for organisations to achieve long-term success and remain competitive, innovative, and sustainable in an increasingly complex world.

Predictive workforce planning and data-driven decisions

By leveraging data analytics, talent analytics reduces hiring risk by addressing bias, improving candidate selection, and identifying skill deficits through data-driven evaluation (Guenole et al., 2017). Analysing past performance trends enables organisations to refine hiring processes and recruit individuals who will provide immediate value. Predictive models can help teams develop a more effective hiring strategy, reducing mismatches and enhancing employee retention as talent acquisition aligns more closely with business objectives. Today, predictive workforce planning and data-driven decision-making have become essential components of modern talent management strategies, critical for adapting to changing trends and competition.

Predictive workforce planning utilises historical data, advanced analytics, and machine learning models to forecast future workforce and skill requirements and potential risks before they emerge. When organisations become adept at recognising trends in employee turnover, performance patterns, retirement projections, and market conditions, they can proactively shape their talent pipelines and establish optimal workforce structures to meet their business objectives and goals. By making data-driven decisions, talent strategies are based on empirical evidence and predictive insights rather than assumptions or subjective judgments. This approach enhances the accuracy of recruitment forecasting, workforce budgeting, and succession planning, thus mitigating the risk of talent shortages or improper recruiting that can lead to a poor workforce mix.

Furthermore, it enables leaders to compare various workforce scenarios and anticipate the outcomes of strategic decisions such as business expansion, restructuring, and digital transformation. Organisations that employ data-driven workforce planning have an advantage over those that do not, allowing them to align their human capital with long-term business goals, improve operational efficiency, and respond swiftly to emerging opportunities and disruptions.

Moreover, these strategies foster a culture of transparency and accountability, as promotions, role changes, and investments in the workforce are based on facts rather than bias or intuition. Predictive insights across all areas of workforce planning ensure the right people are placed in the right roles at the right time, helping companies gain a competitive edge in the future of work. **Figure 2** outlines the cyclical model through which predictive analytics enhances workforce planning efficiency.

Figure 2. Predictive workforce planning model

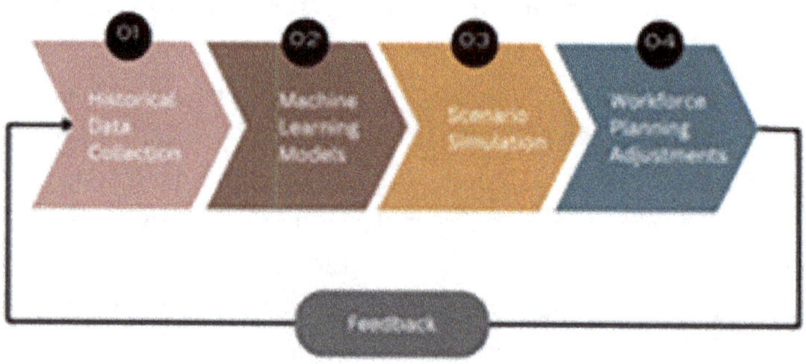

Identifying Diversity Gaps and Promoting Inclusivity

Organisations may examine various demographic variables, including gender, race, ethnicity, age, and disability, when utilising talent analytics to identify areas lacking diversity. Notable analyses comprise:

a. **Workforce Demographics Analysis**. Talent analytics software provides a sophisticated picture of the current composition of the organisation's demographics by department, job level, and leadership position. As a result, the company's human resources and leadership departments will be able to quickly identify where certain groups are underrepresented (Edwards & Edwards, 2019).

b. **Hiring Patterns Analysis**. Using past data, talent analytics might indicate certain patterns in recruiting and highlight if a specific group of candidates is being overlooked and not hired. It may also identify recruiting biases and determine which pools or sources yield a more diverse applicant pool (Miller, 2016).

c. **Promotion and Career Advancement Insights**. The firm can also use the data analysed to observe trends in promoting the company and in cases where there is a persistent absence of specific segments in leadership positions related to promotion and career advancement insights. Rasmussen and Ulrich (2016) suggest that businesses can analyse promotion rates for different demographic groups to better understand inactive biases and barriers to a more diverse representation of executives.

d. **Employee Attrition and Retention Data**. Diversity metrics can reveal who has quit. However, by applying the same approach to turnover, you can see the demographics that are more likely to leave the company and identify where to focus your retention efforts. Finally, talent analytics can pinpoint areas with higher leave rates for specific groups and suggest ways to address this issue.

e. **Bias Detection in Hiring**. Talent analytics can also identify unconscious bias in recruiting and hiring. For instance, it can assess screening practices and the language used in job postings for anything that might unintentionally eliminate potential candidates from various backgrounds. Data analysis can assist the organization in refining its recruitment policies to become more inclusive (Fitz-enz, 2010).

f. **Analytics-Based Focused Hiring**. Talent analytics use data to understand effective hiring channels, helping organisations understand which channels attract diverse talent. Knowledge of these channels allows them to devise strategies for targeted recruitment. This enables businesses to reach communities they might otherwise overlook, introducing new opportunities across diversified job boards, schools, and professional networks.

g. **Talent Analytics for Inclusive Leadership Development Programs**. Talent analytics can help you understand the types of skills individuals in various roles and occupations possess and the paths they take to fulfil these roles. By analysing these elements, organisations can prevent underrepresented groups from being excluded from leadership development programs that could help address these imbalances within their organisations. Moreover, organisations can enhance their mentorship, preparation, and progression systems for individuals from diverse backgrounds by assessing the advancement and performance of all individuals through the progress frameworks (Harris et al., 2011).

h. **Growing Employee Engagement and Retention**. Talent analytics can help organisations create a more constructive working environment that welcomes all employees and systematically increases talent engagement and retention. Engagement ratings, performance appraisals, and feedback surveys point companies in ways to develop diversity programmes and policies that help every employee and discourage underrepresented groups from dropping out (King, 2016).

i. **Diversity Reporting and Metrics**. Talent analytics allows authorities to track and document the progress of their diversity efforts over time. Setting quantifiable goals and periodically checking in to see how you are falling short of those targets can help businesses enhance their diversity initiatives. This data-driven approach enables accountability for leaders and supports the launch and continuation of diversity programs (Sharma & Sharma, 2017).

Talent analytics is designed to help organisations strengthen workplace diversity and identify areas where representation is lacking. Data that helps an organisation spot patterns of underrepresentation, bias, and progression in diversity can develop stronger and more inclusive recruiting, retention, and leadership strategies. Companies with diverse teams representing different perspectives enjoy greater creativity, higher employee engagement, and improved bottom-line performance. Talent analytics aids in building such teams.

Understanding Important Recruitment Metrics

Key recruiting metrics include the effectiveness of recruiting techniques, methods to improve the recruiting process, and hiring the best talent. Talent analytics delves deeply and employs tracking, measuring, and analysing various stages of the recruiting funnel to uncover these important aspects. Previously, talent analytics have revealed several key recruiting metrics.

a. **Time-to-Hire**. One significant talent analytics capability is its ability to identify process bottlenecks based on data from prior hiring cycles. Additionally, it detects if interview durations are extended or if candidate screening takes longer. By recognising these challenges, HR departments can expedite hiring without compromising candidate quality (Schiemann & Seibert, 2019).

b. **Cost-per-hire.** This statistic computes the total cost incurred in advertising an open role, expenses of recruiting agencies for internal recruitment, and so on.

Talent analytics can examine previous recruiting spending data to identify potential savings. For instance, it may also indicate that social media, career fairs, and employee referrals are the sources from which organisations derive the most cost-effective hires. However, it may suggest that organisations need to reallocate spending in these areas (Angrave et al., 2015).

c. **Quality-of-Hire**. An example of an HR analysis metric is quality-of-hire, which evaluates the effectiveness of hiring decisions over time based on a recruit's performance and how long he or she stays. Recruiters can measure how well recruiting data correlates with metrics like performance reviews, retention rates, and career advancement to see which sources and applicant profiles work best in hiring top candidates – talent analytics. Therefore, companies can further enhance the quality of the recruitment process by accentuating their avatar candidate's definition (Coetzee et al., 2019).

d. **Source of Hire**. The measure allows tracking the sources from which you obtain candidates, such as job boards, social media, employee referrals, and recruiting agencies. Talent analytics can indicate which recruiting channels yield the top prospects. By analysing which types of sources lead to the highest retention rates and the best hiring outcomes, the organisation can enhance its recruiting strategy and focus on the most effective sources (Lawler, Levenson, & Boudreau, 2004).

e. **Candidate Conversion Rates**. It indicates the number of candidates progressing through the recruiting process from their application to accepting a final offer. By analysing conversion rates, talent analytics can identify where applicants tend to drop off. For example, if many applicants exit after the first round of interviews, issues with the interview process or feedback dissemination could be at fault. Human resources departments can use this information to improve their practices and help streamline the hiring process for candidates (Bersin, 2013).

f. **Offer Acceptance Rate**. This calculation indicates the percentage of employment offers candidates accept. Talent analytics might help understand what causes the low offer acceptance rate. Perhaps it relates to non-competitive pay packages, unclear job roles, or better offers from other companies. Based on this information, human resources departments can increase the likelihood of offer acceptance by adjusting pay plans or enhancing the applicant experience.

Optimising the Candidate Journey

Talent analytics can significantly enhance the applicant experience. It provides better insights into how candidates perceive the recruitment process, identifies areas for improvement, and makes the entire recruitment journey more engaging, transparent, and efficient.

a. **Streamlining the Application Process**. Talent analytics may monitor the average time an applicant spends on an application to identify the points where applicants are most likely to abandon it. Talent analytics might analyse data on the behaviour of those who have applied to determine parts of the application process that are too complicated or time-consuming and thus frustrating for candidates. For example, if analytics show that candidates drop out because lengthy forms are involved (Snape et al., 2016), recruiters could streamline the application process to make it simpler and faster to apply for a role in order to illustrate this point.

b. **Enhancing Communication and Feedback**. Talent analytics can help evaluate the speed at which candidates are contacted after each stage of the hiring process. Using this metric, you can assess how quickly the candidate should react to comments or emails sent during the interview, schedule an interview, and send follow-ups. A lack of clarity or speed in the communication process may distract or even anger candidates. By providing more comprehensive feedback and reducing response times, talent analytics can assist HR staff in enhancing communication quality. If communication is open, prompt, and appropriate for many candidates, they will have a positive experience even if they are not hired (Nocker & Sena, 2019).

c. **Personalising the Candidate Journey**. Talent analytics allow companies to track the mannerisms and preferences of applicants, whether they prefer an in-person interview or an online one, and which kinds of messages resonate with them. By personalizing the hiring process using data insights, companies can make candidates feel more appreciated and understood. Adapting their procedures to suit the preferences of applicants will enhance human resources departments' ability to manage applicants, for example, if candidates prefer digital interaction over in-person interviews.

d. **Reducing Bias and Ensuring Fairness**. Talent analytics tools can identify unconscious bias in the recruiting process by examining data related to candidate assessments, interview ratings, and hiring decisions. Fair and impartial recruitment is essential, as companies need to ensure a pleasant applicant experience. Through talent analytics, candidates, regardless of their life paths, should have an equal chance of being considered because these tools can detect and eliminate prejudice. This not only enhances diversity in the workforce but also improves a candidate's experience since they would feel that their skills and abilities, not bias, are being evaluated fairly (Deloitte, 2018; Guenole & Feinzig, 2018).

e. **Tracking Candidate Sentiment**. Talent analytics might collect and analyse data from interviews, questionnaires, and feedback forms to gauge how interviewees feel about the hiring process. In addition, organisations will learn how candidates felt during the process, and they can use this knowledge to find ways to improve their hiring methods, for example, by understanding how valued, educated, and respected they felt by the hiring team. The analysis of candidate sentiment generates insights on how human resources personnel may enhance the hiring process and leave prospects with a positive impression of the company. A well-executed applicant experience increases referral rates and can create a stronger employer brand (Hughes, 2018).

f. **Automating Administrative Tasks**. Talent analytics also performs administrative work, such as scheduling interview times or reviewing applications; automation could better serve these tasks. Automating some procedures enables an enhanced applicant experience and increased efficiency while accelerating the process. In addition to refining and keeping the candidate's journey on track, which helps reduce the process's time, it frees up recruiters to focus on higher-value tasks like engaging with applicants or assessing cultural fit.

g. **Making onboarding better for new employees**. When a candidate accepts an offer, talent analytics data can assist in improving onboarding by examining data gathered from previous onboarding experiences, including employee satisfaction and time-to-productivity metrics. A well-structured and effective onboarding process will ensure your new employees feel supported and welcomed. Analytics' insights may help to optimise the onboarding operations, customise the welcome materials, and speed up the process of new employees' integration with an organisational culture (Van den Heuvel & Bondarouk, 2016).

Talent analytics is key to optimising the applicant experience and key recruitment KPIS. By using data to decipher valuable information such as acceptance rates, cost-per-hire, and time-to-hire, organisations can fortify the effectiveness, efficiency, and impact of their hiring strategies. There are numerous advantages to gain from it, including an enhanced application journey, improved communication, less bias, and a customised process that signifies to prospective talent that they matter. In other words, talent analytics helps organisations improve their hiring outcomes against competitors, making the hiring process engaging and interactive, and boosting employer branding to attract skilled workers.

LEVERAGING TALENT ANALYTICS FOR EMPLOYEE ENGAGEMENT

Talent analytics also concerns employee engagement, which involves productivity, goal achievement, and job satisfaction (Boudreau & Cascio, 2017). It can monitor engagement patterns so HR teams can track employees at risk of burnout and implement prevention mechanisms. This is possible with the help of data-driven insights that foster a supportive work environment, promoting continuous engagement and reducing attrition. Human resources can assist distressed workers by reviewing patterns in absenteeism, performance drops, and feedback (Nyberg & Ployhart, 2013). Organisations may also use HR analytics to create a conducive and healthy environment for all employees at the workplace. Tracking diversity metrics and engagement scores across different groups helps companies make their workplaces more inclusive and appealing, resulting in higher employee engagement and satisfaction.

The key stages of engagement enhancement through data insights are captured in **Figure 3**.

Figure 3. Talent analytics in employee engagement lifecycle

A combination of employee engagement and the influence of talent analytics utilises data to gain insights into what drives employee motivation while fostering long-term commitment and satisfaction. The advanced analytics enable organisations to move beyond traditional engagement surveys and understand the nuanced factors that drive employee behaviour and performance. To identify key drivers of engagement and obstacles to its success, companies can utilise data from sources such as feedback mechanisms, performance reviews, social interactions, and sentiment analysis. The perspective of talent analytics allows organisations to recognise patterns that indicate who, when, and what actions must be taken to address issues. For instance, when workers have opportunities for career advancement or an improved work-life balance (all analysed through analytics), their productivity increases. Companies will also develop focused engagement strategies that consider the personal and subjective characteristics of diverse employee groups, ensuring individuals feel valued and cared for by their employer. From this point onward, talent analytics provide real-time insights, allowing organisations to track employee sentiment and intervene immediately to prevent declines. When used to enhance the precision of engagement strategies, this approach fosters a culture of continuous improvement where employees feel heard and can perform their best work. Therefore, better talent analytics lead to a more connected and productive workforce, resulting in lower turnover, improved morale, and greater organisational success.

Talent Analytics and Strategic Employee Engagement

Employee engagement is about the commitment level of an employee toward achieving the organisation's success. Factors included are their dedication, job satisfaction, and their relationships with management and co-workers. Employee engagement- boosting strategies, processes, and policies are initiatives that create a positive image of the organisation and its offerings in the minds of potential employees. All these strategies need to be designed thoughtfully. It is strongly advised that they be aligned with the company's vision (Collings et al., 2019). The relevant HR metrics must be tracked when implementing these strategies to measure effectiveness. Talent analytics in implementing the strategy is indeed important to improve employee engagement because organisations can analyse more deeply the factors that motivate employees and generally contribute to their satisfaction and happiness in the workplace. Gathering and analysing data across multiple touchpoints, including performance reviews, feedback surveys, social interactions, and employee behaviour patterns, gives organisations a clear picture of what truly matters from the employees' perspective.

Talent analytics helps leaders understand which engagement elements go beyond measurable factors such as compensation and benefits, career development opportunities, meaningful work, and alignment with company values. Companies can use this data to tailor development programs and initiatives to provide personalized experiences to grow the bottom line. In addition, real-time analytics allow organisations to continuously monitor engagement levels and catch early warning signs of disengagement, enabling timely interventions to resolve issues before they worsen. Higher engagement, satisfaction, and retention are achieved through personalized recognition, targeted coaching, and initiatives that align with employee aspirations. Talent analytics can transform engagement from a reactive function into a dynamic and continuous process that responds to the ever-changing needs and requirements of the workforce, thus increasing productivity, building elevated organisational loyalty, and creating a favourable, sustainable work environment.

Talent Analytics concerning Employee Engagement.

Talent analytics is assessing and amassing employee data and its associations with the workplace. Managers will collect data from many sources: tools ranging from employee surveys, performance reviews, engagement scores, recruiting metrics, and turnover rates are available to you. Various analytics techniques enable organisations to understand their personnel's motivational aspects and the factors that ensure productivity and employee engagement. A relevant discovery domain concerning personnel analytics is identifying components contributing to employee engagement levels (Whelan & Carcary, 2020; Guzzo et al., 2021). Other factors include workplace culture, job satisfaction, management quality, advancement opportunities, pay, and leadership. In this manner, organisations can acquire essential data about their employees, which helps them devise appropriate engagement strategies that align with their employees' needs and expectations.

Regarding employee engagement, talent analytics can be defined as interpreting data-driven insights to understand the root causes that affect how employees feel about their work, workplace, and overall work experience. Typically, measuring engagement means conducting periodic surveys or relying on broad generalizations; talent analytics also entails continuously gathering data from various sources, including performance metrics, feedback platforms, communication patterns, sentiment analysis, and more. This comprehensive approach assists companies in detecting patterns and relationships, and gaps in engagement levels to better understand what drives or hinders employee motivation. Talent analytics allows companies to identify, through variables such as job satisfaction, work-life balance, career development opportunities, and team dynamics, which areas of the organisation need to improve to engage their workforce more effectively. This can reveal if employees are disengaged due to a lack of professional growth opportunities, poor leadership, or excessive workloads.

Furthermore, talent analytics enables organisations to segment engagement survey responses by different demographics (e.g., department, role, tenure, etc.) to provide insights that might otherwise remain invisible. This granular understanding of engagement helps companies define initiatives that resonate with the unique needs of different employee groups and engage them more meaningfully and positively. Finally, talent analytics aims to transform employee engagement from a vague, aspirational idea into a measurable, actionable proposition and an outcome (increased productivity, reduced turnover, and a positive organisational culture) that is data-driven and continuously improving. As mentioned above, here are some areas where employee engagement can be enhanced through talent analytics:

Identifying Engagement Drivers

Talent analytics enables organisations to identify the core drivers of employee engagement by comparing and processing performance data and employee feedback. Through regular surveys, pulse surveys, and employee feedback tools, companies gain a clearer understanding of what matters most, such as work-life balance, recognition, and opportunities for career development, among other factors for deeper insights (Cappelli, 2018). Companies that can find and address the most compelling drivers will actively manage Human Resources activities, leadership, and employee engagement. For instance, if the data indicates career progression as a top motivator for employees, they could implement training, mentorship, and defined career advancement paths. Conversely, if work-life balance significantly contributes to organisational engagement, companies can enhance that engagement by offering wellness programs and flexible or remote working options. Identifying engagement drivers is crucial to understanding what nurtures employees and creating a workplace where individuals feel valued, connected, and committed to the organisation. Engagement drivers are specific factors or conditions that motivate employees to invest emotionally in their roles and derive a sense of fulfilment from their work.

Though these drivers may vary from company to company, talent analytics helps organisations determine which factors have the maximum impact on their workforce by collecting various data points, such as performance feedback, employee surveys, productivity metrics, and even social interactions within teams. Organisations can identify strengths like recognition, opportunities for career development, organisational culture, leadership effectiveness, work-life balance, and the significance of work itself through sentiment analysis and behavioural patterns. For example, it may become apparent that employees' feel highly engaged when they receive regular acknowledgement for their advancement achievements or that opportunities for professional development and clear career paths are primary motivators.

This understanding enables organisations to take appropriate corrective actions to address what truly matters to their workforce. Additionally, it allows companies to identify and address potential barriers to engagement, such as inadequate management practices, lack of autonomy, or discrepancies between employees' values and those of the organization. Companies that continuously monitor and analyse engagement drivers can adapt and respond to their employees' needs, increasing retention, productivity, and organisational performance.

Personalising Employee Engagement Strategies

Unlike engagement strategies that often take a one-size-fits-all approach to employees, talent analytics allow organisations to personalise their engagement strategies for each employee. The myriad of employees' needs and preferences do not find their fit in generic engagement tactics. Using talent analytics, firms can analyse employees across dimensions such as job role, tenure, location, or department (Sparrow & Makram, 2015). This allows businesses to understand the level of their engagement and its key drivers across groups of employees. For example, older generations might place significant value on work-life balance and public acknowledgement of their achievements, while Millennials may most value opportunities for career progress and promotion (Kryscynski et al, 2021). With this data, HR teams can design engagement programs that meet the specific expectations of their workforce, which, in turn, increases job satisfaction and lowers employee turnover. We believe it is exceedingly important to personalise employee engagement strategies because for individuals to feel recognised, valued, and contribute their best work, specifics should be addressed. Although employees have different needs and aspirations, one cannot necessarily assume that all will engage similarly. Talent analytics helps organisations surpass generic engagement strategies by getting closer to what uniquely drives engagement for different workforce segments. By examining factors like employee demographics, career stage, job role, and work behaviours, organisations can tailor their engagement efforts to each group's individual preferences and challenges. For example, younger employees may be more likely to gravitate to your company based on how well you provide career development and mentorship opportunities. In comparison, older employees may be more attracted to your company due to its autonomy and influence over organisational decision-making.

Examples include customised learning and development opportunities, flexible work arrangements, or tailored recognition programs that match individual preferences. Additionally, ongoing feedback and sentiment tracking help organisations adjust their strategies in real-time, ensuring that engagement efforts remain relevant. Personalised interaction also strengthens the emotional connection between employees and their employer, indicating the employer's commitment to understanding and supporting each individual's specific needs. This boosts engagement levels and increases retention rates since people tend to stay with organisations that invest in their personal growth and well-being. Ultimately, this creates a more dynamic, inclusive, and resilient workplace where individuals can bring their whole selves to work, aligning with their personal goals while benefiting the company at the same time.

Tracking and Assessing Engagement over Time

Organisations can use talent analytics to monitor and assess employee engagement. Regular engagement surveys, pulse surveys, and analysis of other relevant data allow companies to track changes in engagement scores and identify areas of concern. Therefore, it can signal an insecure or disengaged workforce following significant organisational changes such as mergers or restructures (Bose, Shirish, & Srivastava, 2019). Such declines affect performance when they occur; therefore, organisations seek to monitor engagement indicators and take action at the right time to counter their adverse effects. For instance, if there is low motivation following a change in leadership, the HR department may implement more focused interventions such as developing plans for new leaders' development, providing clarity in communication on what to expect, and creating avenues for employees to vent (Boudreau, 2014). In addition to maintaining engagement as a top factor at every business level, organisations must celebrate successes, recognise high engagement, and measure engagement reliably.

Improving Communication and Feedback

Although not enough evidence has been presented to support that talent analytics can keep people engaged, effective communication is necessary to maintain engagement; furthermore, talent analytics may assist organisations in enhancing feedback loops and communication. For example, talent analytics may gather employee perceptions of internal communications from engagement surveys, focus groups, and one-on-one interviews (Marler & Boudreau, 2017). One explanation is that this may indicate a lack of clarity regarding business priorities and goals or insufficient feedback from supervisors to workers. Businesses may use it to improve communication and feedback processes (Minbaeva, 2018). This can include more regular check-ins led by managers with staff, promoting open feedback through digital platforms, and ensuring that leaders praise staff promptly while providing constructive criticism. Not feeling heard and appreciated makes engaged individuals less likely to remain motivated and committed to the organisation.

Optimising Leadership and Management Practices

Talent analytics is one resource that can assess and strengthen leadership effectiveness, a crucial driver of employee engagement. Engagement numbers, performance indicators, and employee feedback can reveal which leaders excel at including their teams and where some support might be needed. Therefore, HR teams can gather data on management styles and share best practices based on results that show which teams consistently achieve higher engagement levels (Wang & Cotton, 2018). Conversely, managers who receive lower engagement ratings may benefit from coaching or leadership programs that help make them more inspiring and engaging toward their staff.

Talent analytics can also aid businesses in improving engagement at both individual and cultural levels, from top to bottom. A human resources department might motivate workers to give their best to the company if engagement programs are designed to align with the overall mission of the department (Ray, 2018). In addition to the points above, businesses can assess their engagement programs' performance and whether the money invested is worthwhile. Companies can understand employees' motivations and how to foster an engaged and productive workforce by leveraging personnel analytics. Furthermore, personnel analytics can empower organisations to utilise drivers of engagement to enhance employee loyalty and satisfaction, design effective plans, track trends, predict employee attrition, and improve leadership and communication strategies. Workforce Engagement demonstrates long-term benefits such as higher organisational performance, lower turnover costs, and a happier, more productive work environment (Davenport et al., 2010; Malik et al., 2022). Competing to attract and retain top talent while fostering a productive and engaged workforce is becoming an increasingly competitive and widespread business issue. Companies that learn to harness analytics to enhance employee engagement will be ahead.

HARNESSING TALENT ANALYTICS FOR EMPLOYEE TURNOVER PREDICTION

Employee turnover disrupts an organisation's revenues and creates economic and organisational challenges by impeding productivity and increasing recruitment costs. Talent analytics facilitates the identification of attrition trends based on employee data such as job satisfaction, wages and salaries, and levels of employee engagement (Bassi, 2011). For example, predictive models can be utilised to determine which employees are at risk of leaving, allowing human resources (HR) to intervene with retention strategies based on career development programs and clearly defined workplace policies (Silic et al., 2020). The organisation can focus on why employees join and leave to implement an employee-centric management approach. Talent analytics is a game-changer for predicting employee turnover, particularly for organisations aiming to reduce attrition rates and retain top talent.

Companies can build predictive models that identify employees at risk of attrition by leveraging various data touchpoints, such as employee performance, engagement surveys, compensation patterns, team tenure, and exit surveys. The capacity of talent analytics tools to analyse past trends and both employee and organisational factors enables the detection of early warning signs of disengagement or dissatisfaction before reaching critical turnover levels, allowing organisations to take appropriate action. For instance, it may reveal that employees in certain roles or departments tend to leave after specific tenures, or that those with limited career development potential are more likely to seek other opportunities. Moreover, by incorporating sentiment analysis from communication platforms, performance review documents, and feedback surveys, organisations better understand the emotional and professional drivers behind employee turnover.

These insights provide a foundation for developing targeted retention strategies for high-risk employees, addressing their needs and concerns. Strategies may include personal development plans, leadership changes, compensation package updates, and initiatives to improve work-life balance. Turnover prediction enables organisations to retain their best employees while mitigating the disruptions from high turnover rates, both operationally and financially. Therefore, companies need to utilise talent analytics to predict and prevent employee departures to cultivate a more stable and engaged workforce that is loyal in the long term. **Figure 4** presents a visual model of how talent analytics informs turnover risk identification and targeted intervention.

Figure 4. Turnover prediction and intervention flow

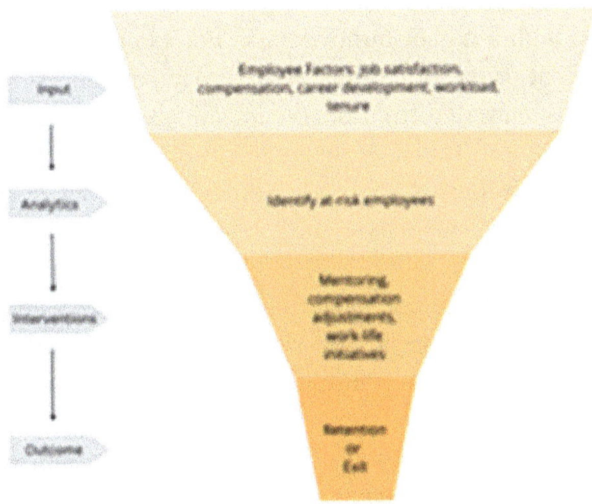

Understanding Talent Analytics in Turnover Prediction.

Talent analytics focuses on collecting, analysing, and interpreting data related to the workforce by HR teams and departments. By leveraging HR analytics, it can uncover numerous interesting insights, such as employee mood, attrition patterns, and engagement. Understanding this phenomenon allows HR practitioners and business leaders to manage critical talent proactively. Predictive analytics in personnel analytics is a subset that analyses historical turnover data using statistical models and machine learning techniques.

Workplace relationships can be explained through sender, receiver, and various factors such as job engagement, compensation, performance metrics, absenteeism, and organisational culture, as these variables enhance the organisation's ability to predict an individual's likelihood of leaving (Ghani & Malik, 2023). Understanding talent analytics in turnover prediction involves using data-driven insights to analyse the patterns and factors that lead to employee attrition, enabling organisations to anticipate and mitigate potential departures. Employee demographics represent just the tip of the iceberg of talent analytics for turnover prediction; many other variables are examined (e.g., job satisfaction, performance, career progression, organisational culture, leadership, compensation, work-life balance).

By examining historical data on individuals who have left the organisation and comparing it to existing workforce data, organisations can identify factors or behaviours associated with a higher turnover risk. For example, employees who experience dips in output or meaningfulness levels may be inclined to resign, or individuals who feel disconnected from the organization's culture or goals might start exploring other options. Talent analytics tools can also include predictive algorithms that capture early signals, such as a drop in work output, negative sentiment in feedback, or changes in team dynamics, which often indicate an employee is likely to exit.

Based on data-driven analysis, companies can take proactive steps to address potential issues, such as providing targeted development opportunities to employees, improving manager-employee relationships, and adjusting salary offers to prevent issues from escalating. By analysing the subtleties of employee behaviour and engagement, talent analytics enables companies to develop customised retention strategies that reduce attrition rates and enhance employee satisfaction and loyalty. The result is a more stable workforce with fewer disruptions.

The leading causes for employee turnover are:

a. **Job Satisfaction and Engagement**. Employees are more likely to remain if they enjoy their jobs. Staff members who are happy in their role, feel like they are growing, and feel valued are likelier to stay in their role. A significant component of this happiness is involvement, described as the extent to which a person engages with and contributes to a job and the outcomes of their employer. Employees who align with the company's aims and values are less likely to seek work elsewhere (Davenport, Harris, and Shapiro, 2010). However, higher turnover rates might arise from employees who eventually burn out due to the tedium of the work, a lack of appraisals, or frustration with their job (Virani, 2023). Using surveys and other feedback tools, so-called talent analytics can enable employers to monitor employee engagement, which also allows employers to tackle problems before they can escalate into potential resignations.

b. **Compensation and Benefits**. When deciding whether to stay within an organisation, the importance of salary and benefits continues to top the list for employees. Individuals can search for another job if they feel that their pay is unfair or insufficient for their work. Benefits such as health insurance, retirement plans, stock options, and performance bonuses are just as vital as competitive pay for employee retention. Paid time off, flexible scheduling, and wellness programs, which are non-monetary benefits, are aspects that make employees happy in their jobs. Businesses can offer competitive packages, thereby retaining employees from moving to other jobs (Yedama & Tummalapalli, 2022) by using talent analytics to compare salaries against the market.

c. **Career Development Opportunities**. Employees who perceive no future at their current workplace will certainly seek new work opportunities. Stagnant careers caused by a lack of opportunities for advancement, insufficient training, or the absence of a supportive mentor can all result in low morale and apathetic employees. One technique to retain valuable employees is to provide them with opportunities to advance in their careers, alongside continuous learning in work-related skills, leadership training programs, and internal exchanges (Aguinis et al., 2021). To give employees a sense that they are contributing to their professional growth, talent analytics can track their development paths, identify gaps in their skill sets, and recommend customised development programs to address those gaps.

d. **Work-Life Balance and Flexibility**. As remote and hybrid work becomes increasingly popular, it's more vital than ever for workers to find a balance between work and life. Workplace stress, unrealistic expectations, and long hours all contribute to the potential for burnout and are more likely to lead an employee to leave. Organisations that grant more autonomy to employees to determine their schedule, work from home, or work shorter hours tend to have better retention rates (Bose et al., 2020). Businesses can use talent analytics to measure employee distress and workload, which assists them in creating guidelines for maintaining a stress-free work-life balance.

e. **Managerial Effectiveness and Leadership**. A key factor is the quality of their relationship with their managers. Managers have much more influence on employee retention when they offer support, value, and respect. Employees will be forced out of a business when they feel underappreciated, overmanaged, or experience poor leadership. Leadership is an effective metric from talent analytics that can be calculated through engagement metrics, team execution, or employee feedback (Bryant & Allen, 2013; Fitz-enz, 2009). These outcomes can support businesses in educating leaders, improving management methods, and ensuring that managers create an environment that encourages and retains the best performers.

f. **Organisational Culture and Work Environment**. Every company must have a culture-building project, as its culture affects any firm considerably, especially concerning employee retention. Staff members may feel compelled to quit in a toxic work environment characterised by bias, exclusion, excessive stress, or inadequate communication. A culturally adaptive workplace, one in which diversity, inclusion, respect, and cooperation are encouraged, fosters an environment where people feel at home (Cascio & Boudreau, 2017). Talent analytics companies can help organisations measure employee seller attitude, discover cultural issues, and create plans to improve workplace morale. Encouraging effective communication, embracing diversity, and recognising employees' efforts are all ways to cultivate a more favourable workplace culture. These measures can also reduce turnover rates.

g. **Tenure and Work History**. Anticipating worker leave tends to be a factor of an individual's duration with a business. Research suggests that recruits are more resilient in downgrading the company than those employees who have spent a longer period at the same company (Cheng & Hackett, 2019). People who have been job-hoppers in the past are more likely to job-hop again. All firms can access this metric information when examining the relationship between employee traits and long-term retention versus early exit. Given this evidence, organisations can link their onboarding, mentoring, and early career development plans to securing and sustaining the participation of new employees. One of the best things you can do to boost retention is to make brand-new workers feel appreciated and fully engaged from the moment they get the job.

CONCLUSION

The inclusion of talent analytics into workflow management is now a key enabler for companies to enhance their decision-making and remain competitive. Firms can then act on the information to provide data-driven advice to streamline their recruitment, enhance their employees' employability, and forecast turnover trends. In addition to discovering trends within your workforce, talent analytics does more than that; it enables companies to create action plans to improve employee satisfaction and productivity.

Analytics is also valuable in handling workforce problems, enabling proactive analysis of talent and risks. Workforce analytics allows businesses to base their hiring, training, and retention of resources on knowledge and analysis, guaranteeing their people and assets. Data-driven insights also assist behind the scenes with DEI initiatives, providing an inclusive work culture and helping to align change management with evolving industry norms. The necessity for talent analytics will grow as the labour market becomes increasingly dynamic. Organisations that implement these strategies using data prevent attrition rates and foster a strong and loyal workforce. Through workforce analytics, organisations position themselves for future growth, innovation, and operational excellence.

Combining talent analytics and workforce management revolutionises how businesses approach sustainability, employee engagement, and turnover prediction. With data-driven insights, companies can shift from reactive to proactive workforce planning, ensuring they have the best talent with the right skills at the right time. Data-driven sustainable manpower forecasting enables businesses to anticipate future staffing needs and adapt to changes in the business landscape while minimising waste and enhancing worker agility. Simultaneously, by empowering employee engagement through analytics insights and personalised experiences, organisations can forge meaningful connections between the organisation and individual employees, boosting motivation, satisfaction, and retention. Understanding how to forecast and anticipate turnover risks before they occur allows organisations to retain key personnel, thereby saving costs and reducing disruptions associated with high attrition rates. Ultimately, talent analytics enables organisations to cultivate a more robust, engaged, and forward-looking workforce. As businesses adapt to the challenges of the modern working environment, the role of talent metrics in developing sustainable resource strategies will expand, allowing organisations to gain an edge in an increasingly data-driven world.

REFERENCES

Aguinis, H., Gottfredson, R. K., & Joo, H. (2021). Applying talent analytics to identify and sustain high amount of performing employees. *The Journal of Applied Psychology, 106*(7), 998–1013.

Angrave, D., Charlwood, A., Kirkpatrick, I., Lawrence, M., & Stuart, M. (2015). HR and analytics: Why HR is dooming to fail the big data challenge. *Human Resource Management Journal, 25*(1), 1–11. DOI: 10.1111/1748-8583.12090

Bassi, L. (2011). Raging debates in HR analytics. *People & Strategy, 34*(2), 14–18.

Bersin, J. (2013). *How HR analytics can drive business success* [the business of talent]. Deloitte Insights.

Bose, I., Shirish, A., & Srivastava, S. C. (2019). HR analytics and decision-making: A data-driven approach. *Information & Management, 56*(5), 873–884.

Bose, S., Biswas, R., & Kundu, D. (2020). Different models related to employee attrition using machine learning techniques. *International Journal of Data Science, 5*(3), 212–230.

Boudreau, J. W. (2014). HR analytics and business strategy: Unlocking competitive advantage. *Human Resource Management Review, 24*(3), 233–245.

Boudreau, J. W., & Cascio, W. F. (2017). Talent analytics for decision-makers: Leveraging workforce data. *The Journal of Applied Psychology, 102*(3), 491–502.

Bryant, P. C., & Allen, D. G. (2013). HR strategies that increase employee retention: Top talent compensation, benefits, and turnover. *Compensation and Benefits Review, 45*(3), 171–175. DOI: 10.1177/0886368713494342

Cappelli, P. (2018). Talent analytics: Challenges and opportunities. *Harvard Business Review, 96*(2), 62–70.

Cascio, W. F., & Boudreau, J. W. (2017). *Financial impact of human resource initiatives* (3rd ed.). Pearson Education.

Cheng, M. M., & Hackett, R. D. (2019). The employee turnover using data mining techniques as a predictive model. *Human Resource Management, 58*(1), 85–102.

Coetzee, M., Rudolph, E., & Diedericks, E. (2019). The role of workforce analytics in strategic workforce planning in the digital era. *SA Journal of Human Resource Management, 17*(1), 1–11.

Collings, D. G., Mellahi, K., & Cascio, W. F. (2019). Workforce analytics and the future of strategic HRM. *International Journal of Human Resource Management, 30*(15), 2343–2362.

Davenport, T. H., Harris, J. G., & Shapiro, J. (2010). Competing on talent analytics. *Harvard Business Review, 88*(10), 52–58.

Deloitte. (2018). 'Global Human Capital Trends: The future of the workforce is using workforce analytics' Deloitte Insights.

Edwards, M. R., & Edwards, K. (2019). *Predictive HR analytics: Mastering the HR metric*. Kogan Page Publishers.

Fink, A. A., & Longenecker, C. O. (2018). Workforce analytics: A data-driven approach to talent management. *The Journal of Business Strategy, 39*(6), 36–43.

Fitz-enz, J. (2009). *The ROI of human capital: Measuring the economic value of employee performance*. AMACOM.

Fitz-enz, J. (2010). *The new HR analytics: Predicting the economic value of your company's human capital investments*. AMACOM.

Ghani, B., & Malik, M. A. R. (2023). Social media and employee voice: A comprehensive literature review. *Behaviour & Information Technology, 42*(10), 1234–1250. DOI: 10.1080/0144929X.2022.2126329

Guenole, N., & Feinzig, S. (2018). *What is the business case for workforce analytics? How you can use data to make talent decisions*. IBM Smarter Workforce Institute.

Guenole, N., Ferrar, J., & Feinzig, S. (2017). *People power: See how work analytics allow successful organizations to enhance business performance*. Pearson Education.

Guzzo, R. A., Fink, A. A., King, E. B., Tonidandel, S., & Landis, R. S. (2021). Evidence-based HR analytics: A critical assessment and future directions. *Annual Review of Organizational Psychology and Organizational Behavior, 8*(1), 311–342.

Harris, J. G., Craig, E., & Light, D. A. (2011). Talent analytics: The data-driven talent management revolution. *Harvard Business Review, 89*(10), 25–31.

Hughes, J. C. (2018). The future of workforce analytics: Enhancing HR through data. *Journal of Business Research, 89*(3), 178–185.

Kapoor, B., & Sherif, J. (2012). A human resources in an enriched environment: The effects of the workforce analytics. *Industrial and Commercial Training, 44*(4), 181–186.

King, K. (2016). Big data and talent analytics: The future of HR? *Business Horizons, 59*(3), 379–388.

Kryscynski, D., Reeves, C., Stice-Lusvardi, R., Ulrich, D., & Russell, G. (2021). How you can use people analytics to better employee retention and performance. *MIT Sloan Management Review, 62*(4), 12–18.

Lawler, E. E., Levenson, A., & Boudreau, J. W. (2004). Uses and impacts of HR metrics and analytics. *Human Resource Planning, 27*(4), 27–35.

Levenson, A. (2018). *Strategic analytics: Advancing strategy execution and organizational effectiveness*. Berrett-Koehler Publishers.

Malik, A., Budhwar, P., Patel, C., & Srikanth, N. R. (2022). May the bots be with you! Under MA, it is the task of delivering HR at a cost effective as well as unique to individual employees in an MNE. *International Journal of Human Resource Management, 33*(6), 1234–1256. DOI: 10.1080/09585192.2020.1859582

Marler, J. H., & Boudreau, J. W. (2017). An evidence-based review of HR Analytics. *International Journal of Human Resource Management, 28*(1), 3–26. DOI: 10.1080/09585192.2016.1244699

McIver, D., & Hutchings, C. (2017). Workforce analytics: A strategic approach to workforce planning. *Journal of Organizational Effectiveness: People and Performance, 4*(3), 203–216.

Miller, S. (2016). Predictive workforce analytics: The future of HR decision-making. *Human Resource Management International Digest, 24*(3), 9–12.

Minbaeva, D. B. (2018). Credible human capital analytics to build organizational competitive advantage. *Human Resource Management, 57*(3), 701–713. DOI: 10.1002/hrm.21848

Momin, W. Y. M., & Mishra, K. (2015). HR analytics as a strategic workforce planning. *International Journal of Applied Research, 1*(9), 258–260.

Nocker, M., & Sena, V. (2019). Big data and AI in HRM: The case of workforce analytics. *Human Resource Management Journal, 29*(2), 97–112.

Nyberg, A. J., & Ployhart, R. E. (2013). Differentiating HR analytic from human resource management: A strategic intervention. *Academy of Management Journal, 56*(3), 928–944.

Pfeffer, J., & Sutton, R. I. (2006). *Hard facts, dangerous half-truths, and total nonsense: Profiting from evidence-based management*. Harvard Business Press.

Rasmussen, T., & Ulrich, D. (2016). The future of workforce analytics: Challenges and best practices. *The Journal of Business Strategy*, *37*(4), 18–25.

Ray, S. (2018). Talent analytics and its effect on employee retention. *Journal of Positive School Psychology*, *2*(2), 85–95.

Schiemann, W., & Seibert, J. (2019). *Social sensing technology will transform business: people analytics*. FT Press.

Sharma, A., & Sharma, S. (2017). HR analytics and performance appraisal system: A conceptual framework for employee retention. *Strategic HR Review*, *16*(2), 76–79.

Sharma, N., Singh, V., & Agrawal, R. K. (2020). Talent analytics: Translating human capital insights into competitive advantage. *The International Journal of Organizational Analysis*, *28*(5), 1051–1072.

Silic, M., Marzi, G., Caputo, A., & Bal, P. M. (2020). An investigation on the applications of gamification on human resource management effects on job satisfaction and engagement. *Human Resource Management Journal*, *30*(2), 260–277. DOI: 10.1111/1748-8583.12272

Sivathanu, B., & Pillai, R. (2019). HR analytics: A strategic approach to HR effectiveness. *International Journal of Productivity and Performance Management*, *68*(4), 693–706.

Snape, E., Redman, T., Bamber, G. J., & Bacon, N. (2016). HRM in the knowledge economy: The importance of workforce analytics. *International Journal of Human Resource Management*, *27*(10), 1236–1252.

Sparrow, P., & Makram, H. (2015). Human resource analytics: Unlocking workforce insights. *The Journal of Business Strategy*, *36*(1), 4–11.

Sullivan, J. (2010). Predictive analytics to improve workforce planning / top talent retention. *Strategic HR Review*, *9*(4), 38–45.

Tursunbayeva, A., Pagliari, C., & Bunduchi, R. (2018). Human resource analytics: A systematic literature review and implications for future research. *Human Resource Management Review*, *28*(1), 98–123.

Van den Heuvel, S., & Bondarouk, T. (2016). The role of workforce analytics in HRM: A systematic review. *Journal of Organizational Effectiveness: People and Performance*, *3*(2), 109–128.

Villeda, M., & McCamey, R. (2021). Candidate experience and its cycle in the hiring process: An analysis of student employees. *Southwestern Business Administration Journal*, *20*, 10–20.

Virani, F. (2023). Application of HR analytics in business. *Met Management Review, 10*(1), 15–27.

Wang, W., & Cotton, R. D. (2018). The study of sports labor is the case of moneyball to social capital inside the clubhouse. *Industrial & Labor Relations Review, 71*(4), 853–877.

Whelan, E., & Carcary, M. (2020). Workforce analysis effectiveness using HR analysis models. *HRM Journal, 41*(1), 77–92.

Yedama, N. K., & Tummalapalli, H. K. (2022). HR analytics as a moderating role in effective employee engagement and its outcomes. *NeuroQuantology : An Interdisciplinary Journal of Neuroscience and Quantum Physics, 20*(8), 4913–4920.

Chapter 14
Societal Change and Economic Transformation Through AI

Arun Agrawal
http://orcid.org/0000-0001-7233-6660
Institute of Technology and Management, Gwalior, India

R. Soumya
http://orcid.org/0009-0008-0387-544X
Dayananda Sagar Business Academy, Udayapura, India

B. R. Roopashree
http://orcid.org/0009-0007-7248-3602
Surana College, India

P. T. Rajeshwari
http://orcid.org/0009-0000-1195-6831
School of Commerce, Mount Carmel College, Bangalore. India.

Manoj Kumar Jhariya
http://orcid.org/0009-0006-1414-0559
Mangalayatan University, Jabalpur, India

Charanjeet Dadiyala
http://orcid.org/0000-0001-6191-4904
Ramdeobaba University, Nagpur, India

Deepak Gupta
http://orcid.org/0000-0003-3929-1362
Institute of Technology and Management, Gwalior, India

Pradeep Yadav
http://orcid.org/0000-0003-1073-7076
Institute of Technology and Management, Gwalior, India

EXECUTIVE SUMMARY

Artificial Intelligence (AI) is transforming societies by reshaping economies, democracies, and public services. This paper explores AI's dual role as both an enabler of progress and a source of new challenges. It examines its impact on labor markets, governance, healthcare, education, and urban development, highlighting both opportunities and risks such as bias, inequality, and misinformation. Through international cooperation, ethical frameworks, and inclusive policies, AI can be

DOI: 10.4018/979-8-3373-3867-5.ch014

guided toward enhancing human well-being. Real-world case studies from Estonia and India demonstrate how AI can strengthen democracy and public services when developed responsibly.

1. INTRODUCTION

Artificial Intelligence (AI) is changing more than just the economy. It is also deeply affecting how democratic societies and governments function (Helbing, 2018). As AI becomes part of everyday life, it is starting to shape how people receive information, make decisions, and interact with public institutions. AI is now being used in many areas of government, including public service delivery, policy planning, and even citizen engagement. These changes can make governments more efficient, responsive, and able to serve people better. AI helps in organizing and analyzing large amounts of data quickly. This can help leaders understand what people need and where problems exist. For example, city officials can use AI to plan better transport routes, track pollution levels, or respond to emergencies faster. In some countries, governments use AI chatbots to answer questions from the public, making it easier for people to get help and services. AI can also support online voting systems, improve language access, and make public meetings more inclusive. Besides making services faster and smarter, AI can help people become more involved in democracy. AI-powered tools can show citizens how government decisions may affect them, suggest ways to take part in public discussions, or help draft policies through digital platforms. This can increase civic engagement and allow more people to share their views in a simple, direct way (Duberry, 2022).

However, while AI brings many opportunities, it also comes with serious risks. One major concern is the spread of false information. AI can create realistic but fake videos, known as deepfakes, and generate fake news articles that look real. These tools can be used to trick people, spread lies, or damage trust in elections and leaders. When people can't tell what is true and what is not, it becomes harder to make good decisions or have honest debates. Another risk is bias. AI systems learn from the data they are given, and if that data has built-in unfairness or gaps, the AI can repeat or even increase that bias (Klaassen, 2024). For example, a hiring tool or a facial recognition system could treat some groups unfairly if the training data doesn't reflect diversity. This can lead to unfair treatment and discrimination, which weakens public trust. There is also concern over who controls these powerful AI tools. In many cases, private tech companies develop and run the systems used by governments. These companies may not always be fully transparent or accountable to the public. If decisions are made by AI systems without clear oversight, it can lead to a lack of fairness and make it hard for people to question or challenge those decisions. This can harm democracy by giving too much power to a few organizations.

To protect democratic values, it is important to create strong rules and policies for the use of AI. These rules should make sure that AI systems are fair, transparent, and used in ways that benefit the public. Governments must set standards for how data is collected, stored, and used. They should also make sure people can understand how AI makes decisions, especially in areas that affect their rights or opportunities (Leslie et al., 2021). Public involvement is also key. Citizens should have a say in how AI is used in society. Governments can support this by holding public discussions, sharing information in simple language, and involving a wide range of voices in policy-making. Schools and community groups should also teach people about AI, so they can use it wisely and understand both its risks and benefits (Duberry, 2022). International cooperation is another important step. Since AI is used across borders, countries must work together to set shared rules and stop harmful uses of AI (ÓhÉigeartaigh et al., 2020), such as spreading fake political content or using AI tools to control people unfairly. Global frameworks can help keep AI safe and useful for everyone.

AI can support democracy if it is used with care, fairness, and public oversight. It can improve services, increase civic participation, and help governments solve problems more effectively. But without proper rules, transparency, and accountability, it can also harm trust, increase inequality, and limit people's voices. The goal should be to build AI systems that support freedom, fairness, and the common good. By doing this, societies can use AI not just to make life easier, but also to strengthen democracy for all.

2. ECONOMIC TRANSFORMATION: LABOR MARKETS AND PRODUCTIVITY

AI is reshaping the global economy. It is changing how businesses operate and how people work. Companies use AI to complete tasks more quickly and with greater accuracy. This shift is making many industries more efficient. Research shows that industries adopting AI report nearly five times higher growth in worker productivity (Dumay et al., 2024). This highlights AI's potential to drive strong economic progress. However, rising productivity also brings challenges. When machines complete tasks faster, fewer human workers may be needed. This can create job losses in some sectors. At the same time, new kinds of skills are becoming essential. Routine work is slowly being replaced by more complex, technology-driven roles. These changes must be examined carefully to avoid long-term risks. It is equally important to understand how workers will be affected by this shift. Job security, wages, and career opportunities may all change. The transition could be difficult for people without access to new training or education. Companies and governments must step in to manage this impact. Support programs can play a key role in easing the change. For example, workers may need new training in data analysis, problem-solving, or digital tools. Education systems must also adapt to prepare students for an AI-driven future. Planning at the policy level is essential to ensure economic growth does not harm social stability.

2.1. Labor Market Disruption and Adaptation

AI is changing the job market in clear and fast-moving ways. One major trend is the growing demand for technology-related jobs. Data shows that the share of jobs in STEM fields, such as software development and data analysis, increased from 6.5 percent in 2010 to nearly 10 percent by 2024 (Arhimah et al., 2025). This shows a strong shift toward work that depends more on technical knowledge. At the same time, many companies are planning to reduce their workforce. Around 40 percent of employers expect to cut jobs in areas where AI can take over tasks (Chhibber et al., 2025). This raises serious concerns about job loss and the need to prepare for future changes. AI's effect on employment is not the same for everyone. It varies by sector, skill level, and age group. Reports from different regions in the United States show that workers in manufacturing and low-skill service jobs are most at risk. People in middle-skill roles, those not in STEM fields, and individuals who are either young or nearing retirement also face higher chances of being replaced (Pizzinelli & Tavares, 2025). This uneven pattern may make social and economic gaps worse. Without early and thoughtful action, some groups may be left behind.

However, the shift is not only negative. There is also growth in roles that work alongside AI. These jobs support the use of intelligent systems rather than being replaced by them. In fact, AI can help grow the economy by speeding up innovation and opening the door to brand-new industries. This kind of growth creates new jobs that did not exist before. These jobs often require new types of knowledge and training. Because of these changes, learning new skills becomes very important. Workers will need to gain new knowledge or improve their current skills to stay competitive. Programs for reskilling and upskilling are key to helping people move into better roles. These efforts must focus not just on technical skills but also on problem solving, communication, and adaptability. Governments, businesses, and schools all have a role to play in offering these learning opportunities.

AI is bringing both progress and challenges to the labor market. It is increasing demand for skilled workers while putting others at risk. The changes are happening fast and are affecting some groups more than others. But with the right plans in place, such as training programs and support for affected workers, it is possible to reduce the harm and increase the benefits. Planning now can help make the future of work more fair and full of opportunity.

2.2. Skills Evolution and Human Capital Development

AI is rapidly transforming the nature of work and the skills required to succeed in the job market. Earlier, people could complete their formal education and rely on the same knowledge throughout their careers. However, in the AI-driven world, skills become outdated very quickly. Therefore, individuals must continuously update their knowledge and abilities to remain relevant. This concept is known as lifelong learning, and it is becoming essential for career success (Morris, 2024).

For example, in the past, a teacher only needed subject knowledge and basic teaching methods. Today, teachers are expected to use AI-based tools, online platforms, and digital assessment systems. If they do not learn these technologies, they may struggle to perform effectively. Similarly, a doctor who learns to use AI-based diagnostic tools can provide faster and more accurate treatment, improving both job performance and career growth.

AI-related skills are highly demanded in the labor market, and this demand is reflected in higher wages. Professionals with skills in machine learning, data analysis, robotics, and AI programming often earn significantly more than those without such skills. For instance, a data scientist or AI engineer may earn double the salary of a traditional IT worker. This happens because companies value employees who can use AI to improve productivity and innovation, and there are still limited numbers of such skilled professionals.

However, the increasing demand for AI skills can also create social and economic challenges. Workers who lack digital and AI skills may face job loss or lower wages, leading to a growing gap between skilled and unskilled workers. For example, automation in factories may replace manual laborers, while technicians who can operate AI-driven machines will remain in demand. This situation can increase inequality if access to AI education is limited to certain groups, such as urban or wealthy populations. To prevent this digital divide, it is important to make AI education and training widely accessible. Schools, universities, employers, and governments must collaborate to build strong learning systems that support skill development at every stage of life. Schools should introduce digital literacy and AI concepts early in education. Employers should provide regular training programs to help workers adapt to new technologies. Governments can support citizens through free online courses, scholarships, and skill development initiatives. Flexible and inclusive learning opportunities are also crucial. Many people cannot attend full-time universities due to work or financial constraints. Online courses, short-term certification programs, workplace training, and community learning centers can help individuals learn at their own pace. For example, a farmer can learn how AI-based weather prediction apps work, and a shop owner can learn to use AI-powered inventory systems. These flexible learning options make skill development possible for people from all backgrounds.

AI is reshaping skills, careers, and human capital development. Continuous learning and skill updating are necessary for individuals to remain competitive in the workforce. Inclusive and flexible education systems can reduce inequality and ensure that everyone benefits from technological progress. By investing in lifelong learning and accessible training, societies can build a skilled workforce that is prepared for the AI-driven future.

3. SOCIETAL TRANSFORMATION: DEMOCRACY AND GOVERNANCE

AI is transforming democratic societies and governance. It improves information sharing, decision-making, public services, and citizen participation. However, AI can produce biased outcomes, spread confusion, and weaken trust in elections and leaders. Concerns also exist over who controls AI systems and whether they are transparent and accountable. To safeguard democracy, AI must be governed by clear, fair, and transparent regulations that promote the public good and protect citizens' voices.

3.1. Democratic Challenges and Electoral Integrity

The growing link between AI and democratic systems is raising serious concerns, especially about election interference and misinformation. AI can be used to create deepfakes, fake news, and targeted propaganda, which can manipulate public opinion, mislead voters, and undermine trust in democratic institutions. Advanced AI tools can now be used by harmful groups to shape public opinion, disrupt voting systems, and create confusion. This puts democratic values at serious risk (Selvakumar et al., 2025). Tools such as deepfakes, fake news campaigns, and AI-generated content make it hard for voters to know what is true. As a result, people may struggle to make informed decisions during elections.

Some steps have been taken to address this danger. In 2024, several leading AI companies signed the Tech Accord to Combat Deceptive Use of AI in Elections (Soon & Quek, 2024). This agreement focuses on reducing the spread of misleading AI content, especially during election periods. It also supports better ways to detect fake materials and promote accurate information. However, these efforts are voluntary. They do not yet provide full protection or long-term solutions to the larger problems posed by AI in democratic systems.

The issue is not limited to elections. It also affects how democratic systems function overall. Large tech companies now play a powerful role in shaping how information is shared and understood. These companies make important decisions about what content is seen, promoted, or removed. Yet, they do not answer to voters or public institutions. This shift in power raises serious questions about fairness, responsibility, and who gets to make decisions in a digital society (Lin, 2024).

Democracy is built on the ideas of equal voice, transparency, and accountability. But in AI-driven societies, these values can be weakened if private companies have too much control over public conversations. The growing influence of technology corporations without public oversight may create a system where decisions are guided more by profit than by public interest.

To protect democratic values, stronger actions are needed. Laws and policies must ensure that AI is used responsibly, especially in public communication and election settings. Governments and civil groups must also work together to educate citizens, build trust, and promote media literacy.

AI can help society in many ways, but it also brings serious risks to democracy. Addressing these risks requires cooperation, clear rules, and public awareness. Only then can democratic systems remain strong in an AI-influenced world.

3.2. Governance Innovation and Institutional Adaptation

AI presents important opportunities for improving governance and strengthening democratic institutions. One key approach is the development of publicly owned AI systems, which can help ensure that AI technologies serve the public interest rather than only private companies. When governments and communities participate in designing and managing AI systems, they can promote fairness, transparency, and accountability. This approach can reduce the dominance of large technology corporations and ensure that AI is used for social welfare, public services, and policy development (Iosad et al., 2024).

For example, governments can use public AI systems to improve healthcare delivery, education planning, and social welfare distribution. If such systems are publicly controlled, citizens can trust that their data is protected and that decisions are not driven by profit. This model supports democratic values such as equality, participation, and accountability, while still allowing societies to benefit from technological innovation.

Another important concept is dynamic governance, which focuses on adapting institutions to rapid technological change. Instead of trying to restrict or slow down AI development, dynamic governance encourages governments to use AI responsibly and intelligently. Institutions must become flexible and responsive so they can adjust policies as technology evolves. AI can assist policymakers by analyzing large datasets, predicting outcomes, and supporting evidence-based decisions. However, AI should not replace human judgment. Human oversight is essential to ensure ethical decision-making and prevent bias or misuse (Gambrell, 2025).

For instance, AI tools can help governments predict economic trends or manage public resources more efficiently, but final decisions should remain in human hands. Proper design, ethical frameworks, and accountability mechanisms are necessary to ensure that AI strengthens rather than undermines democratic governance.

Because AI is a global technology, international cooperation is also crucial. Countries must work together to create shared standards and regulations for AI development and use. This includes defining acceptable uses of AI, assessing risks, ensuring equitable access, and preventing harmful applications such as misinformation or surveillance abuse. Global discussions on generative AI highlight the need for international frameworks that reflect shared ethical values and human rights principles (Jin et al., 2025).

For example, international organizations and governments can collaborate to develop global AI governance guidelines, similar to agreements on climate change or cybersecurity. Such cooperation can help reduce technological inequalities between developed and developing countries and promote responsible AI use worldwide.

AI does not necessarily threaten democracy. When governed properly, it can improve transparency, efficiency, and public trust in institutions. Public ownership of AI systems, dynamic governance models, and international cooperation are essential strategies for ensuring that AI strengthens democratic societies rather than weakening them. By adapting institutions and policies to technological change, governments can harness AI's potential while protecting democratic values and citizen rights (Iosad et al., 2024; Gambrell, 2025; Jin et al., 2025).

4. SECTORAL TRANSFORMATIONS: HEALTHCARE, EDUCATION, AND URBAN DEVELOPMENT

AI's transformative impact extends across multiple sectors, each experiencing unique challenges and opportunities that collectively reshape societal structures and individual experiences.

4.1. Healthcare Revolution

The use of AI in healthcare shows how technology can improve access to medical knowledge and services. AI-powered tools are helping doctors make better decisions and allowing more people to receive quality care. In areas where there are few medical specialists, these tools can be especially helpful (Khan et al., 2025). For example, machine learning systems are now able to detect certain cancers, eye diseases, and other health problems with accuracy equal to or even better than human doctors. This means patients in remote or underserved areas can benefit from early diagnosis and timely treatment.

While these developments offer great promise, they also raise important concerns. Not all healthcare systems have the resources to adopt AI. Countries or hospitals with more money and technology will likely move ahead faster. This can lead to new gaps between healthcare providers who use AI effectively and those who do not. As a result, some people may receive much better care than others simply based on where they live or how much support their health system receives.

Another issue is dependency. If healthcare workers rely too much on AI, they may begin to lose important skills or trust technology too much. This can affect the quality of care, especially when AI systems make mistakes or are used without proper oversight. It is essential that humans remain in control and use AI as a tool rather than a replacement.

To ensure that AI helps more people, efforts must focus on fairness and inclusion. This means making AI tools available to low-resource settings and training healthcare workers to use them effectively. It also means creating clear policies to guide how AI is used in medical settings.

AI can make healthcare smarter and more widely available. But for its benefits to reach everyone, it must be used in ways that promote equality, support human judgment, and strengthen global healthcare systems rather than divide them.

4.2. Educational Transformation

AI is bringing a major shift to the world of education. Traditional teaching methods often follow a fixed structure, where all students receive the same lessons in the same way. This approach does not always support individual learning needs. AI is helping to change this by enabling more personalized learning. Intelligent tutoring systems can adapt lessons based on a student's strengths, weaknesses, and pace of learning. These systems offer continuous feedback, helping students improve with targeted guidance. As a result, learners receive support that feels more like a one-on-one tutoring experience, which can make learning more effective and engaging (Zootzky & Pfeiffer, 2024).

Beyond the classroom, AI is also influencing how we understand education and the nature of knowledge itself. As AI tools become capable of generating detailed analysis and creative outputs, the role of human learning is changing. Educational systems can no longer focus only on memorizing facts or following fixed steps.

Instead, they must help students build skills that AI cannot replace. These include critical thinking, creativity, emotional intelligence, ethical reasoning, and the ability to work with others. These uniquely human abilities are essential in an AI-driven world (Petrova, 2023).

Teachers continue to play an important role in this transformation. While AI can provide personalized content, it cannot replace the human connection and mentorship that teachers offer. In the future, teachers may focus more on coaching, guiding, and helping students think more deeply about the material. They can also teach students how to use AI tools responsibly and think critically about the information they receive from digital sources (Ashraf & Mustafa, 2025).

To fully benefit from AI in education, schools must provide equal access to technology and training for both students and educators. They must also focus on developing thoughtful policies that ensure AI tools support learning without widening existing gaps.

AI has the power to make education more inclusive, responsive, and future-ready if guided wisely.

4.3. Urban Development and Smart Cities

The integration of AI into urban planning and city management is reshaping how cities function and grow. AI technologies offer the ability to make urban areas more efficient, responsive, and sustainable. Smart systems can manage traffic flow, reduce congestion, and improve road safety by analyzing real-time data from cameras, sensors, and connected vehicles. AI can also help cities use energy more efficiently by predicting demand and adjusting supply, which leads to cost savings and lower environmental impact. In public services, AI can support better waste management, faster emergency response, and more accurate forecasting of city needs. These improvements have the potential to greatly enhance the quality of life for people living in urban environments (Kutkov et al., 2025).

One major area of change is transportation. The rise of autonomous vehicles and AI-guided public transport systems is set to transform how people move around cities. These changes could reduce travel time, improve accessibility, and influence the design of future urban spaces. Streets, parking areas, and public zones may be redesigned to support new mobility patterns, making cities more walkable and livable (Ortega-Fernández et al., 2020).

Despite these benefits, there are important concerns to address. The vision of a smart city depends heavily on collecting and analyzing large amounts of data. This includes information about people's movements, behaviors, and even personal habits. While this data can help improve services, it also raises serious privacy issues. Without clear rules and safeguards, constant monitoring can lead to unwanted surveillance and misuse of personal information (Mehmood et al., 2024).

There are also challenges around fairness and democratic involvement. Decisions based on AI systems may not always reflect the needs or voices of local communities. If technology companies and city planners make choices without public input, it may weaken community control over urban life.

To build cities that are both smart and just, it is essential to balance innovation with human rights. Cities must create transparent policies that protect privacy, ensure ethical data use, and include residents in decision-making. AI should serve the public, not control it.

AI can help cities become more sustainable and efficient. But for smart cities to succeed, technology must be used in ways that respect privacy, promote equity, and support democratic values.

5. CASE STUDIES

5.1. Estonia as a Digital State

Estonia's pioneering approach to integrating AI into public governance demonstrates the transformative potential of ethically governed AI systems in strengthening democratic institutions and public trust. Recognized as the world's most advanced digital society, Estonia has implemented its ambitious KrattAI strategy to develop interoperable AI agents that serve citizens across multiple government services, creating a comprehensive ecosystem of digital public administration. The country has successfully deployed over 80 AI solutions within government operations, revolutionizing how citizens interact with public services through intelligent systems that manage complex tasks such as public transportation routing, tax filing processes, and visa application processing (Mishra et al., 2024). Perhaps most significantly, Estonia's AI-powered electronic health records system has transformed healthcare delivery by enabling doctors to access patient information securely and instantaneously, resulting in improved diagnostic accuracy and accelerated treatment timelines that directly benefit citizen health outcomes.

The implementation of these AI systems has generated measurable improvements in both operational efficiency and citizen satisfaction, demonstrating that technology can enhance rather than diminish democratic governance when properly designed and implemented. Government staff have reported significant reductions in administrative workload, allowing them to focus on more complex, human-centered tasks that require empathy, creativity, and nuanced judgment rather than routine data processing. Simultaneously, citizens have experienced faster, more accurate services that reduce bureaucratic friction and improve their overall interaction with government institutions. This enhanced service delivery has strengthened public trust in digital governance, creating a positive feedback loop where citizens become more willing to engage with digital public services and participate in democratic processes.

Estonia's success illustrates several critical principles for effective AI governance in democratic societies. First, the emphasis on publicly owned and ethically governed AI systems ensures that AI serves broad public interests rather than narrow commercial objectives, maintaining democratic accountability over technological development and deployment. Second, the integration of transparent policy frameworks alongside AI implementation creates clear guidelines for system operation while maintaining citizen oversight and trust. Third, the interoperable nature of Estonia's AI agents prevents the creation of isolated technological silos, instead fostering a cohesive digital ecosystem that enhances government effectiveness while preserving institutional coherence. This comprehensive approach demonstrates that when paired with robust ethical frameworks and transparent governance structures, AI can serve as a powerful tool for democratic innovation, enhancing both the efficiency of public services and the quality of citizen-state relationships in ways that strengthen rather than undermine democratic institutions and values.

5.2. eSanjeevani and DRISTI Initiatives

India's innovative deployment of AI in rural healthcare through initiatives like eSanjeevani and DRISTI (Diagnostic Research and Imaging System for Tribal India) exemplifies how strategically designed AI systems can address healthcare inequalities and expand access to specialized medical care in underserved regions. Confronting the persistent challenge of specialist shortages in rural and tribal areas, the Indian government has leveraged AI-powered telemedicine and diagnostic tools to bridge the gap between urban medical expertise and remote populations who have historically lacked access to quality healthcare services. The eSanjeevani platform has revolutionized healthcare delivery by enabling remote consultations through telemedicine infrastructure supported by sophisticated AI diagnostic tools that assist healthcare providers in making accurate diagnoses and treatment recommendations, effectively extending the reach of limited medical personnel across vast geographic distances. Simultaneously, the DRISTI program, developed under the leadership of the Indian Council of Medical Research (ICMR), employs advanced AI image analysis capabilities to detect critical conditions including eye diseases, tuberculosis, and other prevalent health issues among tribal populations, providing early screening and intervention opportunities that were previously unavailable in these remote communities.

The quantitative impact of these AI-driven healthcare initiatives demonstrates their transformative potential for addressing systemic healthcare inequities, with eSanjeevani alone facilitating over 140 million telemedicine consultations as of 2024, representing an unprecedented scale of remote healthcare delivery that has fundamentally altered the healthcare landscape for millions of rural Indians. This massive reach has simultaneously reduced the overwhelming burden on overworked medical personnel in urban centers while dramatically improving early detection capabilities and care delivery timelines in hard-to-reach areas where traditional healthcare infrastructure remains limited or nonexistent. The success of these programs lies not merely in their technological sophistication but in their thoughtful integration of AI capabilities with existing healthcare systems, ensuring that AI enhances rather than replaces human medical judgment while making specialized expertise accessible to populations who might otherwise go without proper medical attention.

India's approach offers crucial insights into how AI can serve as a powerful tool for healthcare equity when implemented with deliberate attention to inclusion and social justice. The model demonstrates that AI's potential to reduce healthcare inequalities requires more than technological innovation alone; it demands sustained government commitment, substantial infrastructure investment, and most importantly, inclusion-focused design principles that prioritize the needs of marginalized and underserved populations. By combining telemedicine platforms with AI-assisted diagnostics and targeting specific vulnerable communities like tribal populations, India has created a replicable framework showing how developing nations can harness AI to leapfrog traditional healthcare infrastructure limitations and achieve more equitable health outcomes across diverse geographic and socioeconomic contexts.

6. CHALLENGES AND PATHWAYS FORWARD

The transition to an AI-enhanced society presents significant challenges that require coordinated responses from multiple stakeholders. Economic inequality, social fragmentation, and governance deficits represent key areas requiring proactive intervention.

6.1. Addressing Inequality and Inclusion

One of the most pressing concerns in the age of AI is the risk of deepening existing inequalities. As AI becomes more integrated into daily life, the gap between those with access to AI tools and those without may widen. This divide is not only about who can use AI but also about who understands it. Differences in geography, education, and income levels are already shaping how people benefit from these technologies. Without targeted efforts to close these gaps, the digital divide could grow into a long-lasting form of inequality, affecting entire generations (Lainjo, 2020).

To prevent this, strong and inclusive strategies are needed. Public investment in digital infrastructure is crucial, especially in rural and underserved regions. Every person should have access to reliable internet and modern devices. In addition, education systems must evolve to include AI literacy as a basic skill. Schools, colleges, and community programs should offer training that helps people understand how AI works and how to use it in real life. Policymakers must also ensure that the economic benefits of AI are widely shared, not just concentrated in a few regions or industries (Challoumis, 2024).

As AI changes how people work, it also challenges the traditional structure of employment. Many jobs may disappear or require new skills. To support those affected, social safety nets must be updated. Options like universal basic income, job retraining, and portable benefits can help people adapt to the new economy. These programs provide financial support and create opportunities for individuals to reskill and find meaningful work.

The outcome of the AI revolution depends heavily on how societies respond to these changes. If thoughtful policies are put in place, AI can lead to more equal opportunities and improved living standards. But if the transition is poorly managed, it may result in greater inequality and division.

In conclusion, managing AI's impact on inequality requires action on multiple fronts—education, infrastructure, employment, and economic policy. The goal should be to ensure that the benefits of AI reach everyone, not just a privileged few.

6.2. Building Ethical AI Ecosystems

Building ethical AI systems is a shared responsibility that requires input from many different groups. Technologists, policymakers, civil society organizations, and communities directly affected by AI must all work together. When AI tools are designed through inclusive and participatory processes, they are more likely to reflect a wide range of values and needs. This helps ensure that AI does not only serve the interests of large companies but also addresses public concerns such as fairness, safety, and equality (Martínez-García, 2022).

A key part of ethical AI development is involving people who will be impacted by the technology. This includes workers, students, healthcare users, and marginalized communities. Their voices can highlight potential harms or unintended effects that developers may not foresee. Including these perspectives early in the design process improves trust and leads to systems that are more just and responsive to real-world needs.

Alongside inclusive design, strong regulatory frameworks are essential. These rules must protect individual rights and social values while still allowing space for innovation and progress. This is not a simple task. Too much restriction could slow useful discoveries, while too little oversight may lead to misuse, bias, or harm. Therefore, a careful and flexible approach is required.

Laws and guidelines must evolve with the pace of technological change. Traditional regulatory systems often move slowly, but AI is developing rapidly. Governments and institutions need adaptive tools and review mechanisms that keep up. They should also promote openness by requiring developers to explain how their systems work and make decisions. Transparency, accountability, and fairness must remain central to any legal or ethical framework.

In addition, global cooperation is important. AI does not stop at national borders, so ethical standards and regulations should be shared across countries. Working together internationally helps create consistency and reduces the risk of harmful practices being moved to areas with weaker protections.

6.3. International Cooperation and Global Governance

The global reach of AI makes international cooperation essential for effective governance. AI technologies are not confined by borders, and their impact is felt across countries, industries, and societies. As a result, there is a growing need for shared rules, safety guidelines, and ethical standards that apply globally. Without coordinated efforts, countries may compete to relax regulations in an attempt to gain an edge in AI development. This could lead to a "race to the bottom" where safety, fairness, and public interest are compromised. To avoid this, countries must work together to develop frameworks that ensure AI is developed and used responsibly, and that its benefits are shared broadly.

Such cooperation should aim to promote global public goods solutions that improve human well-being on a large scale, such as healthcare access, climate solutions, and education. Global agreements on AI ethics, safety protocols, and data usage can help build trust and accountability while avoiding harmful uses of the technology.

However, managing AI is not just about setting technical rules. It also involves deeper issues of fairness and global inclusion. Many developing countries lack the resources and infrastructure to keep up with rapid AI advancements. If left unaddressed, this imbalance could widen existing global inequalities. For international AI governance to be fair, all countries must have a seat at the table.

To support participation from developing nations, efforts must focus on technology transfer, capacity building, and institutional support. Wealthier countries and global organizations can help by sharing knowledge, investing in education and infrastructure, and making AI tools accessible to all. Inclusive international institutions are needed to guide these efforts and ensure that policies consider the needs of countries at different stages of development.

Ultimately, effective AI governance requires a balance between innovation and responsibility, competition and cooperation, national interest and global welfare. By creating shared goals and working together, the global community can shape AI in ways that respect human rights, reduce inequalities, and unlock opportunities for all.

7. CONCLUSION

The transformation of society and economy through AI represents both humanity's greatest opportunity and its most significant challenge in the 21st century. The evidence presented demonstrates that AI's impact extends far beyond technological advancement to fundamental questions about work, democracy, equity, and human flourishing.

Success in navigating this transformation requires recognition that technological development and social progress are not automatically aligned. Deliberate choices about AI development priorities, governance structures, and benefit distribution will determine whether AI serves to enhance human capabilities and social welfare or exacerbate existing problems and create new forms of exclusion.

The path forward demands unprecedented collaboration across sectors, disciplines, and national boundaries. Policymakers, technologists, educators, and civil society organizations must work together to ensure that AI development serves human values and contributes to a more equitable and sustainable future.

The window for shaping AI's societal impact remains open, but it will not remain so indefinitely. The choices made in the coming years will largely determine whether future generations inherit an AI-enhanced society that serves human flourishing or one that prioritizes efficiency over equity and technological capability over human agency. The responsibility for making these choices wisely belongs to all of us.

REFERENCES

Arhimah, T., Thompson, M., & Cudjoe-Mensah, Y. M. (2025). Disparities in access to educational technology and its impact on performance across socio-economic and racial groups in US public schools.

Ashraf, Z. A., & Mustafa, N. (2025). Role of AI in transforming society. In *Intersection of Human Rights and AI in Healthcare* (pp. 431–452). IGI Global Scientific Publishing.

Challoumis, C. (2024). AI and economic inequality—addressing the challenges ahead. In *XVIII International Scientific Conference* (pp. 120–155). Dortmund, Germany.

Chhibber, S., Rajkumar, S. R., & Dassanayake, S. (2025). Will artificial intelligence reshape the global workforce by 2030? *Blockchain, Artificial Intelligence, and Future Research, 1*(1), 35–51. DOI: 10.70211/bafr.v1i1.178

Duberry, J. (2022). Artificial intelligence and democracy: Risks and promises of AI-mediated citizen–government relations. In *Artificial intelligence and democracy*. Edward Elgar Publishing. DOI: 10.4337/9781788977319

Dumay, J., Ricceri, F., & Guthrie AM, J. (2024). Australian PwC affair: An international perspective. *Journal of Behavioural Economics and Social Systems, 6*(1). Advance online publication. DOI: 10.54337/ojs.bess.v6i1.8721

Gambrell, D. (2025, June). AI for e-governance: Combining artificial intelligence and collective intelligence to develop evidence-based AI policy. In *2025 Eleventh International Conference on eDemocracy & eGovernment (ICEDEG)* (pp. 317–324). IEEE Computer Society. DOI: 10.1109/ICEDEG65568.2025.11081634

Helbing, D. (2018). Societal, economic, ethical and legal challenges of the digital revolution. In *Towards digital enlightenment* (pp. 47–72). Springer.

Iosad, A., Railton, D., & Westgarth, T. (2024). *Governing in the age of AI: A new model to transform the state*. Tony Blair Institute for Global Change.

Jin, Y., Yan, L., Echeverria, V., Gašević, D., & Martinez-Maldonado, R. (2025). Generative AI in higher education. *Computers and Education: Artificial Intelligence, 8*, 100348.

Khan, S., Majdalawieh, M., Kharadi, D., Verma, T., Farhin, T., & Kumar, A. (2025). From digital disruption to AI revolution. *Artificial Intelligence in Medicine and Healthcare, 31*.

Klaassen, G. (2024). *Confronting bias in artificial intelligence: Building transparent, diverse, and ethical AI systems.*

Kutkov, O., Zolotov, A., Akimova, L., & Akimov, O. (2025). Digital transformation of social governance. *Economics. Finance and Management Review*, (1), 17–28.

Lainjo, B. (2020). The global social dynamics and inequalities of artificial intelligence. *Int. J. Innov. Sci. Res. Rev*, *5*, 4966–4974.

Leslie, D., Burr, C., Aitken, M., Cowls, J., Katell, M., & Briggs, M. (2021). Artificial intelligence, human rights, democracy, and the rule of law: A primer. *arXiv preprint arXiv:2104.04147.*

Lin, T. A. (2024). "Democratizing AI" and the concern of algorithmic injustice. *Philosophy & Technology*, *37*(3), 103. DOI: 10.1007/s13347-024-00792-2

Martínez-García, A. N. (2022). Artificial intelligence for sustainable complex socio-technical-economic ecosystems. *Computation (Basel, Switzerland)*, *10*(6), 95. DOI: 10.3390/computation10060095

Mehmood, R., Yigitcanlar, T., & Corchado, J. M. (2024). Smart technologies for sustainable urban and regional development. *Sustainability (Basel)*, *16*(3), 1171. DOI: 10.3390/su16031171

Mishra, A. K., Tyagi, A. K., Dananjayan, S., Rajavat, A., Rawat, H., & Rawat, A. (2024). Revolutionizing government operations. In *Conversational Artificial Intelligence* (pp. 607–634). DOI: 10.1002/9781394200801.ch34

Morris, T. H. (2024). Four dimensions of self-directed learning. *Adult Education Quarterly*, *74*(3), 236–254. DOI: 10.1177/07417136231217453

ÓhÉigeartaigh, S. S., Whittlestone, J., Liu, Y., Zeng, Y., & Liu, Z.ÓhÉigeartaigh. (2020). Overcoming barriers to cross-cultural cooperation in AI ethics and governance. *Philosophy & Technology*, *33*(4), 571–593. DOI: 10.1007/s13347-020-00402-x

Ortega-Fernández, A., Martín-Rojas, R., & García-Morales, V. J. (2020). Artificial intelligence in the urban environment. *Sustainability (Basel)*, *12*(19), 7860. DOI: 10.3390/su12197860

Petrova, T. (2023). Digital and social transformation in education. *Проблеми на постмодерността*, *13*(3), 384–393.

Pizzinelli, C., & Tavares, M. M. (2025). AI and the future of work in an aging economy.

Selvakumar, P., Sharma, R., Kunnathully, K., Satyanarayana, P., Singh, K., & Manjunath, T. C. (2025). AI technologies for enhancing democratic processes. In *Democracy and Democratization in the Age of AI* (pp. 133–152). IGI Global Scientific Publishing. DOI: 10.4018/979-8-3693-8749-8.ch008

Soon, C. A. R. O. L., & Quek, S. A. M. A. N. T. H. A. (2024). Safeguarding elections from threats posed by artificial intelligence.

Zootzky, G., & Pfeiffer, A. (2024). Educational transformation through AI. In *INTED2024 Proceedings* (pp. 1202–1207). IATED.

Chapter 15
Technology and AI Professionals

M. Mayuranathan
http://orcid.org/0009-0006-4681-4503
SRM Valliammai Engineering College, India

T. C. Manjunath
http://orcid.org/0000-0003-2545-9160
Rajarajeswari College of Engineering, India

P. Selvakumar
http://orcid.org/0000-0002-3650-4548
Department of Science and Humanities, Nehru Institute of Technology, Coimbatore, India

P. Sudheer
http://orcid.org/0009-0005-1912-6636
CVR College of Engineering, India

B. Maheshwar Rao
http://orcid.org/0009-0006-0659-4876
Sri Balaji University, Pune, India

R. Shanmugaa Priyaa
Sathyabama Institute of Science and Technology, India

EXECUTIVE SUMMARY

In the 21st century, few forces have reshaped the world of work as profoundly as technology and artificial intelligence (AI). What once seemed the domain of science fiction—machines learning from data, robots performing complex surgeries, or algorithms writing poetry—has now become everyday reality. From the factory floor to the executive boardroom, technological advancements are transforming how tasks are performed, how decisions are made, and how value is created. but also enhancing human capabilities, enabling better insights, faster communication, and more personalized customer experiences. real-time analysis, and predictive modeling to stay competitive in fast-evolving markets. Human resource departments are using AI to streamline recruitment, identify employee engagement trends, and even predict

DOI: 10.4018/979-8-3373-3867-5.ch015

potential attrition. Marketing teams are leveraging algorithms to target customers with pinpoint accuracy, while finance departments utilize AI tools to detect fraud, analyze investment opportunities, and manage risk more efficiently.

THE RISE OF TECHNOLOGY AND AI IN THE WORKPLACE

In the 21st century, few forces have reshaped the world of work as profoundly as technology and artificial intelligence (AI). What once seemed the domain of science fiction—machines learning from data, robots performing complex surgeries, or algorithms writing poetry—has now become everyday reality. From the factory floor to the executive boardroom, technological advancements are transforming how tasks are performed, how decisions are made, and how value is created. but also enhancing human capabilities, enabling better insights, faster communication, and more personalized customer experiences. real-time analysis, and predictive modeling to stay competitive in fast-evolving markets. Human resource departments are using AI to streamline recruitment, identify employee engagement trends, and even predict potential attrition.(Agrawal et al., 2019) Marketing teams are leveraging algorithms to target customers with pinpoint accuracy, while finance departments utilize AI tools to detect fraud, analyze investment opportunities, and manage risk more efficiently. Even healthcare, a sector traditionally reliant on human judgment, has begun to embrace AI for diagnostic support, patient monitoring, and personalized treatment plans.access to new technologies and those without—may also exacerbate existing inequalities in the workforce. Moreover, the deployment of AI systems raises critical issues about transparency, accountability, and control. How do we ensure that these tools are used responsibly? Who is liable when AI systems fail or cause harm? Can machines ever truly replicate human intuition, empathy, and ethics?The growing prominence of AI and technology in the workplace also demands a rethinking of traditional job structures and performance metrics. Roles that once had clearly defined boundaries are becoming more fluid, with hybrid positions emerging at the intersection of technology and human expertise. For instance, data scientists are now expected to understand business strategy, while marketing professionals are increasingly required to interpret complex data sets. Teams are becoming more interdisciplinary, and decision-making is becoming more collaborative and informed by real-time insights. The traditional hierarchical structure of organizations is giving way to more agile, networked models that prioritize adaptability and innovation. (Baruffaldi et al., 2020) In this new environment, soft skills—such as creativity, emotional intelligence, and communication—are becoming as critical as technical know-how.Moreover, the rise of remote work, powered by digital collaboration tools and AI-driven platforms, has redefined the very concept of the workplace.

Employees are no longer confined to physical offices; work can now be performed from virtually anywhere, at any time. changes thoughtfully, ensuring that the benefits of remote and hybrid work models are equitably distributed and do not come at the cost of employee well-being. These technologies promise to open new frontiers of innovation, but they also call for vigilant oversight and proactive governance. As workplaces become more digitally driven, the core of successful organizations will be their ability to foster a culture of continuous learning, inclusivity, and ethical responsibility. The transformation we are witnessing is not just technological—it is cultural, social, and fundamentally human. The future of work is being written in real-time, and it is up to us to ensure that it leads to a more empowered, equitable, and intelligent workforce.

THE ROLE OF TECHNOLOGY AND AI PROFESSIONALS: DRIVING INNOVATION AND GROWTH

In today's increasingly digital world, technology and AI professionals have emerged as pivotal agents of transformation, innovation, and growth across all industries. These individuals are not just technicians behind the scenes—they are strategic partners, creative thinkers, and change agents responsible for shaping the trajectory of modern enterprises. From designing intelligent systems that streamline operations to building platforms that redefine user experiences, far beyond writing code or managing(Bessen, 2019) IT infrastructure—they are now central to identifying new opportunities, solving complex problems, and driving sustainable innovation. In sectors like healthcare, finance, logistics, education, retail, and manufacturing, these experts are instrumental in creating intelligent solutions that improve efficiency, reduce costs, and open up entirely new revenue streams. (Bessen, 2016)For instance, data scientists and AI engineers are enabling predictive analytics in healthcare to anticipate patient needs and personalize treatments, while machine learning engineers are optimizing supply chain operations in logistics companies to improve delivery times and minimize waste. In marketing, AI professionals build recommendation engines that personalize content, increasing user engagement and sales. The impact of their work is broad, far-reaching, and often invisible to the end user, but its influence on productivity and competitiveness is undeniable.Beyond technical proficiency, successful AI and tech professionals possess a unique blend of analytical thinking, problem-solving abilities, and strategic vision. They are expected to bridge the gap between technical solutions and business objectives, ensuring that innovation aligns with organizational goals. of innovation-driven environments. Their role also involves educating stakeholders on the potential and limitations of technology, thereby managing expectations and promoting responsible adoption of AI-driven tools.Technology and AI professionals also serve as catalysts for organizational agility and adaptability. In an era marked by rapid technological change, companies must be able to pivot quickly and respond to new challenges with innovation and resilience. Tech professionals help facilitate this agility by building scalable, flexible systems that can evolve with business needs. (Carnevale et al., 2014)They implement automation tools that free up human workers to focus on creative and strategic tasks, foster the adoption of cloud technologies that enable remote collaboration, and develop AI-powered platforms that support real-time decision-making.

Their work helps organizations stay ahead of the curve, capitalize on emerging trends, and future-proof their operations against disruption. learning engineer, data scientist, cloud architect, and AI ethicist didn't exist a decade ago, and now they are among the most in-demand positions. Startups led by innovative tech professionals are disrupting traditional markets, creating competition that drives efficiency and lowers costs. On the public sector side, governments are increasingly relying on tech experts to develop smart infrastructure, enhance public services, and drive digital transformation initiatives that improve citizen engagement and resource management. In this way, the contributions of technology professionals extend far beyond individual companies—they shape economies, influence public policy, and impact global development.The rise of open-source communities, knowledge-sharing platforms, and collaborative innovation has further amplified the influence of technology professionals. Platforms such as GitHub, Stack (Dawson et al., 2021)Overflow, and AI-focused research forums have created ecosystems where knowledge only sharpen their own skills but also drive the collective evolution of the field. generative AI, edge computing, and the metaverse. They will be called upon to lead digital transformation efforts, redesign outdated systems, and envision new ways to use technology for social good. Their ability to think critically, act ethically, and innovate continuously will determine how effectively we can navigate the opportunities and risks of the digital age.s, providing ongoing learning opportunities, and offering career pathways that reward innovation and collaboration. Education systems must also adapt, placing a stronger emphasis on interdisciplinary learning that combines technical skills with ethics, communication, and business acumen. Governments, too, have a role to play by funding STEM initiatives, supporting research, and creating policies that promote fair and responsible technology use.In conclusion, technology and AI professionals are at the heart of modern innovation and economic growth. Their work not only transforms the way businesses operate but also shapes the future of societies. As stewards of one of the most powerful forces of our time, they carry a responsibility that extends beyond their organizations—to the economy, to communities, and to future generations. Empowering these professionals with the tools, knowledge, and ethical frameworks they need will be essential to building a world where technology serves humanity, rather than the other way around.

THE SKILLS AND QUALIFICATIONS REQUIRED FOR TECHNOLOGY AND AI PROFESSIONALS

In an era increasingly shaped by digital transformation and artificial intelligence, the demand for highly skilled technology and AI professionals has surged dramatically. (Felten et al., 2018)These roles are not only foundational to innovation and competitive advantage, but they are also crucial for addressing complex global challenges, optimizing operations, and enabling future-ready strategies across industries. To thrive in this evolving landscape, professionals must possess a . Many roles, especially those involving advanced AI model development or research, may also require a master's degree or PhD in fields like machine learning, robotics, applied mathematics, or computational neuroscience. Coursework in algorithms, data structures, probability, statistics, calculus, linear algebra, and optimization lays the groundwork for understanding how AI systems function and how to build them responsibly. In addition to formal education, certifications from respected organizations such as Google, Microsoft, IBM, or Coursera in areas like AI engineering, data science, cloud computing, and cybersecurity can enhance a candidate's credentials and demonstrate specialization in a specific area.Beyond theoretical knowledge, practical technical skills are essential for success in technology and AI roles. Proficiency in programming languages is non-negotiable, with Python being the most widely used language in frameworks is critical, especially for training models, handling large datasets, and deploying AI solutions. Knowledge of database systems, SQL, NoSQL, data warehousing, and data pipeline creation is also essential for data engineers and analysts. Additionally, familiarity with cloud platforms like AWS, Microsoft Azure, and Google Cloud Platform is becoming increasingly important, as organizations shift toward scalable and remote infrastructures. Tools such as Docker, Kubernetes, and Jenkins are commonly used in DevOps and MLOps environments, allowing teams to automate workflows, containerize applications, and ensure seamless deployment of AI systems into production environments.

Apart from machine learning, today's AI professionals are often expected to possess expertise in related technologies, including For instance, those working on language models must understand transformer architectures, tokenization techniques, and attention mechanisms, while those in computer vision should be proficient in convolutional neural networksan understanding of cybersecurity principles, ethical hacking, and data protection is vital in ensuring that systems are safe, secure, and compliant with evolving regulations.However, technical mastery alone is not sufficient. (Felten et al., 2021)As AI and technology projects become more interdisciplinary and collaborative, soft skills are increasingly important for success. One of the most critical soft skills is communication— Collaboration and teamwork are equally vital, as most tech initiatives require coordination across departments including product, design, marketing, legal, and operations. The ability to work well in cross-functional teams, adapt to various working styles, and resolve conflicts constructively makes a significant difference in delivering successful projects. errors, troubleshoot bugs, and optimize models in environments with incomplete data or ambiguous requirements. Innovative thinking, combined with an iterative mindset, helps in finding creative solutions and improving system performance. Project management skills, such as time management, resource allocation, and agile methodologies (Scrum, Kanban, etc.), enable professionals to stay organized and meet deadlines efficiently. Attention to detail is particularly important in roles involving data labeling, model evaluation, and security protocols, where small oversights can lead to significant consequences.One of the emerging and indispensable requirements in AI roles is ethical awareness and responsibility. As AI systems gain influence in decision-making across sensitive way that respects human rights and societal values. This ethical perspective should be complemented by a commitment to lifelong learning, as the field of technology and AI changes rapidly with each new breakthrough.Globalization and the shift toward hybrid or remote work environments also necessitate cultural competency and adaptability. AI professionals may find themselves collaborating with teams from effectively to changing tools, shifting priorities, or evolving project scopes—a vital trait in fast-paced tech environments. (Felten et al., 2019)To support their development, many AI and tech professionals engage in continuous learning networks. Active participation in communities such as Kaggle, GitHub, and AI forums not only builds technical competence but also enhances visibility and peer learning. Mentorship and coaching, whether as mentors or mentees, further enrich their professional growth and contribute to a culture of shared knowledge and innovation.

EMERGING TRENDS IN TECHNOLOGY AND AI

These domains, once considered experimental or niche, are now integral to the digital strategies of businesses, governments, and academic institutions. As we step further into the age of intelligent systems, understanding the emerging trends within these disciplines is essential to anticipate future innovations and the opportunities they present. The convergence of these technologies, combined with advances in computational power, big data availability, and open-source platforms, is propelling us toward a more connected, automated, and intelligent world.Machine Learning continues to be at the heart of AI advancements, evolving far beyond traditional supervised and unsupervised techniques. Today, cutting-edge ML models are capable of handling unstructured data, making real-time decisions, and learning continuously with minimal human intervention. One major trend within ML is automated machine learning (AutoML), which enables non-experts to build sophisticated models by automating the process of feature selection, model selection, and hyperparameter tuning. This democratization of ML is expanding access and accelerating deployment across organizations. Another significant development is federated learning, security—especially critical in sectors like healthcare and finance.Moreover, reinforcement learning autonomous vehicles, game AI, and dynamic pricing. Unlike traditional ML, RL learns optimal behavior through trial and error, making it highly effective in complex, real-time environments. Self-supervised learning is also gaining attention as a powerful alternative to labor-intensive labeled data, allowing models to learn from vast amounts of unlabeled information—an approach used prominently in training large language models. Additionally, TinyML, which focuses on deploying ML models on edge devices with limited resources, is enabling intelligent features in low-power applications like wearable devices, smart home appliances, and industrial sensors.Simultaneously,(Gibbons and Waldman, 2004) Natural Language Processing (NLP) has experienced explosive growth, largely driven by the These models can generate human-like text, engage in multi-turn conversations, and even assist in content creation, programming, and legal analysis. LLMs are being fine-tuned for domain-specific applications, from medical diagnostics to legal research, demonstrating their versatility and economic potential.A key emerging area within NLP is multimodal AI, which combines text, images, audio, and video to understand and generate richer content.

This is exemplified by models that can understand a user's spoken request, interpret visual context, and respond appropriately—greatly enhancing user experience. Another trend is conversational (Gibbons and Waldman, 2006)AI and voice interfaces, with applications in virtual assistants, customer service bots, and smart devices. These systems are becoming increasingly natural, responsive, and context-aware, thanks to advancements in intent recognition, sentiment detection, and dialogue management 3D computer vision and spatial computing, machines can now understand depth, movement, and physical spaces in three dimensions, enabling more immersive and interactive digital environments. Generative AI within computer vision—through tools like DALL·E, MidJourney, and Stable Diffusion—is pushing the boundaries of creativity, allowing users to generate high-quality images from textual prompts. This not only redefines artistic expression but also introduces new applications in advertising, design, and content creation.The fusion of ML, NLP, and computer vision is giving rise to intelligent automation, where systems can analyze data, make decisions, and take action with minimal human intervention. This has significant implications for sectors like manufacturing, logistics, and financial services, where —enhancing the efficiency and quality of care. In retail, computer vision and NLP together power cashier-less stores and personalized shopping experiences. AI-enhanced cybersecurity is being developed to proactively detect and respond to threats. Neuroscience-inspired AI models aim to emulate more closely how the human brain learns and adapts, potentially leading to more generalizable and robust AI systems. Meanwhile, AI's role in sustainability—optimizing energy usage, reducing emissions, and monitoring environmental changes—is gaining traction as organizations prioritize environmental responsibility.intelligent, adaptive, and human-centered systems.(Goos et al., 2014).

THE IMPACT OF TECHNOLOGY AND AI ON INDUSTRIES

The rise of advanced technology and artificial intelligence (AI) is profoundly reshaping industries across the globe, driving innovation, improving efficiency, and redefining business models. As AI systems evolve to process massive datasets, make predictions, and learn autonomously, their integration into sectors such as healthcare, finance, and transportation has become a transformative force.AI-powered systems such as IBM Watson have assisted physicians by suggesting potential diagnoses and treatment protocols based on the latest medical literature. Additionally, robotic surgeries guided by AI offer enhanced precision and reduced recovery times. The emergence of wearable devices and remote monitoring tools, often paired with AI, enables real-time patient tracking and proactive care. to ensure the safe deployment of AI in sensitive healthcare contexts.In the financial industry, AI has become indispensable for enhancing operational efficiency, risk management, and customer experience. Algorithms now drive fraud detection by identifying anomalies in real-time transactions. AI is also at the core of algorithmic trading, where machines execute complex trades within milliseconds based on market trends and predictive analytics. Robo-advisors are offering personalized investment strategies to retail investors, often at a fraction of the cost of traditional advisory services. Moreover, natural language processing (NLP) enables financial institutions to automate customer service via AI-driven chatbots and virtual assistants. Risk assessment and credit scoring are also being refined through machine learning, which evaluates non-traditional data sources to assess a borrower's creditworthiness. Despite these advances, financial institutions must carefully navigate ethical implications, particularly around data privacy, explainability of algorithms, and the potential for automation to displace human jobs.The transportation sector is undergoing a radical transformation, largely driven by AI and automation technologies. Self-driving vehicles, powered by computer vision, sensor fusion, and deep learning, are being developed and tested by companies like Tesla, Waymo, and Uber. These autonomous systems promise to reduce traffic accidents, lower emissions, and increase mobility deployment of autonomous vehicles and AI-driven infrastructure raises concerns around cybersecurity, liability in accidents, and the societal impacts of job displacement in driving and delivery occupations.Beyond these three sectors, retail, manufacturing, education, and agriculture are also seeing significant changes due to AI and technology integration. In retail,(Hershbein and Kahn, 2018) AI powers recommendation engines, personalized marketing, and inventory management. Amazon, for example, uses AI to predict what customers will buy, enabling just-in-time delivery and efficient warehouse automation. Brick-and-mortar retailers are adopting smart checkout systems, in-store analytics, and AI-powered customer service to remain competitive in a digital-first world. Quality control is increasingly automated, with AI-enabled vision systems identifying defects more accurately than the human eye. These innovations not only boost efficiency but also support sustainability by reducing waste and energy consumption.In agriculture, AI and technology are enhancing crop management, soil analysis, and pest detection. Precision farming uses AI to monitor field conditions and apply water, fertilizers, and pesticides only where needed, increasing yields while minimizing environmental impact.

THE FUTURE OF WORK: HOW TECHNOLOGY AND AI ARE CHANGING THE JOB MARKET

These changes are reshaping not only how we work but also where, when, and even why we work. From automation and digital platforms to remote collaboration tools and AI-powered decision-making systems, related to job displacement, inequality, and the urgent need for upskilling and reskilling the global workforce. One of the most significant shifts in the job market is the increasing automation of routine tasks. Repetitive, rule-based jobs, particularly in manufacturing, logistics, and administrative sectors, are being replaced or augmented by machines. Robotics, AI algorithms, and software bots can now perform tasks ranging from data entry and inventory management to assembly line operations with greater speed, accuracy, and efficiency than humans. For example, in warehouses, autonomous robots are optimizing order fulfillment and reducing delivery times, while in offices, robotic process automation (RPA) tools are streamlining back-office functions. This trend is not limited to blue-collar roles—white-collar professions, such as legal research, accounting, and journalism, are also being impacted as AI begins to handle analytical and creative functions once considered immune to automation.business operations, the demand for human oversight, interpretation, and strategic implementation of these technologies increases.(Jin and Waldman, 2019) Moreover, industries like green energy, biotechnology, and space exploration are opening new frontiers for employment, driven by innovation and the urgent need to address global challenges such as climate change Tools like Zoom, Microsoft Teams, and Slack have made it possible for teams to collaborate effectively from anywhere in the world. This shift has redefined the concept of the workplace, allowing greater flexibility and work-life balance for employees while enabling companies to access a global talent pool. At the same time, it has spurred discussions about digital burnout, isolation, and the importance of building organizational culture in virtual environments. Companies are now rethinking office spaces, employee engagement strategies, and performance measurement in this new work paradigm.The gig economy and platform-based work are also reshaping employment norms. Digital platforms such as Uber, Upwork, Fiverr, and DoorDash have enabled millions to participate in freelance and contract work. This model offers autonomy and flexibility, especially appealing to younger generations seeking non-traditional career paths. need for new labor protections, portable benefits, and fair compensation structures to support this evolving work-force.Given these dynamics, the need for upskilling and reskilling has never been more critical.

The World Economic Forum estimates that by 2025, half of all employees will require reskilling due to automation and technological advancements. Lifelong learning is becoming the norm as professionals must continually adapt to new tools, methodologies, and business models. Educational institutions(Lane and Saint-Martin, 2021), governments, and employers all play a role in facilitating this transition. Online learning platforms such as Coursera, edX, LinkedIn Learning, and Khan Academy are helping bridge the skills gap by offering accessible, affordable, and flexible education. Corporate training programs are also evolving, focusing not only on technical skills but also on soft skills like critical thinking, communication, and emotional intelligence—capabilities that are uniquely human and difficult to replicate through (Madgule et al., 2023)AI.Inequality and access to opportunity, however, remain significant concerns in this transition. The digital divide—both in terms of access to technology and digital literacy—can widen existing socioeconomic gaps. Workers in low-income communities or developing countries may face greater risks of job loss and fewer opportunities for reskilling. Addressing this imbalance Moreover, youth and education systems must prepare the next generation for jobs that may not yet exist. Traditional curricula are being reevaluated in favor of more dynamic, interdisciplinary learning experiences that emphasize adaptability, problem-solving, and innovation. Schools and universities are starting to incorporate coding, AI literacy, and digital ethics into their programs, helping students understand and navigate the future In addition to skill development, mental health and well-being have emerged as central concerns in the evolving workplace.

The fast pace of change, coupled with job insecurity and the pressure to constantly adapt, can contribute to anxiety and stress. Companies are increasingly investing in mental health support, employee wellness programs, and more empathetic management practices to foster a resilient workforce. Ensuring that technological progress does not come at the expense of human well-being is essential for long-term sustainability.(Nolan, 2021)The future of work also invites questions about purpose and meaning. As machines take over more routine functions, workers are seeking roles that offer a sense of contribution and fulfillment. Employers that align their mission with broader social and environmental goals are better positioned to attract and retain talent, particularly among millennials and Gen Z employees. This shift from purely transactional work relationships to more values-driven engagement reflects a deeper transformation in the nature of work itself.(Qian et al., 2020)Government and policy interventions will be pivotal in managing this transition. Universal basic income (UBI), shorter workweeks, job guarantees, and expanded social safety nets are being discussed as potential solutions to support workers during times of disruption. Tax incentives for companies that invest in workforce development and fair labor practices could also encourage responsible adoption of technology. At the international level, cooperation on AI governance, labor standards, and digital infrastructure will be crucial to ensure that the benefits of technological progress are distributed equitably.(Raj and Seamans, 2019)In conclusion, technology and AI are undoubtedly reshaping the future of work in complex and far-reaching ways. They offer unprecedented opportunities for innovation, productivity, and human potential, but they also challenge traditional employment structures and demand a rethinking of how society supports its workers. The path forward requires collaboration among governments, businesses, educators, and individuals to build a job market that is inclusive, adaptive, and resilient. Embracing lifelong learning, prioritizing well-being, and fostering human-AI collaboration will be essential to thriving in this new era of work. As we navigate this transition, the goal must be not only to survive the changes but to use them as a catalyst for creating a more meaningful, equitable, and sustainable world of work.

Figure 1. Applications of AI in technology

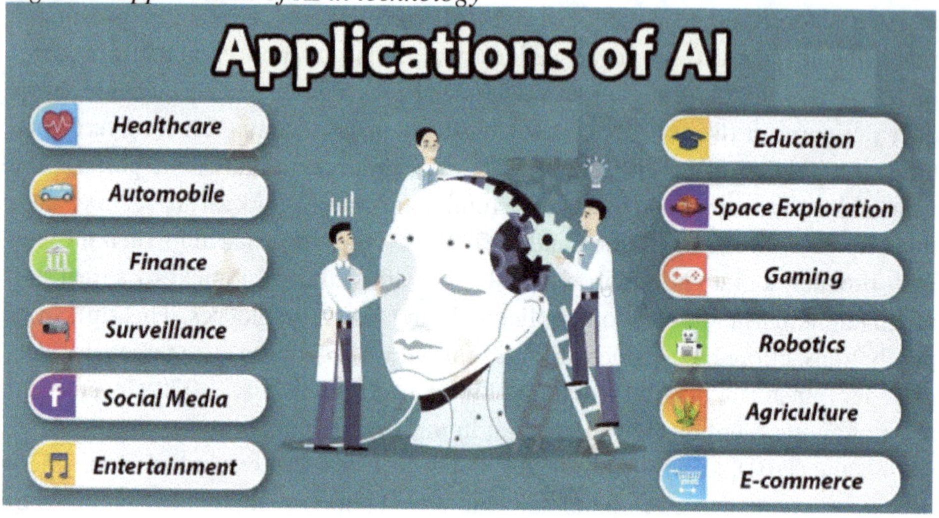

TECHNOLOGY AND AI IN HEALTHCARE

AI systems can identify early signs of cancer, including lung, breast, and skin cancers, often before visible symptoms manifest. These tools analyze imaging data at a pixel level, recognizing subtle patterns that might escape the human eye. Similarly(Ramakrishnan et al., 2022), AI has been instrumental in analyzing pathology slides to detect cell abnormalities, enabling early intervention and improving patient outcomes. In genomics, AI facilitates the interpretation of complex genetic data to identify mutations linked to rare genetic disorders, thereby enhancing the precision of diagnosis and paving the way for personalized medicine.In terms of treatment, AI and technology are redefining how care is delivered. amounts of clinical data to recommend the most effective treatments while minimizing adverse effects. For example, in oncology, AI algorithms help oncologists select optimal chemotherapy regimens or targeted therapies by analyzing the genetic profile of a tumor. Robotic-assisted surgeries, powered by dexterity and control. Additionally, AI contributes to drug discovery and development by analyzing molecular structures and predicting the efficacy and safety of new compounds. This significantly shortens the drug development cycle, lowers costs, and accelerates the time-to-market for life-saving medications.Patient care has also undergone a dramatic transformation through the implementation of AI and digital technologies. hese systems not only enhance accessibility but also relieve the burden on healthcare professionals by managing routine inquiries and facilitating remote monitoring. Telemedicine platforms, bolstered by AI-driven diagnostic support tools, enable patients to deterioration and prompt timely medical interventions. Remote patient monitoring systems are increasingly used in chronic disease management, allowing for real-time adjustments to treatment plans and reducing the need for hospital visits.Moreover, AI enhances clinical decision-making by providing physicians with evidence-based recommendations and risk assessments. patient outcomes and prevent complications. For example, AI can forecast the likelihood of hospital readmissions, sepsis onset, or disease progression, enabling preemptive actions that improve prognosis and reduce healthcare costs. transcribing and organizing clinical notes through voice recognition and natural language processing. This reduces physician burnout associated with administrative burdens and ensures that patient records are more accurate and up-to-date.(Squicciarini and Nachtigall, 2021) Furthermore, AI-driven resource management systems help hospitals optimize staff allocation, manage bed occupancy, and forecast supply chain needs, enhancing the overall efficiency of healthcare delivery.. Therefore, transparency in algorithm development, continuous validation, and ethical oversight are crucial. The need for explainability in AI decision-making is also vital in a clinical setting, as physicians must understand and trust the recommendations provided by these systems.In conclusion, the use of technology and AI in healthcare is reshaping the entire ecosystem of medicine, offering transformative benefits in diagnosis, treatment, and patient care. By improving accuracy, efficiency, and personalization, AI enhances clinical outcomes and empowers both patients and providers. While challenges related to ethics, privacy, and integration remain, the continued evolution and responsible application of AI hold the promise of a healthier, more connected, and more responsive healthcare future.

CAREER PATHS FOR TECHNOLOGY AND AI PROFESSIONALS

The rapid advancement of technology and artificial intelligence (AI) has created an ever-expanding array of career opportunities for professionals in this field.(Sreenivasulu et al., 2022) As AI continues to permeate every sector—from healthcare and finance to education, manufacturing, and entertainment—the demand for skilled professionals has grown exponentially. Careers in technology and AI are not only diverse in nature but also offer lucrative compensation and long-term growth potential, making them some of the most attractive options in today's job market. At the heart of this ecosystem are several high-demand job roles, each requiring a unique set of skills, educational background, and area of expertise.One of the most prominent and foundational roles is that of a machine learning engineer. These professionals design, build, and maintain machine learning models that allow computers to learn from and make decisions based on data. They typically have a background in computer science, mathematics, or statistics and are proficient in programming languages such as Python, R, and Java. Their work involves data preprocessing, algorithm development, model training, and deployment. Machine learning engineers earn an average annual salary ranging from $100,000 to $160,000 in the United States, with higher salaries possible in tech hubs like San Francisco or New York, and in specialized industries such as finance or defense. Related to this role is the data scientist, who focuses more on extracting insights from data using statistical analysis and machine learning techniques. Data scientists help organizations make data-driven decisions and often work closely with business stakeholders. Their average salary typically ranges from $90,000 to $150,000, depending on experience and industry. These roles are particularly important as AI systems become more influential in decision-making processes affecting privacy, civil rights, and social equity. Careers in this field may be found in government agencies, NGOs, universities, or corporate ethics teams. Salaries here can vary significantly, generally falling in the range of $70,000 to $130,000, with leadership or consulting roles earning more. Similarly, AI product managers act as the bridge between technical teams and business stakeholders, guiding the development of AI-powered products.(Tolan et al., 2021) They are responsible for market research, feature prioritization, roadmapping, and ensuring the alignment of AI technologies with customer needs. These professionals often have both technical knowledge and strong business acumen. The average salary for AI product managers typically ranges from $120,000 to $180,000, often bolstered by performance bonuses and equity.Robotics engineers are another specialized group of AI professionals who design and program intelligent machines used in manufacturing, healthcare, space exploration, and consumer electronics. These roles require knowledge of hardware design, embedded systems, AI algorithms, and real-time control systems. (Sugumaran et al., 2024)With robotics becoming more central to industries such as logistics, agriculture, and autonomous vehicles, the demand for robotics engineers is soaring. They generally earn between $90,000 and $160,000, depending on the complexity of the projects and industry. Similarly, professionals working in natural language processing (NLP) develop systems that understand and generate human language, powering applications like chatbots, translation services, and voice assistants. As NLP technologies become more integrated into daily life, demand for these experts continues to rise. NLP engineers and researchers can command salaries from $100,000 to $170,000 or more.

In terms of growth opportunities, the field of AI and technology is expected to remain one of the fastest-growing employment sectors globally. According to reports from the World Economic Forum and McKinsey, millions of new jobs are projected to be created in AI and related technologies over the next decade. As organizations in every industry strive to become more data-driven and efficient, the demand for AI professionals is far outpacing the current supply of skilled workers. This creates significant upward mobility for those entering the field, with ample room for specialization and leadership. Many professionals begin as junior engineers or analysts and quickly progress to senior, lead, or managerial roles, often within a few years. Furthermore, AI professionals frequently move into entrepreneurship, founding startups that address niche problems with innovative AI solutions. Venture capital funding for AI startups continues to grow, offering opportunities for both financial success and meaningful impact.Another attractive aspect of AI and tech careers is the flexibility and variety of work environments. Professionals can choose to work in large multinational corporations, agile startups, research institutions, government agencies, or as independent contractors. Many roles offer remote or hybrid options, enabling a better work-life balance and access to global opportunities. Additionally, the interdisciplinary nature of AI allows professionals to work across domains, combining their technical skills with interests in healthcare, education, finance, art, or sustainability. For example, (Vijayakumar et al., 2024)AI specialists may collaborate with doctors to improve diagnostic tools, or with environmental scientists to monitor climate change. This cross-pollination of ideas fosters innovation and keeps the work intellectually stimulating.To enter the field, aspiring AI professionals typically pursue degrees in computer science, data science, mathematics, or engineering, though many also transition from fields such as physics, economics, or linguistics. Increasingly, alternative pathways such as coding bootcamps, online courses, certifications (e.g., from Coursera, edX, or Google), and self-study are becoming viable routes into the profession, especially for roles in data science and machine learning engineering. Continuous learning is essential in this fast-paced domain, as new tools, frameworks, and methodologies emerge regularly. Technologies like TensorFlow, PyTorch, Keras, scikit-learn, and Hugging Face's Transformers are widely used and considered industry standards, and proficiency in cloud platforms like AWS, Azure, and Google Cloud is often required.In conclusion, careers in technology and AI offer dynamic, high-paying, and intellectually rewarding opportunities with strong long-term growth potential. Whether through hands-on development, research, product management, ethics, or consulting, AI professionals are at the forefront of innovation, shaping the future across virtually every sector. As demand for talent continues to rise, individuals who invest in developing their skills and staying abreast of technological trends will find themselves well-positioned for a fulfilling and impactful career in one of the most exciting fields of the 21st century.

UPSKILLING AND RESKILLING FOR TECHNOLOGY AND AI PROFESSIONALS

As the pace of innovation accelerates, the need for continuous upskilling and reskilling has become essential for technology and AI professionals aiming to stay relevant in an ever-evolving digital landscape. The rapid emergence of new tools, frameworks, languages, and methodologies, coupled with the increasing integration of artificial intelligence across all sectors, demands that professionals not only maintain their existing skills but also acquire new ones to adapt to shifting roles and responsibilities. Unlike traditional career paths where degrees and initial training sufficed for years, modern tech and AI careers require a mindset of lifelong learning. Emerging technologies like generative AI, quantum computing, blockchain, edge computing, and advanced robotics have redefined what it means to be a tech-savvy professional, and organizations are prioritizing talent that can evolve alongside these innovations.One of the primary drivers of this shift is the short shelf life of technical skills. According to various industry studies, the average half-life of a tech skill is now just 2–3 years, meaning that knowledge acquired today may become outdated within a short period. For AI professionals, this is particularly true due to the rapid evolution of models, frameworks, and APIs. Online learning platforms such as Coursera, edX, Udacity, DataCamp, and Pluralsight offer flexible, self-paced courses in (Webb, 2020)Assembly, or Flatiron School offer immersive, mentor-supported experiences that prepare learners for real-world roles.In addition to technical certifications, there is growing recognition of the need for cross-functional and soft skills in technology roles. AI professionals are expected to work closely with product managers, designers, ethicists, and business leaders, requiring strong communication, problem-solving, and ethical reasoning abilities. As a result, many upskilling programs now include components on AI ethics, responsible AI development, and collaborative workflows, which are vital in ensuring that AI systems are fair, transparent, and aligned with human values. Institutions like MIT, Stanford, and Harvard offer short courses and micro-certifications on AI governance, fairness, and legal implications, equipping professionals to take on interdisciplinary leadership roles. Government and nonprofit initiatives are also playing a pivotal role in expanding access to upskilling and reskilling opportunities. Programs like Grow with Google, AI4ALL, and the Microsoft Global Skills Initiative aim to democratize access to digital skills training, especially for underrepresented groups. Public-private partnerships are launching reskilling hubs and innovation centers to help displaced workers transition into high-demand tech roles. Countries like Singapore, Germany, and Canada have national strategies supporting lifelong learning through subsidized programs, tax incentives, and digital skills passports, setting a global precedent for future-ready workforces.

NETWORKING AND COMMUNITY BUILDING FOR TECHNOLOGY AND AI PROFESSIONALS

In the rapidly evolving landscape of technology and artificial intelligence (AI), the significance of networking and community building has grown tremendously. For professionals working in such dynamic and often complex fields, staying connected to peers, mentors, thought leaders, and collaborators is not only beneficial—it's essential. Unlike traditional professions where linear career paths and well-defined roles are the norm, tech and AI fields thrive on collaboration, knowledge exchange, and open innovation. In addition to global conferences, local meetups and user groups play a crucial role in community engagement and grassroots networking. Platforms like Meetup.com, Eventbrite, and TechEvents—such as San Francisco, London, Berlin, Toronto, Bangalore, and Singapore—have become hubs for these gatherings, but online options have ensured that even those in remote or underserved areas can participate. The accessibility and diversity of perspectives offered by these events contribute to richer conversations, cross-disciplinary innovation, and stronger professional bonds.Online forums and communities are perhaps the most consistent and scalable ways to stay connected and engaged. Platforms like GitHub, Stack Overflow, Reddit, Hugging Face forums, Kaggle, AI Alignment Forum, and LinkedIn have become indispensable tools for AI and tech professionals.

Active participation in such forums helps professionals build reputations, stay updated on technical issues, and find collaborators for projects or research.Social media platforms such as Twitter (now X), LinkedIn, and Discord have also become essential tools for real-time networking and thought leadership. On LinkedIn, professionals can share articles, post achievements, or engage in meaningful discussions about AI ethics, emerging trends, or new frameworks. Twitter is a hotspot for real-time commentary during events, rapid sharing of research papers, and community threads that distill complex ideas into digestible insights. Discord and Slack channels, often hosted by communities such as Women in AI, AI Global, Data Science Society, and Fast.ai, provide space for in-depth discussions, mentorship, resource sharing, and live coding sessions. These initiatives foster inclusive ecosystems where diverse voices contribute to innovation, help close opportunity gaps, and build stronger, more empathetic professional communities. Events like Hack the North, ETHGlobal, Kaggle Days, and AI Hackathons hosted by MIT, Stanford, and other leading institutions bring together multidisciplinary teams to tackle real-world problems using AI. These time-bound events promote creative thinking, rapid prototyping, and cross-functional teamwork. Participants often find mentors, co-founders, or job offers through these immersive experiences, making them ideal for both early-career professionals and seasoned experts looking to expand their networks.Community engagement also helps professionals stay updated on ethical, legal, and societal issues in AI. As AI adoption increases, so does the need for discussions around AI safety, bias, explainability, privacy, and accountability. Forums like Partnership on AI, AI Now Institute, and Montreal AI Ethics Institute create spaces for thoughtful dialogue and research on these pressing concerns. Engaging with these communities ensures that tech professionals are not only building capable systems but also responsible and inclusive ones.Importantly, networking and community involvement also contribute to career advancement. Many job opportunities, especially in competitive fields like AI research or software engineering at top tech companies, come through referrals and personal connections. Hiring managers often look for candidates who are engaged in their fields, contribute to open-source or research, and show initiative in self-learning. A strong professional network can provide insider knowledge about company culture, hiring practices, and upcoming roles. Additionally, community involvement can lead to speaking engagements, invitations to panels, or teaching opportunities—further boosting one's professional profile.

CHALLENGES FACING TECHNOLOGY AND AI PROFESSIONALS

As technology and artificial intelligence (AI) continue to reshape the world at an unprecedented pace, professionals in these fields are not only navigating a landscape of innovation but also grappling with a growing set of complex challenges. While AI and automation present vast opportunities, they also bring significant responsibilities and risks that technology and AI professionals must address proactively. Among the most pressing issues are job displacement, algorithmic bias, and ethical dilemmas, all of which intersect with broader concerns around data privacy, regulation, public trust, and professional accountability. Understanding these challenges is essential for current and aspiring professionals to not only succeed in their careers but to contribute to the development of technology that is fair, responsible, and sustainable.One of the most discussed concerns is job displacement caused by automation and AI-driven systems. . While AI creates new roles, such as machine learning engineers, AI product managers, and data scientists, it also renders many traditional jobs obsolete or drastically changes their nature. For instance, roles in manufacturing, transportation, and even legal and financial services are at risk of automation. This shift requires AI professionals to think not only about the efficiency of automation but also its social consequences. Responsible development includes anticipating the downstream impact of their innovations and collaborating with policymakers, educators, and organizations to support reskilling initiatives and career transition strategies for displaced workers. This results in an uneven distribution of opportunities, often favoring professionals in urban centers or developed countries.

Addressing this requires AI professionals and industry leaders to advocate for inclusive education, open-source tools, community-driven initiatives, and international collaboration to democratize access to AI knowledge and resources.

Technology and AI professionals must confront this reality head-on by implementing bias detection, fairness auditing, and data diversification strategies. However, addressing bias is not a one-time fix; it requires continuous monitoring and ethical reflection throughout the entire AI development lifecycle. AI professionals must navigate the tension between accuracy and interpretability, exploring solutions such as model distillation, interpretable machine learning, and post-hoc explanation tools like LIME and SHAP. But even with these tools, there is still a communication gap between developers and non-technical stakeholders—another area where professionals must improve to build responsible systems. can also introduce complexity and compliance burdens for professionals. Navigating shifting legal landscapes requires AI professionals to stay informed, adapt quickly, and often collaborate with legal and compliance teams. At the same time, they must balance innovation with caution, ensuring that new products meet ethical standards while remaining competitive in a global marketplaceadversarial training, differential privacy, watermarking, and robust authentication systems to protect AI models and their outputs. However, staying ahead of bad actors is a constant arms race, and it requires a collective effort across the tech industry, academia, and government agencies.Another often overlooked challenge is the mental and emotional strain experienced by tech and AI professionals. Constant pressure to innovate, long hours, imposter syndrome, and ethical dilemmas can contribute to burnout and decision fatigue. Professionals in this field are frequently asked to shoulder enormous responsibility with limited guidance or support. Building a sustainable career in AI thus also means advocating for mental health awareness, work-life balance, and a supportive community culture within organizations and professional networks.

OPPORTUNITIES FOR TECHNOLOGY AND AI PROFESSIONALS

The rise of artificial intelligence (AI) and advanced technologies has unlocked a vast and growing array of opportunities for technology professionals, placing them at the forefront of shaping the future. As digital transformation accelerates across every sector—from healthcare and finance to education, logistics, entertainment, and sustainability—the demand for innovative, skilled, and forward-thinking professionals in AI and technology continues to skyrocket. These opportunities go far beyond traditional technical roles. Today's tech and AI professionals can become innovators, entrepreneurs, and leaders, driving real-world change, creating high-impact solutions, and influencing global economic and societal progress.One of the most exciting domains for tech professionals is innovation, where they have the chance to develop and apply cutting-edge solutions to solve complex problems. The rise of AI-as-a-Service (AIaaS) models and low-code/no-code platforms has also lowered barriers to entry, enabling technologists to launch products and platforms with fewer resources and faster go-to-market strategies. Investors, including venture capital firms and government innovation funds, are increasingly backing AI startups, recognizing the transformative potential of such technologies. Professionals with a blend of technical depth, user-centric design, and business strategy can carve out niche solutions that scale globally—turning startups into impactful ventures. Many leading companies today, such as OpenAI, DeepMind, UiPath, and DataRobot, were born from the entrepreneurial vision of technologists who understood AI's potential. Opportunities also abound in leadership and strategic roles. As organizations across industries implement AI-driven systems, there is a growing need for professionals who can bridge the gap between technical executio multidisciplinary teams. Professionals who grow into leadership roles are also tasked with ensuring that AI initiatives are implemented ethically, sustainably, and in ways that benefit all stakeholders. This makes leadership in technology not only a path to influence and organizational impact but also a chance to shape policy, culture, and social outcomes.The global demand for AI and technology expertise has created abundant career opportunities in both established corporations and emerging sectors. Multinational companies such as Google, Microsoft, Amazon, IBM, Apple, Meta, and Tesla are constantly expanding their AI teams, offering roles in research, engineering, operations, ethics, and product development.

Simultaneously, industries like healthcare, manufacturing, agriculture, logistics, and energy are recruiting tech talent to power smart automation, predictive maintenance, and AI-based decision-making systems. AI professionals also find roles in non-traditional sectors such as legal tech, fashion tech, real estate, insurance, and the arts, where digital disruption is opening new frontiers. Governments and nonprofits are hiring tech talent to develop public services, disaster prediction systems, smart governance tools, and educational platforms—proving that AI and technology careers are not confined to Silicon Valley or private industry alone. With the expansion of remote work and global collaboration, professionals are no longer limited by geography. AI researchers in India can work with companies in the U.S.; developers in Nigeria can contribute to open-source projects used in Europe. This global interconnectedness creates a borderless job market, providing access to international clients, diverse teams, and a wide variety of projects. Professionals can freelance, consult, join distributed teams, or even build digital products from anywhere, creating flexible and highly personalized career paths. Remote work also promotes the democratization of opportunity, allowing talent from underserved or underrepresented regions to participate in the global AI revolution.or those interested in research and academia, the opportunities are equally vast. As the societal impact of AI becomes more significant, professionals who understand both the technical and human dimensions of AI are needed to shape regulations, develop ethical frameworks, and lead responsible AI initiatives. Organizations such as the OECD, UNESCO, World Economic Forum, and Partnership on AI are hiring experts to advise on ethical standards, bias mitigation, and algorithmic accountability. Likewise, corporations are appointing ethics officers and creating responsible AI teams to ensure their systems are trustworthy and transparent. Tech professionals with a background in law, social sciences, or philosophy—alongside technical expertise—can become powerful advocates and thought leaders in this emerging space. for public health, AI-driven crop optimization in developing countries, real-time translation services for global communication, and smart systems for water and energy conservation. Working on mission-driven technology not only offers career fulfillment but also allows professionals to contribute to solutions that uplift communities and drive positive change on a global scale.

RECOMMENDATIONS FOR TECHNOLOGY AND AI PROFESSIONALS

The field of technology and artificial intelligence (AI) is evolving at an unprecedented pace, creating vast opportunities and challenges for professionals who want to stay ahead of the curve. As AI technologies continue to transform industries and daily life, it is crucial for technology professionals to proactively develop their careers, adapt to changing skill sets, and seize emerging opportunities. Below are several key recommendations for technology and AI professionals aimed at fostering long-term career growth, ensuring technical proficiency, and embracing the changing landscape of the digital economy. These suggestions not only provide a roadmap for navigating the evolving landscape but also highlight the importance of building a well-rounded skill set, cultivating leadership qualities, and engaging in continuous learning knowledge and adapt to new tools, frameworks, and methodologies. One of the primary ways to achieve this is by engaging in continuous upskilling.master new programming languages, software tools, or AI algorithms. Formal education, such as graduate degrees or specialized certifications in AI, machine learning, or data science, can also play a pivotal role in further enhancing one's qualifications.. Professionals who can quickly pivot to master new technologies or integrate them with AI solutions will enjoy a significant competitive advantage.Moreover, professionals should learn interdisciplinary skills. AI is not just a technical field—it intersects with domains such as ethics, business management, psychology, sociology, and law.

Understanding the broader implications of AI on society and business will make technology professionals more valuable assets and will ensure they have a well-rounded perspective when solving complex problems.professionals need to translate complex technical concepts into understandable terms for non-technical stakeholders, including executives, policymakers, and the general public. This is especially true for those working in AI development roles, where the ability to communicate the potential benefits, risks, and limitations of AI is paramount.AI professionals should focus on developing leadership and teamwork abilities to effectively collaborate with cross-functional teams. The nature of AI projects often involves diverse expertise from data scientists, engineers, designers, business analysts, and legal advisors.

Strong interpersonal and leadership skills will allow AI professionals to coordinate efforts, navigate potential conflicts, and ensure that projects run smoothly. In addition, having business acumen is becoming increasingly important, especially for those looking to take on leadership or managerial roles. Understanding how AI can drive business value and transform operations across sectors is crucial for making strategic decisions.While general AI knowledge is important, technology professionals are increasingly expected to develop specialized expertise in niche areas of AI. Specialization allows professionals to differentiate themselves in a competitive job market and become recognized experts in their fields. Some potential areas of focus include:By building expertise in a specific domain, AI professionals can position themselves as leaders in their field. This can open up opportunities for more senior roles or research positions that require deep technical knowledge. Gaining advanced certifications, attending specialized conferences, or publishing research papers in academic journals will also help in cementing a professional's status as an authority in their chosen area.Networking is an essential component of career development, particularly for those working in fast-evolving fields like AI. Technology professionals should engage with the broader AI and tech communities by attending industry events, conferences, and meetups. Participating in these events provides opportunities to learn from thought leaders, share insights, and form valuable connections that can lead to collaborative projects, job opportunities, and mentorship.Building a strong online presence through platforms such as LinkedIn, GitHub, or Kaggle (for data science challenges) is also vital.

CONCLUSION

As we stand at the intersection, the role of technology and AI professionals is evolving from that of problem-solvers and innovators to that of visionaries, architects of progress, and stewards of humanity's digital destiny. AI professionals are not merely responding to change—they are creating it, shaping tomorrow's world through code, data, and design. and beyond—are undergoing rapid digital transformation. AI professionals will be instrumental in driving innovation in personalized medicine, smart infrastructure, green energy solutions, ethical automation, and human-AI collaboration systems. Whether working in research labs developing general AI systems, at startups designing next-gen platforms, or in multinational companies leading enterprise-wide transformations, professionals will find a diverse range of roles that challenge their minds and amplify their impact. The continued integration of AI into daily life will generate millions of new jobs in areas like AI ethics, machine learning operations (MLOps), explainable AI, and augmented intelligence systems, requiring a fusion of technical, analytical, creative, and human-centered thinking.At the same time, the future will require professionals to engage deeply with complex challenges and responsibilities. As AI systems gain decision-making power, questions surrounding bias, fairness, privacy, autonomy, and accountability will grow more urgent. Technology professionals will be called upon to develop solutions that are not only powerful but also transparent, inclusive, and just. They will need to design with empathy, ensure accessibility, and advocate for responsible governance, helping to bridge the growing divide between technological capabilities and ethical standards. As such, the future of the profession lies not only in technical proficiency but in multidisciplinary collaboration—where ethics, law, philosophy, sociology, and the arts intersect with computer science and engineering. The ability to rapidly acquire skills, apply them in novel contexts, and collaborate across domains will set apart those who lead from those who follow. Training, upskilling, and cross-functional learning will be essential not just for career survival, but for advancement and leadership in the AI-powered economy.Furthermore, the global nature of AI development presents both a challenge and an opportunity. Talent is now borderless. Collaboration across continents is the norm, not the exception. This interconnectedness empowers professionals to work on international teams, contribute to open-source ecosystems, and participate in global conversations about the future of AI. It also means that success will require cultural intelligence, humility, and respect for diverse perspectives. The future will favor professionals who can navigate global networks, appreciate ethical and regulatory nuances across regions, and build solutions that resonate universally. startups that challenge norms and create real-world impact. Whether solving problems in healthcare, agriculture, finance, or education, the entrepreneurial path offers a chance to turn ideas into action and shape markets, industries, and even societal behavior.where creativity, collaboration, and experimentation thrive. As the AI revolution matures, leadership will require more than just experience; it will demand vision, courage, and a commitment to building technology that serves the greater good. complex technical ideas into language that non-experts can understand. Professionals who can educate, listen, and collaborate with non-technical stakeholders—from policymakers and journalists to educators and community leaders—will play a crucial role in aligning AI development with democratic values and societal needs.Additionally, the intersection of technology with sustainability and climate resilience presents a frontier of profound importance. AI professionals are uniquely positioned to address global challenges such as climate modeling, disaster prediction, energy optimization, and sustainable agriculture. The future will demand that professionals design solutions not only for economic gain but for planetary survival. Those who align their work with sustainability goals—leveraging AI for environmental monitoring, emissions tracking, and ecological preservation—will become critical agents in humanity's effort to build a livable future.

REFERENCES

Agrawal, A., Gans, J., & Goldfarb, A. (Eds.). (2019). *8. Artificial Intelligence, Automation, and Work*. University of Chicago Press.

Baruffaldi, S., van Beuzekom, B., Dernis, H., Harhoff, D., Rao, N., Rosenfeld, D., ... (2020). Identifying and Measuring Developments in Artificial Intelligence: Making the Impossible Possible. Available online at: https://www.oecd-ilibrary.org/science-and-technology/identifying-and-measuring-developments-in-artificial-intelligence_5f65ff7e-en

Bessen, J. (2016). How Computer Automation Affects Occupations: Technology, Jobs, and Skills. Boston University School of Law, Law and Economics Research Paper 15-49. Available online at: https://scholarship.law.bu.edu/faculty_scholarship/813

Bessen, J. (2019). Automation and jobs: When technology boosts employment. *Economic Policy*, *34*(100), 589–626. DOI: 10.1093/epolic/eiaa001

Carnevale, A. P., Jayasundera, T., & Repnikov, D. (2014). *Understanding online job ads data. Center on Education and the Workforce*. Georgetown University., Available online at https://cew.georgetown.edu/wp-content/uploads/2014/11/OCLM.Tech_.Web_.pdf

Dawson, N., Rizoiu, M., & Williams, M. (2021). Skill-driven recommendations for job transition pathways. *PLoS One*, *16*(8), e0254722. DOI: 10.1371/journal.pone.0254722

Felten, E., Raj, M., & Seamans, R. (2018). A method to link advances in artificial intelligence to occupational abilities. *AEA Papers and Proceedings. American Economic Association*, *108*, 54–57. DOI: 10.1257/pandp.20181021

Felten, E., Raj, M., & Seamans, R. (2021). Occupational, industry, and geographic exposure to artificial intelligence: A novel dataset and its potential uses. *Strategic Management Journal*, *42*(12), 2195–2217. DOI: 10.1002/smj.3286

Felten, E. W., Raj, M., & Seamans, R. (2019). *The Occupational Impact of Artificial Intelligence: Labor, Skills, and Polarization*. NYU Stern School of Business.

Gibbons, R., & Waldman, M. (2004). Task-specific human capital. *The American Economic Review*, *94*(2), 203–207. DOI: 10.1257/0002828041301579

Gibbons, R., & Waldman, M. (2006). Enriching a theory of wage and promotion dynamics inside firms. *Journal of Labor Economics*, *24*(1), 59–107. DOI: 10.1086/497819

Goos, M., Manning, A., & Salomons, A. (2014). Explaining job polarization: Routine-biased technological change and offshoring. *The American Economic Review, 104*(8), 2509–2526. DOI: 10.1257/aer.104.8.2509

Hershbein, B., & Kahn, L. (2018). Do recessions accelerate routine-biased technological change? Evidence from vacancy postings. *The American Economic Review, 108*(7), 1737–1772. DOI: 10.1257/aer.20161570

Jin, X., & Waldman, M. (2019). Lateral moves, promotions, and task-specific human capital: Theory and evidence. *Journal of Law Economics and Organization, 36*, 1–46. DOI: 10.1093/jleo/ewz017

Lane, M., & Saint-Martin, A. (2021). The Impact of Artificial Intelligence on the Labour Market: What Do We Know So Far? OECD Social, Employment and Migration Working Papers, No. 256. Paris: OECD Publishing.

Mahadev Madgule, N. (2023). Vinayaka, Yeshwant M. Sonkhaskar, Dhiren Ramanbhai Patel, R. Karthikeyan, P. Selvakumar,(2023). Mechanical properties and microstructure of activated TIG welded similar joints of Inconel alloys by desirability approaches. *Materials Today: Proceedings, 77*, 528–533. DOI: 10.1016/j.matpr.2022.12.250

Nolan, A. (2021). Making life easier, richer and healthier: Robots, their future and the roles of public policy.

Qian, M., Saunders, A., & Ahrens, M. (2020). In Chishti, S., Bhatti, S. A., Datoo, A., & Indjic, D. (Eds.), *"Mapping legaltech adoption and skill demand," in The Legal Tech Book: The Legal Technology Handbook for Investors, Entrepreneurs and FinTech Visionaries* (pp. 211–214). John Wiley and Sons.

Raj, M., & Seamans, R. (2019). Primer on artificial intelligence and robotics. *J. Organ. Des., 8*(1), 11. DOI: 10.1186/s41469-019-0050-0

Ramakrishnan, T., Mohan Gift, M. D., Chitradevi, S., Jegan, R., & Subha Hency Jose, P. Nagaraja, Rajneesh Sharma H.N., Selvakumar P., Sintayehu Mekuria Hailegiorgis, (2022). "Study of Numerous Resins Used in Polymer Matrix Composite Materials", Advances in Materials Science and Engineering, vol. 2022, Article ID 1088926, 8 pages, 2022. DOI: 10.1155/2022/1088926

Squicciarini, M., & Nachtigall, H. (2021). Demand for AI skills in jobs: Evidence from online job postings, OECD Science, Technology and Industry Working Papers, No. 2021/03. Paris: OECD Publishing. DOI: 10.1787/18151965

Sreenivasulu, A., & Manimozhi, T. Satheesh kumar P., Selvakumar P. and Singh P.,(2022). "The Model of Smart Sensing Device For Sensitive Nanoclusters Modification in Sensing Properties," 2022 2nd International Conference on Advance Computing and Innovative Technologies in Engineering (ICACITE), Greater Noida, India, 2022, pp. 1043-1047, DOI: 10.1109/ICACITE53722.2022.9823846

Sugumaran, K. M. D., Pandiyarajan V., Y. B S, Selvakumar P. and M. S, (2024). "Analysis of Electromyography Signals for Control of Mechanical Prosthesis using Machine Learning Techniques," 2024 2nd International Conference on Intelligent Data Communication Technologies and Internet of Things (IDCIoT), Bengaluru, India, 2024, pp. 1059-1067, DOI: 10.1109/IDCIoT59759.2024.10467707

Tolan, S., Pesole, A., Martínez-Plumed, F., Fernández-Macías, E., Hernández-Orallo, J., & Gómez, E. (2021). Measuring the occupational impact of AI: Tasks, cognitive abilities and AI benchmarks. *Journal of Artificial Intelligence Research, 71*, 191–236. DOI: 10.1613/jair.1.12647

Vijayakumar, G., Rajkumar, M., Rajiv Chandar, N., Selvakumar, P., & Duraisamy, R. (2024). Muniyandi Rajkumar, Rajiv Chandar N, Selvakumar P and Ramesh Duraisamy, (2024). Environmentally friendly TDS removal from waste water by electrochemical ion exchange batch-type recirculation (EIR) technique. *Environmental Science. Water Research & Technology, 10*(4), 826–835. DOI: 10.1039/D3EW00793F

Webb, M. (2020). The Impact of Artificial Intelligence on the Labor Market. Working Paper. Standford University. Available online at: https://web.stanford.edu/

Chapter 16
The Dual Challenge of Genetically Modified Crops for the Environment and Farmers' Rights

Ananya Pandey
http://orcid.org/0000-0002-2419-6314
Christ University, Bangalore, India

EXECUTIVE SUMMARY

The potential environmental benefits of genetically modified (GM) crops are accompanied by worries about ecological dangers and the degradation of farmers' rights. The relationship between genetically modified crop technology, environmental sustainability, and seed sovereignty laws is critically examined in this chapter. Certain genetically modified features may result in biodiversity loss, soil degradation, and genetic contamination, even though they can help minimize pesticide use and increase climate resistance. Furthermore, traditional farming methods are frequently undermined by the spread of intellectual property regimes, which restrict farmers' capacity to share and conserve seeds. Diverse socio-legal results are illustrated by case studies from Africa, the USA, and India, exposing a gap in global governance. To guarantee that GM technologies are in line with ecological integrity and farmers' autonomy, the chapter advocates for a multifaceted policy framework that balances innovation and justice, encourages participatory regulation, and funds interdisciplinary research.

DOI: 10.4018/979-8-3373-3867-5.ch016

INTRODUCTION

Plants whose genetic material has been purposefully altered through biotechnology to express desired qualities like pest resistance, herbicide tolerance, or enhanced nutritional value are referred to as genetically modified or genetically engineered crops. Genetic modification makes it possible to transfer particular genes across species boundaries, in contrast to traditional breeding, which depends on the natural recombination of genes within species. With the commercial launch of crops like genetically modified maize, Roundup Ready soybeans, and Bt cotton in the 1990s, this invention gained significant traction (James, 2014). The development of molecular biology and biotechnology is closely linked to the history of genetic modification in agriculture. The commercialization of genetically modified crops took place in the mid-1990s, following the initial field testing of genetically modified plants in the 1980s. The use of genetically modified crops has grown significantly since then. By 2020, genetically modified crops were grown on more than 190 million hectares in more than 25 countries, according to the International Service for the Acquisition of Agri-biotech Applications (ISAAA) (ISAAA, 2020). Herbicide-tolerant soybean, insect-resistant cotton, and maize are the most commonly grown genetically modified crops, and the leading producers are the United States, Brazil, Argentina, Canada, and India. However, genetically modified technology has not spread evenly throughout the world. The European Union (EU) has taken a cautious approach, citing health and environmental concerns, whereas nations like the United States and Brazil have welcomed genetically modified crops with few limitations. Similar to this, certain African nations—like South Africa and Sudan—have embraced genetically modified crops, while others are wary or opposed because of concerns about biosafety, ethics, and sovereignty (Chambers & Smyth, 2021). Thus, political, legal, and cultural issues influence the spread of genetically modified crops in addition to technological and commercial ones.

Putting the Dual Challenge in Perspective

The emergence of genetically modified crop technology poses two challenges: balancing scientific progress with the preservation of farmers' rights, as well as weighing the possible environmental benefits against the ecological concerns involved. On the one hand, proponents of genetically modified crops contend that, in the face of climate change, they can increase food security, boost yields, and decrease the need for pesticides (Qaim, 2020). However, detractors draw attention to serious environmental issues, including the emergence of weeds and pests with increased resistance, biodiversity loss, and the unknowable long-term ecological consequences of gene flow to non-target species (Hilbeck et al., 2015). At the same time, the spread of genetically modified crops has significant effects on farmers' independence and seed sovereignty. Corporate dominance over the global seed industry has grown as a result of the extensive implementation of intellectual property rights (IPRs), such as patents and plant variety protections, on genetically modified seeds. Restrictive license agreements frequently prevent farmers, especially in the Global South, from replanting, sharing, or conserving genetically modified seeds (Kloppenburg, 2010). Traditional farming methods that have been maintained for many generations and are essential to community-based seed systems and biodiversity preservation are in danger due to these limitations. Furthermore, the concepts of informed choice and participatory governance are compromised when genetically modified crops are introduced without sufficient consultation or consent procedures. Smallholder farmers are susceptible to market pressures and reliance on international seed companies, and they frequently do not have access to objective information concerning genetically modified technologies (Shiva, 2016). Farmers are excluded from decisions that have a direct impact on their livelihoods and cultural customs due to this dynamic, which produces imbalances in knowledge and power.

Therefore, the twofold issue is not just evaluating the ecological effects of genetically modified crops but also challenging the ethical and legal frameworks that govern their use. To gain a thorough understanding, one must look at the complex relationships between biotechnology, environmental sustainability, and social justice rather than merely the "pro-genetically modified" versus "anti-genetically modified" dichotomy. Through two interconnected lenses—environmental sustainability and farmers' rights—this chapter aims to examine the multiple challenges presented by genetically modified crops. Its first goal is to assess the ecological aspects of growing genetically modified crops, taking into account both the risks to ecosystems and biodiversity as well as any potential benefits to sustainable agriculture. Analyzing scholarly discussions on insect resistance, soil health, non-target impacts, and gene flow is part of this. With an emphasis on how they impact farmers' autonomy, access to seeds, and cultural rights, the second chapter critically analyzes the legal and policy frameworks governing genetically modified crops. The chapter examines whether the current regulatory frameworks effectively safeguard farmers' rights in the face of expanding corporate power, drawing on international accords such as the International Treaty on Plant Genetic Resources for Food and Agriculture (ITPGRFA) and the Cartagena Protocol on Biosafety. The chapter advances a more comprehensive understanding of how biotechnology governance might be made more ecologically conscious and egalitarian by linking these two fields. It promotes a fair system that protects farmers' rights and the environment, particularly in areas with inadequate legal protections and noticeable power imbalances. The chapter concludes by highlighting the significance of inclusive, transparent, and participatory methods to genetically modified crop regulation that respect ecological boundaries and preserve the knowledge and dignity of agricultural communities.

ENVIRONMENTAL IMPLICATIONS OF GENETICALLY MODIFIED CROPS

Genetically modified crops' effects on the environment are still a topic of discussion in the farming, scientific, and policy communities. Critics point to unforeseen ecological repercussions and governance issues, while supporters highlight the potential advantages of biotechnology in addressing food security and climate resiliency. This section looks at the limitations of current regulatory control as well as the environmental benefits and risks of genetically modified crops.

Possible Advantages

The decrease in pesticide use is one of the most commonly mentioned environmental benefits of genetically modified crops, particularly when it comes to insect-resistant cultivars like Bt cotton and Bt maize. Bacillus thuringiensis (Bt)-derived toxins produced by these crops can lessen the demand for chemical insecticides. According to a number of studies, Bt crops significantly reduced the amount and frequency of pesticide applications (Klümper & Qaim, 2014). In addition to saving farmers money on inputs, this change lessens the amount of pesticide runoff into soil and water, which may be advantageous for aquatic ecosystems. The increased yield and drought tolerance of genetically modified crops, especially in climate change-exacerbated environments, is another claimed environmental benefit. For example, during times of water constraint, drought-tolerant genetically modified maize cultivars created in the United States and sub-Saharan Africa have shown modest yield stability (Nuccio et al., 2018). The incorporation of stress-resilient characteristics is regarded as a crucial innovation for agricultural adaptation tactics, even though the yield benefits differ depending on the region and crop type. Additionally, genetically modified technology has made it easier to implement no-till and soil conservation techniques, particularly in crops that can withstand herbicides like Roundup Ready soybeans. No-till farming improves moisture retention, lowers soil erosion, and helps sequester carbon. The spread of genetically modified soybeans in nations like Argentina and the United States has been strongly linked to a shift to conservation agriculture, which is in line with more general objectives for mitigating climate change (Brookes & Barfoot, 2020).

Hazards to the Environment

Notwithstanding these advantages, genetically modified crops carry considerable ecological concerns, some of which may materialize over time and at landscape dimensions. The rise of resistant pests and superweeds is one major worry. Particularly in North and South America, glyphosate-resistant weed species have evolved as a result of an over-reliance on herbicide-tolerant crops and ongoing glyphosate use (Duke & Powles, 2009). In a similar vein, the widespread use of Bt crops without appropriate refuge measures has led to populations of insects that are resistant to the technology, endangering its long-term viability. The loss of biodiversity and gene flow to wild relatives is a serious worry as well. If conventional landraces and cultivars are displaced by genetically modified crops, crop genetic diversity may be diminished. Furthermore, transgenes may be introduced into unmanaged ecosystems through accidental cross-pollination between genetically modified crops and their wild or weedy cousins, which could change the dynamics of natural evolution (Ellstrand et al., 2013). In centers of origin and variety, where wild relatives are crucial for future crop breeding and ecological resilience, this kind of gene flow is especially concerning. Furthermore, genetically modified crops may have an effect on soil biota and non-target creatures, such as helpful insects like bees and butterflies. Although Bt toxins are usually thought to be specific, some research has shown that they may have sub-lethal effects on pollinators and non-target Lepidoptera (Hofmann et al., 2014). Additionally, birds and invertebrates that depend on field-edge biodiversity may find their habitat availability disrupted by the cumulative effects of herbicide-based weed management in genetically modified systems.

Scientific Uncertainty and Regulatory Oversight

Inadequate risk evaluations and monitoring systems further complicate the environmental regulation of genetically modified crops. Numerous regulatory bodies depend on limited field studies and pre-commercialization experiments, which might not adequately represent the ecological complexity of the real world. Particularly in nations without strong biosafety agencies, post-release environmental monitoring is frequently inadequate or nonexistent (Jasanoff, 2005). In view of scientific uncertainty, the precautionary principle, which is fundamental to EU biosafety regulation, requires a thorough risk assessment prior to genetically modified clearance. However, the burden of proof and regulatory thresholds vary greatly among nations, therefore this principle is not consistently implemented worldwide. Industry-driven data predominates in some jurisdictions' approval processes, which raises questions regarding openness and conflicts of interest (Hilbeck et al., 2015). Furthermore, there is also scientific ambiguity surrounding long-term ecological repercussions, such as cumulative and synergistic effects across landscapes. Adaptive biosafety rules can be informed by independent, long-term ecological research that fills up these knowledge gaps. Assessing acute toxicity is only one aspect of the problem; other aspects include comprehending resistance limits, wider ecosystem dynamics, and unforeseen repercussions of genetic changes.

NEXUS BETWEEN GENETICALLY MODIFIED CROPS AND FARMERS RIGHTS

A significant change in the legal and economic standing of seeds has resulted from the commercialization of genetically modified crops, especially with the introduction of intellectual property rights (IPRs). Seeds are now considered proprietary assets rather than a shared legacy due to the introduction of patents and Plant Variety Protection (PVP) systems. In contrast to conventional seeds, genetically modified seeds are frequently protected by patent regulations, which means that farmers are not allowed to save, replant, or exchange these seeds without the patent holder's consent (Kloppenburg, 2010). The long-standing custom of storing seeds, which is essential to traditional farming methods and agricultural sustainability, is directly threatened by this change. The case of Monsanto Canada Inc. v. Schmeiser (2004) is among the most representative examples of the conflict between IPRs and farmers' autonomy. Monsanto filed a lawsuit against Canadian farmer Percy Schmeiser in this case for allegedly cultivating its trademarked Roundup Ready canola without a permit. Schmeiser maintained that natural processes like wind and cross-pollination had unintentionally contaminated his fields with the seeds. Nevertheless, the Supreme Court of Canada decided in favor of Monsanto, holding that regardless of origin or intent, the mere existence of patented genes in Schmeiser's crops amounted to infringement. By reaffirming corporate rights over seeds, even in situations of unintentional use, this decision established a global precedent (Magnus, 2008). Furthermore, farmers' rights to reuse protected varieties are restricted by Plant Variety Protection regimes, which are frequently in line with the norms of the International Union for the Protection of New Varieties of Plants (UPOV). The 1991 Act significantly reduces the seed-saving exemptions offered by some UPOV versions (such as UPOV 1978), frequently omitting smallholder methods that are prevalent in the Global South (De Jonge, 2014). As a result, the growth of Plant Variety Protection and patent regimes has shifted the power structure in favor of biotech companies, undermining farmers' traditional agricultural expertise and seed sovereignty.

Displacement and Dependency

Farmers are becoming more and more reliant on agro-biotech companies for chemical inputs, seeds, and fertilizer as a result of the extensive adoption of genetically modified crops. The market for genetically modified seeds is dominated by multinational corporations like Bayer-Monsanto, Syngenta, and Corteva, who impose stringent licensing requirements that prohibit farmers from storing or distributing seeds (Howard, 2015). In addition to limiting farmers' autonomy, this vertical integration entails ongoing input expenses, which are particularly onerous for small-scale and resource-poor farmers. Traditional crop varieties have also been displaced in several areas as a result of the adoption of genetically modified crops. Native seed systems and agroecological methods have been marginalized as a result of genetically modified monocultures' intentional promotion of homogeneity over variation. According to studies conducted in India, the adoption of Bt cotton, while initially lucrative for many farmers, ultimately led to the loss of indigenous cotton types and increased farmers' susceptibility to ecological stress and market instability (Stone, 2011). Extreme instances of farmer misery and suicide have been connected to the ecological and financial strains associated with genetically modified seed reliance, especially in areas with inadequate safety nets and market protections (Gruère et al., 2008). There are ramifications beyond economics when varietal diversity declines. In rural communities, where seed exchange is not merely a commercial activity but also a social practice connected to identity, customs, and resilience, it upends the ecological and cultural fabric. Therefore, farming communities suffer a material and symbolic loss when proprietary genetically modified seeds replace varied seed systems.

Consent and Biosafety Regulations

Biosafety is another crucial aspect of genetically modified crop governance, especially in relation to farmers' rights to information, consultation, and protection from negative effects. A global framework for the safe handling and application of living modified organisms (LMOs), including genetically modified crops, is provided by the Cartagena Protocol on Biosafety (Secretariat of the Convention on Biological Diversity, 2000), a supplemental accord to the Convention on Biological Diversity. Particularly for nations receiving transboundary GMOs, it requires prior informed consent procedures and highlights the precautionary principle (Secretariat of the CBD, 2000). The Cartagena Protocol has, however, been applied unevenly. Biosafety laws are either insufficiently developed or poorly implemented in many developing nations, which restricts farmers' ability to effectively regulate the introduction of genetically modified crops. Furthermore, only government organizations or technical specialists are frequently consulted during decision-making processes, leaving farmers out. This exclusion undercuts farmers' rights to consent or not to technologies that impact their livelihoods and runs counter to the protocol's goal of fostering participatory governance (Sharma, 2021). In reality, biosafety evaluations frequently overlook socioeconomic and cultural effects in favor of technical dangers like gene flow or allergenicity. This technocratic approach ignores how genetically modified technologies are integrated in regional ecological and social contexts and marginalizes farmer opinions. Additionally, nations that have enacted pro-genetically modified laws under corporate pressure frequently ignore the opinions of opposing farmers, particularly in the Global South, which goes against the principle of free, prior, and informed consent (Lander, 2017). There is continuous work to develop inclusive, rights-based biosafety frameworks. Community-level biosafety measures that incorporate participatory monitoring and traditional knowledge systems are supported by certain civil society organizations. These strategies seek to reposition farmers as owners of rights rather than as passive consumers of innovation and democratize technology governance.

LEGAL AND POLICY FRAMEWORK

A complex network of international treaties, national legal systems, and normative frameworks are involved in the regulation of genetically modified crops and the protection of farmers' rights. The dual imperatives of biotechnology governance—fostering innovation and safeguarding ecological sustainability and farmers' autonomy—are critically examined in this section along with how national and international legal systems handle them. Even if frameworks like the TRIPS Agreement and the International Treaty on Plant Genetic Resources for Food and Agriculture (ITPGRFA) seek to organize intellectual property rights and access and benefit-sharing, gaps and inconsistencies between regimes still present serious difficulties.

International Law

The Agreement on Trade-Related Aspects of Intellectual Property Rights (TRIPS) and the International Treaty on Plant Genetic Resources for Food and Agriculture (ITPGRFA) are two of the most significant international legal frameworks affecting genetically modified crops and farmers' rights. Adopted by the Food and Agriculture Organization (FAO) in 2001, the ITPGRFA creates a Multilateral System (MLS) for equitable benefit-sharing and easier access to plant genetic resources for food and agriculture (PGRFA) (FAO, 2009). It expressly acknowledges farmers' rights, such as the ability to participate in decision-making, save, use, exchange, and sell farm-saved seeds, as well as the ability to profit from PGRFA. National laws, however, govern these rights, which results in differing interpretations and applications (Andersen, 2013). Although the Treaty seeks to safeguard food security and preserve agrobiodiversity, it does not contain any legally binding procedures to align these objectives with intellectual property regulations, which frequently limit the practical practice of seed preservation. On the other hand, the TRIPS Agreement, which is overseen by the World Trade Organization, requires that member nations protect plant varieties' intellectual property through patents, an effective sui generis system, or both (World Trade Organization, 1994, Article 27.3(b)). TRIPS has drawn a lot of criticism for eroding seed sovereignty, especially in poor nations, and giving corporate breeders' rights precedence over traditional seed methods (Shiva, 2001). Many nations lack the institutional capacity or political desire to take advantage of TRIPS' flexibilities, which include exemptions from patent rights and sui generis systems, in order to support smallholder farmers (Correa, 2000). Another important instrument under the Convention on Biological Diversity (CBD) is the Cartagena Protocol on Biosafety, which regulates the transboundary movement of living modified organisms (LMOs), including genetically modified crops. Although its enforcement mechanisms are still lacking and its scope does not directly address farmers' rights linked to intellectual property rights, it does highlight the precautionary principle and prior informed consent (CBD Secretariat, 2000).

National Strategies

Different legal cultures, development objectives, and public sentiments have led to different responses from national regulatory systems to genetically modified technologies and farmers' rights. This diversity is demonstrated through a comparative study of the United States (USA), the European Union (EU), and India.

India

The Protection of Plant Varieties and Farmers' Rights Act (PPV&FR Act), 2001, which was passed in accordance with the sui generis clause of the TRIPS Agreement, acknowledges the rights of farmers in India. With the exception of branded seed, the Act permits farmers to conserve, use, sow, re-sow, exchange, and sell seed from protected kinds (Government of India, 2001). However, there are legal issues when this regulation coexists with the Seed Act and patent laws, especially when it comes to genetically modified seeds like Bt cotton (Sahai, 2003). The Environment Protection Act (EPA), 1986, governs India's biosafety framework, which includes risk assessment processes for genetically modified crops. However, issues with openness and farmer engagement still exist.

European Union

Regarding genetically modified crops, the EU takes a cautious and limited approach. Labeling, traceability, and thorough environmental risk evaluations are necessary. A number of EU nations have outright prohibited genetically modified agriculture (European Commission, 2021). Instead of having a single Farmers' Rights law, the EU depends on Plant Variety Protection through national laws and the Community Plant Variety Office (CPVO), which mostly limits seed saving to licensed use, frequently at a cost (Louwaars et al., 2005). However, some of the hazards connected to the acceptance of genetically modified products are mitigated by robust consumer and environmental protections.

United States of America

Over 90% of corn, soy, and cotton planted in the USA are genetically modified crops, demonstrating the country's pro-biotechnology stance (USDA, 2022). Utility patents, which forbid seed saving and allow lawsuits against farmers who repurpose protected seeds, are a strict means of enforcing intellectual property rights (Janis & Kesan, 2002). Farmers work under private contracts with biotech businesses; there is no federal law that recognizes their rights similar to the ITPGRFA. The FDA, EPA, and USDA regulate genetically modified crops, with a greater emphasis on product safety than on ethical or social issues.

Gaps and Inconsistencies

Despite the availability of several frameworks, human rights-based approaches to agriculture and intellectual property regimes can have conflicting duties. While the ITPGRFA calls for the protection of farmers' rights, TRIPS requires nations to uphold the rights of breeders. However, the national discretion clause and soft law structure of ITPGRFA reduce its normative strength, meaning that farmers' claims are not as strongly enforced (Andersen, 2013). Further disenfranchisement results from the fact that the majority of legal systems do not expressly acknowledge farmers' traditional knowledge as intellectual property. The absence of standardized biosafety standards is another important gap. Trade disputes and inconsistent genetically modified crop approvals between nations are caused by differences in risk assessment processes, labeling regulations, and public participation standards. Global regulatory coherence may be undermined, for example, if a genetically modified crop that has been approved in the USA is prohibited in the EU because of conflicting safety assessments (Jasanoff, 2005). Additionally, farmers in the Global South have no access to participatory governance frameworks or legal remedies, and they are frequently left out of decision-making processes pertaining to the adoption of genetically modified. An uneven biotechnology system that prioritizes corporate actors over environmental justice and peasant rights is a result of this regulatory fragmentation.

Case Studies

India: The Debate Over Bt Cotton and Farmers' Suicides

An important development in agricultural biotechnology in the Global South was India's 2002 adoption of Bt cotton. Bt cotton was marketed as a remedy for crop failures caused by pests because it was genetically modified to produce a toxin from Bacillus thuringiensis that deters bollworms. Pesticide use apparently decreased and initial yields improved, but smallholders' long-term socioeconomic results have been complicated and controversial. The claimed connection between Bt cotton and farmer suicides is one of the most hotly contested topics in India. According to researchers like Shiva (2005) and Gutierrez et al. (2015), the high price of genetically modified seeds, along with unstable markets and input-intensive farming methods, drove indebted farmers to despair. Because Bt seeds were proprietary and mostly under Monsanto's (now Bayer's) control, farmers were unable to save seeds, which resulted in yearly repurchases and growing dependence. Furthermore, the long-term effectiveness of Bt cotton has been weakened by reports of pest resistance and the return of secondary pests, increasing farmer susceptibility (Kranthi & Stone, 2020). The situation is made more difficult by licensing issues. The Indian government intervened in the market to set price caps and protect the public interest as a result of Monsanto's royalties for Bt characteristics. The conflicts between national food security requirements and global IPR holders are brought to light by these court cases. India's biosafety framework still lacks strong mechanisms for farmer participation, seed failure compensation, and transparency in risk assessments, despite regulatory pushbacks.

USA: Legal Difficulties and IPR Enforcement

The legal environment in the United States is different from that in India in that biotech companies' rights over genetically modified seeds are well-protected by intellectual property legislation. Because utility patents are strictly enforced, farmers in the United States are typically not allowed to save and replant copyrighted seeds. The power of biotech corporations to assert patent rights over genetically modified organisms was upheld in the historic case of Monsanto Co. v. Geertson Seed Farms, 561 U.S. 139 (2010). Monsanto Canada Inc. v. Schmeiser, [2004] 1

S.C.R. 902, is another case that serves as an example of how farmers can be held accountable for growing proprietary seeds, even if those seeds were brought in by cross-contamination. Despite being Canadian, this case has international significance. The customary practice of storing seeds has been severely restricted by such judicial precedents, undermining what are globally recognized as Farmers' Rights under the ITPGRFA (FAO, 2009). With a strong emphasis on promoting innovation through robust patent protections, the United States lacks a comprehensive legal framework to acknowledge or defend farmers' rights. This asymmetry essentially consolidates seed management in corporate hands by leaving small and independent farmers with little options when they clash with biotech businesses (Howard, 2015).

Africa: Farmer Mobilization, Regulation, and Resistance

The way that farmers and regulators react to genetically modified crops varies throughout Africa. While some nations, like Burkina Faso, have retracted their genetically modified policies following unfavorable results, other nations, like Ghana and South Africa, have actively sought the acceptance of biotechnology. The example of Burkina Faso is especially illuminating; following years of growing Bt cotton, the government phased out genetically modified types because of concerns about fiber quality and cotton producers' discontent (Dowd-Uribe & Schnurr, 2016). Concerns about biosafety, intellectual property rights, and local food sovereignty have been the main causes of civil society opposition and legal challenges to genetically modified crop experiments in Ghana, especially with regard to rice and cowpea. However, research shows a growing socioeconomic divide between resource-poor farmers who lack access to capital and inputs and major commercial growers, even though South Africa is one of the continent's most tolerant genetically modified markets (Schnurr & Mujabi-Mujuzi, 2017). The tension between native knowledge systems and foreign technical models is a recurring theme in African cultures. Many farmers use agroecological practices, community seed systems, and a variety of cropping techniques that are incompatible with the monoculture model that genetically modified acceptance promotes. Resistance groups highlight the loss of cultural customs and local sovereignty over seeds in addition to the hazards to the environment and human health.

TOWARDS A BALANCED FRAMEWORK

Moving beyond dichotomous stances that frame the discussion as pro- or anti-genetically modified is crucial as the worldwide debate over genetically modified crops heats up. A balanced governance structure that balances innovation and justice, upholds farmers' rights, and guarantees strong environmental protections is urgently needed instead. Multidisciplinary expertise, participatory procedures, and several legal systems must all be included in such a framework.

Balancing Equity and Innovation

Developing a biotechnology paradigm that takes into account the demands and voices of public-interest researchers, smallholder farmers, and indigenous groups is the problem of equitable innovation. The institutionalization of participatory technology assessments (PTAs) is one of the most practical strategies. By including stakeholders early in the research and innovation process, PTAs seek to democratize science and technology decision-making, especially for those most impacted by the implementation of GM technologies (Stirling, 2008). PTAs can lessen technical lock-ins and promote socially conscious innovation through local trials, farmer-scientist discussions, and public surveys. Additionally, R&D in the public sector is essential to preventing corporate consolidation in the biotech sector. Public R&D institutions have the ability to prioritize crops that are vital to food security and customize discoveries to a variety of agroecological situations, unlike private research that is motivated by profit. For example, the Indian Council of Agricultural Research (ICAR) and other organizations have developed a number of non-genetically modified bio-inputs that improve soil health and pest resistance in India (Kumar & Pandey, 2022). The existing disparity in biotech governance can be addressed by increasing public financing and encouraging cooperative research among academic institutions, farmers, and civil society. Open-source biotechnology is another paradigm-shifting example. This paradigm, which draws inspiration from the open-source software movement, promotes genetic resources and data that are freely available for use, sharing, and improvement without being constrained by intellectual property laws (Hope, 2008). Open access can encourage regional innovation while adhering to ethical standards, as shown by initiatives such as the Biological Innovation for Open Society (BiOS) Foundation. Open-source biotech gives underserved populations the chance to innovate independently and defy reliance on large businesses.

Increasing the Rights of Farmers

The deterioration of farmers' rights, especially their control over seed methods, in the context of genetically modified crops has drawn international attention. Traditional knowledge (TK) and customary practices must be legally recognized as part of a rights-based approach to agricultural innovation. TK is a co-evolving body of knowledge based on generations of ecological adaptation, not just an adjunct to formal science. Farmers' rights, such as the ability to save, use, trade, and sell farm-saved seed, are protected and promoted under the International Treaty on Plant Genetic Resources for Food and Agriculture (ITPGRFA) (FAO, 2009). However, in many jurisdictions, strict intellectual property protections often supersede national laws or fail to adequately apply these commitments (Gautam, 2021). This divide can be closed with the support of legal pluralism, which acknowledges the coexistence of formal statutory law and unofficial customary systems. Sui generis systems and community protocols that are tailored to local requirements can be used as legal instruments to safeguard traditional knowledge. For example, member states are encouraged to respect traditional knowledge and community consent procedures as legal requirements for introducing genetically modified crops by the African Model Law on Safety in Biotechnology (African Union, 2001). Support for agrobiodiversity conservation and community seed banks (CSBs) is also crucial for bolstering the tangible foundation of farmers' rights. By serving as local seed banks, CSBs support climate resilience, seed sovereignty, and on-farm conservation. They are especially useful in fending off the genetic deterioration brought on by monocultures and the dominance of genetically modified crops. Well-supported CSBs boost farmers' negotiating power and maintain the integrity of local food systems, according to studies from Ethiopia, India, and Nepal (Frison, 2020).

Protection of the Environment

Environmental integrity must also be given top priority in a balanced framework, particularly in light of the unknown ecological effects of genetically modified crop deployment. It is recommended that mandatory environmental impact assessments (EIAs) be carried out both before and after a product is released. GMO EIAs, in contrast to traditional EIAs, have to take into consideration cumulative, long-term, and indirect effects, such as effects on non-target organisms, gene flow, and ecosystem services (Hilbeck et al., 2015). However, many nations lack thorough and open EIA procedures for genetically modified crops. Corporate-submitted data is frequently the basis for regulatory decisions, which raises questions about prejudice and conflicts of interest. Therefore, increased openness and data exchange in the biosafety assessment procedure are vital. Regulatory accountability can be improved by open databases, peer-reviewed ecological research, and public access to safety data. Furthermore, when faced with scientific ambiguity, choices should be made based on the precautionary principle, which is incorporated in the Cartagena Protocol on Biosafety (CBD Secretariat, 2000). Furthermore, understanding of howgenetically modified crops interact with local biodiversity can be improved by incorporating indigenous ecological knowledge into environmental assessments. By involving farmers and local people as co-researchers, participatory environmental monitoring can assist detect ecological problems early on and increase public confidence in governance procedures.

CONCLUSION

A paradigm change in contemporary agriculture has been sparked by the introduction of genetically modified crops, raising both concerns and hopes. As this chapter has shown, genetically modified crops pose a dual problem: they raise serious concerns about ecological sustainability, seed sovereignty, and the erosion of farmers' rights, even as they offer the possibility of improved agricultural output and environmental advantages. The implementation of genetically modified technologies is a complex subject with deep ties to legal, sociopolitical, and ecological contexts, as demonstrated by a critical synthesis of the available data.

Key Findings Synthesis

In certain situations, genetically modified crops have provided measurable agronomic advantages such as decreased pesticide use, drought tolerance, and pest resistance (Qaim, 2020). For example, Bt cotton initially increased yields and reduced the need for pesticides in India. However, because of pest resistance, soil erosion, and reliance on outside inputs, these improvements have frequently turned out to be unsustainable (Glover, 2010). Gene flow, biodiversity loss, and unknowable long-term ecological effects continue to be environmental issues (Andow & Zwahlen, 2006). Uneven regulatory supervision and a dearth of thorough, long-term ecological evaluations exacerbate these environmental hazards. The ramifications for human rights and the law are equally alarming. Multinational biotech companies have intentionally leveraged intellectual property rights (IPRs), particularly patents and Plant Variety Protection legislation, to increase their control over seed markets. Ancient customs of preserving, distributing, and exchanging seeds—the foundations of agricultural traditions and community resilience—are put to the test by seed patenting (Kloppenburg, 2010). Legal systems in a number of jurisdictions, including the US and increasingly in nations like Brazil and India, favor corporate interests and technical advancement over environmental conservation and farmer autonomy (Shiva, 2001; Pratap, 2019). Even in the absence of intentional patent infringement, corporate dominance over genetic material can legally disempower farmers, as demonstrated by the seminal Canadian case Monsanto Co. v. Schmeiser. Furthermore, conflicting national obligations result from the legal fragmentation between IPR regimes (like TRIPS) and human rights or environmental frameworks (like the Convention on Biological Diversity [CBD] and the International Treaty on

Plant Genetic Resources for Food and Agriculture [ITPGRFA]) (Chiarolla, 2011). In the face of strict biosafety regulations and proprietary claims, farmers' rights to store, use, exchange, and sell seeds are frequently neglected, particularly in the Global South where regulatory capacity is frequently constrained.

Demand Integrated Governance

Integrated governance—a policy approach that concurrently supports innovation, ecological sustainability, and social equity—is desperately needed to negotiate these interconnected difficulties. The traditional division of "pro-genetically modified vs. anti-genetically modified" arguments must give way to inclusive, participatory frameworks that acknowledge the wide range of stakeholders impacted by genetically modified technologies. Fair access to technology, farmer agency, and environmental protection should be given top priority under a multifaceted policy framework. By incorporating protections like mandatory licensing, benefit-sharing arrangements, and the preservation of traditional knowledge, legal procedures should balance IPRs with farmers' rights (Brush, 2005). To make sure that the deployment of genetically modified does not violate local biodiversity or community sovereignty, national biosafety regulations must be harmonized with international commitments under the ITPGRFA and the Cartagena Protocol. In order to provide farmer cooperatives, indigenous groups, and civil society organizations a significant say in decision-making, such governance must be democratic and decentralized. In order to lessen reliance on corporate inputs and promote resilience within smallholder systems, this also calls for public investment in agroecological research and open-source biotechnology alternatives (Lacey, 2005).

Prospects for the Future

Interdisciplinary research and inclusive innovation are the way forward. Law, ecology, sociology, and indigenous knowledge systems must all be incorporated into a comprehensive understanding of genetically modified crops. In order to evaluate long-term ecological effects, socioeconomic inequality, and cultural displacement, research should go beyond productivist measurements. Future research must examine the advantages and hazards of genetically modified technologies in particular contexts. Agricultural biotechnology should be adapted to regional agro-ecological conditions and cultural customs rather than advocating for a universal solution. More sustainable and morally sound solutions may be provided by collaborative innovation, in which farmers, scientists, and legislators co-design technologies (Stone, 2011). At the same time, policy changes are required to close the gap between justice and innovation. This entails updating seed laws to take into account unofficial seed systems, bringing biosafety regulations into compliance with the Free, Prior, and Informed Consent (FPIC) principles, and encouraging community-based monitoring of the effects of genetically modified organisms. To enable developing nations to negotiate more equitable terms in biotechnology governance, international institutions must support South-South collaboration and capacity-building. Essentially, genetically modified crops represent both opportunity and risk. A just and sustainable model of biotechnology governance is essential as the world's agricultural sector struggles with issues including food hunger, market consolidation, and climate change. One that does not compromise environmental integrity in the name of innovation or diminish the rights of those who have long nurtured, conserved, and shared biodiversity. Social fairness, legal pluralism, ecological ethics, and scientific progress must all be ingrained in the future of genetically modified agriculture.

REFERENCES

African Union. (2001). *African Model Law on Safety in Biotechnology*. AU Commission.

Andersen, R. (2013). *Plant genetic resources: Farmers' rights and the law*. Routledge.

Andow, D. A., & Zwahlen, C. (2006). Assessing environmental risks of transgenic plants. *Ecology Letters*, *9*(2), 196–214. DOI: 10.1111/j.1461-0248.2005.00846.x

Brookes, G., & Barfoot, P. (2020). *Genetically modified crops: global socio-economic and environmental impacts 1996–2018*. PG Economics Ltd.

Brush, S. B. (2005). *Farmers' rights and protection of traditional agricultural knowledge*. Washington, DC: CAPRi.

Chambers, J., & Smyth, S. J. (2021). Adoption and acceptance of genetically modified crops in the United States and the European Union. *Frontiers in Plant Science*, *12*, 748229. DOI: 10.3389/fpls.2021.748229

Chiarolla, C. (2011). *Intellectual Property, Agriculture and Global Food Security: The Privatization of Crop Diversity*. Edward Elgar Publishing. DOI: 10.4337/9781849807340

Correa, C. M. (2000). *Options for the implementation of farmers' rights at the national level*. South Centre.

De Jonge, B. (2014). *Plant variety protection and farmers' rights: Towards a new balance*. Routledge.

Dowd-Uribe, B., & Schnurr, M. A. (2016). Burkina Faso's reversal on genetically modified cotton and the implications for Africa. *African Affairs*, *115*(458), 161–172. DOI: 10.1093/afraf/adv063

Duke, S. O., & Powles, S. B. (2009). Glyphosate-resistant weeds and crops. *Pest Management Science*, *65*(4), 317–318. DOI: 10.1002/ps.1561

Ellstrand, N. C., Prentice, H. C., & Hancock, J. F. (2013). Gene flow and introgression from domesticated plants into their wild relatives. *Annual Review of Ecology and Systematics*, *30*(1), 539–563. DOI: 10.1146/annurev.ecolsys.30.1.539

European Commission. (2021). *EU authorization process for GMOs*. https://food.ec.europa.eu

FAO. (2009). *International Treaty on Plant Genetic Resources for Food and Agriculture*. FAO.

Frison, E. (2020). *Agrobiodiversity: The Key to Sustainable and Resilient Food Systems*. Global Commission on Biodiversity for Food and Agriculture.

Gautam, P. (2021). Reconciling TRIPS and Farmers' Rights: A South Asian Perspective. *The Journal of World Intellectual Property, 24*(3), 325–340.

Glover, D. (2010). The corporate shaping of GM crops as a technology for the poor. *The Journal of Peasant Studies, 37*(1), 67–90. DOI: 10.1080/03066150903498754

Government of India. (2001). *The Protection of Plant Varieties and Farmers' Rights Act*. Ministry of Agriculture.

Gruère, G. P., Mehta-Bhatt, P., & Sengupta, D. (2008). Bt cotton and farmer suicides in India: Reviewing the evidence. *International Food Policy Research Institute Discussion Paper 00808*. https://doi.org/DOI: 10.2499/0896291682

Hilbeck, A., Binimelis, R., Defarge, N., Steinbrecher, R., Székács, A., Wickson, F., Antoniou, M., Bereano, P. L., Clark, E. A., Hansen, M., Novotny, E., Heinemann, J., Meyer, H., Shiva, V., & Wynne, B. (2015). No scientific consensus on GMO safety. *Environmental Sciences Europe, 27*(1), 4. DOI: 10.1186/s12302-014-0034-1

Hofmann, F., Otto, M., & Wosniok, W. (2014). Effects of Bt maize on non-target organisms and the environment. *Environmental Sciences Europe, 26*(1), 1–13.

Hope, J. (2008). *Biobazaar: The Open Source Revolution and Biotechnology*. Harvard University Press. DOI: 10.4159/9780674033603

Howard, P. H. (2015). Intellectual property and consolidation in the seed industry. *Crop Science, 55*(6), 2489–2495. DOI: 10.2135/cropsci2014.09.0669

ISAAA. (2020). *Global Status of Commercialized Biotech/GM Crops: 2019*. ISAAA Brief No. 55. International Service for the Acquisition of Agri-biotech Applications. https://www.isaaa.org

James, C. (2014). *Global status of commercialized biotech/GM crops: 2014*. ISAAA Brief No. 49.

Janis, M. D., & Kesan, J. P. (2002). U.S. Plant Variety Protection: Sound and fury...? *Houston Law Review, 39*(3), 727–779.

Jasanoff, S. (2005). *Designs on nature: Science and democracy in Europe and the United States*. Princeton University Press. DOI: 10.1515/9781400837311

Kloppenburg, J. (2010). Impeding dispossession, enabling repossession: Biological open source and the recovery of seed sovereignty. *Journal of Agrarian Change, 10*(3), 367–388. DOI: 10.1111/j.1471-0366.2010.00275.x

Klümper, W., & Qaim, M. (2014). A meta-analysis of the impacts of genetically modified crops. *PLoS One*, *9*(11), e111629. DOI: 10.1371/journal.pone.0111629

Kranthi, K. R., & Stone, G. D. (2020). Long-term impacts of Bt cotton in India. *Nature Plants*, *6*(3), 188–196. DOI: 10.1038/s41477-020-0615-5

Kumar, R., & Pandey, V. (2022). Public Sector Research in Indian Agriculture: Opportunities for Democratizing Biotech. *Asian Biotechnology and Development Review*, *24*(2), 11–30.

Lacey, H. (2005). *Is Science Value Free? Values and Scientific Understanding*. Routledge. DOI: 10.4324/9780203983195

Lander, J. (2017). Corporate power and biosafety regulation: South America and the EU compared. *Third World Quarterly*, *38*(10), 2330–2347. DOI: 10.1080/01436597.2017.1334555

Louwaars, N. P., Dons, H., van Overwalle, G., Raven, H., Arundel, A., Eaton, D., & Nelis, A. (2005). *Breeding business: The future of plant breeding in the light of developments in patent rights and plant breeder's rights*. CGN Report 2005-01.

Magnus, M. (2008). *Biotech patent law: Protecting innovation, not farmers*. Environmental Law Institute.

Nuccio, M. L., Paul, M. J., Bate, N. J., Cohn, J., & Cutler, S. R. (2018). Where are the drought tolerant crops? An assessment of more than two decades of plant biotechnology effort in crop improvement. *Plant Science*, *273*, 110–119. DOI: 10.1016/j.plantsci.2018.01.020

Pratap, S. (2019). Bt Cotton and the myth of enhanced farmers' income: Evidence from Maharashtra. *Economic and Political Weekly*, *54*(36), 30–36.

Qaim, M. (2020). Role of new plant breeding technologies for food security and sustainable agricultural development. *Applied Economic Perspectives and Policy*, *42*(2), 129–150. DOI: 10.1002/aepp.13044

Sahai, S. (2003). The Bt cotton story: The ethics of science and its reportage. *Current Science*, *84*(8), 974–975.

Schnurr, M. A., & Mujabi-Mujuzi, S. (2017). Stakeholder perspectives on the regulation of genetically modified crops in Uganda. *Journal of Environmental Policy and Planning*, *19*(3), 213–226. DOI: 10.1080/1523908X.2016.1210907

Secretariat, C. B. D. (2000). *Cartagena Protocol on Biosafety to the Convention on Biological Diversity*. Secretariat of the Convention on Biological Diversity.

Secretariat of the Convention on Biological Diversity. (2000). *Cartagena Protocol on Biosafety to the Convention on Biological Diversity*. https://www.cbd.int/doc/legal/cartagena-protocol-en.pdf

Sharma, D. (2021). Farmers and biosafety governance in India: The limits of participation. *Asian Biotechnology and Development Review*, *23*(2), 1–18.

Shiva, V. (2001). *Protect or plunder? Understanding intellectual property rights*. Zed Books.

Shiva, V. (2005). *The seeds of suicide: The ecological and human costs of seed monopolies*. Navdanya.

Shiva, V. (2016). *Who really feeds the world? The failures of agribusiness and the promise of agroecology*. North Atlantic Books.

Stirling, A. (2008). "Opening Up" and "Closing Down": Power, Participation, and Pluralism in the Social Appraisal of Technology. *Science, Technology & Human Values*, *33*(2), 262–294. DOI: 10.1177/0162243907311265

Stone, G. D. (2011). Field versus farm in Warangal: Bt cotton, higher yields, and larger questions. *World Development*, *39*(3), 387–398. DOI: 10.1016/j.worlddev.2010.09.008

United States Department of Agriculture (USDA). (2022). *Adoption of genetically engineered crops in the U.S.* https://www.ers.usda.gov

World Trade Organization. (1994). *Agreement on Trade-Related Aspects of Intellectual Property Rights*. https://www.wto.org

KEY TERMS AND DEFINITIONS

Biosafety: A set of policies and practices that aim to prevent potential risks to human health and the environment resulting from the development, release, and use of genetically modified organisms (GMOs), typically through regulatory oversight and risk assessment.

Farmers' Rights: A set of entitlements recognized under international and national laws that protect the rights of farmers to save, use, exchange, and sell farm-saved seeds and to participate in decisions regarding plant genetic resources, particularly in relation to traditional knowledge and biodiversity.

Genetically Modified (GM) Crops: Crops that have been altered at the genetic level using biotechnology to express desired traits such as pest resistance, herbicide tolerance, or improved yield. These modifications often involve the insertion of genes from other species.

Intellectual Property Rights (IPRs): Legal protections granted to inventors and creators, including patents and plant variety protections, which in the context of GM crops can restrict the use and distribution of genetically modified seeds by farmers.

Seed Sovereignty: The right of farmers and indigenous communities to breed, exchange, and preserve seeds free from corporate control or intellectual property restrictions, ensuring autonomy over agricultural practices and food systems.

About the Contributors

Munir Ahmad is a seasoned professional in the realm of Spatial Data Infrastructure (SDI), Geo-Information Productions, Information Systems, and Information Governance, boasting over 25 years of dedicated experience in the field. With a PhD in Computer Science, Dr. Ahmad's expertise spans Spatial Data Production, Management, Processing, Analysis, Visualization, and Quality Control. Throughout his career, Dr. Ahmad has been deeply involved in the development and deployment of SDI systems specially in the context of Pakistan, leveraging his proficiency in Spatial Database Design, Web, Mobile & Desktop GIS, and Geo Web Services Architecture. His contributions to Volunteered Geographic Information (VGI) and Open Source Geoportal & Metadata Portal have significantly enriched the geospatial community. As a trainer and researcher, Dr. Ahmad has authored over 50 publications, advancing the industry's knowledge base and fostering innovation in Geo-Tech, Data Governance, and Information Infrastructure, and Emerging Technologies. His commitment to Research and Development (R&D) is evident in his role as a dedicated educator and mentor in the field.

Ameer Asra Ahmed hails from a family of educationists and holds a PhD degree in the field of Organizational Behaviour and Human Resource Management from Jain University. She also holds an MBA degree specialising in Human Resource Management. She holds more than 18 years of teaching experience and is currently working as an Associate Professor at the MBA Department in Dayananda Sagar College of Arts, Science and Commerce . She is an ardent researcher who has authored several original research papers in several National and International Journals both Scopus indexed as well as UGC care listed and other peer reviewed journals. She holds more than 13 best paper awards to her credit and has presented more than 30 papers in National and International conferences. She is also the winner of the National case writing competition organized by Confederation of Indian Industries (CII) for her case on “Trans-friendly or Transphobic” and has published several cases. She strongly believes that Business Schools should focus on inculcating a research culture among management students as most of the business problems in the current scenario can be overcome only through Research.

Andi Subhan Amir asa@unhas.ac.id Department of Communication Studies Universitas Hasanuddin Andi Subhan Amir is a faculty member at the Department of Communication Science, Faculty of Social and Political Sciences, Universitas Hasanuddin. He earned his Bachelor's degree in Communication Science from Universitas Hasanuddin, followed by a Master's degree in Mass Communication from the university's Graduate School. He completed his doctoral studies at the Faculty of Communication Science, Universitas Padjadjaran. In addition to his academic role as a lecturer and researcher, ASA—as he is commonly known—is actively involved in several professional organizations, including ISKI (Ikatan Sarjana Komunikasi Indonesia), ASPIKOM (Asosiasi Pendidikan Ilmu Komunikasi), and APEPINDO (Asosiasi Peneliti dan Penulis Indonesia). He has authored numerous scholarly works, including books, journal articles, and conference proceedings, published both nationally and internationally. His publications are accessible through his Google Scholar and SINTA profiles

Yasir Ansari, born in 1989 in Hyderabad, Sindh, Pakistan, is a dedicated Sub Engineer with a passion for preserving and celebrating the rich cultural heritage of Sindh. With over 13 years of experience in the Culture Tourism Antiquities and Archives Department, Ansari has been instrumental in various projects aimed at conserving and promoting the province's historical legacy. Ansari's educational background in Civil Engineering and General History has equipped him with a unique blend of skills, enabling him to approach heritage preservation with a holistic perspective. His associate degree in Civil Engineering has provided him with a solid foundation in construction and restoration, while his master's degree in General History has deepened his understanding of the cultural and historical significance of Sindh's heritage sites. Beyond his professional endeavors, Ansari is an avid enthusiast of cultural heritage, often visiting heritage sites and collecting data on Sindh's cultural legacy. His ultimate goal is to safeguard this legacy for future generations, ensuring that the province's historical treasures remain a source of pride and inspiration for years to come. Ansari's future projects include the execution and supervision of schemes for heritage site conservation, restoration, and rehabilitation, as well as the establishment of libraries, cultural complexes, tourist complexes, and museums. Through his tireless efforts, Yasir Ansari is poised to leave an indelible mark on the cultural landscape of Sindh, inspiring a new generation of heritage enthusiasts and professionals.

Roopa Shree B.R is an accomplished academician and researcher with over 14 years of teaching experience in Management, specializing in Marketing, Entrepreneurship, and Finance. She is currently serving at Surana College (Autonomous), PG Centre, Bengaluru, where she heads the Institute Innovation Council (IIC) and leads entrepreneurship-related initiatives. She has also held roles such as HOD – Commerce and Principal In-Charge, demonstrating strong academic leadership at Dayananda Sagar Business Academy. She earned her PhD in Marketing (VTU) with research focused on consumer buying behavior towards organic food products in Bengaluru. She holds an MBA in Finance & Marketing, M. Com from KSOU, is UGC-NET qualified, and has further specialized with diplomas in HRM and Women Entrepreneurship. Dr. Roopa has published extensively in Scopus-indexed and UGC-recognized journals and has presented papers at national and international conferences on entrepreneurship, consumer behaviour, and sustainable business practices. She has also authored three textbooks in the fields of Business Regulations and Retail Management and was granted a UK Design Patent (2025) for an AI-enabled f inance analytics device. As a certified Entrepreneurship Educator by the Wadhwani Foundation, she has actively mentored students, coordinated entrepreneurship development activities, and contributed to incubation and innovation initiatives. She was recognized with the Silver Global Jury Award (2021) by Wadhwani Foundation for evaluating global startup proposals and received the WEGROW Research Excellence Award (2025). Her expertise lies in entrepreneurship development, innovation ecosystem building, brand management, Services marketing, Retail Management and rural marketing. Through her leadership at Surana's IIC and INSPIRE – the Entrepreneurship Club, she is committed to fostering an entrepreneurial mindset among students and strengthening the innovation ecosystem within higher education.

Charanjeet Dadiyala (Ph.D. (CSE)) currently working as Assistant Professor in Ramdeobaba University, Nagpur. He has a Ph.D. in Computer Science and Engineering in Multivariate Multi-sourced Prediction Model and its accuracy improvement using Machine Learning and Deep Learning techniques. He has more than 15 years of teaching experience and has published more than 16 research papers in reputed International Journals and Conferences. His research interests are in Cyber Security, Pattern Recognition, Machine Learning, Artificial Intelligence and Web Technologies.

I Nyoman Darmayasa is a lecturer (Professor on Accounting and Tax) and researcher in the Accounting Department, Bali State Polytechnic, Indonesia. He holds a doctoral degree in accounting, specializing in taxation, from Brawijaya University, and honored cum laude grade. His research expertise relates to green taxation, green accounting, and green auditing. He also appointed be a reviewer in the international reputable journals published by Elsevier, European Academy of Management and Business Economics, EnPress Publisher, LLC, and Cogent. I Nyoman Darmayasa is also a certified specialist in Chartered Accountant (CA), Bersertifikat Konsultan Pajak (BKP), Certified Professional Management Accountant (CPMA), Certified Public Accountant (CPA), and ASEAN CPA. He is a partner in the Public Accounting Firm and handle numerous of international tax clients

Deepak Gupta is a distinguished academician with over 20 years of teaching experience and expertise in Computer Science and Engineering. He holds a Ph.D. in Computer Engineering and has an extensive research portfolio, including many international journal papers, multiple conference proceedings, and several books. His research interests span machine learning, artificial intelligence, and data mining. Currently, Dr. Gupta serves as an Associate Professor and Head of Department of CSE (Emerging Branches) at ITM Gwalior, MP, India. He has also contributed significantly to the field through patents and copyrights and actively engages as a reviewer, conference chair and editor.

Rusdiana Junaid Rosejunaid246@gmail.com +6281243011777 Universitas Cokroaminoto Palopo Jl. Latamacelling No. 19 Kota Palopo, Sulawesi Selatan Indonesia Prof. Dr. Rusdiana Junaid, Grad.Dipl. in TESOL., M.Hum., M.A., is a distinguished academic leader and scholar in the field of English language education, applied linguistics, and cultural studies. Currently serving as the Rector of the Institute of Health and Business Kurnia Jaya Persada Palopo, she brings decades of academic, administrative, and international experience to her role. She holds multiple postgraduate degrees in English Language Studies and Applied Linguistics from Hasanuddin University and Curtin University, Australia, where she also completed specialized training in TESOL. Her professional development includes participation in international programs such as the SUSI Program at New York University, the JICA-sponsored Lesson Study Training in Japan, and the Ph.D. Sandwich Program with Griffith University, Australia. Prof. Rusdiana has held various leadership positions, including Dean of the Faculty of Education and Dean of Computer Engineering at Universitas Cokroaminoto Palopo. Her academic interests center on language teaching and learning, language studies, and cultural studies. She is actively involved in professional organizations such as TEFLIN, WALS, ALSI, and MLI. In addition to her teaching and research roles, she contributes as an assessor in national academic quality assurance programs, including PPG, BKD, JAFUNG, and LAMDIK

Sapna Kumar is an Assistant Professor at Chandigarh College of Technology, where she teaches Human Resource Management domain subjects to BBA and MBA students. She is currently pursuing her Ph.D. in Human Resource Management from Himachal Pradesh University, Shimla. Her academic interests include employee engagement, organizational behavior, and strategic HR practices, with a focus on applying research to enhance HR effectiveness in modern organizations.

Balu L. is a seasoned academic and administrator with over 23 years of experience in teaching, research, and leadership in higher education. He holds a Ph.D. from Bharathiar University, along with an M.Phil., MBA, and PGDIM. His career includes significant roles at renowned institutions such as Christ (Deemed to be University), Presidency University, and BMSIT&M, Bengaluru. Currently, he serves as the Principal of Dayananda Sagar College of Arts, Science & Commerce. Dr. Balu has been instrumental in designing and launching several undergraduate and postgraduate programs aligned with Industry 4.0, including BBA Aviation Management and MBA in Financial Technology. As a research supervisor, he has guided multiple PhD scholars and has authored one academic book. His contributions to academia include 67 international journal publications, over 120 paper presentations, and leadership in organizing academic conferences and development programs. Recognized for his excellence, he has received awards such as "Best Faculty in HR & OB" for 12 consecutive years and "Principal Par Excellence" in 2024. Notably, he played a key role in building the School of Commerce at Presidency University from the ground up, expanding it to 2,320 students and 50 faculty members. His leadership continues to impact higher education significantly.

K. Lalitha is an Assistant Professor in the Department of Computer Science and Engineering at Santhiram Engineering College, Nandyal, Andhra Pradesh, India. She received her Master of Technology in Computer Science and Engineering from Vaagdevi Institute of Technology & Science, Proddatur, Andhra Pradesh, India. Her research interests include machine learning, data mining, and healthcare informatics. She has published multiple research articles in reputed journals.

M. Mayuranathan, is working as an Associate Professor in the Department of Computer Science and Engineering, SRM Valliammai Engineering College, Chengalpattu. Having 20+ years of Experience in Teaching and 1+ year of Industrial Experience. He holds Ph.D., in Computer Science and Engineering from Anna University. Research work interest include Cloud Security using AI and Machine Learning Algorithms. His Area of Interest includes Security, Image Processing and Blockchain. He has published around 23 International Journals, 3 Patents, 1 Book named "Machine Learning using Python" and 2 Book Chapters. He has presented several International and National Conferences. He is an active member of ISTE and CSI.

Durga Madhab Mahapatra is an Associate Professor in the Department of Commerce at North-Eastern Hill University (NEHU), Shillong, India. With a distinguished academic career spanning over two decades, Dr. Mahapatra has made significant contributions to the fields of Management and E-Commerce has developed a strong research portfolio that bridges theory and practice, particularly in the areas of marketing management, consumer behavior, rural entrepreneurship, and sustainable development. Dr. Mahapatra is widely recognized for his interdisciplinary approach and has published extensively in national and international peer-reviewed journals. His current research interests include digital transformation in commerce, tribal entrepreneurship, inclusive business models, and the socio-economic dynamics of the North-Eastern region of India. He has also actively participated in national conferences and UGC-sponsored seminars and has contributed chapters to edited volumes on contemporary issues in Management, E-commerce and E-Learning.

T.C. Manjunath was born on 6th February 1967. He did his B.E. from RV College of Engg. in 1989 (B'lore Univ), M.E. in Robotics & Automation from Govt.'s LD College of Engg., (Gujarat Univ., Ahmedabad) in 1992 with FCD-First Rank & PhD in Systems & Control Engg. from IIT Bombay in the year 2007, got best research scholar award for the entire IITB. He is currently working as the Dean Research (R & D) and as Professor in Dept. of Computer Science & Engg. with specialization in IoT, Cyber Security, Blockchain Technology in Rajarajeswari College of Engineering, Bengaluru, Karnataka. He has got a teaching (academic), research & administrative experience of more than 35+ years (10 years as Principal & 8 years as HoD, 1 year as Dean Research & rest as faculty) and has published more than 1500+ research papers in various national & international journals & conferences, with 175+ patents, 100+ book-chapters, 25 awards, 100s of Keynote talks and also published 25 text books in various field of science, engineering & technology, completed projects worth Rs. 9 Crores till date & guided 10 PhD scholars in VTU. He is a member of 30 Professional Society Chapters and is a fellow of IE, IETE, AMIEE, Sr. Member of IEEE and a chartered engineer.

Anumeha Mathur is a dynamic and accomplished academic professional with over 18 years of extensive experience in teaching, research, and curriculum development in the field of marketing. Currently serving as Assistant Professor (Marketing) and Program Coordinator – BBA at the School of Management and Commerce, KR Mangalam University, she brings deep expertise in Consumer Behaviour, Brand Management, Integrated Marketing Communication and HR.

Her academic journey includes teaching role at esteemed institutions like St. Kabir Institute of Professional Studies, Nirma University, and Skylark School of Business Technology, among others. She has consistently contributed to student success through the development of innovative and practical teaching methodologies and corporate readiness programs. Dr. Mathur is also an active researcher, with multiple publications, conference presentations, and patents to her credit. She holds important institutional roles, including SRC Member, University IPR Cell Member, and Editorial Board Member of the SOMC Newsletter.

Nitish Kumar Minz is a multidisciplinary researcher and academic editor currently pursuing his MBA at Vellore Institute of Technology, Vellore (AACSB & NAAC A++ accredited). He holds a background in commerce and has authored several research papers and book chapters published in Scopus and Web of Science-indexed journals. His areas of expertise include human resource management, artificial intelligence, sustainability, gender equity, digital transformation, and cybersecurity. His current research focuses on AI-driven inclusive hiring, digitalization in higher education HRM, and entrepreneurship for women's economic resilience in the Global South. Nitish serves as the Managing Editor of the International Journal of Convergent Research (IJCR), overseeing editorial operations and indexing initiatives. Nitish's scholarly contributions have earned him accolades such as the Chancellor's Excellence Award and Best Paper Presenter recognition at multiple conferences. Deeply committed to bridging research, policy, and practice, he strives to contribute meaningful insights to academia and society through innovation-driven, inclusive, and sustainability-focused scholarship.

O. Bhaskaru is currently working as an Assistant Professor in the Department of Computer Science and Engineering at Vignan's Foundation for Science, Technology and Research, Guntur, Andhra Pradesh. He received his Ph.D. in Computer Science and Engineering from KL University in 2023. He obtained his Master of Technology in Computer Science and Engineering during 2007–2009 from R.G.M. College of Engineering and Technology, affiliated with JNTU Anantapur, Andhra Pradesh.

P. Selvakumar is currently an Associate Professor in the Department of Science and Humanities at Nehru Institute of Technology, Coimbatore, Tamil Nadu, India. Prior to joining Nehru Institute of Technology, he held positions as an Assistant Professor in the Department of Science and Humanities various engineering colleges in Coimbatore, Tamil Nadu, India, spanning from 2011 to 2023. Dr.P. Selvakumar's academic and research interests lie primarily in the field of phytochemistry. He has made significant contributions to his field, with an impressive record that includes 30 journal publications, 12 patents, and 20 conference papers. Additionally, he has organized 5 seminars and conferences, further demonstrating his commitment to academic and scientific exchange. Throughout his career, Dr. P.Selvakumar has been recognized for his dedication and excellence in teaching, having been honored with several awards, including the Best Teacher Awards. He holds a prominent position in the academic community, contributing actively to research.

P. Sudheer is a Senior Assistant Professor in the Department of Computer Science and Engineering (Artificial Intelligence & Machine Learning) at CVR College of Engineering, Hyderabad, Telangana (Postal Code: 501510). With a strong academic and research background, he specializes in the fields of image processing, deep learning, and machine learning. His dedication to teaching and innovation in emerging technologies has made him a valuable contributor to the department. Passionate about guiding students and advancing research, P. Sudheer continually works towards integrating cutting-edge AI/ML methodologies into both academics and practical applications.

Vinish P is an accomplished academician, currently working as Associate Professor at the Department of Management Studies, Dayananda Sagar College of Arts, Science, and Commerce in Bengaluru. With a rich academic tenure spanning 16 years, he brings a wealth of experience in both teaching and research. Dr. Vinish holds a Master's in MBA with a specialization in Marketing, a Ph.D. in Management from Visvesvaraya Technological University, and a Bachelor's in Computer Science from Mangalore University. His areas of expertise encompass Business Analytics, Quantitative Techniques, Business Statistics, and Marketing Research. Apart from his teaching duties, he successfully authored a substantial number of research articles in Scopus, Web of Science, and ABDC-indexed journals, while also presenting research papers at both national and international conferences. Dr. Vinish has also undertaken two minor research projects delving into the realms of entrepreneurship and organizational behavior in education.

Ananya Pandey is a Research Scholar in School of Law at Christ University, Bangalore. She has her research interests in the field of Constitutional Law, Environment Law, Human Rights, Food Security, Intellectual Property Law and Jurisprudence.

R. Bhuvaneswari working as an Assistant Professor of English at Dr.Mahalingam College of Engineering and Technology, Pollachi. To her credit she completed 10 NPTEL / SWAYAM and published few articles in Scopus indexed journals.

Shanmugaa priyaa is an Indian Author, combines her deep technical knowledge with a strong desire to educate and inspire students., currently working as an

Assistant Professor in the Department of Computer Science & Engineering at Sathyabama Institute of Science and Technology, Chennai, India. She has completed her Master of Engineering in Computer Science and Engineering from Sathyabama Institute of science and technology in 2016 and She has completed her Bachelor of Engineering in Computer Science and Engineering from Maamallan Institute of Science and Technology, Chennai, Tamil Nadu, India in 2014. She has Industrial experience (Cognizant) for close to 4 years. Her research area includes Data Privacy and Security and Machine Learning. She has published many articles in peer reviewed journals and presented paper in national and international conference

R. Velmurugan presently working as an Associate Professor in Commerce, Karpagam Academy of Higher Education, Coimbatore. He started his career as a Project Fellow under UGC Sponsored Major Research Project at NGM College, Pollachi. He has 18 years of teaching experience has 15 years of research experience. To his credit he produced 22 Ph.D. Scholars and 5 M.Phil. Scholars. At present 1 scholar submitter his thesis, 6 Ph.D. Scholars are under his guidance. Moreover, to his credit he published 168 articles in various International Journals, of which 85 articles are published in Scopus Indexed Journals and 15 articles in Web of Science and 76 articles in edited volumes. He also participates and presented 27 papers in various International Seminar / Conference and 54 National Seminar / Conference. He acted as an external examiner for various M.Phil. and Ph.D. Viva voce examinations. He acted as a Vice Chancellor nominee for Doctoral Committee Expert at Bharathiar University, Coimbatore and Periyar University, Salem. He acted as a Chairperson at various National Level Conferences. He also acted as an Expert for Syllabus Scrutiny Committee, Question Paper Scrutiny Committee and Expert members for Board of Studies at various reputed Colleges. Considering his meritorious contribution, he received awards like Best Paper Presenter, Best Research Supervisor and Best Faculty Awards from various research foundations and councils. He too acted as a resource person for 27 Guest Lectures, 30 Workshops and 10 faculty development programmes.

B. Maheshwar Rao is an Assistant Professor at Sri Balaji University, Pune, where he contributes his academic expertise and research-driven approach to higher education. Dr. Rao is dedicated to delivering quality education through a blend of theoretical knowledge and practical insights. His academic pursuits are complemented by active participation in research, seminars, and academic development programs. Known for his student-centric teaching methodology and commitment to academic excellence, Dr. Rao plays a key role in shaping the learning environment at Sri Balaji University.

K. S. Shibani Shankar Ray is an Assistant Professor at Rajiv Gandhi National Aviation University, Fursatganj, Amethi. He is a scholar-practitioner at the intersection of strategy, policy, and behavioural science. With an MBA from IIM Indore and a doctoral research in Marketing Management, his research explores heuristics in strategic decision-making, stakeholder engagement in sustainability, and digital health systems. He has taught across premier institutions and delivered flagship programs on women's financial leadership and rural entrepreneurship. Shibani has worked with various renowned corporate houses, bringing rich field insights into his classrooms and publications. His writing appears in Empirical Economics Letters, Technology in Society, and IGI Global volumes on AI, blended learning, and sustainable e-commerce. A recipient of multiple national awards, Shibani combines academic rigour with on-ground impact, driven by a commitment to inclusive development and transformative pedagogy.

José De Jesús Reyes-Sánchez, Ph.D. in senior management, has six master's degrees, in education, in management, professional soccer technique, in physical preparation, in professional soccer, in physical rehabilitation sciences, in sports sciences, as well as in coaching and integral well-being, who is a research professor at the TECNM Instituto Tecnológico Superior De Fresnillo, with more than 20 years of teaching experience, PRODEP profile and coordinator of the academic body with vast experience in conferences and workshops, currently novelist and writer.

Rismawati is a distinguished academic and consultant with a robust focus on sustainability reporting. She currently holds the position of lecturer and Head of the Quality Assurance Institute at Universitas Muhammadiyah Palopo, where she has been pivotal in ensuring the quality of university processes and outputs since February 2020. Additionally, she serves as an Assurer for Sustainability Reporting at the National Center for Sustainability Reporting in Jakarta, specializing in the evaluation of sustainability reports for mining companies across Indonesia. Her academic qualifications are extensive, comprising a Bachelor's degree in Economics and Accounting, a Master's degree in Accounting Science, and a Doctorate in Accounting from Universitas Brawijaya, Malang. Rismawati is also a certified specialist in sustainability reporting, risk management, and tax planning, holding several prestigious certifications including Certified Sustainability Reporting Specialist (CSRS), Certified Risk Management Practitioner (CRMP), Certified Management Accountant (CMA) and Certified Enterprise Risk Analysis (CERA). In her professional capacity, she has provided consultancy services in financial management and tax compliance for companies such as PT. Reski Barito Timur and PT. Helay Raya. Furthermore, she has authored multiple publications on Social Accounting, Sustainability Accounting, Management Accounting and CSR, contributing significantly to the academic community. Her interests in reading, writing, and travel reflect her commitment to lifelong learning and professional growth in her field.

Bijaya Laxmi Rout is an Assistant Professor and researcher affiliated with Fakir Mohan Autonomous College, Balasore, Odisha. With a strong background in Management, she has contributed extensively to the field through her teaching, research, and academic publications. Her scholarly interests include gender studies, rural development, language pedagogy, public policy, etc., and she is known for her insightful analyses rooted in regional and socio-cultural contexts. Bijaya Laxmi Rout actively engages in curriculum development and student mentoring and regularly participates in national and international seminars and workshops. She is deeply committed to promoting inclusive education and interdisciplinary research. Her work often reflects a balanced integration of theoretical knowledge and practical relevance, particularly in addressing issues pertinent to Odisha and the wider eastern Indian region.

S. Senthilkumar, currently working as Assistant Professor in Finance and Management, Skyline University, Nigeria. His qualifications are MBA, M.Com, M.Phil, MS, and PhD. He has rich experience in teaching and academic of 18.2 years. He had published 58 papers Publications in National and International Journals and Proceedings. He Authored 4 books in Research Methodology, Corporate Finance, Principles of Accounting and Business Policy & Strategic management. Participated and presented 62 papers in National & International Seminars and Conferences. He acted as resource person and Guest lecture around 25 Programmemes. He guided 225 projects in M.B.A., 36 M.Phil, and 9 PhD. He got Authorized Guide ship for PhD & M.Phil from Indian Universities such as Anna University, Karpagam University, Bharathiar University, Periyar Manimai University and AMIET University and Vinayaka Mission University and Bahir Dar University, Ethiopia. He performed as Foreign examiner for evaluating PhD Thesis around 18 Thesis of Indian universities such as Bharathiar University, Visvesvaraya Technological University, University of Mumbai, MS University and Bharathidasan university.

Zakir Hossen Shaikh is an Assistant Professor, Department of Accounting and Finance, School of Business Administration, Kingdom University, Bahrain. Prior to this, he worked more than 28 years in commercial and academic industry. He has published numerous articles in referred journals and presented many papers in various conferences, both local and abroad exclusively in the different area of Accounting, management and Islamic Banking and Finance. He has also participated in a variety of seminars, forums, workshops and international conferences. He obtained his Ph.D. (Accounting and Finance) from India in 2018. His doctoral thesis explored the entrepreneurial phenomenon from an Islamic perspective and argued for profit and loss sharing (PLS) contracts as viable alternatives to conventional interest-based financing instruments. He has a Bachelor degree in Commerce and holds Master degree in Commerce, Business Administration & Finance and Control.

Soumya R is a distinguished academician, researcher, and innovator whose career spans over a decade of teaching, research, leadership, and knowledge creation. She currently serves as an Associate Professor at Surana College (Autonomous), Bengaluru, and is also a Postdoctoral Fellow at the Indian Council of Social Science Research (ICSSR), hosted at Maharani Cluster University. Alongside her academic roles, she is the Research Cell Coordinator at Surana College, where she fosters a culture of inquiry, innovation, and student research. Early Life and Education Born on April 23, 1988, in Bengaluru, Dr. Soumya pursued a multidisciplinary academic path that reflects her diverse interests and commitment to lifelong learning. She holds a Ph.D. in Management from Bangalore University (2016–2020) and is a UGC-NET JRF awardee in Management (2017). Her educational qualifications further include an MBA from Visvesvaraya Technological University, a B.Ed. and B.A. from Bangalore University, and a B.Com from Karnataka State Open University. She is also pursuing her M.Com at Bangalore University (2025–2027). Academic and Teaching Career Dr. Soumya began her teaching journey as a Lecturer at Shushruthi Institute of Management Studies in 2011, followed by faculty positions at Oxbridge Business College and BGS Institute of Management Studies. Her academic career reached a new milestone with her appointment as an Associate Professor at Surana College (Autonomous) in 2024. In addition, she has enriched her teaching profile as a visiting faculty at premier institutions such as Maharani's Arts College for Women, Government First Grade College, Peenya, and Government First Grade College, Malleshwaram. Over the years, she has taught a wide range of subjects including Human Resource Management, Organizational Behaviour, International Business, Intellectual Property Rights, Marketing Management, Financial Systems and Markets, and Global Talent Management. Research and Publications Her postdoctoral research with ICSSR focuses on Entrepreneurship Skill Development Programmes and MSME Sustainability, reflecting her passion for entrepreneurship, innovation, and financial systems. She has authored over 25 research papers in reputed Scopus, UGC-CARE, and peer-reviewed journals, covering areas such as financial literacy, HR analytics, digital marketing, organizational culture, leadership models, and startup ecosystems. Some of her widely cited works include: Assessment of Digital Marketing Strategies in the AI Era (Scopus, 2024) Entrepreneurship Programs & MSMEs (UGC-CARE, 2024) Women Entrepreneurship and Gender Dynamics in Startups (2023) Work-Life Balance in Doctors (Scopus, 2022) She has also presented her research at numerous national and international conferences in India, Singapore, and beyond. Books and Authorship Dr. Soumya has authored influential books, including: Skill Education and Entrepreneurship Development (AG Publishing House, 2024) Predictive Analytics in HR (Red Unicorn Publishing, 2025) Cultural Identity in the Digital Age (Book Chapter, AG Publishing House, 2025) Her works bridge the gap between theory and practice, particularly in entrepreneurship, HR, and cultural studies. Patents and Innovation A prolific innovator, Dr. Soumya has published patents in the areas of cross-cultural management, AI-driven event management platforms, and workplace diversity analytics. These patents underscore her pioneering role in integrating technology with management research and higher education. Awards and Recognition Dr. Soumya's contributions have been recognized with numerous accolades, including: Innovative Researcher Award (2025) – International Conference on IPR, Mumbai Best IP Researcher Award (2025) – Bakliwal Foundation College, Vashi Global Eminent Researcher Award (2023) Best Paper Presentation Award (2024) Winner of multiple essay competitions She has also been honoured as a Guest of Honour and Keynote Speaker at several academic forums and national workshops. Leadership and Service Beyond research and teaching, Dr. Soumya is a dynamic academic leader. She is the Founder and Coordinator of the Student Research Club – Thinkspire and the Commerce Club at Surana College. She has convened national-level workshops on IPR, served as an Advisory Committee Member for INNOBTE 2025, and contributed as a Reviewer for IEEE conferences and as an Editorial Board Member for journals in HRM and Entrepreneurship. Her professional expertise spans curriculum development, research writing, academic event coordination, digital pedagogy, data analysis (SPSS/AMOS), cross-cultural management, and entrepreneurship development. Personal Life A multilingual scholar, she is fluent in English, Kannada, Hindi, and Tamil. Dr. Soumya resides in Bengaluru with a strong commitment to academia, innovation, and social impact.

J. Sudarvel working as an Assistant Professor of Management at Karpagam Academy of Higher Education. He produced five Ph.D. Scholars and four Ph.D. Scholars are under his guidance. Further, to his credit he published 36 articles in Scopus indexed journals and published more than 50 articles in international journals. He is acting as a Subject Experts in Board of studies of various autonomous colleges.

Remi Thomas is a dedicated academic and industry practitioner committed to preparing students for real-world challenges through experiential learning and strategic mentoring. With over 12 years of cross-functional expertise in Marketing, Business Development, Ed-Tech, Operations Management, Tourism,

Communication, and Entrepreneurship, Remi brings a rich blend of industry insight and academic rigor to the classroom. Currently serving as an Assistant Professor at Vishwakarma University, he undertakes both academic and administrative roles while also contributing significantly to the university's brand-building initiatives. He actively supports student success through his responsibilities as a Placement Coordinator and Student Coordinator, fostering opportunities for career readiness and leadership. Remi has published six research papers and has presented at numerous national and international conferences in the fields of Tourism and Management. His career trajectory includes the establishment of Distance Learning and Technical Training Centers, collaboration with universities, and setting up State Learning Centers—initiatives that have enabled him to mentor and positively impact the lives of over 1000 students across diverse domains and age groups. With a clear vision to bridge the gap between academia and industry, Remi continues to empower students by channeling their potential into purposeful and impactful careers.

Neeraj Kumar Vats is an Assistant Professor in the Department of Management & Commerce at Maharishi Markandeshwar (Deemed to be University), Mullana, Haryana. He holds a Ph.D. in Management and an MBA with dual specializations in Finance and Marketing. With over nine years of combined academic and industry experience, he teaches courses including Financial Accounting, Finance for Everyone, and Accounting for Managers.

Javaid Ahmad Wagay Javaid8973@gmail.com +919541155179. Department of Library and Information Science University of Kashmir Hazratbal; Country india; Postal code 19006; City Srinagar; State Jammu and Kashmir Javaid Ahmad Wagay from kashmir india is a dedicated researcher with a Master's degree in Library and Information Science from the University of Kashmir. He has also completed a Bachelor of Education (B.Ed) from the same institution. Javaid brings a diverse range of expertise to his field, including bibliometrics, scientometrics, sentiment analysis, artificial intelligence, Islamic banking, electronic resources, and cloud computing. His multidisciplinary interests and deep analytical skills make him a valuable contributor to both the academic and technological

Index

A

adaptive learning systems 4, 7, 36, 257, 277, 283
AI Augmentation 118
AI Ethics 22, 24, 42, 61, 88, 90, 96, 140, 224, 253, 264, 272, 274, 393, 396, 414, 415, 416, 421
AI in Education 5, 18, 20, 21, 22, 24, 26, 28, 29, 42, 66, 129, 130, 135, 141, 145, 194, 197, 200, 202, 203, 205, 206, 207, 224, 225, 230, 236, 239, 388
AI in Human Capital 39, 42, 55, 62, 246
AI in Recruitment 70, 75, 86, 89, 295
AI-integrated learning 127, 189, 196, 218
Amazon 64, 76, 79, 87, 94, 99, 100, 101, 102, 103, 104, 105, 106, 107, 108, 109, 110, 111, 112, 113, 114, 115, 116, 117, 118, 119, 120, 121, 122, 128, 141, 407, 418
Artificial Intelligence (AI) 1, 2, 3, 6, 11, 16, 19, 23, 26, 29, 31, 32, 34, 35, 39, 42, 44, 46, 50, 55, 59, 64, 65, 66, 67, 69, 70, 75, 78, 81, 84, 86, 89, 91, 94, 95, 97, 99, 100, 101, 102, 103, 104, 105, 106, 107, 108, 109, 110, 113, 114, 116, 117, 118, 119, 122, 123, 125, 126, 129, 145, 164, 165, 185, 187, 190, 192, 194, 198, 200, 202, 206, 209, 210, 212, 214, 215, 218, 219, 220, 221, 222, 223, 225, 226, 227, 229, 231, 232, 233, 234, 235, 236, 238, 239, 240, 241, 242, 243, 245, 246, 249, 251, 255, 271, 279, 282, 285, 286, 287, 298, 299, 304, 310, 311, 312, 316, 331, 332, 341, 347, 352, 379, 380, 395, 396, 397, 399, 400, 403, 406, 411, 414, 415, 416, 417, 419, 423, 424, 425

B

Biodiversity 427, 428, 429, 431, 440, 441, 442, 443, 445, 447
Biosafety 428, 429, 431, 432, 433, 434, 435, 436, 437, 438, 440, 442, 443, 446, 447

C

Competency-Based Learning (CBL) 209, 211, 212, 214, 215, 216, 217, 219, 221, 222, 223, 225, 227, 229, 230, 231
Consumer Behavior 149, 150, 151, 153, 160, 161

D

data privacy 1, 16, 19, 20, 27, 34, 56, 69, 71, 87, 92, 100, 117, 126, 131, 136, 189, 192, 198, 200, 202, 204, 205, 214, 221, 222, 231, 259, 267, 269, 277, 299, 406, 416
Democracy 380, 381, 384, 385, 386, 394, 395, 396, 397, 445
Digital Inclusion 225, 234, 236
Digital Transformation 3, 14, 32, 74, 84, 94, 105, 114, 118, 119, 127, 128, 150, 219, 220, 232, 233, 256, 265, 272, 283, 289, 293, 297, 308, 312, 316, 336, 338, 343, 356, 396, 402, 403, 417, 421

E

educational equity 129
Emotional Intelligence 3, 4, 6, 12, 15, 103, 166, 169, 170, 172, 173, 174, 175, 176, 177, 178, 181, 185, 210, 211, 215, 220, 241, 257, 266, 286, 309, 388, 400, 408
Empirical Research 60, 63, 230
Employee Engagement 74, 100, 104, 106, 109, 111, 113, 114, 117, 118, 119, 246, 254, 256, 268, 289, 298, 304, 350, 351, 354, 355, 358, 361, 362, 363, 364, 365, 366, 367, 368, 370, 373, 378, 399, 400, 408

Employee Retention 77, 91, 102, 112, 352, 355, 371, 372, 374, 376, 377
Employer Branding 69, 70, 71, 72, 73, 77, 83, 84, 85, 86, 91, 92, 93, 94, 95, 97, 320, 361
Environmental Sustainability 25, 27, 28, 343, 350, 427, 429
Ethical AI 15, 21, 31, 42, 60, 80, 89, 90, 115, 116, 119, 140, 167, 183, 227, 269, 271, 273, 279, 280, 306, 392, 396
Ethical Governance 39, 91, 103, 118, 209, 230, 259, 270, 273, 296, 306, 316
Ethical Reasoning 25, 117, 125, 145, 211, 218, 254, 388, 414
Explainable AI (XAI) 17, 19, 54, 67, 80, 87, 89, 163, 166, 180, 185, 186, 253, 269, 275, 295, 325, 421

F

Faculty Development 32, 34, 36, 37, 42, 43, 44, 55, 57, 60, 64, 67, 68, 127, 138, 139, 145
Farmers' Rights 427, 444, 445, 447
F&B 149, 150, 151, 160, 161
Foundational Learning 1, 2, 3, 4, 5, 6, 7, 8, 9, 10, 11, 14, 15, 19, 23, 25, 26, 28
Future-Ready Human Capital 209, 211, 212, 215, 218, 225, 227, 230, 231

G

Genetically Modified Crops 427, 428, 429, 430, 431, 432, 433, 434, 435, 436, 438, 439, 440, 441, 442, 443, 444, 446
Governance 18, 19, 20, 22, 26, 27, 32, 39, 41, 42, 49, 58, 59, 60, 61, 71, 72, 80, 86, 88, 90, 91, 100, 103, 114, 116, 117, 118, 119, 132, 136, 144, 183, 209, 222, 223, 224, 225, 229, 230, 231, 249, 259, 263, 264, 266, 267, 269, 270, 271, 273, 275, 277, 280, 285, 296, 297, 306, 308, 316, 319, 322, 323, 324, 326, 330, 331, 334, 335, 336, 337, 338, 339, 344, 379, 384, 385, 386, 389, 390, 391, 393, 394, 395, 396, 401, 409, 414, 418, 421, 427, 429, 430, 433, 434, 436, 438, 439, 441, 442, 443, 447

H

Hospitality 285, 286, 287, 288, 290, 291, 292, 293, 294, 297, 298, 299, 300, 301, 303, 304, 305, 306, 307, 308, 309, 310, 311, 319, 336
HR analytics 65, 96, 246, 253, 272, 349, 350, 362, 369, 374, 375, 376, 377, 378
Human Capital 31, 32, 33, 34, 35, 37, 38, 39, 40, 42, 44, 45, 46, 48, 50, 52, 53, 55, 59, 60, 61, 62, 66, 68, 72, 74, 93, 94, 96, 101, 102, 103, 108, 111, 121, 122, 123, 125, 182, 209, 211, 212, 215, 218, 225, 227, 229, 230, 231, 245, 246, 247, 248, 249, 255, 260, 261, 262, 279, 282, 284, 286, 306, 315, 316, 325, 350, 351, 354, 356, 375, 376, 377, 383, 384, 423, 424
Human Resource Management 33, 34, 35, 55, 58, 65, 70, 91, 94, 96, 97, 99, 100, 101, 102, 103, 104, 110, 116, 118, 122, 168, 184, 249, 282, 283, 374, 375, 376, 377

I

Infrastructure Finance 245, 246, 247, 248, 260, 265, 266, 268, 279
Intellectual Property 317, 339, 427, 429, 432, 434, 435, 436, 437, 438, 439, 440, 441, 444, 445, 447, 448
Intelligent Systems 4, 115, 122, 190, 215, 265, 269, 278, 291, 382, 389, 401, 404

L

Labor Markets 4, 13, 17, 21, 23, 26, 28, 221, 329, 379, 381
Learner-Centered Education 194
Legal Frameworks 20, 326, 335, 429, 434
Lifelong Learning 1, 2, 3, 6, 11, 12, 14, 21, 22, 23, 26, 27, 28, 125, 127, 128, 143, 145, 239, 260, 261, 262, 307, 383, 384, 404, 408, 409, 414

72, 73, 74, 86, 89, 90, 91, 92

N

Neurodigitality 334, 335

O

Organizational Learning 315, 321, 322, 323, 324, 344

P

People Analytics 245, 246, 247, 248, 249, 250, 251, 252, 253, 254, 265, 266, 279, 280, 282, 283, 335, 376, 377
personalized learning 32, 101, 103, 108, 112, 133, 134, 138, 140, 141, 190, 191, 192, 193, 194, 196, 198, 199, 200, 201, 203, 206, 207, 211, 221, 231, 246, 252, 257, 259, 266, 276, 301, 311, 320, 337, 387
Personalized Learning Systems 112
Psychometric Profiling 163, 164, 166, 168, 176, 178, 180, 182, 183, 185
Public Services 379, 380, 384, 385, 388, 389, 390, 402, 418

R

RapidMiner 149, 150, 152, 154, 155, 160, 162
Reskilling 2, 14, 21, 23, 26, 100, 101, 116, 119, 127, 182, 237, 252, 285, 287, 290, 292, 306, 308, 311, 382, 407, 408, 414, 416

S

Seed Sovereignty 427, 429, 432, 435, 440, 441, 445, 448
Service Speed 149, 150, 160
Smart Technologies 135, 396
Strategic Talent Acquisition 69, 70, 71, 72, 73, 74, 86, 89, 90, 91, 92

T

Take-Away Coffee 149, 150, 151
Talent Analytics 64, 102, 103, 163, 349, 350, 351, 352, 353, 354, 355, 357, 358, 359, 360, 361, 362, 363, 364, 365, 366, 367, 368, 369, 370, 371, 372, 373, 374, 375, 376, 377
Talent DNA 163, 164, 165, 166, 167, 168, 170, 171, 173, 174, 175, 176, 178, 179, 180, 181, 182, 184, 185, 186
Talent Economy 125, 272
Talent Mobility 109, 182, 186, 221
Technology and AI Professionals 399, 401, 402, 403, 411, 414, 415, 416, 417, 419, 420
Trait Activation Theory 163, 166, 177, 179, 180, 181, 185
Turnover Prediction 351, 368, 369, 370, 373

W

Workforce Analytics 34, 67, 68, 76, 245, 295, 298, 303, 350, 372, 373, 374, 375, 376, 377
Workforce Development 1, 81, 99, 109, 111, 118, 218, 225, 236, 249, 262, 266, 275, 291, 307, 409
Workforce Diversity and Inclusion 72, 91, 121
Workforce Engagement 368
Workforce Forecasting 72
Workforce Planning 21, 31, 32, 33, 35, 37, 38, 39, 42, 72, 73, 76, 90, 102, 113, 116, 228, 246, 253, 261, 277, 280, 285, 295, 299, 303, 307, 308, 355, 356, 373, 374, 376, 377
Workforce Readiness 8, 13, 14
Workforce Transformation 254

www.ingramcontent.com/pod-product-compliance
Lightning Source LLC
LaVergne TN
LVHW062331300926
849161LV00007B/1658